The cable diameter is $36\frac{3}{8}$ inches.

The height of the tower above the roadway is 500 feet.

The total weight of steel used is 83,000 tons.

The two main cables are made of 80,000 miles of wire.

CALIFORNIA
HSP Math

Harcourt
SCHOOL PUBLISHERS

Visit *The Learning Site!*
www.harcourtschool.com

Requests for permission to make copies of any part of the work should be addressed to School Permissions and Copyrights, Harcourt, Inc., 6277 Sea Harbor Drive, Orlando, Florida 32887-6777.
Fax: 407-345-2418.

Printed in the United States of America

ISBN 13: 978-0-15-354170-4
ISBN 10: 0-15-354170-9

5 6 7 8 9 10 0914 16 15 14 13 12 11 10 09

CALIFORNIA HSP Math

Mathematics Advisor

Tom Roby
Associate Professor of Mathematics
Director, Quantitative
    Learning Center
University of Connecticut
Storrs, Connecticut

Senior Authors

Evan M. Maletsky
Professor Emeritus
Montclair State University
Upper Montclair, New Jersey

Joyce McLeod
Visiting Professor, Retired
Rollins College
Winter Park, Florida

Authors

Angela G. Andrews
Assistant Professor,
    Math Education
National-Louis University
Lisle, Illinois

Juli K. Dixon
Associate Professor of
    Mathematics Education
University of Central Florida
Orlando, Florida

Vicki Newman
Classroom Teacher
McGaugh Elementary School
Los Alamitos Unified
    School District
Seal Beach, California

Robin C. Scarcella
Professor and Director
Program of Academic English
    and ESL
University of California, Irvine
Irvine, California

David G. Wright
Professor
Department of Mathematics
Brigham Young University
Provo, Utah

Jennie M. Bennett
Mathematics Teacher
Houston Independent
    School District
Houston, Texas

Lynda Luckie
Director, K–12 Mathematics
Gwinnett County Public Schools
Suwanee, Georgia

Karen S. Norwood
Associate Professor of
    Mathematics Education
North Carolina State University
Raleigh, North Carolina

Janet K. Scheer
Executive Director
Create-A-Vision
Foster City, California

Tom Roby
Associate Professor
    of Mathematics
Director, Quantitative
    Learning Center
University of Connecticut
Storrs, Connecticut

Program Consultants and Specialists

Russell Gersten
Director, Instructional
    Research Group
Long Beach, California
Professor Emeritus of
    Special Education
University of Oregon
Eugene, Oregon

Michael DiSpezio
Writer and On-Air Host,
    JASON Project
North Falmouth, Massachusetts

Tyrone Howard
Assistant Professor
    UCLA Graduate School
    of Education
Information Studies
University of California
    at Los Angeles
Los Angeles, California

Lydia Song
Program Specialist, Mathematics
Orange County Department
    of Education
Costa Mesa, California

Rebecca Valbuena
Language Development Specialist
Stanton Elementary School
Glendora, California

Understand Whole Numbers and Operations

UNIT 2

Multiplication and Division Facts

6 Algebra: Use Multiplication and Division Facts 134

UNIT 3

Multiply by 1- and 2-Digit Numbers

9 Multiply by 2-Digit Numbers 216

MATH ON LOCATION

Photos from
The Futures Channel
with California
Chapter Projects and
VOCABULARY POWER 173

READ Math
WORKSHOP 189

WRITE Math
WORKSHOP 223

 GO ONLINE Technology

Harcourt Mega Math: Chapter 7, p. 194; Chapter 8, p. 210; Chapter 9, p. 221, Extra Practice: pp. 194, 210, 232
The Harcourt Learning Site: www.harcourtschool.com
Multimedia Math Glossary: www.harcourtschool.com/hspmath

The World Almanac for Kids

Space Travel 238

12 Number Theory and Patterns 286

MATH ON LOCATION

Photos from The Futures Channel with California Chapter Projects and **VOCABULARY POWER** 241

READ Math WORKSHOP 251

WRITE Math WORKSHOP 295

GO ONLINE Technology

Harcourt Mega Math: Chapter 10, p. 250; Chapter 11, p. 276; Chapter 12, p. 294, Extra Practice: pp. 260, 280, 308
The Harcourt Learning Site: www.harcourtschool.com
Multimedia Math Glossary: www.harcourtschool.com/hspmath

The World Almanac for Kids

Collecting Labels. 314

UNIT 5

Data and Algebra

MATH ON LOCATION

Photos from The Futures Channel with California Chapter Projects and **VOCABULARY POWER** 317

READ Math WORKSHOP 381

WRITE Math WORKSHOP 365

GO ONLINE   Technology

Harcourt Mega Math: Chapter 13, p. 331; Chapter 14, p. 354; Chapter 15, p. 399, Extra Practice: pp. 336, 366, 402
The Harcourt Learning Site: www.harcourtschool.com
Multimedia Math Glossary: www.harcourtschool.com/hspmath

The World Almanac for Kids

Waves and Weather 408

UNIT 6

Fractions and Decimals

16 Understand Fractions and Mixed Numbers 412

17 Add and Subtract Like Fractions and Mixed Numbers 442

22 Solid Figures 564

UNIT 8

Measurement and Probability

MATH ON LOCATION

Photos from The Futures Channel with California Chapter Projects and **VOCABULARY POWER** 587

READ Math WORKSHOP 619

WRITE Math WORKSHOP 637

 Technology

Harcourt Mega Math: Chapter 23, p. 602; Chapter 24, pp. 610, 636, Extra Practice: pp. 620, 646
The Harcourt Learning Site: www.harcourtschool.com
Multimedia Math Glossary: www.harcourtschool.com/hspmath

🐻

The World Almanac for Kids

Birthday Rocks 652

TALK, READ, and WRITE
About Math

Mathematics is a language of numbers, words, and symbols.

This year you will learn ways to communicate about math as you **talk**, **read**, and **write** about what you are learning.

The table and the bar graph show the speeds of some of the fastest steel roller coasters in the United States.

Steel Roller Coasters

Roller Coaster	Park	Speed (in miles per hour)
Kingda Ka	Six Flags Great Adventure Jackson, New Jersey	128
Top Thrill Dragster	Cedar Point Sandusky, Ohio	120
Superman: The Escape	Six Flags Magic Mountain Valencia, California	100
Millennium Force	Cedar Point Sandusky, Ohio	93
Titan	Six Flags Over Texas Arlington, Texas	85
Phantom's Revenge	Kennywood West Mifflin, Pennsylvania	82

Steel Roller Coasters

Roller Coasters: Kingda Ka, Millennium Force, Phantom's Revenge, Superman: The Escape, Titan, Top Thrill Dragster

Speed (in miles per hour): 0 10 20 30 40 50 60 70 80 90 100 110 120 130

TALK Math

Talk about the table and the bar graph.

1. What information is in the table but is not in the bar graph?

2. What is the difference in the way the data are organized in the table and on the bar graph?

3. What do the numbers along the bottom of the bar graph represent?

4. Why is it important that the spaces between the numbers on the bar graph are the same size?

Read the data in the table and on the bar graph.

4. In what city and state is the fastest roller coaster located?

5. What is the difference in speed of Superman: The Great Escape and Phantom's Revenge?

6. What is the difference in speed of the two roller coasters in Sandusky, Ohio?

7. Which two roller coasters have a difference in speed of 35 miles per hour?

WRITE Math ▶

Write a problem about the bar graph.

This year you will write many problems. When you see **Pose a Problem**, you look at a problem on the page and use it to write your own problem.

In your problem you can
- change the numbers or some of the information.
- exchange the known and unknown information.
- write an open-ended problem that can have more than one correct answer.

These problems are examples of ways you can pose your own problem. Solve each problem.

Problem How much faster is the Kingda Ka than the Millennium Force?

● **Change the Numbers or Information**
How much faster is the Millennium Force than the Titan?

● **Exchange the Known and Unknown Information**
The speed of the Millennium Force is 93 miles per hour. Which roller coaster has a speed that is 27 miles per hour faster than the Millennium Force?

● **Make the Problem Open-Ended**
Name a roller coaster with a speed between 90 and 125 miles per hour?

Pose a Problem Chose one of the three ways to write a new problem. Use the information in the table and on the bar graph.

1 Understand Whole Numbers and Operations

Math on Location

1 Flowers are packaged by the dozen and prepared for shipment to flower businesses.

2 Flowering plants must be watered and cared for until they are shipped to customers.

3 Florists make arrangements by combining specific numbers of different colors.

VOCABULARY POWER

TALK Math

What math is used in **Math on Location**? How could you find if there are more red flowers or yellow flowers prepared for shipment?

READ Math

REVIEW VOCABULARY You learned the words below last year. How do these words relate to **Math on Location**?

compare to describe whether numbers are equal to, less than, or greater than each other

estimate to find an answer that is close to the exact amount

greater than (>) a symbol used to compare two numbers, with the greater number given first

less than (<) a symbol used to compare two numbers, with the lesser number given first

WRITE Math

Copy and complete the table using the word pairs shown below. Use what you know about numbers and operations.

addition, subtraction   addition, sum   odd, even

subtraction, count backward   regroup, compare

digit, place value   fact family, number sentence

subtraction, difference   sum, difference   compare, order

greater than, less than   sum, total

Same	Opposite	Go Together	Not Related
	addition subtraction		

GO ONLINE
Technology
Multimedia Math Glossary link at
www.harcourtschool.com/hspmath

1 Understand Place Value

The Big Idea The position of a digit determines its value.

Investigate

Each year, scientists count California sea lion pups. What are some ways to compare the numbers of pups for the years shown in the table?

California Sea Lion Pups

Year	Population
2000	49,337
2001	49,032
2002	45,431
2003	36,451
2004	43,386
2005	48,277

CALIFORNIA FAST FACT

California sea lions are playful and friendly animals. They are also strong swimmers. They can reach speeds of 25 miles per hour with their powerful flippers.

GO ONLINE

Technology
Student pages are available in the Student eBook.

Show What You Know

Check your understanding of important skills
needed for success in Chapter 1.

▶ **Place Value Through Thousands**

Find the value of the underlined digit.

1. 8<u>2</u>4

2. 59<u>1</u>

3. <u>3</u>74

4. <u>5</u>,312

5. 1,04<u>3</u>

6. 9,<u>2</u>08

7. <u>2</u>,307

8. 7,<u>8</u>61

▶ **Read and Write Whole Numbers Through Thousands**

Write each number in standard form.

9. thirty-five

10. eight hundred four

11. seven thousand, two hundred twenty-one

12. seventy-eight

13. five hundred sixty-three

14. two thousand, forty-six

15. 600 + 40 + 9

16. 3,000 + 200 + 8

17. 5,000 + 700 + 50 + 1

▶ **Compare Whole Numbers Through Thousands**

Compare. Write <, >, or = for each ●.

18. 203 ● 230

19. 65 ● 56

20. 888 ● 881

21. 98 ● 103

22. 5,339 ● 5,393

23. 422 ● 4,222

24. 3,825 ● 5,283

25. 7,881 ● 7,881

VOCABULARY POWER

CHAPTER VOCABULARY

compare
digit
equal to (=)
expanded form
greater than (>)
less than (<)
millions

not equal to (≠)
order
period
place value
standard form
word form

WARM-UP WORDS

period Each group of three digits separated by commas in a multidigit number

standard form A way to write numbers by using digits

expanded form A way to write numbers by showing the value of each digit

word form A way to write numbers by using words

Place Value Through Hundred Thousands

OBJECTIVE: Model, read, write, and identify the place value of whole numbers through hundred thousands.

Learn

PROBLEM The cost of caring for a pet can really add up. Did you know that the average yearly cost to take care of a medium-sized dog is $1,115?

You can use base-ten blocks to show the cost.

Activity

Materials ■ base-ten blocks

Model 1,115 in more than one way.

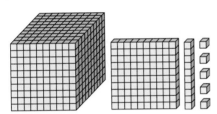

Think: 1 ten = 10 ones

1 thousand 1 hundred 1 ten 5 ones shows 1,115.

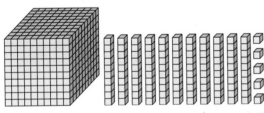

Think: 1 hundred = 10 tens

1 thousand 11 tens 5 ones shows 1,115.

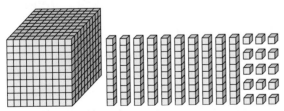

1 thousand 10 tens 15 ones shows 1,115.

• Are these different ways to show 1,115 related? **Explain.**

Quick Review

Write in standard form.

1. 6 tens 5 ones
2. 4 hundreds 2 tens
3. 8 tens 9 ones
4. 7 hundreds 7 ones
5. 5 hundreds 3 tens 1 one

Vocabulary

period

standard form

word form

expanded form

Understand Place Value

In 2004, the number of Labrador retrievers registered with the American Kennel Club was 146,692. What is the value of the digit 4 in 146,692?

A place-value chart can help you understand the value of each digit in a number. The value of a digit depends on its place-value position in the number.

Example Use place value to find the value of a digit.

PERIOD

THOUSANDS			ONES		
Hundreds	Tens	Ones	Hundreds	Tens	Ones
1	4	6,	6	9	2

1 hundred thousand	4 ten thousands	6 thousands	6 hundreds	9 tens	2 ones
$1 \times 100,000$	$4 \times 10,000$	$6 \times 1,000$	6×100	9×10	2×1
100,000	40,000	6,000	600	90	2

← Multiply the digit by its place value to find the value of each digit.

So, the value of the digit 4 is 40,000.

Each group of three digits separated by commas in a multidigit number is called a **period**. Commas separate the periods. Each period has ones, tens, and hundreds in it. The number 146,692 has two periods, ones and thousands.

You can use place value and period names to read 146,692 and to write 146,692 in different forms.

Standard Form: 146,692

Word Form: one hundred forty-six thousand, six hundred ninety-two

Expanded Form: $100,000 + 40,000 + 6,000 + 600 + 90 + 2$

ERROR ALERT

When numbers have zeros, you do not need to write or represent the digit 0 in word form or expanded form.

More Examples

A **Standard form:** 70,186

Word Form: seventy thousand, one hundred eighty-six

Expanded Form: $70,000 + 100 + 80 + 6$

B **Standard Form:** 306,409

Word Form: three hundred six thousand, four hundred nine

Expanded Form: $300,000 + 6,000 + 400 + 9$

1. Name the number shown by the model. What are two other ways can you model this number?

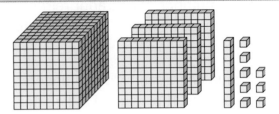

Write each number in two other forms.

✓2. four hundred seven thousand, fifty-one

✓3. 90,000 + 6,000 + 200 + 80 + 1

4. **TALK Math** Explain how you can use the standard form of a number to write the number in word form.

Independent Practice and Problem Solving

Write each number in two other forms.

5. 70,000 + 4,000 + 50 + 6

6. five hundred thousand, two hundred six

7. 981,416

8. 80,308

Complete.

9. 340,680 = three hundred forty __?__ , six hundred eighty = ■ + 40,000 + ■ + 80

10. ■ + 6,000 + 400 + 3 = 56,4■■ = fifty-six thousand, four __?__ three

Write the value of the underlined digit in each number.

11. <u>4</u>35,258

12. 368,<u>1</u>09

13. 5<u>7</u>0,217

14. 129,<u>6</u>34

USE DATA For 15–17, use the table.

15. How many poodles were registered in 2004? Write the number in two other forms.

16. Which breed had nineteen thousand, three hundred ninety-six dogs registered in 2004?

17. Represent the number of Pointers in as many different ways as you can. Use models, pictures, or numbers.

18. **≡FAST FACT** In 2001, an English mastiff set a world record for heaviest dog with a weight of 282 pounds. Describe two different ways that you could use base-ten blocks to show this number.

Dogs Registered by the American Kennel Club in 2004		
	Breed	**Number Registered**
	Bulldogs	19,396
	Pointers	512
	Poodles	32,671
	Pomeranians	21,269

19. **Reasoning** What number is 100 less than the greatest number you can make if you use the digits 2, 3, 4, 5, and 9 exactly once?

CD ROM **Technology** Use Harcourt Mega Math, Fraction Action, *Number Line Mine*, Level A.

20. Reasoning Les wrote a number between 700 and 900 that had one zero. What might the number be?

21. Cameron wrote this sequence of numbers: 437, 447, 457, 467. What pattern do you see?

Achieving the Standards

22. What is the least whole number you can make using the digits 5, 3, 6, and 8? Use each digit exactly once. (Grade 3 NS 1.1)

23. What is 328 ÷ 4? (Grade 3 NS 2.5)

24. Test Prep What is the value of the digit 7 in 473,562?

  A 700

  B 7,000

  C 70,000

  D 700,000

25. What digit is in the hundreds place of 5,873? (Grade 3 O¬n NS 1.3)

26. Test Prep The population of the city where Ben lives is four hundred six thousand, fifty-three. What is this number in standard form?

  A 400,053

  B 400,653

  C 406,053

  D 460,053

Problem Solving and Reasoning

NUMBER SENSE You can name numbers in different ways.

The number of dog bones shown can be named as 1 thousand 3 hundreds 1 ten 2 ones or 500 + 500 + 100 + 100 + 100 + 10 + 2.

Name numbers using numbers and words.	Name numbers using numbers and operation signs.
4,100	**1,247**
4 thousands 1 hundred	1,000 + 200 + 40 + 7
41 hundreds	500 + 500 + 240 + 7
410 tens	1,250 − 3
4,100 ones	1,300 − 53

Name each number using numbers and words.

1. 150   **2.** 705   **3.** 479   **4.** 862   **5.** 2,464

Name each number using numbers and operation signs.

6. 308   **7.** 1,305   **8.** 2,300   **9.** 4,550   **10.** 576

2 Model Millions

OBJECTIVE: Understand the magnitude of numbers through millions.

Investigate

Materials ■ 10-by-10 grid paper ■ crayons ■ tape

A stack of 1 million one-dollar bills is as tall as a nine-story building. One million is the next counting number after 999,999. One million is written as 1,000,000 in standard form.

A Draw a dot in each box in 1 column of the 10-by-10 grid paper. Each dot represents 1 one-dollar bill. How many one-dollar bills does this grid represent?

B Draw a dot in each box of the grid. How many 1 one-dollar bills does one grid represent when filled? Write the number.

C Tape your grid paper to other students' grid papers. Write the number of 1 one-dollar bills that are represented by the sheets of grid paper taped together.

• How many sheets of grid paper will you need to show 1,000 one-dollar bills? 10,000 one-dollar bills? 100,000 one-dollar bills? 1,000,000 one-dollar bills? Write the number of sheets for each.

Draw Conclusions

You can look for a pattern to find how many sheets of grid paper you will need to show 1,000,000 one-dollar bills. Copy and complete the table.

1. What pattern did you use to complete the table? Explain.

2. **Analysis** How can picturing what a model of a million looks like help you better understand the relative size of numbers?

Model Millions	
Total Dollars	Sheets of Paper
100	1
1,000	10
10,000	100
100,000	■
1,000,000	■

O━π NS 1.1 Read and write whole numbers in the millions. *also* NS 1.0, MR 2.0, MR 2.3, MR 2.4, MR 3.2

Connect

The period to the left of thousands is **millions**.
One million is equal to 10 hundred thousands.

You can use place value and period names to help
you read numbers in millions.

In 1989, Pablo Picasso's painting, entitled *Les Noces de Pierrette*,
sold for $51,671,920. Look at the amount paid for the painting
in the place-value chart.

MILLIONS			THOUSANDS			ONES		
Hundreds	Tens	Ones	Hundreds	Tens	Ones	Hundreds	Tens	Ones
	5	1	6	7	1	9	2	0

The number 51,671,920 is read as fifty-one million, six hundred
seventy-one thousand, nine hundred twenty.

• Would the population of a large country be counted in
  thousands or millions? Give some examples of things that can
  be counted in the millions.

Practice

Solve.

1. How many hundreds are in 1,000?

2. How many hundreds are in 10,000?

3. How many thousands are in 100,000?

✓4. How many thousands are in 1,000,000?

**Tell whether each number is large enough to be in the millions
or more. Write *yes* or *no*.**

5. the distance from Earth to the sun in miles

✓6. the number of people in your class

7. the number of grains of sand on a beach

8. the number of bees living in a beehive

9. the number of students riding on a
   school bus

10. the number of people living in the
    United States

Choose the number in which the digit 7 has the greater value.

11. 7,500,000 or 75,000,000

12. 35,007,000 or 35,070,000

13. 19,070,000 or 700,000

14. 237,100,000 or 71,100,000

15. **WRITE Math** ▶ Describe how 10,000 sheets of 10-by-10 grid
    paper and 1,000 thousands blocks are related.

Place Value Through Millions

OBJECTIVE: Read, write, and identify the place value of numbers through millions.

Quick Review

Write the number of hundreds in each.

1. 70,000
2. 100,000
3. 9,000
4. 300,000
5. 50,000

Learn

PROBLEM You can write the number 92,955,628 in standard form, word form, and expanded form.

Example Use place value to write and read numbers in millions.

MILLIONS			THOUSANDS			ONES		
Hundreds	Tens	Ones	Hundreds	Tens	Ones	Hundreds	Tens	Ones
	9	2,	9	5	5,	6	2	8

PERIOD

Standard Form: 92,955,628

Word Form: ninety-two million, nine hundred fifty-five thousand, six hundred twenty-eight

Expanded Form: 90,000,000 + 2,000,000 + 900,000 + 50,000 + 5,000 + 600 + 20 + 8

The distance between the Earth and the sun is about 92,955,628 miles.

More Examples

A **Standard Form:** 5,200,007

Word Form: five million, two hundred thousand, seven

Expanded Form: 5,000,000 + 200,000 + 7

B **Standard Form:** 860,092,170

Word Form: eight hundred sixty million, ninety-two thousand, one hundred seventy

Expanded Form: 800,000,000 + 60,000,000 + 90,000 + 2,000 + 100 + 70

• How do you find the value of the digit 4 in 45,213,073?

Math Idea
You can use place value and period names to read and write numbers in three forms.

Guided Practice

1. How can you use place value and period names to write the number 5,324,904 in word form?

Write each number in two other forms.

✓2. ninety million, four hundred eight thousand, seventeen

✓3. 365,009,058

O┐ NS 1.1 Read and write whole numbers in the millions. *also* NS 1.0, MR 2.0, MR 2.3, MR 2.4, MR 3.2

4. **TALK Math** **Explain** how you can use the expanded form of a number to write the number in standard form.

Independent Practice and Problem Solving

Write each number in two other forms.

5. forty-seven million, five hundred eight thousand

6. two hundred three million, forty thousand, six hundred nineteen

7. 60,570,020

8. 400,000,000 + 60,000 + 5,000 + 100

Use the number 63,145,973.

9. Write the name of the period that has the digits 145.

10. Write the name of the period that has the digits 63.

11. Write the digit in the millions place.

12. Write the value of the digit 6.

Find the sum. Then write the answer in standard form.

13. 4 thousands 3 hundreds 2 ones + 5 thousands 2 tens 4 ones

14. 3 ten thousands 4 hundreds 8 tens + 4 ten thousands

USE DATA For 15–16, use the Average Distance from the Sun picture.

Planet	Venus	Mars	Jupiter	Saturn
Distance (in miles)	67,200,000	141,600,000	483,800,000	890,800,000

15. What is the average distance of Saturn from the sun?

16. Which planet has an average distance of four hundred eighty-three million, eight hundred thousand miles from the sun?

17. **WRITE Math** **Explain** how trading the position of the digit 2 and the digit 4 in 129,304,718 affects the value of the number.

Achieving the Standards

18. If $4 \times 7 = 28$, then what is 7×4? (Grade 3 AF 1.5)

19. What is the value of the digit 7 in 8,751? (O━┓ NS 1.1, p. 4)

20. What is the standard form of seven hundred four thousand, six hundred twenty?
(O━┓ NS 1.1, p. 4)

21. **Test Prep** Which of these is the number 60,008,012?

A sixty thousand, eight hundred, twelve

B six million, eight thousand, twelve

C sixty million, eight hundred, twelve

D sixty million, eight thousand, twelve

Extra Practice on page 24, Set B

Compare Whole Numbers

OBJECTIVE: Compare numbers through millions using base-ten blocks, number lines, and place value.

Learn

PROBLEM Crystal Palace Cave in Alaska is 429 feet deep. French Creek Cave in Montana is 434 feet deep. Which is deeper, Crystal Palace Cave or French Creek Cave?

Example 1 Use base-ten blocks.

To find which cave is deeper, compare 429 and 434.

Compare the values of the blocks in each place-value position from left to right. Keep comparing the blocks until the values are different.

	Hundreds	**Tens**	**Ones**
Model 429.			
Model 434.			

There are the same number of hundreds. 3 tens is greater than 2 tens.

434 > 429

So, French Creek Cave is deeper than Crystal Palace Cave.

Example 2 Use a number line.

Compare 10,408 and 10,433.

10,408   10,433

10,400   10,410   10,420   10,430   10,440   10,450

10,408 is to the left of 10,433.   10,433 is to the right of 10,408.

So, 10,408 is less than 10,433.   So, 10,433 is greater than 10,408.

10,408 < 10,433   10,433 > 10,408

Example 3 Use a place-value chart.

Mammoth Cave National Park in Kentucky had 1,898,822 visitors in 2002 and 1,888,126 visitors in 2004. In which year were there more visitors?

Compare 1,898,822 and 1,888,126.

MILLIONS			THOUSANDS			ONES		
Hundreds	Tens	Ones	Hundreds	Tens	Ones	Hundreds	Tens	Ones
		1,	8	9	8,	8	2	2
		1,	8	8	8,	1	2	6

Step 1

Start with the first place on the left. Compare the millions.

1,898,822

↓   1 = 1

1,888,126

There are the same number of millions.

Step 2

Compare the hundred thousands.

1,898,822

↓   8 = 8

1,888,126

There are the same number of hundred thousands.

Step 3

Compare the ten thousands.

1,898,822

↓   9 > 8

1,888,126

9 ten thousands are greater than 8 ten thousands.
So, 1,898,822 > 1,888,126.

> **Math Idea**
> To compare numbers, start at the left and compare the digits in each place-value position until the digits differ.

So, there were more visitors in 2002.

Example 4 Compare different numbers of digits.

Compare 21,623,785 and 103,317,256. Write >, <, or =.

21,623,785

↑   0 < 1

103,317,256

So, 21,623,785 < 103,317,256.

Example 5 Compare to make a relationship true.

What digits make this relationship true?

26■ ≠ 265   Think: What digits are not equal to 5?

Replace ■ with 0, 1, 2, 3, 4, 6, 7, 8, or 9.

260, 261, 262, 263, 264, 266, 267, 268, and 269 are not equal to 265.

So, the digits 0, 1, 2, 3, 4, 6, 7, 8, or 9 make the relationship true.

1. Use the base-ten blocks to compare 324 and 332. Write the lesser number.

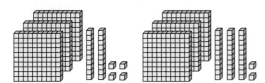

2. Use the number line to compare 5,327 and 5,341. Write the greater number.

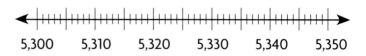

```
5,300   5,310   5,320   5,330   5,340   5,350
```

Compare. Write <, >, or = for each ⬤.

3. 45,595 ⬤ 45,585

✓4. 631,328 ⬤ 640,009

✓5. 528,807,414 ⬤ 5,699,001

6. **TALK Math** **Explain** how to compare 79,308 and 79,354.

Independent Practice and Problem Solving

Use the number line to compare. Write the lesser number.

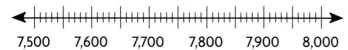

```
7,500   7,600   7,700   7,800   7,900   8,000
```

7. 7,710 or 7,680

8. 7,800 or 7,680

9. 7,584 or 7,616

Compare. Write <, >, or = for each ⬤.

10. 2,212 ⬤ 2,600

11. 41,190 ⬤ 41,090

12. 63,803 ⬤ 6,409

13. 88,304 ⬤ 88,304

14. 5,249,116 ⬤ 41,090

15. 439,064 ⬤ 440,000,438

16. 8,279,314 ⬤ 8,279,299

17. 975,408 ⬤ 912,005,300

18. 7,512,720 ⬤ 8,510,001

Algebra **Find all of the digits that can replace each ■.**

19. 420 ≠ 4■0

20. 7,486 ≠ 7,48■

21. 3,■15 ≠ 3,129

USE DATA For 22–24, use the table.

22. Which ocean trench is deeper, Tonga or Marianas?

23. Which ocean trench has a depth less than 34,000 feet?

24. **Pose a Problem** Write a problem that compares two numbers from the Deepest Ocean Trenches table.

Deepest Ocean Trenches

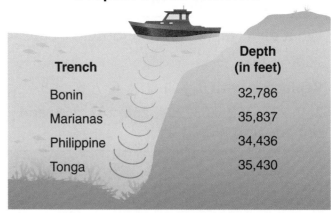

Trench	Depth (in feet)
Bonin	32,786
Marianas	35,837
Philippine	34,436
Tonga	35,430

25. **What's the Error?** Max said that 36,594 is less than 5,980 because 3 is less than 5. Describe Max's error and give the correct answer.

26. **Reasoning** Which is greater, the number that is 1,000 less than 16,892 or the number that is 10,000 less than 26,892. **Explain** how you know.

 Achieving the Standards

27. What is the standard form of twenty thousand, four hundred nine?

    (O━┳ NS 1.1, p. 4)

28. Which has the greatest value? 9,911, 9,191, or 9,119 (Grade 3 NS 1.2)

29. **Test Prep** Which number is greater than 2,105?

    A 2,100   **C** 2,015

    B 2,150   **D** 2,005

30. There are 100 centimeters in 1 meter. How many centimeters are in 4 meters?

    (Grade 3 MG 1.4)

31. **Test Prep** Which number is the least?

    A 50,771   **C** 50,871

    B 50,781   **D** 50,770

MATH POWER   Problem Solving and Reasoning

VISUAL THINKING A **benchmark** is a known number of things that helps you understand the size or amount of a different number of things.

Use the benchmark to choose the best estimate for the number of bats it would take to cover the whole wall of the cave.

To cover the wall, it would take about 4 times the benchmark number.

$10 + 10 + 10 + 10$, or $4 \times 10 = 40$

The most reasonable estimate for the number of bats it would take to cover the entire wall is 40 bats.

10 bats   10, 20, 30, or 40

• Will your estimate be less than, more than, or the same amount as the benchmark number? Explain.

Use the benchmark to choose the best estimate for each amount.

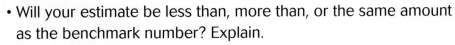

1.

   1,000 worms   500, 750, 1,000, or 1,500

2.

   20 beetles   10, 20, 60 or 120

3.

   200 spiders   50, 100, 200 or 400

5 Order Whole Numbers

OBJECTIVE: Order numbers through millions using base-ten blocks, number lines, and place value.

Learn

PROBLEM Did you know that the giant sequoia is the world's largest kind of tree? Sequoia National Park in California is home to many of the largest sequoias. Three of the largest trees in the park are 275 feet tall, 241 feet tall, and 255 feet tall. Order the heights of the trees from greatest to least.

Example 1 Use base-ten blocks.

Order 275, 241, and 255 from greatest to least.

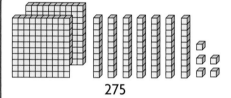 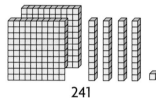 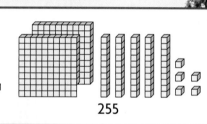

| 275 | 241 | 255 |

Step 1	Step 2	Step 3
Compare the hundreds. There are the same number of hundreds.	Compare the tens. The model for 275 has the most tens, so it is the greatest number.	Compare the tens in 241 and 255. The model for 255 has more tens, so it is greater than 241.

So, from the greatest to least, the numbers are 275, 255, 241.

So, the heights of the trees in order from greatest to least are 275 feet, 255 feet, and 241 feet.

Example 2 Use a number line.

Order 20,650; 21,150; and 20,890 from greatest to least.

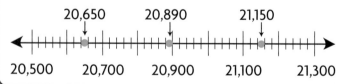

So, the numbers in order from greatest to least are 21,150; 20,890; and 20,650.

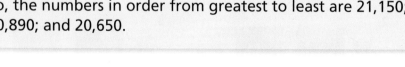

O—n NS 1.2 Order and compare whole numbers and decimals to two places. *also* O—n NS 1.1, AF 1.1, MR 2.0, MR 2.3, MR 2.4, MR 3.2

Example 3 Use place value.

The table shows the number of visitors to Sequoia National Park during three years.

You can order the number of visitors for each year by using a place-value chart.

Order 1,418,519; 1,552,258; and 1,520,835 from least to greatest.

Visitors to Sequoia National Park	
Year	Number of Visitors
2002	1,418,519
2003	1,552,258
2004	1,520,835

Math Idea

When you compare and order numbers you must begin comparing at the greatest place-value position.

MILLIONS			THOUSANDS			ONES		
Hundreds	Tens	Ones	Hundreds	Tens	Ones	Hundreds	Tens	Ones
		1,	4	1	8,	5	1	9
		1,	5	5	2,	2	5	8
		1,	5	2	0,	8	3	5

Step 1

Start with the first place on the left. Compare the millions.

1,418,519
↓   1 = 1
1,552,258
↓
1,520,835

There are the same number of millions.

Step 2

Compare the hundred thousands.

1,418,519
↓   4 < 5
1,552,258
↓
1,520,835

Since 4 < 5, 1,418,519 is the least of the three numbers.

Step 3

Compare the ten thousands in the other two numbers.

1,552,258
↓   5 > 2
1,520,835

Since 5 > 2, 1,552,258 is greater than 1,520,835.

1,418,519 < 1,520,835 < 1,552,258

So, the number of visitors in order from least to greatest are 1,418,519; 1,520,835; and 1,552,258.

• Explain how you would order 102,535,458; 105,236,030; and 120,539,078 from greatest to least.

Guided Practice

1. Use the base-ten blocks to order 1,027; 1,105; and 1,041 from least to greatest.

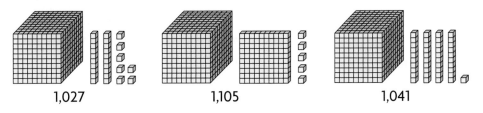

1,027   1,105   1,041

Solve.

2. Use the number line to order 4,788; 4,793; and 4,784 from least to greatest.

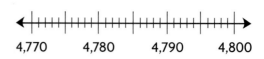

4,770   4,780   4,790   4,800

Write the numbers in order from least to greatest.

✅ 3. 55,997; 57,000; 56,038

✅ 4. 787,925; 1,056,000; 789,100

5. (TALK Math) **Explain** how knowing the number of digits in each number can help you order a set of whole numbers.

Independent Practice **and Problem Solving**

Write the numbers in order from greatest to least.

6. 8,523; 8,538; 8,519

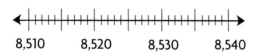

8,510   8,520   8,530   8,540

7. 43,050; 42,938; 42,951

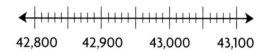

42,800   42,900   43,000   43,100

8. 623,096; 68,999; 621,960

9. 3,452,805; 3,542,805; 542,905

10. 7,122,890; 700,122,089; 70,122,098

11. 939,822; 9,398,820; 9,398,802

12. 430,000,459; 43,000,549; 403,000,456

13. 8,778; 870,780; 878,070; 807,870

Algebra Write all of the digits that can replace each ■.

14. $567 < 5■5 < 582$

15. $3,408 < 3,■30 < 3,540$

16. $52,780 > 5■,790 > 50,120$

17. $4,464,545 > 4,4■3,535 > 4,443,550$

USE DATA For 18–20, use the map.

18. Name the national parks in order from least number of acres to greatest number of acres.

19. Which park has less than 500,000 acres?

20. In a comparison of the number of acres in Yosemite National Park and in Joshua Tree National Park, in which place do the digits first differ?

Yosemite
761,266 acres

Sequoia
402,051 acres

Joshua Tree
789,745 acres

21. **Reasoning** A number has 4 different odd digits. The difference between the greatest digit and the least digit is 6. The number is greater than 2,000 and less than 3,160. What is the number?

22. Janine, Erik, and Mario collect rare coins. Janine has 357 coins, Erik has 361 coins, and Mario has 349 coins. Who has the most coins?

18   (Extra Practice) on page 24, Set D

Technology
Use Harcourt Mega Math, Fraction Action, *Number Line Mine*, Level B.

23. **WRITE Math** What's the Error? Emma ordered three numbers from least to greatest. Her work is shown at the right. Describe her error. Write the numbers in the correct order.

24. **WRITE Math** What's the Question? There are three numbers: 643,251; 633,512; and 633,393. The answer is 633,512.

Emma's Work
○
3258
33,438   6 ‹ 8
33,246   3 ‹ 5
○ So, from least to greatest, the numbers are 33,246; 3,258; 33,438

Achieving the Standards

25. Is it certain, likely, unlikely, or impossible that Independence Day is in July?

(Grade 3 SDAP 1.1)

26. $7 + 9 =$ (Grade 3 🔑 NS 2.1)

27. Test Prep Which shows the numbers in order from least to greatest?

   A 102,397; 102,395; 102,359

   B 216,001; 216,101; 216,010

   C 422,956; 422,596; 422,298

   D 575,029; 575,209; 575,290

28. What is the value of the digit 3 in 638,041,299? (NS 🔑 1.1, p. 10)

29. Test Prep Which shows the numbers in order from greatest to least?

   A 26,495; 26,459; 26,945

   B 60,101; 60,011; 60,110

   C 98,902; 89,902; 89,209

   D 40,005; 40,050; 40,500

MATH POWER — Problem Solving and Reasoning

NUMBER SENSE Numbers are used in many ways.

Counting	Measuring	Locating	Labeling
There are 2,256 books.	The room is 14 feet by 12 feet.	Apartment 605 is on the sixth floor.	The number on his soccer jersey is 17.

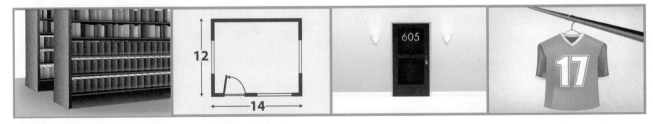

Tell which way each number is used.

1. The lake is 127 feet deep.

2. Ling lives in apartment 533.

3. Max wears the number 34 on his baseball uniform.

4. There were 101,213 fans at a football game.

Problem Solving Workshop
Strategy: Use Logical Reasoning

OBJECTIVE: Solve problems by using the strategy *use logical reasoning*.

Learn the Strategy

Sometimes a problem has clues that help you find the solution. Organizing the clues can help you use logical reasoning to draw conclusions and solve the problem.

Sometimes, the clues can be organized in a list.

Kari, Nora, and June are the only runners in a race. June finishes before Nora. Kari is not last. June is not first.

In what position did each runner finish?

1st	2nd	3rd
Kari	~~Kari~~	~~Kari~~
~~Nora~~	~~Nora~~	Nora
~~June~~	June	~~June~~

Sometimes, the clues can be organized in a Venn diagram.

Ben is thinking of a number from 45 to 60. The sum of the digits is greater than 10. The product of the digits is less than 30.

What number is Ben thinking of?

Sum of Digits >10   Product of Digits <30

59   60   54
56 49   45 51
57 58 47 46 55
   48   50 62 53

Sometimes, the clues can be organized in a table.

Max, Anya, and Troy each have a different kind of pet. The pets are a dog, a cat, and a fish. Troy's pet does not bark or swim. Anya does not have a dog.

What pet does each person have?

	Dog	Cat	Fish
Max	Yes	No	No
Anya	No	No	Yes
Troy	No	Yes	No

TALK Math

Look at the third problem. How many boxes can be filled in using only the clue about Troy's pet? Explain.

NS 1.2 Order and compare whole numbers and decimals to two places. *also* NS 1.1, AF 1.1, MR 1.0, MR 1.1, MR 2.3, MR 2.4, MR 3.2

Use the Strategy

PROBLEM Baseball games were played on Friday, Saturday, and Sunday. The number of people who attended were 32,431; 44,462; and 44,064. The greatest number of people attended Saturday's game. Fewer than 40,000 people attended Sunday's game. How many people attended each day?

Read to Understand

- Use a graphic aid to organize the clues.
- What information is given?

Plan

- What strategy can you use to solve the problem?
  You can use logical reasoning.

Solve

- How can you use the strategy to solve the problem?
  Look at one clue at a time. Make a table to record the information you know, and draw conclusions.

	32,431	44,462	44,064
Friday			
Saturday			
Sunday			

The greatest number of people went to Saturday's game. The greatest number in the problem is 44,462. So, write yes in Saturday's row for 44,462. Write no in the rest of the row for Saturday and the rest of the column for 44,462.

	32,431	44,462	44,064
Friday		No	
Saturday	No	Yes	No
Sunday		No	

Fewer than 40,000 people went to Sunday's game. The only number that is less than 40,000 is 32,431. Write yes in Sunday's row for 32,431 and no in the rest of that row and column.

That leaves one number for Friday, 44,064. Write yes in the table to show this.

	32,431	44,462	44,064
Friday	No	No	Yes
Saturday	No	Yes	No
Sunday	Yes	No	No

So, 44,064 people went to Friday's game; 44,462 people went to Saturday's game; and 32,431 people went to Sunday's game.

Check

- Look back at the problem. Do your work and your answer make sense? Explain.

1. Ed, Nick, Sandra, and Ty collect baseball cards. Ed has less than 500 cards. Sandra has more than 700 cards. Nick has more cards than Sandra. How many baseball cards does each person have?

   First, make a table to organize the information given in the problem.

   Then, use the information given in the problem to complete the table.

   Finally, use logical reasoning to answer the question.

	447	568	703	764
Ed	Yes	No	No	No
Nick	No			
Sandra	No			
Ty	No			

2. Leena, Theo, Chris, Ann, and Bob are waiting in line for hockey tickets. Leena is not first or last. Theo is behind Leena but is not last. Chris is in front of Leena. Ann is behind Bob. In what order are they standing in line?

3. **What if** a basketball team has a score that is a 2-digit number. The sum of the digits is 8. The difference between the digits is 2. The tens digit is less than the ones digit. What is the score?

Problem Solving Strategy Practice

Use logical reasoning to solve.

4. Copy and complete the magic square. Each row and column should have a sum of 12.

2	▪	7
▪	▪	0
▪	1	▪

5. Look at the record crowds list. Richard forgot to write the name of the sport for each crowd. Use these clues to decide what the record crowd is for each sport.

   • Football did not have the smallest record crowd.

   • Soccer's record crowd is greater than 150,000 people.

Record Crowds at a Single Football Game, Baseball Game, and Soccer Game
199,854 people
103,985 people
92,706 people

Mixed Strategy Practice

USE DATA For 6–8, use the information about sports collectors' items shown in the art.

6. Mr. Clay, Mr. Juarez, and Ms. Michaels buy the Annika Sorenstam golf ball, the Tom Brady Super Bowl football, and the Larry Bird signed basketball. Mr. Juarez spends less than $300. Mr. Clay spends more than Ms. Michaels does. Which item does each person buy?

7. **Pose a Problem** Look back at problem 7. Change the items that Mr. Clay wants to buy.

8. **Open-Ended** Mr. Krauss bought a Sandy Koufax baseball card for $135. He used $20-bills, $10-bills, and $5-bills to make exactly $135. The total number of bills that Mr. Krauss used is fewer than 12. What combination of bills might Mr. Krauss have used?

9. Tina saves money to buy a baseball card that costs $30. After 2 weeks, she has $10. After 3 weeks, she has $15. After 4 weeks, she has $20. How long do you think it will take her to save $30?

Choose a STRATEGY

Draw a Diagram or Picture
Make a Model or Act It Out
Make an Organized List
Find a Pattern
Make a Table or Graph
Predict and Test
Work Backward
Solve a Simpler Problem
Write an Equation
Use Logical Reasoning

Babe Ruth signed baseball
Price: $38,157

Wayne Gretzky Hockey Puck
Price: $494

Mickey Mantle game bat
Price: $37,604

Annika Sorenstam golf ball
Price: $287

Larry Bird signed basketball
Price: $326

Tom Brady signed Super Bowl XXIX football
Price: $499

CHALLENGE YOURSELF

More kids than ever before are playing sports. For example, in 2005, an average of 17,500,000 kids were playing soccer, 204,000 were playing lacrosse, and 2,200,000 kids were playing baseball.

10. Mariah plays lacrosse. Compared to soccer and baseball, is she part of a group that has the most kids participating or the least?

11. George is writing down the number of kids that participate in each type of sport. He wrote down the number for football incorrectly. He knows that the number is less than the numbers for soccer and baseball, but more than the number for lacrosse. Could the number be 200,600 or 260,000? **Explain** how you know.

 **Extra Practice**

Set A Write each number in two other forms. (pp. 4–7)

1. 700,000 + 3,000 + 600 + 4

2. 27,683

3. seventy-six thousand, four hundred thirty-two

4. eight hundred ninety-one thousand, two hundred fifty

5. 116,508,906

6. 60,000 + 800 + 90

Set B Use the number 827,916,401. (pp. 10–11)

1. Write the name of the period that has the digits 827.

2. Write the name of the period that has the digits 916.

3. Write the digit in the ten millions place.

4. Write the digit in the thousands place.

5. Write the value of the digit 8.

6. Write the value of the digit 9.

Set C Compare. Write <, >, or = for each ●. (pp. 12–15)

1. 1,409 ● 1,389

2. 6,794 ● 8,005

3. 56,006 ● 56,006

4. 37,106 ● 37,008

5. 10,006 ● 2,789

6. 6,807,043 ● 6,870,034

7. 4,345,119 ● 535,119

8. 88,416 ● 101,871,415

9. 2,124,156 ● 1,124,156

10. Doug's family drove 768 miles on Saturday and 524 miles on Sunday. On which day did they drive farther?

11. During the school book fair, 1,123 books were sold the first week and 1,032 books were sold the second week. During which week were fewer books sold?

Set D Write the numbers in order from least to greatest. (pp. 16–19)

1. 48,004; 48,040; 40,804

2. 30,004; 3,074; 3,704

3. 522,818; 55,945; 600,961

4. 437,408; 428,509; 420,320

5. 221,829,459; 283,000; 2,820,999

6. 5,408,517; 5,460,500; 4,558,590

7. Sales at Toy Mart for three days this week were $2,571; $1,897; and $3,342. Which amount is the greatest?

8. Theater attendance for performances on Friday was 16,207 people, for Saturday was 28,771 people, and for Sunday was 16,270 people. On which day was attendance the least?

Technology
Use Harcourt Mega Math, The Number Games, *Number Line Mine*, Levels A, B.

PRACTICE GAME

Climb the Math Mountain

 Who's Climbing

2 or 3 players

Get Your Climbing Gear!

- Number cards
  (0–9, three of each)
- Coins (a different kind of
  coin for each player)
- Paper

Camp 7

Camp 5

Camp 6

Camp 4

Camp 3

Camp 2

Camp 1

Start Climbing!

■ Each player draws 6 horizontal lines on a sheet of paper. Each line needs to be long enough to fit a number card on it.

■ Each player selects a different kind of coin and places the coin on CAMP 1. Players shuffle the number cards and place them facedown in a stack.

■ The object of the game is to make the greatest number. Players take turns drawing a card and placing it on one of his or her 6 lines until each player has made a 6-digit number.

■ Once a player has placed a number card on a line, it cannot be moved.

■ The player with the greatest number moves his or her coin up the mountain to the next camp. If the numbers are the same, each player moves to the next camp.

■ Players return the number cards to the stack, shuffle them, and repeat the steps to play another round.

■ The first player to reach CAMP 7 wins.

 # Chapter 1 Review/Test

Check Vocabulary and Concepts

Choose the best term from the box.

1. One __?__ is equal to 10 hundred thousands. (O━ NS 1.1, p. 9)

2. In 549,167,001 the digits 1, 6, and 7 are in the same __?__. (O━ NS 1.1, p. 5)

Check Skills

Write each number in two other forms. (O━ NS 1.1, pp. 4–7, 10–11)

3. two hundred thirty-four thousand, one hundred forty-six

4. 78,091

5. 30,000,000 + 600,000 + 8,000 + 500 + 7

6. fifty-three million, seven hundred thousand, eighty

7. 702,655

8. 1,000,000 + 40,000 + 1,000 + 30

Write the value of the underlined digit in each number. (O━ NS 1.1, pp. 4–7)

9. 90,6̲59

10. 5̲01,462

11. 4,7̲15,001

12. 804̲,183,712

13. 3̲42,500,654

Compare. Write <, >, or = for each ●. (O━ NS 1.2, pp. 12–15)

14. 27,985 ● 28,064

15. 523,406 ● 523,406

16. 3,416,125 ● 3,408,926

Write numbers in order from least to greatest. (O━ NS 1.2, pp. 16–19)

17. 207,409; 270,210,009; 27,420

18. 7,029,400; 6,258,414; 6,285,484

Check Problem Solving

Solve. (O━ NS 1.2, MR 2.0, pp. 20–23)

19. George is thinking of a number between 70 and 90. The sum of the digits is less than 12. The product of the digits is greater than 25. What is George's number?

20. ⎡WRITE Math⎤ ▸ Matt and his 3 friends played an electronic game. Their scores are shown at the right. Tina had more than 10,000 points. Rosa had more points than Tina. Sam had less than 5,000 points. How many points did each friend have? Show a table or an organized list that supports your solution.

PLAYER A............8,450

PLAYER B............10,320

PLAYER C............11,080

PLAYER D............4,900

GO ONLINE Technology Use *Online Assessment.*

Enrich • Counting in Other Cultures
Numeration Systems

Our numeration system uses Arabic numerals, or digits 0–9, and is based on groupings of ten. Some ancient cultures had numeration systems that used other numerals or symbols to represent numbers. The table below compares Arabic, Roman, and Egyptian numerals.

Arabic	0	1	2	3	4	5	6	7	8	9	10	50	100	500	1000
Roman		I	II	III	IV	V	VI	VII	VIII	IX	X	L	C	D	M
Egyptian		I	II	III	II II	III II	III III	IIII III	IIII IIII	IIIII IIII	∩		℮		⚱

To write Roman numerals as Arabic numerals:

- Add if the values of the symbols are the same or if they decrease from left to right. A symbol cannot repeat more than 3 times.
- Subtract if a symbol's value is less than the value of the symbol to its right.

Examples

A Write CXIII in Arabic numerals.

Think: C represents 100, X represents 10, and each I represents 1.

So, CXIII is 100 + 10 + 1 + 1 + 1, or 113.

B Write MCD in Arabic numerals.

Think: M represents 1,000, C represents 100, and D represents 500.

Since C < D, CD is 500 − 100, or 400. So, MCD is 1,000 + 400, or 1,400.

To write Egyptian numerals as Arabic numerals: Find the sum of the symbols.

C Write ⚱℮℮III in Arabic numerals.

Think: ⚱ represents 1,000, ℮ represents 100, and I represents 1.

So, ⚱℮℮III is 1,000 + 100 + 100 + 1 + 1 + 1, or 1,203.

D Write ⚱⚱∩∩∩∩∩ in Arabic numerals.

Think: ⚱ represents 1,000, and ∩ represents 10.

So, ⚱⚱∩∩∩∩∩ is 1,000 + 1,000 + 10 + 10 + 10 + 10 + 10, or 2,060.

Try It

Write Roman numerals as Arabic numerals.

1. LXXXVIII **2.** CCXCV **3.** MCMXIV **4.** MMDCIX

Write Egyptian numerals as Arabic numerals.

5. ∩IIII **6.** ℮℮℮∩∩IIIIII **7.** ℮℮℮℮ ℮℮℮℮ ∩∩ IIII **8.** ⚱⚱℮℮∩∩∩∩ ℮℮∩∩

WRITE Math > **Explain** the advantages in writing numbers using the Arabic numeration system compared with using the Roman and Egyptian numeration systems.

Number Sense

1. In 2002, the number of cats in the United States was about seventy-six million, four hundred thirty thousand. What is this number in standard form? (O—n NS 1.1)

A 76,430   **C** 76,430,000

B 76,000,430   **D** 760,430,000

 Test Tip   **Understand the problem.**

See item 2. Be sure you understand what the problem asks. Item 2 asks you to find a set of numbers that is in order from *greatest to least*. So, a list that is in order from least to greatest would be incorrect.

2. Which set of numbers is in order from greatest to least? (O—n NS 1.2)

A 736,849; 739,489; 1,725,089

B 1,725,089; 739,489; 736,849

C 1,725,089; 736,849; 739,489

D 739,489; 736,849; 1,725,089

3. Which of the following is the number 305,082? (O—n NS 1.1)

A 300,000 + 50,000 + 800 + 2

B 300,000 + 50,000 + 80 + 2

C 30,000 + 5,000 + 800 + 2

D 300,000 + 5,000 + 80 + 2

4. **WRITE Math** ▸ Wendy says that 235,340 is exactly 1,000 less than 245,340. Do you agree? **Explain** how you know.

(O—n NS 1.1)

Algebra and Functions

5. The table below shows the number of players needed to make a certain number of volleyball teams.

Volleyball				
Number of Teams	1	2	3	4
Number of Players	6	12	18	24

How many players would be needed to make 8 volleyball teams? (Grade 3 O—n AF 2.1)

A 6   **C** 36

B 32   **D** 48

6. Ms. Gomez bought 24 pens. The pens are in 3 packs with the same number of pens in each pack. Which number sentence shows how to find the number of pens in each pack?

(Grade 3 O—n AF 1.1)

A $24 - 3 = $ ■

B $24 \div 3 = $ ■

C $24 + 3 = $ ■

D $24 \times 3 = $ ■

7. What symbol goes in the box to make this number sentence true? (Grade 3 O—n AF 1.3)

$$4 \ ■ \ 7 = 28$$

A $\times$ **C** $+$

B $\div$ **D** $-$

8. **WRITE Math** ▸ **Explain** how to find the number that makes this number sentence true. (Grade 3 AF 1.2)

$$■ - 5 = 15$$

Measurement and Geometry

9. Which of these is a pentagon?

(Grade 3 ⊙━π MG 2.1)

A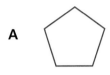

B

C

D

10. What is the area of this figure?

(Grade 3 ⊙━π MG 1.2)

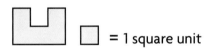 ☐ = 1 square unit

  F 3 square units

  G 4 square units

  H 5 square units

  J 6 square units

11. **WRITE Math** Raul says that an isosceles triangle can also be a right triangle. Do you agree? **Explain** your answer.

(Grade 3 ⊙━π MG 2.2)

Statistics, Data Analysis, and Probability

12. The bar graph shows the number of books Ed read during the past two months. How many books did Ed read in the two months altogether?

(Grade 3 ⊙━π SDAP 1.3)

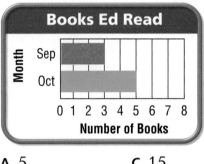

  A 5   **C** 15

  B 8   **D** 20

13. Look at the tally chart. In how many spins did the pointer not stop on blue?

(Grade 3 ⊙━π SDAP 1.2)

Spinner Experiment	
Outcome	**Tally**
Red	|||
Yellow	||||
Blue	⅏ ||||

  F 3   **H** 7

  G 4   **J** 9

14. **WRITE Math** A bag has 3 yellow, 4 red, and 2 blue marbles all the same size. Which term best describes the probability of pulling a blue marble from the bag—*certain, likely, unlikely,* or *impossible*? **Explain** your answer.

(Grade 3 ⊙━π SDAP 1.1)

2 Addition and Subtraction: Mental Math and Estimation

The Big Idea Mental math and estimation are strategies for solving addition and subtraction of multidigit numbers.

CALIFORNIA FAST FACT

The San Diego Symphony plays at Copley Symphony Hall. The hall has seats for 2,252 people. Each year, the Symphony gives more than 100 concerts.

Investigate

Copley Symphony Hall in San Diego holds performances several days a week. Use estimation and the data in the table to write a sales report. Use subtraction in your sales report to compare the numbers of tickets sold each week.

Copley Symphony Hall Performance Ticket Sales		
Section	Week 1	Week 2
Floor Level	4,740	5,304
Grand Tier	648	812
Mezzanine	996	1,224
Balcony	1,208	1,461

GO ONLINE

Technology
Student pages are available in the Student eBook.

Check your understanding of important skills needed for success in Chapter 2.

▶ **Two-Digit Addition and Subtraction**

Find the sum or difference.

1. 22 + 41

2. 58 − 17

3. 26 + 52

4. 79 − 33

5. 61 + 25

6. 45 − 14

7. 34 + 55

8. 29 − 12

▶ **Place Value Through Millions**

Write the value of the underlined digit.

9. 5,3<u>9</u>0

10. <u>7</u>,033

11. 1,72<u>8</u>

12. 6,8<u>3</u>5

13. 8,3<u>9</u>3,781

14. 6,741,<u>4</u>92

15. 1,193,7<u>0</u>3

16. 4,<u>4</u>54,764

17. <u>1</u>,634,142

18. 2,728,<u>9</u>00

19. 3,57<u>2</u>,193

20. 2,467,8<u>4</u>1

▶ **Addition Properties**

Find each sum.

21. $17 + 0 = \blacksquare$

22. $8 + 7 = \blacksquare$
    $7 + 8 = \blacksquare$

23. $4 + (7 + 5) = \blacksquare$
    $(4 + 7) + 5 = \blacksquare$

24. $11 + (1 + 9) = \blacksquare$
    $9 + 12 = \blacksquare$

25. $(3 + 7) + 9 = \blacksquare$
    $3 + (7 + 9) = \blacksquare$

26. $0 + 11 = \blacksquare$

VOCABULARY POWER

CHAPTER VOCABULARY

compatible numbers
difference
estimate
fact family
inverse
inverse operations
round
pattern
sum

WARM-UP WORDS

inverse operations Operations that undo each other. Addition and subtraction are inverse operations.

fact family a set of related addition and subtraction equations

round to replace a number with another number that tells about how many or how much

LESSON

1

ALGEBRA

Relate Addition and Subtraction

OBJECTIVE: Use the inverse relationship between addition and subtraction to solve problems.

Quick Review

1. $9 + 4 = \blacksquare$
2. $12 - 6 = \blacksquare$
3. $7 + 8 = \blacksquare$
4. $11 - 4 = \blacksquare$
5. $5 + 8 = \blacksquare$

Vocabulary

inverse operations

fact family

Learn

PROBLEM Justin can do 8 pull-ups in a row. His older brother Marcus can do 15 pull-ups in a row. How many more pull-ups can Marcus do than Justin?

Addition and subtraction are opposites, or **inverse operations**. One operation undoes the other. A set of related addition and subtraction sentences using the same numbers is a **fact family**.

Example Use the inverse operation and a related fact.
Subtract. $15 - 8$

> Think: $\blacksquare + 8 = 15$
>
> Use a fact family to solve the problem.
>
> $7 + 8 = 15$, so $15 - 8 = 7$.

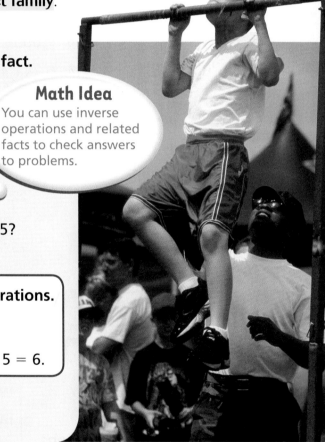

Math Idea
You can use inverse operations and related facts to check answers to problems.

So, Marcus can do 7 more pull-ups than Justin.

• What are the facts in the fact family for 7, 8, and 15?

More Examples Find the missing number.

> **A** Use related facts.
> $13 - \blacksquare = 4$
> Think: $13 - 4 = \blacksquare$
> $13 - 4 = 9$, so $13 - 9 = 4$.

> **B** Use inverse operations.
> $\blacksquare - 5 = 6$
> Think: $5 + 6 = \blacksquare$
> $5 + 6 = 11$, so $11 - 5 = 6$.

• What operation can you use to solve the problem
$\blacksquare + 8 = 12$? Explain.

Guided Practice

1. Keisha did 8 more push-ups than Tara did. Keisha did 17 push-ups. How many push-ups did Tara do? Copy and complete the related addition fact. Then use it to solve the problem.

   $17 - 8 = \blacksquare$

   $8 + \blacksquare = 17$

O→ NS 3.0 Students solve problems involving addition, subtraction, multiplication, and division of whole numbers and understand the relationships among the operations. *also* **AF 1.1, MR 1.1, MR 2.3, MR 2.4, MR 3.2**

Write a related fact. Use it to complete the number sentence.

2. $14 - \blacksquare = 8$ **3.** $5 + \blacksquare = 12$ ✅ **4.** $\blacksquare - 9 = 6$ ✅ **5.** $\blacksquare + 4 = 11$

6. **TALK Math** **Explain** why the fact family with the numbers 8 and 16 only has two number sentences instead of four.

Independent Practice and Problem Solving

Write a related fact. Use it to complete the number sentence.

7. $11 - \blacksquare = 7$ **8.** $\blacksquare + 7 = 13$ **9.** $8 + \blacksquare = 12$ **10.** $\blacksquare + 5 = 11$

11. $\blacksquare - 9 = 8$ **12.** $6 + \blacksquare = 12$ **13.** $10 - \blacksquare = 7$ **14.** $\blacksquare - 3 = 8$

15. $\blacksquare - 4 = 8$ **16.** $3 + \blacksquare = 9$ **17.** $11 - \blacksquare = 2$ **18.** $\blacksquare + 4 = 13$

Write the fact family for each set of numbers.

19. 4, 7, 11   **20.** 5, 5, 10   **21.** 6, 7, 13   **22.** 3, 9, 12

For 23–24, use the pictograph.

23. How many more votes did jumping-jacks get than push-ups? What related facts can you use to solve this problem?

24. If sit-ups gets 4 more votes, how many votes will sit-ups and push-ups have in all?

25. **WRITE Math** **What's the Error?** Jan was asked to write a related fact for $7 + 4 = 11$. She wrote $7 - 4 = 3$. **Explain** why Jan's answer is incorrect. What is the correct answer?

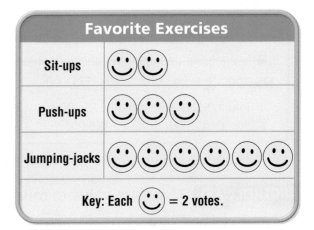

Achieving the Standards

26. A newspaper ad showed these prices: mini-van: $30,010; truck: $29,998; sports car: $30,100. List the prices in order from least to greatest. (O–π NS 1.2, p. 19)

27. What are five numbers that are less than 2,014 but greater than 1,987? (O–π NS 1.2, p. 19)

28. Sean has $3,866 in his college fund. Round the amount in his college fund to the nearest thousand. (Grade 3, NS 1.4)

29. **Test Prep** Which of the following sets of numbers cannot be used to make a fact family?

    A 8, 9, 17   **C** 1, 3, 5

    B 7, 7, 14   **D** 12, 9, 3

Round Whole Numbers Through Millions

OBJECTIVE: Round whole numbers through the millions to the nearest 10, 100, 1,000, 10,000, or 100,000.

Quick Review

Write the value of the underlined digit.

1. 2<u>3</u>4
2. <u>1</u>,547
3. 25,65<u>2</u>
4. 35<u>6</u>,721
5. 1,756,<u>4</u>32

Vocabulary

round

Learn

PROBLEM Each year, immigrants from around the world come to the United States. In 2003, California schools welcomed 175,090 immigrant students.

When you **round** a number, you replace it with a number that tells about how many or about how much. Rounded numbers are often easier to compute. What is 175,090 rounded to the nearest thousand?

ONE WAY Use a number line.

175,090

175,000   175,500   176,000

Think: 175,090 is between 175,000 and 176,000. 175,090 is closer to 175,000 than to 176,000.

So, 175,090 rounded to the nearest thousand is 175,000.

ANOTHER WAY Use place value to round numbers.

Round 175,090 to the nearest hundred thousand.

- Find the place to which you want to round.

- Look at the digit to the right. If the digit to the right is *less than 5*, the digit in the rounding place stays the same. If the digit to the right is *5 or greater*, the digit in the rounding place increases by 1.

- Change all the digits to the right of the rounding place to zero.

Place to be rounded to: hundred thousands
↓
175,090
↓
175,090

The digit in the ten thousands place is 7.

Since 7 > 5, the digit 1 increases by 1.

175,090 → 200,000

So, 175,090 rounded to the nearest hundred thousand is 200,000.

- When might you use rounded numbers instead of exact numbers? Explain.

34

NS 1.3 Round whole numbers through the millions to the nearest ten, hundred, thousand, ten thousand, or hundred thousand. *also* NS 1.0, NS 1.4, MR 2.3, MR 2.4, MR 3.2

Example

The table shows distances immigrants may travel to Houston, Texas, from different cities around the world. About how far do immigrants from London and Frankfurt travel to Houston?

Round the distances below to the nearest thousand miles.

London to Houston   4,860 → 5,000

Frankfurt to Houston   5,245 → 5,000

So, immigrants from London and Frankfurt travel about 5,000 miles to Houston.

Distances Immigrants Travel to Houston, Texas	
From	Distance (in miles)
Bangkok, Thailand	9,253
Frankfurt, Germany	5,245
London, England	4,860
New Delhi, India	8,366
Tel Aviv, Israel	7,079
Tokyo, Japan	6,682

More Examples

Ⓐ Round to the nearest ten thousand.

45,278 is between 40,000 and 50,000.

place to be rounded to ↓   Look at the thousands digit. Since 5 = 5, the digit 4 increases by 1.

4<u>5</u>,278

So, 45,278 rounded to the nearest ten thousand is 50,000.

Ⓑ Round to the nearest hundred thousand.

63,825,914 is between 63,800,000 and 63,900,000.

place to be rounded to ↓   Look at the ten thousands digit. Since 2 < 5, the digit 8 stays the same.

63,8<u>2</u>5,914

So, 63,825,914 rounded to the nearest hundred thousand is 63,800,000.

Ⓒ Round to the nearest hundred.

7,832 is between 7,800 and 7,900.

place to be rounded to ↓   Look at the tens digit. Since 3 < 5, the digit 8 stays the same.

7,8<u>3</u>2

So, 7,832 rounded to the nearest hundred is 7,800.

Ⓓ Round to the nearest ten dollars.

$697 is between $690 and $700.

place to be rounded to ↓   Look at the ones digit. Since 7 > 5, the digit 9 increases by 1. Regroup 10 tens as 1 hundred.

$69<u>7</u>

So, $697 rounded to the nearest ten dollars is $700.

- How does understanding place value help you round numbers?

ERROR ALERT

When you round a 9 to the next digit, remember to regroup to the next place value.

Guided Practice

1. In 2002, a total of 71,105 immigrants came to the United States from India. Use the number line to round this number to the nearest hundred.

71,105
↓

71,100   71,150   71,200

 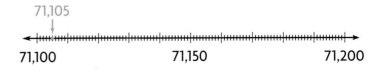

Round each number to the place value of the underlined digit.

2. 3<u>4</u>,567

3. $1,<u>2</u>67

4. $<u>2</u>34

✔**5.** 3,<u>4</u>76,321

Round each number to the nearest ten, hundred, thousand, and hundred thousand.

6. 657,809

7. 709,365

8. 6,442,896

✔**9.** 128,851,342

10. [TALK Math] **Describe** all the numbers that, when rounded to the nearest thousand, are 312,000.

Independent Practice and Problem Solving

Round each number to the place value of the underlined digit.

11. <u>3</u>,769

12. <u>7</u>,507

13. <u>1</u>8,682

14. 57,9<u>4</u>5

15. 11,56<u>4</u>,408

16. 44,<u>7</u>92,300

17. $82,1<u>9</u>2,157

18. $326,19<u>9</u>,814

Round each number to the nearest ten, hundred, thousand, and hundred thousand.

19. 6,144,683

20. 5,351,169

21. 7,826,431

22. 2,332,435

23. 1,943,232

24. 7,899,161

25. 243,346,561

26. 762,974,233

27. Write five numbers that round to 540,000.

28. What is the greatest whole number that rounds to 300,000? What is the least?

29. **Reasoning** Write a number that rounds to 47,000 when rounded to the nearest thousand and to 50,000 when rounded to the nearest ten thousand.

30. ≡**FAST FACT** In 2002, Michigan had 21,787 immigrants. Round this number to the nearest thousand and the nearest ten thousand. Which rounded number is closer to the original number?

USE DATA For 31–32, use the table.

31. Is the number of immigrants from China closer to 61,000 or 62,000?

32. What is the greatest place to which you might round all three numbers?

33. Euro's answer rounds to 7,000. Write three numbers that could be his exact answer.

34. [WRITE Math] **Explain** how to round 982,145 to the nearest hundred thousand.

Immigrants Welcomed to U.S from Selected Countries, 2002

Country	Number
China	61,282
Mexico	219,380
Philippines	51,308

[**Extra Practice** on page 50, Set B]

CD ROM **Technology**
Use Harcourt Mega Math, Fraction Action, *Number Line Mine,* Level C.

35. Diane has 12 oranges. After she gives some to Erin, she has 9 oranges left. Use ▨ to write a number sentence to find how many oranges she gave Erin. Then solve the problem. (AF 1.1, p.32)

36. **Test Prep** Which number rounds to 300,000?

   A 389,001   C 252,348

   B 351,213   D 249,899

37. Write two million, twenty thousand, two hundred ninety in standard form.
   (O━┓ NS 1.1, p. 10)

38. Write the numbers in order from least to greatest: 1,256; 1,526; 1,186; 1,206.
   (O━┓ NS 1.2, p. 16)

39. **Test Prep** To find the rounded number that is closest to 3,264,587, to what place do you round?

Problem Solving and Reasoning

NUMBER SENSE Sometimes rounded numbers are used because you do not need to know exact amounts. At other times, the exact amounts cannot be counted or measured, or they may change often. Which numbers in the paragraph below are rounded?

> The Ellis Island Immigration Museum is open between 9:30 A.M. and 5:00 P.M. Almost 2,000,000 people visit the museum each year. Many visitors take guided tours that last about 50 minutes. There are 3 floors of exhibits at the museum.
> **Think:** Words like *almost* and *about* tell you that a number is rounded.

So, the numbers 2,000,000 and 50 are rounded because they may change often.

Identify any rounded numbers. Explain why you think exact numbers are not used.

1. The museum has taped more than 1,300 interviews with immigrants who passed through Ellis Island. The oldest person interviewed was 106 years old, and the youngest was 46.

2. A ferry ride to Ellis Island costs $11.50 for adults and children 13 and older, $9.50 for seniors, and $4.50 for children 4–12. The ferry ride takes about 10 minutes. Don's mother has $60 to buy ferry tickets for 5 people.

▲ Between 1892 and 1954, about 12,000,000 immigrants entered the U.S. through Ellis Island.

MENTAL MATH
Addition and Subtraction Patterns

OBJECTIVE: Identify and use patterns in addition and subtraction.

Quick Review

1. $5 + 8$
2. $16 - 9$
3. $3 + 9$
4. $12 - 6$
5. $9 + 7$

Learn

PROBLEM The table shows the approximate numbers of plant and animal species in the United States that are threatened, or in danger of becoming extinct. About how many plant and animal species are endangered in all?

It is easy to mentally add or subtract tens, hundreds, thousands, and ten thousands if you use basic facts and a pattern.

Endangered Plant and Animal Species in the United States

Type of Species	Approximate Number
Animals	400
Plants	600

Example Add. $600 + 400$

$6 + 4 = 10$	6 ones + 4 ones = 10 ones $\leftarrow$ basic fact
$60 + 40 = 100$	6 tens + 4 tens = 10 tens
$600 + 400 = 1,000$	6 hundreds + 4 hundreds = 10 hundreds

So, there are about 1,000 threatened or endangered plant and animal species in the United States.

• What pattern do you see in the number sentences above?

Math Idea
As the number of zeros being added increases, the number of zeros in the sum increases. The same is true when you subtract.

More Examples Use a basic fact and a pattern.

A
$14 - 6 = 8 \leftarrow$ basic fact
$140 - 60 = 80$
$1,400 - 600 = 800$
$14,000 - 6,000 = 8,000$

B
$5 + 5 = 10 \leftarrow$ basic fact
$50 + 50 = 100$
$500 + 500 = 1,000$
$5,000 + 5,000 = 10,000$

Guided Practice

1. Write a basic fact that can help you subtract 300 from 1,000 mentally. Use it and a pattern to solve the problem.

$1,000 - 300 = \blacksquare$

Use mental math to complete the pattern.

2. $5 + 8 = 13$
$50 + 80 = \blacksquare$
$500 + 800 = \blacksquare$

3. $12 - 6 = \blacksquare$
$120 - 60 = \blacksquare$
$1,200 - 600 = \blacksquare$

4. $9 + 5 = 14$
$\blacksquare + 50 = 140$
$900 + 500 = \blacksquare$

5. $130 - \blacksquare = 50$
$\blacksquare - 800 = 500$
$13,000 - \blacksquare = 5,000$

6. **TALK Math** **Explain** why $130,000 - 80,000$ is easier to subtract than $924 - 387$.

NS 3.0 Students solve problems involving addition, subtraction, multiplication, and division of whole numbers and understand the relationships among the operations. *also* AF 1.1; MR 1.1, MR 2.0, MR 2.3, MR 2.4, MR 3.2

Use mental math to complete the pattern.

7. ■ + 6 = 10
40 + ■ = 100
400 + 600 = ■
4,000 + 6,000 = ■

8. ■ − 8 = 7
150 − 80 = ■
1,500 − ■ = 700
15,000 − 8,000 = ■

9. ■ − 7 = 7
140 − ■ = 70
■ − 700 = 700
14,000 − 7,000 = ■

10. 9 + 4 = ■
90 + ■ = 130
900 + 400 = ■
■ + 4,000 = 13,000

11. ■ − 6 = 5
110 − 60 = ■
1,100 − ■ = 500
11,000 − 6,000 = ■

12. 3 + ■ = 12
30 + ■ = 120
■ + 900 = 1,200
3,000 + 9,000 = ■

Use mental math patterns to find the sum or difference.

13. 50 + 70

14. 800 + 900

15. 130 − 60

16. 1,100 − 400

17. 7,000 + 9,000

18. 60,000 + 70,000

19. 12,000 − 7,000

20. 110,000 − 80,000

USE DATA For 21–23, use the bar graph.

21. How many more pandas are there in the wild than mountain gorillas and Spanish eagles combined?

22. If the number of mountain gorillas increases by 50 each year, how many will there be in 3 years?

23. **Pose a Problem** Use the information in the graph to write a mental math problem. Have a classmate solve the problem.

24. **WRITE Math** **What's the Error?** Jason thinks the sum of 500 + 900 is 140,000. Describe Jason's mistake and find the correct sum.

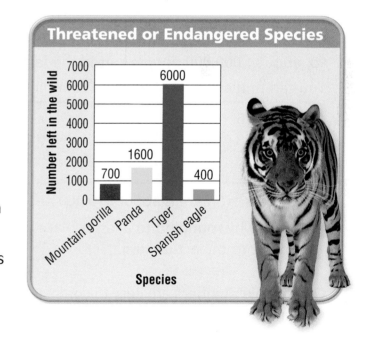

Threatened or Endangered Species

Species

Achieving the Standards

25. What related fact can you use to find the value of ■ in 13 − ■ = 9? (AF 1.1, p. 32)

26. Round 3,017,920 to the nearest thousand. (NS 1.3, p. 34)

27. What is the perimeter of a square with sides measuring 3 feet? (Grade 3 MG 1.3)

28. Which number is represented by ■?

800 + ■ = 1,500

A 70

C 7,000

B 700

D 70,000

MENTAL MATH

Estimate Sums and Differences

OBJECTIVE: Estimate sums and differences.

Learn

PROBLEM In 1995, the Orange County Fair in California had 698,976 visitors. By 2004, attendance had increased by 265,008 visitors. About how many people visited the fair in 2004?

You can estimate to find about how many people.
An **estimate** is a number close to an exact amount.

ONE WAY Use rounding.

Estimate the sum. 698,976 + 265,008

698,976	→	700,000
+ 265,008	→	+ 300,000
		1,000,000

Round each number to the nearest hundred thousand. Then add.

So, about 1,000,000 people visited the fair in 2004.

You can find a closer estimate by rounding to a lesser place.

698,976	→	700,000
+ 265,008	→	+ 270,000
		970,000

Round each number to the nearest ten thousand. Then add.

So, a closer estimate is about 970,000 people.

• Explain why rounding to a lesser place gives a closer estimate to the actual sum.

Compatible numbers are easy to compute mentally. Use properties and compatible numbers to estimate a sum.

ANOTHER WAY Use compatible numbers and properties.

Estimate the sum. 46 + 28 + 67

46 + 28 + 67	Find compatible numbers. **Think:** 40 + 60 = 100
40 + 28 + 60	Use the Commutative Property.
28 + 40 + 60	
28 + (40 + 60)	Use the Associative Property.
28 + 100 = 128	

So, the sum is about 128.

Quick Review

Round to the place of the underlined digit.

1. 8<u>1</u>5
2. <u>9</u>,374
3. 60,<u>2</u>96
4. 1<u>4</u>2,841
5. 9,66<u>4</u>,053

Vocabulary

estimate

compatible numbers

Remember

The Commutative Property of Addition states that you can add two or more numbers in any order and the sum remains the same.
4 + 5 = 5 + 4
The Associative Property of Addition states that you can group numbers in different ways and the sum remains the same.
4 + (6 + 2) = (4 + 6) + 2

40

NS 2.1 Estimate and compute the sum or difference of whole numbers and positive decimals to two places. *also* NS 1.3, MR 2.0, MR 2.1, MR 2.3, MR 2.4, MR 3.2

Estimate Differences

ONE WAY Use rounding.

In 2003, the Orange County Fair had 881,596 visitors. In 1999, there were 724,561 visitors. About how many more visitors came in 2003?

Estimate the difference. 881,596 − 724,561

881,596	→	900,000
− 724,561	→	− 700,000
		200,000

Round each number to the nearest hundred thousand.

So, about 200,000 more visitors came to the fair in 2003.

You can find a closer estimate by rounding to a lesser place.

881,596	→	880,000
− 724,561	→	− 720,000
		160,000

Round each number to the nearest ten thousand.

So, a closer estimate is 160,000 more people.

ANOTHER WAY Use compatible numbers.

In 2002, the Orange County Fair judged 14,623 exhibits and the Humboldt County Fair judged 5,391 exhibits. About how many more exhibits were judged at the Orange County Fair?

Estimate the difference. 14,623 − 5,391

14,623	→	15,000
− 5,391	→	− 5,000
		10,000

Think: 15,000 − 5,000 is easy to compute mentally.

So, the Orange County Fair judged about 10,000 more exhibits.

Guided Practice

1. Estimate 300,612 + 400,285 by rounding to the nearest hundred thousand. Then estimate the sum by rounding to the nearest hundred. Which estimate is closer to the exact sum?

Use rounding to estimate.

2.	12,591	3.	9,362	4.	76,368	5.	429,832	6.	6,362
	+ 36,284		+ 5,781		− 31,842		+ 473,099		− 1,714

Use compatible numbers to estimate.

7.	4,072 + 6,581	**8.**	1,639 − 947	**9.**	28,322 − 16,378	**10.**	37,137 + 69,205	✓**11.**	1,749,206 + 4,222,358

12. **TALK Math** Explain why you can find more than one estimate for a sum or difference.

Independent Practice and Problem Solving

Use rounding to estimate.

13.	7,409 + 6,186	**14.**	8,932 − 5,341	**15.**	267,372 + 542,949	**16.**	64,372 − 18,754	**17.**	814,592 − 273,491
18.	259 + 684	**19.**	746 − 309	**20.**	23,592 + 41,073	**21.**	9,472 − 2,612	**22.**	6,258,942 − 2,735,172

Use compatible numbers to estimate.

23. 10,732 − 8,961   **24.** 1,070 − 508   **25.** 22,579 − 16,067

26. 384 + 225 + 587   **27.** 282 + 25 + 51 + 172   **28.** 2,467 + 511 + 1,124 + 542

Adjust the estimate to make it closer to the exact sum or difference.

29. 7,395 + 4,098
Estimate: 11,000

30. 68,905 − 23,241
Estimate: 50,000

31. 25,319 − 12,946
Estimate: 20,000

32. 327 + 198
Estimate: 500

33. 321,422 + 163,272
Estimate: 500,000

34. 439,957 − 221,893
Estimate: 200,000

USE DATA For 35–38, use the table.

35. There were 249,640 more visitors to the fair in 2005 than in 2000. Estimate the attendance at the fair in 2005.

36. About how many more visitors were there in 2000 than in 1996?

37. Between which two years did the attendance increase by 1,500?

38. Corbin estimated the difference in attendance from 1999 to 2000 to be about 100,000. Give a closer estimate.

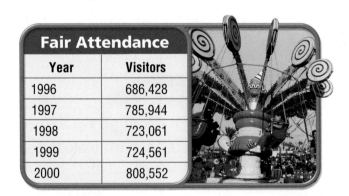

Fair Attendance	
Year	**Visitors**
1996	686,428
1997	785,944
1998	723,061
1999	724,561
2000	808,552

39. **WRITE Math** Explain how a rounded sum compares to the exact sum if the addends are rounded to a lesser place value.

40. A new car costs $28,355. To the nearest $1,000, about how much does the car cost? (O—ᴄ NS 1.3, p. 34)

41. Kevin needs $995 for a school trip. He has saved $582. How much more does he have to save? (Grade 3, NS 2.1)

42. A movie was seen by 8,438 people on Friday, 8,694 people on Saturday, and 8,004 people on Sunday. On which day did the greatest number of people see the movie? (O—ᴄ NS 1.2, p. 12)

43. Test Prep A plane at a height of 32,198 feet drops 14,824 feet to collect weather data. Which is the best estimate of the plane's height when it collects the data?

    A 10,000 feet   **C** 40,000 feet

    B 15,000 feet   **D** 50,000 feet

44. Test Prep This year, students sold 7,342 magazine subscriptions for a fund raiser. Last year they sold 943 fewer subscriptions. About how many subscriptions did they sell in all last year and this year? **Explain** your answer.

 **Problem Solving and Reasoning**

NUMBER SENSE When you estimate, you get either an overestimate or an underestimate. An **overestimate** is greater than the exact answer. An **underestimate** is less than the exact answer.

On opening night, 11,548 people saw a play. The next night, 21,574 people saw it. About how many people saw the play in all?

Estimate the sum. 11,548 + 21,574

Examples

Ⓐ Round to the greater thousand.

$$
\begin{array}{r}
11,548 \rightarrow 12,000 \\
+\ 21,574 \rightarrow +\ 22,000 \\
\hline
34,000
\end{array}
$$

Both rounded addends are greater than the original addends. So, the estimate is an overestimate.

Ⓑ Round to the lesser thousand.

$$
\begin{array}{r}
11,548 \rightarrow 11,000 \\
+\ 21,574 \rightarrow +\ 21,000 \\
\hline
32,000
\end{array}
$$

Both rounded addends are less than the original addends. So, the estimate is an underestimate.

So, between 32,000 and 34,000 people saw the play.

Tell why the estimate is an overestimate or an underestimate.

1. 7,524 + 1,632
Estimate: 10,000

2. 15,104 + 22,301
Estimate: 37,000

3. 2,414 + 1,206
Estimate: 3,000

4. 25,714 + 36,822
Estimate: 70,000

Mental Math Strategies

OBJECTIVE: Use mental math strategies to find sums and differences.

Quick Review

1. $20 + 50$
2. $300 + 800$
3. $1,300 - 400$
4. $1,100 - 600$
5. $7,000 + 2,000$

Learn

PROBLEM The high school choir and orchestra are giving a concert. There are 56 students in the choir. There are 37 students in the orchestra. At the concert, each student has a chair on the stage. How many chairs are needed?

Sometimes you don't need paper and pencil to add or subtract. Use these strategies to help you add or subtract mentally.

ONE WAY Use the *Break Apart* Strategy.

Ⓐ Addition

Find the sum. $56 + 37$

		Think: $56 = 50 + 6$
Add the tens.	$50 + 30 = 80$	$37 = 30 + 7$
Add the ones.	$6 + 7 = 13$	
Add the sums.	$80 + 13 = 93$	

So, 93 chairs are needed.

Ⓑ Subtraction

Find the difference. $76 - 42$

		Think: $76 = 70 + 6$
Subtract the tens.	$70 - 40 = 30$	$42 = 40 + 2$
Subtract the ones.	$6 - 2 = 4$	
Add the differences.	$30 + 4 = 34$	

So, $76 - 42 = 34$.

• Why do you think this strategy is called the break apart strategy?

More Examples

Ⓒ Addition

Find the sum. $235 + 412$

$$200 + 400 = 600$$
$$30 + 10 = 40$$
$$5 + 2 = 7$$
$$600 + 40 + 7 = 647$$

Ⓓ Subtraction

Find the difference. $458 - 136$

$$400 - 100 = 300$$
$$50 - 30 = 20$$
$$8 - 6 = 2$$
$$300 + 20 + 2 = 322$$

NS 2.1 Estimate and compute the sum or difference of whole numbers and positive decimals to two places. *also* O—ℼ NS 3.0, MR 2.2, MR 2.3, MR 2.4, MR 3.2

E Use a *Friendly Number* Strategy

You can change one number to the nearest 10 and then adjust the other number to add or subtract mentally.

Subtraction is easier if the number you subtract is a friendly number. To get a friendly number, increase the number you subtract to the next ten. Then add the same amount to the other number to adjust the answer.

Find the difference. $56 - 38$

Think: Add to 38 to make a number with 0 ones.

Add 2 to 38 to get 40. $38 + 2 = 40$

Add 2 to 56 to adjust the difference. $56 + 2 = 58$

Subtract. $58 - 40 = 18$

So, $56 - 38 = 18$.

- Why do you use the next friendly ten for 38 instead of 56?

F Use a *Swapping* Strategy

When you add numbers, you can swap digits with the same place value. Sometimes this helps you make a friendly number.

Find the sum. $239 + 194$

Think: 194 is close to the friendly number 200.

Swap the ones digits. $234 + 199$

Add 1 to 199 to get 200. $199 + 1 = 200$

Subtract 1 from 234 to adjust the sum. $234 - 1 = 233$

Add. $200 + 233 = 433$

So, $239 + 194 = 433$.

- Explain how to solve the problem by swapping the digits in a different place.

Guided Practice

1. Find $68 + 56$ mentally. Add 2 to 68 to make the next friendly number. Subtract 2 from 56 to adjust the sum. What is the sum?

Add or subtract mentally. Tell the strategy you used.

2. $86 - 43$ 3. $72 + 39$ 4. $62 - 29$ ✓5. $867 - 425$ ✓6. $145 + 213$

7. **TALK Math** Explain how to find $478 - 215$ using mental math.

Independent Practice and Problem Solving

Add or subtract mentally. Tell the strategy you used.

8. $94 - 57$ **9.** $16 + 58$ **10.** $95 + 36$ **11.** $38 + 75$ **12.** $93 - 46$

13. $152 - 79$ **14.** $238 + 431$ **15.** $286 - 159$ **16.** $723 + 142$ **17.** $442 - 238$

18. $758 - 426$ **19.** $384 + 218$ **20.** $276 + 79$ **21.** $576 - 98$ **22.** $726 - 314$

Find the sum or difference.

23. $462 - 18$ **24.** $79 + 42$ **25.** $134 + 112$ **26.** $27 + 335$ **27.** $86 + 63$

28. $656 - 429$ **29.** $64 + 58$ **30.** $47 - 39$ **31.** $211 + 725$ **32.** $137 - 19$

For 33–35, use the table and mental math.

33. How many instruments make up the orchestra?

34. Use mental math to find how many more strings there are than woodwinds and brass combined.

35. Alyvia has 100 instrument stands. How many more does she need so each instrument has a stand?

36. **WRITE Math** ▸ **Explain** how to find $87 - 53$ using the break apart and friendly number strategies. Which is easier to use?

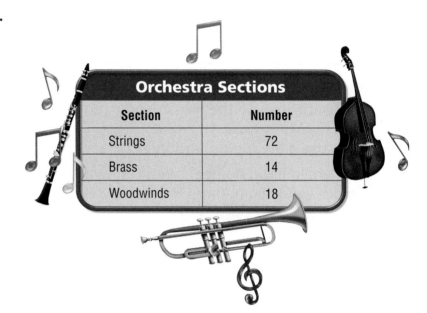

Orchestra Sections

Section	Number
Strings	72
Brass	14
Woodwinds	18

Achieving the Standards

37. Hank's score rounds to 5,400. What is his actual score if the digit in the tens place is 8 and the digit in the ones place is 2? (○━ NS 1.3, p. 34)

38. Vic's class raised $6,980. Ina's class raised $6,890. Which class raised more money? (○━ NS 1.2, p. 12)

39. If Brad tosses two number cubes numbered 1 to 6, is it certain, likely, unlikely, or impossible that both cubes will land on 4? (Grade 3 SDAP 1.1)

40. **Test Prep** Dan wants to buy an apple that costs 48¢ and a banana that costs 45¢. He adds 2¢ to 48¢ to find the total mentally. How should he adjust the sum to find the total?

A add 2¢ to 45¢

B add 5¢ to 45¢

C subtract 2¢ from 45¢

D subtract 5¢ from 45¢

Write to Explain

Writing to explain how you use mental math strategies can help you learn how to add and subtract greater numbers in your head.

Three groups of students are practicing for a dance concert. There are 19 students in the first group, 17 students in the second group, and 12 students in the third group. How many students are practicing?

Read the explanation Ryan gave for his solution.

Tips

To write an explanation:
- Your first sentence should tell what the problem is.
- Use words such as first, next, and finally to explain your steps.
- Use correct math vocabulary.
- Show your computations.
- Write a statement to summarize the answer.

I need to add 19 + 17 + 12. First, I can use the friendly number strategy to add 19 + 17. I add 1 to 19 to make 20 and subtract 1 from 17 to make 16 because I know that the sum of 20 + 16 is the same as the sum of 19 + 17. Add 20 + 16 = 36.

Next, I need to find the sum of 36 + 12. I use the break apart strategy. 36 = 30 + 6 and 12 = 10 + 2. So, I can add the tens and ones to find the sum.

I add 30 + 10 = 40, 6 + 2 = 8, and 40 + 8 = 48. The sum is 48. So, there are 48 students practicing.

Problem Solving Write to explain how you used mental math strategies to solve.

1. There are 18 fourth graders, 14 fifth graders, and 23 sixth graders in the choir. How many students are in the choir?

2. Would you use mental math to subtract 185 − 67?

Problem Solving Workshop
Skill: Estimate or Exact Answer

OBJECTIVE: Solve problems by using the skill *estimate or exact answer*.

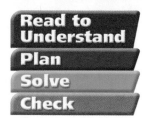

Read to Understand
Plan
Solve
Check

Use the Skill

PROBLEM The safe maximum flying weight of the plane is 1,600 pounds. Is the total weight of the plane, oil, fuel, extra equipment, baggage, and pilot less than 1,600 pounds? How many adult passengers can travel on the loaded plane?

Whether you need an estimate or exact answer depends on the situation.

Step 1   Find the total weight of the loaded plane and pilot.

You do not need to know the exact weight to find if it is less than 1,600 pounds. You can estimate this weight to compare to 1,600 pounds.	Round to the next ten pounds. Then add. $973 + 15 + 20 + 146 + 95 + 150$ ↓ ↓ ↓ ↓ ↓ ↓ $980 + 20 + 20 + 150 + 100 + 150 = 1{,}420$ 1,420 pounds < 1,600 pounds

Light Plane Weights

Item	Weight (in pounds)
Empty plane	973
Oil	15
Extra equipment	20
Fuel	146
Baggage	95
Typical pilot/adult	150
Safe maximum weight	1,600

Step 2   Find how much weight is left for passengers.

Find the difference between the total weight of the loaded plane and the safe maximum flying weight. Use the exact weight to be safe.	Add to find the exact weight of the loaded plane. $973 + 15 + 20 + 146 + 95 + 150 = 1{,}399$ Subtract the exact weight from 1,600. $1{,}600 - 1{,}399 = 201$ There are 201 pounds for adults.

Step 3   Find the number of passengers.

You cannot have more than the safe maximum flying weight, so, find an exact answer.	Add 150 pounds for each adult passenger. The sum must be less than 201 pounds. $150 < 201$, but $150 + 150 > 201$

So, the total weight of the loaded plane is less than 1,600 pounds, and one 150-pound adult passenger can travel on the plane.

Think and Discuss

Explain whether to estimate or find an exact answer. Then solve.

a. If there were no baggage or extra equipment, how many adult passengers could the loaded plane hold?

b. Two bags weigh 95 pounds. If one of them weighs 47 pounds, about how much does the other bag weigh?

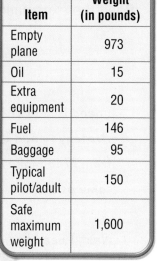

NS 1.4 Decide when a rounded solution is called for and explain why such a solution may be appropriate. *also* NS 2.1, NS 3.0, MR 1.0, MR 1.1, MR 2.0, MR 2.3, MR 2.4, MR 2.5, MR 2.6, MR 3.1 MR 3.2 MR 3.3

Guided Problem Solving

1. Horseshoe Falls in Australia is 502 feet high. Students measured their school and found that it was 210 feet long and 80 feet wide. Which is greater, the height of Horseshoe Falls or the distance around the outside of the school?

   First, decide if you need an estimate or an exact answer.

   Then, decide how you will compare the two numbers.

   Finally, make the comparison.

2. **What if** the students estimated that the school was about 200 feet long and about 100 feet wide? Explain why you should estimate or find an exact answer.

3. To be an airline pilot, you must fly a total of at least 1,500 hours. Dan flew 827 hours last year and 582 hours this year. How many more hours must he fly to be an airline pilot?

Mixed Applications

Explain whether to estimate or find an exact answer. Then solve the problem.

4. The school hallway is 190 feet long. If Carlos walks the length of the school hallway 3 times, will he have walked at least 500 feet? How far will he have walked?

5. The auditorium has 360 seats. There are 189 fourth-grade students and 170 fifth-grade students. If all the fifth-grade students sit in the auditorium, how many seats are left for fourth-grade students?

USE DATA For 6–8, use the bar graph.

6. How many degrees warmer was Meridian's highest January temperature than Greenville's?

7. The difference between the highest and lowest January temperatures at the Jackson station was 57°F. Find Jackson's lowest temperature in January.

8. In 2006, Vicksburg's highest January temperature was about 26°F warmer than normal. What was the normal temperature in Vicksburg in January?

9. **WRITE Math** ▶ **Explain** when you might need an exact answer and when you can estimate.

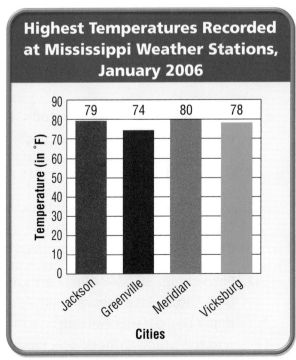

Highest Temperatures Recorded at Mississippi Weather Stations, January 2006

Extra Practice

Set A Write the fact family for each set of numbers. (pp. 32–33)

1. 6, 7, 13   **2.** 8, 6, 14   **3.** 4, 5, 9   **4.** 8, 7, 15

5. 4, 6, 10   **6.** 9, 8, 17   **7.** 5, 6, 11   **8.** 3, 5, 8

Set B Round each number to the place value of the underlined digit. (pp. 34–37)

1. 5<u>6</u>,479   **2.** $8<u>4</u>2   **3.** 2,<u>3</u>52,840   **4.** 917,<u>6</u>21

5. 56<u>9</u>,310   **6.** 4,<u>7</u>98,452   **7.** $42,<u>0</u>87   **8.** 84<u>6</u>,232

Set C Use mental math patterns to find the sum or difference. (pp. 38–39)

1. $40 + 80$ **2.** $900 - 400$ **3.** $1,500 - 800$ **4.** $40,000 + 90,000$

5. $700 - 200$ **6.** $2,400 + 700$ **7.** $16,000 + 3,000$ **8.** $60,000 - 40,000$

Set D Use rounding to estimate. (pp. 40–43)

1. $\begin{array}{r} 7,931 \\ +4,899 \\ \hline \end{array}$ **2.** $\begin{array}{r} 42,061 \\ +21,312 \\ \hline \end{array}$ **3.** $\begin{array}{r} 57,439 \\ -34,377 \\ \hline \end{array}$ **4.** $\begin{array}{r} 29,871 \\ +46,830 \\ \hline \end{array}$

Use compatible numbers to estimate.

5. $2,494 - 570$ **6.** $13,477 - 7,089$ **7.** $47,802 - 18,934$

8. $26 + 27 + 24 + 25$ **9.** $516 + 221 + 356$ **10.** $3,781 + 2,207 + 6,117$

11. Mabel's team collected 4,985 soup labels. Sun's team collected 2,356 soup labels. About how many labels did the teams collect in all?

Set E Add or subtract mentally. Tell the strategy you used. (pp. 44–47)

1. $89 - 37$ **2.** $590 + 275$ **3.** $497 - 308$ **4.** $752 + 244$ **5.** $609 - 292$

6. $614 + 345$ **7.** $489 - 56$ **8.** $380 + 98$ **9.** $677 - 470$ **10.** $393 + 427$

11. Mr. Chase is ordering 249 pencils and 290 erasers. Use mental math to determine the total number of items Mr. Chase is ordering. What strategy did you use?

12. Nikolai has 297 baseball cards. Garreth has 542 cards. Use mental math to find how many more cards Garreth has than Nikolai and tell which strategy you used.

Technology
Use Harcourt Mega Math, Ice Station
Exploration, *Arctic Algebra*, Level G.

Tree Climb

Get Ready!
2 players

Get Set!
- Two-color counters (10 for each player)
- Index cards (20)

FINISH
700,000
200,000

900,000
400,000

50,000
30,000

900
300

700
100

8,000
7,000

9,000
5,000

80,000
60,000

7,000
5,000

90
60

600
200

9,000
4,000

80
50

70
30

700
400

900
200

80
40

900
800

700
600

900
500

START

Climb the Tree!

- Make a set of operation cards. Write + on 10 cards. Write − on the other 10 cards. Shuffle the cards and place them facedown in a stack.

- The first player takes the top card. Use mental math to perform the required operation on the numbers in the first red space. If your answer is correct, place a red counter on the space. If your answer is wrong, your turn is over. Then it is the second player's turn.

- Remember, you can move to the next space only after getting a correct answer.

- Take turns. The first player to climb to the top of the tree wins.

Chapter 2 Review/Test

Check Vocabulary and Concepts

Choose the best term from the box.

VOCABULARY

estimate

inverse operations

regroup

1. Addition and subtraction are opposite or ? (O⊓ NS 3.0 p. 32)

2. When you ? , you find a number that is close to the exact amount. (O⊓ NS 2.1 p. 40)

Check Skills

Write the fact family for each set of numbers. (O⊓ NS 3.0 pp. 32–33)

3. 9, 6, 15   **4.** 2, 9, 11   **5.** 4, 9, 13   **6.** 7, 9, 16

Write a related fact. Use it to complete the number sentence. (O⊓ NS 3.0 pp. 32–33)

7. ■ $- 8 = 6$ **8.** $9 +$ ■ $= 14$ **9.** ■ $+ 4 = 11$ **10.** $12 -$ ■ $= 6$

Round each number to the place value of the underlined digit. (O⊓ NS 1.3 pp. 34–37)

11. $\underline{5}67{,}231$ **12.** $6{,}0\underline{8}1{,}392$ **13.** $7{,}40\underline{9}{,}488$ **14.** $\underline{8}{,}978{,}004$

Use a pattern to find the sum or difference mentally. (O⊓ NS 3.0 pp. 38–39)

15. $70 + 60$ **16.** $8{,}000 - 5{,}000$ **17.** $30{,}000 - 20{,}000$

18. $40{,}000 + 20{,}000$ **19.** $90 - 30$ **20.** $800 + 600$

21. $150{,}000 - 80{,}000$ **22.** $60{,}000 + 50{,}000$ **23.** $21{,}000 - 7{,}000$

Estimate by using rounding or compatible numbers. (NS 2.1 pp. 40–43)

24. $\begin{array}{r} 321 \\ + 198 \\ \hline \end{array}$ **25.** $\begin{array}{r} 6{,}799 \\ - 3{,}856 \\ \hline \end{array}$ **26.** $\begin{array}{r} 34{,}893 \\ - 19{,}877 \\ \hline \end{array}$ **27.** $\begin{array}{r} 67{,}062 \\ + 23{,}219 \\ \hline \end{array}$

Add or subtract mentally. Tell the strategy you used. (NS 2.1 pp. 44–47)

28. $81 + 49$ **29.** $497 - 206$ **30.** $344 - 190$ **31.** $499 + 99$

Check Problem Solving

Solve. Explain why an exact answer or an estimate is needed. (O⊓ NS 1.4, MR 2.5 pp. 48–49)

32. There are 76 students in the third grade and 92 students in the fourth grade. Rachael buys 180 cookies. Does she have enough to give each student one cookie?

33. **◖WRITE Math▸** Mr. Bolton has $7,000. **Explain** how to use estimation to find whether he has enough to buy a satellite dish for $2,459, a set of speakers for $2,359, and a TV for $2,599.

GO ONLINE Technology Use *Online Assessment.*

Enrich • Elapsed Time
IT'S ABOUT TIME

Creative Arts Night was supposed to start at 6:15 P.M. and end at 7:30 P.M. It started 12 minutes late because the band was late. To make up for lost time, Principal Andrews decided not to show the video, which shortened the program to 55 minutes. What time did Creative Arts Night start and end?

Elapsed time is the length of time that passes from the start of an activity to the end of that activity. You can add or subtract to find elapsed time.

Step I	Step 2
Find the new start time.	Find the new end time.
6 hr 15 min ← 6:15 P.M. + 12 min ——————— 6 hr 27 min	6 hr 27 min ← new start time + 55 min Think: 1 hr = 60 min ——————— Rename 6 hr 82 min as 6 hr + 6 hr 82 min 1 hr + 22 min, or 7 hr 22 min.
So, Creative Arts Night started at 6:27 P.M.	So, Creative Arts Night ended at 7:22 P.M.

Clock In

A Find the elapsed time from 6:35 P.M. to 9:15 P.M.	B Find the start time if the end time is 7:35 P.M. and the elapsed time is 42 minutes.
$\overset{8}{\cancel{9}}$ hr $\overset{75}{\cancel{15}}$ min Think: 1 hr = 60 min −6 hr 35 min Rename 9 hr 15 min as ———————— 8 hr 75 min. 2 hr 40 min 60 min + 15 min = 75 min	$\overset{6}{\cancel{7}}$ hr $\overset{95}{\cancel{35}}$ min Think: 1 hr = 60 min − 42 min Rename 7 hr 35 min as ———————— 6 hr 95 min. 6 hr 53 min 60 min + 35 min = 95 min
So, the elapsed time is 2 hr 40 min.	So, the start time is 6:53 P.M.

Track the Time
Write the time for each.

1. **start:** 5:15 A.M.
 end: 7:35 A.M.
 elapsed time: ■

2. **start:** ■
 end: 6:55 P.M.
 elapsed time: 35 min

3. **start:** 2:12 P.M.
 end: ■
 elapsed time: 75 min

Clock Out

WRITE Math ▶ It is 2:15 P.M. Joe has to do chores before his game at 3:00 P.M. It takes Joe 13 minutes to wash dishes, and 20 minutes to clean his room. It takes 15 minutes to ride to the game. Will Joe make it to his game on time? **Explain.**

Number Sense

1. This year's budget for the Community Zoo is one million, two hundred fifty thousand dollars. What is this number in standard form? (O—n NS 1.1)

   A $1,250   **C** $1,250,000

   B $125,000   **D** $125,000,000

2. Which of these is the number 3,000,105? (O—n NS 1.1)

   A three million, one hundred fifteen

   B three thousand, one hundred five

   C three million, one hundred five

   D three hundred thousand, fifteen

 Test Tip **Eliminate choices.**

See item 3. Look at the first two numbers in each answer choice. If the second number is less than the first, eliminate that choice.

3. Which list shows the numbers 1,248; 1,229; 1,237; 3,213; and 4,122 in order from least to greatest?

   (O—n NS 1.2)

   A 1,248; 1,229; 1,237; 3,213; 4,122

   B 1,229; 1,237; 1,248; 3,213; 4,122

   C 1,237; 1,229; 1,248; 3,213; 4,122

   D 3,213; 4,122; 1,237; 1,229; 1,248

4. **WRITE Math** **Explain** how to round 3,749 to the nearest hundred.

   (O—n NS 1.3)

Measurement and Geometry

5. Which rectangle has an area of 20 square units? (Grade 3 O—n MG 1.2)

   A

   B
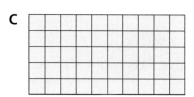

   C

   D

6. What is the name of the polygon shown below? (Grade 3 O—n MG 2.1)

   A square

   B rectangle

   C pentagon

   D octagon

7. **WRITE Math** **Explain** how to find the number of minutes in 3 hours.

   (Grade 3 MG 1.4)

Algebra and Functions

8. Which number is represented by ▪?
(Grade 3 AF 1.2)

$$3 + ▪ > 12?$$

A 4

B 6

C 9

D 10

9. The table shows the relationship between the number of spiders and the number of legs. What is the missing number?
(Grade 3 O—¬ AF 2.1)

Spider Legs				
Spiders	1	2	3	4
Legs	8	16	▪	32

A 19   **C** 24

B 20   **D** 28

10. What might the missing number be in the following pattern? (Grade 3 AF 2.2)

$$50, 46, 42, ▪, 34$$

A 40

B 38

C 37

D 36

11. **WRITE Math** ▸ **Explain** how to find the number that makes the following number sentence true. (Grade 3 AF 1.2)

$$4 \times 5 = 6 + ▪$$

Statistics, Data Analysis, and Probability

12. How likely is it that there will be snow falling in San Diego in April?
(Grade 3 SDAP 1.1)

A certain

B likely

C unlikely

D impossible

13. Which list shows the data from the bar graph below? (Grade 3 O—¬ SDAP 1.3)

A purple 6, blue 7, green 10

B purple 10, blue 7, green 6

C purple 8, blue 5, green 9

D purple 7, blue 10, green 6

14. **WRITE Math** ▸ **Explain** how to record the outcomes of tossing a number cube labeled 1 to 6 20 times. How many possible outcomes are there?
(Grade 3 O—¬ SDAP 1.2)

3 Add and Subtract Whole Numbers

The Big Idea Addition and subtraction of multi-digit numbers is based on single-digit addition and subtraction facts and base-ten and place-value concepts.

Investigate

Every year, the Tournament of Roses parade is held in Pasadena. Different groups design floats made from fresh flowers and other natural materials. In what ways can you use addition and subtraction to compare the numbers of flowers used in these two floats from the 2006 Tournament of Roses parade?

Polar Wonderland Float

Type of Flower	Number
White rose	3,000
Orchid	3,500
Iris	1,500

Pachyderm Parade Float

Type of Flower	Number
Light pink rose	840
Cream/peach rose	480
Hot pink rose	480
Orange rose	960
Red rose	600
Leonida rose	480
Iris	4,800
Orchid	150

CALIFORNIA FAST FACT

The "Memory Lane" float in the 2005 Tournament of Roses parade celebrated family and diversity. The float was 35 feet high and 55 feet long.

GO ONLINE

Technology
Student pages are available in the Student eBook.

Check your understanding of important skills
needed for success in Chapter 3.

▶ **Regroup Tens as Hundreds**

Regroup. Write the missing numbers.

1.

   12 tens = ■ hundred ■ tens

2.

   27 tens = ■ hundreds ■ tens

▶ **Regroup Hundreds as Tens**

Regroup. Write the missing numbers.

3. 2 hundreds = ■ tens

4. 3 hundreds = ■ tens

5. 1 hundred 1 ten = ■ tens

▶ **Two-Digit Addition and Subtraction**

Find the sum or difference.

6. $23 + 46$ 7. $67 - 35$ 8. $13 + 28$ 9. $41 - 17$ 10. $61 - 40$

11. $\begin{array}{r} 29 \\ + 57 \\ \hline \end{array}$ 12. $\begin{array}{r} 31 \\ + 49 \\ \hline \end{array}$ 13. $\begin{array}{r} 52 \\ + 36 \\ \hline \end{array}$ 14. $\begin{array}{r} 87 \\ - 28 \\ \hline \end{array}$ 15. $\begin{array}{r} 73 \\ - 24 \\ \hline \end{array}$

VOCABULARY POWER

CHAPTER VOCABULARY

difference
estimate
regroup
round
sum

WARM-UP WORDS

regroup to exchange amounts of equal value to rename a number

sum the answer to an addition problem

difference the answer to a subtraction problem

LESSON

1 Add and Subtract Through 5-Digit Numbers

OBJECTIVE: Add and subtract through 5-digit numbers.

Quick Review

Tino wants to buy a skateboard that costs $46. He has $28. How much more money does he need?

Learn

PROBLEM In spring, some monarch butterflies fly 1,718 miles from their winter home in Mexico to South Dakota. They fly another 1,042 miles to reach their summer home in Ontario, Canada. How far do the butterflies fly in all?

Example 1

Add. 1,718 + 1,042   **Estimate.** 2,000 + 1,000 = 3,000

Step 1	**Step 2**
Add the ones. Regroup 10 ones. $$\begin{array}{r} \overset{1}{} \\ 1{,}7\,1\,8 \\ +1{,}0\,4\,2 \\ \hline 0 \end{array}$$	Add the tens. $$\begin{array}{r} \overset{1}{} \\ 1{,}7\,1\,8 \\ +1{,}0\,4\,2 \\ \hline 6\,0 \end{array}$$

Step 3	**Step 4**
Add the hundreds. $$\begin{array}{r} 1 \\ 1{,}7\,1\,8 \\ +1{,}0\,4\,2 \\ \hline 7\,6\,0 \end{array}$$	Add the thousands. $$\begin{array}{r} 1 \\ 1{,}7\,1\,8 \\ +1{,}0\,4\,2 \\ \hline 2{,}7\,6\,0 \end{array}$$

So, the butterflies fly 2,760 miles in all. Since 2,760 is close to the estimate of 3,000, the answer is reasonable.

More Examples

A	**B**	**C**
$$\begin{array}{r} \overset{1}{} \\ 3{,}728 \\ +4{,}219 \\ \hline 7{,}947 \end{array}$$	$$\begin{array}{r} \overset{11}{} \\ 27{,}311 \\ +52{,}825 \\ \hline 80{,}136 \end{array}$$	$$\begin{array}{r} \overset{11}{}\,\overset{1}{} \\ 43{,}516 \\ +\ 8{,}736 \\ \hline 52{,}252 \end{array}$$

- Explain how you know when it is not necessary to regroup in addition.

NS 3.1 Demonstrate an understanding Thof, and the ability to use standard algorithms for the addition and subtraction of multidigit numbers. *also* **NS 2.1, NS 3.0, MR 2.0, MR 2.3, MR 2.4, MR 2.6, MR 3.2**

Subtract Through 5-Digit Numbers

In autumn, some monarch butterflies fly 3,825 kilometers from southern Canada to their winter home in central Mexico. A butterfly has flown 1,948 kilometers. How much farther is its winter home?

READ Math

Add to find a total, or how many in all.

Subtract to compare how much more or how much less.

Example 2

Subtract. 3,825 − 1,948   **Estimate.** 4,000 − 2,000 = 2,000

Step 1	Step 2	Step 3	Step 4
Subtract the ones. Regroup 2 tens 5 ones as 1 ten 15 ones.	Subtract the tens. Regroup 8 hundreds 1 ten as 7 hundreds 11 tens.	Subtract the hundreds. Regroup 3 thousands 7 hundreds as 2 thousands 17 hundreds.	Subtract the thousands.
$\begin{array}{r} {\scriptstyle 1\ 15} \\ 3,8\cancel{2}\cancel{5} \\ -1,948 \\ \hline 7 \end{array}$	$\begin{array}{r} {\scriptstyle 11} \\ {\scriptstyle 7\ 1\ 15} \\ 3,8\cancel{2}\cancel{5} \\ -1,948 \\ \hline 77 \end{array}$	$\begin{array}{r} {\scriptstyle 17\ 11} \\ {\scriptstyle 2\ 7\ 1\ 15} \\ 3,8\cancel{2}\cancel{5} \\ -1,948 \\ \hline 877 \end{array}$	$\begin{array}{r} {\scriptstyle 17\ 11} \\ {\scriptstyle 2\ 7\ 1\ 15} \\ 3,8\cancel{2}\cancel{5} \\ -1,948 \\ \hline 1,877 \end{array}$

So, the butterfly's winter home is 1,877 kilometers farther. Since 1,877 is close to the estimate of 2,000, the answer is reasonable.

• How can you use place value to add or subtract multidigit numbers?

More Examples

A
$\begin{array}{r} {\scriptstyle 11} \\ {\scriptstyle 7\ 1\ 13} \\ 78,2\cancel{3}9 \\ -\ 3,782 \\ \hline 74,457 \end{array}$

B
$\begin{array}{r} 7,849 \\ -3,618 \\ \hline 4,231 \end{array}$

C
$\begin{array}{r} {\scriptstyle 10} \\ {\scriptstyle 8\ 0\ 17} \\ \cancel{9},\cancel{1}79 \\ -2,183 \\ \hline 6,996 \end{array}$

Guided Practice

1. Copy each step of the problem at the right. Then tell what is happening in each step.

Step 1
$\begin{array}{r} {\scriptstyle 0\ 14} \\ 7\cancel{1}\cancel{4} \\ -438 \\ \hline 6 \end{array}$

Step 2
$\begin{array}{r} {\scriptstyle 10} \\ {\scriptstyle 6\ 0\ 14} \\ \cancel{7}\cancel{1}\cancel{4} \\ -438 \\ \hline 76 \end{array}$

Step 3
$\begin{array}{r} {\scriptstyle 10} \\ {\scriptstyle 6\ 0\ 14} \\ \cancel{7}\cancel{1}\cancel{4} \\ -438 \\ \hline 276 \end{array}$

Estimate. Then find the sum or difference.

2. $\begin{array}{r} 918 \\ -726 \\ \hline \end{array}$

3. $\begin{array}{r} 6,245 \\ +1,534 \\ \hline \end{array}$

4. $\begin{array}{r} 72,608 \\ +24,193 \\ \hline \end{array}$

✓ 5. $\begin{array}{r} 7,989 \\ -2,358 \\ \hline \end{array}$

✓ 6. $\begin{array}{r} 63,407 \\ +\ 2,936 \\ \hline \end{array}$

7. **TALK Math** Explain how you know which places to regroup to subtract.

Estimate. Then find the sum or difference.

8. 957
    +409

9. 7,345
    −1,213

10. 8,936
    + 385

11. 42,375
    +31,098

12. 9,435
    −4,217

13. 536
    −273

14. 4,892
    + 708

15. 68,473
    − 2,785

16. 7,419
    − 846

17. 6,045
    +1,742

18. 309
    +892

19. 726
    +2,643

20. 8,129
    − 953

21. 57,936
    −32,358

22. 72,983
    − 4,275

23. 6,842
    −2,858

24. 7,123
    +5,739

25. 27,159
    +3,235

26. 12,513
    − 4,628

27. 16,982
    +63,447

★ Algebra Find the missing digit.

28. 9■6
    + 437
    ─────
    1,383

29. 6,532
    − 4,1■5
    ─────
    2,407

30. 4■,158
    −   437
    ─────
    42,721

31. 3,657
    + 2■4
    ─────
    3,901

32. 25,3■1
    + 4,265
    ─────
    29,616

USE DATA For 33–34 and 36, use the table.

33. How many butterflies roosted from September 1 through September 4?

34. How many more butterflies roosted on September 2. than on September 3 and 4 combined?

35. **Reasoning** Add an even 4-digit number and an odd 4-digit number. Is the sum odd or even? **Explain.**

36. **Pose a Problem** Write a problem like problem 33 by changing the dates.

37. **≡FAST FACT** Frederick Urquhart first tagged monarch butterflies in 1937. No one knew where monarchs spent the winter until 1975. How long did it take to find the winter homes after first tagging the butterflies?

38. **WRITE Math** ▶ **What's the Question?** Angelina's nature group counted 622 butterflies roosting on Monday. On Tuesday, they counted 458 butterflies. The answer is 164 butterflies.

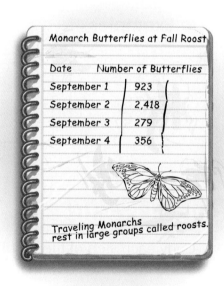

Monarch Butterflies at Fall Roost

Date	Number of Butterflies
September 1	923
September 2	2,418
September 3	279
September 4	356

Traveling Monarchs rest in large groups called roosts.

Extra Practice on page 70, Set A

CD ROM **Technology**
Use Harcourt Mega Math, The Number Games, *Tiny's Think Tank*, Levels A, B, C.

39. When you add two odd numbers, is it certain or impossible that the sum will be odd? (Grade 3 SDAP 1.1)

40. Find the missing number: $5 + \blacksquare = 12$.
(AF 1.1, p. 32)

41. Test Prep Greg has put together 1,372 pieces of his puzzle. He has 1,128 pieces left to finish the puzzle. How many pieces are in the puzzle?

  A 244   **C** 2,490

  B 256   **D** 2,500

42. One Friday, 27,398 people attend a home football game. Round the number to the nearest thousand. (⊶ NS 1.3, p. 34)

43. Test Prep Students collected 875 cans during the first month of their aluminum drive. The second month, they collected 2,155 cans. How many more cans did they collect the second month than the first month? **Explain.**

Problem Solving and Reasoning

VISUAL THINKING You can use a number line to visualize a problem and to help you solve the problem.

Driving from Green Bay, Wisconsin to Wheaton, Illinois, on major highways, you go through Milwaukee, Wisconsin and Wheeling, Illinois. Some of the distances are shown on the number line. What is the distance from Wheeling to Wheaton?

Look at the distances on the number line.

| ← 119 miles → | ← 97 miles → | ? |

Green Bay   Milwaukee   Wheeling   Wheaton

← 243 miles →

Add to find the distance from Green Bay to Wheeling. $119 + 97 = 216$

Subtract to find the distance from Wheeling to Wheaton. $243 - 216 = 27$

So, the distance from Wheeling to Wheaton is 27 miles.

Draw a number line for each problem. Find the distance.

1. *A* to *D* is 185 miles. *B* to *C* is 57 miles. *C* to *D* is 94 miles. Find A to B.

2. *A* to *D* is 278 miles. *A* to *B* is 43 miles. *C* to *D* is 129 miles. Find *B* to *C*.

2 Subtract Across Zeros

OBJECTIVE: Subtract whole numbers across zeros.

Quick Review

1. 7,543 − 3,924
2. 8,351 − 427
3. 6,254 − 1,683
4. 5,832 − 678
5. 3,425 − 1,789

Learn

PROBLEM A volcano is an opening in the earth's crust that erupts hot gases and melted rock called lava. Mount Popocatepetl is an active volcano in central Mexico. One eruption took place in 2005. The Aztec Indians first recorded an eruption in 1347. How many years passed between these two eruptions?

Example **Subtract.** 2,005 − 1,347   **Estimate.** 2,000 − 1,300 = 700

There are not enough ones, tens, or hundreds to subtract, so you have to regroup.

Step 1	Step 2	Step 3	Step 4
Regroup 2 thousands as 1 thousand 10 hundreds.	Regroup 10 hundreds as 9 hundreds 10 tens.	Regroup 10 tens 5 ones as 9 tens 15 ones	Subtract.
1 10 2,̸0̸ 0 5 −1, 3 4 7	1 10 10 2,̸0̸ ̸0̸ 5 −1, 3 4 7	9 9 1 10 10 15 2,̸0̸ ̸0̸ ̸5̸ −1, 3 4 7	9 9 1 10 10 15 2,̸0̸ ̸0̸ ̸5̸ −1, 3 4 7 6 5 8

So, 658 years have passed between the eruptions. Since 658 is close to the estimate 700, it is reasonable.

• In Step 1, why is it necessary to regroup 2 thousands?

ERROR ALERT

Remember that when the bottom digit is greater than the top digit, you need to regroup to subtract. Regroup from the next greater place value to the left that is not 0.

More Examples

A
```
      11
  3  ̸7̸ 10
4,̸2̸ ̸0̸ 8
−2,4 5 2
─────────
 1,7 5 6
```

B
```
  6 10 4 10
7,̸0̸ ̸5̸ ̸0̸
− 3,3 1 9
─────────
 3,7 3 1
```

C
```
        9  9
  8 10 10 10
5̸9̸,̸0̸ ̸0̸ ̸0̸
− 6,8 4 3
──────────
52,1 5 7
```

Guided Practice

1. Copy the problem at the right. Regroup the ones, tens, and hundreds. Then subtract. What is the difference?

```
 200
−165
```

NS 3.1 Demonstrate an understanding of, and the ability to use, standard algorithms for the addition and subtraction of multidigit numbers. also NS 2.1, NS 3.0, MR 2.0, MR 2.3, MR 2.4, MR 2.6, MR 3.2

Estimate. Then find the difference.

2.   706
  − 289

3.   2,030
  −   907

4.   9,000
  − 6,208

⊘5.   26,400
  −21,583

⊘6.   3,000
  − 1,076

7. **TALK Math** Explain why you need to regroup to find
5,010 − 328. What is the difference?

Independent Practice and Problem Solving

Estimate. Then find the difference.

8.   604
  − 238

9.   52,000
  − 6,724

10.   4,200
  − 476

11.   37,005
  − 25,392

12.   4,201
  − 3,050

13.   720
  − 519

14.   6,200
  − 3,685

15.   2,060
  − 1,077

16.   7,000
  − 1,225

17.   41,700
  −32,298

Choose two numbers from the box to make each difference.

| 3,000 | 3,400 | 3,040 | 274 | 2,074 | 2,704 |

18. 1,326

19. 2,766

20. 336

21. 926

22. 2,726

USE DATA For 23–25, use the table.

23. How many years passed between the
eruptions of the Chiginagak and
Veniaminof volcanoes?

24. Which two volcanoes have the greatest
difference in elevation? Find the difference.

25. **WRITE Math** What's the Error? Cole said
Veniaminof is 4,225 feet higher than Aniakchak.
Explain Cole's mistake and describe his error.
How much higher is Veniaminof?

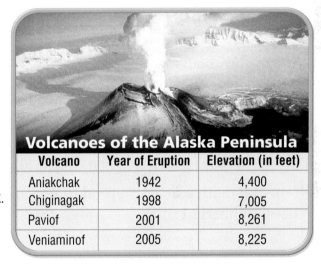

Volcanoes of the Alaska Peninsula

Volcano	Year of Eruption	Elevation (in feet)
Aniakchak	1942	4,400
Chiginagak	1998	7,005
Paviof	2001	8,261
Veniaminof	2005	8,225

Achieving the Standards

26. Write the number four million, five in
standard form. (O⎯π NS 1.1, p. 10)

27. A square sandbox is 9 feet on each side.
What is the perimeter? (Grade 3 MG 1.4)

28. What is 922,382 rounded to the nearest
thousand? (O⎯π NS 1.3, p. 34)

29. Test Prep A movie theater has 3,000
seats. There were 2,682 people at the
first showing of the movie. How many
empty seats were there?

A 318   **C** 1,682

B 428   **D** 5,682

Extra Practice on page 74, Set B

OBJECTIVE: Choose paper and pencil or mental math to add and subtract to greater numbers.

Quick Review

1. $4,350 - 3,199$
2. $7,020 + 460$
3. $2,808 - 704$
4. $9,000 + 3,678$
5. $6,004 - 1,683$

Learn

PROBLEM Uranus is the third-largest planet in the solar system. It has more than 25 known moons. Titania is the largest moon of Uranus. It is 435,910 kilometers from the planet's surface. Oberon is Uranus's most distant moon. It is 147,610 kilometers farther from Uranus than Titania is. How far is Oberon from Uranus?

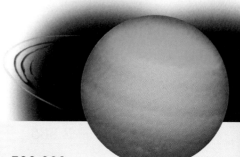

Use paper and pencil.

Add. $435,910 + 147,610$ **Estimate.** $440,000 + 150,000 = 590,000$

Step 1		**Step 2**	
Add the ones, tens, and hundreds. Regroup.	¹ 435,910 +147,610 ─────── 520	Add the thousands. Regroup.	¹ ¹ 435,910 +147,610 ─────── 3,520
Step 3		**Step 4**	
Add the ten thousands and hundred thousands.	¹ ¹ 435,910 +147,610 ─────── 583,520	Subtract to check.	¹² 7 ⁷15 5 8̸ 3,5̸ 2 0 −1 4 7,6 1 0 ───────── 4 3 5,9 1 0

So, Oberon is 583,520 kilometers from Uranus. Since 583,520 is close to the estimate of 590,000, the answer is reasonable.

• Is mental math a good method to use to find the sum of these numbers? Explain.

Math Idea
You can find a sum or difference by using paper and pencil or mental math. Choose the method that works best with the numbers in the problem.

Use mental math.

Add. $41,570 + 4,020$ **Estimate.** $42,000 + 4,000 = 46,000$

Step 1	**Step 2**	**Step 3**
Break apart 4,020 to add. $4,020 = 4,000 + 20$	Add the thousands. $41,570 + 4,000 = 45,570$	Now add the tens. $45,570 + 20 = 45,590$

So, the sum is 45,590. The answer is close to the estimate of 46,000, so 45,590 is reasonable.

• Why is mental math a good method to use to find this sum?

O━┑ NS 3.1 Demonstrate an understanding of, and the ability to use, standard algorithms for the addition and subtraction of multidigit numbers. *also* NS 2.1, O━┑ NS 3.0, MR 2.0, MR 2.3, MR 2.4, MR 2.6, MR 3.0, MR 3.2

Subtract Greater Numbers

The diameter of Uranus is 51,118 kilometers. Neptune, the fourth-largest planet, has a diameter of 49,528 kilometers. How much greater is the diameter of Uranus?

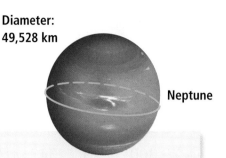

Diameter: 49,528 km

Neptune

Use paper and pencil.

Subtract. 51,118 − 49,528   **Estimate.** 51,000 − 50,000 = 1,000

Step 1		**Step 2**	
Subtract the ones and tens. Regroup.	$\begin{array}{r} {}^{0\,11}5\,1,\!1\,\cancel{1}\,\cancel{1}\,8 \\ -\ 4\,9,\!5\,2\,8 \\ \hline 9\,0 \end{array}$	Subtract the hundreds. Regroup.	$\begin{array}{r} {}^{10}0\,{}^{0}\,{}^{11}5\,\cancel{1},\!\cancel{1}\,\cancel{1}\,8 \\ -\ 4\,9,\!5\,2\,8 \\ \hline 5\,9\,0 \end{array}$
Step 3		**Step 4**	
Subtract the thousands and ten thousands. Regroup.	$\begin{array}{r} {}^{4}\,{}^{\cancel{0}}\,{}^{10}\,{}^{10}\,{}^{\cancel{0}}\,{}^{11}\cancel{5}\,\cancel{1},\!\cancel{1}\,\cancel{1}\,8 \\ -\ 4\,9,\!5\,2\,8 \\ \hline 1,\!5\,9\,0 \end{array}$	Add to check.	$\begin{array}{r} {}^{1\,1}\,{}^{1}49,\!528 \\ +\ 1,\!590 \\ \hline 51,\!118 \end{array}$

So, Uranus's diameter is 1,590 kilometers greater than Neptune's. The answer is close to the estimate of 1,000, so 1,590 is reasonable.

• Can you use mental math to find the difference? Explain.

Use mental math.

Subtract. 39,990 − 38,390   **Estimate.** 40,000 − 38,000 = 2,000

Compare the numbers in each place.

$\begin{array}{r} 39,\!990 \\ -38,\!390 \end{array}$

Think: Each bottom digit is less than or equal to the top digit.

You do not need to regroup to subtract, so you can use place value and mental math.

Step 1	Subtract the ten thousands.	30,000 − 30,000 = 0
Step 2	Subtract the thousands.	9,000 − 8,000 = 1,000
Step 3	Subtract the hundreds, tens, and ones.	990 − 390 = 600
Step 4	Add the differences.	1,000 + 600 = 1,600

So, the difference is 1,600. The answer is close to the estimate of 2,000, so 1,600 is reasonable.

• How do you decide which method to use when adding and subtracting greater numbers?

1. Tell which problem would be easier to solve using mental math. Then find the sum.

    a. 241,156   **b.** 340,100
    +176,812   +204,000

Find the sum or difference. Write the method you used.

2. 76,300	3. 342,007	4. 395,322	5. 84,000	6. 280,000
−41,000	+569,305	− 46,070	−39,075	+300,200

7. **TALK Math** Explain why mental math is a better method for finding 340,000 + 245,600 than for finding 340,000 − 245,600.

Independent Practice and Problem Solving

Find the sum or difference. Write the method you used.

8. 69,004	9. 287,004	10. 506,721	11. 850,540	12. 20,790
− 7,000	+969,506	+ 80,000	−200,540	−10,500

13. 302,700	14. 92,014	15. 58,300	16. 838,672	17. 234,500
+410,000	−86,728	−29,700	+415,059	+302,000

Algebra Find the missing digit.

18. 43■,257	19. 92,■43	20. 53,627	21. 4■7,308	22. 293,148
+253,019	−58,796	−2■,394	+196,321	−14■,325
692,276	33,747	25,233	613,629	146,823

USE DATA For 23–24 and 26, use the table.

23. Which moon is 79,740 miles farther from Uranus than Desdemona?

24. How much farther from Uranus is Belinda than Bianca?

25. **FAST FACT** Uranus was discovered in 1781. The moon Titania was discovered 6 years later. The *Voyager 2* probe discovered another moon, Puck, 198 years after Titania was discovered. What year did *Voyager 2* discover Puck?

26. **WRITE Math** Explain how to find the difference between Ophelia and Rosalind's distances from Uranus by using mental math. Why is mental math the most appropriate method to use?

Some Moons of Uranus

Moon	Distance from Uranus (in miles)
Ariel	118,690
Belinda	46,760
Bianca	36,770
Desdemona	38,950
Miranda	80,390
Ophelia	33,420
Portia	41,070
Rosalind	43,460

27. Nick wants to score 5,000 points in a video game. He has scored 3,752 points. How many more points must he score to reach his goal? (○┑ NS 3.1, p. 62)

28. Mercury is fifty-seven million, nine hundred thousand kilometers from the sun. Write the distance in standard form. (○┑ NS 1.2, p. 10)

29. **Test Prep** The population of San Francisco was 723,959 in 1990. By the 2000 census, the population had grown by 52,774. What was the population of San Francisco in 2000?

30. Manar's bag of marbles has 4 reds and 3 oranges. Kazim has the same number of marbles. He has 3 reds. How many oranges does he have? (Grade 3 AF 1.0)

31. **Test Prep** There are 66,526 kilometers of coastline that border the Indian Ocean. There are 45,389 kilometers of coastline that border the Arctic Ocean. How many more kilometers of coastline border the Indian Ocean?

  A 21,137 kilometers

  B 21,247 kilometers

  C 21,263 kilometers

  D 111,915 kilometers

 **Problem Solving and Reasoning**

NUMBER SENSE A palindrome is a word that reads the same forward or backward. *Mom* and *radar* are word palindromes. There are also number palindromes such as 33, 404, and 2002.

You can use addition to make number palindromes.

Step 1	Step 2	Step 3	Step 4 Keep reversing and adding until you make a palindrome.
Write a number. 348	Reverse the digits. 843	Add the two numbers. 348 + 843 ——— 1,191	348 + 843 ——— 1,191 +1,911 ——— 3,102 +2,013 ——— palindrome → 5,115

Use each number to make a number palindrome.

  1. 421   **2.** 236   **3.** 48   **4.** 637   **5.** 1,384

Problem Solving Workshop
Skill: Too Much/Too Little Information

OBJECTIVE: Solve problems by using the skill *too much/too little information.*

Use the Skill

PROBLEM Marin County in California has 608 miles of city roads, 420 miles of county roads, 90 miles of state highways, and 109 miles of other roads. A road inspector who works from 8:00 A.M. until 4:00 P.M. can examine 60 miles of road each day. How many miles of roads are there to inspect in Marin County?

Sometimes you have too much or too little information to solve a problem. If there is too much, you have to decide what to use. If there is too little, you can't solve the problem.

Step 1	Step 2
Read the problem. Decide what the problem asks you to find. How many miles of road are there to inspect in Marin County?	**Decide what information you need to solve the problem.** The number of miles of each type of road is needed.

Step 3	Step 4
Read the problem again carefully. List the information in the problem. Cross off the information you do not need. • 608 miles of city roads • 420 miles of county roads • 90 miles of state highways • 109 miles of other roads • ~~inspector works from 8:00 A.M. until 4:00 P.M.~~ • ~~inspector can examine 60 miles of road each day~~	**Decide if you have enough information to solve the problem, then solve the problem, if possible.** Add. 608 + 420 + 90 + 109 608 ← miles of city roads 420 ← miles of county roads 90 ← miles of state highways + 109 ← miles of other roads 1,227 ← miles of roads in Marin County

So, there are 1,227 miles of roads to inspect in Marin County.

Think and Discuss

Use the problem above. Tell if you have *too much* or *too little* information. Identify the extra or missing information. Then solve the problem, if possible.

a. The inspector worked 3 days this week. How many miles of roads did he inspect?

b. How long will it take Saskia to drive 90 miles of state highways?

O─┐ NS 3.0 Students solve problems involving addition, subtraction, multiplication, and division of whole numbers and understand the relationships among the operations. *also* **NS 2.1, O─┐ NS 3.1, MR 1.0, MR 1.1, MR 2.0, MR 2.3, MR 2.4, MR 2.6, MR 3.0, MR 3.1, MR 3.2, MR 3.3**

Tell if you have *too much* or *too little information*. Identify the extra or missing information. Then solve the problem, if possible.

| Driving Distances from Sacramento ||
City	Distance (in miles)
Los Angeles	388
Monterey	188
Palm Springs	497
San Diego	509
San Francisco	90
San Jose	126
Santa Cruz	144

1. The table shows the driving distance from Sacramento to some other California cities. How many more miles is the drive from Sacramento to Palm Springs than from Sacramento to San Jose?

   Copy the table. Put a check next to information that you need. Cross out the information you do not need.

   Identify if there is too much or too little information. Solve the problem, if possible.

2. **What if** Problem 1 asked you to find how many more miles the drive from Sacramento to Palm Springs is than the drive from Los Angeles to Sacramento?

3. Alameda County has 3,628 miles of roads. There are 2,945 miles of city roads. There are also county and state highways. How many miles of county roads are there?

Mixed Applications

USE DATA For 4–6, use the map.

4. You want to drive from San Diego to Los Angeles and then to Yosemite. You can travel 400 miles on one tank of gasoline. Can you make the trip on one tank? Explain.

5. How much farther is the drive from Los Angeles to Yosemite than from San Diego to Los Angeles?

6. A park ranger drove from Yosemite to Los Angeles and then to San Diego on Friday. On Sunday, the ranger drove back to Yosemite by the same route. How many miles did the park ranger drive over the weekend?

7. **WRITE Math** Zach spilled some water on a map that showed how far he had to drive to his cousin's house. His cousin's name is Ernest. The distance was smeared. This is what it looked like: | 1, 92 |

   The distance was greater than 1,100 miles and less than 1,400 miles. Find the distance to Zach's cousin's house. Do you have too much or too little information to solve the problem? **Explain.** Then solve the problem, if possible.

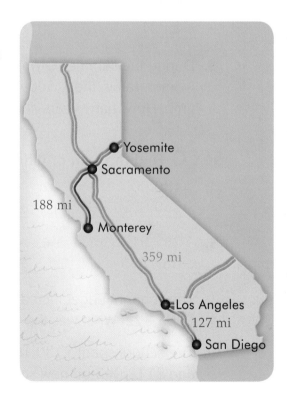

 **Extra Practice**

Set A Estimate. Then find the sum or difference. (pp. 58–61)

1.	2.	3.	4.	5.
563 +261	732 −124	6,409 +3,188	7,698 −2,677	4,898 +3,621

6.	7.	8.	9.	10.
768 −259	6,311 +2,454	7,046 + 889	8,946 −2,889	9,565 −3,178

Find the missing digit.

11.	12.	13.	14.
7▮4 +259 983	3,9▮3 −1,536 2,397	7,367 −6,▮99 868	5,299 − ▮34 4,365

15. Stephanie saved 458 pennies in a jar. Her brother gives her 636 pennies. Does Stephanie have enough pennies to trade for a $10 bill? **Explain.**

Set B Estimate. Then find the difference. (pp. 62–63)

1.	2.	3.	4.
500 −379	4,036 −2,305	3,009 −2,873	6,080 −3,592

5.	6.	7.	8.
4,700 −2,891	5,040 − 398	12,900 − 3,875	20,708 −18,969

9. During the summer Olympic games of 1972, women ran in the 1,500-meter race for the first time. How many years ago was this?

Set C Find the sum or difference. Write the method you used. (pp. 64–67)

1.	2.	3.	4.
430,009 +250,091	675,900 −350,500	900,275 +100,125	825,193 +56,047

5.	6.	7.	8.
357,918 +387,899	779,692 −489,753	468,345 −59,926	324,981 −46,109

9. The school budget increased $29,402 this year to $905,822. What was the school budget last year?

10. The school spent $130,195 on new math books and $112,043 on new social studies books. What was the total amount spent on new books?

CD ROM Technology
Use Harcourt Mega Math, The Number
Games, *Tiny's Think Tank*, Levels B, C.

Who's the Closest?

On Your Mark!
4 players and a referee

Get Set!
• Digit cards (0–9)
• Problem board

Go!

■ Players take turns being the referee. For each round, the referee decides
  • whether to use addition or subtraction,
  • how many digits each number will have,
  • and what the goal will be. For example, the referee might choose the goal *closest to 0*, *closest to 500*, or *closest to 1,000*.

■ Choose a problem board based on the referee's decision.

■ Place the digit cards facedown in a stack.

■ The referee draws a digit card and reads the number aloud. The players write the digit in a blank space on their boards. Once a digit has been written, it may not be erased.

■ The referee continues to draw digit cards, one at a time. Players fill in their boards as the numbers are called.

■ When all the blank spaces on their board have been filled, each player solves his or her own problem. The referee checks to see who is closest to the goal. That player wins the round.

 **Chapter 3 Review/Test**

Check Concepts

1. Would you use mental math or paper and pencil to find
   59,999 + 26,001? **Explain** why you chose that method. (O━n NS 3.1, pp. 64–67)

2. Write a subtraction problem that you could solve using
   mental math. The difference should be greater than 1,000. (O━n NS 3.1, pp. 64–67)

Check Skills

Estimate. Then find the sum or difference. (O━n NS 3.1, pp. 58–61)

3.	4.	5.	6.	7.
462	834	671	3,842	4,293
−268	−356	+167	+1,872	−1,796

Estimate. Find the difference. (O━n NS 3.1, pp. 62–63)

8.	9.	10.	11.
400	508	1,500	4,090
−317	−279	−1,487	−2,305

12.	13.	14.	15.
3,000	3,600	6,003	2,800
−1,604	−2,489	−2,376	− 751

Find the sum or difference. Write the method you used. (O━n NS 3.1, pp. 64–67)

16.	17.	18.	19.
35,907	45,268	35,696	67,036
−24,788	+15,803	+49,682	−29,507

20.	21.	22.	23.
357,742	576,304	405,881	603,711
−247,908	+209,198	−199,633	+ 19,949

Check Problem Solving

Solve. (O━n NS 3.0, MR 1.1, pp. 68–69)

24. Dillon went to the mall with his friends
    and bought a shirt for $13, a pair of
    shoes for $22, and a jacket for $49.
    How much did Dillon spend for both
    the shirt and the jacket?

25. **WRITE Math** In Problem 24, **explain**
    how you decided which information you
    needed to solve the problem and which
    information you did not need.

GO ONLINE Technology Use *Online Assessment.*

Enrich • Use Logical Reasoning
WORK UP OR DOWN

In a number pyramid, each number is found by adding the two numbers below it. In the pyramid at the right, $25 = 10 + 15$, $10 = 2 + 8$, and $15 = 8 + 7$.

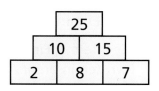

You can find missing numbers in a number pyramid by using addition and subtraction.

To find A: Think $121 + A = 238$,
so $A = 238 - 121 = 117$.

To find B: Think $A + B = 247$,
so $B = 247 - A = 247 - 117 = 130$.

To find C: Think $419 + 532 = C$, so $C = 951$.

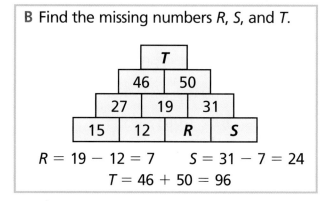

Examples

A Find the missing numbers M and N.

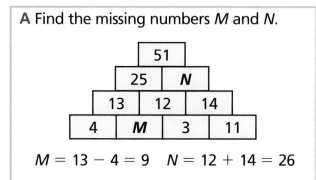

$M = 13 - 4 = 9 \quad N = 12 + 14 = 26$

B Find the missing numbers R, S, and T.

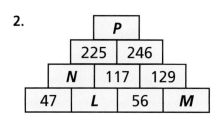

$R = 19 - 12 = 7 \qquad S = 31 - 7 = 24$
$T = 46 + 50 = 96$

Try It

Find the missing numbers.

1.

	Z	
16	19	
11	Y	14
9	2	3	X

2.

	P	
225	246	
N	117	129
47	L	56	M

WRITE Math ▸ **Explain** how you found each missing number in problem 2.

Achieving the Standards
Chapters 1–3

Number Sense

Test Tip Eliminate choices.

See item 1. First, find the lists that are written in order. Then find the one that is ordered from greatest to least.

1. The table shows the number of people attending the Roosevelt High football game. Which list shows the attendence in order from greatest to least?

   (O–n NS 1.2)

Game Attendence				
Week	1	2	3	4
Attendence	1,321	790	1,091	534

   A 1,321; 790; 534; 1,091

   B 1,321; 1,091; 790; 534

   C 790; 1,091; 1,321; 534

   D 534; 790; 1,091; 1,321

2. Kevin's class collected 708 pounds of paper for recycling. Sara's class collected 689 pounds. How many more pounds of paper did Kevin's class collect? (O–n NS 3.1)

   A 19 pounds

   B 21 pounds

   C 119 pounds

   D 121 pounds

3. **WRITE Math** **Explain** how to round 19,654 to the nearest thousand.

   (O–n NS 1.3)

Measurement and Geometry

4. What is the perimeter of a polygon with side lengths of 5 feet, 6 feet, 3 feet, 7 feet, and 9 feet?

   (Grade 3 O–n MG 1.3)

   A 21 feet

   B 25 feet

   C 30 feet

   D 32 feet

5. Which statement about this figure is true? (Grade 3 O–n MG 2.2)

   A It has three equal sides.

   B It has one right angle.

   C It has two equal sides.

   D It has two right angles.

6. What solid figure is shown below?

   (Grade 3 MG 2.5)

   A cylinder

   B pyramid

   C prism

   D cone

7. **WRITE Math** **Describe** the solid objects used to make up this figure.

   (Grade 3 MG 2.6)

Algebra and Functions

8. Which inequality shows 3 times a number is greater than 5 plus 2?

(Grade 3 O━┓ AF 1.1)

A $3 \times \blacksquare < 5 + 2$

B $3 \times \blacksquare = 5 + 2$

C $3 \times \blacksquare > 5 + 2$

D $5 + 2 > 3 \times \blacksquare$

9. The table shows the cost of marbles at four different stores. Which price is the least price per marble?

(Grade 3 O━┓ AF 2.1)

Marble Prices				
Marbles (per Bag)	3	5	6	9
Cost (in Cents)	27	40	42	54

A 3 for 27¢   **C** 6 for 42¢

B 5 for 40¢   **D** 9 for 54¢

10. There are 3 feet in 1 yard. There are 12 inches in 1 foot. How many inches are in 3 yards? (Grade 3 AF 1.4)

A 9 in.   **C** 72 in.

B 36 in.   **D** 108 in.

11. **WRITE Math** **Explain** how you can find $5 \times 7 \times 2$ if you know $5 \times 2 \times 7 = 70$. (Grade 3 AF 1.5)

Statistics, Data Analysis, and Probability

12. Which event is certain to occur?

(Grade 3 SDAP 1.1)

A Pick any two 2-digit numbers, and their sum is less than 200.

B It will snow in your town on April 1.

C A coin toss will show heads.

D Pick any two odd numbers, and their sum is odd.

13. How many possible outcomes are there if you toss a coin?

(Grade 3 O━┓ SDAP 1.2)

A 2   **C** 4

B 3   **D** 5

14. Robin pulls a marble from a bag that has 6 blue, 1 red, 8 yellow, and 10 white marbles all the same size. How many possible outcomes are there?

(Grade 3 O━┓ SDAP 1.2)

A 10

B 6

C 4

D 2

15. **WRITE Math** Suppose you toss a number cube labeled 1 to 6 18 times. **Explain** how to show the outcomes of the experiment in a table.

(Grade 3 O━┓ SDAP 1.3)

4 Algebra: Use Addition and Subtraction

The Big Idea
Properties and the concepts of algebra are used to evaluate expressions and solve addition and subtraction equations.

Investigate
Bowlers play 10 frames, or rounds. Each frame starts with 10 pins standing. A bowler may roll two balls in each frame to try to knock down all the pins. Suppose the first ball knocks down only some of the pins. If 4 pins are left standing, use the equation $4 + p = 10$ to find how many pins were knocked down. What addition or subtraction equations can you write to find the number of pins that could be knocked down by a first ball?

CALIFORNIA FAST FACT

More than 25,000 athletes with disabilities participate in sports through Special Olympics Northern California and Southern California.

GO ONLINE
Technology
Student pages are available in the Student eBook.

Show What You Know

Check your understanding of important skills
needed for success in Chapter 4.

▶ **Addition and Subtraction**

Find the sum or difference.

1. $8 + 5 = \blacksquare$

2. $12 + 7 = \blacksquare$

3. $16 - 3 = \blacksquare$

4. $12 - 9 = \blacksquare$

5. $9 + 8 = \blacksquare$

6. $15 + 7 = \blacksquare$

7. $11 - 3 = \blacksquare$

8. $14 + 5 = \blacksquare$

9. $25 - 8 = \blacksquare$

▶ **Find the Missing Number**

Find the missing number.

10. $5 + \blacksquare = 11$

11. $16 - \blacksquare = 9$

12. $8 + \blacksquare = 15$

13. $13 - \blacksquare = 4$

14. $\blacksquare + 4 = 9$

15. $\blacksquare - 7 = 4$

16. $\blacksquare - 8 = 5$

17. $17 - \blacksquare = 8$

18. $\blacksquare + 6 = 14$

19. $3 + \blacksquare = 10$

20. $\blacksquare - 5 = 9$

21. $\blacksquare + 2 = 11$

▶ **Number Patterns**

Predict the next number in the pattern.

22. 14, 21, 28, 35, $\blacksquare$

23. 6, 13, 20, 27, $\blacksquare$

24. 125, 225, 325, 425, $\blacksquare$

25. 88, 92, 96, 100, $\blacksquare$

26. 35, 30, 25, 20, $\blacksquare$

27. 253, 263, 273, 283, $\blacksquare$

VOCABULARY POWER

CHAPTER VOCABULARY

Associative
 Property
Commutative
 Property
equation
expression
fact family

Identity
 Property
inverse
 operations
parentheses
variable

WARM-UP WORDS

Commutative Property of Addition The property
that states that when the order of two addends is
changed, the sum is the same

Identity Property of Addition The property that
states that when you add zero to any number, the
sum is that number

Addition Properties

OBJECTIVE: Identify and use the properties of addition.

Quick Review

1. $90 + 30$ 2. $82 + 15$
3. $17 + 22$ 4. $9 + 7$
5. $45 + 13$

Vocabulary

Commutative Property

Identity Property

Associative Property

Learn

PROBLEM Jared and Savon collect swirled and clear marbles. They have the same number of marbles. Jared has 38 swirled marbles and 23 clear marbles. Savon has 38 clear marbles. How many swirled marbles does Savon have?

The **Commutative Property of Addition** states that numbers can be added in any order and the sum will be the same.

Example 1 Use the Commutative Property.

Jared's marbles				Savon's marbles		
38 swirled	plus	23 clear	equals	▮ swirled	plus	38 clear
↓	↓	↓	↓	↓	↓	↓
38	+	23	=	▮	+	38

Since $38 + 23 = 23 + 38$, then ▮ = 23.

So, Savon has 23 swirled marbles.

The **Identity Property of Addition** states that when you add zero to any number, the sum is that number.

Example 2 Use the Identity Property.

If Savon has no other swirled marbles, how many swirled marbles does he have in all?
$$23 + 0 = 23$$
$$0 + 23 = 23$$

So, Savon has 23 swirled marbles in all.

The **Associative Property of Addition** states that the way addends are grouped does not change the sum.

> **Math Idea**
> Parentheses ( ) tell which operations to do first.

Example 3 Use the Associative Property.

Matilda has 16 red, 24 yellow, and 18 blue shooter marbles. How many shooter marbles does she have in all?

$$16 + (24 + 18) = (16 + 24) + 18$$
$$= 40 + 18 \qquad \text{Use the Associative Property.}$$
$$= 58 \qquad \text{Use mental math.}$$

So, Matilda has 58 marbles.

 AF 1.0 Students use and interpret variables, mathematical symbols, and properties to write and simplify expressions and sentences. *also* **NS3.1, AF 1.1, O⊸ AF 1.2, O⊸ AF 1.3, MR 1.1, MR 2.3, MR 2.4, MR 3.2**

1. Which shows an example of the Commutative Property?

    $(13 + 17) + 22 = 13 + (17 + 22)$ $46 + 21 = 21 + 46$ $67 + 0 = 67$

Find the missing number. Name the property you used.

2. $73 + \blacksquare = 73$ ✓3. $47 + \blacksquare = 56 + 47$ ✓4. $\blacksquare + (31 + 18) = (24 + 31) + 18$

5. **TALK Math** Explain how to use the Commutative and the Associative Properties to add $62 + 79 + 38$.

Independent Practice and Problem Solving

Find the missing number. Name the property you used.

6. $93 + 28 = 28 + \blacksquare$ 7. $\blacksquare + 0 = 31$ 8. $35 + (42 + \blacksquare) = (35 + 42) + 56$

9. $69 = \blacksquare + 69$ 10. $59 + 85 = \blacksquare + 59$ 11. $(76 + 97) + 19 = 76 + (\blacksquare + 19)$

Change the order or group the addends so that you can add mentally. Find the sum. Name the property you used.

12. $450 + 83 + 50$ 13. $78 + 32 + 46$ 14. $125 + 62 + 75$ 15. $64 + 15 + 36 + 30$

USE DATA For 16–17, use the table.

16. Use the Associative Property to find the total number of green, red, and blue marbles that Serena has.

17. Serena has 10 fewer clay marbles than the total number of green and black marbles. How many clay marbles does she have?

18. **WRITE Math** Explain how you know which addition property to use to solve a problem.

Serena's Marbles	
Color	**Number**
Black	24
Blue	43
Green	26
Red	17

 Achieving the Standards

19. $478 + 236 =$

    (○━ NS 3.1, p. 58)

20. Find the missing number.
    $15 + \blacksquare = 22$ (○━ NS 3.1 p. 58)

21. Round 3,905,441 to the nearest ten thousand. (○━ NS 1.3, p. 34)

22. **Test Prep** Which shows the Associative Property of Addition?

    A $45 + 0 = 45$

    B $12 + 78 = 78 + 12$

    C $84 + (35 + 76) = 84 + (76 + 35)$

    D $(52 + 96) + 63 = 52 + (96 + 63)$

2 Write and Evaluate Expressions

OBJECTIVE: Write and evaluate addition and subtraction expressions.

Vocabulary

expression

Learn

PROBLEM There are 15 clown fish in a tank. The store sells 6 fish. Then it receives a shipment of 8 more fish. How many fish are in the tank after the shipment?

You can write an expression to find the number of fish in the tank. An **expression** is a part of a number sentence that has numbers and operation signs but does not have an equal sign.

Example

Think:	15 fish	minus	6 fish	plus	8 fish
	↓	↓	↓	↓	↓
	(15	−	6)	+	8

Find the value of $(15 − 6) + 8$.

$(15 − 6) + 8$ Subtract 6 from 15.
↓
$9 + 8$ Add 9 and 8.
↓
17

So, there are 17 fish in the tank after the shipment.

Parentheses tell which operation to do first. An expression can have a different value if the parentheses are in different places.

ERROR ALERT

Always do the operation in parentheses first, even if it comes second in the expression.

More Examples Find the value of the expression.

Ⓐ $(18 − 7) + 3$

$(18 − 7) + 3$ Subtract 7 from 18.
↓
$11 + 3$ Add 11 and 3.
↓
14

Ⓑ $18 − (7 + 3)$

$18 − (7 + 3)$ Add 7 to 3.
↓
$18 − 10$ Subtract 10 from 18.
↓
8

• How does where you place the parentheses change the value of the expression $12 − 5 + 2$?

Guided Practice

Tell what you do first. Then find the value of the expression.

1. $9 + (7 - 2)$ **2.** $(6 + 8) + 5$ ✅ **3.** $15 - (5 + 2)$ ✅ **4.** $12 - (8 - 3)$

5. **TALK Math** Explain how finding the value of $(12 - 4) + 6$ is similar to finding the value of $12 - (4 + 6)$. How is it different?

Independent Practice and Problem Solving

Tell what you do first. Then find the value of each expression.

6. $(18 - 12) - 4$ **7.** $17 - (5 + 6)$ **8.** $14 + (7 - 3)$ **9.** $20 - (13 - 3)$

10. $12 + (6 + 2)$ **11.** $(34 - 10) + 16$ **12.** $10 + (2 - 2)$ **13.** $(27 + 3) + 20$

Place the parentheses so the expression has a value of 4.

14. $17 - 4 + 9$ **15.** $32 - 30 + 2$ **16.** $5 - 4 + 3$ **17.** $7 - 2 + 1$

Write an expression. Then find the value of the expression.

18. Lola had $8. She spent $3 on markers and $2 on paper. How much money does she have left?

19. Patrick had 20 stickers. He used 12 of them and then bought 5 more. How many stickers does he have?

20. Colin had 11 tetras in his fish tank. He moved 6 to his sister's tank and then bought 2 more. How many tetras does Colin have now?

21. Chloe had 19 tablets of fish food in a bag. She took 11 out of the bag to feed her fish, but put 3 of them back. How many tablets are in the bag now?

22. There are 9 kiwis on the counter. Matt and Alison each ate 2 kiwis, and then they bought 12 more. How many kiwis are on the counter now?

23. **WRITE Math** Explain how to place parentheses so that the expression $16 - 7 + 4$ has a value of 5.

Achieving the Standards

24. What number makes this number sentence true? (AF 1.0, p. 78)

$$73 + 56 = \blacksquare + 73$$

25. $3{,}012 + 4{,}107 = \bullet\!\!-\!\!n$ (NS 3.0, p. 58)

26. Lana has reviewed 8 of 15 spelling words. Write a number sentence to show the number of words she has left. (Grade 3 AF 1.1)

27. **Test Prep** What is the value of the following expression?

$$17 - (6 + 4)$$

   A 7   **C** 19

   B 15   **D** 27

Extra Practice on page 98, Set B

3 Expressions with Variables

OBJECTIVE: Interpret and evaluate addition and subtraction expressions with variables.

Quick Review

Max has $12. He spends $6 for a movie ticket and $2 for popcorn. Write an expression to show how much money he has left. Find the value of the expression.

Vocabulary

variable

Learn

PROBLEM Jay has some basketball cards. His grandfather gives him 5 new cards. What expression can you write to show how many cards he has now?

A **variable** is a letter or symbol that stands for an unknown number or numbers. These are expressions with variables.

$$\blacksquare + 3 \qquad 12 - \blacksquare \qquad 4 - n \qquad 3 + b - 5$$

Use a variable to show the original number of cards Jay had.

original cards	plus	new cards
↓	↓	↓
$\blacksquare$	$+$	5

So, the expression $\blacksquare + 5$ shows the number of cards Jay has now.

- Why can the expression $n + 5$ also be used to show the number of cards Jay has now?

Examples Find the value of the expression.

Ⓐ $18 - x$ if $x = 6$.

$18 - x$	Replace x with 6.
↓	
$18 - 6$	Subtract 6 from 18.
↓	
12	

So, the value of the expression is 12.

Ⓑ $9 + (y - 7)$ if $y = 15$.

$9 + (y - 7)$	Replace y with 15.
↓	
$9 + (15 - 7)$	Subtract 7 from 15.
↓	
$9 + 8$	Add.
↓	
17	

So, the value of the expression is 17.

Guided Practice

1. Ray has 8 muffins. He eats some of the muffins. Let m be the number of muffins eaten. Write an expression to show how many muffins are left.

AF 1.0 Students use and interpret variables, mathematical symbols, and properties to write and simplify expressions and sentences. *also* **AF 1.1, ⊶ AF 1.2, ⊶ AF 1.3, MR 2.0, MR 2.2, MR 2.3, MR 2.4, MR 3.2**

Write an expression. Choose a variable. Tell what the variable represents.

✅ **2.** Pete hangs 3 posters on the wall. Then he hangs some more posters on the wall.

✅ **3.** Jenna found some shells on the beach. She gave 4 of them to Lance.

4. [**TALK Math**] **Explain** how to find the value of the expression $12 - (5 + n)$ if $n = 3$.

Independent Practice and Problem Solving

Write an expression. Choose a variable. Tell what the variable represents.

5. Denise had some stamps. She used 6 stamps to mail letters.

6. Todd has 20 pages to read. He read some of the pages this morning.

7. Sergio rode his bike to the park. Then he rode 2 miles to the library.

8. Angelique had 16 marbles. She got some more marbles.

Find the value of each expression if $x = 4$ and $y = 5$.

9. $12 - x$ **10.** $y + 8$ **11.** $6 + (y - 2)$ **12.** $13 - (3 + x)$

13. $40 - (x + y)$ **14.** $(y - x) + 11$ **15.** $(y - 5) + 3$ **16.** $21 - (5 - x)$

USE DATA For 17–19, use the table.

17. Jay also has some other sports cards. Write an expression to show the total number of cards Jay has.

18. Jay took his baseball cards and some soccer cards, s, to Eddie's house. Write an expression for the total number of cards. Then use the expression to find the total if $s = 5$.

Jay's Sports Cards

Sport	Number
Baseball	42
Football	26
Hockey	15

19. Jay's grandfather gave him some football cards. Write an expression for the number of football and hockey cards he has now.

20. [**WRITE Math**] ▶ **What's the Error?** Reba said the value of $20 - (9 + w)$ is 20 if $w = 9$. Describe Reba's error. Find the correct value of the expression.

Achieving the Standards

21. $4 + \blacksquare = 11$ (Grade 3 O—n NS 2.0)

22. What is the value of $\blacksquare$? (O—n AF 1.2, p. 80)

$17 - (5 - 2) = \blacksquare$

23. What quadrilateral has 4 equal sides and 4 right angles? (Grade 3 O—n MG 2.3)

24. Test Prep Which is the value of the expression below if $n = 4$?

$$16 - (n + 3)$$

A 9   **C** 12

B 12   **D** 23

Extra Practice on page 98, Set C

LESSON 4

Addition and Subtraction Equations

OBJECTIVE: Write and solve addition and subtraction equations.

Learn

PROBLEM A service dog has completed 4 months of its 9-month training program at Canine Companions. What equation can you write to show how many months the dog has left to finish its training?

An **equation** is a number sentence stating that two amounts are equal.

Example 1 Write an addition equation.

Match the words to write an equation. Use the variable *m* to show the number of months left to finish his training.

4 months	plus	months left	equals	9 months
↓	↓	↓	↓	↓
4	+	*m*	=	9

So, the equation is $4 + m = 9$.

Example 2 Write a subtraction equation.

There are 10 dog biscuits in a bowl. After the dogs eat some, there are 3 dog biscuits left.

Let *b* represent the number of dog biscuits eaten.

10 dog biscuits	minus	dog biscuits eaten	equals	3 dog biscuits left
↓	↓	↓	↓	↓
10	−	*b*	=	3

• **What if** there are 12 dog biscuits in the bowl? After some more dog biscuits are put in the bowl, there are 17 dog biscuits. How would the equation change?

Example 3 Write a problem for the equation $m - 3 = 4$.

m	minus	3	equals	4
↓	↓	↓	↓	↓
money Ben has	−	money Ben spends	=	money Ben has left

After spending $3 for a dog bone, Ben has $4 left. How much money did Ben have to start with?

Quick Review

1. $17 + 6$
2. $25 - 8$
3. $56 + 24$
4. $93 - 32$
5. $73 + 29$

Vocabulary

equation

84

AF 1.0 Students use and interpret variables, mathematical symbols, and properties to write and simplify expressions and sentences. *also* **AF 1.1, O━┓ AF 1.5, MR 2.0, MR 2.4, MR 3.0, MR 3.2, MR 3.3**

Solve Equations

An equation is true if the values on both sides of the equal sign are equal. You solve an equation when you find the value of the variable that makes the equation true.

In the problem, to find how many months the service dog has left to finish its training, you can solve the equation $4 + m = 9$.

 ONE WAY **Use the strategy predict and test.**

Materials ■ Equabeam™ balance

You can use the Equabeam balance to find the number that makes $4 + m = 9$ a true equation.

Step 1	**Step 2**
Show 4 on the left and 9 on the right.	Replace m with 4. Place 4 on the left side.
	$4 + 4 \overset{?}{=} 9$ $8 \neq 9$
	Replace m with 5. Place 5 on the left side.
	$4 + 5 \overset{?}{=} 9$ $9 = 9$ ✔

So, the service dog has 5 months left to finish its training.

ANOTHER WAY **Use mental math.**

Solve.	$14 - d = 8$	Think: 14 minus what number equals 8?
	$d = 6$	
Check:	$14 - 6 \overset{?}{=} 8$	Replace d with 6.
	$8 = 8$ ✔	The equation is true.

So, the value of d is 6.

• How can you check that your equation is true?

Guided Practice

1. Which number, 8 or 9, makes the equation $n + 5 = 14$ true?

Write an equation for each. Choose a variable for the unknown. Tell what the variable represents.

2. A box has 24 pens. There are some blue pens and 8 red pens.

 3. Emil has 18 stamps. After he uses some stamps, he has 12 stamps left.

Solve the equation.

4. $x + 9 = 17$

5. $c - 6 = 7$

6. $15 + \blacksquare = 21$

✓7. $13 - n = 4$

8. **TALK Math** Explain how to make the equation
$20 + a = 29$ true.

Independent Practice and Problem Solving

Write an equation for each. Choose the variable for the unknown. Tell what the variable represents.

9. There are 15 apples in the box. Some are green apples and 9 are red apples.

10. Andrea had some money. She spent $8 and had $4 left.

Solve the equation.

11. $4 + b = 16$

12. $\blacksquare - 5 = 20$

13. $m - 9 = 12$

14. $24 - n = 21$

Write words to match the equation.

15. $m + 5 = 13$

16. $15 - n = 4$

17. $12 - p = 8$

18. $y - 6 = 8$

USE DATA For 19–20, use the table.

19. How many more hearing dogs graduated than service dogs?

20. **Pose a Problem** Write and solve an equation that compares the total number of hearing dogs and service dogs that graduated. Tell what the variable represents.

Graduating Dogs

Month	Hearing	Service
February	8	2
May	5	4
November	9	4

21. **Reasoning** If $6 = m + 4$ and $c + m = 7$, find m and c.

22. **WRITE Math** Compare the values of n for $n + 8 = 12$ and $12 - n = 8$. **Explain** how you solved each equation.

Achieving the Standards

23. If $z = 17$, what is the value of $21 + (35 - z)$? (○━┓ AF 1.2, p. 82)

24. Billy has a bag of red and black marbles. If he randomly picks two marbles, what color combinations might he get?

(Grade 3 ○━┓ SDAP 1.2)

25. $32,908 + 254 = $ (○━┓ NS 3.1, p. 64)

26. **Test Prep** Art class lasts 45 minutes. Students work 35 minutes on their projects, then clean up. Which equation can be used to find how long clean up, c, lasts?

A $35 + c = 45$ C $45 + c = 35$

B $35 - c = 45$ D $c - 45 = 35$

Extra Practice on page 98, Set D

Are We There Yet?

 Reading Skill **Cause and Effect**

Levi's and Cindy's families are meeting at Lake Shasta for vacation. Both families live the same distance from the lake. Levi's family drives 196 miles the first day and 223 miles the second day to reach the lake. If Cindy's family drives 195 miles the first day, how far does Cindy's family drive on the second day to reach the lake?

Cause and effect can help you understand this problem.

Cause	Effect
The first day Cindy's family drove fewer miles.	The second day Cindy's family will drive more miles than Levi's.

Write an equation that shows the distances each family travels. Let d represent the distance Cindy's family drives on the second day.

▲ Lake Shasta has 370 miles of shoreline. It is the largest of all the California lakes.

$$\underset{\substack{\text{first day} \\ \downarrow}}{196} + \underset{\substack{\text{second day} \\ \downarrow}}{223} = \underset{\substack{\text{first day} \\ \downarrow}}{195} + \underset{\substack{\text{second day} \\ \downarrow}}{d}$$

Levi's family   Cindy's family

Compare the numbers in the equation to solve.

• Use mental math to make an addend on the left of the equation the same as the one on the right.

Think: Since 196 is one more than 195, d has to be one more than 223 for the equation to be true.

Problem Solving Use cause and effect to solve.

1. Solve the problem above.

2. Hannah's and Ravi's families plan to camp together near Lake Shasta. They live the same distance from the campground. Hannah's family drives 142 miles on the first day and the rest of the way on the second day. Ravi's family drives 143 miles on the first day and 176 miles on the second day. How far does Hannah's family drive on the second day? Write an equation. Tell what the variable represents, then solve.

LESSON 5

Add Equals to Equals

OBJECTIVE: Keep an equation equal by adding the same amount to both sides.

Quick Review

Solve the equation.

1. $9 + n = 16$
2. $y + 4 = 12$
3. $\blacksquare - 5 = 7$
4. $x - 2 = 8$
5. $14 - a = 10$

Learn

PROBLEM There are 3 poppies in a vase. Agnes puts 4 more poppies in the vase. Then she puts 7 poppies in another vase. Both vases have the same number of poppies. If she puts 2 more poppies in each vase, will the number of poppies in each vase still be equal?

The equation $3 + 4 = 7$ models the number of poppies in each vase. The equation is a true equation because both sides are equal.

$$3 + 4 = 7$$
$$\downarrow \qquad \downarrow$$
$$7 \quad = 7$$

You can use a model to solve the problem.

Remember
In a true equation, the left side and the right side have the same value.

Activity

Materials ■ Equabeam™ balance

Step 1	Step 2	Step 3
Put weights on 3 and on 4 on the left side and a weight on 7 on the right side to show $3 + 4 = 7$ is a true equation.	Put weights on 2 on each side of the balance.	Compare the values of both sides of the equation. Does the balance show that $3 + 4 + 2 = 7 + 2$ is a true equation?

The equation is a true equation.
So, the number of poppies in each vase will still be equal.

• Does adding the same value to both sides keep the equation true? How do you know?

• **What if** Agnes puts 5 more poppies in each vase? Would the number of poppies in each vase still be equal? Explain.

O‒¬ AF 2.1 Know and understand that equals added to equals are equal *also* **AF 1.1, O‒¬ AF 2.0,** MR 2.0, MR 2.2, MR 2.3, MR 2.4, MR 3.2

Add or Subtract Equal Amounts

Examples Tell whether the equations are true.

A Subtract 3 from both sides of $6 - 2 = 4$.

$$6 - 2 = 4$$

Subtract 3 from → $(6 - 2) - 3 = 4 - 3$ ← Subtract 3 from the right side.
the left side.   ↓   ↓   Compare the two sides.
                        1   =   1   ← The equation is true.

So, subtracting 3 from both sides keeps the equation true.

B Add 26 to both sides of $48 = 17 + 31$.

$$48 = 17 + 31$$

Add 26 to the $48 + 26 = (17 + 31) + 26$ ← Add 26 to the right side.
the left side.   ↓   ↓
                       74   =   74   ← Compare the two sides.
                                                  The equation is true.

So, adding 26 to both sides keeps the equation true.

- How can you find the missing value of $9 + 8 + \blacksquare = 17 + 4$?

- **What if** you subtract 5 from both sides of the equation $17 + 31 = 48$? Will the equation still be true? How do you know?

Math Idea
If you add the same amount to or subtract the same amount from both sides of a true equation, the values on both sides are still equal, and the equation is still true.

Guided Practice

1. To add 6 to both sides of the equation $3 + 5 = 8$, write $(3 + 5) + 6 = 8 + 6$. Is the new equation a true equation?

Tell whether the values on both sides of the equation are equal.
Write *yes* or *no*. Explain your answer.

2.
$$3 + 2 + 2 \overset{?}{=} 5 + 2$$

✓ 3.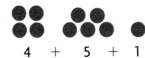
$$4 + 5 + 1 \overset{?}{=} 9 + 2$$

Complete to make the equation true.

4. $13 + 6 = 13 + \blacksquare$

5. $10 + 4 - \blacksquare = 14 - 2$

✓ 6. $9 - \blacksquare + 1 = 6 + 1$

7. **TALK Math** Explain how to show that the equation $12 + 5 = 17$ is still a true equation if 4 is added to both sides of the equation.

Tell whether the values on both sides of the equation are equal.
Write *yes* or *no*. Explain your answer.

8.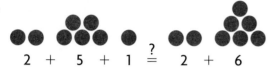

$$2 + 5 + 1 \overset{?}{=} 2 + 6$$

9.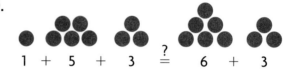

$$1 + 5 + 3 \overset{?}{=} 6 + 3$$

Complete to make the equation true.

10. $12 + 2 + \blacksquare = 14 + 4$

11. $8 - 3 + 9 = \blacksquare + 9$

12. $10 + 5 - 2 = 15 - \blacksquare$

13. $29 + \blacksquare = 29 + 17$

14. $45 - 5 = 40 + 5 - \blacksquare$

15. $19 - \blacksquare + 6 = 10 + 6$

16. $7 + 10 = \blacksquare + 5 + 2$

17. $17 - 8 - 2 = \blacksquare - 2$

18. $20 - 10 - 7 = 10 - \blacksquare$

Add to or subtract from both sides of the equation.
Find the new value.

19. Subtract 3.
$11 - 5 = 6$

20. Add 15.
$9 - 4 = 5$

21. Subtract 12.
$12 + 5 + 19 = 19 + 17$

22. Add 25.
$2 + 5 - 4 = 1 + 2$

23. Subtract 16.
$45 + 12 + 5 = 17 + 40 + 5$

24. Add 7.
$24 - 5 - 11 = 19 - 11$

USE DATA For 25–26, use the information in the art.

25. Jamie and Leanne bought the packets of seeds shown at the right. If Jamie gave 1 packet of seeds to Bob, would they have an equal number of packets left? How many packets would each girl have?

26. Leanne planted the seeds in 3 of her packets. Jamie planted all of her buttercup seeds. Then Leanne bought 4 more packets of larkspur seeds. How many packets of seeds does Jamie need to buy so that she has the same number of packets as Leanne?

27. **FAST FACT** • Every April 6 is California Poppy Day. How many days are there until the next California Poppy Day?

28. **Reasoning** The letters *A* and *B* stand for numbers. If $A - 20 = B - 20$, what can you say about *A* and *B*?

29. **WRITE Math** If you add 5 to both sides of the equation $8 + 16 = 24$ and then you subtract 3 from both sides, will the equation still be true? **Explain** how you know.

30. $8 + \blacksquare = 15$ (AF 1.0, p. 84)

31. Write the number nine million, forty-eight thousand, twenty-six in standard form.

(O— NS 1.1, p. 10)

32. Test Prep Manny has 8 pair of sneakers. His brother, Lamil, has 6 pair of boots and 2 pair of sandals. Manny and Lamil's uncle takes them shopping and buys each boy 2 pair of loafers. Write an equation that shows the number of pair of shoes each boy has. Is the equation true? **Explain.**

33. What is the value of the expression $9 - (7 - 2)$? (O— AF 1.2, p. 80)

34. Test Prep The letters Q and R stand for numbers. If $Q = R$, which statement is true?

A $Q < R$

B $Q - 12 = R - 12$

C $Q + 12 = R$

D $Q + 12 = R - 12$

Problem Solving and Reasoning

ALGEBRA You can use a hundred chart to solve an equation.

Solve. $42 - m = 36$

Step 1

Start at 42. Count back until you reach 36. Color each square as you count back to 36: 41, 40, 39, 38, 37, 36.

Step 2

Count the number of squares colored: 6. This number is the value of m.

Step 3

Check. Replace m with 6.

$42 - 6 \overset{?}{=} 36$

$36 = 36$ ✔ The equation is true.

1	2	3	4	5	6	7	8	9	10
11	12	13	14	15	16	17	18	19	20
21	22	23	24	25	26	27	28	29	30
31	32	33	34	35	36	37	38	39	40
41	42	43	44	45	46	47	48	49	50
51	52	53	54	55	56	57	58	59	60
61	62	63	64	65	66	67	68	69	70
71	72	73	74	75	76	77	78	79	80
81	82	83	84	85	86	87	88	89	90
91	92	93	94	95	96	97	98	99	100

So, the value of m is 6.

• How can you solve the equation $68 + n = 83$ by using the hundred chart?

Use the hundred chart to solve the equation. Check your answer.

    1. $26 + n = 33$ **2.** $b + 12 = 24$ **3.** $20 - y = 18$ **4.** $32 - k = 26$ **5.** $57 - a = 48$

Problem Solving Workshop
Strategy: Work Backward

OBJECTIVE: Solve problems using the strategy *work backward*.

Learn the Strategy

When you work backward to solve a problem, you start with the end result and use the facts in the problem to work back to the beginning of a problem.

Work backward from a total.

There are 16 pelicans at the pier. When more pelicans fly to the pier, there are 20 pelicans. How many more pelicans fly to the pier?

When you add to find a total, you can subtract to work backward to solve.

Write an addition equation to model the problem.

$16 + p = 20$ Let p = number of pelicans that fly to the pier.

To find the value of *p*, work backward.

$20 - 16 = p$

Work backward from an end time.

Raymond and Charity got to the library at 3:45 P.M. It takes 20 minutes to walk to the library from Charity's house, and Raymond got to Charity's house 15 minutes before they left for the library. At what time did Raymond arrive at Charity's house?

Use a model to find the time Raymond arrived at Charity's house.

To find the time Raymond arrived at Charity's house, work backward.

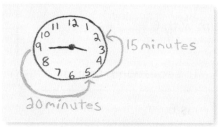

20 minutes

TALK Math

How can you check your answer to the first problem?

AF 1.0 Students use and interpret variables, mathematical symbols, and properties to write and simplify expressions and sentences. *also* **AF 1.1, ○━━ AF 1.2, ○━━ AF 1.3, ○━━ AF 2.0, MR 1.0, MR 2.0, MR 2.3, MR 2.4, MR 2.6, MR 3.1, MR 3.2**

Use the Strategy

PROBLEM A wildlife preserve in Zimbabwe, Africa, has a habitat for lions. The rangers released 8 lions back into the wild and then received 12 lions from another preserve. Now there are 24 lions at the preserve. How many lions did the preserve have before the release?

Read to
Understand
Plan
Solve
Check

Read to Understand

 Reading Skill

- **What information will you use?**

Plan

- **What strategy can you use to solve the problem?**

You can write an equation with a variable. Then solve the problem by working backward.

Solve

- **How can you use the strategy to solve the problem?**

Write an equation with a variable to model the problem.

 Reading Skill Make sure the equation shows the sequence of events.

Think: There were some lions before the release. Eight lions were released. Then the preserve received 12 lions. Now there are 24 lions.

Choose a variable. Let b represent the number of lions before the release. To find the value of b, work backward.

lions before release	→	lions released	→	lions received	→	lions now
b	−	8	+	12	=	24

lions now	→	lions received	→	lions released	→	lions before release
24	−	12	+	8	=	20

So, there were 20 lions before the release.

Check

- **What other strategies could you use to check your answer?**

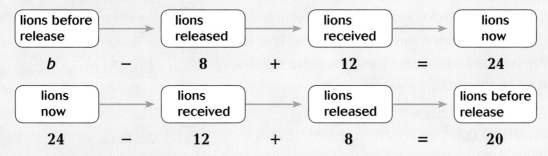

Guided Problem Solving

Read to Understand

Plan

Solve

Check

1. There are many volunteer teams that feed the lions at Léon Preserve. Another preserve needed help, so 10 volunteer teams left. The next day, 4 new volunteer teams arrived and now Léon Preserve has 15 teams. How many teams were there originally?

   First, choose a variable. Tell what the variable represents.

   Let v represent the original number of volunteer teams.

   Next, write an equation.

   $v - 10 + 4 = 15$

   Then, work backward.

   $15 - 4 + 10 = v$

   Finally, solve the equation.

   $21 = v$

2. **What if** 5 volunteer teams left and 11 arrived? How many teams were there originally?

3. Many volunteer teams must patrol and clean the lion preserve. Twelve teams leave the preserve on patrol. Seven teams arrive to clean. There are 23 teams at the preserve now. How many volunteer teams were there originally?

Problem Solving Strategy Practice

Work backward to solve.

4. It costs $2,900 to volunteer for 4 weeks at a lion breeding project. There is an extra cost for each additional week. It costs Jeff $3,500 to volunteer for 5 weeks. How much does each additional week cost?

USE DATA For 5–6, use the table.

5. The mature lions at the preserve are injured lions. When they are healthy again, they are returned to the wild. This year, the preserve has had a total of 11 injured mature lions. How many have been returned to the wild?

6. **WRITE Math** Last week, 7 cubs were moved to the adolescent group, and 4 cubs were born. **Explain** how to find how many cubs the preserve had last week.

7. **FAST FACT** The largest recorded African lion weighed 690 pounds. The difference in weight between the largest lion and an average lion is 120 pounds. How much does an average African lion weigh?

Preserve Lion Population

Age	Number
Cubs	18
Adolescents	14
Mature	2
Older	7

94

Mixed Strategy Practice

8. Daily duties for each animal include grooming, walking, and feeding. If a volunteer is in charge of 7 animals, how many daily duties will the volunteer do?

USE DATA For 9–10, use the bar graph.

9. There were more volunteers for the lion project during the summer than during the spring. If 105 people volunteered in the summer, how many more volunteers were there than in the spring?

10. During a two-week stay at the wildlife preserve in the summer, there were 17 fewer volunteers than the total number for the spring. About how many volunteers were there in the two-week period?

11. **Pose a Problem** Look back at Problem 7. Write a similar problem by exchanging the known and unknown information.

12. **Open-Ended** Zawati Preserve had some volunteers. Some of the volunteers went to other preserves. Zawati Preserve has 12 volunteers left. How many volunteers might have been there to begin with and how many might have left for other preserves?

13. Volunteers rescued a lion, an elephant, and a leopard from traps. They rescued the lion before the leopard. The lion was not the first animal rescued. In what order did the volunteers rescue the animals?

CHALLENGE YOURSELF ───────────

Visitors to the wildlife preserve can take a guided tour to see the animals. There were 373 visitors to the preserve in January and 388 visitors in February.

14. Each month, the preserve had 15 more visitors than the month before. How many visitors did the preserve have in June, July, and August combined?

15. During January, 151 more children than adults visited the preserve. Draw a diagram to find how many adults visited the preserve during January.

Choose a STRATEGY

Draw a Diagram or Picture

Make a Model or Act It Out

Make an Organized List

Find a Pattern

Make a Table or Graph

Predict and Test

Work Backward

Solve a Simpler Problem

Write an Equation

Use Logical Reasoning

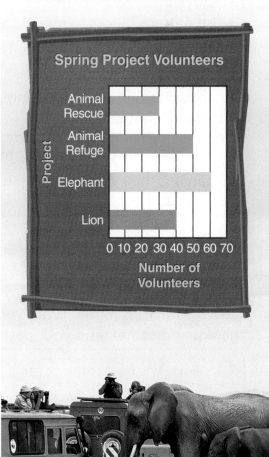

Patterns: Find a Rule

OBJECTIVE: Find a rule for a number relationship and write an equation for the rule.

Quick Review

Add 12 to each number.

1. 6   2. 14
3. 23   4. 35
5. 60

Learn

PROBLEM A pattern of figures is made using triangles 1 unit long on each side. The perimeter of the first figure is 3 units. The second figure has 2 triangles and a perimeter of 4 units. The third figure has 3 triangles and a perimeter of 5 units. Find a rule for the perimeter of a figure using the number of triangles in the figure.

Remember
Perimeter is the distance around a figure.

Activity **Materials** ▪ triangle pattern blocks

Input	Output
t	*p*
1	3
2	4
3	5
4	▪
5	▪

- Use pattern blocks to model the pattern.
- Make an input/output table. The input, *t*, is the number of triangles, and the output, *p*, is the perimeter.
- Look for a pattern in the table. Pattern: The output is 2 more than the input.

So, the rule is the perimeter is 2 more than the number of triangles.

You can use the rule to write an equation. Use variables to show the input and output.

input   output
  ↓   ↓
$t + 2 = p$ **Think:** To find the value of p, add 2 to t.

Examples Find a rule. Write your rule as an equation. Use the equation to extend your pattern.

Ⓐ

Input	*x*	8	10	12	14	16
Output	*y*	4	6	8	▪	▪

Rule: Subtract 4 from *x*.
Equation: $x - 4 = y$

Test your rule for each pair of numbers in the table.

$x - 4 = y$ $x - 4 = y$
$14 - 4 = 10$ $16 - 4 = 12$

So, the next two numbers are 10 and 12.

Ⓑ

Input	*b*	9	17	25	33	▪
Output	*c*	16	24	32	40	48

Rule: Add 7 to *b*.
Equation: $b + 7 = c$

Test your rule for each pair of numbers in the table.

$b + 7 = c$
$41 + 7 = 48$ **Think:** Work backward, b = 48 − 7.

So, the next number is 41.

O━ᴨ AF 1.5 Understand that an equation such as $y = 3x + 5$ is a prescription for determining a second number when a first number is given. *also* **O━ᴨ NS 3.0, AF 1.0, MR 1.1, MR 2.0, MR 2.3, MR 2.4, MR 3.2**

1. Rule: Add 15 to the input. The equation is: $r + 15 = s$. What are the next two numbers in the pattern?

Input	r	7	9	12	16	20	23
Output	s	22	24	27	31	■	■

Find a rule. Write your rule as an equation. Use the equation to extend your pattern.

2.
Input	a	12	25	31	43	59	62	74
Output	b	20	33	39	■	■	■	■

3.
Input	m	62	58	47	31	24	17	9
Output	n	57	53	42	■	■	■	■

4. **TALK Math** **Explain** why it is important to test your rule with all the numbers in an input/output table.

Independent Practice and Problem Solving

Find a rule. Write your rule as an equation. Use the equation to extend your pattern.

5.
Input	x	35	42	63	75	80	97	98
Output	y	24	31	52	■	■	■	■

6.
Input	w	14	21	45	■	■	■	■
Output	x	34	41	65	73	92	100	123

Use the rule and equation to make an input/output table.

7. Add 16 to k.
   $k + 16 = m$

8. Subtract 10 from b.
   $b - 10 = c$

9. Add 23 to f.
   $f + 23 = g$

10. Subtract 17 from x.
    $x - 17 = y$

USE DATA For 11–12, use the table.

11. Find a rule. Write your rule as an equation for the information in the Hot Lunch Accounts table. Use your rule to extend the pattern.

12. **WRITE Math** **What's the Question?** Mabel has $12 on Friday after buying lunch each day that week. The answer is $27.

Hot Lunch Accounts	
Before	**After**
$16	$13
$24	$21
$29	$26
$33	$30

Achieving the Standards

13. $32 - 3 + ■ = 29 + 41$ (○🔒 AF 2.1, p. 88)

14. $3 + 3 + 3 + 3 + 3 + 3 =$
    (Grade 3 NS 2.0)

15. If $h = 9$, what is the value of $26 - (15 - h)$? (○🔒 AF 1.2, p. 82)

16. **Test Prep** Which equation describes the data in the table?

Input	r	14	23	31	39
Output	s	8	17	25	33

   A $r + 6 = s$ **C** $s - 6 = r$

   B $r - 6 = s$ **D** $r + s = 6$

 **Extra Practice**

Set A Find the missing number. Name the property you used. (pp. 78–79)

1. $62 + 46 = 46 + \blacksquare$

2. $53 + (64 + \blacksquare) = (53 + 64) + 19$

3. $\blacksquare + 0 = 92$

4. $98 = \blacksquare + 98$

5. $(23 + 77) + 54 = 23 + (\blacksquare + 54)$

6. $79 + 63 = 63 + \blacksquare$

Set B Tell what you do first. Then find the value of each expression. (pp. 80–81)

1. $11 + (8 - 4)$

2. $24 - (7 + 9)$

3. $(28 - 6) - 9$

4. $35 - (13 - 5)$

5. Donna had 12 books. She donated 8 books to the book fair. Then she bought 3 more books. How many books does she have now? Write an expression. Then tell the value of the expression.

Set C Find the value of each expression if $x = 6$ and $y = 9$. (pp. 82–83)

1. $15 - x$

2. $y - 4$

3. $12 + (y - 3)$

4. $15 - (7 + x)$

5. $x + 9$

6. $17 - y$

7. $24 - (9 - x)$

8. $4 + (y + 8)$

Set D Solve the equation. (pp. 84–87)

1. $9 + n = 17$

2. $\blacksquare - 8 = 15$

3. $n - 15 = 20$

4. $30 - b = 20$

5. $k - 33 = 7$

6. $g + 19 = 25$

7. $41 + m = 59$

8. $9 + \blacksquare = 100$

9. There are 36 mystery and biography books in a box. Some are mysteries, and 9 are biographies. Write an equation with a variable. Tell what the variable represents. Solve the equation.

Set E Complete to make the equation true. (pp. 88–91)

1. $10 + 6 + \blacksquare = 16 + 8$

2. $7 - 4 + 8 = \blacksquare + 8$

3. $12 + 3 - 6 = 15 - \blacksquare$

4. $30 + 11 + \blacksquare = 41 + 17$

5. $58 - 8 = 50 + 8 - \blacksquare$

6. $31 - \blacksquare + 2 = 10 + 2$

Set F Find a rule. Write your rule as an equation. Use the equation to extend your pattern. (pp. 96–97)

1.

Input	x	4	8	12	16	20
Output	y	16	20	24	$\blacksquare$	$\blacksquare$

2.

Input	x	32	47	55	$\blacksquare$	$\blacksquare$
Output	y	23	38	46	73	88

Technology
Use Harcourt Mega Math, Ice Station
Exploration, *Arctic Algebra*, Levels B, F, I, Y.

Variable Race

On Your Mark!
2 players

Get Set!
- Number cube labeled 1 to 6
- Two-color counters (1 for each player)

START

$n + 6$

$n + 2$

$10 - n$

Jump Ahead 2 Spaces

$5 + n$

$n - 1$

$4 + n$

Take Another Turn

$n + 8$

$15 - n$

$9 + n$

$n + 1$

$12 - n$

Go Back 2 Spaces

$3 + n$

$n + 10$

Lose a Turn

$7 + n$

$9 - n$

Go Back 1 Space

$n + 10$

FINISH

Go!

- Decide who will be red and who will be yellow. Put your counters on START. Toss the number cube. The player who rolls the greater number goes first.

- Players take turns tossing the number cube and moving that number of spaces on the game board. If the space has an expression, the player uses the number tossed as the variable to find the value of the expression.

- If the answer is correct, the player leaves the counter in that space. If the answer is incorrect, the player goes back to his or her previous space.

- If a player lands in a space that gives a direction, the player must follow the direction.

- The first player to reach FINISH wins.

 **Chapter 4 Review/Test**

Check Vocabulary and Concepts

Choose the best term from the box.

VOCABULARY

Associative Property

Commutative Property

equation

1. An ___?___ is a number sentence stating that two amounts are equal. (AF 1.0, p. 84)

2. Numbers can be added in any order and the sum will be the same. This is called the ___?___. (AF 1.0, p. 78)

Check Skills

Find the missing number. Name the property you used. (AF 1.0, pp. 78–79)

3. $52 + 28 = 28 + \blacksquare$

4. $\blacksquare + 0 = 67$

5. $28 + (12 + \blacksquare) = (28 + 12) + 38$

Find the value of each expression. (AF 1.0, pp. 80–81, 82–83)

6. $16 + (9 - 5)$

7. $27 - (7 + 8)$

8. $\blacksquare - 12$ if $\blacksquare = 52$

9. $45 - (d + 9)$ if $d = 4$

Solve the equation. (AF 1.0, pp. 84–87)

10. $8 + d = 15$

11. $k - 7 = 35$

12. $n + 21 = 24$

13. $17 - b = 9$

Complete to make the equation true. (O━┓ AF 2.1, pp. 88–91)

14. $19 + 2 + \blacksquare = 21 + 7$

15. $12 - 9 + 9 = \blacksquare + 9$

16. $9 + 9 - 2 = 18 - \blacksquare$

Find a rule. Write your rule as an equation. Use the equation to extend your pattern. (O━┓ AF 1.5, pp. 96–97)

17.

Input	x	23	35	49	56	71
Output	y	36	48	62	$\blacksquare$	$\blacksquare$

18.

Input	x	26	34	46	$\blacksquare$	$\blacksquare$
Output	y	11	19	31	58	77

Check Problem Solving

Solve. (AF 1.0, MR 2.6, pp. 92–95)

19. Ellie had 37 stuffed animals in her collection. Her aunt gave her some more stuffed animals to add to her collection, so now she has 43. How many stuffed animals did her aunt give her?

20. **WRITE Math** ▶ Manuel saved $64 for a new bicycle, including the $18 he earned mowing lawns. Write an equation. **Explain** how to work backward to find how much money Manuel had before he mowed the lawns.

GO ONLINE Technology Use *Online Assessment.*

Enrich • Use Relational Thinking
Baseball Cards

Mike has 27 baseball cards and buys 18 more cards. Laura has the same number of baseball cards as Mike after she buys 19 cards. How many baseball cards did Laura have before she bought 19 cards?

You can write an equation to find the number of baseball cards Laura had.

Mike's	Laura's

27 cards + 18 cards = x cards + 19 cards

$$27 + 18 = x + 19$$

Think: The value of the left side of an equation is the same as the value of the right side.

Use relational thinking to find the value of x without computing.

$27 + 18 = x + 19$
$27 + 18 = 26 + 19$ **Think:** 19 is 1 more than 18, so x is 1 less than 27.
$x = 26$

So, Laura had 26 baseball cards before she bought 19 cards.

All Star Examples

A $12 + 9 = 10 + 8 + n$	**Think:** 10 is 2 less than 12, and 8 is 1 less than 9.	**B** $75 - 36 = 75 - 35 - s$	**Think:** 75 is equal to 75, and 35 is 1 less than 36.
$12 + 9 = 10 + 8 + 3$		$75 - 36 = 75 - 35 - 1$	
$n = 3$		$s = 1$	

So, n is $2 + 1$, or 3.   So, s is 1.

Take a Swing

Use relational thinking to find the value of the variable.

1. $8 + 5 = p + 6$
2. $85 - 25 = 75 - y$
3. $449 + 862 = 450 + b$
4. $100 - 77 = s - 79$
5. $14 + 38 = 14 + 36 + x$
6. $99 - 68 = 99 - 66 - t$
7. $55 + 59 = 50 + 50 + c$
8. $432 - 167 = 432 - 67 - n$
9. $87 + 56 = 86 + 55 + p$

Ninth Inning

WRITE Math **Explain** how you used relational thinking to solve problem 7.

Unit Review/Test
Chapters 1–4

Multiple Choice

1. The table shows daily attendance at some amusement parks in 2004 and 2005.

Daily Amusement Park Attendance	
Year	**Number of Visitors**
2004	899,000
2005	917,000

How many more amusement park visitors were there in 2005 than in 2004? (O━┓ NS 3.1, p. 44)

A 18,000

B 19,000

C 20,000

D 21,000

2. Which number is shown in expanded form? (O━┓ NS 1.1, p. 4)

$90,000 + 3,000 + 600 + 40 + 3$

A 99,643   C 93,064

B 93,643   D 90,364

3. Sherri found a grand piano that costs $29,445. To the nearest thousand, how much does the piano cost? (O━┓ NS 1.3, p. 34)

A $30,000   C $29,000

B $29,500   D $20,000

4. Which digit is in the millions place in 35,970,241? (O━┓ NS 1.1, p. 10)

A 9   C 5

B 7   D 3

5. A flight from San Diego to Austin costs $453 in July and $298 in October. About how much more does the flight cost in July than in October? (NS 2.1, p. 40)

A $50   C $250

B $150   D $800

6. What is the value of the digit 8 in 48,213? (O━┓ NS 1.1, p. 4)

A 8   C 800

B 80   D 8,000

7. Jake had $43. He spent some on music and $3 on a magazine. Now he has $21 left. How much did he spend on music? (NS 2.1, p. 92)

A $24   C $19

B $21   D $17

8. Which statement is not true? (O━┓ AF 2.1, p. 88)

A $27 + 37 + 11 = 64 - 11$

B $27 + 37 + 11 = 64 + 11$

C $27 + 37 - 1 = 64 - 1$

D $27 + 37 + 5 = 64 + 5$

9. Which equation describes the data in the table? (O━┓ AF 1.5, p. 96)

Input	x	5	7	9	11	13
Output	y	14	16	18	20	22

A $x + 8 = y$ C $x + 10 = y$

B $x + 9 = y$ D $x + 11 = y$

GO ONLINE Technology Use *Online Assessment.*

10. Marcos had some comic books. At Cory's Comics he bought 4 more. Now Marcos has 43 comic books in all. Which equation could be used to find how many comic books Marcos had before he went to Cory's Comics? (AF 1.1, p. 84)

A $43 = n + 4$

B $43 = n - 43$

C $43 = n - 4$

D $n = 43 + 4$

11. The table shows the number of cars that used Exit 8 on Trans-State Parkway in different months.

Exit 8 Traffic	
Month	Number of Cars
June	112,451
July	183,612
August	243,519

How many cars in all used Exit 8 during July and August? (O—n NS 3.1, p. 64)

A 425,021

B 426,121

C 426,131

D 427,131

12. Which digit makes the number sentence true? (O—n NS 1.2, p. 12)

$$4,201,351 > 4,20\blacksquare,351$$

A 3

B 2

C 1

D 0

Short Response

13. Alma had 9 CDs. She used some of them to record music. Write an expression to show how many CDs Alma has left. (AF 1.1, p. 82)

14. The first edition of the *Oxford English Dictionary* was published in 1928. The third edition was published online in 2000. How many years after the first edition was the third edition published? (O—n NS 3.1, p. 62)

15. Order the numbers from greatest to least. (O—n NS 1.2, p. 16)

12,413; 13,313; 12,213; 13,113

16. A music group printed 20,000 postcards. They handed out 16,263. Approximately how many postcards were not handed out? (NS 2.1, p. 40)

Extended Response `WRITE Math`

17. Kathleen's computer stores 900 songs. She has 883 songs and wants to add 15 more. Will 15 more songs fit on Kathleen's computer? Do you need an exact answer or an estimate. **Explain.** (O—n NS 1.4, p. 48)

18. **Explain** how the parentheses change the value of each expression. (O—n AF 1.2, p. 80)

$$(27 - 14) + 9$$
$$27 - (14 + 9)$$

19. Is *A* greater than, equal to, or less than *B*? **Explain** how you know. (O—n AF 2.1, p. 88)

$$A + 5 = B$$

Languages at Home in California

MANY LANGUAGES

No one is sure how many languages there are in the world, but there are certainly more than 4,000. Most people in California speak English. However, many people speak other languages, too.

Language Spoken at Home in California

Language	Number of Speakers Over 5 Years Old
Chinese	937,000
English Only	19,125,000
Japanese	161,000
Korean	348,000
Spanish	8,968,000
Vietnamese	428,000

FACT·ACTIVITY

Use the table above to answer the questions.

❶ If you round to the nearest million, which language has about 1 million speakers?

❷ Do more speakers over 5 years old speak Korean or Vietnamese at home?

❸ Which two languages have a number of speakers with the digit 6 in the ten-thousands place?

❹ Which language's number of speakers would round to 300,000?

❺ Which language has the digit 5 in the thousands place?

❻ Write the number of Spanish speakers in word form.

❼ **WRITE Math** Explain how to round the number of Japanese speakers to the nearest hundred thousand.

23 18 9 20 9 14 7
9 14 3 15 4 5

In 1838, the American inventor Samuel F. B. Morse developed a code for sending messages over electrical wires. His code used short pulses (dots) and long pulses (dashes) of electricity to represent letters and numbers. Morse code allows people to communicate over long distances without speaking.

Morse Code

A	B	C	D	E	F	G	H	I	J	K	L	M
.-	-...	-.-.	-..	.	..-.	--.	....	..	.---	-.-	.-..	--

N	O	P	Q	R	S	T	U	V	W	X	Y	Z
-.	---	.--.	--.-	.-.	...	-	..-	...-	.--	-..-	-.--	--..

1	2	3	4	5	6	7	8	9	0
.----	..---	...--	....-	.....	-....	--...	---..	----.	-----

Telegraph operators tap a key like this to send messages in Morse code.

FACT·ACTIVITY

Use codes to answer the questions.

❶ Another name for California is the Golden State. Write California's nickname in Morse code.

❷ The title of this page is written in a simple number code. The chart to the right shows the code used. Use the code to find the title of this page.

❸ Make up your own number code.

► Make a different code using the same 26 letters.

► How can you use number patterns to make a new code?

► How can you use what you know about place value to make up a new code?

► Write a message in your code. Do not put the solution on the page. Have a few classmates try to crack your code!

Number Code			
A = 1	B = 2	C = 3	D = 4
E = 5	F = 6	G = 7	H = 8
I = 9	J = 10	K = 11	L = 12
M = 13	N = 14	O = 15	P = 16
Q = 17	R = 18	S = 19	T = 20
U = 21	V = 22	W = 23	X = 24
Y = 25	Z = 26		

Multiplication and Division Facts

Save the Blackfooted Ferret

Math on Location

1 Many families like this baby black-footed ferret's family of 4 are protected and fed by scientists.

2 Family groups are prepared to live in divided areas in the wild by living in similar, but protected, areas.

3 Protection and preparation equal multiple strong families for a species once considered extinct.

VOCABULARY POWER

TALK Math

Look at the words below the first **Math on Location** photograph. If each family group in the protected area has the same number of ferrets as that family, how could you find the number of ferrets in 6 family groups?

READ Math

REVIEW VOCABULARY You learned the words below when you learned multiplication and division basic facts. How do these words relate to **Math on Location**?

divide to separate into equal groups; the opposite operation of multiplication

fact family a set of related multiplication and division, or addition and subtraction, number sentences

multiply when you combine equal groups, you can multiply to find how many in all; the opposite operation of division

WRITE Math

Copy and complete the Venn diagram below. Use what you know about multiplication and division facts to complete the Venn diagram.

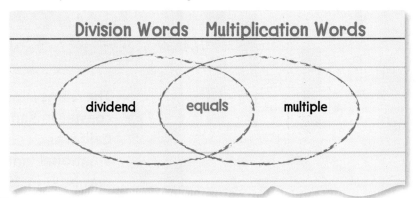

Division Words   Multiplication Words

dividend   equals   multiple

Technology
Multimedia Math Glossary link at
www.harcourtschool.com/hspmath

CHAPTER

5 Multiplication and Division Facts

The Big Idea Basic fact strategies for multiplication and division are based on properties, patterns, and number relationships.

Investigate

Use the bar graph. Suppose there are at least 2 cars on each roller coaster train and each train is filled. What are the possible numbers of cars in each train? Choose a roller coaster, and draw pictures of how the train could look.

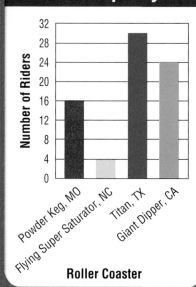

Roller Coaster Train Capacity

Number of Riders

(Bar graph showing: Powder Keg, MO = 16; Flying Super Saturator, NC = 4; Titan, TX = 30; Giant Dipper, CA = 24)

Roller Coaster

CALIFORNIA FAST FACT

The Giant Dipper roller coaster in San Diego, California, considered a national landmark, was built in 1925. A 75-foot drop helps it reach 45 miles per hour on 2,600 feet of track.

GO ONLINE
Technology
Student pages are available in the Student eBook.

**Check your understanding of important skills
needed for success in Chapter 5.**

▶ Meaning of Multiplication

Copy and complete each number sentence.

1.

    ■ groups of ■ = ■

2.

    ■ rows of ■ = ■

3.

    ■ rows of ■ = ■

4.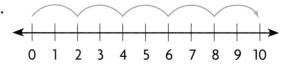

    ■ jumps of ■ = ■

▶ Meaning of Division

Answer the questions for each picture.

5. How many stars are there in all?
6. How many equal groups are there?
7. How many stars are in each group?

8. How many tiles are there in all?
9. How many equal rows are there?
10. How many tiles are in each row?

VOCABULARY POWER

CHAPTER VOCABULARY

addition	inverse
array	operations
divide	multiple
dividend	multiply
divisor	product
fact family	quotient
factor	square number
	subtraction

WARM-UP WORDS

multiply join equal-size groups

divide separate into equal-size groups or find how many in each group

inverse operations operations, such as multiplication and division, that undo each other

fact family a set of related multiplication and division sentences using the same numbers

ALGEBRA
Relate Operations

OBJECTIVE: Relate repeated addition to multiplication and repeated subtraction to division.

Learn

When you **multiply**, you join equal-size groups. When you **divide**, you separate into equal-size groups or you find how many in each group.

PROBLEM The miniature train ride has 6 cars. Each car holds 4 people. How many people at a time can ride the train?

Example 1 Use repeated addition and multiplication.

Draw a picture to show 6 groups of 4.

Add to find how many in all.

Write: $4 + 4 + 4 + 4 + 4 + 4 = 24$

Read: 6 fours equal 24.

Multiply to find how many in all.

Write: $6 \times 4 = 24$, or $\begin{array}{r} 4 \\ \times 6 \\ \hline 24 \end{array}$

Read: 6 times 4 equals 24.

So, 24 people at a time can ride the train.

Example 2 Use repeated subtraction and division.

There are 12 people waiting in line to ride the miniature train. Each car holds 4 people. How many cars will the 12 people fill?

Subtract to find how many equal-size groups. Start with 12. Take away groups of 4 until you reach zero.

Count the number of times you subtract 4.

Write: $12 - 4 - 4 - 4 = 0$

Read: From 12 subtract 4 three times.

Divide to find how many equal-size groups there are.

There are 3 groups of 4.

Write: $12 \div 4 = 3$, or $4\overline{)12}^{\,3}$

Read: 12 divided by 4 equals 3.

So, the 12 people will fill 3 cars.

ERROR ALERT

Remember that the multiplication ($\times$) sign is different from the plus ($+$) sign.
6×4 means 6 groups of 4.
$6 + 4$ means 6 and 4 more.

NS 3.0 Students solve problems involving addition, subtraction, multiplication, and division of whole numbers and understand the relationships among the operations. *also* MR 1.1, MR 2.3, MR 2.4, MR 3.2

Copy and complete.

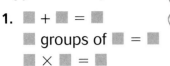

1. ▨ + ▨ = ▨

    ▨ groups of ▨ = ▨

    ▨ × ▨ = ▨

2. 6 − 2 − ▨ − ▨ = ▨

    ▨ ÷ ▨ = ▨

Write the related multiplication or division sentence. Draw a picture that shows the sentence.

3. 5 groups of 6 equal 30.   ✅ 4. 9 − 3 − 3 − 3 = 0   ✅ 5. 3 + 3 + 3 + 3 + 3 = 15

6. **TALK Math** A ride has 4 cars that hold 5 people each. How many people at a time can ride? Show two ways to solve this problem. **Explain** how the two ways are related.

Independent Practice and Problem Solving

Write the related multiplication or division sentence. Draw a picture that shows the sentence.

7. 14 − 7 − 7 = 0

8. 4 + 4 + 4 = 12

9. 12 − 6 − 6 = 0

Reasoning For 10–12, tell whether the number sentence is *true* or *false*. If false, explain how you know.

10. $8 + 8 + 8 + 8 + 8 \overset{?}{=} 5 \times 8$ 11. $3 \times 7 \overset{?}{=} 14 + 7$

12. $5 \times 4 \overset{?}{=} 4 + 4 + 4 + 4$

13. Thirty-six people at a time can ride the Scrambler. Each car holds 3 people. If 8 cars are full and the rest of the cars are empty, how many more people can get on?

14. Sara has 27 tickets. If each ride costs 3 tickets, how many different rides can she go on?

15. Andy says $10 \times 2 = 20$. How can he check his answer?

16. **WRITE Math** Is 2×3 equal to 3×2? Use related addition facts to **explain**.

Achieving the Standards

17. What is the value of $(11 − 7) + 2$?

    (O┑ AF 1.2, p. 80)

18. $5 \times 7 =$ (Grade 3 O┑ NS 2.2)

19. Identify the polygon.

    (Grade 3 O┑ MG 2.1)

20. **Test Prep** Which of these is another way to write $21 − 7 − 7 − 7 = 0$?

    A $21 ÷ 7 = 3$ **C** $7 \times 3 = 21$

    B $21 ÷ 3 = 7$ **D** $7 + 7 = 14$

2

ALGEBRA
Relate Multiplication and Division

OBJECTIVE: Relate multiplication to division.

Quick Review

Write an addition sentence and a multiplication sentence for the picture.

Learn

PROBLEM A box of crayons holds 2 rows of 8 crayons each. How many crayons does the box hold?

Example 1 Use repeated addition.

$2 \times 8 = n$ Think: $2 \times 8 = 8 + 8$, or 16.

↓

$2 \times 8 = 16$

So, the box holds 16 crayons.

Multiplication and division by the same number are opposite operations, or **inverse operations**. One operation undoes the other.

A **fact family**, a set of related multiplication and division sentences using the same numbers, shows this relationship.

factor	factor	**product**	**dividend**	**divisor**	**quotient**	
2	× 8	= 16	16	÷ 8	= 2	← fact family
8	× 2	= 16	16	÷ 2	= 8	for 2, 8, 16

Example 2 Use a related multiplication sentence.

Another box holds 16 crayons. There are 2 crayons of each color. How many colors of crayons are in the box?

$16 \div 2 = n$ Think: $8 \times 2 = 16$, so $16 \div 2 = 8$.

↓

$16 \div 2 = 8$

So, the box holds 8 colors of crayons.

Vocabulary

inverse operations

fact family	dividend
factor	divisor
product	quotient

Guided Practice

Copy and complete the fact family.

1. $4 \times 8 = 32$ $\qquad\qquad$ $32 \div \blacksquare = 4$

$\quad 8 \times \blacksquare = 32$ $\qquad\qquad$ $\blacksquare \div 4 = 8$

O─ NS 3.0 Students solve problems involving addition, subtraction, multiplication, and division of whole numbers and understand the relationships among the operations. *also* **NS 4.0, AF 1.1, MR 1.1, MR 2.2, MR 2.3, MR 2.4, MR 3.1, MR 3.2**

Write the fact family for the set of numbers.

2. 2, 5, 10   **3.** 3, 4, 12   **4.** 2, 6, 12   ✓**5.** 2, 3, 6   ✓**6.** 1, 3, 3

7. [TALK Math] **Explain** how to use a fact family to write the related multiplication and division sentences.

Independent Practice (and Problem Solving)

Write the fact family for the set of numbers.

8. 2, 7, 14   **9.** 1, 4, 4   **10.** 3, 5, 15   **11.** 3, 3, 9   **12.** 5, 6, 30

Find the value of the variable. Then write a related sentence.

13. $24 \div 8 = n$ **14.** $3 \times 10 = c$ **15.** $8 \div 1 = y$ **16.** $36 \div m = 9$ **17.** $7 \times a = 28$

18. $6 \times 1 = b$ **19.** $35 \div 5 = p$ **20.** $18 \div 9 = n$ **21.** $8 \times c = 40$ **22.** $y \div 3 = 7$

USE DATA For 23–24, use the pictograph.

23. What if the crayon factory made 8 different shades of yellow? How many symbols would represent 8 shades in the pictograph?

24. How many different shades of crayon colors does the crayon factory make?

25. ≡**FAST FACT** The average American child will use up about 730 crayons by the age of 10, or about 6 crayons each month. About how many crayons will a child use up in 4 months?

26. [WRITE Math] ▸ **What's the Error?** Dale says that 2×6 is in the same fact family as $6 \div 2$. Is he right? **Explain** why or why not.

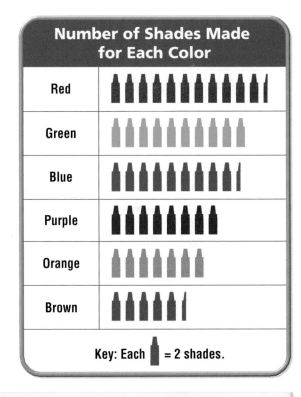

Number of Shades Made for Each Color

Red	
Green	
Blue	
Purple	
Orange	
Brown	

Key: Each 🖍 = 2 shades.

Achieving the Standards

27. Suppose you are asked to pick any one-digit number greater than 10. Is this event certain, likely, unlikely, or impossible? (Grade 3 SDAP 1.1)

28. What is the value of the expression below? (0━┑ AF 1.2, p. 80)

$$24 - (13 - 5)$$

29. What is the missing number in this pattern? (Grade 3, AF 2.2)

2, 4, 6, 8, 10, ■

30. Test Prep Which fact belongs to the same fact family as $4 \times 4 = 16$?

A $4 + 4 = 8$ **C** $16 - 4 = 12$

B $4 \div 4 = 1$ **D** $16 \div 4 = 4$

3 Multiply and Divide Facts Through 5

OBJECTIVE: Multiply and divide facts from 0 through 5.

Quick Review

Write the fact family.

1. 2, 3, 6
2. 1, 3, 3
3. 3, 5, 15
4. 4, 7, 28
5. 2, 9, 18

Learn

Mr. Chen asked his students to use models to show that multiplication and division are inverse operations. This is how they showed their work.

A Amanda made 4 quilt blocks. How many rectangles did she use?

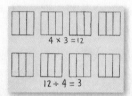

$4 \times 3 = 12$

$12 \div 4 = 3$

First, I made 4 groups of 3 rectangles to get 12 rectangles. Then, to check, I used 12 rectangles and separated them into 4 groups to get 3 in each group.

B Jon's quilt is 2 times as long as Mia's quilt. Mia's quilt is 4 blocks long. How long is Jon's quilt?

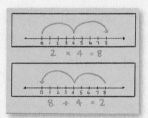

$2 \times 4 = 8$

$8 \div 4 = 2$

I started at 0 on a number line and made 2 jumps of 4 to land at 8. Then, to check, I started at 8 and took 2 jumps of 4 back to 0.

▲ In a rail fence quilt each quilt block is made by sewing 3 rectangular strips together.

C Paul's quilt has 20 blocks, with 4 blocks in each row. How many rows does his quilt have?

$5 \times 4 = 20 \qquad 20 \div 4 = 5$

I made 5 rows of 4 blocks to make 20 blocks. Then, to check, I divided 20 blocks into 4 columns to get 5 in each column.

D Ella used 21 rectangles to make some quilt blocks. How many quilt blocks did she make?

Since there are 3 rectangles in each block, I found 21 by looking down column 3. Then I looked left to find the quotient, 7.

To check, I looked across row 7 and down column 3 to find the product, 21.

$21 \div 3 = 7$, so $7 \times 3 = 21$.

×	0	1	2	3	4	5
0	0	0	0	0	0	0
1	0	1	2	3	4	5
2	0	2	4	6	8	10
3	0	3	6	9	12	15
4	0	4	8	12	16	20
5	0	5	10	15	20	25
6	0	6	12	18	24	30
7	0	7	14	21	28	35
8	0	8	16	24	32	40
9	0	9	18	27	36	45

- **Reasoning** Use the multiplication table to show that $0 \div 5 = 0$. Then use the table to show $5 \div 0 = \blacksquare$ does not make sense.

NS 3.0 Students solve problems involving addition, subtraction, multiplication, and division of whole numbers and understand the relationships among the operations. *also* **AF 1.0, MR 1.1, MR 2.0, MR 2.3, MR 2.4, MR 3.0, MR 3.2, MR 3.3**

Find the product or quotient. Then write a related multiplication or division sentence.

1. $2 \times 5 = n$

2. $6 \div 3 = n$

3. $2 \times 4 = n$

Find the product or quotient.

4. 6×1 **5.** $14 \div 2$ **6.** 8×3 **7.** $36 \div 4$ ✓ **8.** 3×3 ✓ **9.** $15 \div 5$

10. **TALK Math** Explain why division by a number is the inverse of multiplication by that number. Give an example. You may wish to draw a model.

Independent Practice and Problem Solving

Find the product or quotient.

11. 6×2 **12.** $10 \div 1$ **13.** 9×3 **14.** $28 \div 4$ **15.** $27 \div 3$ **16.** 6×5

17. 4×1 **18.** 10×5 **19.** $24 \div 4$ **20.** $16 \div 2$ **21.** 8×4 **22.** $40 \div 4$

★ **Algebra** Find the value of $n \times 4$ for each value of n.

23. $n = 4$ **24.** $n = 1$ **25.** $n = 6$ **26.** $n = 10$ **27.** $n = 5$ **28.** $n = 0$

USE DATA For 29–31, use the quilt block.

29. Maya wants to make 4 quilt blocks like this one. She cut out 4 squares and 8 triangles. How many more triangles does she need to cut out?

30. Enrique's quilt is 2 quilt blocks by 2 quilt blocks. How many squares and triangles did he cut out?

31. **WRITE Math** What's the Question? Davis cut out 28 triangles. The answer is 7 squares.

Achieving the Standards

32. What is the value of x? (AF 1.1, p. 84)

$$x + 9 = 17$$

33. If $2 \times 5 = 10$, what is 5×2? (Grade 3 AF 1.5)

34. Round 4,492,022 to the nearest million.

(O–π NS 1.3, p. 34)

35. **Test Prep** A quilt is 3 quilt blocks wide and 5 quilt blocks long. How many quilt blocks does it have in all?

A 2   C 15

B 8   D 35

Multiply and Divide Facts Through 10

OBJECTIVE: Multiply and divide facts through 10.

Learn

Using strategies can help you learn the multiplication and division facts that you do not know.

PROBLEM A checkerboard has 8 squares on each side. How many squares are on a checkerboard?

To find the product of 8 and 8, you can break apart one of the factors into products you know.

 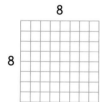 **Activity** **Use the break apart strategy.**

Materials ▪ centimeter grid paper

Multiply. 8×8

Step 1	Step 2	Step 3
Draw a square array that is 8 units wide and 8 units long. Think of the area as 8×8.	Cut apart the array to make two smaller arrays for products you know.	Find the sum of the products of the two smaller arrays.
8 8 [grid]	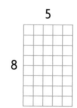 5 3 8 8 8 rows of 5 8 rows of 3 The factor 8 is now 5 plus 3.	$8 \times 5 = 40$ $8 \times 3 = 24$ $40 + 24 = 64$

So, there are 64 squares on a checkerboard.

• **What if** you cut apart the array horizontally? What other ways can you break apart the 8×8 array?

• Use grid paper and the break apart strategy to find 9×7.

• Does the break apart strategy always work? Explain.

NS 3.0 Students solve problems involving addition, subtraction, multiplication, and division of whole numbers and understand the relationships among the operations. *also* **MR 1.1, MR 1.2, MR 2.0, MR 2.2, MR 2.3, MR 2.4, MR 3.0, MR 3.2, MR 3.3**

More Strategies

Use a multiplication table.

Multiply. 7×5

Find the row for the factor, 7. Find the column for the factor, 5.

Look down column 5. The product is found where row 7 and column 5 meet.

×	0	1	2	3	4	5	6	7	8	9	10
0	0	0	0	0	0	0	0	0	0	0	0
1	0	1	2	3	4	5	6	7	8	9	10
2	0	2	4	6	8	10	12	14	16	18	20
3	0	3	6	9	12	15	18	21	24	27	30
4	0	4	8	12	16	20	24	28	32	36	40
5	0	5	10	15	20	25	30	35	40	45	50
6	0	6	12	18	24	30	36	42	48	54	60
7	0	7	14	21	28	35	42	49	56	63	70
8	0	8	16	24	32	40	48	56	64	72	80
9	0	9	18	27	36	45	54	63	72	81	90
10	0	10	20	30	40	50	60	70	80	90	100

So, $7 \times 5 = 35$.

Math Idea
The Commutative Property of Multiplication states that you can multiply any two factors in any order and get the same product. So, if you know that $6 \times 9 = 54$, you also know that $9 \times 6 = 54$. You need to memorize only half of the facts in the multiplication table.

• How can you use the multiplication table to find $70 \div 10$?

Use inverse operations.
Divide. $63 \div 9$
Think: $9 \times 7 = 63$
So, $63 \div 9 = 7$.

Use a pattern.
Divide. $42 \div 6$
Count back from 42 by sixes.
Think: 42, 36, 30, 24, 18, 12, 6, 0
So, $42 \div 6 = 7$.

Use doubles.
Multiply. 8×9
Think: One factor is an even number. $4 + 4 = 8$
$$4 \times 9 = 36$$
$$4 \times 9 = 36$$
$$36 + 36 = 72$$
So, $8 \times 9 = 72$.

Guided Practice

1. Copy the sentences. Use the arrays to complete the sentences.

$4 \times 9 = \blacksquare$
$2 \times 9 = \blacksquare$
$6 \times 9 = \blacksquare + \blacksquare$
So, $6 \times 9 = \blacksquare$.

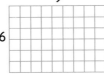
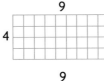

Find the product or quotient. Show the strategy you used.

2. 8×6 **3.** $63 \div 7$ **4.** $30 \div 6$ **5.** 7×6 ✓**6.** $50 \div 5$ ✓**7.** 9×3

8. [**TALK Math**] **Explain** two ways to use strategies to find 8×7.

Independent Practice (and Problem Solving)

Find the product or quotient. Show the strategy you used.

9. $40 \div 4$ **10.** 6×6 **11.** $8\overline{)64}$ **12.** $27 \div 9$ **13.** $56 \div 7$ **14.** 9×10

15. $7\overline{)49}$ **16.** $7\overline{)42}$ **17.** $9 \div 9$ **18.** 10×10 **19.** $8\overline{)80}$ **20.** 9×4

21. $\begin{array}{r} 3 \\ \times\ 7 \\ \hline \end{array}$ **22.** $\begin{array}{r} 10 \\ \times\ 6 \\ \hline \end{array}$ **23.** $\begin{array}{r} 0 \\ \times\ 8 \\ \hline \end{array}$ **24.** $\begin{array}{r} 4 \\ \times\ 7 \\ \hline \end{array}$ **25.** $\begin{array}{r} 9 \\ \times\ 9 \\ \hline \end{array}$ **26.** $\begin{array}{r} 2 \\ \times\ 6 \\ \hline \end{array}$

⭐**Algebra** Find the value of the coins.

27.

Nickels	5	6	7	8	9	10
Cents	25	▨	▨	▨	▨	▨

28.

Dimes	1	2	4	6	8	10
Cents	10	▨	▨	▨	▨	▨

Game 1 Results

ED   TANYA   JAMAL

USE DATA For 29–31, use the Game 1 Results.

29. In checkers, a king is 2 checkers stacked. Tanya has 3 kings. How many single checkers does she have?

30. What is the greatest number of kings that Jamal could have?

31. Ed had the same number of checkers left at the end of each game. He ends the checkers marathon with a total of 45 checkers left. How many games did Ed play?

32. [**WRITE Math**] ▶ Find the missing numbers. Describe the relationships between the products. **Explain** why this happened.

$6 \times 2 = $ ▨
$6 \times 4 = $ ▨
$6 \times 8 = $ ▨
$6 \times 16 = $ ▨

🐻 Achieving the Standards

33. $5 + 9 = 9 + $ ▨ (AF 1.0, p. 78)

34. The numbers in the pattern increase by the same amount each time. What is the missing number in this pattern?

(Grade 3 AF 2.2)

$$3, 6, 9, \blacksquare, 15$$

35. Find the value of $3 + (n - 1)$ if $n = 4$.

(O━┓ AF 1.2, p. 82)

36. Test Prep $42 \div 7 = $

   A 6   **C** 35

   B 7   **D** 49

🖸 **Technology**
Use Harcourt Mega Math, The Number
ROM   Games, *Up, Up, and Array*, Levels B, C, F, G.

Are You Game?

Reading Skill Visualize

A growing number of kids are having fun playing chess. Many are joining clubs, playing in tournaments, and even competing online.

Maya's chess club has 6 members. The club will play 24 games this weekend. Each member plays the same number of games. How many games will each club member play this weekend?

Visualizing the information given in a problem can help you understand the situation. When you visualize, you picture something in your mind.

The United States Chess Federation has about 100,000 members, and more than half of them are kids. Ten-year old fourth grader Daniel Naroditsky from California, swept his section at the 2005 National K–12/ Collegiate Chess Championship with a perfect 7–0 score.

Make a list of models that can be used to help solve the problem, and then picture each model in your mind.

↓

Think about which model best represents the situation.

↓

Picture the situation in your mind. Then draw a picture.

Models
groups of objects
number line
array
multiplication table

Problem Solving Visualize to understand the problem.

1. Solve the problem above.

2. Barney and Lauren are playing a card-matching game. Before they begin, they place 42 cards facedown in rows and columns. If they place 7 cards in each row, how many columns of cards do they have?

Chapter 5   119

5 Multiplication Table Through 12

OBJECTIVE: Multiply and divide facts through 12.

Quick Review

1. 10×9
2. 8×7
3. 0×10
4. 2×8
5. 9×9

Investigate

Materials ■ blank multiplication table

You can use patterns and strategies to help you complete a multiplication table for the facts of 11 and 12. Copy the table.

Remember

The Zero Property states that the product of 0 and any number is 0. The Identity Property states that the product of 1 and any number is that number.

×	0	1	2	3	4	5	6	7	8	9	10	11	12
0	0	0	0	0	0	0	0	0	0	0	0	■	■
1	0	1	2	3	4	5	6	7	8	9	10	■	■
2	0	2	4	6	8	10	12	14	16	18	20	■	■
3	0	3	6	9	12	15	18	21	24	27	30	■	■
4	0	4	8	12	16	20	24	28	32	36	40	■	■
5	0	5	10	15	20	25	30	35	40	45	50	■	■
6	0	6	12	18	24	30	36	42	48	54	60	■	■
7	0	7	14	21	28	35	42	49	56	63	70	■	■
8	0	8	16	24	32	40	48	56	64	72	80	■	■
9	0	9	18	27	36	45	54	63	72	81	90	■	■
10	0	10	20	30	40	50	60	70	80	90	100	■	■
11	■	■	■	■	■	■	■	■	■	■	■	■	■
12	■	■	■	■	■	■	■	■	■	■	■	■	■

A Use the Zero Property to complete the row and column for 0. Use the Identity Property to complete the row and column for 1.

B Use doubles to complete the row and column for 2.

C Count on to complete the rows and columns for 3 through 10.

D Use the break apart strategy to find 11×11, 11×12, and 12×12.

E Now complete the rest of the table.

Draw Conclusions

1. Compare your break apart strategy to find 12×12 with your classmates' break apart strategies. What can you conclude?

2. **Application** What strategy could you use to find the product of 20 and 5? Find the product. Describe the strategy you used.

NS 3.0 Students solve problems involving addition, subtraction, multiplication, and division of whole numbers and understand the relationships among the operations. *also* **MR 1.1, MR 1.2, MR 2.0, MR 2.3, MR 2.4, MR 3.0, MR 3.2, MR 3.3**

Connect

You can also use a multiplication table to find the quotient in a division problem.

Divide. $56 \div 8 = \blacksquare$

Think: $8 \times \blacksquare = 56$

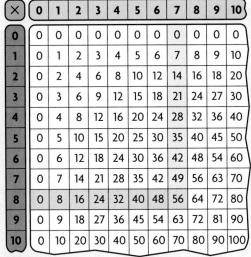

Step 1

Find the row for the given factor, 8.

Step 2

Look across to find the product, 56.

Step 3

Look up to find the missing factor, 7.

So, $56 \div 8 = 7$.

In Step 1, the divisor is the given factor in the related multiplication fact. In Step 2, the dividend is the product. The quotient is the missing factor.

- How do you know that you can use the multiplication fact $8 \times 7 = 56$ to find $56 \div 8$?

TALK Math

How do strategies and patterns help you learn multiplication facts?

Practice

Find the product or quotient. Show the strategy you used.

1. 6×11
2. 12×10
3. $77 \div 11$
4. 10×11
5. 11×12
6. $48 \div 12$
7. 3×12
8. $60 \div 12$
9. 11×4
10. 11×3
11. $96 \div 12$
12. 9×11
13. $132 \div 11$
14. 5×11
15. 12×12
16. $121 \div 11$
17. 6×12
18. 7×11

Algebra Use the rule to find the missing numbers.

19. Multiply the input by 11.

Input	Output
1	■
10	■
11	■
12	■

20. Multiply the input by 12.

Input	Output
2	■
■	48
5	■
■	120

21. Divide the input by 11.

Input	Output
22	■
44	■
66	■
■	8

22. Divide the input by 12.

Input	Output
36	■
72	■
■	9
■	12

23. **WRITE Math** What could be the missing factors in $\star \times \blacktriangle = 48$? Find as many factor pairs as you can. **Explain** how you found these factors.

LESSON 6

Patterns on the Multiplication Table

OBJECTIVE: Identify patterns on the multiplication table.

Quick Review

Name the pattern unit.

1. 1, 2, 3, 1, 2, 3, 1, 2, 3
2. 2, 4, 2, 4, 2, 4, 2, 4
3. 3, 0, 7, 3, 0, 7, 3, 0, 7
4. 8, 5, 8, 5, 8, 5, 8, 5
5. 6, 5, 4, 6, 5, 4, 6, 5, 4

Vocabulary

square number

multiple

Learn

You can use a multiplication table to explore number patterns.

Activity **Materials** ■ multiplication table

- Find 4 × 4. Circle the product.

- Shade the squares for all the products above the row for 4 and to the left of the column for 4. Look at the array you shaded. What shape do you see?

A number that can be modeled with a square array is called a square number. A **square number** is a number that is the product of any number and itself.

- Continue multiplying to find the other square numbers in the table. Circle the square numbers. What do you see?

- Compare the numbers to the left of and above each square number. What pattern do you see?

A **multiple** is the product of a given whole number and another whole number. To find the multiples of 4, look at the row or the column for the factor 4.

- List the multiples of 4 shown in the table. What patterns do you see?

- Look at the multiples of 1, 3, 5, 7, 9, and 11. What patterns do you see?

×	0	1	2	3	4	5	6	7	8	9	10	11	12
0	0	0	0	0	0	0	0	0	0	0	0	0	0
1	0	1	2	3	4	5	6	7	8	9	10	11	12
2	0	2	4	6	8	10	12	14	16	18	20	22	24
3	0	3	6	9	12	15	18	21	24	27	30	33	36
4	0	4	8	12	16	20	24	28	32	36	40	44	48
5	0	5	10	15	20	25	30	35	40	45	50	55	60
6	0	6	12	18	24	30	36	42	48	54	60	66	72
7	0	7	14	21	28	35	42	49	56	63	70	77	84
8	0	8	16	24	32	40	48	56	64	72	80	88	96
9	0	9	18	27	36	45	54	63	72	81	90	99	108
10	0	10	20	30	40	50	60	70	80	90	100	110	120
11	0	11	22	33	44	55	66	77	88	99	110	121	132
12	0	12	24	36	48	60	72	84	96	108	120	132	144

Guided Practice

1. Use the array to find the square number. ■ × ■ = ■

Find the square number.

2. 6 × 6   3. 2 × 2   4. 9 × 9   5. 1 × 1   6. 4 × 4   7. 11 × 11

 NS 3.0 Students solve problems involving addition, subtraction, multiplication, and division of whole numbers and understand the relationships among the operations. *also* **MR 1.1, MR 2.0, MR 2.3, MR 2.4, MR 3.2**

Use the multiplication table.

8. What pattern do you see in the multiples of 5?

9. Which multiples have only even numbers?

10. **TALK Math** **Explain** how patterns in the multiplication table can help you remember multiplication facts.

Independent Practice and Problem Solving

Find the square number.

11. 3×3

12. 6×6

13. 8×8

14. 10×10

15. 7×7

16. 12×12

Use the multiplication table.

17. What pattern do you see in the multiples of 8?

18. What pattern do you see in the first 9 multiples of 10?

19. What pattern do you see in the ones digits of multiples of 2?

20. What pattern do you see in the multiples of 4 and multiples of 12?

Reasoning Write *true* or *false*. If the statement is false, explain why.

21. All of the multiples of 6 are multiples of 3.

22. For any multiple of 5, the ones digit is 5.

USE DATA For 23–25, use the Facts of Nine table.

23. How does the pattern of the tens digits in the products relate to the pattern of the factors?

24. How do the digits of each product relate to the factor 9?

25. **Explain** how you can use the patterns to find 9×9 without using the table.

26. Use the rule *3 less than 2 times the number* to make a pattern. Start with 4. What is the fifth number in the pattern?

27. **WRITE Math** Look at the multiples of 2 and 4 in the multiplication table. **Explain** how they are alike and how they are different.

Facts of Nine
$1 \times 9 = 9$
$2 \times 9 = 18$
$3 \times 9 = 27$
$4 \times 9 = 36$
$5 \times 9 = 45$
$6 \times 9 = 54$
$7 \times 9 = 63$
$8 \times 9 = 72$
$9 \times 9 = 81$
$10 \times 9 = 90$

Achieving the Standards

28. Would you measure the length of a goldfish in inches, in feet, or in miles?
(Grade 3 MG 1.1)

29. Write a division fact in the same fact family as $5 \times 9 = 45$. (0⌐¬ NS 3.0, p. 112)

30. $11 \times 10 =$ (0⌐¬ NS 3.0, p. 120)

31. **Test Prep** Which number has multiples that are double the multiples of 4?

 A 2   **B** 4   **C** 6   **D** 8

Extra Practice on page 128, Set E

Problem Solving Workshop
Skill: Choose the Operation

OBJECTIVE: Solve problems by using the skill *choose the operation*.

Use the Skill

PROBLEM Nancy is baking cookies to take to a party. There will be 12 people at the party. She mixes enough cookie dough for each person to have 4 cookies. Then she bakes the cookies on cookie sheets for 11 minutes. How many cookies will Nancy bake in all?

This chart will help you decide which operation you can use to solve the problem.

Add	Join groups of the same or different sizes
Subtract	Take away or compare groups
Multiply	Join equal-size groups
Divide	Separate into equal-size groups or find how many in each group

Since Nancy bakes 12 equal groups of 4 cookies, you can multiply to find how many cookies she will bake in all.

number of people		number of cookies for each person		total number of cookies
↓		↓		↓
12	×	4	=	48

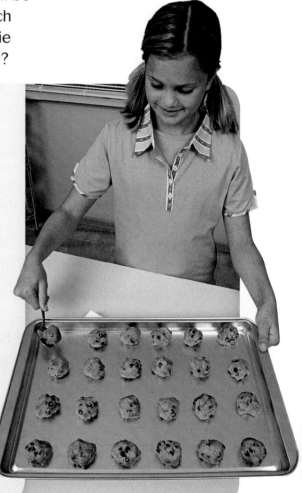

So, Nancy will bake 48 cookies in all.

• What other operation could you use to solve this problem? Explain how you solved the problem.

Think and Discuss

Tell which operation you would use to solve the problem. Explain your choice. Solve the problem.

a. The Sandwich Shop served 3,275 lunches in May and served 4,250 lunches in June. How many lunches did the Shop serve in all?

b. Raul's class made $200 from this year's bake sale. Last year, the class made $178. How much more did they make this year?

c. The cafeteria served 132 pizza lunches. Each pizza was cut into 12 slices. If each student received 1 slice, how many pizzas were served?

O—┓ **NS 3.0** Students solve problems involving addition, subtraction, multiplication, and division of whole numbers and understand the relationships among the operations. *also* O—┓ NS 3.1, MR 1.0, MR 1.1, MR 2.0, MR 2.3, MR 2.4, MR 2.6, MR 3.0, MR 3.1, MR 3.2

Guided Problem Solving

Read to
Understand
Plan
Solve
Check

Tell which operation you would use to solve the problem.
Then solve the problem.

1. Russell made 36 ounces of trail mix to take on a hiking trip. He poured equal amounts of the trail mix into 4 bags. How many ounces of trail mix are in each bag?

   Think: What operation can you use to find how many ounces of trail mix are in each bag?

ounces of trail mix	number of bags	amount in each bag
↓	↓	↓
36 ÷	4 =	■

2. **What if** Russell poured equal amounts of the trail mix into 6 bags? How many ounces of trail mix would be in each bag?

3. The hiking trip is on Friday. On Thursday, the high temperature was 67°F. Russell hopes that it will be 8° warmer on Friday. What temperature is Russell hoping for?

Mixed Applications

USE DATA For 4–7, use the information in the picture.

4. Donald wants to place flower bouquets on 6 tables. How much will the flower bouquets cost in all?

5. Sonya bought 3 boxes of crackers. What number sentence can be used to find the total amount of money Sonya spent on 1 box of crackers?

6. Art wants to send out 24 invitations for his party. How many boxes of cards will he need? How much will they cost?

7. Look at Mr. Hill's shopping list. What information is needed to find the total amount of money he spent at the grocery store?

8. **Pose a Problem** Write a word problem for the number sentence $48 ÷ 12 = n$. Then solve the problem.

9. **WRITE Math** Orange Park charges $11 per day per person. Deer Park charges $2 per hour per person. Help Lisa choose the less expensive park to hold her picnic if 12 people come to the picnic for 5 hours. **Explain** how you decided.

Shopping List

3 boxes of crackers
2 gallons of orange juice
2 loaves of bread
1 bouquet of flowers

ALGEBRA
Find Missing Factors

OBJECTIVE: Use multiplication and division to find missing factors.

Quick Review

Write the fact family.

1. 2, 5, 10   2. 3, 6, 18
3. 5, 7, 35   4. 6, 8, 48
5. 9, 9, 81

Learn

PROBLEM A basketball club has 10 members. How many teams of 5 players each can play at the same time?

When you know the product and one factor, you can use a model or a fact family to help you find the missing factor.

■ × 5 = 10   Think: What number times 5 equals 10?

ONE WAY Use a model.

Draw 10 counters in rows of 5. Count the number of rows to find the missing factor. There are 2 rows of 5 counters.

ANOTHER WAY Use a fact family.

Use a related division sentence to find the missing factor.
10 ÷ 5 = 2, so 2 × 5 = 10. The missing factor is 2.

So, 2 teams can play at the same time.

Remember
A variable is a symbol or letter that stands for a number or numbers you don't know.

More Examples Find the missing factors.

A   ★ × 8 = 56   Think: What number times 8 equals 56?
          ★ = 7

Check: $7 \times 8 \stackrel{?}{=} 56$ Replace ★ with 7. The sentence is true.
       56 = 56 ✔

The missing factor is 7.

B   9 × n = 45   Think: 9 times what number equals 45?
          n = 5

Check: $9 \times 5 \stackrel{?}{=} 45$ Replace n with 5. The sentence is true.
       45 = 45 ✔

The missing factor is 5.

• How could you use division to solve Examples A and B?

Guided Practice

1. The first factor in a multiplication sentence is 3, and the product is 30. Use the model to find the missing factor.

   3 × ■ = 30

AF 1.1 Use letters, boxes, or other symbols to stand for any number in simple expressions or equations (e.g., demonstrate an understanding and the use of the concept of a variable). also NS 3.0, NS 4.0, MR 1.1, MR 2.0, MR 2.3, MR 2.4, MR 3.2

Find the missing factor.

2. $n \times 5 = 55$　　　　**3.** $6 \times \blacktriangledown = 72$　　　☑**4.** $10 \times g = 70$　　　☑**5.** $\blacksquare \times 11 = 132$

6. [**TALK Math**] **Explain** the relationship between factors and products. Use an example to show what you mean.

Independent Practice and Problem Solving

Find the missing factor.

7. $\blacksquare \times 2 = 18$　　　**8.** $12 \times p = 12$　　　**9.** $\bigstar \times 9 = 72$　　　**10.** $11 \times r = 110$

11. $g \times 10 = 120$　　**12.** $4 \times d = 32$　　　**13.** $7 \times n = 63$　　　**14.** $c \times 10 = 50$

15. $\blacksquare \times 3 = 40 - 4$　**16.** $7 \times \blacksquare = 43 + 6$　　**17.** $3 \times \blacksquare = 19 + 5$　**18.** $\blacksquare \times 8 = 20 - 4$

USE DATA For 19–21, use the table.

19. Each football team has 1 coach. Three teams and their coaches are arranged for a photograph. How many people are in the photograph?

20. Reasoning In a game, 2 basketball teams play against each other. You want to find out how many players are on the court during a game. In a multiplication sentence, will the answer be a product or a factor?

21. Pose a Problem Look back at Problem 19. Write a similar problem by exchanging the known and unknown numbers.

Sports Team	
Sport	**Players**
Baseball	9
Basketball	5
Football	11
Ice Hockey	6
Soccer	11
Volleyball	6

22. High school basketball games last 32 minutes. There are 4 quarters in each game. Write a number sentence that can be used to find the number of minutes in each quarter.

23. [**WRITE Math**] ▸ A sports team needs to reserve a field for a game. The players collect $88 in all to pay for the field. Each player paid $8. **Explain** how to find how many players are on the team.

Achieving the Standards

24. A spinner has a green section, a red section, and a yellow section. List the possible outcomes for spinning the pointer. (Grade 3 O━🔑 SDAP 1.2)

25. $3 + 2 = \blacksquare + 3$ (AF 1.0, p. 78)

26. What is the value of n in $11 - n = 8$?

(AF 1.1, p. 84)

27. Test Prep What is the missing factor in $12 \times m = 36$?

A 2

B 3

C 6

D 12

Extra Practice on page 128, Set F　　　　　　　　　　　　　　　　　　　　　Chapter 5 **127**

 # Extra Practice

Set A Write the related multiplication or division sentence.
Draw a picture that shows the sentence. (pp. 110–111)

1. $16 - 8 - 8 = 0$
2. $4 + 4 + 4 + 4 + 4 = 20$
3. $6 + 6 + 6 + 6 = 24$

4. $3 + 3 + 3 + 3 = 12$
5. $7 + 7 + 7 + 7 + 7 = 35$
6. $27 - 9 - 9 - 9 = 0$

Set B Write the fact family for the set of numbers. (pp. 112–113)

1. 4, 5, 20
2. 3, 4, 12
3. 5, 9, 45
4. 6, 7, 42
5. 8, 9, 72

Set C Find the product or quotient. (pp. 114–115)

1. 8×2
2. 6×4
3. $21 \div 3$
4. 8×5
5. $4 \div 4$
6. $18 \div 3$

7. A roller coaster at an amusement park has 8 cars. Each car can hold 4 people. How many people can ride the roller coaster on one trip?

Set D Find the product or quotient. Show the strategy you used. (pp. 116–119)

1. $36 \div 9$
2. 7×8
3. 7×6
4. $7 \overline{)63}$
5. $30 \div 6$
6. 8×10

7. 5×9
8. $8 \overline{)48}$
9. 9×8
10. $7 \overline{)14}$
11. 9×9
12. $6 \overline{)54}$

13. There are 49 students going on a field trip to the planetarium. Each van can hold 7 students. How many vans are needed?

Set E Use the multiplication table on page 122. (pp. 122–123)

1. What pattern do you see in the ones digits of multiples of 5?
2. What pattern do you see in the multiples of 3 and 9?
3. What pattern do you see in the multiples of 2 and 3?

Set F Find the missing factor. (pp. 126–127)

1. $2 \times m = 24$
2. $6 \times w = 36$
3. $c \times 9 = 72$
4. $g \times 6 = 66$

5. $\blacksquare \times 3 = 17 + 1$
6. $5 \times \bigstar = 33 - 3$
7. $4 \times \blacksquare = 32 + 4$
8. $8 \times \blacktriangle = 65 - 1$

9. Carlos read the same number of pages in his 60-page book each day for 1 week. After the week, he still had 4 pages to read. How many pages did Carlos read each day?

Technology
Use Harcourt Mega Math, The Number Games, *Up, Up, and Array*, Levels A, B, C, D, E, F, G, H, I.

HOPSCOTCH FACTS

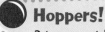

● Hoppers!
2 teams, at least 2 players on each team

○ Get Set!
- Number cards (1–12, two sets)
- Two-color counters (1 for each team)

● Hop! . . . .

■ Players shuffle each set of number cards and place them facedown in two stacks.

■ Teams take turns. A player chooses one card from each stack. A teammate uses those numbers to write a basic multiplication or division fact sentence.

■ If the fact sentence is correct, the team places a counter on 1. The cards are placed in discard stacks.

■ If a player makes an incorrect fact sentence on the first or second turn, that team loses a turn. If a player makes an incorrect fact sentence after his or her team has hopped past 2 on the game board, that team moves its counter back two spaces.

■ On each turn, teammates trade roles.

■ If all the number cards are used, players shuffle each set and place them facedown to use again.

■ The first team to reach 10 wins.

 Chapter 5 Review/Test

Check Vocabulary and Concepts

Choose the best term from the box.

1. A ___?___ is the product of any number and itself. (O▬ NS 3.0, p. 122)

2. In $36 \div 9 = 4$, 4 is the ___?___. (O▬ NS 3.0, p. 112)

3. The answer to a multiplication problem is called the ___?___.

   (O▬ NS 3.0, p. 112)

Check Skills

Write the related multiplication or division sentence.
Draw a picture that shows the sentence. (O▬ NS 3.0, pp. 110–111)

4. $10 - 5 - 5 = 0$ 5. $3 + 3 + 3 = 9$ 6. $12 - 12 = 0$ 7. $2 + 2 + 2 = 6$

Find the value of the variable. (O▬ NS 3.0, pp. 112–113, 126–127)

8. $24 \div 2 = y$ 9. $48 \div 6 = w$ 10. $56 \div 7 = a$ 11. $99 \div 9 = v$

12. $k \times 12 = 60$ 13. $108 \div 9 = b$ 14. $g \times 6 = 42$ 15. $72 \div e = 9$

Find the product or quotient. (O▬ NS 3.0, pp. 114–115, 116–119, 120–121)

16. 3×6 17. 12×4 18. $4\overline{)28}$ 19. $60 \div 5$ 20. 6×6

21. 7×12 22. $33 \div 11$ 23. 5×3 24. 8×8 25. $8\overline{)96}$

26. 4×8 27. $5\overline{)50}$ 28. $9 \div 9$ 29. $9\overline{)45}$ 30. 6×7

Check Problem Solving

Solve. (O▬ NS 3.0, MR 1.1, pp. 124–125)

31. Ed collected cans for recycling. He collected 79 cans last week and 114 cans this week. How many more cans did he collect this week than last week?

32. Maria needs 8 ounces of nuts to make 1 batch of cookies. How many ounces of nuts will she need to make 5 batches of cookies?

33. ▐WRITE Math▶ There are 12 baseball bats in each shipping carton. Would you use addition or multiplication to find the number of baseball bats in 6 shipping cartons? **Explain.**

GO **Technology** Use *Online Assessment.*
ONLINE

Enrich • Number Relationships
EVEN or Odd?

Eric is making smoothies for his family. Some family members want 2 cups of blueberries, and some want 3 cups of blueberries in their smoothies. Will Eric use an even or odd number of cups when he makes the smoothies?

Is the product even or odd when you multiply two even numbers? two odd numbers? an even number and an odd number?

Examples

A Even × Even	B Odd × Odd	C Even × Odd
$2 \times 2 = 4$	$3 \times 1 = 3$	$2 \times 1 = 2$
$2 \times 4 = 8$	$3 \times 3 = 9$	$2 \times 3 = 6$
$2 \times 6 = 12$	$3 \times 5 = 15$	$2 \times 5 = 10$

So, if Eric uses 2 cups for an even number of people, he will use an even number of cups in all. If he uses 3 cups for an odd number of people, he will use an odd number of cups in all. If he uses 2 cups for an odd number of people, he will use an even number of cups in all.

• Is the product even or odd when you multiply three even numbers?
• Is the product even or odd when you multiply three odd numbers?

Try It

Tell whether the product is _even_ or _odd_.

1. 4×7 **2.** 5×9 **3.** 6×8 **4.** 9×7

5. 8×6 **6.** $8 \times 4 \times 6$ **7.** $7 \times 9 \times 5$ **8.** $4 \times 6 \times 2$

9. Is the product even or odd when you multiply 5 by an even number? an odd number? **Explain**.

10. Is the product even or odd when you multiply two even numbers and an odd number? **Explain**.

 WRITE Math Explain how you can tell whether a product of two or more numbers will be even or odd.

Number Sense

1. There are 9 spiders in the terrarium. Each spider has 8 legs. How many legs are there in all? (O━ NS 3.0)

   A 72

   B 80

   C 88

   D 96

2. Round 3,219,754 to the nearest hundred. (O━ NS 1.3)

   A 3,220,000

   B 3,219,800

   C 3,219,700

   D 3,200,000

3. The new baseball stadium has 5,213 seats. That is 3,928 more seats than the old stadium had. How many seats did the old stadium have? (O━ NS 3.1)

   A 2,295

   B 2,285

   C 1,295

   D 1,285

4. **WRITE Math** Molly has 6 loaves of bread. Each loaf of bread has 10 slices. **Explain** how to find how many slices of bread there are in all.

   (O━ NS 3.0)

Algebra and Functions

5. What is the value of the expression $24 + n$ if $n = 2$? (AF 1.1)

   A 48   **C** 22

   B 26   **D** 12

6. Look at the problem below.

$$\blacksquare + 5 = \blacklozenge$$

   If $\blacklozenge = 16$, what is $\blacksquare$? (O━ AF 1.5)

   A 9

   B 10

   C 11

   D 21

7. What number is represented by y? (AF 1.1)

$$5 \times y = 40$$

   A 8

   B 9

   C 10

   D 12

8. **WRITE Math** Paula has 12 flowers. The table shows the number of petals in different numbers of flowers.

Flower Petals				
Flowers	2	4	6	7
Petals	22	44	66	77

   Explain how to find the total number of petals in Paula's flowers.

   (Grade 3 O━ AF 2.1)

Measurement and Geometry

9. Which statement is true about the right triangle shown below? (Grade 3 O━n MG 2.2)

  A The triangle has 1 obtuse angle.

  B The triangle has 1 right angle.

  C The triangle has 2 right angles.

  D The triangle has 3 acute angles.

10. The music room is shaped like a rectangle 30 feet long and 20 feet wide.

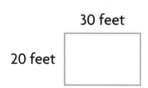

30 feet

20 feet

What is the perimeter of the room?

(Grade 3 O━n MG 1.3)

  A 30 feet

  B 50 feet

  C 100 feet

  D 600 feet

11. Which unit would you use to measure the length of a playground? (Grade 3 MG 1.1)

  A kilometer   **C** gram

  B liter   **D** meter

12. [WRITE Math] **Explain** the difference between a cone and a pyramid.

Statistics, Data Analysis, and Probability

Test Tip **Get the information you need.**

See Item 13. You need to know how many different outcomes are possible when Marian tosses the coin.

13. Marian played a coin-tossing game. The table shows the results.

Coin Toss	
Outcome	**Number**
Heads	12
Tails	12

If Marian tosses the coin again, what are the chances that the result will be heads?

(Grade 3 O━n SDAP 1.2]

  A 1 out of 12   **C** 1 out of 3

  B 1 out of 4   **D** 1 out of 2

14. [WRITE Math] The pointer of Jack's spinner stopped on yellow 6 times, green 2 times, and red 4 times.

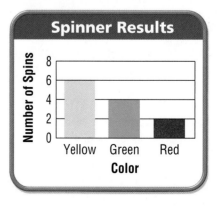

Explain how you would change the graph to show the results. (Grade 3 O━n SDAP 1.3)

6 Algebra: Use Multiplication and Division Facts

The Big Idea Properties and the concepts of algebra are used to evaluate expressions and solve multiplication and division equations.

CALIFORNIA FAST FACT

Charles Schulz created the comic strip *Peanuts*. You can see nearly 6,000 of his drawings at the Charles Schulz Museum in Santa Rosa. Also, there is this mural made up of 2- by 8-inch comic-strip tiles.

Investigate

There are 12 members of the *Peanuts* gang. The expressions 6 + 6 and 3 × 4 both equal 12. Write three different expressions that equal the number of cartoon panels shown here, using two or more operations. Explain how you decided whether you should use parentheses.

Technology
Student pages are available in the Student eBook.

Check your understanding of important skills
needed for success in Chapter 6.

▶ **Use a Rule**

Copy and complete each table.

1.

Team	2	3	4	5	6
Players	12	18	24	▨	▨

Rule: Multiply the number of
teams by 6.

2.

Dimes	4	5	6	7	8
Pennies	40	50	▨	70	▨

Rule: Multiply the number of
dimes by 10.

3.

Legs	12	16	20	24	28
Cows	3	4	5	▨	▨

Rule: Divide the number of
legs by 4.

4.

Inches	12	24	36	48	60
Feet	1	2	▨	4	▨

Rule: Divide the number of
inches by 12.

▶ **Fact Families**

Copy and complete each number sentence.

5. $5 \times 3 = $ ▨
$15 \div $ ▨ $ = 3$

6. $6 \times 7 = $ ▨
$42 \div $ ▨ $ = 7$

7. $4 \times 9 = $ ▨
$36 \div $ ▨ $ = 9$

8. $7 \times 9 = $ ▨
$63 \div $ ▨ $ = 9$

▶ **Addition and Subtraction Equations**

Solve the equation by using mental math. Check your solution.

9. $n + 8 = 13$

10. $9 - n = 6$

11. $n + 6 = 14$

12. $12 - n = 3$

VOCABULARY POWER

CHAPTER VOCABULARY

Associative
   Property
Commutative
   Property
Distributive
   Property
equation
expression

Identity
   Property
order of
   operations
parentheses
variable
Zero Property

WARM-UP WORDS

Zero Property the property that states that the
product of 0 and any number is 0

Identity Property the property that states that the
product of any number and 1 is that number

Commutative Property the property that states
that when the order of two factors is changed, the
product is the same

Multiplication Properties

OBJECTIVE: Identify and use the properties of multiplication.

Quick Review

1. 3×1
2. 5×3
3. 2×6
4. 7×0
5. 8×2

Learn

The properties of multiplication can help you find products of two or more factors.

Vocabulary

Zero Property

Identity Property

Commutative Property

Associative Property

Distributive Property

MULTIPLICATION PROPERTIES

The **Zero Property** states that the product of 0 and any number is 0.

$$3 \times 0 = 0$$

The **Identity Property** states that the product of 1 and any number is that number.

$$1 \times 3 = 3$$

The **Commutative Property** states that you can multiply two factors in either order and get the same product.

$$2 \times 3 = 6 \qquad 3 \times 2 = 6$$

The **Associative Property** states that you can group factors in different ways and get the same product. Use parentheses ( ) to group the factors you multiply first.

$$(4 \times 2) \times 3 = 24 \qquad 4 \times (2 \times 3) = 24$$

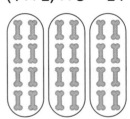

• Use counters to show two ways you can group $3 \times 2 \times 5$ to find the product. Are the products the same? Explain. Make a drawing to record your models.

Example 1 Use the properties to find the missing factor.

A ■ $\times 12 = 0$
$0 \times 12 = 0$ — Zero Property

So, ■ = 0.

B $9 \times$ ■ $= 8 \times 9$
$9 \times 8 = 8 \times 9$ — Commutative Property

So, ■ = 8.

AF 1.0 Students use and interpret variables, mathematical symbols, and properties to write and simplify expressions and sentences. *also* NS 3.0, AF 1.1, AF 1.2, AF 1.3, MR 1.1, MR 1.2, MR 2.3, MR 2.4, MR 3.2

The Distributive Property

PROBLEM At the pet store, the rabbits are in a pen that is 4 feet wide by 12 feet long. What is the area of the pen?

Activity Use the Distributive Property.

Materials ■ square tiles

The **Distributive Property** states that multiplying a sum by a number is the same as multiplying each addend by the number and then adding the products.

Remember
Area is the number of square units needed to cover a flat surface.

area = 2 × 3, or 6, square units

Multiply. 4 × 12

Step 1	Step 2	Step 3
Make a model to find 4 × 12. Use square tiles to build an array. 12 4 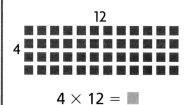 4 × 12 = ▪	Break apart the array to make two smaller arrays for products you know. 10 2 4 4 × (10 + 2)	Use the Distributive Property to show the sum of two products. (4 × 10) + (4 × 2) ↓ ↓ 40 + 8 = 48

So, the area of the pen is 48 square feet.

Using the properties can help you solve problems mentally.

Example 2 Use the properties and mental math.

Ⓐ Find 8 × 12.

$$8 \times 12 = 8 \times (10 + 2)$$
$$= (8 \times 10) + (8 \times 2)$$
$$= 80 + 16$$
$$= 96$$

Think: 12 = 10 + 2
Distributive Property

Ⓑ Find 5 × 5 × 2.

$$5 \times 5 \times 2 = 5 \times (5 \times 2)$$ Associative Property
$$= 5 \times 10$$
$$= 50$$

Ⓒ Find 2 × 7 × 5.

$$2 \times 7 \times 5 = 2 \times 5 \times 7$$ Commutative Property
$$= (2 \times 5) \times 7$$ Associative Property
$$= 10 \times 7$$
$$= 70$$

• How can you group the factors to multiply 5 × 2 × 8?

• Is 27 × (48 − 48) = 0 true? **Explain** how you can easily see this.

1. Use the Associative Property to find the missing factor.
   $(12 \times \blacksquare) \times 4 = 12 \times (3 \times 4)$

Use the properties and mental math to find the product.

2. $1 \times 56 \times 1$ 3. $24 \times 0 \times 6$ ✓4. $8 \times 3 \times 3$ ✓5. 7×12

6. **TALK Math** **Explain** how the Commutative Property is true for 4×8 and 8×4. Make a model or draw a picture.

Independent Practice and Problem Solving

Use the properties and mental math to find the product.

7. $9 \times 7 \times 0$ 8. $2 \times 4 \times 7$ 9. $8 \times 5 \times 2$ 10. $6 \times 9 \times 1$

Find the missing number. Name the property you used.

11. $8 \times 6 = 6 \times \blacksquare$ 12. $5 \times 12 = (5 \times 10) + (5 \times \blacksquare)$ 13. $(4 \times 5) \times 2 = 4 \times (\blacksquare \times 2)$

Make a model and use the Distributive Property to find the product.

14. 5×12 15. 3×12 16. 6×12 17. 12×9

Show two ways to group by using parentheses. Find the product.

18. $3 \times 2 \times 5$ 19. $8 \times 7 \times 1$ 20. $7 \times 0 \times 2$ 21. $2 \times 6 \times 2$

22. There are 2 tables, each with 3 tanks with 5 fish in each. There are also 3 tables, each with 2 tanks with 5 fish in each. Are the quantities the same? **Explain.**

23. There are 9 tanks with 11 tetras in each and 12 tanks with 7 mollies in each. Are there more tetras or mollies? How many more?

24. **Pose a Problem** Write a problem that can be solved using the product $(4 \times 2) \times 8$.

25. **WRITE Math** **What's the Question?** The product is 19. **Explain** how you know.

Achieving the Standards

26. $18 + 36 =$ (O—n NS 3.0, p. 44)

27. $42 \div 7 =$ (O—n NS 3.0, p. 116)

28. What is 324,946 rounded to the nearest ten thousand? (O—n NS 1.3, p. 34)

29. **Test Prep** Which is the missing number?
    $$7 \times \blacksquare = (7 \times 10) + (7 \times 2)$$
    A 2   **C** 12
    B 10   **D** 20

Write to Prove or Disprove

Sometimes, you must evaluate whether a number sentence or math idea is true or false. You can use what you know about operations and properties to prove or disprove whether the multiplication properties are true for division.

Sharon's group wants to know if the Commutative Property is true for division. The members of her group wrote this explanation to show what they learned.

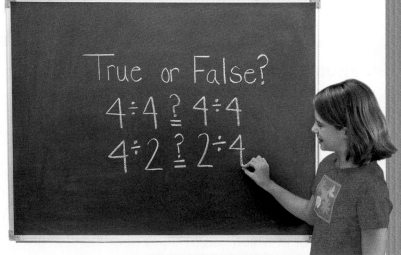

We can try different division problems to find out if the Commutative Property works for division. We decided to try $6 \div 6$ and $6 \div 3$.

First, we asked if $6 \div 6 \overset{?}{=} 6 \div 6$. Both quotients equal 1. So, the number sentence is true, and the Commutative Property works for this division problem.

Next, we asked if $6 \div 3 \overset{?}{=} 3 \div 6$. In this example, the divisor and the dividend are different numbers. $6 \div 3 = 2$ and $3 \div 6 = \frac{3}{6}$. The quotients 2 and $\frac{3}{6}$ are not equal. So, this number sentence is false.

Finally, our group members agreed that since the second number sentence is false, division is not commutative.

Tips

To write to prove or disprove:

- Use correct math vocabulary.
- State the math idea you are proving or disproving.
- Decide on at least two examples to use to test your idea.
- Show your computations, and explain what you learned about each of your examples.
- To prove, every case needs to be tested. To disprove, only one false case is needed.
- Show your reasoning by making a conclusion about each example.
- Finally, write a conclusion that states whether you proved or disproved the math idea you were testing.

Problem Solving Write to prove or disprove each property for division.

1. Zero Property

2. Identity Property

2 Order of Operations

OBJECTIVE: Use the order of operations to find the value of expressions.

Quick Review

1. 8×6
2. $28 \div 4$
3. $56 \div 7$
4. $45 + 28$
5. $91 - 34$

Vocabulary

order of operations

Investigate

PROBLEM At a visit to the Los Angeles Times Festival of Books, Corey buys 1 book for $6 and 2 books for $4 each. She pays with a $20 bill. How much money does she have left?

You can write the expression $20 - 6 - 2 \times 4$ to solve the problem.

Remember
An expression is part of a number sentence that has numbers and operation signs but does not have an equal sign.

Before you solve this problem, investigate how the order in which you perform operations might change the answer.

A Make a list of all the possible orders you can use to find the value of the expression $4 + 16 \div 4 - 2$.

B Use each order in your list to find the value of the expression. Use paper and pencil.

Draw Conclusions

1. Did following different orders change the value of the expression?

2. Compare all of the values you found. Do all the values make sense? Explain.

3. How does the order in which you perform the operations change the value of an expression that has more than one type of operation?

4. **Synthesis** What advantage is there in setting an order of operations that everyone follows?

AF 1.0 Students use and interpret variables, mathematical symbols, and properties to write and simplify expressions and sentences. *also* NS 3.0, MR 2.0, MR 2.3, MR 2.4, MR 3.2

Connect

When solving problems with more than one type of operation, you need to know which operation to do first. A special set of rules, called the **order of operations**, gives the order in which calculations are done in an expression.

First, multiply and divide from left to right.

Then, add and subtract from left to right.

Now, use the order of operations to solve the problem.

Find the value of $20 - 6 - 2 \times 4$.

Step 1		Step 2		Step 3	
$20 - 6 - 2 \times 4$	Multiply from left to right.	$20 - 6 - 8$	Next, subtract from left to right.	$14 - 8$	Then, subtract again.
$20 - 6 - 8$		$14 - 8$		6	

So, Corey has $6 left.

• How did the order of operations help you solve this problem?

Examples

A $12 + 15 \div 3$ Divide from
$12 + 5$ left to right.
17 Then add.

B $32 - 10 + 6$ Add and
$22 + 6$ subtract from
28 left to right.

TALK Math

What operation should you do first to find the values of $12 - 6 \div 2$ and $12 \div 6 - 2$? What is the value of each expression?

Practice

Write *correct* if the operations are listed in the correct order. If not correct, write the correct order of operations.

1. $4 + 5 \times 2$ Multiply, add

✓**2.** $8 \div 4 \times 2$ Multiply, divide

3. $12 + 16 \div 4$ Add, divide

4. $9 + 2 \times 3 - 1$ Add, multiply, subtract

Follow the order of operations to find the value of each expression.

5. $6 + 9 \div 3$

6. $3 \times 6 \div 2$

7. $49 \div 7 + 5$

✓**8.** $36 - 4 + 8 \div 4$

9. $8 + 27 \div 9 - 2$

10. $9 \times 7 + 4$

11. $45 \div 5 - 6$

12. $8 \times 9 - 4 + 12$

Reasoning Use the numbers listed to make a true number sentence.

13. 2, 6, and 5
$\blacksquare + \blacksquare \times \blacksquare = 16$

14. 4, 12, and 18
$\blacksquare - \blacksquare \div \blacksquare = 15$

15. 8, 9, and 7
$\blacksquare \times \blacksquare - \blacksquare = 47$

16. **WRITE Math** Is $4 + 8 \times 3$ equal to $4 + 3 \times 8$? **Explain** how you know without finding the value of each expression.

Quick Review
1. $9 + 3 \times 6$
2. $15 - 8 \div 2$
3. $20 \div 4 - 3$
4. $7 \times 6 - 3 \times 5$
5. $36 \div 4 + 8 \times 2$

Learn

You already know how to use the order of operations to evaluate an expression with more than one type of operation. Some expressions may contain parentheses. In an expression that contains parentheses, you do what is in the parentheses first.

First, perform any operations in parentheses.
Next, multiply and divide from left to right.
Then, add and subtract from left to right.

California
thrasher ▶

Example 1 Use the order of operations.

A David is a bird watcher. He saw 8 California thrashers during the week. On each day of the weekend, he saw 3 more thrashers. How many thrashers did he see in all?

$8 + (2 \times 3)$ **Think:** 8 thrashers plus 2 days times 3 thrashers each day
↓
$8 +$ 6 Do what is in the parentheses first.
↓
14 Then add.

RANGE MAP
California Thrasher
Toxostoma curvirostre

Legend ☐ Year-round

So, David saw 14 California thrashers in all.

B David saw 8 California quail on Monday and another 2 on Tuesday. By the end of the week, he had seen 3 times as many quail as he saw on Monday and Tuesday together. How many quail did he see in all?

$(8 + 2) \times 3$ **Think:** 3 times the total of 8 quail and 2 quail
↓
10 $\times 3$ Do what is in the parentheses first.
↓
30 Then multiply.

◀ California quail

RANGE MAP
California Quail
Calipepla gambelii

So, David saw 30 California quail in all.

• Find the value of $8 + 2 \times 3$. How is this expression like $8 + (2 \times 3)$ and $(8 + 2) \times 3$? How is it different?

Legend ☐ Year-round

○━┓ AF 1.2 Interpret and evaluate mathematical expressions that now use parentheses. *also*
○━┓ NS 3.0, AF 1.0, ○━┓ AF 1.3, MR 2.3, MR 2.4, MR 3.2

Match Words and Expressions

You can match words to an expression or you can write an expression to match words.

▲ California towhee

RANGE MAP
California Towhee
Pipilo chlorurus

Legend ☐ Year-round

Example 2 Match the words to an expression. Then find the value of the expression.

Jill counted California towhees in 2 trees. Each tree had 5 birds in it. Then 3 birds from each tree flew away. How many towhees were left?

Which expression matches the meaning of the words?

Think: The 2 trees, which had 5 birds in each, now have 3 fewer birds in each tree.

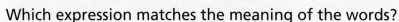

$(2 \times 5) - 3$ ← First, find the total number of birds in the trees, and then subtract the number that flew away.

$2 \times (5 - 3)$ ← First, find the number of birds left in each tree, and then find the total number left.

$(2 \times 5) - 3$ **Does not match the meaning.**

$2 \times (5 - 3)$ **Matches the meaning.**

To find how many towhees are left, follow the order of operations.

$2 \times (5 - 3)$ Do what is in the parentheses first.
   ↓
$2 \times$ 2   Then multiply.
 ↓
 4

So, there were 4 California towhees left.

Math Idea
Parentheses help you find the correct value of an expression with more than one type of operation. The meaning of the words in a problem will tell you where to place the parentheses.

Example 3 Write an expression to match the words. Then find the value of the expression.

Ella saw 6 California quail in each of 3 trees. She also saw 4 western bluebirds. How many more quail did she see than western bluebirds?

$(6 \times 3) - 4$ ← 6 quail each in 3 trees and 4 fewer bluebirds

To find how many more quail Ella saw, follow the order of operations.

$(6 \times 3) - 4$ Do what is in the parentheses first.
  ↓
  18   − 4   Then subtract.
    ↓
   14

So, Ella saw 14 more California quail than western bluebirds.

• Explain why the position of the parentheses is important.

Western bluebird ▶

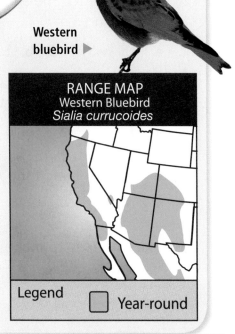

RANGE MAP
Western Bluebird
Sialia currucoides

Legend ☐ Year-round

1. Which placement of the parentheses gives the value of 35?

   a. $5 \times (9 - 2)$ **b.** $(5 \times 9) - 2$

Follow the order of operations to find the value of each expression.

2. $3 \times 6 - (2 + 4) \div 2$ 3. $3 \times (6 - 2) + 4 \div 2$ ✓ 4. $3 \times (6 - 2 + 4) \div 2$

Choose the expression that matches the words.

5. Brooke had $7 and then worked 3 hours for $6 an hour.

   a. $(7 + 3) \times 6$ **b.** $7 + (3 \times 6)$

✓ 6. Savon had 4 pages with 5 stamps on each one. He used 3 stamps.

   a. $(4 \times 5) - 3$ **b.** $4 \times (5 \times 3)$

7. **TALK Math** Explain why the values of $8 + 6 \div 2$ and $(8 + 6) \div 2$ are different. What is the value of each expression?

Independent Practice and Problem Solving

Follow the order of operations to find the value of each expression.

8. $45 - 9 \div 3$

9. $30 + 2 \times (6 - 4)$

10. $(45 - 9) \div 3$

11. $36 - (4 + 8) \div 4$

12. $8 + 6 \times 5 - 2$

13. $(28 - 8) \div 4 + 6$

14. $5 \times (9 - 4) + (12 \div 6)$

15. $18 - (5 \times 3)$

16. $(36 \div 4) + (10 - 5)$

17. $(3 \times 8) \div (6 + 6)$

18. $(9 - 6) \times (8 - 5 + 3)$

19. $(12 \times 3) \div (8 - 4)$

Choose the expression that matches the words.

20. Ariel had $15. She spent $3 and then was given $5.

    a. $(15 - 3) + 5$ **b.** $15 - (3 + 5)$

21. Billy had 50¢. He gave 4 nickels to his brother.

    a. $50 - (4 \times 5)$ **b.** $(50 - 4) \times 5$

22. Sam worked 6 hours a day for 4 days. He worked 5 hours on the fifth day.

    a. $(6 \times 4) + 5$ **b.** $6 \times (4 + 5)$

23. Jessica bought 2 tickets for $8 each. She paid $1 in sales tax.

    a. $2 \times (8 + 1)$ **b.** $(2 \times 8) + 1$

Write words to match the expression.

24. $4 \times (5 + 3)$ 25. $(10 + 2) \times 6$ 26. $6 \times (5 - 3)$ 27. $(7 \times 2) - 12$

Use parentheses to make the number sentence true.

28. $34 + 6 \div 5 = 8$

29. $7 \times 6 - 3 = 21$

30. $14 - 4 + 8 \div 2 = 8$

31. $7 \times 6 + 6 - 2 = 82$

32. $5 + 6 \times 2 = 22$

33. $9 - 6 \times 6 \div 2 = 9$

34. Lila saw 8 quail in each of 3 trees and 4 towhees in each of 2 trees. How many more quail did she see than towhees?

35. Pose a Problem Write a problem to match the expression $4 \times (8 - 3)$.

36. Trevor saw 4 California horned larks in his first hour of bird-watching. The second hour, he saw 1 more than twice the number he saw in the first hour. Write an expression for the number of horned larks he saw in the second hour. How many horned larks did he see in all?

37. **WRITE Math** ▸ When you evaluate $6 + 6$ and 3×4, both expressions equal 12. What other names for 12 can you write that use only numbers less than 10 and at least three different operations? **Explain** how you decided whether you should use parentheses.

Achieving the Standards

38. Find the value of $w + 26$ if $w = 17$.
(AF 1.1, p. 82)

39. A bird sanctuary has 8 birds in each giant cage. If there are 56 birds, how many cages are there? (O━┓ NS 3.0, p. 116)

40. Test Prep Find the value of the expression.

$$4 \times (9 - 5) - 1$$

41. ▪ $\times 6 = 6 \times 9$ (AF 1.1, p. 136)

42. Test Prep Which expression has a value of 28?

A $(16 - 2) \times 2$

B $16 - 2 \times 2$

C $16 + 4 \div 2 + 8$

D $(16 + 2) \div 2 + 8$

Problem Solving [connects to] Social Studies

California National Historic Trail

The California National Historic Trail traces some routes that pioneers took on the journey west to California. More than 200,000 pioneers traveled the trails from 1840 to 1859.

Write an expression to match the words. Then find the value of the expression.

1. A pioneer traveled 3 miles per hour for 3 hours in the morning. Then he traveled 5 miles in the afternoon and 3 miles in the evening. How far did he travel?

2. A family traveled 7 miles in the morning, 2 miles per hour for 4 hours in the afternoon, and then 1 more mile in the evening. How far did the family travel?

▲ Pioneers traveled at a rate of about 16 miles per day along trails such as this one.

Write and Evaluate Expressions

OBJECTIVE: Write and evaluate multiplication and division expressions with variables.

Learn

PROBLEM Diana collects stamps. She has 5 times as many stamps in her collection now as when she started the collection. Write an expression for the number of stamps she has now. Then find how many stamps she has now if she started with 3 stamps.

Example 1

ONE WAY Use a model.

Use pattern blocks to model the expression.

> Let ⬡ represent the number of stamps Diana started her collection with, and let ■ represent 1 stamp.
>
> ⬡ ⬡ ⬡ ⬡ ⬡   ← number of stamps she has now
>
> Since she started with 3 stamps, replace each ⬡ with 3 ■s.
>
> ⬡ ⬡ ⬡ ⬡ ⬡
> ↓ ↓ ↓ ↓ ↓
> ■■■ ■■■ ■■■ ■■■ ■■■ = 15

ANOTHER WAY Use a variable.

Write an expression with a variable.

> Let n represent the number of stamps Diana started her collection with.
>
> $5 \times n$ ← number of stamps she has now
>
> Find the value of $5 \times n$ if $n = 3$.
>
> $5 \times n$
> ↓
> 5×3 Replace n with 3, since she started with 3 stamps.
> ↓
> 15

Remember
A variable can stand for any number. You can use any letter as a variable.

So, Diana has 15 stamps in her collection now.

• How could you use the Associative Property to rewrite and then to find the value of $(d \times 4) \times 3$ if $d = 6$?

AF 1.0 Students use and interpret variables, mathematical symbols, and properties to write and simplify expressions and sentences. *also* ⊙—ন NS 3.0, AF 1.1, MR 1.1, MR 2.3, MR 2.4. MR 3.2

Example 2

Carl keeps his stamps in a stamp album. He fills a page with 24 stamps in equal rows. Write an expression for the number of stamps in 1 row. Then find how many stamps are in each row if he puts the stamps in 4 rows.

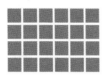

ONE WAY Use a model.

Use pattern blocks to model the expression.

> Use 24 ■s to represent 24 stamps.
>
> Put the ■s into 4 equal rows.

ANOTHER WAY Use a variable.

Write an expression with a variable.

> Let *r* represent the number of equal rows of stamps.
>
> 24 ÷ *r*   ← number of stamps in each row
>
> Find the value of 24 ÷ *r* if *r* = 4.
>
> 24 ÷ *r*
> ↓
> 24 ÷ 4   Replace *r* with 4 since
> ↓   there are 4 equal rows.
> 6

So, Carl put 6 stamps in each row.

READ Math

These multiplication phrases have the same meaning:

- 4 groups each with *n* objects
- $4 \times n$
- 4 times a number, *n*

These division phrases have the same meaning:

- *n* objects separated into 6 groups
- $n \div 6$
- a number, *n*, divided by 6

Example 3 Write an expression to match the words. Then find the value of the expression.

A Carl spent $10 on some stamps. Write an expression for the price of 1 stamp.

total cost ÷ among a number of stamps
   ↓   ↓
   10   ÷   *s*   ← *s* is the number of stamps.

Suppose he bought 5 stamps.

   10 ÷ *s*
      ↓
   10 ÷ 5   Replace *s* with 5.
      ↓
      2

So, Carl spent $2 on each stamp.

B Carl bought some $3 stamps. Write an expression for the total amount he spent.

a number of stamps × price of each stamp
      ↓   ↓
      s   ×   3   ← *s* is the number of stamps.

Suppose he bought 8 stamps.

   s × 3
   ↓
   8 × 3   Replace *s* with 8.
      ↓
      24

So, Carl spent $24 for 8 stamps.

1. There are 2 boxes of crayons, with *c* crayons in each box. Find the total number of crayons, $2 \times c$, if $c = 8$.

Write an expression that matches the words.

2. 3 times a number of words, *w*, in a spelling list

✅ 3. a handful of keys, *k*, divided equally and put on 4 key chains

Find the value of the expression.

4. $2 \times p$ if $p = 9$ 5. $6 \times w$ if $w = 7$ 6. $40 \div m$ if $m = 5$ ✅ 7. $s \div 3$ if $s = 27$

8. **TALK Math** **Explain** how to find the value of $8 \times k$ and $36 \div k$ if $k = 4$.

Independent Practice (and Problem Solving

Write an expression that matches the words.

9. the price of some toys, *t*, at $5 each

10. several pages, *p*, that have 10 stickers each

11. a number of books, *b*, divided equally and put on 6 shelves

12. 16 miniature cars divided equally into a number of display cases, *c*

Find the value of the expression.

13. $c \times 8$ if $c = 3$ 14. $9 \times y$ if $y = 7$ 15. $v \div 8$ if $v = 32$ 16. $25 \div q$ if $q = 5$

17. $a \div 2$ if $a = 12$ 18. $b \times 4$ if $b = 8$ 19. $72 \div b$ if $b = 9$ 20. $7 \times r$ if $r = 8$

Match the expression with the words.

21. $9 \div y$ 22. $6 \times (y \times 3)$ 23. $9 \times y$ 24. $(6 \div y) + 3$

   a. 6 times the product of *y* and 3

   b. the dividend of 9 divided by *y*

   c. 6 divided by *y*, and add 3

   d. 9 times *y*

Find the value of each expression if $n = 7$. Then write $<$, $>$, or $=$.

25. $59 - 58$ ● $n \div 7$ 26. 9×3 ● $42 \div n$ 27. $4 \times n$ ● $26 + 4$

28. Angela buys some sheets of stamps. Each sheet has 10 stamps. Write an expression for the number of stamps she buys. How many more stamps are on 9 sheets than on 6 sheets?

29. **≡FAST FACT** In 1932, it cost 3¢ to mail a letter. By 2006, the price was 3 pennies more than 12 times as much. How much did it cost to mail a letter in 2006?

Extra Practice on page 164, Set C

30. Reasoning Use the Commutative and Associative Properties to rewrite and then to find $(5 \times n) \times 2$ if $n = 9$. **Explain** how you found your answer.

31. **WRITE Math** ▸ **What's the Error?** Blaine claims that $w \times 8$ is 16 if $w = 8$. What error might Blaine have made? Write the correct answer.

Achieving the Standards

32. What number is represented by n?

(AF 1.1, p. 84)

$$n + 7 = 14$$

33. How many pairs of parallel sides does this figure appear to have? (Grade 3 **O━┓** MG 2.3)

34. Test Prep Which is the value of the expression $36 \div t$ if $t = 4$?

A 9   **C** 40

B 32   **D** 144

35. Show two ways to use parentheses to group $6 \times 2 \times 3$. Find the product.

(**O━┓** AF 1.3, p. 136)

36. Test Prep Dan has 6 times as many coins as Suzie. Let s represent the number of coins Suzie has. Which expression shows the number of coins Dan has?

A $6 + s$

B $6 - s$

C $6 \times s$

D $6 \div s$

Problem Solving connects to Art

Since 1934, the United States Postal Service has sold special stamps to raise money to buy wetlands for the National Wildlife Refuge System. Each year there is an art contest. The two winning pictures are used on Federal Duck Stamps. Each Federal Duck Stamp sells for $15. In 1989, the Junior Duck Stamp program was started for students from kindergarten through high school.

Write an expression that matches the words.

1. the total of 2 stamps on each Artist Commemorative card, c

2. the price of a number of First Day Cover envelopes, e, that cost $25 each

Each Junior Duck Stamp, s, cost $5. Find the total cost for the number of stamps.

3. $s = 8$ **4.** $s = 5$ **5.** $s = 7$

▲ A winning stamp from 2005

5 Multiplication and Division Equations

OBJECTIVE: Write and solve multiplication and division equations.

Learn

PROBLEM Sofie is making a number of bracelets to sell at the school craft fair. Each bracelet uses 6 beads. She has 24 beads. What equation can you write to find the number of bracelets she can make?

> **Remember**
> An equation is a number sentence that shows that two amounts are equal.

Example 1 Write multiplication equations.

A The number of bracelets with 6 beads each is 24 beads.

$$b \times 6 = 24 \quad \leftarrow b \text{ is the number of bracelets.}$$

So, the equation is $b \times 6 = 24$.

If the missing information changes, the equation changes.

B 4 bracelets times the number of beads is 24 beads.

$$4 \times n = 24 \quad \leftarrow n \text{ is the number of beads.}$$

C 4 bracelets with 6 beads each is the total number of beads.

$$4 \times 6 = t \quad \leftarrow t \text{ is the total number of beads.}$$

Example 2 Write division equations.

Ethan pays $12 to make spin-art pictures. Each picture costs $4 to make. What equation can you write to find the number of pictures he can make?

A $12 divided equally among the number of pictures is $4.

$$12 \div p = 4 \quad \leftarrow p \text{ is the number of pictures.}$$

So, the equation is $12 \div p = 4$.

B The total cost divided equally among 3 pictures is $4.

$$t \div 3 = 4 \quad \leftarrow t \text{ is the total cost of the pictures.}$$

C $12 divided equally among 3 pictures is the cost of each picture.

$$12 \div 3 = c \quad \leftarrow c \text{ is the cost for each picture.}$$

AF 1.1 Use letters, boxes, or other symbols to stand for any number in simple expressions or equations (e.g., demonstrate an understanding and the use of the concept of a variable). *also* **NS 3.0, AF 1.0, MR 1.1, MR 2.3, MR 2.4, MR 2.6, MR 3.1, MR 3.2**

Solve Equations

You can solve equations by using different strategies and methods.

 ONE WAY **Use the strategy *predict and test*.**

Materials ■ EquaBeam Balance™

Use the EquaBeam Balance to solve $10 \div n = 2$.

> Place a weight on 10 on the left side.
>
> Predict how many weights you need to place on 2 on the right side to restore balance.
>
> Test your prediction. Repeat until you restore balance.

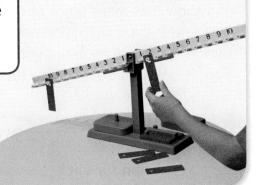

- How many weights do you need to place on 2? What is the value of n?

- Predict the value of b in $9 \times b = 18$. Test your prediction. What is the value of b?

ANOTHER WAY **Use the properties and mental math.**

A $\quad m \times 7 = 28$ **Think:** What number times 7 equals 28?

$\quad\quad\quad m = 4$

Check: $4 \times 7 \overset{?}{=} 28$ Replace m with 4.

$\quad\quad\quad\quad 28 = 28$ ✔   The equation is true. The value of m is 4.

B $\quad 32 \div g = 4$ **Think:** 32 divided by what number equals 4?

$\quad\quad\quad g = 8$

Check: $32 \div 8 \overset{?}{=} 4$ Replace g with 8.

$\quad\quad\quad\quad 4 = 4$ ✔   The equation is true. The value of g is 8.

C $\quad 4 \times h \times 2 = 16$

$\quad\quad 4 \times 2 \times h = 16$ Use the Commutative Property.

$\quad\quad\quad\quad 8 \times h = 16$ Use the Associative Property.

$\quad\quad\quad\quad\quad\quad h = 2$ **Think:** 8 times what number equals 16?

Check: $4 \times 2 \times 2 \overset{?}{=} 16$ Replace h with 2.

$\quad\quad\quad\quad\quad 16 = 16$ ✔   The equation is true. The value of $h = 2$.

Guided Practice

1. Choose the equation that shows the total number of clay animals, a, divided equally among 4 shelves is 8 animals each.

   a. $4 \div a = 8$ **b.** $a \div 4 = 8$ **c.** $8 \div 4 = a$

Write an equation for each. Choose a variable for the unknown. Tell what the variable represents.

2. An equal amount of money for each of 6 hand-painted hats is a total of $30.

☑ 3. The total number of rings divided equally among 4 friends is 2 rings for each friend.

Solve the equation.

4. $3 \times n = 21$

5. $d \div 6 = 8$

6. $z \div 5 = 4$

☑ 7. $a \times 7 = 63$

8. **TALK Math** Jill buys 15 pins at the fair. Her sister buys 3 pins. To show how many times as many pins Jill buys than her sister, Jill writes $3 \times r = 15$, and her sister writes $15 \div r = 3$. Is the value of r the same in both equations? **Explain** how the equations are alike and how they are different.

Independent Practice and Problem Solving

Write an equation for each. Choose a variable for the unknown. Tell what the variable represents.

9. Three knitted scarves at an equal cost for each is a total cost of $27.

10. 12 potholders divided equally among a number of bags is 3 potholders each.

11. The same number of necklaces in each of 6 boxes makes a total of 42 necklaces.

12. The total number of toys divided equally among 6 shelves is 9 toys on each shelf.

Solve the equation.

13. $4 \times n = 32$

14. $c \div 7 = 7$

15. $p \times 5 = 35$

16. $9 = k \div 3$

17. $m \div 8 = 7$

18. $6 = 54 \div n$

19. $3 \times h \times 2 = 18$

20. $2 \times n \times 6 = 60$

USE DATA For 21–22, use the picture.

21. **What if** Tommy made 12 more teddy bears? How could he arrange them on the shelves so that each shelf has the same number of bears?

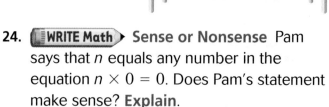
Tommy's Handmade Bears

22. Tommy sells 24 bears. He sells 8 bears each hour. Write an equation to find how many hours it takes him to sell the bears. Solve the equation.

23. **Reasoning** Find the values of a and b in these equations. **Explain** how you found the value of a and b.
$$a \times 6 = 18 \text{ and } a \times b = 12$$

24. **WRITE Math** Sense or Nonsense Pam says that n equals any number in the equation $n \times 0 = 0$. Does Pam's statement make sense? **Explain**.

Technology
Use Harcourt Mega Math, Ice Station
Exploration, *Arctic Algebra*, Levels F, T.

Extra Practice on page 164, Set D

25. Find the value of the expression.
(**O—π** AF 1.2, p. 142)

$$(4 + 2) \times 3$$

26. Toss a coin 10 times. Make a tally table to show the results. (Grade 3 **O—π** SDAP 1.2)

27. Test Prep What is the value of *a*?

$$a \times 4 = 36$$

A 8   **C** 32

B 9   **D** 40

28. Megan has 27 buttons. Each shirt needs 3 buttons. How many shirts can she sew buttons on? (**O—π** NS 3.0, p. 116)

29. Test Prep If $n = 2$, which equation below can be used to find the value of *n*?

A $14 \div n = 16$

B $8 \div n = 10$

C $2 \div n = 4$

D $18 \div n = 9$

MATH POWER — Problem Solving and Reasoning

ALGEBRA Sometimes you can use a number line to solve an equation.

A **Solve.** $n \times 4 = 12$

- Draw a number line.
- Start at 0. Skip count by fours to 12.

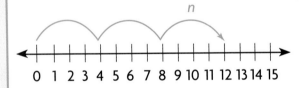

- Count the number of skips. This is the value of *n*.
- $n = 3$

Check: $3 \times 4 \overset{?}{=} 12$ Replace *n* with 3.
$\ 12 = 12$ ✔   The equation is true.

So, the value of *n* is 3.

B **Solve.** $12 \div n = 6$

- Draw a number line.
- Start at 12. Count back by sixes to 0.

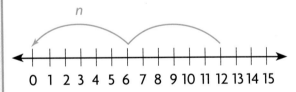

- Count the number of skips. This is the value of *n*.
- $n = 2$

Check: $12 \div 2 \overset{?}{=} 6$ Replace *n* with 2.
$\ 6 = 6$ ✔   The equation is true.

So, the value of *n* is 2.

Use a number line to solve the equation. Check your solution.

1. $n \times 6 = 24$

2. $g \times 9 = 27$

3. $12 \div y = 3$

4. $21 \div d = 3$

5. $16 \div n = 2$

6. $a \times 5 = 30$

6 Multiply Equals by Equals

OBJECTIVE: Keep an equation equal by multiplying the same amount to both sides.

Learn

PROBLEM Angie picks 5 Gala apples and 4 Elstar apples to put in her basket. Cedric picks 9 Macintosh apples to put in his basket. Do Angie and Cedric have the same number of apples?

An equation is a number sentence that shows that two amounts are equal. You can use the equation $5 + 4 = 9$ to model the number of apples in Angie's and Cedric's baskets.

▶ More than 20 types of apples are grown in California.

ONE WAY Use a model.

Materials ■ EquaBeam Balance™

Use the balance to test whether both sides of the equation are equal.

> Model $5 + 4 = 9$ on the balance. Place weights on 5 and 4 on the left side and a weight on 9 on the right side.
>
> • Compare the two sides. Are the values equal? Explain.

So, Angie and Cedric have the same number of apples.

When Angie and Cedric finish picking apples, they each have 3 times as many apples in their baskets as when they started. Do Angie and Cedric still have the same number of apples? How many apples are in each basket now?

> Multiply both sides by 3. Put a total of 3 weights on each number on the balance.
>
> • Compare the two sides. Are the values equal? Explain.
>
> • What equation does the balance show now? Is the equation true? Explain.

So, Angie and Cedric still have the same number of apples. There are 27 apples in each basket now.

• **What if** you multiply the equation $5 + 4 = 9$ on one side by 3 and the other side by 4? Compare the two sides. Is the equation true? Explain.

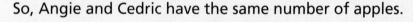

○━┓ AF 2.2 Know and understand that equals multiplied by equals are equal. *also* ○━┓ NS 3.0, AF 1.1, ○━┓ AF 1.2, ○━┓ AF 2.0, MR 1.1, MR 2.3, MR 2.4, MR 3.2

Multiply both sides of the equation by the given number.
Find the values.

A $8 = 2 \times 4$; multiply by 7.

$$8 = 2 \times 4$$
$$8 \times 7 = (2 \times 4) \times 7 \quad \leftarrow \text{Multiply by 7.}$$
$$\downarrow \qquad\qquad \downarrow$$
$$56 \quad = \quad 56$$

B $1 + 2 = 6 - 3$; multiply by 4.

$$1 + 2 = 6 - 3$$
$$(1 + 2) \times 4 = (6 - 3) \times 4 \quad \leftarrow \text{Multiply by 4.}$$
$$\downarrow \qquad\qquad \downarrow$$
$$3 \times 4 \quad = \quad 3 \times 4$$
$$\downarrow \qquad\qquad \downarrow$$
$$12 \quad = \quad 12$$

C $2 \times 3 = 24 \div 4$; multiply by 5.

$$2 \times 3 = 24 \div 4$$
$$(2 \times 3) \times 5 = (24 \div 4) \times 5 \quad \leftarrow \text{Multiply by 5.}$$
$$\downarrow \qquad\qquad \downarrow$$
$$6 \times 5 \quad = \quad 6 \times 5$$
$$\downarrow \qquad\qquad \downarrow$$
$$30 \quad = \quad 30$$

D $35 \div 7 = 14 - 9$; multiply by 8.

$$35 \div 7 = 14 - 9$$
$$(35 \div 7) \times 8 = (14 - 9) \times 8 \quad \leftarrow \text{Multiply by 8.}$$
$$\downarrow \qquad\qquad \downarrow$$
$$5 \times 8 \quad = \quad 5 \times 8$$
$$\downarrow \qquad\qquad \downarrow$$
$$40 \quad = \quad 40$$

- What number makes the equation $(9 - 4) \times 6 = 5 \times \blacksquare$ true? How do you know?

- Divide both sides of $8 \times 3 = 30 - 6$ by 4. Do the values stay equal? Explain.

- **Reasoning** If you add, subtract, multiply, or divide both sides of an equation by the same number except 0, will the equation stay true? Show an example of each operation to explain.

Math Idea

If you add, subtract, multiply, or divide (except by 0) both sides of an equation by the same number, the values of both sides may change but stay equal.

Guided Practice

1. To multiply both sides of the equation $1 + 6 = 14 \div 2$ by 3, write $(1 + 6) \times 3 = (14 \div 2) \times 3$. Then follow the order of operations to find the value of each side of the equation. What are the values? Did the values stay equal?

Tell whether each equation is true. If not, explain why.

2. $(7 + 4) \times 6 \stackrel{?}{=} 3 \times 6$ 　　3. $(9 - 5) \times 8 \stackrel{?}{=} (2 \times 2) \times 8$ 　　✓4. $(3 \times 3) \times 6 \stackrel{?}{=} (36 \div 4) \times 7$

Multiply both sides of the equation by the given number. Find the new values.

5. $6 = 3 \times 2$; multiply by 9.

✓6. $12 - 4 = 40 \div 5$; multiply by 3.

7. **TALK Math** Explain why the values of the sides stay equal when you multiply both sides of the equation $10 + 2 = 24 \div 2$ by 3.

Independent Practice and Problem Solving

Tell whether each equation is true. If not, explain why.

8. $(12 - 6) \times 2 \overset{?}{=} 6 \times 2$

9. $(3 + 4) \times 5 \overset{?}{=} (21 \div 3) \times 6$

10. $(8 \times 1) \times 9 \overset{?}{=} (4 \times 2) \times 9$

11. $(4 + 2) \times 7 \overset{?}{=} (9 - 3) \times 7$

12. $(56 \div 8) \times 3 \overset{?}{=} (63 \div 7) \times 3$

13. $(42 \div 6) \times 8 \overset{?}{=} 7 \times (2 \times 4)$

Multiply both sides of the equation by the given number. Find the new values.

14. $16 - 9 = 5 + 2$; multiply by 3.

15. $16 \div 4 = 2 \times 2$; multiply by 5.

16. $3 \times 3 = 45 \div 5$; multiply by 8.

17. $14 - 8 = 42 \div 7$; multiply by 4.

What number makes the equation true?

18. $(16 \div 8) \times 9 = 2 \times \blacksquare$

19. $(1 + 5) \times 3 = \blacksquare \times 3$

20. $(10 - 5) \times \blacksquare = 5 \times 4$

21. $(6 \times 2) \times 7 = \blacksquare \times 7$

22. $(8 - 2) \times 4 = (2 \times b) \times 4$

23. $(3 + b) \times 6 = (2 \times 4) \times 6$

USE DATA For 24–25, use the table.

24. Keisha picks the same total number of apples as Eric. She picked only one type of apple. She has 5 times as many of this type of apple as Eric has of this type. Which type of apple does Keisha pick?

25. Scott and Paul start with the same number of apples. Scott has 3 times as many Braeburn apples as Eric. Paul has the same number of Granny Smith apples as Eric. Both Scott and Paul fill their baskets with 4 times as many apples as they started with. Write an equation to show how many apples Scott and Paul have now. Do they still have the same number of apples?

26. **WRITE Math** Explain why the equation $9 - 2 \times 4 \overset{?}{=} (9 - 2) \times 4$ is not true.

Apples in Eric's Basket	
Type	Number
Golden Delicious	4
Red Delicious	3
Braeburn	2
Granny Smith	6

Extra Practice on page 164, Set E

27. What is the value of the expression?
(O━ AF 1.2, p. 142)

$$4 \times 9 - (8 + 2)$$

28. What is 74,629,386 rounded to the nearest hundred thousand? (O━ NS 1.3, p. 34)

29. Test Prep What number goes into the box to make this number sentence true? **Explain** how you know.

$$(4 + 5) \times 3 = (18 \div \blacksquare) \times 3$$

30. What is a rule for the table? (O━ AF 1.5, p. 96)

Input	a	7	9	12	16
Output	b	11	13	16	20

31. Test Prep The letters M and N stand for numbers. If $M \times 5 = N \times 5$, which statement is true?

A $M < N$ **C** $M = 5 \times N$

B $M = N$ **D** $M > 5 \times N$

Problem Solving and Reasoning

ALGEBRA An equation shows a relationship between two quantities that are equal. An **inequality** shows a relationship between two quantities that are not equal.

A balance scale can help you determine whether two expressions show an equation or an inequality. The scale for an equation is balanced and for an inequality is not balanced.

> **READ Math**
>
> Read = as "equal to."
> Read < as "is less than."
> Read > as "is greater than."

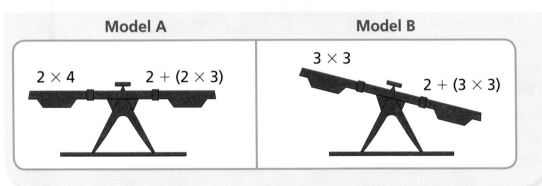

Model A — 2×4 and $2 + (2 \times 3)$

Model B — 3×3 and $2 + (3 \times 3)$

For 1–2, use the models.

1. Which model shows an equation? Which model shows an inequality? **Explain.**

2. Use =, >, or < to write an equation or inequality that describes each model.

3. Reasoning How can you change $(4 + 6) \times 3 > (2 + 2) \times 3$ to make the inequality an equation? **Explain.**

Problem Solving Workshop
Strategy: Predict and Test

OBJECTIVE: Solve problems using the strategy *predict and test*.

Learn the Strategy

Sometimes, you can make an educated prediction to solve a problem and then test your prediction to see whether it fits the problem conditions. It is a good strategy to use when one condition depends on another condition.

Make a list to record your predictions.

What are three consecutive numbers whose sum is 15?

Think: The sum is less than 20, so the addends must be 1-digit numbers.

> Predict 1: 2+3+4=9 too low
> Predict 2: 3+4+5=12 too low
> Predict 3: 4+5+6=15 ✓

Make a table to record your predictions.

Mary is thinking of two numbers. The sum of the numbers is 15, and the difference of the numbers is 3. What are Mary's numbers?

Think: Write two equations, $m + n = 15$ and $m - n = 3$.

Predict	Test		Does It Check?
	Sum: m+n=15	Difference: m−n=3	
m=8 n=7	8+7=15	8−7=1	The sum is 15. The difference is 1. too low
m=12 n=3	12+3=15	12−3=9	The sum is 15. The difference is 9. too high
m=9 n=6	9+6=15	9−6=3	The sum is 15. ✓ The difference is 3. ✓

Draw a picture to record your predictions.

Write 2, 3, 4, and 5 in each outer circle so the sum of the numbers across and down are equal.

Prediction 1: $2 + 1 + 4 = 7$ and
$\qquad 3 + 1 + 5 = 9$

Prediction 2: $3 + 1 + 4 = 8$ and
$\qquad 2 + 1 + 5 = 8$ ✔

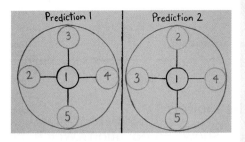

To use the strategy, make a prediction, test your prediction, and then revise the prediction until all conditions in the problem are met.

TALK Math

How can you use the first prediction to make a better prediction?

 AF 1.1 Use letters, boxes, or other symbols to stand for any number in simple expressions or equations (e.g., demonstrate an understanding and the use of the concept of a variable). *also* ⟵ NS 3.0, MR 1.0, MR 1.1, MR 2.0, MR 2.3, MR 2.4, MR 3.0, MR 3.1, MR 3.2, MR 3.3

Use the Strategy

PROBLEM On rainy days, Raul likes to solve riddles. He found this riddle in a book about numbers.

The product of two numbers is 24. Their sum is 11. What are the numbers?

Read to Understand

 Reading Skill

- Identify the details given.

- Are there details you will not use? If so, what?

Plan

- **What strategy can you use to solve the problem?**

  You can predict and test to solve the problem.

Solve

- **How can you use the strategy to solve the problem?**

  Make a table to record your predictions.

  Think: What are the factors of 24? Write two equations to test your predictions.

  Use what you know about multiplication facts to make a prediction. Check your prediction and test another pair of factors, if needed. Predict and test until all the problem conditions are met.

  So, the numbers are 3 and 8.

Predict	Test		Does It Check?
	Product: $a \times b = 24$	Sum: $a + b = 11$	
$a = 2$ $b = 12$	$2 \times 12 = 24$	$2 + 12 = 14$	The product is 24. The sum is 14. too high
$a = 4$ $b = 6$	$4 \times 6 = 24$	$4 + 6 = 10$	The product is 24. The sum is 10. too low
$a = 3$ $b = 8$	$3 \times 8 = 24$	$3 + 8 = 11$	The product is 24. ✔ The sum is 11. ✔

Check

- **How do you know your answer is correct?**
- **What other strategy could you use to solve the problem?**

1. Erica is thinking of two numbers. The difference of the two numbers is 5. The product of the numbers is 24. What are Erica's numbers?

   First, make a table.

   Next, make a prediction based on the facts.

   Then, adjust and predict again until you find the two numbers.

Predict	Test		Does It Check?
	Difference $a - b = 5$	**Product** $a \times b = 24$	
$a = 6$ $b = 1$	$6 - 1 = 5$	$6 \times 1 = 6$	The difference is 5. The product is 6. too low

2. **What if** the product of the two numbers is 36? What would Erica's numbers be?

3. Marc likes to solve word scrambles and mazes. Yesterday he solved 10 word scrambles and mazes in all. He solved 2 more word scrambles than mazes. How many word scrambles did Marc solve yesterday?

Problem Solving Strategy Practice

Predict and test to solve.

4. Tina and Larry played a memory game. Tina scored twice as many points as Larry did. Together they scored 30 points. How many points did Tina score?

5. Marie bought two puzzle books. Together the books cost $17. One book costs $3 more than the other. How much did each book cost?

USE DATA For 6–8, copy and complete the puzzle.

6. Write 2 in the center circle. Write 3, 6, 4, and 8 in the outer circles so that the products across and down are equal.

7. Write 3 in the center circle. Write 2, 4, 6, and 8 in the outer circles so the sums across and down are equal.

8. Write 4 in the center circle. Write 2, 3, 6, and 9 in the outer circles so the products across and down are equal.

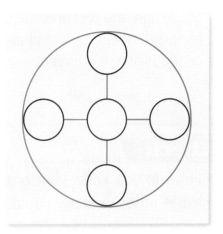

9. André is thinking of a number. The number times itself is less than 150 but greater than 75. The sum of the number and itself is less than 20. What is the number?

10. **WRITE Math** **Sense or Nonsense** Maria says that the sum of two numbers is 6 and their product is 5. Does Maria's statement make sense? **Explain.**

Mixed Strategy Practice

USE DATA For 11–15, copy and complete the table.

	Sum	Product	Difference	Two Numbers
11.	14	48	■	■, ■
12.	11	■	5	■, ■
13.	12	35	■	■, ■
14.	■	40	6	■, ■
15.	15	■	9	■, ■

Choose a STRATEGY

Draw a Diagram or Picture

Make a Model or Act It Out

Make an Organized List

Find a Pattern

Make a Table or Graph

Predict and Test

Work Backward

Solve a Simpler Problem

Write an Equation

Use Logical Reasoning

16. Jimmy designed a maze made up of triangles. If you can move only forward, and never retrace your steps, how many different ways can you walk through his maze?

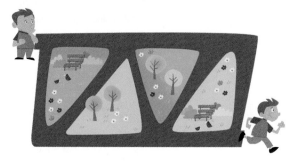

17. Patty, Rex, Jan, and Tara were waiting in line for their riddle cards at the corn maze. Tara was behind Rex. Patty was not next to Jan. Jan was first in line. Patty was between Rex and Tara. In what order were they standing in line?

18. Pose a Problem Look back at Problem 9. Write a similar riddle.

19. Open-Ended John is thinking of two odd numbers that add up to 26. What could John's numbers be?

▼ Two and one-half miles of maze in the shape of Wisconsin was cut into 10 acres of corn near Janesville, Wisconsin.

CHALLENGE YOURSELF

Ryan is working on number puzzles in a book. It takes him 2 minutes to complete a puzzle rated *Easy*, and 3 minutes to complete one rated *Hard*.

20. On Monday, Ryan worked for 25 minutes and completed a total of 11 puzzles. How many *Hard* puzzles did he complete? How many *Easy* ones?

21. On Tuesday, Ryan worked for 30 minutes and completed the same number of *Easy* puzzles as *Hard* ones. **Explain** how you can find how many *Easy* and how many *Hard* puzzles Ryan completed on Tuesday.

8 Patterns: Find a Rule

OBJECTIVE: Find a rule for a number relationship and write an equation for the rule.

Quick Review

1. 5×7
2. 8×6
3. $32 \div 4$
4. $63 \div 9$
5. $3 \times 6 + 2$

Learn

PROBLEM One gallon of milk equals 4 quarts of milk, 2 gallons equal 8 quarts, and 3 gallons equal 12 quarts. How many quarts of milk do 4 gallons equal?

You can use an input/output table to find a rule that relates the number of gallons to the number of quarts.

Input (gallons)	Output (quarts)
1	4
2	8
3	12
4	■

Find a pattern to help you find a rule.

Pattern: Each output is the input multiplied by 4.

Rule: Multiply the input by 4.
← Input: 4   Output: $4 \times 4 = 16$

▲ One cow can produce more than 188 gallons of milk in a month.

So, 4 gallons equal 16 quarts of milk.

You can write an equation to show the rule.
Use variables to show the input and output.

input (gallons) output (quarts)
↓   ↓
$$g \times 4 = q$$

Think of the equation as a rule.
To find the value of q, multiply g by 4.

ERROR ALERT

A rule must work for each pair of numbers in the table. Be sure to test your rule with each pair of numbers in the table.

Examples

A Find a rule. Write your rule as an equation. Use the equation to find the next number in your pattern.

Input, b	Output, c	Think:
14	2	$14 \div 7 = 2$
28	4	$28 \div 7 = 4$
42	6	$42 \div 7 = 6$
56	■	← $56 \div 7 = 8$

Pattern: Each output is the input divided by 7.
Rule: Divide b by 7.
Equation: $b \div 7 = c$

So, the next number in your pattern is 8.

B Use the equation $(n \times 3) + 5 = p$ to complete the table.

First, multiply n by 3.

Then, add 5 to the result.

Input, n	4	5	6	7	8	9
Output, p	17	20	23	26	■	■

$(8 \times 3) + 5 = 29$
$(9 \times 3) + 5 = 32$

So, the next two numbers are 29 and 32.

AF 1.5 Understand that an equation such as $y = 3x + 5$ is a prescription for determining a second number when a first number is given. *also* **NS 3.0, AF 1.1, AF 1.3, AF 1.4, MR 1.1, MR 2.3, MR 2.4, MR 3.2, MR 3.3**

Guided Practice

1. The rule is multiply w by 6. The equation is $w \times 6 = z$. What is the next number in the pattern?

Input, w	4	5	6	7	8
Output, z	24	30	36	42	■

Find a rule. Write your rule as an equation. Use your rule to find the missing numbers.

2.
Input, b	90	70	60	50	30	20	10
Output, c	9	7	6	■	■	■	■

3.
Input, r	2	3	5	6	8	9	10
Output, s	18	27	45	■	■	■	■

4. **TALK Math** Explain how to use the table to write an equation to find the distance in miles, d, a truck travels on g gallons of gas. Use the equation to complete the table.

Input, g	1	2	3	4
Output, d	12	24	36	■

Independent Practice and Problem Solving

Find a rule. Write your rule as an equation. Use your rule to find the missing numbers.

5.
Input, x	14	28	42	56	70	77	84
Output, y	2	4	6	■	■	■	■

6.
Input, d	3	4	6	■	■	■	11
Output, f	15	20	30	40	45	50	55

Use the rule and the equation to make an input/output table.

7. Divide k by 10.
$k \div 10 = m$

8. Multiply c by 12.
$c \times 12 = d$

9. Multiply f by 4, add 7.
$(f \times 4) + 7 = g$

10. Divide p by 5, subtract 2.
$(p \div 5) - 2 = q$

USE DATA For 11–12, use the food pyramid for kids.

11. How many cups of milk should a kid drink in 2, 3, 4, and 5 days? Make an input/output table. Write an equation to solve.

12. **WRITE Math** Explain how to find a rule and write an equation for the total number of ounces of grain a kid should eat in 3 days.

◀ For an 1,800-calorie diet, you need to eat or drink the amount shown from each group every day.

Grains	Vegetables	Fruits	Milk	Meat & Beans
6 ounces	$2\frac{1}{2}$ cups	$1\frac{1}{2}$ cups	3 cups	5 ounces

Achieving the Standards

13. What is the value of p? (AF 1.1, p. 84)

$$15 - p = 8$$

14. $4 \times 10 =$ ⬤━ NS 3.0, p. 116)

15. $(10 - 2) \times 7 =$ ⬤━ AF 1.3, p. 142)

16. **Test Prep** What equation shows a rule for the table?

Input, q (quarts)	3	6	9
Output, p (pints)	6	12	18

Extra Practice on page 164, Set F

 **Extra Practice**

Set A Use the properties and mental math to find the product (pp. 136–139)

1. $2 \times 7 \times 5$ **2.** $2 \times 0 \times 31$ **3.** $1 \times 6 \times 7$ **4.** $3 \times 8 \times 2$

5. $8 \times 1 \times 7$ **6.** $5 \times 4 \times 1$ **7.** $5 \times 9 \times 2$ **8.** $3 \times 0 \times 34$

9. A grocery store received a shipment of 2 crates, each with 10 cases of juice boxes. There are 5 juice boxes in each case. How many juice boxes did the grocery store receive?

Set B Follow the order of operations
to find the value of each expression. (pp. 142–145)

1. $28 - 4 \div 2$ **2.** $25 + 15 \div (2 + 3)$ **3.** $5 \times (6 - 3) + 9$ **4.** $28 - (5 + 3) \div 4$

5. $16 + 4 \times (3 + 7)$ **6.** $(22 - 1) \div 7$ **7.** $(9 + 18) \div 3$ **8.** $36 \div 9 - 4$

Set C Find the value of the expression. (pp. 146–149)

1. $d \times 9$ if $d = 6$ **2.** $f \div 7$ if $f = 49$ **3.** $6 \times n$ if $n = 8$ **4.** $56 \div q$ if $q = 7$

5. $n \times 8$ if $n = 5$ **6.** $63 \div m$ if $m = 9$ **7.** $9 \times s$ if $s = 8$ **8.** $w \div 9$ if $w = 36$

9. Allison pasted 10 pictures on each of n pages in her album. Write an expression to show the total number of pictures in the album.

Set D Solve the equation. (pp. 150–153)

1. $3 \times n = 21$ **2.** $c \div 9 = 1$ **3.** $t \times 4 = 28$ **4.** $h \div 4 = 10$

5. $r \div 6 = 5$ **6.** $56 \div m = 7$ **7.** $3 \times w \times 3 = 36$ **8.** $3 \times n \times 4 = 24$

Set E Tell whether each equation is true. If not, explain why. (pp. 154–157)

1. $(12 - 4) \times 8 \overset{?}{=} 8 \times 3$ **2.** $(5 + 4) \times 4 \overset{?}{=} (30 \div 10) \times 12$

3. $(8 + 7) \div 3 \overset{?}{=} (5 \times 3) \div 5$ **4.** $(56 \div 8) \times 3 \overset{?}{=} (63 \div 7) \times 3$

Set F Find a rule. Write your rule as an equation.
Use your rule to find the missing numbers. (pp. 162–163)

1.

Input, *a*	6	12	18	24	30
Output, *b*	1	2	3	■	■

2.

Input, *m*	4	5	6	■	■
Output, *n*	32	40	48	56	64

Technology
Use Harcourt Mega Math, Ice Station
Exploration, *Arctic Algebra,* Levels F, H, K, Q, T.

Equation Connection

On Your Mark!
2 players

Get Set!
Index cards (20)

A player turned over these two cards. The values of *n* do not match. So, the player will turn the cards facedown, and it will be the other player's turn.

$6 \div n = 3$ $10 \div n = 2$

Go!

- Each player takes 10 index cards. One player will write 10 mutliplication equations, and the other will write 10 division equations. All the equations should use *n* as a variable, and the value of *n* in each should be a whole number from 1 to 10.

- Mix the cards together. Place them facedown in 4 rows of 5 cards each.

- Decide who will play first. The first player turns over 2 cards. If both equations have the same value of *n*, the player keeps the cards. If they are not the same, the player turns them facedown again.

- Take turns until all the cards have been matched. The player with the greater number of cards wins.

 **Chapter 6 Review/Test**

Check Vocabulary and Concepts

Choose the best term from the box.

VOCABULARY

Associative Property
Commutative Property
Identity Property
Zero Property

1. The ? states that when the order of two factors is changed, the product is the same. (AF 1.0, p. 136)

2. The ? states that the product of 0 and any number is 0. (AF 1.0, p. 136)

3. The ? states that you can group factors in different ways and still get the same product. (AF 1.0, p. 136)

Check Skills

Follow the order of operations to find the value of each expression. (O—🔑 AF 1.2, pp. 140–141, 142–145)

4. $25 - 10 \div 2$ 5. $11 + 1 \times (7 - 3)$ 6. $3 \times (8 - 6) + 7$ 7. $14 - (3 + 9) \div 6$

Write an expression that matches the words. (AF 1.0, pp. 146–149)

8. a number of toys, t, divided equally among 8 cats

9. several binders, b, that have 3 rings each

Solve the equation. (AF 1.1, pp. 150–153)

10. $7 \times n = 56$ 11. $d \div 6 = 4$ 12. $w \times 6 = 30$ 13. $p \div 6 = 7$

14. $k \div 4 = 2$ 15. $35 \div m = 7$ 16. $3 \times h \times 3 = 45$ 17. $4 \times n \times 5 = 40$

Tell whether each equation is true. If not, explain why. (O—🔑 AF 2.2, pp. 154–157)

18. $(4 \times 4) \times 4 \stackrel{?}{=} (8 + 8) \times 4$

19. $(24 \div 4) \times 10 \stackrel{?}{=} (2 \times 6) \times 10$

20. $(10 + 6) \div 4 \stackrel{?}{=} (36 \div 3) \div 3$

21. $(14 - 9) + 3 \stackrel{?}{=} (40 \div 8) - 3$

Find a rule. Write your rule as an equation. Use your rule to find the missing numbers. (O—🔑 AF 1.5, pp. 162–163)

22.

Input, x	20	25	30	35	40
Output, y	4	5	6	■	■

23.

Input, n	3	4	5	■	■
Output, m	27	36	45	54	63

Check Problem Solving

Solve. (O—🔑 AF 1.1, MR 1.1, pp. 158–161)

24. The sum of the two numbers is 17. Their product is 72. What are the numbers?

25. **WRITE Math** ▸ The product of two numbers is one less than their sum. **Describe** what you know about the numbers.

GO ONLINE **Technology** Use *Online Assessment.*

Enrich • Predict Patterns
Growing, Growing, Growing

You can use diagrams, tables, and equations to predict patterns.

Each square table can seat 1 student on a side. How many students can sit at 4 tables placed end-to-end? What equation can you use to predict the number of students who can sit at any number of tables placed end-to-end?

Input, t	1	2	3	4
Output, s	4	6	8	▣

Complete the input/output table to predict the number of students who can sit at 4 tables placed end-to-end. Write an equation for the number of students who can sit at any number of tables placed end-to-end.

$(2 \times t) + 2 = s$ **Think:** Each table seats 2 students plus 1 student at each end.

The equation $(2 \times t) + 2 = s$ predicts the number of students who can sit at any number of tables pushed together. So, 10 students can sit at 4 tables placed end-to-end.

Try It

Copy and complete the table for the pattern. Then write an equation to predict the number of objects in the nth design of the pattern.

1.

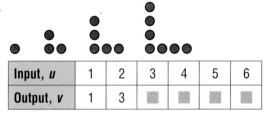

Input, u	1	2	3	4	5	6
Output, v	1	3	▣	▣	▣	▣

2.

		Row 1
		Row 2
		Row 3
		Row 4

Input, r	1	2	3	4	5	6
Output, c	2	4	▣	▣	▣	▣

3.

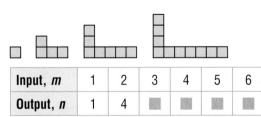

Input, m	1	2	3	4	5	6
Output, n	1	4	▣	▣	▣	▣

4.

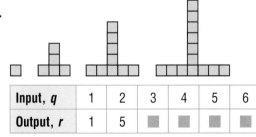

Input, q	1	2	3	4	5	6
Output, r	1	5	▣	▣	▣	▣

WRITE Math ▶ **Explain** how you can predict the number of students who can sit at 14 tables placed end-to-end by using the equation $(2 \times t) + 2 = s$.

Multiple Choice

1. Reena wrote the equation $y = 3 \times k$ as the rule for taxi fares outside the city. The fare is y, and the number of kilometers traveled is k. What is the taxi fare for a 9-kilometer trip? (AF 1.5, p. 162)

   A $9

   B $15

   C $18

   D $27

2. What number goes in the box to make this number sentence true?

   (O➜ NS 3.0, p. 116)

   $$6 \times 8 = 4 \times 4 \times ▪$$

   A 6   **C** 3

   B 4   **D** 2

3. Jamal weighs twice as much as his brother. If m represents Jamal's weight, which expression shows how much his brother weighs? (AF 1.1, p. 146)

   A $m \div 2$

   B $m + 2$

   C $m - 2$

   D $m \times 2$

4. What is the value of the expression below if $t = 8$? (O➜ AF 1.2, p. 142)

   $$48 \div (t + 4) \times 5$$

   A 50   **C** 10

   B 20   **D** 4

5. The salespeople at Ultimate Used Cars sold 32 cars in 4 days. The same numbers of cars were sold each day. How many cars were sold each day?

   (O➜ NS 3.0, p. 116)

   A 4   **C** 12

   B 8   **D** 24

6. The Ortiz family bought 3 milkshakes. The Lott family bought 3 one-scoop cones and 4 sundaes. Which expression shows how much more money the Lott family spent than the Ortiz family? (O➜ AF 1.3, p. 142)

Cones	
1 Scoop	$2
2 Scoops	$3
Sundae	$4
Milkshake	$3

   A $(3 \times 2) + 4 - (3 \times 3)$

   B $(3 \times 2) + (4 \times 4) + (3 \times 3)$

   C $(3 \times 2 + 4) \times (4 - 3) \times 3$

   D $(3 \times 2) + (4 \times 4) - (3 \times 3)$

7. What number goes in the box to make this number sentence true?

   (AF 1.1, p. 126)

   $$▪ \times 5 = 21 + 9$$

   A 3

   B 5

   C 6

   D 10

GO ONLINE Technology Use *Online Assessment.*

8. Which number sentence is not in the same fact family as $6 \times 9 = \blacksquare$?

(AF 1.1, p. 112)

A $\blacksquare \div 9 = 6$

B $\blacksquare \div 6 = 9$

C $9 \times \blacksquare = 6$

D $9 \times 6 = \blacksquare$

9. The letters A and N stand for numbers. If $A \times 5 = N \times 5$, which statement is true? (O━ AF 2.2, p. 154)

A $A > N$

B $A < N$

C $A = N$

D $A \neq N$

10. Natasha is reading a book. The book is 99 pages long. How many pages must Natasha read each day to finish the book in 9 days? (O━ NS 3.0, p. 120)

A 8

B 9

C 10

D 11

11. Which number is represented by g?

(AF 1.1, p. 150)

$$g \div 12 = 7$$

A 96

B 84

C 74

D 72

Short Response

12. Let p represent the original price of a poster. Write an expression to show its sale price. (AF 1.1, p. 146)

> Giant Sale!!!
> All Prices Cut in Half

13. Add parentheses to the following expression so that its value is 28. (O━ AF 1.3, p. 142)

$$9 + 5 \times 2$$

14. Look at the problem below.

$$y = x \div 2$$

If $y = 10$, what is x? (O━ AF 1.5, p. 162)

15. Mrs. Lin buys 11 boxes of party invitations. Each box has 12 invitations. How many invitations does Mrs. Lin buy in all? (O━ NS 3.0, p. 120)

Extended Response ⟨WRITE Math⟩

16. **Explain** how to find the value of the expression $42 \div 6 + (5 - 3)$.

(O━ AF 1.3, p. 142)

17. There are 3 times as many girls as boys in a ballet class. There are 12 girls in the class. **Explain** how to write an equation to find the number of boys in the ballet class.

(AF 1.1, p. 150)

18. **Explain** how you know what number makes this number sentence $6 \times n = 6 \times (3 + 4)$ true.

(O━ AF 2.2, p. 154)

Gold Rush!

OFF TO CALIFORNIA

In 1848, gold was discovered in California. Many people rushed to California to seek their fortunes. The gold-seekers were called "forty-niners" because most left home in 1849.

The first forty-niners came by sea but most arrived in covered wagons from the East by way of the Oregon Trail and the California Trail. They carried supplies for their long and difficult journey to California.

Supply List (for one person)

9 pounds coffee	12 pounds bacon
2 pounds tea	5 pounds vegetables
20 pounds corn meal	40 pounds sugar

FACT·ACTIVITY

Use the Supply List to answer the questions.

1. How many pounds of vegetables were needed for 5 people?

2. If 8 people traveled in one wagon, how many pounds of tea should they have brought?

3. How many forty-niners would 27 pounds of coffee serve on their journey?

4. On good days, forty-niners would travel 10 miles a day. How far might they have traveled in 7 days?

5. **WRITE Math** Suppose 3 people traveled in one wagon and they had 24 pounds of bacon. Did they have enough bacon for everyone? **Explain** how you know.

PLANNING AHEAD

Forty-niners needed to bring everything with them as they made the long journey to California. Store owners selling supplies could make big profits. One famous shop keeper made canvas pants for the miners, which are still popular today. His name was Levi Strauss, the man whose pants later became known as blue jeans!

FACT·ACTIVITY

The table below shows some food supplies in 1849.

Suppose your family is going by covered wagon to California in 1849. Your wagon can carry about 2,100 pounds.

► Decide which food supplies each family member will need. Make a list of the items and number of pounds each family member will bring.

► Find the total pounds of each item for your entire family. Now find the total amount of pounds that will be loaded into the wagon. Make sure the total amount of pounds does not go over 2,100 pounds.

► If the total pounds of items is less than 2,100 pounds, add more items to get as close to 2,100 pounds as possible.

Some Food Supplies in 1849	
bacon	coffee
cornmeal	sugar
vegetables	tea

3 Multiply by 1- and 2-Digit Numbers

Math on Location

1

Meals are developed so astronauts have a balanced diet eating 4 pounds of food and 10 cups of water each day.

2

Over 200 dishes, such as these scrambled eggs, are prepared through a process called freeze-drying.

3

The packages for a menu cycle of 10 days or longer are boxed for storage in the space module.

VOCABULARY POWER

TALK Math

What math do you see in the **Math on Location** photographs? How can you find how many pounds of food and how much water the astronauts have in 30 days?

READ Math

REVIEW VOCABULARY You learned the words below when you learned about multiplication facts. How do these words relate to **Math on Location**?

factor a number that is multiplied by another number to find a product

multiple the product of a given whole number and another whole number

product the answer to a multiplication problem

WRITE Math

Copy and complete a word definition map like the one below. Use what you know about multiplication to answer the questions.

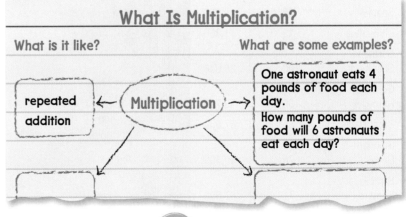

What Is Multiplication?

What is it like?		What are some examples?
repeated addition ←	Multiplication →	One astronaut eats 4 pounds of food each day. How many pounds of food will 6 astronauts eat each day?

Technology
Multimedia Math Glossary link at
www.harcourtschool.com/hspmath

7 Multiply by 1-Digit Numbers

The Big Idea
Multiplication of multi-digit whole numbers is based on place value and the basic multiplication facts.

Investigate
Dogs come in many different sizes. Use the data from the table. What are some ways can you use multiplication to compare the sizes of these dogs?

Average Dog Sizes

	Height (in centimeters)	Weight (in grams)
American Cocker Spaniel	38	10,800
Chihuahua	12	1,800
German Shepherd	60	36,000
Golden Retriever	60	33,750
Great Dane	81	67,500
Standard Dachshund	20	10,800
Saint Bernard	71	67,500

CALIFORNIA FAST FACT

Gibson, a Great Dane, is the world's tallest dog. He is more than 107 centimeters tall. When he stands on his hind legs, he is more than 213 centimeters tall. Gibson lives in Grass Valley, California.

GO ONLINE

Technology
Student pages are available in the Student eBook.

Show What You Know

Check your understanding of important skills needed for success in Chapter 7.

▶ **Regroup Tens and Ones**

Regroup. Write the missing numbers.

1. 3 tens 14 ones = ■ tens 4 ones

2. 5 tens 21 ones = ■ tens ■ one

3. 7 tens ■ ones = 8 tens 3 ones

4. ■ tens 28 ones = 6 tens 8 ones

▶ **Multiplication Facts**

Find the product.

5. 6×3 **6.** 4×4 **7.** 5×9 **8.** 6×2

9. 8×7 **10.** 9×8 **11.** 7×4 **12.** 0×5

▶ **Model Multiplication**

Write a multiplication sentence for each model.

13.   **14.**   **15.**

VOCABULARY POWER

CHAPTER VOCABULARY

array
compatible
    numbers
estimate
factor
mental math
multiple

partial
    product
pattern
product
regroup
round

WARM-UP WORDS

multiple the product of a given whole number and another whole number

partial product a method of multiplying in which the ones, tens, hundreds, and so on are multiplied separately and then the products are added together

compatible numbers numbers that are easy to compute mentally

MENTAL MATH
Multiplication Patterns
OBJECTIVE: Use a basic fact and a pattern to multiply mentally.

Quick Review
1. 7×9 2. 3×4
3. 2×5 4. 6×6
5. 8×3

Learn

It is easy to multiply whole numbers mentally by multiples of 10, 100, and 1,000 if you know the basic facts.

PROBLEM Moe's Sun Fun rents 400 body boards each month. How many body boards do they rent in 6 months?

Example Use mental math to multiply. 6×400

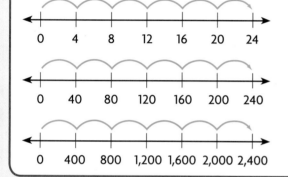

Multplication can be thought of as repeated addition.

| 0 | 4 | 8 | 12 | 16 | 20 | 24 |

$6 \times 4 = 24$ ← basic fact

| 0 | 40 | 80 | 120 | 160 | 200 | 240 |

$6 \times 40 = 240$

| 0 | 400 | 800 | 1,200 | 1,600 | 2,000 | 2,400 |

$6 \times 400 = 2,400$

So, Moe's Sun Fun rents 2,400 body boards in 6 months.

• What pattern do you see in the number sentences?

More Examples

A Basic fact with a pattern
$4 \times 7 = 28$ ← basic fact
$4 \times 70 = 280$
$4 \times 700 = 2,800$
$4 \times 7,000 = 28,000$

B Basic fact with a zero
$8 \times 5 = 40$ ← basic fact
$8 \times 50 = 400$
$8 \times 500 = 4,000$
$8 \times 5,000 = 40,000$

Math Idea
As the number of zeros in a factor increases, the number of zeros in the product increases.

Guided Practice

1. What basic multiplication fact does this picture represent? Use it to find 7×30 and $7 \times 3,000$.

| 0 | 3 | 6 | 9 | 12 | 15 | 18 | 21 |

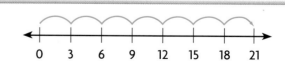

NS 3.0 Students solve problems involving addition, subtraction, multiplication, and division of whole numbers and understand the relationships among the operations. *also* AF 1.1, MR 1.1, MR 2.2, MR 2.3, MR 2.4, MR 3.2, MR 3.3

Use mental math to complete the pattern.

2. $4 \times 8 = 32$
$4 \times 80 = \blacksquare$
$4 \times 800 = \blacksquare$

3. $6 \times 2 = 12$
$6 \times 20 = \blacksquare$
$6 \times 200 = \blacksquare$

✓4. $9 \times 6 = \blacksquare$
$9 \times 60 = \blacksquare$
$9 \times 600 = \blacksquare$

✓5. $4 \times 5 = 20$
$4 \times \blacksquare = 200$
$4 \times 500 = \blacksquare$

6. **TALK Math** Explain how to use a basic fact and a pattern to find $9 \times 7,000$.

Independent Practice and Problem Solving

Use mental math to complete the pattern.

7. $3 \times 7 = 21$
$3 \times 70 = \blacksquare$
$3 \times 700 = \blacksquare$
$3 \times 7,000 = \blacksquare$

8. $10 \times 2 = \blacksquare$
$10 \times 20 = \blacksquare$
$10 \times 200 = \blacksquare$
$10 \times 2,000 = \blacksquare$

9. $3 \times 9 = 27$
$3 \times 90 = \blacksquare$
$3 \times \blacksquare = 2,700$
$3 \times 9,000 = \blacksquare$

10. $12 \times 5 = 60$
$12 \times \blacksquare = 600$
$12 \times 500 = \blacksquare$
$12 \times \blacksquare = 60,000$

Use patterns and mental math to find the product.

11. 9×700

12. $6 \times 8,000$

13. 7×700

14. $5 \times 9,000$

15. 5×40

16. 8×900

17. $9 \times 9,000$

18. $4 \times 3,000$

Algebra Find the value of n.

19. $9 \times 80 = n$

20. $5 \times n = 3,000$

21. $7 \times n = 56,000$

22. $n \times n = 100$

USE DATA For 23–24, use the table.

23. Make an input/output table to find the cost (*c*) to rent surfboards for different numbers of days (*d*). Write an equation to show a rule.

24. **WRITE Math** Gary rented snorkeling gear and swim fins for 2 weeks. Sue rented swim fins and a wetsuit for 9 days. Sue paid more than Gary. **Explain** why this happened.

Beach Rentals

Item	Per Hour	Per Day	Per Week
Surfboard	$10	$20	$85
Skimboard	$5	$18	$60
Snorkeling Gear	$5	$18	$65
Swim Fins	$3	$8	$25
Wetsuit	$5	$15	$50

Achieving the Standards

25. What is 150,810 rounded to the nearest thousand? (○━┓ NS 1.3, p. 34)

26. Estimate $313 + 45$ by rounding both numbers to the nearest ten. (○━┓ NS 1.3, p. 34)

27. One side of a square is 8 feet long. What are the lengths of the other sides?
(Grade 3 ○━┓ MG 2.3)

28. **Test Prep** Which number is missing from this equation? $4 \times \blacksquare = 12,000$

MENTAL MATH

Estimate Products

OBJECTIVE: Estimate products by rounding factors and using compatible numbers and then finding the product mentally.

Quick Review

Write the basic fact shown on the number line.

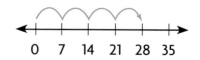

0   7   14   21   28   35

Learn

Sometimes you can solve a problem by finding an estimate.

PROBLEM An African elephant is the largest living land mammal. It uses its trunk to pick up objects that weigh up to 3 times as much as a 175-pound person. About how much weight can an African elephant pick up with its trunk?

ONE WAY **Use rounding and mental math.**

Estimate. 3×175

Step 1	Step 2
Round the greater factor to the nearest hundred. 3×175 $\downarrow$ 3×200	Use mental math. $3 \times 2 = 6$ ← basic fact $3 \times 20 = 60$ $3 \times 200 = 600$

So, an African elephant can pick up about 600 pounds with its trunk.

ANOTHER WAY **Use compatible numbers and mental math.**

In one day, an African elephant eats 9 bags of food. Each bag weighs 57 pounds. How many pounds of food does the elephant eat?

Estimate. 9×57

Step 1	Step 2
Find compatible numbers. 9×57 $\downarrow$ 10×50	Use mental math. $10 \times 5 = 50$ ← basic fact $10 \times 50 = 500$

▲ An elephant can reach as high as 23 feet with its trunk.

So, the African elephant eats about 500 pounds of food.

More Examples Estimate the products.

A Compatible numbers	**B** Nearest thousand	**C** Nearest dollar
9×129 $\downarrow$ $10 \times 130 = 1,300$	$5 \times 7,441$ $\downarrow$ $5 \times 7,000 = 35,000$	$7 \times \$6.68$ $\downarrow$ $7 \times \$7 = \$49$

• How could you use a number line to estimate 4×62?

0—π **NS 1.3** Round whole numbers through the millions to the nearest ten, hundred, thousand, ten thousand, or hundred thousand. *also* 0—π **NS 1.4,** 0—π **NS 3.0, MR 2.3, MR 2.4, MR 2.1**

Round the greater factor. Then use mental math to estimate the product.

1. 4×32 **2.** 7×98 **3.** 5×182 **4.** 3×415 ✓ **5.** $6 \times \$3.25$

Estimate the product. Write the method.

6. 8×42 **7.** 2×67 **8.** 6×281 **9.** $9 \times 6,221$ ✓ **10.** $7 \times \$7.59$

11. **TALK Math** **Explain** how you know whether an estimate of 560 is less than or greater than the exact product of 8 times 72.

Independent Practice and Problem Solving

Estimate the product. Write the method.

12. 4×37 **13.** 6×23 **14.** 5×630 **15.** $3 \times 1,914$

16. $4 \times \$9.78$ **17.** 9×23 **18.** 4×47 **19.** $9 \times \$8.81$

20. 89×3 **21.** 709×4 **22.** $2,509 \times 7$ **23.** $\$545 \times 8$

USE DATA For 24–26, use the graph.

24. About how many more pounds of food do 5 monkeys eat in 6 weeks than 5 wallabies?

25. **Pose a Problem** Use the information in the graph to write a problem. Have a classmate solve the problem.

26. **WRITE Math** **What's the Error?** Tracy says that 8 lemurs eat about 160 pounds of food per week. Is she correct? **Explain.**

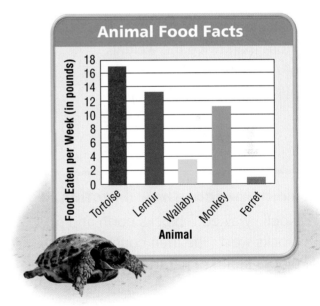

Achieving the Standards

27. If Holly buys 12 bags of apples. Each bag holds 4 apples. How many apples did Holly buy? (O—π NS 3.0, p. 120)

28. $8 \times 8,000 =$ (O—π NS 3.0, p. 176)

29. Frieda tosses a number cube labeled 1 to 6. What different numbers might come up? (Grade 3 O—π SDAP 1.2)

30. **Test Prep** Which number sentence would give the best estimate for 9×758?

  A $9 \times 600 =$ ■

  B $9 \times 700 =$ ■

  C $9 \times 800 =$ ■

  D $9 \times 900 =$ ■

Problem Solving Workshop
Strategy: Draw a Diagram

OBJECTIVE: Solve problems by using the strategy *draw a diagram.*

Learn the Strategy

Drawing a diagram or picture can help you understand a problem. It also sometimes makes the solution visible. You can use different types of diagrams to show different types of problems.

A diagram can show position.

Sally threw the softball 135 feet. Arturo threw it 155 feet, and Joe threw it 140 feet.

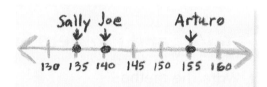

A diagram can show size.

Matt's puppy weighs 2 pounds more than twice the weight of Ann's puppy. Together the puppies weigh 26 pounds.

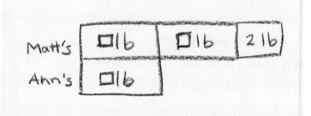

A diagram can show direction.

Noelle walked 5 blocks north and 5 blocks west. She then continued 3 blocks south to her friend's house.

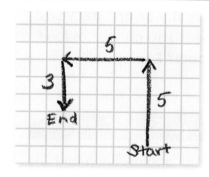

TALK Math

What are some questions that can be answered by using each of the diagrams shown above?

To draw a diagram, carefully follow the information or action given in the problem. Keep the diagram simple. Label the parts to show what they represent.

NS 3.0 Students solve problems involving addition, subtraction, multiplication, and division of whole numbers and understand the relationships among the operations. *also* MR 1.0, MR 2.3, MR 2.4, MR 3.1, MR 3.2

Use the Strategy

PROBLEM At the sea park, one section in the stadium has 9 rows with 32 seats in each row. In the center of each of the first 6 rows, 8 seats are in the splash zone. How many seats are not in the splash zone?

Read to Understand
Plan
Solve
Check

Read to Understand

Reading Skill

• Summarize what you are asked to find.
• What information will you use?

Plan

• **What strategy can you use to solve the problem?**
You can draw a diagram to help you solve the problem.

Solve

• **How can you use the strategy to solve the problem?**
Draw a diagram of the section.

Draw an array that shows 9 rows of 32 seats. In the center, outline an array that shows 6 rows of 8 seats for the splash zone.

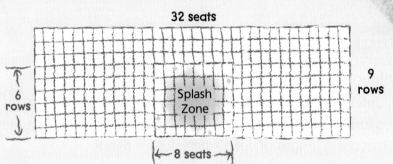

Find the total number of seats in the section.

$$\begin{array}{r} 32 \\ \times\ 9 \\ \hline 288 \end{array}$$ ← total number of seats

Find the number of seats in the splash zone.

$$\begin{array}{r} 8 \\ \times\ 6 \\ \hline 48 \end{array}$$ ← number of seats in splash zone

Then, find the number of seats **not** in the splash zone.

$$\begin{array}{r} 288 \\ -\ 48 \\ \hline 240 \end{array}$$ ← total number of seats
← number of seats in splash zone
← number of seats **not** in splash zone

So, 240 seats are not in the splash zone.

Check

• **How can you check your answer?**
• **What other ways could you solve the problem?**

Guided Problem Solving

Read to Understand
Plan
Solve
Check

1. The seats in Section A and Section B of the stadium are all taken for the last show of the day. Section A has 8 rows of 14 seats each. Section B has 6 rows of 16 seats each. How many people are seated in Sections A and B for the last show?

    First, draw a diagram.

    Then, find the number of seats in each section.

    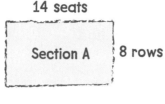

    14 seats | Section A | 8 rows

    16 seats | Section B | 6 rows

    Finally, find the total number of seats.

    Section A: $8 \times 14 = $ ■   Section B: $6 \times 16 = $ ■

✓ 2. **What if** Sections A and B in Problem 1 each had 7 rows? How many people would have been seated?

✓ 3. Carol, Juan, Tami, and Brad are the first four people in line to see the Open Ocean exhibit. Carol is not first in line. Tami has at least two people ahead of her in line. Juan is third. Give the order of the four in line.

Problem Solving Strategy Practice

Draw a diagram to solve.

4. Matt, Julio, and Frank each bought a toy fish. Matt's fish is 10 inches longer than Julio's fish. Frank's fish is 2 inches longer than twice the length of Julio's fish. Julio's fish is 12 inches long. Find the length of each toy fish.

USE DATA For 5–6, use the graph.

5. Mr. Torres took his students to the dolphin show. Each row in the stadium had 11 seats. One adult sat at each end of a row, and each group of 4 students was seated between 2 adults. Mr. Torres sat in a row by himself. How many adults were there?

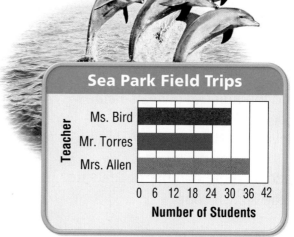

Sea Park Field Trips

Teacher: Ms. Bird, Mr. Torres, Mrs. Allen

Number of Students: 0 6 12 18 24 30 36 42

6. **WRITE Math** ▸ Another section of the stadium has rows of 24 seats each. Describe at least two ways Mrs. Allen's class can sit if an equal number of students sit in each row.

7. Joan and Kim have a total of $31 to spend on school supplies. Kim has $1 more than twice the amount Joan has. How much money does each of them have to spend?

Mixed Strategy Practice

USE DATA For 8–12, use the information in the picture.

8. How many Pilot whales laid end to end would it take to be longer than one Blue Whale?

9. A Gray whale is 43 feet long. List the whales shown in order from the greatest difference in length from the length of the Gray whale to the least difference in length.

10. Mr. Jeremy owns a car that is 12 feet long. How many cars like Mr. Jeremy's parked end to end would equal the length of a Bowhead whale?

11. **Pose a Problem** Look back at Problem 9. Write a similar problem by changing the type of whale and the number.

12. **Open-Ended** Write three different expressions that equal the length of the Fin whale, using one or more operations.

CHALLENGE YOURSELF

Stan researched whale populations and found that there are about **150,000 fin whales and 14,000 blue whales in the world.**

13. The number of blue whales is about 2,000 more than 3 times the number of right whales. About how many right whales are there?

14. There are about 10,000 humpback and 8,000 bowhead whales in the world. **Explain** how you can find the difference between the number of fin whales and the total number of blue, humpback, and bowhead whales.

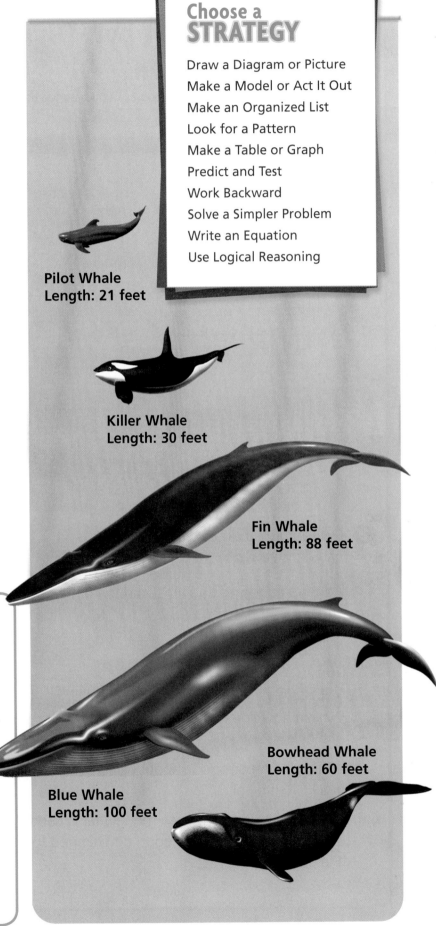

Choose a
STRATEGY

Draw a Diagram or Picture
Make a Model or Act It Out
Make an Organized List
Look for a Pattern
Make a Table or Graph
Predict and Test
Work Backward
Solve a Simpler Problem
Write an Equation
Use Logical Reasoning

Pilot Whale
Length: 21 feet

Killer Whale
Length: 30 feet

Fin Whale
Length: 88 feet

Bowhead Whale
Length: 60 feet

Blue Whale
Length: 100 feet

4 Model 3-Digit by 1-Digit Multiplication

OBJECTIVE: Model multiplication by using base-ten blocks.

Quick Review

Estimate the product.

1. 3×18
2. 6×79
3. 4×192
4. 7×319
5. 8×597

Investigate

Materials ■ base-ten blocks

You can use base-ten blocks to multiply a 3-digit by a 1-digit number.

Ⓐ Model 3×123 using base-ten blocks.

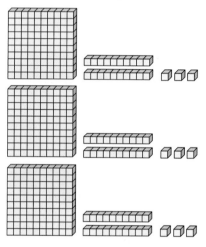

Ⓑ Gather the hundreds, gather the tens, and gather the ones.

Ⓒ Add the hundreds, the tens, and the ones to find the product.

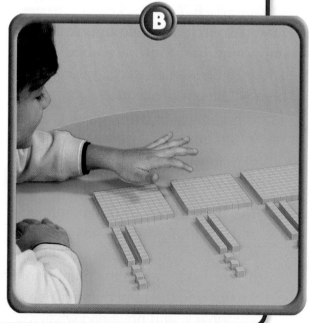

Draw Conclusions

1. How does your model show the 1-digit factor?

2. Explain how you found the total number of blocks.

3. What can you conclude about using base-ten blocks to multiply?

4. **Application** Explain how a model that is used to find 3×123 would need to be changed to find 5×123.

NS 3.0 Students solve problems involving addition, subtraction, multiplication, and division of whole numbers and understand the relationships among the operations. *also* NS 1.0, MR 2.3, MR 2.4, MR 3.2

You can also use base-ten blocks to model multiplication with regrouping.

Multiply. 2 × 136

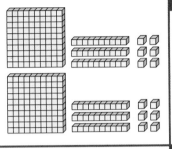

Step 1

Model 2 groups of 136.

Step 2

Combine the ones.
2 × 6 ones =
12 ones.
Regroup 12 ones as
1 ten 2 ones.

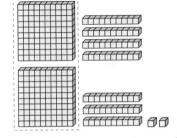
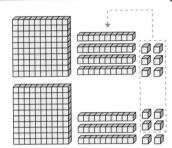

Step 3

Combine the tens.
2 × 3 tens =
6 tens
6 tens + 1 ten =
7 tens.

Step 4

Combine the hundreds.
2 × 1 hundred =
2 hundreds
Record the total.
200 + 70 + 2 = 272

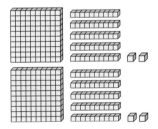

So, 2 × 136 = 272.

TALK Math

How do base-ten blocks show that multiplication and addition are related?

Practice

Find the product.

1.
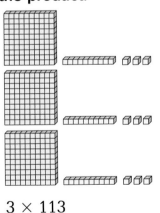

3 × 113

2.
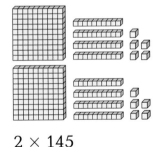

2 × 145

✓ 3.

2 × 152

Use base-ten blocks to model the product. Record your answer.

4. 2 × 144   **5.** 3 × 233   **6.** 4 × 212   ✓**7.** 2 × 432

8. 3 × 126   **9.** 4 × 621   **10.** 7 × 435   **11.** 6 × 432

12. **WRITE Math** ▶ **Explain** how base-ten blocks can help you determine if you will need to regroup.

5 Record 3-Digit by 1-Digit Multiplication

OBJECTIVE: Find products using place value, regrouping, and partial products.

Quick Review

1. 4 × 35   2. 7 × 22
3. 8 × 62   4. 6 × 55
5. 9 × 41

Vocabulary

partial products

Learn

PROBLEM Meg has 256 minutes of songs stored on her portable music player. If Meg doubles the size of her music collection, how many minutes of music will she have?

Example 1

Multiply. 2 × 256   **Estimate.** 2 × 250 = 500

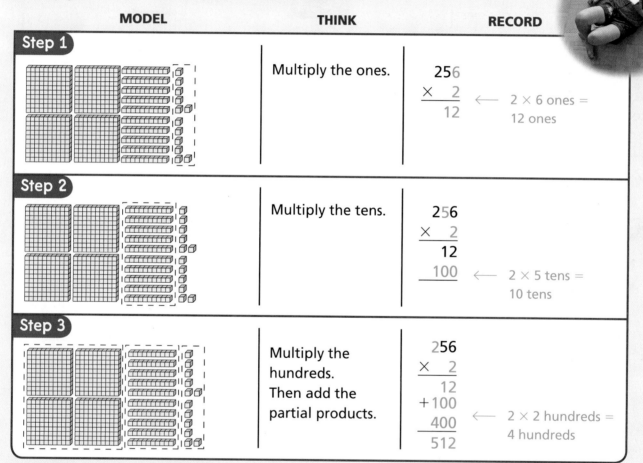

	MODEL	THINK	RECORD
Step 1		Multiply the ones.	256 × 2 12 ← 2 × 6 ones = 12 ones
Step 2		Multiply the tens.	256 × 2 12 100 ← 2 × 5 tens = 10 tens
Step 3		Multiply the hundreds. Then add the partial products.	256 × 2 12 +100 400 ← 2 × 2 hundreds = 4 hundreds 512

So, Meg will have 512 minutes of music. Since 512 is close to the estimate of 500, it is reasonable.

Using **partial products** is a method of multiplying in which the ones, tens, and hundreds are multiplied separately and then the products are added together.

NS 3.0 Students solve problems involving addition, subtraction, multiplication, and division of whole numbers and understand the relationships among the operations: *also* **NS 1.3, AF 1.1, MR 1.1, MR 1.2, MR 2.3, MR 2.4, MR 3.2**

Example 2 Use place value and regrouping.

Multiply. 2 × 172   **Estimate.** 2 × 200 = 400

MODEL	THINK	RECORD

Step 1

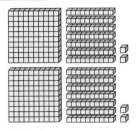

Multiply the ones.
2 × 2 ones = 4 ones

$$\begin{array}{r} 172 \\ \times\ \ \ 2 \\ \hline 4 \end{array}$$ ← 2 × 2 ones = 4 ones

Step 2

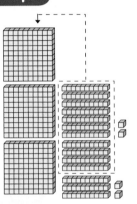

Multiply the tens.
2 × 7 tens = 14 tens
Regroup the 14 tens.

$$\begin{array}{r} {\scriptstyle 1} \\ 172 \\ \times\ \ \ 2 \\ \hline 44 \end{array}$$ Regroup 14 tens as 1 hundred 4 tens

Step 3

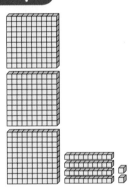

Multiply the hundreds.
2 × 1 hundred = 2 hundreds
Add the regrouped hundred.
2 hundreds + 1 hundred = 3 hundred

$$\begin{array}{r} {\scriptstyle 1} \\ 172 \\ \times\ \ \ 2 \\ \hline 344 \end{array}$$ 2 × 1 hundred = 2 hundreds.

So, 2 × 172 = 344.

Example 3 Use place value and expanded form.

Multiply. 6 × 543   **Estimate.** 6 × 500 = 3,000

Step 1	Step 2	Step 3
Write 543 in expanded form 543 = 500 + 40 + 3	Multiply each addend by 6. Think: 6 × 500 6 × 40 6 × 3 ↓ ↓ ↓ 3,000 + 240 + 18	Add the partial products. 3,000 + 240 + 18 = 3,258

So, 6 × 543 = 3,258.

1. The model shows 2×137. Find the partial products.

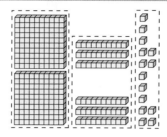

$2 \times 137 = \blacksquare + \blacksquare + \blacksquare = \blacksquare$

Estimate. Then record the product.

2. 5×213 3. 3×195 4. 4×471 ✔ 5. 7×332 ✔ 6. 6×534

7. **TALK Math** **Explain** how using place value and expanded form to break apart a multiplication problem makes finding the product simpler.

Independent Practice and Problem Solving

Estimate. Then record the product.

8. 5×355 9. 8×112 10. 7×211 11. 6×626 12. 9×473

★**Algebra** **Find the missing digit.**

13.
$$\begin{array}{r} 7\blacksquare3 \\ \times\quad 2 \\ \hline 1,486 \end{array}$$

14.
$$\begin{array}{r} 248 \\ \times\quad 3 \\ \hline \blacksquare44 \end{array}$$

15.
$$\begin{array}{r} 395 \\ \times\quad \blacksquare \\ \hline 2,370 \end{array}$$

16.
$$\begin{array}{r} 421 \\ \times\quad 9 \\ \hline 3,7\blacksquare9 \end{array}$$

17.
$$\begin{array}{r} \blacksquare86 \\ \times\quad 7 \\ \hline 5,502 \end{array}$$

18. Look at the picture. Jerome has 832 songs on his player. Tina has 5 times as many songs. How many more songs can Jerome add to his player than Tina can add to hers?

19. **WRITE Math** **What's the Error?** Hal says the greatest 3-digit by 1-digit product is 8,891. Is he correct? **Explain.**

Get Sound
Portable Media Player

Up to 85 hours of movies or up to 9,000 songs.
Battery life for audio: 22 hours

Achieving the Standards

20. $7 \times 5 =$ (O⟋ NS 3.0, p. 120)

21. Use base-ten blocks to find 2×155.
(O⟋ NS 3.2, 184)

22. What shapes make up the pyramid shown? (Grade 3 MG 2.5)

23. **Test Prep** Which expression shows how to multiply 5×381 using place value and expanded form ?

A $5 \times 3 + 5 \times 8 + 5 \times 1$

B $5 \times 300 + 5 \times 800 + 5 \times 100$

C $5 \times 300 + 5 \times 80 + 5 \times 1$

D $5 \times 300 + 5 \times 80 + 5 \times 10$

Miles of Trails

Reading Skill Use Graphic Aids

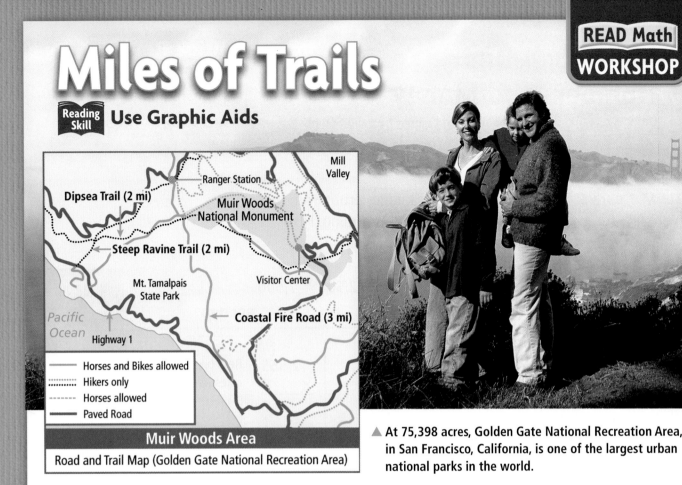

Muir Woods Area

Road and Trail Map (Golden Gate National Recreation Area)

Dipsea Trail (2 mi)

Ranger Station

Mill Valley

Muir Woods National Monument

Steep Ravine Trail (2 mi)

Mt. Tamalpais State Park

Visitor Center

Pacific Ocean

Highway 1

Coastal Fire Road (3 mi)

— Horses and Bikes allowed
.... Hikers only
- - - - - Horses allowed
— Paved Road

▲ At 75,398 acres, Golden Gate National Recreation Area, in San Francisco, California, is one of the largest urban national parks in the world.

Golden Gate National Recreation Area in San Francisco, California, offers a variety of activities for families. Daily exercise helps people think better, sleep better, and maintain a healthy weight. The table shows the number of calories a 75-pound person might burn in one hour.

Calories Burned per Hour	
Activity	**Number of Calories**
Bicycling	350
Hiking	260
Horseback riding	165
Rock climbing	480

Problem Solving Use the graphic aids. Use the information to solve the problems.

1. Jason went horseback riding for 2 hours and rock climbing for 3 hours. About how many calories did he burn?

2. Which activity burns about 3 times as many calories as horseback riding?

3. On a camping trip, Jason and his parents hiked the Coastal Fire Road, Dipsea Trail, and Steep Ravine Trail each day for 4 days. About how many miles did they hike in all?

4. **WRITE Math** Jason wants to compare the lengths of the trails in the Muir Woods National Monument area. Which graphic aid would you use to show the lengths: a table, a picture, a bar graph, or a map? **Explain** your answer.

Chapter 7　189

Multiply 4-Digit Numbers and Money

OBJECTIVE: Multiply 4-digit numbers and money by 1-digit numbers.

Learn

PROBLEM Nearly 2,555 liters of water per minute erupt from the Clepsydra Geyser, in Yellowstone National Park, Wyoming. How many liters of water erupt in 3 minutes?

Example 1 **Multiply.** $3 \times 2,555$ **Estimate.** $3 \times 2,500 = 7,500$

THINK	RECORD
Step 1 Multiply the ones. 3×5 ones $= 15$ ones. Regroup the 15 ones.	$\begin{array}{r} {\scriptstyle 1} \\ 2{,}55\underline{5} \\ \times \quad 3 \\ \hline 5 \end{array}$ Regroup 15 ones as 1 ten 5 ones.
Step 2 Multiply the tens. 3×5 tens $= 15$ tens. Add the regrouped ten. 15 tens $+$ 1 ten $= 16$ tens. Regroup the 16 tens.	$\begin{array}{r} {\scriptstyle 1\ 1} \\ 2{,}555 \\ \times \quad 3 \\ \hline 65 \end{array}$ Regroup 16 tens as 1 hundred 6 tens.
Step 3 Multiply the hundreds. 3×5 hundreds $= 15$ hundreds. Add the regrouped hundred. 15 hundreds $+$ 1 hundred $= 16$ hundreds. Regroup 16 hundreds.	$\begin{array}{r} {\scriptstyle 1\ 11} \\ 2{,}555 \\ \times \quad 3 \\ \hline 665 \end{array}$ Regroup 16 hundreds as 1 thousand 6 hundreds.
Step 4 Multiply the thousands. 3×2 thousands $= 6$ thousands. Add the regrouped thousand. 6 thousands $+$ 1 thousand $= 7$ thousands	$\begin{array}{r} {\scriptstyle 1\ 11} \\ 2{,}555 \\ \times \quad 3 \\ \hline 7{,}665 \end{array}$

So, nearly 7,665 liters of water erupt in 3 minutes.

Since 7,665 is close to the estimate of 7,500, it is reasonable.

Example 2 **Multiply dollars and cents.**

$\begin{array}{r} \$85.76 \\ \times \quad 9 \\ \hline \end{array}$ $\rightarrow$ $\begin{array}{r} 8576 \\ \times \quad 9 \\ \hline 77184 \end{array}$ Multiply the same way you multiply whole numbers. $\rightarrow$ $\begin{array}{r} {\scriptstyle 5\ 6\ 5} \\ \$8576 \\ \times \quad 9 \\ \hline \$771.84 \end{array}$ Write the product in dollars and cents.

▲ The most powerful eruptions from Clepsydra Geyser can reach a height of 40 feet. A geyser is a hot spring that erupts, throwing water into the air.

NS 3.0 Students solve problems involving addition, subtraction, multiplication, and division of whole numbers and understand the relationships among the operations. *also* NS 1.3, MR 2.1, MR 2.3, MR 2.4, MR 3.2

Guided Practice

1. Tell what is happening in each step of the problem.

   Step 1 $\overset{2}{1{,}2\overset{}{7}4}$ Step 2 $\overset{42}{1{,}274}$ Step 3 $\overset{1\ 42}{1{,}274}$ Step 4 $\overset{1\ 42}{1{,}274}$

   $\begin{array}{r} \times\ \ \ 6 \\ \hline 4 \end{array}$ $\begin{array}{r} \times\ \ \ 6 \\ \hline 44 \end{array}$ $\begin{array}{r} \times\ \ \ 6 \\ \hline 644 \end{array}$ $\begin{array}{r} \times\ \ \ 6 \\ \hline 7{,}644 \end{array}$

Estimate. Then find the product.

2. $\begin{array}{r} 1{,}924 \\ \times\ \ \ \ 2 \\ \hline \end{array}$
3. $\begin{array}{r} 5{,}183 \\ \times\ \ \ \ 4 \\ \hline \end{array}$
4. $\begin{array}{r} 1{,}235 \\ \times\ \ \ \ 7 \\ \hline \end{array}$
5. $\begin{array}{r} \$2{,}853 \\ \times\ \ \ \ 6 \\ \hline \end{array}$
6. $\begin{array}{r} \$13.24 \\ \times\ \ \ \ 7 \\ \hline \end{array}$

7. **TALK Math** **Explain** how many digits the product $4 \times 1{,}861$ will have.

Independent Practice and Problem Solving

Estimate. Then find the product.

8. $\begin{array}{r} 2{,}743 \\ \times\ \ \ \ 2 \\ \hline \end{array}$
9. $\begin{array}{r} 7{,}214 \\ \times\ \ \ \ 5 \\ \hline \end{array}$
10. $\begin{array}{r} \$33.16 \\ \times\ \ \ \ 8 \\ \hline \end{array}$
11. $\begin{array}{r} \$2{,}519 \\ \times\ \ \ \ 7 \\ \hline \end{array}$
12. $\begin{array}{r} \$41.23 \\ \times\ \ \ \ 6 \\ \hline \end{array}$

13. $\begin{array}{r} 8{,}251 \\ \times\ \ \ \ 3 \\ \hline \end{array}$
14. $\begin{array}{r} \$1{,}893 \\ \times\ \ \ \ 4 \\ \hline \end{array}$
15. $\begin{array}{r} 2{,}481 \\ \times\ \ \ \ 5 \\ \hline \end{array}$
16. $\begin{array}{r} \$91.42 \\ \times\ \ \ \ 8 \\ \hline \end{array}$
17. $\begin{array}{r} 3{,}286 \\ \times\ \ \ \ 9 \\ \hline \end{array}$

Compare. Write <, >, or = for each ●.

18. $5 \times \$1{,}852$ ● $4 \times \$2{,}315$
19. $6 \times 8{,}167$ ● $5 \times 9{,}834$
20. $4 \times 3{,}956$ ● $2 \times 7{,}692$

21. How would you find $7 \times 2{,}198$ by using partial products?

22. What number is 150 more than 5 times 4,892?

23. Emily bought 3 shirts for $11.99 each as souvenirs. She paid with a $50 bill. How much change did she receive?

24. **WRITE Math** **Sense or Nonsense** Joe says the product of 4-digit number and a 1-digit number is always a 4-digit number. Does Joe's statement make sense? **Explain.**

Achieving the Standards

25. $6 \times 145 =$ (○━ NS 3.0, p. 190)

26. $(42 - 12) + (7 \times 8) =$ (○━ AF 1.2, p. 142)

27. Estimate 4×672. (○━ NS 3.0, p. 179)

28. **Test Prep** It is 2,462 miles from Los Angeles to New York City. What is the round-trip distance?

   A 4,824 miles   C 5,824 miles

   B 4,924 miles   D 5,924 miles

Multiply with Zeros

OBJECTIVE: Multiply numbers with zeros by 1 digit numbers.

Quick Review

Lynn has 127 stickers. Jose has 3 times as many stickers as Lynn has. How many stickers does Jose have?

Learn

PROBLEM Carl has gone on the same trip for the last 5 years. The round-trip distance is 1,082 miles. What is the total number of miles his family has driven on this trip in the last 5 years?

Boston, MA
Hartford, CT
New York, NY
Hopedale, OH

Example 1 Multiply. $5 \times 1,082$ Estimate. $5 \times 1,000 = 5,000$

Step 1

Multiply the ones.
Regroup the ones.

$$\begin{array}{r} \overset{1}{1,082} \\ \times\ \ \ \ 5 \\ \hline 0 \end{array}$$

Regroup 10 ones as 1 ten 0 ones.

Step 2

Multiply the tens.
Add the regrouped tens.
Regroup the tens.

$$\begin{array}{r} \overset{41}{1,082} \\ \times\ \ \ \ 5 \\ \hline 10 \end{array}$$

Regroup 41 tens as 4 hundreds 1 ten.

Step 3

Multiply the hundreds.
Add the regrouped hundreds.

$$\begin{array}{r} \overset{41}{1,082} \\ \times\ \ \ \ 5 \\ \hline 410 \end{array}$$

5×0 hundreds = 0 hundreds
0 hundreds + 4 hundreds = 4 hundreds

Step 4

Multiply the thousands.

$$\begin{array}{r} \overset{41}{1,082} \\ \times\ \ \ \ 5 \\ \hline 5,410 \end{array}$$

ERROR ALERT

In Step 3, the 4 hundreds above the 0 hundreds have to be added after multiplying 5 by 0 hundreds.

So, Carl has driven 5,410 miles. Since 5,410 is close to the estimate of 5,000, it is reasonable.

More Examples

A Use paper and pencil.

$$\begin{array}{r} \overset{5}{5,009} \\ \times\ \ \ \ 6 \\ \hline 30,054 \end{array}$$

B Multiply dollars and cents.

$$\begin{array}{r} \$98.20 \\ \times\ \ \ \ 4 \end{array} \rightarrow \begin{array}{r} 9820 \\ \times\ \ \ \ 4 \end{array}$$

Multiply the same way you multiply whole numbers. →

$$\begin{array}{r} \$98.20 \\ \times\ \ \ \ 4 \\ \hline \$392.80 \end{array}$$

Write the product in dollars and cents.

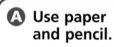 NS 3.0 Students solve problems involving addition, subtraction, multiplication, and division of whole numbers and understand the relationships among the operations. *also* NS 1.0, MR 2.0, MR 2.3, MR 2.4, MR 3.2

Guided Practice

1. Copy the problem at the right. Multiply the ones, then regroup. Multiply the tens, then regroup. Multiply the hundreds. Do you have to regroup? Then multiply the thousands. What is the product?

$$\begin{array}{r} 1{,}032 \\ \times \quad 6 \\ \hline \end{array}$$

Estimate. Then find the product.

2. $\begin{array}{r} 1{,}304 \\ \times \quad 3 \\ \hline \end{array}$

3. $\begin{array}{r} 4{,}002 \\ \times \quad 4 \\ \hline \end{array}$

4. $\begin{array}{r} \$53.50 \\ \times \quad 6 \\ \hline \end{array}$

✓5. $\begin{array}{r} \$10.20 \\ \times \quad 7 \\ \hline \end{array}$

✓6. $\begin{array}{r} \$4{,}046 \\ \times \quad 2 \\ \hline \end{array}$

7. **TALK Math** Explain how you can find $6 \times 2{,}430$.

Independent Practice and Problem Solving

Estimate. Then find the product.

8. $\begin{array}{r} 1{,}603 \\ \times \quad 3 \\ \hline \end{array}$

9. $\begin{array}{r} 2{,}019 \\ \times \quad 7 \\ \hline \end{array}$

10. $\begin{array}{r} \$50.06 \\ \times \quad 2 \\ \hline \end{array}$

11. $\begin{array}{r} 8{,}505 \\ \times \quad 4 \\ \hline \end{array}$

12. $\begin{array}{r} \$40.20 \\ \times \quad 6 \\ \hline \end{array}$

13. $1 \times 7{,}014$

14. $5 \times \$90.02$

15. $4 \times 2{,}806$

16. $3 \times 5{,}050$

17. $8 \times 8{,}109$

USE DATA For 18–19, use the picture.

18. Carl took the elevator from the lobby to the 86th floor and back 3 times. What is the total number of feet he traveled?

19. ≡**FAST FACT** The Empire State Building is 1,454 feet tall. A builder wants to build a skyscraper that is 100 feet less than twice as tall as the Empire State Building. What will be the height of the skyscraper?

20. **WRITE Math** What's the Question? Don, Kay, and Jane each have 3 rolls of film. They can take 24 pictures with each roll. The answer is 216 pictures.

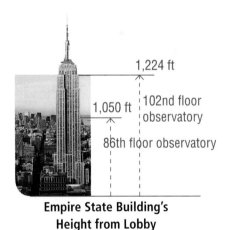

Empire State Building's Height from Lobby

- 1,224 ft
- 1,050 ft — 102nd floor observatory
- 86th floor observatory

Achieving the Standards

21. Write 430,607 in expanded form.
    (O━┓ NS 1.1, p. 4)

22. $3 \times (12 + 3) - 8 =$ (O━┓ AF 1.2, p. 142)

23. What digit is in the hundred thousands place in 6,701,320? (O━┓ NS 1.1, p. 10)

24. **Test Prep** A store wants to buy 1,052 pairs of socks for $2 each. How much will the socks cost?

    A $2,004   C $2,104

    B $2,014   D $3,014

Extra Practice

Set A Use mental math to complete the pattern. (pp. 176–177)

1. $6 \times 4 = 24$
   $6 \times 40 = \blacksquare$
   $6 \times 400 = \blacksquare$
   $6 \times 4{,}000 = \blacksquare$

2. $5 \times 8 = \blacksquare$
   $5 \times 80 = \blacksquare$
   $5 \times 800 = \blacksquare$
   $5 \times 8{,}000 = \blacksquare$

3. $9 \times 9 = 81$
   $9 \times \blacksquare = 810$
   $9 \times 900 = \blacksquare$
   $9 \times \blacksquare = 81{,}000$

4. $7 \times \blacksquare = 42$
   $7 \times 60 = \blacksquare$
   $7 \times \blacksquare = 4{,}200$
   $7 \times 6{,}000 = \blacksquare$

Set B Estimate the product. Write the method. (pp. 178–179)

1. 3×56

2. $8 \times \$21$

3. 2×865

4. $5 \times \$6.89$

5. $7 \times 4{,}133$

6. $\begin{array}{r} \$59 \\ \times\ \ 4 \\ \hline \end{array}$

7. $\begin{array}{r} 82 \\ \times\ \ 9 \\ \hline \end{array}$

8. $\begin{array}{r} 876 \\ \times\ \ 8 \\ \hline \end{array}$

9. $\begin{array}{r} \$5{,}236 \\ \times\ \ \ \ \ 6 \\ \hline \end{array}$

10. $\begin{array}{r} 3{,}462 \\ \times\ \ \ \ \ 5 \\ \hline \end{array}$

Set C Estimate. Then record the product. (pp. 186–189)

1. 3×245

2. 6×472

3. 5×774

4. 7×384

5. 8×261

6. 9×562

7. 8×346

8. 4×783

9. 6×385

10. 7×643

11. Emma plans to burn 4 songs on a CD. Each song is 2 minutes 40 seconds long. What is the total time, in seconds, for the 4 songs?

12. Leo has 3 movies on DVD. Each movie is 137 minutes long. How long are all 3 movies?

Set D Estimate. Then find the product. (pp. 190–191)

1. $\begin{array}{r} 3{,}418 \\ \times\ \ \ \ \ 5 \\ \hline \end{array}$

2. $\begin{array}{r} \$6{,}552 \\ \times\ \ \ \ \ 7 \\ \hline \end{array}$

3. $\begin{array}{r} 8{,}735 \\ \times\ \ \ \ \ 6 \\ \hline \end{array}$

4. $\begin{array}{r} \$32.19 \\ \times\ \ \ \ \ 4 \\ \hline \end{array}$

5. $\begin{array}{r} 6{,}437 \\ \times\ \ \ \ \ 8 \\ \hline \end{array}$

6. $6 \times \$4{,}627$

7. $3 \times \$91.76$

8. $5 \times 7{,}794$

9. $8 \times 1{,}866$

10. $4 \times \$5{,}689$

Set E Estimate. Then find the product. (pp. 192–193)

1. $\begin{array}{r} 6{,}036 \\ \times\ \ \ \ \ 7 \\ \hline \end{array}$

2. $\begin{array}{r} 3{,}700 \\ \times\ \ \ \ \ 4 \\ \hline \end{array}$

3. $\begin{array}{r} \$9{,}006 \\ \times\ \ \ \ \ 5 \\ \hline \end{array}$

4. $\begin{array}{r} 3{,}408 \\ \times\ \ \ \ \ 9 \\ \hline \end{array}$

5. $\begin{array}{r} \$40.06 \\ \times\ \ \ \ \ 3 \\ \hline \end{array}$

6. $4 \times \$60.56$

7. $8 \times 5{,}007$

8. $9 \times 3{,}080$

9. $6 \times 4{,}500$

10. $7 \times \$6{,}078$

11. Julie bought 6 cans of paint for $10.25 each. How much did she pay for the paint?

12. Calvin is buying 3 boxes of blank CDs for $12.09 each. How much will he pay for the CDs?

CD ROM **Technology**
Use Harcourt Mega Math, The Number Games, *Buggy Bargains*, Level J.

Multiplication Marathon

On Your Mark!
2 players

Get Set!
- Number cards (0–9, four of each)
- 2 coins

START

WATER

FINISH

GO!

- Players shuffle the number cards and place them facedown in a stack.

- Each player selects a different coin and places the coin on START.

- Players take turns drawing three number cards from the stack.

- Players use the cards to make and solve a 2-digit by 1-digit multiplication problem.

- The player with the greater product moves his or her coin one space.

- Once both players reach the WATER table, each draws four number cards and makes and solves a 3-digit by 1-digit multiplication problem.

- The first player to reach the FINISH line wins.

Check Vocabulary and Concepts

Choose the best term from the box.

> **VOCABULARY**
>
> estimate
>
> multiply
>
> partial products

1. To find the product of a 3-digit number and a 1-digit number, you can multiply the ones, tens, and hundreds separately, and then add the _?_ together. (0—ᴚ NS 3.0, p. 186)

2. You can _?_ to find a number that is close to the exact amount. (0—ᴚ NS 1.3, p. 178)

Check Skills

Use mental math to complete the pattern. (0—ᴚ NS 3.0, p. 176–177)

3. $2 \times 4 = 8$
   $2 \times 40 = ▪$
   $2 \times 400 = ▪$
   $2 \times 4,000 = ▪$

4. $3 \times 6 = ▪$
   $3 \times ▪ = 180$
   $3 \times 600 = ▪$
   $3 \times ▪ = 18,000$

5. $10 \times 7 = ▪$
   $10 \times 70 = ▪$
   $10 \times ▪ = 7,000$
   $10 \times 7,000 = ▪$

6. $8 \times 9 = ▪$
   $8 \times ▪ = 720$
   $8 \times 900 = ▪$
   $8 \times 9,000 = ▪$

Estimate the product. Write the method. (0—ᴚ NS 3.0, p. 178–179)

7. 8×26

8. 9×539

9. $4 \times 1,561$

10. $6 \times \$7.22$

11. $7 \times \$654$

Estimate. Then find the product. (0—ᴚ NS 3.0, p. 186–189, 190–191, 192–193)

12. $\begin{array}{r} 43 \\ \times\ 6 \\ \hline \end{array}$

13. $\begin{array}{r} 199 \\ \times\ 7 \\ \hline \end{array}$

14. $\begin{array}{r} 2,004 \\ \times\ 9 \\ \hline \end{array}$

15. $\begin{array}{r} 5,286 \\ \times\ 4 \\ \hline \end{array}$

16. $\begin{array}{r} 56 \\ \times\ 6 \\ \hline \end{array}$

17. $\begin{array}{r} \$802 \\ \times\ 6 \\ \hline \end{array}$

18. $\begin{array}{r} 93 \\ \times\ 7 \\ \hline \end{array}$

19. $\begin{array}{r} \$24.04 \\ \times\ 8 \\ \hline \end{array}$

20. 4×84

21. 8×207

22. $9 \times \$638$

23. $4 \times \$5.65$

Check Problem Solving

Solve. (0—ᴚ NS 3.0, MR, 2.3 p. 180–183)

24. Section A of the theater has 4 rows of 18 seats each. Kathy's class has reserved the 14 seats in the center of each of the first 3 rows. How many seats in Section A are NOT reserved?

25. **WRITE Math** June is arranging 4 rows of 24 souvenirs each. If 12 of the souvenirs are toy whales, how many of the souvenirs are NOT toy whales? **Show** how her arrangement might look.

GO ONLINE **Technology** Use *Online Assessment.*

Enrich • Distributive Property
Run for Fun

Each student in the Running Club plans to run for 35 minutes, 5 days a week. How many total minutes will each student run per week?

You can use mental math and the **Distributive Property** of Multiplication to find the product. The property states that multiplying a sum by a number is the same as multiplying each addend by the number and then adding the products.

Find 5×35.

$5 \times 35 = 5 \times (30 + 5)$ Think: $35 = 30 + 5$
$\quad\quad\quad = (5 \times 30) + (5 \times 5)$ Use the Distributive Property.
$\quad\quad\quad = 150 + 25$
$\quad\quad\quad = 175$

So, each student will run a total of 175 minutes per week.

Warm Up

A Find 7×94.

Think: $94 = 90 + 4$

$7 \times 94 = 7 \times (90 + 4)$
$\quad\quad\quad = (7 \times 90) + (7 \times 4)$
$\quad\quad\quad = 630 + 28$
$\quad\quad\quad = 658$

B Find 3×132.

Think: $132 = 100 + 30 + 2$

$3 \times 132 = 3 \times (100 + 30 + 2)$
$\quad\quad\quad\quad = (3 \times 100) + (3 \times 30) + (3 \times 2)$
$\quad\quad\quad\quad = 300 + 90 + 6$
$\quad\quad\quad\quad = 396$

Work Out

Use mental math and the Distributive Property to find the product.

1. 6×31
2. 4×92
3. 3×124
4. 5×318
5. 4×212
6. 5×240
7. $8 \times 2{,}005$
8. $6 \times 4{,}052$

9. Monica has dance class twice a week. Each class is 55 minutes long. How many minutes does Monica spend in class each week?

10. The Swim Club has 14 members. Each day, they swim 4 laps to warm up. How many warm-up laps do the members swim each week?

Cool Down

WRITE Math **Explain** why using the Distributive Property makes finding a product easier.

Number Sense

1. In 2003, there were 45,033 beagles and 52,530 golden retrievers registered with the American Kennel Club. How many more golden retrievers were registered than beagles? (NS 3.1)

   A 7,497

   B 7,507

   C 17,507

   D 97,563

Test Tip **Eliminate choices.**

See item 2. You can eliminate choices that do not have the digit 6 in the tens place. Then start at the left, and compare the digits in each place-value position until the digits differ.

2. Maggie drew the five cards with the numbers shown below.

6	8	2	4	0

   If she uses each card only once, what is the greatest number possible with the digit 6 in the tens place? (NS 1.1)

   A 84,260

   B 48,620

   C 82,460

   D 86,420

3. **WRITE Math** ▶ **Explain** how to round 9,327 to the nearest thousand.

   (NS 1.3)

Algebra and Functions

4. The table below shows the cost of hot dogs at Hot Dog Haven.

Hot Dog Prices				
Number of Hot Dogs	1	2	3	4
Price	$2	$4	$6	$8

   Which expression shows how to find the cost of 14 hot dogs? (AF 1.1)

   A $14 - 2$

   B $14 + 2$

   C $14 \div 2$

   D 14×2

5. Tim sells potatoes by the bag. The table shows how many pounds are in each bag.

Potatoes				
Number of Bags	3	5	7	8
Number of Pounds	30	50	70	▨

   If Tim sells 8 bags of potatoes, how many pounds of potatoes is that? (AF 1.1)

   A 10 pounds

   B 80 pounds

   C 140 pounds

   D 160 pounds

6. **WRITE Math** ▶ **Explain** how you can use multiplication to find the number that makes this equation true. (AF 1.1)

$$\blacksquare \div 12 = 12$$

Measurement and Geometry

7. James drew the figures below.

Which statement is true? (Grade 3 O—¬ MG 2.1)

A They are all quadrilaterals.

B They have the same perimeter.

C They all have the same area.

D They all have sides that are the same length.

8. Which of these figures is a hexagon?
(Grade 3 O—¬ MG 2.1)

A

B

C

D

9. **⬛WRITE Math**▶ Karen is drawing a rectangle. She says that it has 2 right angles and 2 angles less than a right angle. Do you agree? **Explain** why or why not. (Grade 3 O—¬ MG 2.3)

Statistics, Data Analysis, and Probability

10. Elena made a bar graph to show the results of her marble experiment.

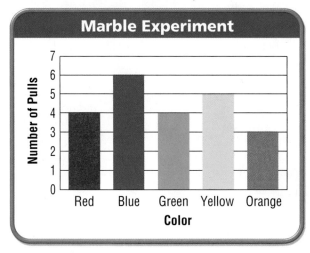

How many blue and yellow marbles did Elena pull? (Grade 3 O—¬ SDAP 1.3)

A 9

C 11

B 10

D 22

11. Look at the spinner.

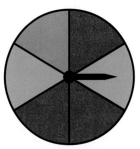

What is the probability of the pointer stopping on green? (Grade 3 SDAP 1.0)

A 1 out of 4

C 2 out of 2

B 2 out of 4

D 2 out of 6

12. **⬛WRITE Math**▶ Pat is tossing a coin in the air. Predict how it will land. **Explain.**
(Grade 3 SDAP 1.0)

8 Understand 2-Digit Multiplication

The Big Idea Multiplying by multiples of ten builds proficiency with mental math and estimation.

CALIFORNIA
FAST
FACT

More than 4,000,000 tons of grapes are grown in Napa Valley, California each year. Many are dried to make raisins. Almost all raisins in the United States come from California.

Investigate

Suppose you want to buy 50 grapevine plants of different sizes. How many of each size can you buy if you must buy at least 10 of each size shown in the graph? Estimate the total amount you would spend.

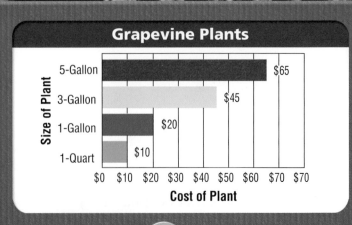

Grapevine Plants

Size of Plant	Cost of Plant
5-Gallon	$65
3-Gallon	$45
1-Gallon	$20
1-Quart	$10

Cost of Plant: $0 $10 $20 $30 $40 $50 $60 $70 $70

GO ONLINE
Technology
Student pages are available in the Student eBook.

Check your understanding of important skills needed for success in Chapter 8.

▶ **Multiply by Tens and Hundreds**

Find the product.

1. 3×10
2. 7×100
3. 2×600
4. 6×90

5. 4×80
6. 9×300
7. 7×50
8. 3×200

9. 4×300
10. 5×60
11. 8×100
12. 5×500

▶ **Estimate Products**

Estimate the product.

13. $\begin{array}{r} 54 \\ \times\ 4 \\ \hline \end{array}$
14. $\begin{array}{r} 41 \\ \times\ 5 \\ \hline \end{array}$
15. $\begin{array}{r} 88 \\ \times\ 7 \\ \hline \end{array}$
16. $\begin{array}{r} 63 \\ \times\ 2 \\ \hline \end{array}$

17. $\begin{array}{r} 102 \\ \times\ \ 3 \\ \hline \end{array}$
18. $\begin{array}{r} 844 \\ \times\ \ 6 \\ \hline \end{array}$
19. $\begin{array}{r} 581 \\ \times\ \ 3 \\ \hline \end{array}$
20. $\begin{array}{r} 496 \\ \times\ \ 7 \\ \hline \end{array}$

▶ **Multiply 2-Digit by 1-Digit Numbers**

Estimate. Then find the product.

21. $\begin{array}{r} 38 \\ \times\ 4 \\ \hline \end{array}$
22. $\begin{array}{r} 17 \\ \times\ 7 \\ \hline \end{array}$
23. $\begin{array}{r} 61 \\ \times\ 3 \\ \hline \end{array}$
24. $\begin{array}{r} 46 \\ \times\ 5 \\ \hline \end{array}$

25. $\begin{array}{r} 72 \\ \times\ 9 \\ \hline \end{array}$
26. $\begin{array}{r} 89 \\ \times\ 2 \\ \hline \end{array}$
27. $\begin{array}{r} 55 \\ \times\ 8 \\ \hline \end{array}$
28. $\begin{array}{r} 27 \\ \times\ 6 \\ \hline \end{array}$

VOCABULARY POWER

CHAPTER VOCABULARY

compatible numbers
estimate
multiple
partial product
product
regroup
round

WARM-UP WORDS

multiple the product of a given whole number and another whole number

compatible numbers numbers that are easy to compute mentally

partial product a method of multiplying in which the ones, tens, hundreds, and so on are multiplied separately and then the products are added together

MENTAL MATH
Multiplication Patterns

OBJECTIVE: Use a basic fact and a pattern to multiply mentally by multiples of 10, 100, and 1,000.

Learn

PROBLEM The actual size of an adult bumblebee is about 12 millimeters long. The photo shows part of the bee under a microscope at 10 times its actual size. What would the length of the bee appear to be at a magnification of 100 times its actual size?

Example 1 Multiply. 12×100

Use what you know about 1-digit multiplication to help you multiply by 2-digit numbers. The number lines show repeated addition.

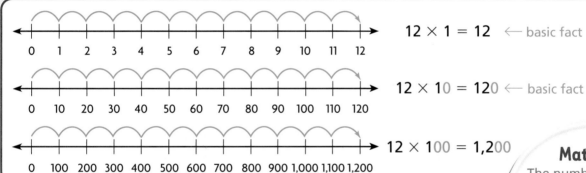

$12 \times 1 = 12$ ← basic fact

$12 \times 10 = 120$ ← basic fact

$12 \times 100 = 1,200$

So, the bumblebee would appear to be 1,200 millimeters long.

• What pattern do you see in the number sentences?

> **Math Idea**
> The number of zeros in the factors should match the number of zeros in the product, unless the product of the basic fact has a zero.

More Examples

A **Basic fact and a pattern**

$6 \times 9 = 54$ ← basic fact
$60 \times 90 = 5,400$
$60 \times 900 = 54,000$

B **Basic fact with a zero and a pattern**

$10 \times 10 = 100$ ← basic fact
$10 \times 100 = 1,000$
$10 \times 1,000 = 10,000$

Guided Practice

1. What product does this number line show?
   Use it to find 12×20 and 12×200.

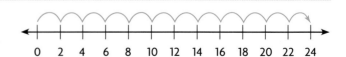

O—□ NS 3.3 Solve problems involving multiplication of multidigit numbers by two-digit numbers. *also* AF 1.1, MR 1.1, MR 1.2, MR 2.3, MR 2.4, MR 3.2, MR 3.3

Use patterns and mental math to find the product.

2. 10×400 **3.** 11×60 **4.** 12×900 **5.** $11 \times 1,000$ **6.** $12 \times 6,000$

7. **TALK Math** Explain how to find $11 \times 4,000$ by using basic facts and patterns.

Independent Practice and Problem Solving

Use patterns and mental math to find the product.

8. 11×50 **9.** 10×20 **10.** 12×700 **11.** 12×600 **12.** $11 \times 8,000$

13. $30 \times 6,000$ **14.** 40×900 **15.** $10 \times 5,000$ **16.** 70×80 **17.** $20 \times 3,000$

Algebra Copy and complete the tables by using mental math.

18. 1 roll = 50 dimes

Rolls	20	30	40	50	60
Dimes	1,000	▓	▓	▓	▓

19. 1 roll = 40 quarters

Rolls	20	30	40	50	60
Quarters	800	▓	▓	▓	▓

×	6	70	800	9,000
20. 60	360	▓	▓	▓
21. 70	▓	4,900	▓	▓

×	6	70	800	9,000
22. 80	▓	▓	64,000	▓
23. 90	▓	▓	▓	810,000

USE DATA For 24–25, use the table.

24. **What if** you wanted to magnify a carpenter bee by 9,000? What would the length be?

25. If you magnified a termite 4,000 times and a wasp 3,000 times, which insect would appear longer? How much longer?

26. **Reasoning** How can you use what you know about 1-digit multiplication patterns to multiply by a 2-digit number?

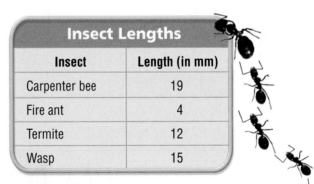

Insect Lengths

Insect	Length (in mm)
Carpenter bee	19
Fire ant	4
Termite	12
Wasp	15

27. **WRITE Math** Explain what the product of any factor times 100 always has.

Achieving the Standards

28. What are the possible outcomes if you roll a number cube labeled 1 through 6?

(Grade 3 ⬦ SDAP 1.2)

29. What is the value of the 6 in 6,345?

(NS 1.0, p. 4)

30. $7 \times \$38.25 =$ (⬦ NS 3.0, p. 190)

31. **Test Prep** How many zeros are in the product of $50 \times 10,000$?

    A 4   **C** 6

    B 5   **D** 7

Extra Practice on page 210, Set A

LESSON 2

Multiply by Tens

OBJECTIVE: Multiply 2-digit numbers by multiples of ten using place value and mental math.

Quick Review

1. 0×10
2. 2×0
3. 3×10
4. 4×100
5. $5 \times 1,000$

Learn

PROBLEM Animation for a computer-drawn cartoon takes about 15 frames per second. How many frames would need to be drawn for a 60-second cartoon?

ONE WAY Use place value.

Multiply. 15×60

THINK	RECORD
Step 1 Multiply the ones. Place a zero in the ones place.	$\begin{array}{r} 15 \\ \times\ 60 \\ \hline 0 \end{array}$ ← 0 ones × 15 = 0 ones
Step 2 Multiply the tens.	$\begin{array}{r} 15 \\ \times\ 60 \\ \hline 900 \end{array}$ ← 6 tens × 15 = 90 tens

So, 900 frames would need to be drawn for a 60-second cartoon.

ANOTHER WAY Use mental math.

Multiply. 16×40
You can use halving and doubling.

Step 1	**Step 2**
Find half of 16 and double 40. $16 \div 2 = 8$ and $40 \times 2 = 80$	Multiply. $8 \times 80 = 640$

So, $16 \times 40 = 640$.

- What is another way that you can use halving and doubling to multiply 16×40?

> **Math Idea**
> When you multiply a whole number by a multiple of ten, the digit in the ones place of the product is always zero.

Guided Practice

1. Multiply 18×20. Tell what method you chose. What is the first step to find the product? What is the second step?

NS 3.3 Solve problems involving multiplication of multidigit numbers by two-digit numbers. *also* AF 1.1, MR 1.1, MR 2.3, MR 2.4, MR 3.0, MR 3.2, MR 3.3

Choose a method. Then find the product.

2. 15×10 **3.** 19×20 **4.** 34×40 ✓**5.** 78×60 ✓**6.** 90×18

7. [TALK Math] **Explain** which method of multiplying 2-digit numbers by multiples of ten you prefer, and give reasons why.

Independent Practice and Problem Solving

Choose a method. Then find the product.

8. 55×70 **9.** 64×30 **10.** 49×50 **11.** 88×20 **12.** 89×60

13. 20×27 **14.** 50×46 **15.** 30×68 **16.** 92×90 **17.** 40×77

Algebra Find the missing digit.

18. $64 \times 40 = 2,56\blacksquare$ **19.** $29 \times 50 = 1,\blacktriangle50$ **20.** $3\bigstar \times 47 = 1,410$

21. $\bullet7 \times 90 = 5,130$ **22.** $20 \times \blacksquare9 = 1,980$ **23.** $20 \times 8\blacktriangle = 1,740$

USE DATA For 24–27, use the table.

24. How many frames did it take to produce 50 seconds of *Pinocchio*?

25. Are there more frames in 10 seconds of *The Flintstones* or 14 seconds of *The Enchanted Drawing*?

26. Write a multiplication problem that shows the total number of frames in 30 seconds of Little Nemo.

27. Pose a Problem Look back at Problem 24. Write a similar problem by changing the animated production and the number.

Animated Productions		
Title	Date Released	Frames per Second
The Enchanted Drawing©	1900	20
Little Nemo©	1911	16
Snow White and the Seven Dwarfs©	1937	24
Pinocchio©	1940	19
The Flintstones™	1960–1966	24

28. [WRITE Math] **What's the Error?** Tanya says that the product of a multiple of ten and a multiple of ten will always have only one zero. Is she correct? **Explain.**

Achieving the Standards

29. Which of the following has the greater value, 5,006,719 or 5,017,691?

(O⚷ NS 1.2, p. 12)

30. Estimate 48×9. (O⚷ NS 3.0, p. 178)

31. $5 \times 387 =$ (O⚷ NS 3.0, p. 186)

32. Test Prep Jade jogs 10 miles a week. How many miles will she jog in a year?

A 520 miles

B 530 miles

C 600 miles

D 620 miles

Extra Practice on page 210, Set B

MENTAL MATH

Estimate Products

OBJECTIVE: Estimate products by rounding factors and compatible numbers.

Learn

PROBLEM The average number of times a refrigerator door is opened during one week is 266 times. About how many times is it opened during one year?

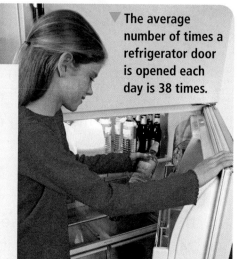

▼ The average number of times a refrigerator door is opened each day is 38 times.

ONE WAY Use rounding and mental math.

Estimate. 52×266.

Step 1	Step 2
Round each factor. $\quad$ 52 × 266 $\quad$ **Think:** There $\quad$ ↓ $\quad$ ↓ $\quad$ are 52 weeks $\quad$ 50 × 300 $\quad$ in a year.	Use mental math. $\quad 5 \times 3 = 15$ $\quad 50 \times 30 = 1{,}500$ $\quad 50 \times 300 = 15{,}000$

So, the refrigerator door is opened about 15,000 times during one year.

• Will the actual number of times the refrigerator is opened in a year be greater than or less than 15,000? Explain.

ANOTHER WAY Use compatible numbers and mental math.

Compatible numbers are numbers that are easy to compute mentally.

Step 1	Step 2
52 × 266 $\quad$ **Think:** 50 × 30 $\quad$ ↓ $\quad$ ↓ $\quad$ is easy to compute $\quad$ 50 × 300 $\quad$ mentally.	Multiply. $\quad$ If $\quad 5 \times 30 = 150$ and $\quad\quad\quad 50 \times 30 = 1{,}500$ $\quad$ Then $50 \times 300 = 15{,}000$

Remember

To round a number:
• Find the place to which you want to round. Look at the digit to its right.
• If the digit is less than 5, the digit in the rounding place stays the same.
• If the digit is 5 or greater, the digit in the rounding place increases by 1.
• Change all digits to the right of the rounding place to 0.

More Examples Estimate the products.

A Nearest ten	**B** Nearest hundred and nearest ten	**C** Compatible numbers
$\begin{array}{r}\$57\\ \times\ 83\end{array} \rightarrow \begin{array}{r}\$60\\ \times\ 80\\ \hline \$4{,}800\end{array}$	$\begin{array}{r}654\\ \times\ 19\end{array} \rightarrow \begin{array}{r}700\\ \times\ 20\\ \hline 14{,}000\end{array}$	$\begin{array}{r}815\\ \times\ 36\end{array} \rightarrow \begin{array}{r}800\\ \times\ \ 40\\ \hline 32{,}000\end{array}$

• Why are the products for rounding different from the products for compatible numbers?

NS 3.3 Solve problems involving multiplication of multidigit numbers by two-digit numbers. *also* NS 1.3, NS 3.2, MR 2.1, MR 2.3, MR 2.4, MR3.2, MR3.3

1. To estimate the product 62×28 by rounding, how would you round the factors? What would the estimated product be?

Choose the method. Estimate the product.

2. 96×34 **3.** $\$39 \times 26$ **4.** 78×74 ✓**5.** $\$23 \times 62$ ✓**6.** 41×178

7. **TALK Math** **Explain** how you know if your estimate will be greater than or less than the exact answer when you are estimating a product.

Independent Practice and Problem Solving

Choose the method. Estimate the product.

8. 54×73 **9.** 34×80 **10.** 67×23 **11.** 56×27 **12.** 19×45

13. 61×318 **14.** 52×680 **15.** 26×448 **16.** 69×573 **17.** 24×393

18. 51×61 **19.** 28×31 **20.** 74×85 **21.** 55×39 **22.** 81×94

USE DATA For 23 and 25, use the data on page 206.

23. Len has two refrigerators in his house. About how many times in a 2 week period are the refrigerator doors opened?

24. New refrigerators cost about $97 per year to run. About how much will it have cost to run by the time it is 25 years old?

25. Mel wants to find how many times his refrigerator door is opened during the month of May. Find the total number of times for the month. Will the actual number of times be more than or less than 1,200? **Explain.**

26. **≣FAST FACT** The average person in the United States eats about 23 quarts of ice cream each year. There are 27 students in Kay's class. About how many quarts of ice cream did Kay's class eat last year?

27. **Reasoning What's the Question?** I am thinking of two numbers that are multiples of ten. The answer is 2,800.

28. **WRITE Math** **Explain** how you can estimate 19×123 using compatible numbers.

Achieving the Standards

29. What number makes this number sentence true? (○╍ AF 2.2, p. 154)

$$(5 - 3) \times 6 = 2 \times \blacksquare$$

30. $12 \times 4,000 =$ (○╍ NS 3.3, p. 202)

31. $38 \times 50 =$ (○╍ NS 3.2, p. 204)

32. **Test Prep** Choose the best estimate for the product 75×231.

A 24,000   **C** 16,000

B 21,000   **D** 1,600

Extra Practice on page 210, Set C

Problem Solving Workshop
Skill: Multistep Problems

OBJECTIVE: Solve problems by using the skill *multistep problems*.

Use the Skill

PROBLEM The Chicago World's Fair of 1893 introduced the first Ferris wheel. It had 36 cars. Each car could carry 60 passengers. The Pacific Wheel in Santa Monica, California, can carry 6 passengers in each of its 20 cars. How many more passengers could the first Ferris wheel carry?

First, find the total number of people each wheel can hold.

	number of cars ↓		capacity of each car ↓	total capacity ↓
1893 Ferris wheel	36	×	60	= 2,160
Pacific Wheel	20	×	6	= 120

Then, find out how many more the 1893 Ferris wheel could carry. Then subtract: $2,160 - 120 = 2,040$

So, the first 1893 Ferris wheel could carry 2,040 more passengers.

- Look back at the problem. Does your answer make sense? Explain how you know.

▲ The Ferris wheel at Chicago World's Fair was 250 feet tall.

Think and Discuss

What steps would you take to solve the problem? Solve the problem.

a. Gold braid comes in 15-foot rolls and costs $25 per foot. Silver braid comes in 31-foot rolls and costs $12 per foot. What is the total cost of one roll of each type of braid?

b. Ms. Kimble teaches 6 music classes of 20 students each school day. In her Monday classes, 80 of the students are fourth graders. How many students are not fourth graders?

c. In one class, Mr. Thacker handed out 14 sheets of construction paper to each of the 20 students. He had 40 sheets of construction paper left over. How many sheets of construction paper did he start with?

▲ The Pacific Wheel is the world's first solar powered Ferris wheel. It is 130 feet tall.

O—ɳ **NS 3.2** Demonstrate an understanding of, and the ability to use, standard algorithms for multiplying a multidigit number by a two-digit number and for dividing a multidigit number by a one-digit number; use relationships between them to simplify computations and to check results. *also* O—ɳ **NS 3.1,**
O—ɳ **NS 3.3, MR 1.0, MR 2.0, MR 2.3, MR 2.4, MR 3.0, MR 3.1, MR 3.2, MR 3.3**

Guided Problem Solving

Read to Understand
Plan
Solve
Check

1. A small Ferris wheel at a carnival makes a complete trip around in 20 seconds. Julia rode the Ferris wheel for 20 trips. Alexa rode it for 25 trips. How much longer was Alexa on the Ferris wheel?

   What steps do you need to take to solve the problem?

   First, find the amount of time each girl was on the Ferris wheel.

   Then subtract the amount of time that Julia was on the Ferris wheel from the amount of time that Alexa was on it.

   Solve the problem.

2. **What if** the Ferris wheel made a complete trip every 30 seconds? How much longer was Alexa on it than Julia was?

3. Rides at a carnival cost $2 each. There were 20 rides. A group of 22 students went on every ride once. How much money was spent to ride all of the rides?

Mixed Applications

USE DATA For 4–6, use the table.

4. Maya and Carla want to go to the carnival each night for a week. Each girl has $75. Do they have enough to attend every night?

5. The Terrell family has 4 people. How much will it cost to go to the carnival if they go on Saturday?

6. How much more will Robert spend if he goes to the carnival on Friday and Saturday than if he goes on Monday and Wednesday?

7. Zora ran 2 laps around the gym the first week, 4 laps the second week, 8 laps the third week, and 16 laps the fourth week. If the pattern continues, how many laps will she run in the fifth week?

8. **WRITE Math** Chen strung paper lanterns across the patio to the kitchen and then 10 feet down the hallway. At the end of the hallway, she strung the lanterns 6 feet into her playroom. She strung a total of 24 feet of lanterns. How long was the section from the patio to the kitchen? **Explain.**

Carnival Admission
One-Night Tickets

Night	Cost
Monday through Wednesday	$12
Thursday through Friday	$15
Saturday	$20

 **Extra Practice**

Set A Use mental math and patterns to find the product. (pp. 202–203)

1. 10×30
2. 11×400
3. 12×200
4. 11×700
5. $11 \times 6,000$

6. $40 \times 5,000$
7. 50×60
8. $12 \times 9,000$
9. 10×800
10. $70 \times 3,000$

11. The actual length of a wasp is 15 millimeters. How long would the wasp appear to be under a microscope at a magnification of 200 times its actual size?

Set B Choose a method. Then find the product. (pp. 204–205)

1. $\begin{array}{r} 14 \\ \times\ 60 \\ \hline \end{array}$
2. $\begin{array}{r} 28 \\ \times\ 30 \\ \hline \end{array}$
3. $\begin{array}{r} 36 \\ \times\ 50 \\ \hline \end{array}$
4. $\begin{array}{r} 47 \\ \times\ 80 \\ \hline \end{array}$
5. $\begin{array}{r} 56 \\ \times\ 70 \\ \hline \end{array}$

6. $\begin{array}{r} 77 \\ \times\ 30 \\ \hline \end{array}$
7. $\begin{array}{r} 49 \\ \times\ 40 \\ \hline \end{array}$
8. $\begin{array}{r} 67 \\ \times\ 30 \\ \hline \end{array}$
9. $\begin{array}{r} 89 \\ \times\ 50 \\ \hline \end{array}$
10. $\begin{array}{r} 38 \\ \times\ 90 \\ \hline \end{array}$

11. 20×63
12. 38×80
13. 50×25
14. 54×60
15. 36×40

16. Ms. Michaels has 30 packages of construction paper. Each package has 25 sheets of paper. How many sheets of paper does she have?

Set C Choose the method. Estimate the product. (pp. 206–207)

1. 63×24
2. 48×57
3. 32×21
4. 59×68
5. 37×49

6. 32×43
7. 61×458
8. 297×37
9. 29×378
10. 32×201

11. 33×56
12. 29×687
13. 33×799
14. 78×67
15. 48×607

16. A drawbridge opens 19 times each week. About how many times does the drawbridge open in one year?

CD ROM **Technology**
Use Harcourt Mega Math, The Number Games, *Up, Up, and Array,* Levels I, K.

Triangle Products

 Get Ready!
2 teams, 2 players each

Get Set!
Two-color counters

95 × 90

70 × 40

57 × 60   11 × 80

12 × 80   33 × 60

11 × 900   86 × 50   97 × 20

200 × 8   60 × 90   92 × 30

43 × 70   74 × 50   17 × 40   12 × 500

18 × 20   12 × 300   70 × 80   62 × 40

10 × 600   11 × 40   15 × 30   9 × 300   37 × 100

 Play!

■ Decide which team will be red and which will be yellow. Yellow goes first, and then teams take turns.

■ One player places a counter on one of the individual triangles. The teammate finds the product. If the product is correct, the counter stays on the game board. If the product is incorrect, the counter is removed.

■ For each turn, teammates should trade roles.

■ A team may try or retry any triangle whose product has not been found.

■ When all the individual triangles on the board have been claimed, the game is over. The team with more counters on the game board wins.

 # Chapter 8 Review/Test

Check Concepts

1. Explain how to use mental math to find 12×50. (O—n NS 3.3, pp. 202–203)

2. What is the pattern when multiplying a number by a multiple of ten? Give an example of the pattern. (O—n NS 3.3, pp. 204–205)

3. Explain how to find the product by halving and doubling: 14×30. (O—n NS 3.3, pp. 204–205)

Check Skills

Choose a method. Then find the product. (O—n NS 3.3, pp. 204–205)

4. 38×40	5. 65×20	6. 45×70	7. 54×60	8. 38×30
9. 61×40	10. 77×50	11. 82×40	12. 76×80	13. 57×70
14. 67×90	15. 63×60	16. 81×70	17. 39×90	18. 99×60

Choose the method. Estimate the product. (O—n NS 3.3, pp. 206–207)

19. 36×47	20. 58×34	21. 76×38	22. 92×24	23. 42×73
24. 405×28	25. 624×36	26. 18×763	27. 64×26	28. 509×49

Check Problem Solving

Solve. (O—n NS 3.2, MR 2.3, pp. 208–209)

29. Allison's parents put $175 each month into her college fund account. How much do they put in the account during 1 year?

30. Steve measured the length of the art room to be 10 yards. What is the length of the art room in inches?

31. Sandy sold 35 adult tickets and 48 child tickets for the breakfast. An adult ticket costs $6.50 and a child ticket costs $3.50. How much did Sandy collect for the tickets?

32. Ms. Slater estimated the cost of textbooks per student in her class as $285. She has 28 students in her class. Estimate the total cost of textbooks for her class.

33. **WRITE Math** ▸ List the steps needed to find the product 46×63.

GO ONLINE **Technology** Use *Online Assessment.*

Enrich • Use Multiplication Properties
TAKE A SEAT

There are 6 sections of seats in Bianca's school auditorium. Each section has 15 groups of seats. Each group has 50 seats. How many seats are there in the auditorium?

You can use the Commutative and Associative Properties of Multiplication to make partial products that end in 0.

The Commutative Property of Multiplication states the order in which you multiply does not change the product. The Associative Property of Multiplication states the way in which you group the factors does not change the product.

Stage

Multiply. $6 \times 15 \times 50$

$6 \times 15 \times 50 = 6 \times 50 \times 15 \longleftarrow$ Commutative Property

$\qquad = 300 \times 15$

$\qquad = 4,500$

So, the auditorium has 4,500 seats.

Opening Act
Use mental math to find the value.

A Associative Property

$(14 \times 25) \times 8 = 14 \times (25 \times 8)$

$\qquad = 14 \times 200$

$\qquad = 2,800$

B Commutative Property

$3 \times 37 \times 10 = 3 \times 10 \times 37$

$\qquad = 30 \times 37$

$\qquad = 1,110$

Perform
Use mental math to find the value.

1. $3 \times 11 \times 30$
2. $5 \times (20 \times 35)$
3. $6 \times 32 \times 50$
4. $8 \times (25 \times 60)$

5. $(90 \times 4) \times 25$
6. $10 \times 12 \times 7$
7. $5 \times 40 \times 18$
8. $(21 \times 7) \times 80$

9. There are 13 members on the swim team. Each member swims 20 laps at practice. If they practice 5 days a week, how many laps does the team swim each week?

10. An apartment building has 8 floors. Each apartment has 12 windows, and there are 10 apartments on a floor. How many windows are there in the building?

Encore!

WRITE Math ▸ **Explain** how using the properties make it easier to multiply 3 factors mentally.

Number Sense

1. Which of these is the number 1,203,000? (O-n NS 1.1)

   A one million, two hundred thirty thousand

   B one million, two hundred three thousand

   C one million, two hundred thousand, three

   D one million, two hundred three

2. $45,073 - 6,285 =$ (O-n NS 3.1)

   A 38,678

   B 38,698

   C 38,788

   D 38,898

3. Henry wrote this list of numbers ordered from least to greatest.

   $$4,807; \ 4,877; \ 4,890; \ 4,902$$

   He forgot to include the number 4,897. Where should this number be placed in his list? (O-n NS 1.2)

   A first

   B second

   C third

   D fourth

4. **WRITE Math** Explain how to round 6,461,220 to the nearest hundred thousand. (O-n NS 1.3)

Algebra and Functions

5. Kathleen is baking 3 batches of cookies and 4 batches of brownies. She needs 2 sticks of butter for each batch of cookies. Which expression below could be used to find how much butter Kathleen needs? (O-n AF 1.3)

   A $(3 \times 4) \times 2$

   B $(3 \times 4) + 2$

   C $3 + (4 \times 2)$

   D $(3 + 4) \times 2$

6. The table shows about how many Slovenian tolars you would receive in 2005 for different numbers of U.S. dollars.

Slovenian Tolars			
Number of Tolars	193	386	■
Number of Dollars	1	2	3

   Which equation shows the number of tolars you would receive for 3 U.S. dollars? (AF 1.1)

   A $x = 193 \times 3$

   B $x = 193 \div 3$

   C $x = 193 + 193$

   D $x = 193$

7. **WRITE Math** Look at the equation below. (O-n AF 2.2)

   $$x \times 12 = y \times 12$$

   Is x greater than, less than, or equal to y? **Explain** how you know.

Measurement and Geometry

8. Tiffany drew a triangle with three equal sides.

   Which statement about Tiffany's triangle is true? (Grade 3 MG 2.2)

   A It has at least one right angle.

   B It has at least two right angles.

   C It is a right triangle.

   D It is an equilateral triangle.

9. David's bedroom is a square.

   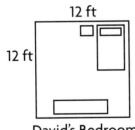

   David's Bedroom

   What is the perimeter of David's bedroom? (Grade 3 MG 1.3)

   A 144 feet

   B 48 feet

   C 24 feet

   D 12 feet

10. **WRITE Math** **Explain** the difference between a pentagon and a hexagon.

    (Grade 3 MG 2.1)

Statistics, Data Analysis, and Probability

Test Tip **Check your work.**
See item 11. Count the tally marks to find the chart that shows the correct results.

11. A coin landed on heads 7 times and on tails 6 times. Which tally table shows these data? (Grade 3 SDAP 1.2)

    A

Coin Toss Results	
Heads	JHT II
Tails	JHT I

    B

Coin Toss Results	
Heads	JHT II
Tails	JHT JHT I

    C

Coin Toss Results	
Heads	JHT I
Tails	JHT II

    D

Coin Toss Results	
Heads	JHT I
Tails	JHT JHT I

12. **WRITE Math** **Explain** how you would make a bar graph to show the results of the experiment in item 11.

    (Grade 3 SDAP 1.3)

9 Multiply by 2-Digit Numbers

The Big Idea Multiplication of multi-digit whole numbers is based on place value and the basic multiplication facts.

CALIFORNIA FAST FACT

Angel Island is in San Francisco Bay. It used to be called the "Ellis Island of the West." It was the first stop for immigrants to the U.S. from the Pacific Basin, Asia, and Russia.

Investigate

The sculpture in the photo is called *American Flag of Faces*. It is at the Ellis Island Immigration Museum. From one angle, you see faces of immigrants. From another angle, you see a flag. As you walk, what you see changes from faces to a flag and back again. The sculpture has 13 rows and 29 columns of blocks with 2 photos on each block. How can you break apart 13 x 29 to find the number of blocks in sculpture?

- American Flag of Faces
  by Pablo Delano

  Height: 9 feet
  Width: 16 feet 6¾ inches
  Depth: 3 feet 2 inches

- The sculpture is made of clear plastic blocks. As a viewer moves, the flag appears to be waving.

GO ONLINE
Technology
Student pages are available in the Student eBook.

216

Show What You Know

**Check your understanding of important skills
needed for success in Chapter 9.**

▶ **Distributive Property**

Make a model and use the Distributive Property to find
the product.

1. 6×12 **2.** 15×4 **3.** 8×14

▶ **Multiply 3- and 4-Digit Numbers by 1-Digit Numbers**

Find the product.

4. 723
  $\times\ \ 6$

5. $3{,}642$
  $\times\ \ \ \ 2$

6. 236
  $\times\ \ 8$

7. 917
  $\times\ \ 5$

8. $4{,}853$
  $\times\ \ \ \ 7$

9. $1{,}019$
  $\times\ \ \ \ 3$

▶ **Multiply by Tens**

Find the product.

10. 70
  $\times\ 3$

11. 50
  $\times\ 6$

12. 80
  $\times\ 8$

13. 60
  $\times\ 7$

14. 90
  $\times\ 9$

15. 40
  $\times\ 5$

VOCABULARY POWER

CHAPTER VOCABULARY

addend
Distributive Property
partial product
product

WARM-UP WORDS

Distributive Property the property that states
that multiplying a sum by a number is the same as
multiplying each addend by the number and then
adding the products

partial product a method of multiplying in which
the ones, tens, hundreds, and so on are multiplied
separately and then the products are added together

addend a number that is added to another in an
addition problem

LESSON 1

Model 2-Digit by 2-Digit Multiplication

OBJECTIVE: Model multiplication by using arrays.

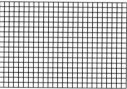 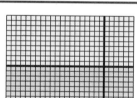

Learn

PROBLEM Matthew's family owns an apple orchard. The orchard has 17 rows of trees with 26 trees in each row. What is the total number of trees in the orchard?

You can make a model and break apart factors to make it easier to find the product.

Activity

Materials ■ grid paper ■ base-ten blocks ■ color pencils

Step 1

Outline a rectangle that is 17 units wide and 26 units long. Think of the area as 17 × 26.

Step 2

Break apart the model into smaller arrays to show factors that are easy to multiply.

Step 3

Find the number of squares in each of the smaller arrays. Add the partial products.

42 + 60 + 200 + 140 = 442

So, there are 442 trees in the orchard.

• **What if** the orchard plants 2 more rows with 26 trees in each? How many more trees would there be in the orchard?

Quick Review

Estimate the product.

1. 21 × 18
2. 59 × 28
3. 19 × 39
4. 27 × 52
5. 303 × 49

○━ NS 3.3 Solve problems involving multiplication of multidigit numbers by two-digit numbers.
also ○━ NS 3.2, MR 1.2, MR 2.3, MR 2.4, MR 3.2

Guided Practice

1. Copy and complete each step of the problem at the right. Then tell what is happening in each step.

  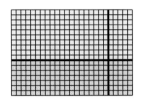

Step 1 **Step 2** **Step 3**

■ + ■ + ■ + ■

Use the model and partial products to solve.

2. 23×16 ✅ 3. 18×19 ✅ 4. 25×17

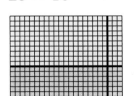 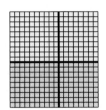 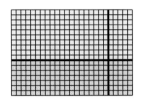

5. **TALK Math** Explain how breaking apart a model makes finding a product easier.

Independent Practice and Problem Solving

Use the model and partial products to solve.

6. 14×24 7. 17×22 8. 28×16

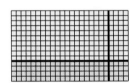 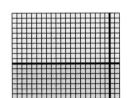 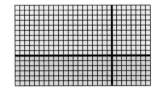

9. **⬛FAST FACT** Each person in the United States eats an average of 65 fresh apples a year. How many apples do three families of 4 eat each year?

10. Apples harvested from an average tree can fill 20 bushel-sized boxes. If 1 row of Matthew's family orchard has 17 trees, how many boxes of apples can one row fill?

11. One tree uses the energy of 50 leaves to produce one apple. How many leaves does it take to produce 15 apples?

12. **WRITE Math** Explain how to find 37×28 by using a model.

Achieving the Standards

13. There are 4 cups in 1 quart. How many cups are in 20 quarts? (Grade 3 MG 1.4)

14. $278 \times 4 =$ (0⎯⊓ NS3.D, p. 186)

15. **Test Prep** What product is shown by the model?

Record 2-Digit by 2-Digit Multiplication

OBJECTIVE: Find products by using partial products and place value.

Quick Review

1. 9×80
2. 2×67
3. 4×21
4. 7×15
5. 6×36

Learn

PROBLEM The amount of time it takes you to burn without sunscreen multiplied by the SPF number of your sunscreen tells you how long you can stay in the sun safely. Without sunscreen, Aaron will burn in about 15 minutes if the UV index is 8. If Aaron puts on lotion with SPF 45, how long can he stay in the sun?

ONE WAY **Use arrays and partial products.**

Multiply. 15×45 **Estimate.** $20 \times 40 = 800$

MODEL	THINK	RECORD
Step 1	Multiply the ones by the ones.	$\begin{array}{r} 45 \\ \times 15 \\ \hline 25 \end{array}$ → 5×5 ones = 25 ones
Step 2	Multiply the tens by the ones.	$\begin{array}{r} 45 \\ \times 15 \\ \hline 25 \\ 200 \end{array}$ → 5×4 tens = 20 tens
Step 3	Multiply the ones by the tens.	$\begin{array}{r} 45 \\ \times 15 \\ \hline 25 \\ 200 \\ 50 \end{array}$ → 10×5 ones = 50 ones
Step 4	Multiply the tens by the tens. Then add the partial products.	$\begin{array}{r} 45 \\ \times 15 \\ \hline 25 \\ 200 \\ 50 \\ +400 \\ \hline 675 \end{array}$ → 10×4 tens = 40 tens

▲ Sunscreen is labeled with a sun protection factor level, or SPF level. Checking the UV index, or the intensity of the sun for the day, can help you determine what level of sun protection you need.

So, if Aaron puts on SPF 45, he can stay in the sun for 675 minutes. Since 675 is close to the estimate of 800, it is reasonable.

O—¬ NS 3.2 Demonstrate an understanding of, and the ability to use, standard algorithms for multiplying a multidigit number by a two-digit number and for dividing a multidigit number by a one-digit number; use relationships between them to simplify computations and to check results. *also* O—¬ NS 3.3, MR 2.1, MR 2.3, MR 2.4, MR 3.1, MR 3.2

Example 1 Use place value.

Multiply. 32 × 31 **Estimate.** 30 × 30 = 900

Step 1	Step 2	Step 3
Think of 32 as 3 tens 2 ones. Multiply by 2 ones.	Multiply by 3 tens, or 30.	Add the partial products.
31 ×32 → 2 × 31 62	31 ×32 → 30 × 31 62 930	31 ×32 62 +930 992

So, 32 × 31 is 992. Since 992 is close to the estimate of 900, it is reasonable.

Example 2 Use place value with regrouping.

Multiply. 57 × 43 **Estimate.** 60 × 40 = 2,400

Step 1	Step 2	Step 3
Think of 57 as 5 tens 7 ones. Multiply by 7 ones.	Multiply by 5 tens, or 50.	Add the partial products.
2 43 ×57 → 7 × 43 301	¹2̸ 43 ×57 → 50 × 43 301 2150	¹2̸ 43 ×57 301 +2150 2,451

So, 57 × 43 is 2,451. Since 2,451 is close to the estimate of 2,400 it is reasonable.

Guided Practice

1. Which product will you find first when you multiply 29 × 54 by using partial products? Which product will you find next? Find the product.

Estimate. Then choose either method to find the product.

2. 15
×17

3. 21
×19

4. 34
×43

✓5. 76
×31

✓6. 89
×47

7. **TALK Math** Explain how you know in which place to begin when you multiply by 2-digit numbers.

Technology
Use Harcourt Mega Math, The Number Games, *Up, Up, and Array,* Level K.

Independent Practice and Problem Solving

Estimate. Then choose either method to find the product.

8. 36
    ×14

9. 63
    ×42

10. $82
    × 29

11. 71
    ×13

12. 57
    ×79

13. $75
    × 32

14. 80
    ×27

15. 55
    ×48

16. $25
    × 25

17. 41
    ×98

18. 19 × 41

19. $33 × 17

20. 28 × 39

21. 52 × 61

22. 82 × $65

23. 76 × 24

24. 82 × 97

25. 15 × 43

26. 45 × $90

27. 35 × 53

USE DATA For 28–30, use the bar graph.

28. Last year, Sun Beach Parasail had 17 riders on each rainy day. How many riders in all parasailed last year on rainy days?

29. Sun Beach Parasail had 15 riders on each cold day. How many riders in all parasailed last year on cold days?

30. **Pose a Problem** Look back at problem 29. Make the problem more open-ended.

31. Last week, Sheila planted 12 rows of seedlings with 15 seedlings in each row. This week, she planted 50 more seedlings. How many seedlings did she plant in all?

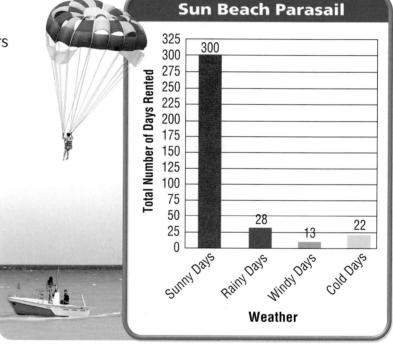

32. **Reasoning** Use the digits 1, 2, 3, and 5 to make two 2-digit numbers that will have the greatest product. Find the product.

33. **WRITE Math** Write a paragraph telling the method you like to use to multiply 2-digit numbers. **Explain** why you use this method.

Achieving the Standards

34. What kind of triangle has exactly two equal sides? (Grade 3 O—n MG 2.2)

35. 7 × 328 =   (O—n NS 3.0, p. 186)

36. A group of 25 students each jumped rope for 30 minutes. How many minutes did the students jump rope in all?

(O—n NS 3.3, p. 204)

37. **Test Prep** Dave bought 18 shrubs to plant in his garden. Each shrub cost $14. How much did the shrubs cost in all?

A $182   C $225

B $222   D $252

Write to Explain

Writing an explanation helps you describe the steps you use to solve a problem.

David knows that the distance around the Earth is divided into 24 equal time zones—one zone for each hour of the day. Each time zone measures about 1,036 miles at the equator. David uses this information to solve this problem: What is the distance around the Earth at the equator?

Read David's explanation of how he used multiplication to find the answer.

Multiply the number of time zones by the measure of each time zone to find the answer.

$$24 \times 1,036$$

First, break apart 1,036 into 1,000 + 30 + 6.

Then, multiply each addend by 24.

$$(24 \times 1,000) + (24 \times 30) + (24 \times 6)$$
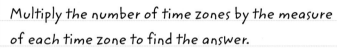
$$24,000 \quad + \quad 720 \quad + \quad 144$$

Finally, find the sum of 24,000 + 720 + 144. The sum is 24,864.

So, the distance around the Earth at the equator is about 24,864 miles.

Tips

- To write an explanation:
- First, identify the question.
- Then use time-order words, such as first, next, then, and finally to explain the steps in your answer.
- Use correct math vocabulary.
- Show all necessary computations.
- State your answer in the last sentence.

Problem Solving **Explain how to solve each problem.**

1. One degree of longitude is about 111 kilometers wide at the equator. What is the distance between two cities along the equator that are 12 degrees of longitude apart?

2. Each time zone spans 15 degrees of longitude. At the equator, each degree of longitude spans 60 nautical miles. How many nautical miles are in a time zone at the equator?

Multiply 2- and 3-Digit Numbers and Money

OBJECTIVE: Multiply 2- and 3-digit numbers and money by 2-digit numbers.

Learn

PROBLEM In 1914, Henry Ford streamlined the assembly line to make a Model T Ford car in 93 minutes. How many minutes did it take to make 105 Model Ts?

Example 1 Use place value.
Multiply. 93×105 **Estimate.** $90 \times 100 = 9,000$

THINK	RECORD
Multiply the ones. Multiply the tens. Add the partial products.	$\begin{array}{r} \overset{4}{\cancel{1}}05 \\ \times\ 93 \\ \hline 315 \leftarrow 3 \times 105 \\ +9450 \leftarrow 90 \times 105 \\ \hline 9,765 \end{array}$

So, it took 9,765 minutes to make 105 Model T Fords.

▲ The first production Model T Ford was assembled at the Piquette Avenue Plant in Detroit on October 1, 1908.

Multiply money the way you multiply whole numbers.

Math Idea
Use what you know about 1-digit multiplication to multiply a 2-digit number by 2- and 3-digit numbers.

Example 2 Multiply money amounts.
Multiply. $50 \times \$4.35$ **Estimate.** $50 \times \$5 = \$250$

Step 1	Step 2	Step 3
Multiply the ones.	Multiply the tens.	Then add the partial products. Place the decimal to write the product in dollars and cents.
$\begin{array}{r} \$4.35 \\ \times\ \ 50 \\ \hline 0\ 00 \leftarrow 0 \times 435 \end{array}$ These zeros can be omitted.	$\begin{array}{r} \overset{1\ 2}{\$4.}35 \\ \times\ \ 50 \\ \hline 0\ 00 \\ 217\ 50 \leftarrow 50 \times 435 \end{array}$	$\begin{array}{r} \$4.35 \\ \times\ \ 50 \\ \hline 0\ 00 \\ +217\ 50 \\ \hline \$217.50 \end{array}$

So, $50 \times \$4.35$ is $217.50.

 ○━ NS 3.2 Demonstrate an understanding of, and the ability to use, standard algorithms for multiplying a multidigit number by a two-digit number and for dividing a multidigit number by a one-digit number; use relationships between them to simplify computations and to check results. *also* NS 1.0, ○━ NS 1.3, NS 3.3, AF 1.1, MR 2.1, MR 2.3, MR 2.4, MR 3.0, MR 3.2

Different Ways to Multiply

You can use different ways to multiply and still get the correct answer. Both Shawn and Patty solved 67×436 correctly, but they used different ways.

Look at Shawn's paper.

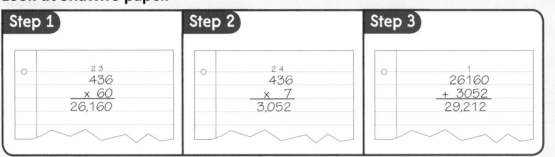

Step 1	Step 2	Step 3
$\begin{array}{r} {\scriptstyle 2\,3} \\ 436 \\ \times\ \ 60 \\ \hline 26{,}160 \end{array}$	$\begin{array}{r} {\scriptstyle 2\,4} \\ 436 \\ \times\ \ \ 7 \\ \hline 3{,}052 \end{array}$	$\begin{array}{r} {\scriptstyle 1} \\ 26160 \\ +\ 3052 \\ \hline 29{,}212 \end{array}$

So, Shawn's answer is $67 \times 436 = 29{,}212$.

• What method did Shawn use to solve the problem?

Look at Patty's paper.

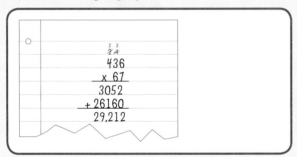

$\begin{array}{r} {\scriptstyle 2\,3} \\ {\scriptstyle 2\,4} \\ 436 \\ \times\ \ 67 \\ \hline 3052 \\ +\ 26160 \\ \hline 29{,}212 \end{array}$

So, Patty also found $67 \times 436 = 29{,}212$.

• What method did Patty use to solve the problem?

• **What if** the problem were $67 \times \$4.36$? What would the product be? Explain.

Guided Practice

1. What is the first partial product when you multiply 40×956? What numbers would you multiply next? Find the product.

Estimate. Then find the product.

2.	3.	4.	5.	6.
$\begin{array}{r} 168 \\ \times\ 53 \end{array}$	$\begin{array}{r} 540 \\ \times\ 19 \end{array}$	$\begin{array}{r} 58 \\ \times\ 76 \end{array}$	$\begin{array}{r} \$3.99 \\ \times\ \ \ 30 \end{array}$	$\begin{array}{r} 901 \\ \times\ 27 \end{array}$

7. **TALK Math** **Explain** why you can omit zeros when you multiply 20×348.

Estimate. Then find the product.

8. 308 × 47	**9.** 92 × 87	**10.** 627 × 25	**11.** 145 × 80	**12.** $2.59 × 13

13. 34 × 654   **14.** 17 × 429   **15.** 42 × $136   **16.** 62 × 427   **17.** 57 × $9.87

18. 55 × 668   **19.** 75 × $2.01   **20.** 92 × 547   **21.** 67 × 54   **22.** 73 × $6.81

REASONING Use each factor in the box only once.
Estimate the products to find the missing factors.

11	44	59	32	12	18

23. The product is between 100 and 150.

■ ■
×■ ■

24. The product is between 700 and 800.

■ ■
×■ ■

25. The product is between 1,500 and 2,000.

■ ■
×■ ■

Algebra Write a rule. Find the missing number.

26.

Number of hours, *h*	5	10	15	20	25
Number of minutes, *m*	300	600	900	■	■

27.

Number of years, *y*	12	14	16	18	20
Number of days, *d*	4,380	5,110	■	6,570	■

USE DATA For 28–30, use the pictures.

28. The hobby shop sold 34 radio remote 4WD monster trucks last year. How much did the truck bring in sales?

29. Less than $1,000 worth of off-road buggies were sold last year. What was the maximum number of this type of car sold?

30. Which costs more, 23 off-road buggies or 21 sports cars? How much more?

31. Reasoning Laura found 67 × 436 by multiplying and subtracting. Show how Laura found the product.

32. (**WRITE Math**) **What's the Error?** Barry says the product of 80 and 729 is 5,832. Is he correct? **Explain.**

33. Is the following event certain, likely, unlikely, or impossible? (Grade 3 SDAP 1.1)

The sum of two one-digit numbers is less than 20.

34. Kevin drove 62 miles an hour for 12 hours. How far did he drive?

(NS 3.3, p. 220)

35. Estimate 36 × 24. (NS 3.0, p. 178)

36. **Test Prep** Last year, Rick ordered 45 pizzas for $9.99 each. How much did he spend on pizzas in all?

A $449.55   **C** $450.00

B $449.65   **D** $459.55

37. **Test Prep** How many seconds are there in 12 minutes?

A 72 seconds   **C** 288 seconds

B 84 seconds   **D** 720 seconds

Problem Solving connects to Science

Solar Power

The same amount of energy that it takes to operate a hair dryer can power a solar car for an entire day. Full size solar racers can run all day at about 40–50 miles per hour (mph) or as fast as 80 miles per hour for two hours if a battery pack is used.

College teams build solar cars and compete in the annual American Solar Challenge competition. In 2005, 10 teams competed in the 2,495-mile race from Austin, Texas, to Calgary, Alberta, Canada.

The table shows the first six stages of the route and the mileage for each stage.

Use the information above to solve the problems.

1. If a team averaged 45 miles per hour for 6 hours for one of the stages, find which stage it might be. How do you know?

2. What is the total number of miles traveled by all cars during the first six stages of the race?

3. **Challenge** A hair dryer uses about 1,100 watts of energy to operate for an entire day. How many watts would it take to power a solar car for 1 week?

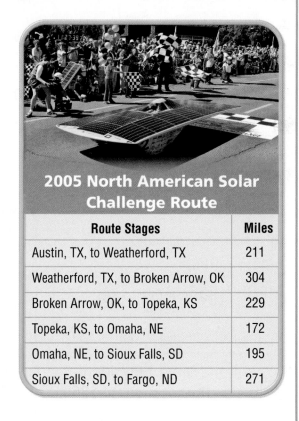

2005 North American Solar Challenge Route

Route Stages	Miles
Austin, TX, to Weatherford, TX	211
Weatherford, TX, to Broken Arrow, OK	304
Broken Arrow, OK, to Topeka, KS	229
Topeka, KS, to Omaha, NE	172
Omaha, NE, to Sioux Falls, SD	195
Sioux Falls, SD, to Fargo, ND	271

4 Multiply Greater Numbers

OBJECTIVE: Multiply greater numbers by 2-digit numbers.

Quick Review

1. 10×36
2. 12×75
3. 35×21
4. 54×78
5. 43×18

Learn

PROBLEM At the Ronald Reagan Presidential Library and Museum store, a book about Ronald Reagan costs $25.99. How much will it cost to purchase 12 books?

ONE WAY Use paper and pencil.

Multiply. $12 \times \$25.99$.   **Estimate.** $12 \times \$30 = \$360$

Step 1	Step 2	Step 3
Multiply the ones.	Multiply the tens.	Add the products. Write the total in dollars and cents.
$\begin{array}{r} \overset{11\ 1}{\$25.99} \\ \times \quad 12 \\ \hline 5198 \end{array}$	$\begin{array}{r} \$25.99 \\ \times \quad 12 \\ \hline 5198 \\ 259\,90 \end{array}$	$\begin{array}{r} \$25.99 \\ \times \quad 12 \\ \hline 5198 \\ + \ 259\,90 \\ \hline \$311.88 \end{array}$

ANOTHER WAY Use mental math.

Step 1	Step 2
Think: $25.99 rounds to $26. Break apart 26 into easier factors and find the product of 12×26. $(12 \times \$20) + (12 \times \$6)$ $\downarrow \qquad\qquad \downarrow$ $\$240 \quad + \quad \$72 = \$312$	Think: Rounding added 1 cent to each book, or 12 cents for the 12 books. Subtract 12 cents from the total. $\$312.00 - \$0.12 = \$311.88$

So, 12 books about President Reagan cost $311.88. Since $311.88 is close to the estimate of $360, the answer is reasonable.

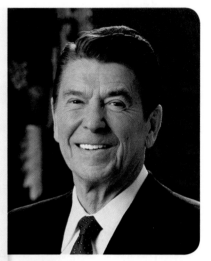

▲ The Ronald Reagan Presidential Library and Museum is in Simi Valley, California. Ronald Reagan was President of the United States from 1981 to 1989.

Guided Practice

1. How can you break apart the factor 41 to find $41 \times 1{,}111$ using mental math? Show how to find the product.

O—┑ NS 3.2 Demonstrate an understanding of, and the ability to use, standard algorithms for multiplying a multidigit number by a two-digit number and for dividing a multidigit number by a one-digit number; use relationships between them to simplify computations and to check results. *also* O—┑ NS 3.1, O—┑ NS 3.3, MR 2.1, MR 2.3, MR 2.4, MR 3.1, MR 3.2

Estimate. Then find the product. Write the method you used.

2. 125
× 4

3. 768
× 30

4. 962
× 57

☑ **5.** 3,500
× 21

☑ **6.** 5,464
× 46

7. [**TALK Math**] **Explain** the difference between finding products using paper and pencil and finding products by using mental math.

Independent Practice and Problem Solving

Estimate. Then find the product. Write the method you used.

8. 532
× 27

9. 843
× 74

10. 950
× 90

11. 2,526
× 57

12. 8,002
× 75

13. $4.97 × 17

14. 20 × $7.34

15. $5.14 × 98

16. 52 × $1.52

17. 27 × $8.01

18. $5.56 × 18

19. 10 × $36.29

20. $10 × 4,730

21. 194 × $0.39

22. 46 × $45.70

23. At the presidential library Garrett bought some postcards that cost 55 cents and some stamps that cost 70 cents. He spent $5. How many of each did he buy?

24. Model kits of Air Force One are sold for $9.95 in the gift shop. If the shop sold 16 in one day, how much money did the kits bring in?

25. A magazine company has 2,367 customers. Each customer is sent 2 issues per month. How many magazines does the company send out each year?

26. A sandwich shop ordered 35 boxes of napkins. Each box holds 265 napkins. How many more napkins would the store have gotten if 39 boxes had been ordered?

27. **Reasoning** Explain how you can use mental math to find 50 × $30.01.

28. [**WRITE Math**] **What's the Error?** Louisa says that 40 × 3,210 is 12,840. Describe and correct her error.

Achieving the Standards

29. There are 25 students in each class at Panther Run Elementary School. There are 35 classes. How many students are in the school? (O─ⁿ NS 3.3, p. 220)

30. 2,000 − 1,384 = (O─ⁿ NS 3.1, p. 62)

31. 16 ÷ 8 = (O─ⁿ NS 3.2, p. 120)

32. **Test Prep** Which shows how to use mental math to find 16 × 140?

A (10 × 140) + (6 × 140)

B (10 × 100) + (6 × 40)

C (4 × 140) + (6 × 140)

D (4 × 70) + (4 × 70)

(Extra Practice) on page 232, Set C

Problem Solving Workshop
Skill: Evaluate Reasonableness

OBJECTIVE: Solve problems by using the skill *evaluate reasonableness*.

Read to Understand
Plan
Solve
Check

Use the Skill

PROBLEM Jawan runs a horse farm. He buys 5,824 pounds of feed each year for each large horse. How much feed does he need in a year for his 18 large horses?

The table shows whether your estimated answer for a multiplication problem will be greater than or less than the actual answer.

Type Of Number		Number In The Problem		Estimate
compatible		greater than		greater than the actual answer
compatible		less than		less than the actual answer
rounded	→	up from	→	greater than the actual answer
rounded		down from		less than the actual answer
rounded		up and down from		close to the actual answer

Multiply. $18 \times 5,824$
Estimate by rounding. $20 \times 6,000 = 120,000$

$$
\begin{array}{r}
^{6\ 1\ 3} \\
5{,}824 \\
\times\quad 18 \\
\hline
46\ 592 \\
+\ 58\ 240 \\
\hline
104{,}832
\end{array}
$$

So, Jawan will need 104,832 pounds of feed in one year for 18 horses.

- Compare your answer to your estimate.
  Is this answer reasonable? How do you know?

Think and Discuss

Solve. Then evaluate the reasonableness of your answer. Explain.

a. It takes 1 pound of cotton to make 650 one-hundred dollar bills. Is it reasonable to say that 2,500 one-hundred dollar bills can be made with 5 pounds of cotton?

b. It takes 1 pound of cotton to make 16 handkerchiefs. Is it reasonable to say that 1,200 handkerchiefs can be made with 750 pounds of cotton?

230

NS 3.3 Solve problems involving multiplication of multidigit numbers by two-digit numbers.
also NS 1.3, NS 3.2, MR 2.1, MR 2.3, MR 2.4, MR 2.6, MR 3.1, MR 3.2

Solve. Then evaluate the reasonableness of your answer. Explain.

1. Radar, the world's tallest living horse, consumes 18 pounds of commercial feed and 40 pounds of hay a day. How much total commercial feed and hay does Radar need for a year?

   First, add the amounts of the two types of feed.

   Next, multiply the amount of feed by the number of days in a year.

   Solve the problem.

   How will you know if your answer is reasonable?

2. **What if** the commercial feed cost $5 per pound? How much would a year's worth of commercial feed cost?

3. The Bureau of Land Management sponsors wild horse adoptions in which people can bid for horses at auction. Toni wants to adopt 4 wild horses. The fee to adopt each horse is $185. Toni estimates that the cost of caring for each horse is about $1,000 per year. Is it reasonable to say that it will cost Toni $4,800 to adopt and care for the 4 horses for the year?

Mixed Applications

4. Jana needs to make 456 color copies of a flyer. The printer can make 24 color copies in one minute. Is it reasonable to say that Jana can make all the copies in 19 minutes? Explain.

5. Reese leaves her house in Pittsburgh, Pennsylvania, to pick up Frieda. Then they begin a day trip across Route 40, the historic National Road. They drive 30 miles to Wheeling, West Virginia, where they visit Victorian Old Town. Then they drive 73 miles to Zanesville, Ohio, to visit the National Ceramic Museum. The entire trip covers 106 miles. How far is Reese's house from Frieda's house?

6. **WRITE Math** ▶ **What's the Question?** A survey found that children ages 2 to 18 spend from 20 to 33 minutes a day playing video games. Angelina spends 20 minutes a day playing video games. The answer is 2 hours.

Extra Practice

Set A Use the model and partial products to solve. (pp. 218–219)

1. 15×21

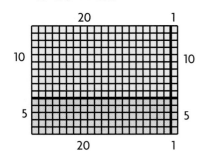

2. 24×14

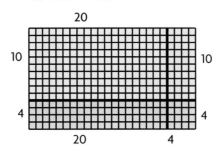

3. 18×23

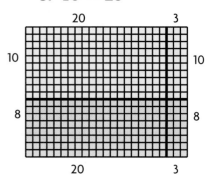

Set B Estimate. Then choose either method to find the product. (pp. 220–223)

1. 14 $\times$ 60	**2.** 28 $\times$ 30	**3.** 36 $\times$ 50	**4.** 47 $\times$ 80
5. 56 $\times$ 70	**6.** 34 $\times$ 28	**7.** 73 $\times$ 35	**8.** 88 $\times$ 32

9. Morgan rides her bike 15 miles a week for exercise. What is the total number of miles Morgan rides in a year?

Set C Estimate. Then find the product. (pp. 224–227)

1. 34×16 **2.** 81×47 **3.** $75 \times \$53$ **4.** 22×68 **5.** $19 \times \$39$

6. 23×94 **7.** 48×66 **8.** $26 \times \$78$ **9.** 51×97 **10.** 72×45

11. Members of the garden club pay $35 in dues each year. The club has 70 members. How much was paid in dues for the year?

Set D Estimate. Then find the product.
Write the method you used. (pp. 228–229)

1. 34×364 **2.** 56×409 **3.** 70×560 **4.** $38 \times 4,375$ **5.** $47 \times 8,003$

Find the product.

6. $35 \times \$6.43$ **7.** $\$5.71 \times 54$ **8.** $67 \times \$6.08$ **9.** $\$7.26 \times 48$ **10.** $93 \times \$3.78$

11. $\$6.41 \times 19$ **12.** $\$25.71 \times 10$ **13.** $6,840 \times \$10$ **14.** $267 \times \$0.52$ **15.** $\$83.30 \times 35$

16. Maxi is buying frames for her photos. Each frame costs $4.39. How much do 12 frames cost?

PRACTICE GAME

On Target

 Get Ready!

2, 3, or 4 players, and a referee

Get Set!

- 2 number cubes, each labeled 1 to 6
- Coins (a different kind of coin for each player)

START

FINISH

Play!

■ The referee chooses a target range for a product. The target range numbers must have 3 digits. The difference between the two numbers must be 100. For example, the range could be 731 to 831, or 509 to 609.

■ The referee then tosses both number cubes, one at a time, to find a starting number. The number on the first cube is the tens digit of the starting number. The number on the second cube is the ones digit.

■ Each player writes the starting number as the first factor of a multiplication problem.

■ Each player then predicts a second factor that will give a product within the target range, and finds the product.

■ The referee checks each product. Each player whose correct product falls within the target range moves 1 spot on the game board.

■ The player that reaches the end first, wins.

Check Concepts

1. Explain how to break apart models to multiply by 2-digit numbers. (O━ NS 3.3, pp. 218–219)

2. Why is estimation important when multiplying geater numbers? (O━ NS 3.2, pp. 224–227)

3. How do you decide whether to use paper and pencil or mental math to solve a multiplication problem? (O━ NS 3.2, pp. 228–229)

Check Skills

Estimate. Then find the product. (O━ NS 3.2, pp. 220–223, 224–227, 228–229)

4. $37 $\times$ 81	5. 63 $\times$ 48	6. 241 $\times$ 25	7. 73 $\times$ 49	8. 508 $\times$ 27
9. 58 $\times$ 39	10. 87 $\times$ 44	11. $5.67 $\times$ 35	12. 607 $\times$ 46	13. $2.89 $\times$ 28
14. $861 $\times$ 17	15. $254 $\times$ 16	16. $467 $\times$ 36	17. $615 $\times$ 18	18. $365 $\times$ 24

19. $56 \times \$578$ 20. $30 \times \$4,862$ 21. $\$690 \times 47$ 22. $\$1.57 \times 49$ 23. $\$23.70 \times 26$

24. $\$67.13 \times 40$ 25. $78 \times \$5,216$ 26. $\$298 \times 41$ 27. $\$4.93 \times 77$ 28. $\$35.81 \times 75$

Check Problem Solving

Solve. (O━ NS 3.2, MR 3.1, pp. 230-231)

29. Rosie practices piano for 75 minutes a day. Is it reasonable to say that in one month she practices for 22,000 minutes? **Explain.**

30. George buys 26 dozen eggs for the Community Pancake Breakfast. How many eggs does he buy? Is it reasonable to say George bought 300 eggs? **Explain.**

31. Sandy sold 32 adult tickets and 48 child tickets for the breakfast. An adult ticket costs $6, and a child ticket costs $3. Is it reasonable to say she collected more than $300 for the tickets? **Explain.**

32. Each level of a parking garage holds 112 cars. There are 4 garages with 6 levels in each garage. Is it reasonable to say 3,500 cars can be parked in all the garages? **Explain.**

33. ⟦**WRITE Math**⟩ List the steps needed to find 46×63.

Enrich • Lattice Multiplication
LATTICE WORK

Lattice multiplication was introduced in Europe about 800 years ago, and is a way to multiply greater numbers. It's called *lattice* multiplication because of the lattice, or grid, on which the multiplication is recorded.

Multiply. 82×74

Step 1

Draw a 2 × 2 lattice. Then write 82 across the top and 74 down the right side. Write × above 7. Draw a diagonal line through each of the boxes.

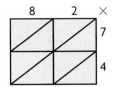

Step 2

For each box, multiply the number at the top of that column by the number at the right of the row. Write the tens digit above the diagonal and the ones digit below it. If a product has only one digit, write a zero above the diagonal.

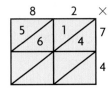

Step 3

Add along the diagonals. Start with the lower right corner. If needed regroup to the next diagonal. Write the sums along the bottom and left side of the lattice.

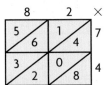

Step 4

Read the product by moving down the left side and across the bottom.

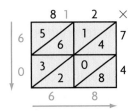

So, $82 \times 74 = 6{,}068.$

Try It

Use lattice multiplication to find the product.

1. 48×39
2. 67×54
3. 182×23
4. 352×24
5. 278×37
6. $1{,}708 \times 42$
7. $2{,}394 \times 42$
8. $4{,}316 \times 65$

WRITE Math ▶ **Explain** how lattice multiplication makes it easier to multiply greater numbers.

Multiple Choice

1. Ben's family sold 2,000 toy cars this year at the flea market. They charged $4 for each car. How much money did they receive? (O┳ NS 3.0, p. 176)

   A $800

   B $8,000

   C $80,000

   D $800,000

2. Sue buys 20 packages of hamburger buns for the school picnic. Each package has 8 buns. How many buns does Sue buy? (O┳ NS 3.0, p. 176)

   A 160

   B 180

   C 200

   D 240

3. Monte watched 5 history videos for his history project. Each video was 115 minutes long. Which equation can be used to find the total number of minutes Monte spent watching the videos? (AF 1.1, p. 188)

   A $115 - 5 = $ ▨

   B $5 + 115 = $ ▨

   C $115 \div 5 = $ ▨

   D $5 \times 115 = $ ▨

4. $6 \times 2,317 = $ (O┳ NS 3.0, p. 176)

   A 13,902

   B 13,800

   C 2,323

   D 2,311

5. Which pair of numbers best completes the equation? (O┳ NS 3.2, p. 204)

   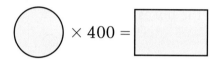

   $$\bigcirc \times 400 = \boxed{}$$

   A $\left(60\right)$ and $\boxed{2,400}$

   B $\left(60\right)$ and $\boxed{24,000}$

   C $\left(6\right)$ and $\boxed{24,000}$

   D $\left(600\right)$ and $\boxed{24,000}$

6. There are 54 cases of baseballs in a warehouse. Each case contains 24 baseballs. Which is the best estimate for the number of baseballs in the warehouse? (O┳ NS 3.3, p. 204)

   A 30

   B 70

   C 100

   D 1,000

GO ONLINE Technology Use *Online Assessment.*

7. The box office sold 79 tickets at $16.45 each for today's performance of the puppet show. How much money did the box office collect? (O━┓ NS 3.3, p. 224)

A $62.55

B $95.45

C $866.55

D $1,299.55

8. Lily's Laundromat has 20 washing machines. Each machine can wash about 50 loads of laundry each week. About how many loads of laundry can be washed each week at Lily's?

(O━┓ NS 3.3, p. 204)

A 100

B 1,000

C 10,000

D 100,000

9. Mr. Sanders bought 2 oak trees and 3 birch trees for his landscape business.

Jackson's Nursery Tree Sale	
Tree	**Price**
Maple	$175
Oak	$229
Birch	$155

Which expression can be used to find the total amount he spent? (O━┓ NS 3.3, p. 208)

A $(229 \times 3) + (175 \times 2)$

B $(229 \times 2) + (175 \times 3)$

C $(229 \times 3) + (155 \times 2)$

D $(229 \times 2) + (155 \times 3)$

Short Response

10. Photo Plus charges $1.05 to print a large digital photo. How much will Sasha pay to have 8 large digital photos printed?

(O━┓ NS 3.0, p. 190)

11. One section of bleachers in a school gymnasium has 17 rows. Each row can seat 42 people. Find the greatest number of people who can sit in that section.

(O━┓ NS 3.3, p. 220)

12. Last year, Rosewood Middle School bought 15 new desks for every classroom. There are 23 classrooms. How many new desks did the school buy in all?

(O━┓ NS 3.3, p. 220)

Extended Response [WRITE Math] ▶

13. Mr. Valdez earns $22 an hour. Last week he worked 37 hours. Did Mr. Valdez earn more than or less than $1,000 last week? **Explain** how you can tell without calculating an exact answer.

(O━┓ NS 3.2, p. 230)

14. The problem below shows part of the product 4×283. How many tens does the digit in the tens place of the product show? What two digits are missing? **Explain** how to find them. (O━┓ NS 3.2, p. 186)

$$\begin{array}{r} 283 \\ \times\ 4 \\ \hline \blacksquare,\blacksquare 32 \end{array}$$

15. Use each of the digits 3, 5, 7, and 9 once to make a three-digit factor and a one-digit factor that will give the greatest product possible. **Explain** how you found your answer. (O━┓ NS 3.2, p. 186)

Space Travel

HUMANS IN SPACE

The SKETCH Gallery at the California Science Center in Los Angeles features objects from space flights by U.S. astronauts. One object is a moon rock. Former astronaut Buzz Aldrin donated to the museum a lucite-encased moon rock collected during the *Apollo 11* mission.

Buzz Aldrin was the lunar module pilot on the mission that landed on the moon on July 20, 1969. He and mission commander Neil Armstrong spent over two hours walking on the lunar surface. The command module pilot, Michael Collins, remained in orbit around the moon until Armstrong and Aldrin returned.

Neil Armstrong

Buzz Aldrin

The *Apollo* lunar module was about 21 feet tall and 14 feet wide.

FACT·ACTIVITY

Use the data on this page to answer the questions.

1. The *Apollo 11* astronauts collected about 49 pounds of soil and rock samples. About how many ounces was this?
   Think: 1 pound = 16 ounces

2. The SKETCH Gallery has also displayed a space suit worn by the three *Apollo 16* astronauts on a mission to the moon in April 1972. The space suit has 21 layers and weighs 185 pounds. How many pounds would 3 space suits be?

3. *Apollo 12* landed on the moon on November 18, 1969. About how many months later after the *Apollo 11* moon landing was this? About how many days?

4. **WRITE Math** Explain how you would find the *Apollo* lunar module's height and width in inches.

SUIT UP FOR SPACE

The *Apollo* space suits were each one piece. Each member of the 3-person crew had 3 suits: a flight suit, a training suit, and a backup suit. The 2 backup astronauts had 2 suits each: a flight suit and a training suit.

Today's shuttle space suits are made in parts. The parts, such as a space helmet, can be made in different sizes.

Space helmets must provide oxygen for breathing, protection from extreme temperatures, and a visor to reflect harmful rays from the sun. Space helmets can include a slot for fruit and cereal snacks and adjustable blinders to block out the sun.

FACT·ACTIVITY

Use the information on this page to answer the questions.

1. How many space suits were needed for one *Apollo* flight?

2. How many would have been needed for 12 *Apollo* flights?

Use the diagram. Design, draw, and label your own space helmet for a mission to Mars.

▶ Will your helmet have visors and lights? How many of each?

▶ How many parts will be needed in all?

▶ Choose the number of astronauts to join you. What is the total number of helmet parts needed?

▶ Describe some extra items you would include in your own space helmet. How many parts will your helmet have? How many will you and your crew need in all?

▶ If 4 missions like yours can be sent at the same time, what is the total number of helmet parts needed?

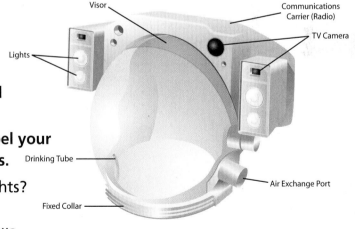

Labels: Visor, Communications Carrier (Radio), TV Camera, Lights, Drinking Tube, Air Exchange Port, Fixed Collar

4 Divide by 1-Digit Divisors

Math on Location

1

These actors live on a ranch near Hollywood. The fee paid to use them in movies pays for their hay.

2

The director of the movie has a budget of $250 to rent a stagecoach for 3 days.

3

The actors, both human and animal, are ready for this scene. Lights, camera, action!

VOCABULARY POWER

TALK Math

Look at the **Math on Location** photographs. How can you find how much it costs the director to rent a stagecoach for one day?

READ Math

REVIEW VOCABULARY You learned the words below when you learned about division facts. How do these words relate to **Math on Location**?

divide to separate into equal groups; the opposite operation of multiplication

factor a number that is multiplied by another number to find a product

quotient the number, not including the remainder, that results from dividing.

WRITE Math

Copy and complete the word knowledge chart below. Mark the division words you know now with a check mark. Use a star to show the new words you know at the end of the unit.

Word	I Know	Sounds Familiar	Don't Know
divisor	✔		
dividend		✔	
quotient			
remainder			
compatible numbers			

GO ONLINE

Technology
Multimedia Math Glossary link at
www.harcourtschool.com/hspmath

10 Understand Division

The Big Idea Division tells how many groups or how many in each group, is related to repeated subtraction, and is the inverse of multiplication.

CALIFORNIA FAST FACT

The Arcata to Ferndale World Championship Kinetic Sculpture Race is a three-day, 40-mile trip on land, water, mud, and sand in a rolling, floating human-powered artwork.

Investigate

Suppose each person following the Kinetic Sculpture Race watched only one part of the race. Use the data shown in the table. For each part, how many equal-size groups of fewer than 10 people might have watched of the race? How could you use models to justify your answer?

Kinetic Sculpture Race Course	
Part of Race	Number of People
Land	348
Water	108
Mud	60
Sand	256

Technology
Student pages are available in the Student eBook.

Show What You Know

Check your understanding of important skills
needed for success in Chapter 10.

▶ **2-Digit Subtraction**

Find the difference.

1. 47
   −26

2. 23
   −14

3. 76
   −34

4. 83
   −31

5. 54
   −39

6. 63 − 26   7. 39 − 17   8. 96 − 29   9. 31 − 20   10. 73 − 52

▶ **Model Division**

Write the division fact that each picture represents.

11.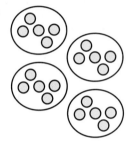

12.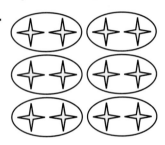

13.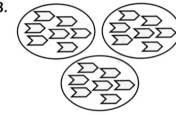

▶ **Division Facts**

Find the quotient.

14. 54 ÷ 6   15. 8)‾72‾   16. 42 ÷ 6   17. 24 ÷ 3   18. 5)‾40‾

19. 6)‾18‾   20. 27 ÷ 9   21. 8)‾32‾   22. 4)‾28‾   23. 63 ÷ 7

VOCABULARY POWER

CHAPTER VOCABULARY	WARM-UP WORDS
compatible numbers **dividend** **divisor** **estimate** **mental math** **quotient** **remainder**	**remainder** the amount left over when a number cannot be divided equally **dividend** the number that is to be divided in a division problem **divisor** the number that divides the dividend

 **LESSON**

1 Divide with Remainders

OBJECTIVE: Divide whole numbers that do not divide evenly.

Quick Review

1. $27 \div 9$ 2. 4×7
3. 3×8 4. $5\overline{)25}$
5. $3\overline{)12}$

Vocabulary

remainder

Learn

Sometimes a number cannot be divided evenly. The amount left over is called the **remainder**.

PROBLEM Three friends are playing a game of dominoes. There are 28 dominoes in the set. If each player receives the same number of dominoes, how many dominoes will each player get? How many dominoes will be left over?

 HANDS ON

Activity Make a model.
Materials ■ counters

Divide 28 by 3. Write $28 \div 3$ or $3\overline{)28}$.

Step 1	Step 2
Use 28 counters. 	Draw 3 circles. Divide the 28 counters into 3 equal groups. The counter left over is the remainder. 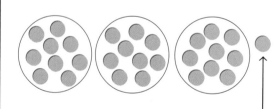 remainder The quotient is 9 and the remainder is 1.

So, each player will get 9 dominoes. There will be 1 domino left over.

• Why does the remainder have to be less than the divisor?

ERROR ALERT

If the remainder is greater than the divisor, keep dividing the counters evenly until the remainder is less than the divisor.

Guided Practice

1. Use counters to model $17 \div 5$. Draw ■ circles. Place ■ counters in each circle. The quotient is ■. The remainder is ■.

  NS 3.4 Solve problems involving division of multidigit numbers by one-digit numbers. *also* **NS 3.0,** **NS 3.2, MR 2.3, MR 2.4, MR 3.0, MR 3.2, MR 3.3**

Use counters to find the quotient and remainder.

2. $15 \div 6$ **3.** $26 \div 7$ **4.** $19 \div 4$ ✓ **5.** $24 \div 5$ ✓ **6.** $42 \div 5$

7. (**TALK Math**) **Explain** how you know when there will be a remainder in a division problem.

Independent Practice and Problem Solving

Use counters to find the quotient and remainder.

8. $18 \div 7$ **9.** $17 \div 5$ **10.** $21 \div 6$ **11.** $22 \div 4$ **12.** $56 \div 9$

Divide. You may wish to use counters or draw a picture to help.

13. $26 \div 3$ **14.** $6\overline{)37}$ **15.** $67 \div 9$ **16.** $3\overline{)47}$ **17.** $5\overline{)41}$

⭐ **Algebra** Find the missing value.

18. $26 \div 4 = 6 \text{ r} \blacksquare$ **19.** $43 \div 8 = \blacksquare \text{ r}3$ **20.** $\blacksquare \div 5 = 4 \text{ r}2$ **21.** $32 \div \blacksquare = 10 \text{ r}2$

USE DATA For 22–24, use the table.

22. Which set will have the greatest number of dominoes left over if 5 players equally divide the dominoes in each set?

23. Seven players divided a set of dominoes so that each had the same number. There were dominoes left over. Which set did they use? **Explain** your answer.

24. Some students are using a double twelve set. Each student has 11 dominoes. There are 3 dominoes left over. How many students are playing the game?

Domino Sets	
Name of Set	Number of Dominoes
Double Six	28
Double Nine	55
Double Twelve	91

25. (**WRITE Math**) **What's the Error?** Frank says that the model represents $4\overline{)13}$. What is his error? Draw a correct model.

Achieving the Standards

26. $24 \times 51 = $ (O─╖ NS 3.2, p. 220)

27. Which is greater: 7,432 or 7,423? (O─╖ NS 1.2, p. 12)

28. Toss a number cube labeled 1 to 6 fifty times. Record the results and display them in a line plot. (Grade 3 O─╖ SDAP 1.3)

29. Test Prep Which problem does the model describe?

   A $14 \div 2$ **C** $12 \div 4$

   B $3\overline{)14}$ **D** $2\overline{)14}$

(Extra Practice) on page 260, Set A

2 Model 2-Digit by 1-Digit Division

OBJECTIVE: Model division by using base-ten blocks.

Quick Review

1. 3×8
2. $12 \div 2$
3. 7×9
4. 6×8
5. $54 \div 6$

Investigate

Materials ■ base-ten blocks

The school lunchroom is serving 72 peaches on 3 trays. Each tray has the same number of peaches. How many peaches are on each tray?

You can use base-ten blocks to find the number of objects in equal groups.

A Use base-ten blocks to model the 72 peaches. Show 72 as 7 tens 2 ones. Draw three circles.

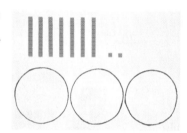

B Place an equal number of tens into each group.

C If there are any tens left, regroup them as ones. Place an equal number of ones into each group.

D Count the number of tens and ones in each group to find the number of peaches on each tray. Record your answer.

Draw Conclusions

1. Why did you draw 3 circles in Step A?

2. Why do you need to regroup in Step C?

3. How many peaches are on each tray?

4. How can you check your answer?

5. **Synthesis** What if there are 96 peaches and 4 trays? How can you use base-ten blocks to find how many peaches will be on each tray?

NS 3.4 Solve problems involving division of multidigit numbers by one-digit numbers. *also* NS 3.0, NS 3.2, MR 2.0, MR 2.3, MR 2.4, MR 3.2

Connect

You can use base-ten blocks to model division with remainders.

Miguel's robot kit has 46 mechanical parts. He can build 4 matching robots with the parts. How many parts does Miguel need for each robot? How many parts will be left over?

Step 1

Show 46 as 4 tens 6 ones.

Step 2

Draw 4 circles. Place 1 ten in each circle.

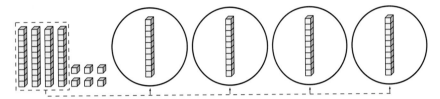

Step 3

Place 1 one in each circle. Count how many ones are left over.

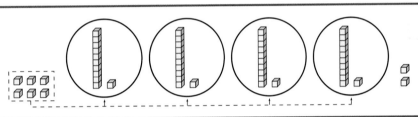

So, each robot needs 11 parts. There will be 2 parts left over.

TALK Math

Explain the steps to model $48 \div 3$ using base-ten blocks.

Practice

Use base-ten blocks to find the quotient and remainder.

1. $2\overline{)84}$ 2. $96 \div 6$ 3. $99 \div 8$ 4. $5\overline{)67}$ 5. $84 \div 3$

6. $2\overline{)52}$ 7. $26 \div 4$ 8. $5\overline{)81}$ 9. $44 \div 3$ ✓10. $7\overline{)84}$

Divide. You may wish to use base-ten blocks.

11. $52 \div 4$ 12. $5\overline{)48}$ 13. $87 \div 7$ 14. $6\overline{)77}$ ✓15. $97 \div 6$

16. $3\overline{)22}$ 17. $3\overline{)72}$ 18. $40 \div 6$ 19. $23 \div 9$ 20. $5\overline{)88}$

21. **WRITE Math** Explain how to model the quotient for $73 \div 5$.

Record 2-Digit by 1-Digit Division

OBJECTIVE: Divide 2-digit numbers by 1-digit numbers.

Learn

PROBLEM Raul, Jeremy, and Manuel have collected 53 baseball cards. They want to divide them equally. How many cards will each of the 3 boys get? How many cards will be left over?

Example 1

Divide 53 by 3. Write 53 ÷ 3 or 3)53.

	MODEL	THINK	RECORD
Step 1		Divide the 5 tens. The difference, 2, must be less than the divisor.	$\begin{array}{r} 1 \\ 3\overline{)53} \\ -3 \\ \hline 2 \end{array}$ Divide. 5 ÷ 3 Multiply. 1 × 3 Subtract. 5 − 3 Compare. 2 < 3
Step 2		Bring down the 3 ones. Regroup 2 tens 3 ones as 23 ones. Then divide the 23 ones. Write the remainder next to the quotient.	$\begin{array}{r} 17\ r2 \\ 3\overline{)53} \\ -3\downarrow \\ \hline 23 \\ -21 \\ \hline 2 \end{array}$ Divide. 23 ÷ 3 Multiply. 7 × 3 Subtract. 23 − 21 Compare. 2 < 3
Step 3		To check, multiply the quotient by the divisor. Then add the remainder.	$\begin{array}{r} 17 \\ \times\ 3 \\ \hline 51 \\ +\ 2 \\ \hline 53 \end{array}$ quotient divisor remainder dividend

▲ In 1947 Jackie Robinson became the first African American to play on a major league baseball team.

JACKIE ROBINSON 2b of BROOKLYN DODGERS

So, each boy gets 17 cards with 2 left over.

- **What if** the remainder is equal to or greater than the divisor? What should you do?

- What conclusion can you make if you compare the quotient to the dividend when you divide whole numbers?

Math Idea

The order of division is as follows:
> Divide
> Multiply
> Subtract
> Compare

Repeat this order until the division is complete.

○━┓ **NS 3.2** Demonstrate an understanding of, and the ability to use, standard algorithms for multiplying a multidigit number by a two-digit number and for dividing a multidigit number by a one-digit number; use relationships between them to simplify computations and to check results. *also* ○━┓ NS 3.0, ○━┓ NS 3.4, MR 2.3, MR 2.4, MR 3.2

Example 2

Divide 46 by 2. Write $46 \div 2$ or $2\overline{)46}$.

MODEL	THINK	RECORD
Step 1 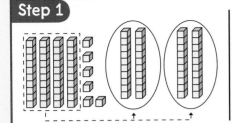	Divide the 4 tens. The difference, 0, must be less than the divisor.	$\begin{array}{r} 2 \\ 2\overline{)46} \\ -4 \\ \hline 0 \end{array}$ Divide. $4 \div 2$ Multiply. 2×2 Subtract. $4 - 4$ Compare. $0 < 2$
Step 2 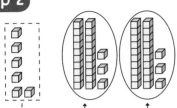	Bring down the 6 ones. Then divide the 6 ones.	$\begin{array}{r} 23 \\ 2\overline{)46} \\ -4\downarrow \\ \hline 06 \\ -6 \\ \hline 0 \end{array}$ Divide. $6 \div 2$ Multiply. 2×3 Subtract. $6 - 6$ Compare. $0 < 2$
Step 3	To check, multiply the quotient by the divisor.	$\begin{array}{r} 23 \\ \times\ 2 \\ \hline 46 \end{array}$ quotient divisor dividend

More Examples

A $99 \div 4$

$$\begin{array}{r} 24\ r3 \\ 4\overline{)99} \\ -8\downarrow \\ \hline 19 \\ -16 \\ \hline 3 \end{array}$$

B $91 \div 7$

$$\begin{array}{r} 13 \\ 7\overline{)91} \\ -7\downarrow \\ \hline 21 \\ -21 \\ \hline 0 \end{array}$$

Guided Practice

1. What is $49 \div 3$? Make a model to solve, and then record.

Divide and record.

2. $4\overline{)59}$ 3. $2\overline{)68}$ 4. $3\overline{)76}$ ✓ 5. $5\overline{)85}$ ✓ 6. $8\overline{)93}$

7. **TALK Math** **Explain** how to use multiplication to check a division problem.

Divide and record.

8. $2\overline{)33}$
9. $7\overline{)91}$
10. $4\overline{)55}$
11. $9\overline{)94}$
12. $6\overline{)78}$

13. $93 \div 6$
14. $64 \div 4$
15. $77 \div 3$
16. $82 \div 8$
17. $90 \div 6$

18. $7\overline{)86}$
19. $59 \div 4$
20. $5\overline{)80}$
21. $96 \div 3$
22. $6\overline{)50}$

Use multiplication to check each answer.

23. $93 \div 2 = 46$ r1
24. $44 \div 5 = 8$ r4
25. $63 \div 3 = 21$
26. $78 \div 7 = 11$ r1

★Algebra Copy and complete each table.

27.

Number of Feet	3	39	45	63	75
Number of Yards	1	13	▪	▪	▪

28.

Number of Days	7	77	84	91	98
Number of Weeks	1	11	▪	▪	▪

29. Fifty-six students signed up for baseball. The coach divided them into 4 equal teams. How many students are on each team?

30. Mr. Ro gave 81 golf tees to 7 golfers. Each golfer gets the same number of tees. How many did each get? How many are left over?

31. **≣FAST FACT** The highest scoring NFL game was November 27, 1966. The winning team scored 72 points! If touchdowns are worth 6 points, how many touchdowns could the team have scored?

32. **WRITE Math** ▸ Write a set of directions to **explain** how to solve $47 \div 4$.

Achieving the Standards

33. $72 \div 9 = $ (O━π NS 3.0, p. 116)

34. $25 \times \$1.49 = $ (O━π NS 3.2, p. 224)

35. Jonah earned 4,007 points playing a game. Felicity earned 2,398 fewer points. How many points did Felicity earn?

(O━π NS 3.1, p. 62)

36. **Test Prep** Jared and his two brothers divided a package of 75 building blocks equally. How many blocks did each receive?

A 23

B 25

C 72

D 78

CD ROM **Technology**
Use Harcourt Mega Math, The Number Games, *Up, Up, and Array*, Level M.

Soccer Games

Reading Skill **Draw Conclusions**

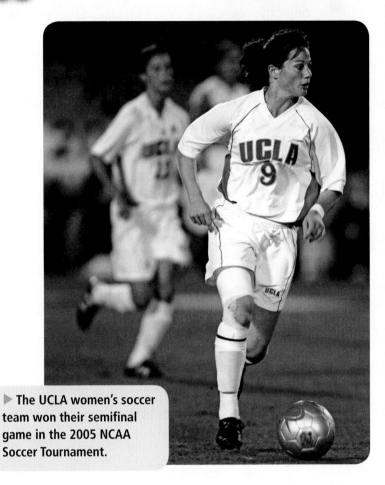

There are 64 teams playing in the Women's NCAA Division I Soccer Tournament. The teams that win each round advance to the next round. The rounds are: first round, second round, third round, quarterfinals, semifinals, and championship. How many games will be played in the tournament?

You can draw conclusions from the data in a problem to help you solve it.

What I know: Two teams play against each other in each game. For each game in each round, there can be only one winner.

▶ The UCLA women's soccer team won their semifinal game in the 2005 NCAA Soccer Tournament.

Conclusion: So, dividing the total number of teams by 2 will give you the number of games in each round. Repeat until only one game remains.

Draw a diagram or make an organized list to keep track of the number of games played in each round. Add the total number of games in each round to find how many games are played in the Women's NCAA Division I Soccer Tournament.

Problem Solving Draw conclusions to solve the problem.

1. Solve the problem above.

2. If there were 32 teams playing in the tournament, how many games would be played in round 2?

3. **Explain** what conclusion you can draw about how many games the winning team will play to win the tournament.

LESSON 4

Problem Solving Workshop
Strategy: Compare Strategies

OBJECTIVE: Compare different strategies to solve problems.

Read to Understand
Plan
Solve
Check

Use the Strategy

PROBLEM Evan's dog weighs 3 times as much as Oxana's dog. Together the dogs weigh 64 pounds. How much does Evan's dog weigh?

Read to Understand

Reading Skill

• Summarize what you are asked to find.

• What information is given?

Plan

• What strategy can you use to solve the problem?

You can draw a diagram or you can predict and test.

Solve

• How can you use each strategy to solve the problem?

Draw a Diagram

Draw a diagram that represents the relationship between the weights of the two dogs.

Evan's: [ ] lb [ ] lb [ ] lb } Total weight
Oxana's: [ ] lb   is 64 pounds.

Divide 64 by 4 to find the value of each equal part. $64 \div 4 = 16$

Each part is 16 pounds.

Add three parts to find the weight of Evan's dog. $16 + 16 + 16 = 48$

So, Evan's dog weighs 48 pounds.

Predict and Test

Predict and test to find the weight of each dog. Oxana's dog weighs ■. Evan's dog weighs $3 \times$ ■. So, ■ $+ (3 \times$ ■$) = 64$.

Predict		Test	Does It Check?
Oxana's dog: ■	Evan's dog: $3 \times$ ■	Total Weight ■ $+ (3 \times$ ■$) = 64$	Compare to 64
13	39	$13 + (3 \times 13) = 52$	$52 < 64$ no
14	42	$14 + (3 \times 14) = 56$	$56 < 64$ no
15	45	$15 + (3 \times 15) = 60$	$60 < 64$ no
16	48	$16 + (3 \times 16) = 64$	$64 = 64$ yes ✔
17	51	$17 + (3 \times 17) = 68$	$68 > 64$ no

■ = 16 pounds. Multiply 3 by 16 to find the weight of Evan's dog.

$3 \times 16 = 48$

Check

• Which strategy was more helpful? Explain.

0— NS 3.2 Demonstrate an understanding of, and the ability to use, standard algorithms for multiplying a multidigit number by a two-digit number and for dividing a multidigit number by a one-digit number; use relationships between them to simplify computations and to check results. *also* **0—** NS 3.4, MR 1.0, MR 2.0, MR 2.2, MR 2.3, MR 2.4, MR 2.6, MR 3.1, MR 3.2

Guided Problem Solving

1. Mia's dog weighs 4 times as much as her rabbit. Together the pets weigh 90 pounds. How much does Mia's dog weigh?

   First, decide whether to draw a diagram or work backward to find the dog's weight.

   Draw a Diagram

   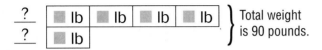

   Find the value of each part. Add to find the dog's weight.

   Predict and Test

   ■ = weight of rabbit
   (4 × ■) = weight of dog
   ■ +(4 × ■) = 90

   Predict and test to find the value of ■. Then multiply 4 × ■ to find the weight of Mia's dog.

2. **What if** Mia's dog weighs 5 times as much as the rabbit. Together the pets weigh 60 pounds. How much does the dog weigh?

3. Ari runs a training school for pet actors. Last year he trained 3 times as many dogs as cats. If the total number of dogs and cats he trained last year is 84, how many cats did he train?

Mixed Strategy Practice

4. The Grant family paid $220 to attend a dog show for two days. Adult tickets were 3 times the cost of children's tickets. The Grants bought 3 adult tickets and 2 children's tickets. How much did they pay for each ticket?

USE DATA For 5–6, use the pictures.

5. Petra walked four of the dogs in the picture. The second dog is half as tall as the first. The third dog is 9 inches taller than the second. The last dog is 8 inches taller than the third. The last dog is the Irish setter. Which dog did Petra walk first?

6. **WRITE Math** A teacup poodle is 6 inches tall. **Explain** how to find how many teacup poodles you would have to stand on top of each other to reach the height of the Labrador retriever.

Choose a
STRATEGY

Draw a Diagram or Picture
Make a Model or Act It Out
Make an Organized List
Find a Pattern
Make a Table or Graph
Predict and Test
Work Backward
Solve a Simpler Problem
Write an Equation
Use Logical Reasoning

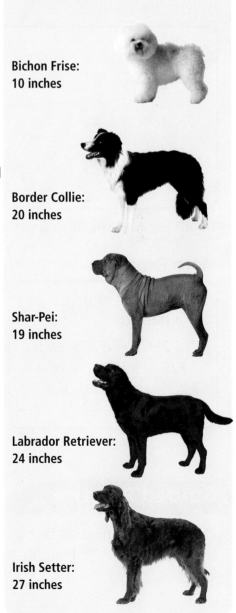

Bichon Frise:
10 inches

Border Collie:
20 inches

Shar-Pei:
19 inches

Labrador Retriever:
24 inches

Irish Setter:
27 inches

5

MENTAL MATH
Division Patterns

OBJECTIVE: Use a basic fact and a pattern to divide mentally.

Quick Review

Jay ran a total of 40 miles in January. Each time that he ran, he ran 5 miles. How many times did Jay run?

Learn

If you know basic facts, you can use them to divide multiples of 10, 100, or 1,000 mentally.

PROBLEM Trams take people to the top of the Gateway Arch in St. Louis, Missouri. If a tram makes 6 trips, it can carry a total of 240 people. How many people fit in a tram?

Example Use a basic fact and a pattern.
Divide. $240 \div 6$

> Think: 24 divided by 6 is 4.
>
> $24 \div 6 = 4$ ← basic fact
>
> $240 \div 6 = 40$
>
> $2,400 \div 6 = 400$

On a clear day, you can see 30 miles in any direction from the top of the arch.

Math Idea
As the number of zeros in the dividend increases, so does the number of zeros in the quotient.

So, 40 people will fit in a tram.

More Examples

A Basic fact and a pattern

$72 \div 9 = 8$ ← basic fact
$720 \div 9 = 80$
$7,200 \div 9 = 800$
$72,000 \div 9 = 8,000$

B Basic fact with a zero and a pattern

$30 \div 6 = 5$ ← basic fact
$300 \div 6 = 50$
$3,000 \div 6 = 500$
$30,000 \div 6 = 5,000$

C Basic fact with a zero and a pattern

$40 \div 10 = 4$ ← basic fact
$400 \div 10 = 40$
$4,000 \div 10 = 400$
$40,000 \div 10 = 4,000$

Guided Practice

1. What basic division fact can you use to find $90 \div 3$ and $9,000 \div 3$? Find $90 \div 3$ and $9,000 \div 3$.

○–╖ NS 3.4 Solve problems involving division of multidigit numbers by one-digit numbers.
also ○–╖ NS 3.2, AF 1.0, MR 2.3, MR 2.4, MR 3.0, MR 3.2, MR 3.3

Use mental math to complete the pattern.

2. $32 \div 8 = 4$
$320 \div 8 = \blacksquare$
$3,200 \div 8 = \blacksquare$

3. $28 \div 4 = \blacksquare$
$280 \div 4 = \blacksquare$
$2,800 \div 4 = \blacksquare$

✓4. $90 \div 9 = \blacksquare$
$900 \div 9 = \blacksquare$
$9,000 \div 9 = \blacksquare$

✓5. $64 \div 8 = \blacksquare$
$640 \div 8 = \blacksquare$
$6,400 \div 8 = \blacksquare$

6. (TALK Math) **Explain** how to use division facts you know to solve division problems with zeros at the end of the dividend.

Independent Practice and Problem Solving

Use mental math to complete the pattern.

7. $27 \div 9 = 3$
$270 \div 9 = \blacksquare$
$2,700 \div 9 = \blacksquare$
$27,000 \div 9 = \blacksquare$

8. $20 \div 5 = \blacksquare$
$200 \div 5 = \blacksquare$
$2,000 \div 5 = \blacksquare$
$20,000 \div 5 = \blacksquare$

9. $42 \div 7 = \blacksquare$
$\blacksquare \div 7 = 60$
$4,200 \div 7 = \blacksquare$
$\blacksquare \div 7 = 6,000$

10. $\blacksquare \div 3 = 2$
$60 \div 3 = \blacksquare$
$\blacksquare \div 3 = 200$
$6,000 \div 3 = \blacksquare$

Use mental math and patterns to find the quotient.

11. $120 \div 2$ **12.** $8,100 \div 9$ **13.** $400 \div 8$ **14.** $27,000 \div 3$

⭐**Algebra** **Find the value of** n.

15. $360 \div 6 = n$ **16.** $6,300 \div n = 700$ **17.** $24,000 \div n = 3,000$ **18.** $n \div 7 = 1,000$

USE DATA For 19–20, use the sign.

19. A camp paid $5,600 for a group of 15-year-olds to ride the tram. How many tickets did the camp buy?

20. Fae paid $280 for youth tickets and $90 for children's tickets. How many of each kind of ticket did she buy?

21. (WRITE Math) **Explain** why there is one more zero in the dividend than in the quotient when you find $40,000 \div 5$.

TRAM TICKETS	
Type	**Cost**
Adults	**$10**
Youth 13-16	**$7**
Children 3-12	**$3**

 ## Achieving the Standards

22. Round 37,629 to the nearest ten thousand. (○━ NS 1.3, p. 34)

23. What is the value of the expression below? (○━ AF 1.2, p. 142)

$$(15 - 6) \times (18 \div 6)$$

24. $75 \div 9 =$ (○━ NS 3.2, p. 244)

25. Test Prep The zoo sold 210 train tickets. The train made 7 trips. If the train was full each trip, how many people rode on the train each trip?

A 3   **C** 30
B 7   **D** 70

LESSON

6

MENTAL MATH
Estimate Quotients

OBJECTIVE: Estimate quotients by using rounding and compatible numbers, and then find the estimated quotient mentally.

Quick Review

1. $21,000 \div 3$
2. $2,100 \div 3$
3. $210 \div 3$
4. $21 \div 3$
5. $21,000 \div 7$

Learn

PROBLEM A hummingbird beats its wings 6,240 times in 2 minutes. About how many times does it beat its wings in 1 minute?

Estimate. $6,240 \div 2$

ONE WAY Use rounding.

Step 1	**Step 2**
Round the dividend to the nearest thousand. $$6,240 \div 2$$ $$\downarrow$$ $$6,000 \div 2$$	Use mental math. $$6 \div 2 = 3 \leftarrow \text{basic fact}$$ $$60 \div 2 = 30$$ $$600 \div 2 = 300$$ $$6,000 \div 2 = 3,000$$

So, a hummingbird beats its wings about 3,000 times in 1 minute.

▲ Hummingbirds visit more than 1,000 flowers a day!

ANOTHER WAY Use compatible numbers.

Step 1	**Step 2**
Find compatible numbers for 6,240 that can be divided evenly by 2. Think: $6 \div 2 = 3$ and $8 \div 2 = 4$ You can use 6,000 or 8,000 for 6,240.	Use mental math. $$6,000 \div 2 = 3,000$$ $$8,000 \div 2 = 4,000$$

So, a hummingbird beats its wings between 3,000 and 4,000 times in 1 minute.

More Examples Estimate using compatible numbers.

Ⓐ $558 \div 6$

Think: $54 \div 6 = 9$ and $60 \div 6 = 10$
You can use 540 or 600 for 558.
$540 \div 6 = 90$ and $600 \div 6 = 100$

So, both 90 and 100 are reasonable estimates.

Ⓑ $5,363 \div 9$

Think: $45 \div 9 = 5$ and $54 \div 9 = 6$
You can use 4,500 or 5,400 for 5,363.
$4,500 \div 9 = 500$ and $5,400 \div 9 = 600$.

So, both 500 and 600 are reasonable estimates.

  NS 3.4 Solve problems involving division of multidigit numbers by one-digit numbers
also **NS 1.3, MR 2.3, MR 2.4, MR 3.2**

Guided Practice

1. Round the dividend to the nearest 100. Use mental math to estimate the quotient.

$263 \div 3$

Estimate the quotient.

2. $362 \div 4$ **3.** $798 \div 2$ **4.** $499 \div 7$ ✓**5.** $147 \div 3$ ✓**6.** $4,522 \div 9$

7. **TALK Math** **Explain** how you know whether your estimate is greater than or less than the exact quotient.

Independent Practice and Problem Solving

Estimate the quotient.

8. $498 \div 5$ **9.** $740 \div 7$ **10.** $5,402 \div 6$ **11.** $823 \div 9$ **12.** $3,337 \div 3$

Estimate to compare. Write <, >, or = for each ●.

13. $613 \div 3 \; ● \; 581 \div 2$ **14.** $364 \div 4 \; ● \; 117 \div 6$ **15.** $2,718 \div 8 \; ● \; 963 \div 2$

USE DATA For 16–19, use the table.

16. About how many times does a damselfly's wings beat in 1 minute?

17. About how many times does a scorpion fly's wings beat in 2 minutes?

18. About how many more times does an Aeschnid dragonfly's wings beat in 1 minute than a large white butterfly's wings?

19. **WRITE Math** **What's the Question?** The answer is about 700 beats in 1 minute.

Insect Wing Beats in 3 Minutes	
Insect	**Number of Wing Beats**
Aeschnid Dragonfly	6,840
Damselfly	2,880
Large White Butterfly	2,160
Scorpion Fly	5,040

Achieving the Standards

20. What digit is in the tens place in 78,247?
(NS 1.0, p. 4)

21. Identify the solid figure. (Grade 3 MG 2.5)

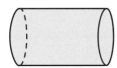

22. $18 \times 26 =$ (O▬ NS 3.2, p.220)

23. **Test Prep** A hummingbird's heart beats 3,782 times in 3 minutes. About how many times does its heart beat in 1 minute?

A 600   **C** 2,000

B 1,200   **D** 4,000

Place the First Digit

OBJECTIVE: Place the first digit in a quotient by estimating or using place value.

Quick Review

Yen put 791 caps in 9 boxes. He put about the same number in each box. About how many caps were in each box?

Learn

PROBLEM Tamiqua has a bunch of 8 black-eyed susans. In all, she counts 168 petals on her flowers. If all the flowers have the same number of petals, how many petals are on one flower?

ONE WAY Divide 168 by 8.

Step 1	Step 2	Step 3
Use compatible numbers to estimate to place the first digit.	Divide the 16 tens.	Bring down the 8 ones. Divide the 8 ones.
Think: $8\overline{)160}^{20}$ or $8\overline{)240}^{30}$	$\begin{array}{r} 2 \\ 8\overline{)168} \\ -16 \\ \hline 0 \end{array}$ Divide. $8\overline{)16}$ Multiply. 8×2 Subtract. $16 - 16$ Compare. $0 < 8$	$\begin{array}{r} 21 \\ 8\overline{)168} \\ -16\downarrow \\ \hline 8 \\ -8 \\ \hline 0 \end{array}$ Divide. $8\overline{)8}$ Multiply. 8×1 Subtract. $8 - 8$ Compare. $0 < 8$
$8\overline{)168}$ So, the first digit is in the tens place.		

ANOTHER WAY Use place value. Divide 423 by 5.

Step 1	Step 2	Step 3
Use place value to place the first digit. Look at the hundreds.	Divide 42 tens.	Bring down 3 ones. Divide the 23 ones.
$5\overline{)423}$ $4 < 5$, so look at the tens.	$\begin{array}{r} 8 \\ 5\overline{)423} \\ -40 \\ \hline 2 \end{array}$ Divide. $5\overline{)42}$ Multiply. 5×8 Subtract. $42 - 40$ Compare. $2 < 5$	$\begin{array}{r} 84\ r3 \\ 5\overline{)423} \\ -40\downarrow \\ \hline 23 \\ -20 \\ \hline 3 \end{array}$ Divide. $5\overline{)23}$ Multiply. 5×4 Subtract. $23 - 20$ Compare. $3 < 8$
$5\overline{)423}$ $42 > 5$, so use 42 tens. Place the first digit in the tens place.		

ERROR ALERT

If you cannot divide the divisor into the first digit of the dividend, the quotient begins at the next place value to the right.

So, there are 21 petals on one flower.

Guided Practice

1. Use place value to place the first digit. Where should you place the first digit? Divide.

   $4\overline{)459}$

NS 3.2 Demonstrate an understanding of, and the ability to use, standard algorithms for multiplying a multidigit number by a two-digit number and for dividing a multidigit number by a one-digit number; use relationships between them to simplify computations and to check results. *also* **NS 3.4, MR 2.3, MR 2.4, MR 3.0, MR 3.2, MR 3.3**

Tell where to place the first digit. Then divide.

2. $7\overline{)228}$ **3.** $922 \div 4$ **4.** $777 \div 3$ ✓**5.** $6\overline{)126}$ ✓**6.** $809 \div 8$

7. [TALK Math] **Explain** why the first digit in the quotient $233 \div 3$ is in the tens place.

Independent Practice and Problem Solving

Tell where to place the first digit. Then divide.

8. $2\overline{)145}$ **9.** $455 \div 5$ **10.** $6\overline{)779}$ **11.** $132 \div 7$ **12.** $3\overline{)945}$

Divide.

13. $923 \div 8$ **14.** $2\overline{)184}$ **15.** $329 \div 5$ **16.** $4\overline{)608}$ **17.** $992 \div 9$

⭐**Algebra** **Find the missing digit.**

18. $426 \div 6 = 7\blacksquare$ **19.** $633 \div 7 = 9\blacksquare \text{ r3}$ **20.** $662 \div 3 = \blacksquare 20 \text{ r2}$

USE DATA **For 21–22, use the garden plan.**

21. If Ty has 125 daisy plants, how many plants will be left if he plants an equal number in each daisy section?

22. Lillie has a total of 56 flowers. She has 14 irises. The rest are ivy and sedum. She has twice as many ivy as sedums. How many sedum plants does she have?

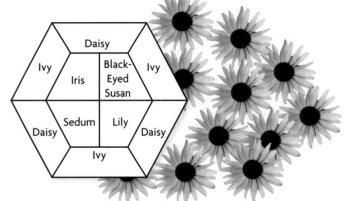

23. **Reasoning** If the dividend is 3 digits and you place the first digit in the tens place, what does that tell you about the divisor?

24. [WRITE Math] **Explain** how you can determine the number of digits in the quotient $726 \div 9$ without dividing.

🐻 Achieving the Standards

25. Use compatible numbers to estimate $165 \div 4$. (O━┓ NS 3.4, p. 256)

26. Is it certain or impossible that you will to toss a number greater than 7 on a number cube labeled 1 to 6?

(Grade 3 SDAP 1.1)

27. $36 - 32 =$ (O━┓ NS 3.1, p. 58)

28. **Test Prep** In which place is the first digit in the quotient $497 \div 2$?

  A thousands   **C** tens

  B hundreds   **D** ones

(Extra Practice) on page 360, Set E

 **Extra Practice**

Set A Use counters to find the quotient and remainder. (pp. 244–245)

1. 26 ÷ 8
2. 22 ÷ 3
3. 29 ÷ 6
4. 38 ÷ 9

Divide. You may wish to use counters or draw a picture to help.

5. 55 ÷ 7
6. 5)‾5‾8‾
7. 49 ÷ 6
8. 4)‾5‾1‾

9. Use the table at the right. Singh divides a bag of each brand of marbles into 6 equal groups. From which brand does he have the greatest number of marbles left over?

10. Use the table at the right. Marni makes 5 equal groups from a bag of each brand. For which brand of marbles will she have marbles left over?

Marbles	
Brand	**Marbles per Bag**
Kit's Cat's Eye	50
Smoothie	65
Clear as Glass	36

Set B Choose a method. Then divide and record. (pp. 248–251)

1. 88 ÷ 7
2. 8)‾9‾8‾
3. 65 ÷ 4
4. 5)‾6‾7‾
5. 79 ÷ 6

6. 4)‾6‾3‾
7. 57 ÷ 2
8. 6)‾9‾5‾
9. 76 ÷ 3
10. 84 ÷ 5

Set C Use mental math and patterns to find the quotient. (pp. 254–255)

1. 150 ÷ 3
2. 4,500 ÷ 5
3. 64,000 ÷ 8
4. 4,900 ÷ 7
5. 3,600 ÷ 4

6. 2,400 ÷ 3
7. 36,000 ÷ 9
8. 630 ÷ 7
9. 2,800 ÷ 4
10. 5,600 ÷ 7

11. Alan pays $320 for admission tickets to a theme park. If he buys 8 tickets, how much does he pay per ticket?

Set D Estimate the quotient. (pp. 256–257)

1. 299 ÷ 3
2. 680 ÷ 5
3. 5,402 ÷ 6
4. 64,622 ÷ 8
5. 4,211 ÷ 6

6. 301 ÷ 5
7. 549 ÷ 6
8. 624 ÷ 7
9. 333 ÷ 8
10. 791 ÷ 8

Set E Tell where to place the first digit. Then divide. (pp. 258–259)

1. 3)‾3‾5‾8‾
2. 909 ÷ 6
3. 325 ÷ 4
4. 7)‾6‾5‾3‾
5. 525 ÷ 4

6. 8)‾9‾7‾1‾
7. 457 ÷ 3
8. 621 ÷ 7
9. 5)‾4‾9‾1‾
10. 918 ÷ 7

Technology
Use Harcourt Mega Math, The Number
CD ROM Games, *Tiny's ThinkTank,* Level K.

Divide All Five

Players
2 players

Materials
- 2-color counters
- Number cube labeled 1 to 6

35	27	64	81	90
76	50	28	41	52
49	43	39	56	4
18	82	70	60	12
65	32	26	24	80

How to Play

■ The object is to cover 5 numbers in a row—across, down, or diagonally.

■ Decide who will use yellow counters and who will use red counters.

■ Players take turns. Toss the number cube. The player places his or her counter on the game board over any number that is divided evenly by the number tossed.

■ If 1 is tossed, place a counter on any number still showing. If a number is tossed that does not divide evenly into one of the numbers still showing, the player loses his or her turn.

■ The first player to cover five numbers in a row wins.

 Chapter 10 Review/Test

Check Vocabulary and Concepts

Choose the best term from the box.

VOCABULARY
quotient
remainder

1. When a number cannot be divided evenly, the amount left over is called the __?__ . (NS 3.4, pp. 244–245)

For 2–5, use counters to find the quotient and remainder. (O—¬ NS 3.2, pp. 244–245)

2. $37 \div 6$ 3. $44 \div 8$ 4. $23 \div 5$ 5. $38 \div 4$

Check Skills

Choose a method. Then divide and record. (O—¬ NS 3.2, pp. 248–251)

6. $62 \div 3$ 7. $71 \div 5$ 8. $4\overline{)72}$ 9. $8\overline{)98}$

Use mental math and patterns to find the quotient. (O—¬ NS 3.2, pp. 254–255)

10. $1,500 \div 3$ 11. $5,400 \div 9$ 12. $360 \div 6$ 13. $56,000 \div 8$

14. $490 \div 7$ 15. $480 \div 6$ 16. $7,200 \div 8$ 17. $1,600 \div 4$

Estimate the quotient. (O—¬ NS 3.4, pp. 256–257)

18. $4,601 \div 9$ 19. $63,999 \div 8$ 20. $4,061 \div 5$ 21. $349 \div 7$

Tell where to place the first digit. Then divide. (O—¬ NS 3.2, pp. 258–259)

22. $161 \div 4$ 23. $342 \div 5$ 24. $6\overline{)276}$ 25. $736 \div 3$ 26. $7\overline{)652}$

27. $8\overline{)672}$ 28. $843 \div 7$ 29. $260 \div 3$ 30. $5\overline{)371}$ 31. $821 \div 4$

Check Problem Solving

Solve. (O—¬ NS 3.2, MR 2.6, pp. 252–253)

32. Pauline has 64 stuffed animals. She wants to put them on 3 shelves. If she puts the same number on each shelf, how many stuffed animals will be left over?

33. **WRITE Math** ▸ Sari weighs 8 times as much as her little brother. Together they weigh 108 pounds. **Explain** how you can draw a diagram to find how much Sari weighs.

GO ONLINE Technology Use *Online Assessment.*

Enrich • Short Division
Maple Trees

The state tree of Wisconsin is the sugar maple. Sugar maple trees produce sap that is used for maple syrup.

A farmer sold 582 pints of maple syrup to 3 stores. Each store bought the same number of pints. How many pints of maple syrup did each store buy?

You can use short division to find the quotient. Short division uses mental math to solve problems. You write only the quotients and the remainders.

▲ One sugar maple tree produces about 20 gallons of sap in the spring, which makes 2 quarts of maple syrup.

Divide. $582 \div 3$ **Estimate.** $600 \div 3 = 200$

Step 1	Step 2	Step 3
Divide the hundreds.	Divide the tens.	Divide the ones.
$\begin{array}{r} 1 \\ 3\overline{)5} \\ -3 \\ \hline 2 \end{array}$ Think: 5 divided by 3 is 1 with a remainder of 2.	$\begin{array}{r} 9 \\ 3\overline{)28} \\ -27 \\ \hline 1 \end{array}$ Think: 28 divided by 3 is 9 with a remainder of 1.	$\begin{array}{r} 4 \\ 3\overline{)12} \\ -12 \\ \hline 0 \end{array}$ Think: 12 divided by 3 is 4.
Write 1 in the quotient. Write 2 in the tens place.	Write 9 in the quotient. Write 1 in the ones place.	Write 4 in the quotient.
$\begin{array}{r} 1 \\ 3\overline{)5\,^28\,2} \end{array}$	$\begin{array}{r} 1\ 9 \\ 3\overline{)5\,^28\,^12} \end{array}$	$\begin{array}{r} 1\ 9\ 4 \\ 3\overline{)5\,^28\,^12} \end{array}$

So, each store bought 194 pints of maple syrup. 194 is close to 200, so the answer is reasonable.

Golden Examples

A $\begin{array}{r} 1\ 4\ 8 \\ 5\overline{)7\,^24\,^40} \end{array}$	B $\begin{array}{r} 1\ 3\ 5 \\ 3\overline{)4\,^10\,^15} \end{array}$	C $\begin{array}{r} 2\ 0\ 8 \\ 4\overline{)83\,^32} \end{array}$

Sample It

Use short division to find the quotient.

1. $534 \div 2$
2. $784 \div 4$
3. $810 \div 6$
4. $816 \div 2$

5. $531 \div 3$
6. $903 \div 7$
7. $952 \div 4$
8. $746 \div 2$

Think About It

WRITE Math ▶ **Explain** how short division makes it easy to find $741 \div 3$.

Measurement and Geometry

1. Darren draws a triangle on his paper. He says all three sides of his triangle are the same length. Which statement is not true about Darren's triangle?

(Grade 3 O─┓ MG 2.2)

   A It is an isosceles triangle.

   B It has three acute angles.

   C It is an equilateral triangle.

   D It has no right angles.

2. Which figure is a pyramid?

(Grade 3 MG 2.5)

A   **C**

B   **D**

3. Which of these would you measure in meters? (Grade 3 MG 1.1)

   A the length of the playground

   B the length of a stapler

   C the distance between San Francisco and Sacramento

   D the width of a paper clip

4. **WRITE Math** ▶ Romeo drew a figure that has 2 pairs of parallel sides but no right angles. What figure could he have drawn? **Explain** your answer and draw an example.

(Grade 3 O─┓ MG 2.3)

Number Sense

5. In 2005, the population of San Bernardino County was one million, nine hundred sixty-three thousand, five hundred thirty-five. What is this number in standard form? (O─┓ NS 1.1)

   A 196,535

   B 1,000,935

   C 1,963,535

   D 1,900,500,035

> **Test Tip** Check your work.
>
> See Item 6. If your answer does not match any of the choices, check your computation.

6. Movie tickets at Cinema City cost $12 per person. How much money is collected for 252 tickets? (O─┓ NS 3.3)

   A $21   **C** $2,700

   B $756   **D** $3,024

7. $5{,}603 - 2{,}497 =$ (O─┓ NS 3.1)

   A 2,296   **C** 3,206

   B 3,106   **D** 3,294

8. **WRITE Math** ▶ Will solved this division problem.

$$\frac{16\ r2}{6\overline{)98}}$$

Is his answer correct? **Explain** how to check the answer. (O─┓ NS 3.2)

Statistics, Data Analysis, and Probability

9. Michael tossed a coin 25 times. Which statement is certain? (Grade 3 SDAP 1.1)

   A The coin landed on heads 25 times.

   B The coin landed on tails 25 times.

   C The coin landed on tails 12 times.

   D The coin landed on either heads or tails each time.

10. Jada tossed a number cube labeled 1 to 6 twenty-five times. Her results are shown in this line plot.

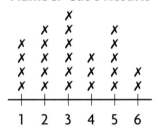

Number Cube Results

Number Tossed

How many times did Jada toss a number greater than 4? (Grade 3 SDAP 1.2)

   A 3

   B 5

   C 7

   D 10

11. WRITE Math ▶ Hugh spun a pointer 15 times. The pointer landed on green 6 times, red 3 times, blue 4 times, and yellow 2 times. Show his results in a bar graph. (Grade 3 SDAP 1.3)

Algebra and Functions

12. If m plus n equals 19, which of the following equations is not true? (AF 2.1)

   A $m + n + 12 = 31$

   B $m + n + 5 = 14$

   C $m + n + 8 = 27$

   D $m + n + 10 = 29$

13. What is the value of the expression? (AF 1.2)

$$(6 + 5) \times (6 - 4)$$

   A 62

   B 22

   C 16

   D 11

14. Which number is represented by n? (AF 1.1)

$$3 \times n = 87$$

   A 26

   B 27

   C 28

   D 29

15. WRITE Math ▶ **Explain** how adding parentheses to the expression changes the value. (AF 1.3)

$$12 + 5 \times 3 - 21$$

$$(12 + 5) \times 3 - 21$$

11 Practice Division

The Big Idea Fluency with basic division facts is based on using patterns and the inverse relationships to recall quotients.

CALIFORNIA FAST FACT

An octopus has eight arms and lives in the sea. The giant octopus is the largest. It can be 23 feet across. The California octopus is the smallest, less than an inch across.

Investigate

An octopus can fill its body with water. Then it can move fast by shooting out the water like a jet. An octopus can also move by using its arms to walk very slowly. Pick a number of centimeters an octopus might walk. How can you find the time it would take each octopus in the graph to walk that distance?

Octopus Walking Speed

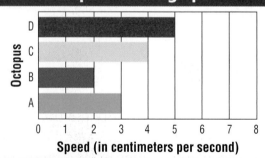

Speed (in centimeters per second)

GO ONLINE

Technology
Student pages are available in the Student eBook.

Check your understanding of important skills
needed for success in Chapter 11.

▶ **Estimate Quotients**

Estimate the quotient.

1. 86 ÷ 3   **2.** 424 ÷ 7   **3.** 338 ÷ 8   **4.** 1,210 ÷ 4

5. 2,605 ÷ 5   **6.** 1,420 ÷ 2   **7.** 4,316 ÷ 2   **8.** 275 ÷ 6

▶ **2-Digit By 1-Digit Division**

Use the model to find the quotient and remainder.

9.

25 ÷ 4 = ■

10.
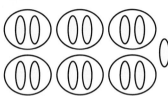

13 ÷ 6 = ■

11.

17 ÷ 5 = ■

12.

33 ÷ 6 = ■

▶ **Place Value Through Thousands**

Tell the value of the underlined digit.

13. 28,9<u>4</u>3   **14.** 19,08<u>2</u>   **15.** 961,<u>3</u>54   **16.** 263,<u>8</u>95

VOCABULARY POWER

CHAPTER VOCABULARY

dividend
divisor
quotient
remainder

WARM-UP WORDS

dividend the number that is to be divided in a division problem

divisor the number that divides the dividend

quotient the number, not including the remainder, that results from dividing

Problem Solving Workshop
Skill: Interpret the Remainder

OBJECTIVE: Solve problems by using the skill *interpret the remainder*.

Read to Understand
Plan
Solve
Check

Use the Skill

PROBLEM There are 95 people with reservations for a guided raft trip on the Nenana River in Denali National Park in Alaska. Each raft holds 6 people. How many rafts are needed for the 95 people? How many rafts will be full? How many people will be in a raft that is not full?

When a division problem has a remainder, you interpret the remainder based on the situation and the question.

Divide. $95 \div 6$

$$
\begin{array}{r}
15\ \text{r}5 \\
6)\overline{95} \\
-\underline{6} \\
35 \\
-\underline{30} \\
5
\end{array}
$$

A Increase quotient by 1.	**B** Quotient stays the same. Drop the remainder.	**C** Use the remainder as the answer.
How many rafts are needed?	How many rafts will be full?	How many people will be in a raft that is not full?
Think: Since 15 rafts only hold 90 people, one more raft is needed. So, drop the remainder, and increase the quotient by 1.	Think: A raft holds 6 people. Drop the remainder because 5 people do not fill a raft.	Think: The remainder is the answer.
So, 16 rafts are needed.	So, 15 rafts will be full.	So, 5 people will be in a raft that is not full.

Think and Discuss

Solve the problem. Explain how you interpreted the remainder.

Another river guide company has rafts that hold 8 people. On Saturday, 99 people will take river trips.

a. How many rafts are needed to take them on river trips?

b. Will each raft be full? If not, how many people will be in the raft that is not full?

O—π NS 3.4 Solve problems involving division of multidigit numbers by one-digit numbers. *also* O—π NS 3.0, O—π NS 3.2, MR 1.0, MR 2.0, MR 2.3, MR 2.4, MR 3.0, MR 3.1, MR 3.2, MR 3.3

Guided Problem Solving

Solve. Write *a*, *b*, or *c*, to explain how to interpret the remainder.

    a. Quotient stays the same. Drop the remainder.

    b. Increase the quotient by 1.

    c. Use the remainder as the answer.

1. A group of 57 people is camping in Denali National Park. Each tent holds 5 people. How many tents are needed for all of the campers?

    First, divide.

    Think: 57 ÷ 5

    Then, look back at the problem to see how to interpret the remainder.

2. **What if** you were asked how many tents will be full? How would your answer be different from your answer to Problem 1?

3. Guides lead groups of 9 people on biking tours in the park. There are 96 people who decided to go on the tours. How many people will be on a tour that is not full? Interpret the remainder.

Mixed Applications

USE DATA For 4–6, use the table. On float trips, the guides take 6 passengers in each raft.

4. How many rafts are needed for the Saturday afternoon trips? Will all of the rafts on Saturday afternoon be full? **Explain.**

5. On which day were more trips taken? How many more trips were taken?

6. By the end of the week, the guides took 12 times as many people on float trips as were booked for the Sunday morning trips. How many people took float trips that week?

7. On Saturday morning, the temperature during the first trip was 63°F. The temperature during the first trip on Sunday was 7°F cooler. What was the temperature on Sunday?

8. **WRITE Math** ▸ A company signed 67 people up for float trips. If 8 people fit in a raft, how many rafts do they need? **Explain** whether you need an exact answer or estimate, and then solve.

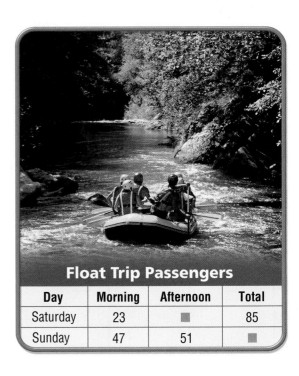

Float Trip Passengers

Day	Morning	Afternoon	Total
Saturday	23	■	85
Sunday	47	51	■

2 Divide 3-Digit Numbers and Money

OBJECTIVE: Divide 3-digit numbers including money amounts by 1-digit numbers.

Learn

PROBLEM President Dwight D. Eisenhower liked vegetable soup so much, that he created his own recipe. One recipe makes about 193 ounces of soup. How many 8-ounce bowls can be filled by using 193 ounces of soup?

Example 1 Divide 193 by 8. Write $8\overline{)193}$.

Step 1	Step 2	Step 3	Step 4
Estimate by rounding. **Think:** 193 is about 200, and 8 is about 10. $200 \div 10 = 20$ ▪ $8\overline{)193}$ Place the first digit in the tens place.	Divide the 19 tens. $\begin{array}{r} 2 \\ 8\overline{)193} \\ -16 \\ \hline 3 \end{array}$ Divide. Multiply. Subtract. Compare.	Bring down the 3 ones. Divide the 33 ones. $\begin{array}{r} 24\ r1 \\ 8\overline{)193} \\ -16\downarrow \\ \hline 33 \\ -\ 32 \\ \hline 1 \end{array}$ Divide. Multiply. Subtract. Compare.	To check, multiply the quotient by the divisor and add the remainder. $\begin{array}{r} 24 \\ \times\ 8 \\ \hline 192 \\ +\ 1 \\ \hline 193 \end{array}$ quotient divisor remainder dividend

So, 24 8-ounce bowls can be filled using 193 ounces. There will be 1 ounce left over.

Example 2 Divide 756 by 6. Write $6\overline{)756}$.

Step 1	Step 2	Step 3	Step 4
Use division facts for 6 to find compatible numbers for 756. $\underline{100}\quad\quad \underline{200}$ **Think:** $6\overline{)600}$ or $6\overline{)1,200}$ The quotient is between 100 and 200. So, place the first digit in the hundreds place.	Divide the 7 hundreds. $\begin{array}{r} 1 \\ 6\overline{)756} \\ -6 \end{array}$	Bring down the 5 tens. Divide the 15 tens. $\begin{array}{r} 12 \\ 6\overline{)756} \\ -6\downarrow \\ \hline 15 \\ -12 \\ \hline 3 \end{array}$	Bring down the 6 ones. Divide the 36 ones. $\begin{array}{r} 126 \\ 6\overline{)756} \\ -6 \\ \hline 15 \\ -12\downarrow \\ \hline 36 \\ -\ 36 \\ \hline 0 \end{array}$

So, $756 \div 6 = 126$. Since 126 is between 100 and 200, the answer is reasonable.

○━┓ NS 3.2 Demonstrate an understanding of, and the ability to use, standard algorithms for multiplying a multidigit number by a two-digit number and for dividing a multidigit number by a one-digit number; use relationships between them to simplify computations and to check results. *also* ○━┓ NS 3.0, ○━┓ NS 3.4, MR 2.1, MR 2.3, MR 2.4, MR 3.0, MR 3.1, MR 3.2, MR 3.3

Divide Money

Divide money amounts as you would divide whole numbers.

Example 3

At Ed's Electronics, 4 stereo speakers are on sale for $168. How much does 1 speaker cost?

Divide $168 by 4. Write 4)$168.

Step 1	**Step 2**	**Step 3**
Use place value to place the first digit. Look at the hundreds	Divide.	Multiply to check.
4)$168 1 < 4, so look at the tens.	$\begin{array}{r} \$\ 42 \\ 4\overline{)\$168} \\ -\ 16\downarrow \\ \hline 08 \\ -\ \ 8 \\ \hline 0 \end{array}$ Divide. Multiply. Subtract. Compare.	$\begin{array}{r} \$42 \\ \times\ \ \ 4 \\ \hline \$168 \end{array}$ quotient divisor dividend
▨ 16 > 4, so use 16 tens. 4)$168 Place the first digit in the tens place.		

So, one speaker costs $42.

• How do you know if the answer is reasonable?

Example 4

At the grocery store, 3 cans of green beans are on sale for $2.59. What is the cost of 1 can of green beans?

Divide $2.59 by 3. Write 3)$2.59.

$\begin{array}{r} \$0.86\ r1 \\ 3\overline{)\$2.59} \\ -2\,4\downarrow \\ \hline 19 \\ -18 \\ \hline 1 \end{array}$ Divide money amounts as you divide whole numbers. Write the quotient in dollars and cents.

A store cannot charge parts of a cent. It increases a quotient to the next cent. $0.86 r1 is increased to $0.87.

So, the cost of 1 can of green beans is $0.87.

• **What if** the store sells 5 cans of green beans for $4.29? How much does 1 can cost?

Guided Practice

1. To find $456 \div 8$, what two compatible numbers can you use for 456? Divide the compatible numbers. In which place do you place the first digit of the quotient?

Divide and check.

2. 4)329   **3.** $7.23 ÷ 3   **4.** 7)655   ✅ **5.** 924 ÷ 8   ✅ **6.** 6)$5.82

7. [TALK Math] **Explain** how to place the first digit in Exercise 5.

Independent Practice and Problem Solving

Divide and check.

8. 188 ÷ 2   **9.** 7)$8.26   **10.** 854 ÷ 6   **11.** 3)112   **12.** $7.98 ÷ 6

13. $332 ÷ 4   **14.** 5)725   **15.** 766 ÷ 8   **16.** 5)$845   **17.** 3)$9.48

18. 4)298   **19.** 2)$2.23   **20.** 9)$1.89   **21.** $1.25 ÷ 4   **22.** 292 ÷ 8

23. 2)483   **24.** 528 ÷ 7   **25.** 3)$4.83   **26.** $746 ÷ 5   **27.** 829 ÷ 9

⭐**Algebra** Find the missing digit.

28.   ■7
     5)485

29.   31 r1
     ■)125

30.   95 r4
     6)■74

31.   35 r■
     9)317

32.   45 r6
     7)3■1

33.   229 r1
     ■)688

34.   49 r5
     6)29■

35.   ■1 r1
     8)89

USE DATA For 36–40, use the table.

36. How much does 1 pound of cabbage cost at Krammer's?

37. How much does 1 pound of potatoes cost at Food Tiger?

38. How much do 3 pounds of carrots cost at Krammer's?

39. How much do 2 pounds of onions cost at Food Tiger?

40. **Pose a Problem** Look back at Problem 36. Exchange the known and unknown information. Then solve the problem.

41. **Explain** how to use compatible numbers to solve the problem 283 ÷ 9.

43. [WRITE Math] **What's the Error?** Describe the error, and then show the correct way to divide.

```
   751
7)526
 -49↓
   36
  -35
    1
```

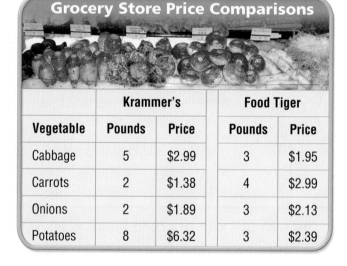

Grocery Store Price Comparisons

Vegetable	Krammer's		Food Tiger	
	Pounds	Price	Pounds	Price
Cabbage	5	$2.99	3	$1.95
Carrots	2	$1.38	4	$2.99
Onions	2	$1.89	3	$2.13
Potatoes	8	$6.32	3	$2.39

42. **Reasoning** Which has the greater quotient, 654 ÷ 2 or 654 ÷ 3? **Explain** how you know.

272 (Extra Practice) on page 280, Set A

44. What is the probability of tossing a coin that lands on tails? (Grade 3 SDAP 1.1)

45. 61 ÷ 3 =   (O━┓ NS 3.2, p. 248)

46. Test Prep 643 ÷ 7 =

   A 91 r6   **C** 92 r6

   B 92   **D** 916

47. In which place is the first digit of the quotient in 816 ÷ 6? (O━┓ NS 3.2 , p. 258)

48. Test Prep Three cans of tennis balls are on sale this week for $5.67. How much will it cost to buy one can of tennis balls?

Problem Solving [connects to] Science

Power plants convert other forms of energy into electricity so we can heat, cool, and light our homes and use televisions and other household appliances. The table shows the estimated weekly use and cost for some household appliances.

Cost of Using Some Household Appliances		
Appliance	**Estimated Weekly Use**	**Estimated Weekly Cost**
Dishwasher	7 loads	$1.26
Washing Machine	6 washes in hot wash/warm rinse with electric water heater	$4.80
Washing Machine	6 washes in warm wash/cold rinse with electric water heater	$1.80
Clothes Dryer	6 loads	$2.70
Refrigerator	7 days constant	$1.12

Use the table to solve the problems.

1. How much does it cost to run the dishwasher for one load?

2. How much does it cost to run the refrigerator for one day?

3. How much does it cost to do one load in the washing machine using hot wash/warm rinse?

4. How much does it cost to dry 8 loads of laundry in the clothes dryer?

5. Explain how you can find how much it costs to run the refrigerator for 3 days.

Zeros in Division

OBJECTIVE: Divide 3-digit numbers by 1-digit numbers when there are zeros in the quotient.

Quick Review

Malcom has 23 quarts of spaghetti sauce. Each jar holds 2 quarts. How many jars does he need for the spaghetti sauce?

Learn

PROBLEM Mr. Bing collects 324 treasures for his backyard treasure hunt. He needs 3 treasures for each student who participates. How many students can participate?

Example

Divide 324 by 3. Write $3\overline{)324}$

Step 1	Step 2	Step 3	Step 4
Estimate to place the first digit in the quotient. **Think:** $\frac{100}{3\overline{)300}}$ or $\frac{200}{3\overline{)600}}$ ■ So, place the first digit in the hundreds place. $3\overline{)324}$	Divide the 3 hundreds. $\begin{array}{r} 1 \\ 3\overline{)324} \\ -3 \\ \hline 0 \end{array}$	Bring down the 2 tens. Divide the 2 tens. $\begin{array}{r} 10 \\ 3\overline{)324} \\ -3\downarrow \\ \hline 02 \\ -0 \\ \hline 2 \end{array}$ The divisor 3 is greater than 2, so write a 0 in the quotient.	Bring down the 4 ones. Divide the 24 ones. $\begin{array}{r} 108 \\ 3\overline{)324} \\ -3 \\ \hline 02 \\ -0\downarrow \\ \hline 24 \\ -24 \\ \hline 0 \end{array}$

So, 108 students can participate in the backyard treasure hunt.

• **What if** Mr. Bing had 420 treasures? How many students could participate?

More Examples

Ⓐ Divide with Zeros

$$\begin{array}{r} 102\ r1 \\ 4\overline{)409} \\ -4 \\ \hline 00 \\ -0 \\ \hline 09 \\ -8 \\ \hline 1 \end{array}$$

CHECK

102	quotient
× 4	divisor
408	
+ 1	remainder
409	dividend

Ⓑ Divide Money

$$\begin{array}{r} \$104 \\ 5\overline{)\$520} \\ -5 \\ \hline 02 \\ -0 \\ \hline 20 \\ -20 \\ \hline 0 \end{array}$$

CHECK

$\overset{2}{\$}104$	quotient
× 5	divisor
$520	dividend

 ○━ NS 3.2 Demonstrate an understanding of, and the ability to use, standard algorithms for multiplying a multidigit number by a two-digit number and for dividing a multidigit number by a one-digit number; use relationships between them to simplify computations and to check results. *also* **○━** NS 3.0, **○━** NS 3.4, MR 2.1, MR 2.3, MR 2.4, MR 3.0, MR 3.2, MR 3.3

Correcting Quotients

The fourth-grade science classes displayed their treasures on tables for nature night. They put the same number of treasures on each table. There were 480 animal treasures on 6 tables. How many treasures were on each table?

Look at Ethan's paper. Ethan divided 480 by 6.

Ethan

$$6\overline{)480} \quad \begin{array}{c} 8 \\ \hline \end{array}$$
$$-48$$
$$0$$

- Describe Ethan's error. Find the correct number of treasures per table.

- Explain how basic facts and patterns could have helped Ethan find the correct answer.

Students who found plant and mineral treasures displayed 424 treasures on 4 tables. How many did they display on each table?

Look at Ava's paper. Ava divided 424 by 4.

Ava

$$4\overline{)424} \quad \begin{array}{c} 16 \\ \hline \end{array}$$
$$-4$$
$$24$$
$$-24$$
$$0$$

- Describe Ava's error. Find the correct number of treasures per table.

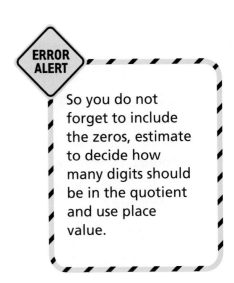

ERROR ALERT

So you do not forget to include the zeros, estimate to decide how many digits should be in the quotient and use place value.

Guided Practice

1. Copy the problem at the right. Estimate to place the first digit. Divide the hundreds. Divide the tens. Do you need to write a zero in the quotient? Then divide the ones. What is the quotient?

$$2\overline{)210}$$

Write the number of digits in each quotient.

2. $360 \div 4$ **3.** $714 \div 7$ **4.** $3\overline{)420}$ **5.** $8\overline{)960}$ ✓**6.** $400 \div 5$

Divide and check.

7. $5\overline{)305}$ **8.** $803 \div 4$ **9.** $6\overline{)840}$ **10.** $901 \div 2$ ✓**11.** $9\overline{)927}$

12. **TALK Math** Think about the problem $216 \div 2$. **Explain** how you know there will be a 0 in the quotient.

Independent Practice and Problem Solving

Write the number of digits in each quotient.

13. $7\overline{)560}$ **14.** $282 \div 4$ **15.** $3\overline{)510}$ **16.** $7\overline{)805}$ **17.** $540 \div 6$

Divide and check.

18. $5\overline{)601}$ **19.** $860 \div 2$ **20.** $8\overline{)704}$ **21.** $609 \div 3$ **22.** $9\overline{)919}$

23. $283 \div 4$ **24.** $763 \div 7$ **25.** $870 \div 3$ **26.** $6\overline{)724}$ **27.** $407 \div 5$

28. $4\overline{)700}$ **29.** $3\overline{)325}$ **30.** $417 \div 2$ **31.** $470 \div 5$ **32.** $306 \div 3$

Algebra Find the missing value.

33. $701 \div 2 = \blacksquare$ **34.** $\blacksquare \div 5 = 106 \text{ r}2$ **35.** $901 \div 3 = \blacksquare \text{ r} \blacksquare$ **36.** $207 \div \blacksquare = 51 \text{ r}3$

37. Anna is making papier-mâché rabbits for a nature celebration. It takes 240 strips of paper to make 8 rabbits. How many strips of paper does Anna need per rabbit?

38. **Reasoning** The Science Center wants to display 110 science projects. Each display area holds 45 projects. Will all of the projects fit in the 2 areas? **Explain.**

39. It takes 606 folds for Brian to make 6 praying mantis origami figures. It takes 540 folds to make 6 Gila lizard figures. How many more folds does Brian do to make one praying mantis than one Gila lizard?

40. Jeri is painting cherry blossoms. She plans to make 5 blossoms. If she spends the same amount of time on each blossom, she should finish in 100 minutes. How long will it take to paint one cherry blossom?

41. **FAST FACT** Japanese legend says that folding a thousand cranes brings good health or peace. Mai made 864 origami cranes in 8 months. If she made the same number of cranes each month, how many cranes did she make in one month?

42. **WRITE Math** **What's the Question?** Jolie's forest fun book tells about different beaver lodges and gives the amount of time it takes a beaver to build one. The answer is 103 hours for each beaver lodge.

Technology
Use Harcourt Mega Math, The Number Games, *Up, Up, and Array,* Level P.

Extra Practice on page 280, Set B

43. $873 \div 3 =$ (○➟ NS 3.2, p. 270)

44. $269 \div 6 =$ (○➟ NS 3.2, p. 270)

45. Test Prep A total of 654 students will count turtle nests at 6 sites. The same number of students will be at each site. How many students will be at one site?

  A 190   **C** 109

  B 119   **D** 19

46. What number goes into the box to make the number sentence true? (○➟ AF 2.2, p. 154)

$$(9 - 7) \times 6 = 3 \times \blacksquare$$

47. Test Prep $562 \div 7 =$

  A 8 r2   **C** 82

  B 80 r2   **D** 802

MATH POWER — Problem Solving and Reasoning

NUMBER SENSE When you estimate quotients, an underestimate gives you a quotient that is less than the actual quotient. An overestimate gives you a quotient that is more than the actual quotient.

Kari pays $105 for 3 DVDs on how to plant a garden. Estimate the cost of each DVD. Compare the estimate to the actual cost.

The actual cost of each DVD is $105 \div 3$, or $35.

ONE WAY Underestimate.

> **Think:** 90 is close to 105. 90 and 3 are compatible numbers since $9 \div 3 = 3$.
>
> $90 \div 3 = 30$ ← underestimate

So, the estimate of $30 is less than the actual cost of $35 since 90 is less than 105.

ANOTHER WAY Overestimate.

> **Think:** 120 is close to 105. 120 and 3 are compatible numbers since $12 \div 3 = 4$.
>
> $120 \div 3 = 40$ ← overestimate

So, the estimate of $40 is greater than the actual cost of $35 since 120 is greater than 105.

Tell whether the estimate is an underestimate or an overestimate. Then compare the estimate to the actual quotient.

1. A community center has 120 volunteers in 8 animal rescue teams. Each team has the same number of volunteers.

Estimate: $160 \div 8 = 20$ volunteers per team

2. Justin sells 330 pinecone bird feeders at the flea market in 3 hours. He sells the same number each hour.

Estimate: $300 \div 3 = 100$ feeders per hour

LESSON 4 Divide Greater Numbers

OBJECTIVE: Divide greater numbers.

Quick Review

1. $42 \div 6$
2. $28 \div 7$
3. $36 \div 4$
4. $50 \div 5$
5. $72 \div 9$

Learn

PROBLEM There are about 2,580 different species of marine animals, birds, and fish in the Gulf of Maine. A photographic team took pictures of every species during a 6-month period. If the team took the same number of pictures each month, about how many species did the team photograph in 1 month?

Choose a method that works easily for the numbers given.

Example 1 Use paper and pencil.

Divide. $2,580 \div 6$

Step 1	Step 2	Step 3	Step 4
Estimate to place the first digit in the quotient. **Think:** $\frac{400}{6)2,400}$ or $\frac{500}{6)3,000}$ ▪ So, place the first digit in the hundreds place. $6)\overline{2,580}$	Divide the 25 hundreds. $\begin{array}{r} 4 \\ 6)\overline{2,580} \\ -24 \\ \hline 1 \end{array}$	Bring down the 8 tens. Divide the 18 tens. $\begin{array}{r} 43 \\ 6)\overline{2,580} \\ -24\downarrow \\ \hline 18 \\ -18 \\ \hline 0 \end{array}$	Bring down the 0 ones. Divide the 0 ones. $\begin{array}{r} 430 \\ 6)\overline{2,580} \\ -24 \\ \hline 18 \\ -18\downarrow \\ \hline 00 \end{array}$

So, the team photographed about 430 species in 1 month.

Example 2 Use mental math.

Divide. $1,824 \div 6$.

Think: $1,824 = 1,800 + 24$

$1,800 \div 6 = 300$
$24 \div 6 = 4$
$300 + 4 = 304$

So, $1,824 \div 6 = 304$.

• When can you use mental math to divide?

• In Example 1, is mental math a good method to use? Explain.

Math Idea

You divide by using paper and pencil or by using mental math. Choose the method that works best with the numbers in the problem.

O—¬ NS 3.2 Demonstrate an understanding of, and the ability to use, standard algorithms for multiplying a multidigit number by a two-digit number and for dividing a multidigit number by a one-digit number; use relationships between them to simplify computations and to check results. *also* O—¬ NS 3.0, O—¬ NS 3.4, MR 2.3, MR 2.4, MR 3.0, MR 3.2, MR 3.3

PRACTICE GAME

Divide to Win

START

N W E S

FINISH

● **Go!**

■ A player shuffles the number cards and places them facedown in a stack.

■ Each player selects a different coin and places the coin on START.

■ The first player draws three number cards from the stack. The three cards make up a three-digit dividend.

■ The player chooses a divisor from 1 to 9.

■ The player finds the quotient to the division problem. If the quotient is between 40 and 61, the player moves forward one square. If not, the player stays on the same square.

■ Players take turns. The first player to reach FINISH wins.

 # Chapter 11 Review/Test

Check Concepts

1. **Explain** how to find the number of digits in the quotient of a division problem. (O—¬ NS 3.2, p. 274)

2. **Explain** the error in this problem and find the correct quotient. (O—¬ NS 3.2, p. 270)

$$
\begin{array}{r}
15 \\
5\overline{)525} \\
-5 \\
\hline
025 \\
-25 \\
\hline
0
\end{array}
$$

Check Skills

Divide and check. (O—¬ NS 3.2, pp. 270–273, 274–277, 278–279)

3. $384 \div 4$
4. $6\overline{)252}$
5. $561 \div 6$
6. $801 \div 7$

7. $246 \div 6$
8. $4\overline{)601}$
9. $920 \div 8$
10. $3\overline{)\$5.61}$

11. $\$4.29 \div 3$
12. $3\overline{)928}$
13. $1{,}539 \div 5$
14. $5\overline{)\$6.45}$

15. $6{,}305 \div 6$
16. $7\overline{)2{,}163}$
17. $7{,}261 \div 3$
18. $4\overline{)\$9.28}$

Write the number of digits in the quotient. (O—¬ NS 3.2, pp. 274–277)

19. $7{,}605 \div 6$
20. $426 \div 5$
21. $2{,}198 \div 3$
22. $7\overline{)\$483}$

Check Problem Solving

Solve. (O—¬ NS 3.4, MR 3.1, pp. 268–269)

23. Taylor has 686 stamps. He wants to put 6 stamps on each page of an album. How many pages will he need for his stamps?

24. Scott has enough film to take 72 photos during his vacation. He wants to take the same number of photos of each of 5 monuments he will visit. How many photos should he take of each monument?

25. **WRITE Math** ▶ The fourth grade donated 526 tulip bulbs to be planted around the school. If they are going to plant the same number of bulbs in each of 8 flower beds, how many bulbs will be left over? **Explain** how you interpreted the remainder.

GO ONLINE **Technology** Use *Online Assessment.*

Enrich • Mental Math: Multiplication and Division
USE YOUR HEAD

The Math Club members are practicing for a "fast math" competition in which they can only compute mentally. Their teacher asks them to find $112 \div 5 \times 15$. How can they use mental math to solve the problem?

Multiplication and division are inverse operations. If you multiply and divide by the same number, one operation undoes the other.

$2 \times 15 \div 15 = 2$ ← Dividing by 15 undoes multiplying by 15.

$40 \div 3 \times 3 = 40$ ← Multiplying by 3 undoes dividing by 3.

Team Strategy
Use mental math to find $112 \div 5 \times 15$.

$112 \div 5 \times 15$	$= 112 \div 5 \times (5 \times 3)$	Factor 15. $5 \times 3 = 15$
		The parentheses show that you are multiplying by 5 and by 3
	$= 112 \div 5 \times 5 \times 3$	Dividing by 5 undoes multiplying by 5. $112 \div 5 \times 5 = 112$
	$= 112 \times 3$	Compute mentally. Multiply by 3.
	$= 336$	

So, $112 \div 5 \times 15 = 336$.

Team Practice
Find the value of the expression.

1. $132 \div 2 \times 6$
2. $243 \div 3 \times 9$
3. $302 \div 4 \times 8$
4. $133 \div 7 \times 14$
5. $212 \div 4 \times 16$
6. $408 \div 8 \times 24$
7. $602 \div 25 \times 75$
8. $315 \div 15 \times 45$

Team Discussion
 **Explain** how to use the Associative Property and mental math to find $312 \div 9 \times 18$.

Measurement and Geometry

1. Which figure is an octagon?
(Grade 3 ⊶ MG 2.1)

A

B

C

D

2. Which statement about an equilateral triangle is true? (Grade 3 ⊶ MG 2.2)

A It has a right angle.

B All sides are the same length.

C Only two sides are the same length.

D All the sides are of different lengths.

3. Mel watched a movie that was 3 hours long. How long was the movie in minutes? (Grade 3 MG 1.4)

A 180 minutes   **C** 60 minutes

B 120 minutes   **D** 45 minutes

4. **⫿WRITE Math** ▸ **Explain** how to find the perimeter of this figure.
(Grade 3 ⊶ MG 1.3)

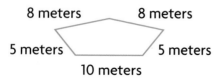

8 meters   8 meters

5 meters   5 meters

10 meters

Number Sense

5. $3{,}849 \div 7 =$ (⊶ NS 3.2)

A 4,149 r6   **C** 547

B 549 r6   **D** 507

 Test Tip **Choose the answer.**

See Item 6. If your answer does not match any of the choices, check your computation. Be sure you chose the correct operation.

6. Frank has 38 DVDs. He paid $12 for each of them. How much did he pay for all of his DVDs? (⊶ NS 3.3)

A $50   **C** $114

B $60   **D** $456

7. A new office complex cost seven hundred fifty million dollars to build. What is this number in standard form?
(⊶ NS 1.1)

A $700,050

B $750,000

C $705,000,000

D $750,000,000

8. **⫿WRITE Math** ▸ Cori has 261 CDs. Each storage case holds 8 CDs. How many storage cases does she need for all of her CDs? **Explain** how to interpret the remainder. (⊶ NS 3.4)

Statistics, Data Analysis, and Probability

9. Tim has a bag containing these 6 equal-sized cards.

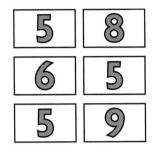

He pulls one of the cards from the bag. How likely is it that he pulls a 6?

(Grade 3 SDAP 1.1)

A certain

B likely

C unlikely

D impossible

10. WRITE Math ▶ Kelly recorded how many times each number came up when she tossed a number cube labeled 1 to 6 fifteen times. She started a line plot to show the results.

Number Cube Results

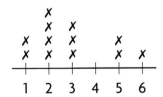

Outcome

Kelly has not yet recorded the number of times the outcome was a 4. **Explain** how Kelly should complete the line plot.

(Grade 3 O⚯ SDAP 1.3)

Algebra and Functions

11. What number goes in the box to make this number sentence true? (O⚯ AF 2.2)

$$(4 + 5) \times 8 = 9 \times \blacksquare$$

A 4

B 5

C 8

D 9

12. What is the value of the expression?
(O⚯ AF 1.2)

$$(18 + 3) - (5 \times 3)$$

A 6   **C** 42

B 8   **D** 48

13. Daniel earns $12 for each car he washes. He earned $96 washing cars this week. Which equation shows how to find the number of cars, n, that he washed? (AF 1.1)

A $96 \times 12 = n$

B $96 \div 12 = n$

C $96 - 12 = n$

D $12 + 96 = n$

14. WRITE Math ▶ Find the missing numbers.

Input, x	1	2	■	4	5
Output, y	4	8	12	■	20

Explain the relationship between the ordered pairs. Write a rule for the table as an equation. (O⚯ AF 1.5)

12 Number Theory and Patterns

The Big Idea The study of number theory builds understanding of factors, multiples, prime numbers, and composite numbers; patterns can be generalized with words and symbols.

CALIFORNIA FAST FACT

Coulter pine trees grow in southern California. They can grow to be 70 feet tall. Their pinecones are the heaviest in the world—they can weigh 5 pounds!

Investigate

The Fibonacci pattern is a special pattern. It follows this rule: add the previous two numbers to get the next number. On most pinecones, the number of spirals follows the Fibonacci pattern. Follow the rule to make your own Fibonacci pattern. Choose any two numbers less than 10 to start. Then find the relationship between the sum of the first ten numbers and the seventh number in your pattern.

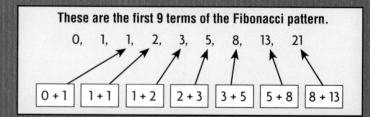

These are the first 9 terms of the Fibonacci pattern.

0, 1, 1, 2, 3, 5, 8, 13, 21

| 0 + 1 | 1 + 1 | 1 + 2 | 2 + 3 | 3 + 5 | 5 + 8 | 8 + 13 |

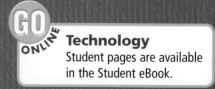

GO ONLINE

Technology
Student pages are available in the Student eBook.

Check your understanding of important skills
needed for success in Chapter 12.

▶ **Arrays**

Use the array to find the product.

1.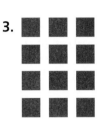

   ▨ rows of ▨ = ▨
   ▨ × ▨ = ▨

2.

   ▨ rows of ▨ = ▨
   ▨ × ▨ = ▨

3.

   ▨ rows of ▨ = ▨
   ▨ × ▨ = ▨

▶ **Multiplication Facts**

Find the product.

4. $\begin{array}{r} 8 \\ \times 6 \\ \hline \end{array}$	5. $\begin{array}{r} 11 \\ \times 4 \\ \hline \end{array}$	6. $\begin{array}{r} 2 \\ \times 8 \\ \hline \end{array}$	7. $\begin{array}{r} 9 \\ \times 5 \\ \hline \end{array}$
8. $\begin{array}{r} 3 \\ \times 7 \\ \hline \end{array}$	9. $\begin{array}{r} 5 \\ \times 6 \\ \hline \end{array}$	10. $\begin{array}{r} 12 \\ \times 5 \\ \hline \end{array}$	11. $\begin{array}{r} 7 \\ \times 7 \\ \hline \end{array}$

▶ **Number Patterns**

Write a rule for each pattern. Then find the missing numbers.

12. 3, 6, 9, 12, ▨, ▨, ▨

13. 42, 36, 30, 24, ▨, ▨, ▨

14. 18, 27, 36, 45, ▨, ▨, ▨

15. 36, 32, 28, 24, ▨, ▨, ▨

VOCABULARY POWER

CHAPTER VOCABULARY

array
composite
   number
equation
factor
factor tree
multiple
pattern
prime
   factor
prime
   number
product

WARM-UP WORDS

prime number a number that has only two factors: 1 and itself

composite number a whole number that has more than two factors

prime factor a factor that is a prime number

Factors and Multiples

OBJECTIVE: Find factors and multiples using arrays and number lines.

Quick Review

1. 8×4
2. 6×7
3. 2×9
4. 5×5
5. 3×10

Learn

A factor is a number multiplied by another number to find a product. Every whole number greater than 1 has at least two factors, that number and 1.

$$18 = 1 \times 18 \qquad 7 = 7 \times 1 \qquad 342 = 1 \times 342$$

↑   ↑

factor factor

Many numbers can be broken into factors in different ways.

$$16 = 1 \times 16 \qquad 16 = 4 \times 4 \qquad 16 = 2 \times 8$$

Activity

Materials ■ square tiles ■ grid paper

Make arrays to show all the factors of 24.

- Use all 24 tiles to make an array. Record the array on grid paper. Write the factors shown by the array.

12

2

$2 \times 12 = 24$

Factors: 2, 12

- Make as many different arrays as you can with 24 tiles. Record the arrays on grid paper and write the factors shown.

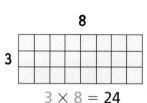

8

3

$3 \times 8 = 24$

Factors: 3, 8

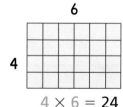

6

4

$4 \times 6 = 24$

Factors: 4, 6

24

1

$1 \times 24 = 24$

Factors: 1, 24

So, the factors of 24 are 1, 2, 3, 4, 6, 8, 12, and 24.

- Can you arrange the tiles in each array another way and show the same factors? Explain.

ERROR ALERT

Don't forget to list 1 and the number itself as factors.

NS 4.0 Students know how to factor small whole numbers. *also* **NS 4.1, MR 1.1, MR 2.0, MR 2.3, MR 2.4, MR 3.0, MR 3.2, MR 3.3**

Find Multiples

To find multiples of any counting number, skip-count or multiply by the counting numbers 1, 2, 3, and so on.

PROBLEM Rachel has a new charm bracelet with 20 links. She put a charm on each link that is a multiple of 3. Which links have charms?

> **Math Idea**
> A multiple of a number is any product that has that number as a factor. The number of multiples a number has is endless.

ONE WAY Make a model.

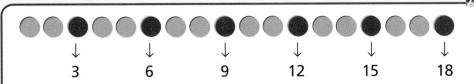

↓ 3   ↓ 6   ↓ 9   ↓ 12   ↓ 15   ↓ 18

The numbers of the red counters are all multiples of 3.

So, the 3rd, 6th, 9th, 12th, 15th, and 18th links have charms.

- **What if** the bracelet had 27 links? Which other links would have charms?

ANOTHER WAY Multiply and make a list.

Find the first six multiples of 4.

$1 \times 4 = 4 \quad 2 \times 4 = 8 \quad 3 \times 4 = 12 \quad 4 \times 4 = 16 \quad 5 \times 4 = 20 \quad 6 \times 4 = 24$

So, the first six multiples of 4 are 4, 8, 12, 16, 20, and 24.

- Explain how you know that 30 is a multiple of 5.
- Can a number that is a multiple of 3 have 5 as a factor? Explain.

Guided Practice

1. Use the arrays to name the factors of 12.

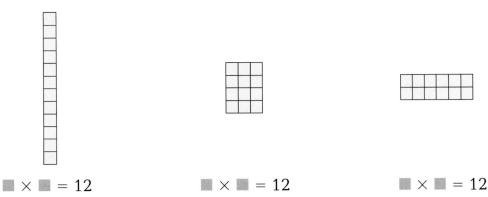

■ × ■ = 12   ■ × ■ = 12   ■ × ■ = 12

The factors of 12 are 1, ■, 3, ■, 6, and ■.

Use arrays to find all the factors of each product.

2. 20   **3.** 5   **4.** 49   **5.** 28   ✓**6.** 25

List the first ten multiples of each number.

7. 6   **8.** 2   **9.** 11   **10.** 4   ✓**11.** 8

12. **TALK Math** Explain how the numbers 3 and 12 are related. Use the words *factor* and *multiple* in your explanation.

Independent Practice and Problem Solving

Use arrays to find all the factors of each product.

13. 30   **14.** 42   **15.** 9   **16.** 50   **17.** 33

18. 64   **19.** 21   **20.** 75   **21.** 18   **22.** 17

List the first ten multiples of each number.

23. 9   **24.** 1   **25.** 7   **26.** 10   **27.** 12

28. 3   **29.** 13   **30.** 5   **31.** 20   **32.** 25

Is **6** a factor of each number? Write *yes* or *no*.

33. 6   **34.** 16   **35.** 48   **36.** 24   **37.** 18

Is **36** a multiple of each number? Write *yes* or *no*.

38. 8   **39.** 9   **40.** 18   **41.** 36   **42.** 5

Algebra Find the missing multiple.

43. 4, 8, ▨, 16   **44.** 7, 14, 21, ▨   **45.** 5, ▨, 15, 20   **46.** 9, 18, 27, ▨

USE DATA For 47–48, copy and complete the Venn diagram. Then use it to solve the problems.

47. What multiples of 4 are not factors of 48?

48. What factors of 48 are also multiples of 4?

49. Kia paid $40 for two charms. The price of each charm was a multiple of $4. What are the possible prices for the charms?

50. **WRITE Math** What's the Question? The answer is 1, 2, 3, 6, 9, and 18.

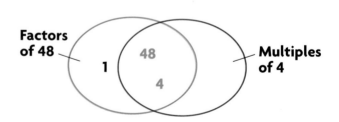

Factors of 48   1   48   4   Multiples of 4

51. Ray had 321 marbles. He lost 17. How many marbles were left? (○—n NS 3.1, p. 58)

52. Evan has 93 action figures. How many shelves will he need if he puts 3 action figures on each shelf? (○—n NS 3.2, p. 248)

53. An array has 4 rows with 3 tiles in each row. How many tiles are there in all?

(Grade 3 ○—n NS 2.3)

54. Test Prep What multiple of 9 is also a factor of 9?

55. Test Prep Ana is arranging 9 photos in equal rows. In what ways can she arrange the photos?

A rows of 1, 3, or 6

B rows of 1, 2, or 9

C rows of 1, 3, or 9

D rows of 3, 6, or 9

 **Problem Solving and Reasoning**

LOGICAL REASONING Starting June 1, an ice-cream truck visits Sasha's street every 3 days and Brad's street every 5 days. What are the first 2 days the truck visits both streets on the same day?

The days the ice-cream truck visits both streets on the same day are common multiples of 3 and 5.

A **common multiple** is a multiple of two or more numbers. You can use a number line to find common multiples.

S	M	T	W	T	F	S
1	2	3	4	5	6	7
8	9	10	11	12	13	14
15	16	17	18	19	20	21
22	23	24	25	26	27	28
29	30					

Example Use a number line.

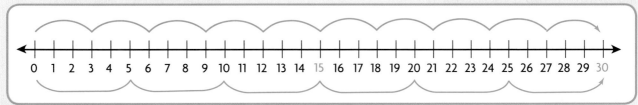

So, the first 2 days the truck visits both streets are June 15 and 30.

List the first six multiples of each. Find the common multiples.

1. 2 and 4   **2.** 9 and 12   **3.** 4 and 8   **4.** 3 and 5

5. 3 and 6   **6.** 2 and 5   **7.** 3 and 9   **8.** 5 and 10

Prime and Composite Numbers

OBJECTIVE: Identify whether a number is prime or composite by using arrays.

Learn

PROBLEM Linda has 7 postcards. She wants to arrange them in equal rows on her bulletin board. How many ways can Linda arrange the postcards?

Activity 1

Materials ■ square tiles

Make all the arrays you can with 7 square tiles to show all the factors of 7.

7×1

1×7

■ ■ ■ ■ ■ ■ ■

1 row of 7 postcards

■
■
■
■
■
■
■

7 rows of 1 postcard

So, Linda can arrange 7 postcards in exactly two ways.

The number 7 has only two factors, 1 and 7. A whole number greater than 1 that has only two factors, 1 and itself, is a **prime number**. So, 7 is a prime number.

• Is 9 a prime number? Explain.

• Name a number between 10 and 20 that is prime.

> **Math Idea**
> The number 1 is neither prime nor composite because it has only one factor, 1.

○━ NS 4.2 Know that numbers such as 2, 3, 5, 7, and 11 do not have any factors except 1 and themselves and that such numbers are called prime numbers. *also* NS 4.0, NS 4.1, MR 1.1, MR 2.0, MR 2.3, MR 2.4, MR 3.2

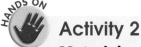

Activity 2

Materials ■ square tiles

Make all the arrays you can with 6 square tiles to show all the factors of 6.

| 2 × 3 | 3 × 2 | 1 × 6 | 6 × 1 |

The factors of 6 are 1, 2, 3, and 6. A whole number greater than 1 that has more than two factors is a **composite number**. So, 6 is a composite number.

Every whole number greater than 1 is either prime or composite. You can tell whether a number is prime or composite by making all the arrays you can for that number.

Activity 3

Materials ■ square tiles

- Use square tiles to make all the arrays you can for the numbers 2 through 11.
- Record the arrays and factors in a table. Write *prime* or *composite* for each number.
- How can you tell whether a number is prime or composite by looking at the Factors column of the table?

Number	Arrays	Factors	Prime or Composite?
2		1, 2	prime
3		1, 3	prime
4		1, 2, 4	composite
5			

Guided Practice

1. Use the arrays to find the factors of 12. Is 12 *prime* or *composite*?

| 1 × ■ | ■ × 4 | 2 × ■ |

Make arrays to find the factors. Write *prime* or *composite* for each number.

2. 14   **3.** 17   **4.** 36   ✓**5.** 39   ✓**6.** 43

7. [TALK Math] **Explain** how prime and composite numbers are alike. Explain how they are different.

Independent Practice (and Problem Solving)

Make arrays to find the factors. Write *prime* or *composite* for each number.

8. 21   **9.** 16   **10.** 23   **11.** 32   **12.** 13

13. 19   **14.** 44   **15.** 28   **16.** 30   **17.** 34

Write *prime* or *composite* for each number.

18. 4   **19.** 48   **20.** 2   **21.** 49   **22.** 11

23. 50   **24.** 45   **25.** 15   **26.** 5   **27.** 31

28. 22   **29.** 7   **30.** 42   **31.** 35   **32.** 29

USE DATA For 33–34, use the picture of stamps.

33. What other ways could the stamps be arranged in equal rows?

34. Is 25 prime or composite? **Explain.**

35. **Reasoning** I am a composite number greater than 10 but less than 20. All of my factors are odd numbers. Two of my factors are prime numbers. What number am I?

36. [WRITE Math] **What's the Error?** Marco listed the first five prime numbers as 2, 3, 7, 11, and 13. Describe his error. Write the correct answer.

Achieving the Standards

37. Jean has 15 boxes of cookies to sell. There are 22 cookies in each box. How many cookies does she have?

(O━┓ NS 3.3, p. 220)

38. What number goes into the box to make this number sentence true? (O━┓ AF 2.2, p. 142)

$$(4 - 2) \times 5 = 2 \times \blacksquare$$

39. How many different ways can you write 15 as the product of two numbers?

(NS 4.1, p. 288)

40. **Test Prep** Which is a composite number?

A 1   **C** 33

B 31   **D** 43

CD ROM **Technology** Use Harcourt Mega Math, Ice Station Exploration, *Arctic Algebra*, Levels O, W.

Justify an Answer

Sometimes you need to provide an argument to justify an answer. Look at the question to identify the important words. Words such as *all* and *only* are key words to help you develop your argument.

Lisa was asked the question, "Are *all* multiples of the prime number 7 composite?" She answered "No," and wrote this argument to defend her answer.

All multiples of the prime number 7 are not composite numbers.
First, I found some multiples of 7.

$$7 \times 1 = 7 \qquad 7 \times 2 = 14 \qquad 7 \times 3 = 21$$

Then, I noticed that the first multiple of 7 is 7. The number 7 is a prime number because it has only two factors, 1 and 7.

So, because I found one example of a multiple of 7 that is not a composite number, my answer is correct.

Tips

- First, state your answer.
- Next, show several examples and decide whether each example supports your answer.
- Write an explanation about how each example relates to your answer.
- Write a statement that summarizes the reason for your answer.

Problem Solving Make mathematical arguments to justify the answer.

1. Are all odd numbers prime?

2. Are all the factors of 4 also factors of 12?

3. Are all multiples of the prime number 5 prime?

4. Why is 2 the only prime number that is even?

Factor Whole Numbers

OBJECTIVE: Find factors using arrays.

Quick Review

Compare. Write $<$, $>$, or $=$ for each ●.

1. 3×6 ● 3×5
2. 9×4 ● 6×6
3. 2×12 ● 4×10
4. 8×3 ● 6×4
5. 7×4 ● 3×9

Learn

Many whole numbers can be broken down into factors in different ways.

$18 = 2 \times 9$ $18 = 3 \times 6$ $18 = 18 \times 1$

You can also show some whole numbers as the product of two or more factors.

$18 = 2 \times (3 \times 3)$ $18 = 3 \times (2 \times 3)$ $18 = (9 \times 2) \times 1$

◄ You can explore factors and products with The Multiplication Machine at The Exploratorium, a hands-on science museum, in San Francisco, California.

 HANDS ON

Activity Use arrays to break down 36 into factors.
Materials ■ grid paper ■ scissors

Step 1	Step 2	Step 3
Outline a rectangle that has 36 squares.	Cut the rectangle into two equal parts.	Cut apart each array into equal parts to find more factors.
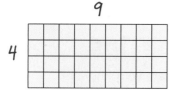	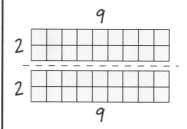	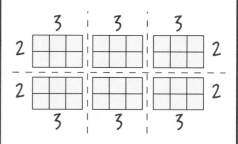
This array shows 4×9. $36 = 4 \times 9$	There are 2 equal arrays. Each array is 2×9. $36 = 2 \times (2 \times 9)$	There are 6 equal arrays. Each array is 2×3. $36 = 6 \times (2 \times 3)$

So, 36 can be shown as 4×9, $2 \times (2 \times 9)$, and $6 \times (2 \times 3)$.

• What is another array you could have used in Step 1?

Guided Practice

1. Use the arrays to complete the equation: $16 = ■ \times (■ \times 2)$.

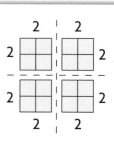

NS 4.1 Understand that many whole numbers break down in different ways (e.g. $12 = 4 \times 3 = 2 \times 6 = 2 \times 2 \times 3$). *also* NS 4.0, MR 1.2, MR 2.0, MR 2.3, MR 2.4, MR 3.2

Write a multiplication equation for the arrays shown.

2.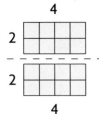

✓3.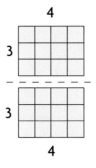

✓4.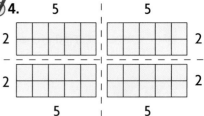

5. **TALK Math** **Explain** a way you can break apart the arrays in Problem 3 to write a different equation with three factors.

Independent Practice and Problem Solving

Write a multiplication equation for the arrays shown.

6.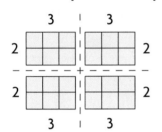

7.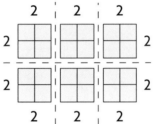

8.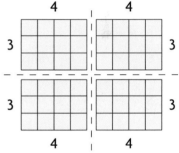

For 9–10, use the array at the right.

9. What number does the array show? What are two different ways to break apart the array?

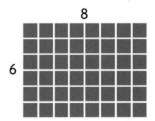

10. **Reasoning** Could you make a square array using all the tiles at the right? **Explain.**

11. What are some different ways you can write 60 as a product of two or more factors?

12. **WRITE Math** **Explain** how arrays can help you break down the number 20 into its factors. You may use grid paper to help.

LESSON 4

Find Prime Factors

OBJECTIVE: Find prime factors using factor trees.

Learn

Every composite number can be written as the product of prime numbers. A factor that is a prime number is a **prime factor**. You can use a **factor tree** to find the prime factors of a number.

Quick Review

Write *prime* or *composite*.

1. 37   2. 21
3. 33   4. 19
5. 26

Vocabulary

prime factor

factor tree

Example 1 Make a factor tree to find the prime factors of 36.

Choose any two factors of 36 and continue factoring until only prime factors are left.

ONE WAY   Use 6×6.

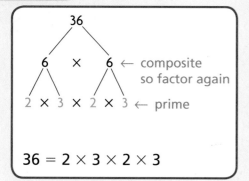

$$36 = 2 \times 3 \times 2 \times 3$$

ANOTHER WAY   Use 4×9.

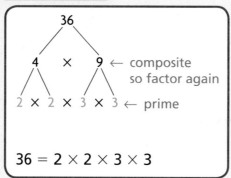

$$36 = 2 \times 2 \times 3 \times 3$$

Write the factors from least to greatest.
So, $36 = 2 \times 2 \times 3 \times 3$.

• Does it matter which two factors you use in the first branch of a factor tree? Explain.

More Examples

A Prime factors of 44

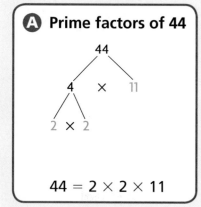

$$44 = 2 \times 2 \times 11$$

B Prime factors of 27

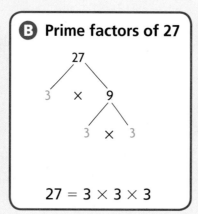

$$27 = 3 \times 3 \times 3$$

C Prime factors of 28

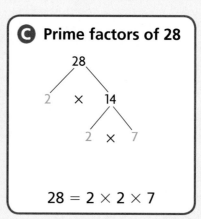

$$28 = 2 \times 2 \times 7$$

O–¬ NS 4.2 Know that numbers such as 2, 3, 5, 7, and 11 do not have any factors except 1 and themselves and that such numbers are called prime numbers. *also* **NS 4.0, NS 4.1, MR 1.1, MR 1.2, MR 2.3, MR 2.4, MR 3.2**

Guided Practice

1. Copy and complete the factor tree to find the prime factors of 18.

    $18 = \blacksquare \times \blacksquare \times \blacksquare$

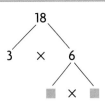

Make a factor tree to find the prime factors.

2. 6   **3.** 30   **4.** 42   **5.** 24   ✅**6.** 10   ✅**7.** 8

8. **[TALK Math]** **Explain** how you know when a factor tree is complete.

Independent Practice and Problem Solving

Make a factor tree to find the prime factors.

9. 16   **10.** 21   **11.** 44   **12.** 50   **13.** 25   **14.** 32

15. 19   **16.** 22   **17.** 15   **18.** 20   **19.** 48   **20.** 49

21. Each of these expressions represents 24. Copy the expressions. Circle all the prime numbers.

    2×12 3×8 $2 \times 3 \times 4$ $2 \times 2 \times 6$ 4×6 $2 \times 2 \times 2 \times 3$ 1×24

22. I am an even number between 12 and 20. I am the product of two prime numbers. What number am I?

23. **≡FAST FACT** A mother blue whale weighs about 120 tons. Her baby weighs about 8 tons. How many times as heavy as the baby is the mother?

24. **Reasoning** How many times greater is the product of the three smallest prime numbers than the product of the two smallest prime numbers?

25. **[WRITE Math]** **What's the Error?** Nick says the prime factors of 48 are $2 \times 2 \times 3 \times 4$. Correct Nick's error.

Achieving the Standards

26. Write the next three numbers in the pattern. (Grade 3 AF 2.2)

    9, 18, 27, 36, $\blacksquare$, $\blacksquare$, $\blacksquare$

27. There are 6 red blocks and 1 blue block in a bag. All blocks are the same size. Is it certain, likely, unlikely, or impossible that a red block will be pulled?

    (Grade 3 SDAP 1.1)

28. Write all the prime numbers greater than 10 and less than 20. (0━π NS 4.2, p. 292)

29. **Test Prep** Which of these is another way to write the product 10×5 ?

    A $2 \times 2 \times 5$ **C** $2 \times 5 \times 5$

    B $2 \times 3 \times 3$ **D** $5 \times 5 \times 5$

Extra Practice on page 308, Set D

Number Patterns

OBJECTIVE: Identify, describe, extend, and make patterns.

Learn

PROBLEM Morgan counts as he juggles three balls. He tosses the red ball on the count of 3, 6, 9, and 12. What numbers will he count for the next two tosses of the red ball?

Example 1

Find a rule. Then find the next two numbers in your pattern.

3, 6, 9, 12, $\blacksquare$, $\blacksquare$

Step 1	Step 2
Think: What rule changes 3 to 6? Try multiply by 2 because $3 \times 2 = 6$. Test: $6 \times 2 \neq 9$ Try add 3 because $3 + 3 = 6$. Test: $6 + 3 = 9 \qquad 9 + 3 = 12$ The rule add 3 works.	Use the rule to find the next two numbers in the pattern. $+3 \quad +3 \quad +3 \quad +3 \quad +3$ 3, 6, 9, 12, 15, 18 $12 + 3 = 15 \qquad 15 + 3 = 18$

So, he will count 15, 18 for the next two tosses of the red ball.

If a number pattern increases, try addition or multiplication. If it decreases, try subtraction or division.

Example 2

Find a rule. Then find the missing numbers in your pattern.

35, 31, 27, $\blacksquare$, 19, 15, $\blacksquare$

Step 1	Step 2
Write a rule for the pattern. Try subtract 4. 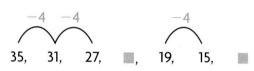 The rule subtract 4 works.	Use the rule to find the missing numbers in your pattern. 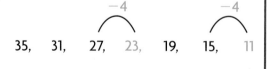

So, the missing numbers are 23 and 11.

• Look at this pattern: 1, 2, 4, $\blacksquare$. If the missing number is 8, what is a rule for a pattern? If the missing number is 7, what is a rule for a pattern?

NS 3.0 Students solve problems involving addition, subtraction, multiplication, and division of whole numbers and understand the relationships among the operations. *also* **MR 1.1, MR 2.3, MR 2.4, MR 3.0, MR 3.2**

Find and Make Patterns

The rules for some patterns have more than one operation. When numbers in a pattern increase **and** decrease, try two operations.

Math Idea

You can use the strategy *find a possible pattern* to help. Compare each number with the next.

Example 3 Use two operations.

Find a rule. Then find the next two numbers in your pattern.
5, 1, 10, 2, 20, 4, 40, ■, ■

Step 1

Write a rule for the pattern.
Try divide by 5, multiply by 10.

$$\div 5 \quad \times 10 \quad \div 5 \quad \times 10 \quad \div 5 \quad \times 10$$

5,　1,　10,　2,　20,　4,　40

The rule divide by 5, multiply by 10 works.

Step 2

Use your rule to find the missing numbers.
$40 \div 5 = 8$
$8 \times 10 = 80$

So, the next two numbers in the pattern are 8 and 80.

Example 4 Make a pattern.

Use the rule *add 13, multiply by 4* to make a pattern.
Start with 1. Find the next three numbers in the pattern.

Step 1	
Find the second number in the pattern: Add 13 to 1.	$1 + 13 = 14$
Step 2	
Find the third number in the pattern: Multiply the sum by 4.	$4 \times 14 = 56$
Step 3	
Find the fourth number in the pattern: Add 13 to the product.	$56 + 13 = 69$

So, the next three numbers in the pattern are 14, 56, and 69.

Guided Practice

1. What are the next two numbers in the pattern?

$$-2 \quad -2 \quad -2$$

58,　56,　54,　52,　■,　■

A rule is ___?___.
$52 - ■ = ■$
$■ - 2 = ■$

So, the next two numbers in your pattern are ■ and ■.

Find a rule. Then find the next two numbers in your pattern.

✅ **2.** 18, 28, 38, 48, ▪, ▪

✅ **3.** 4, 7, 5, 8, 6, 9, 7, ▪, ▪

4. [TALK Math] **Explain** how to find missing numbers in a number pattern.

Independent Practice and Problem Solving

Find a rule. Then find the next two numbers in your pattern.

5. 775, 675, 575, 475, ▪, ▪

6. 160, 80, 40, 20, ▪, ▪

7. 47, 52, 51, 56, 55, 60, 59, ▪, ▪

8. 99, 95, 98, 94, 97, 93, 96, ▪, ▪

Algebra **Find a rule. Then find the missing numbers in your pattern.**

9. 2, 4, ▪, 16, 32, 64

10. 46, 40, ▪, 28, 22, ▪, 10

11. ▪, 130, 145, 160, 175, ▪

12. ▪, ▪, 485, 480, 475, 470

Use the rule to make a number pattern. Write the first four numbers in the pattern.

13. Rule: Divide by 2. Start with 24.

14. Rule: Subtract 8. Start with 72.

15. Rule: Add 3, subtract 2. Start with 16.

16. Jordan is juggling 3 balls. He starts by keeping one ball in his hand and tossing 2 balls into the air. The diagram shows how many balls are in the air and in his hand with each toss. How many balls will be in the air and in his hand with the next toss?

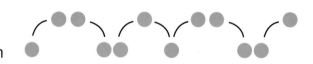

17. Carolyn counts as she juggles 4 balls. She tosses the red ball on the count of 4, 8, 12, and 16. What numbers will she count when she tosses the next two red balls?

18. **Reasoning** Look at the following number pattern. 2, 4, 8, ▪ What is a rule for the pattern if the missing number is 14? What is a rule for the pattern if the missing number is 16?

19. **Pose a Problem** Make a number pattern. Write the first six numbers. Have a classmate write a rule for your pattern and use that rule to find the next two numbers.

20. [WRITE Math] **Explain** how you can tell by looking at a pattern that a rule for the pattern might have two operations.

21. How many times did Evan toss heads?

(Grade 3 O━━ SDAP 1.2)

Evan's Coin Tosses	
Heads	
Tails	JHT JHT

22. Test Prep Which of the following describes a possible rule for this pattern?

2, 4, 8, 10, 20, 22, 44

A Add 2.

B Multiply by 2.

C Add 2, add 4.

D Add 2, multiply by 2.

23. Which is greater, 547,683 or 547,638?

(O━━ NS 1.2, p. 12)

24. Use a factor tree to find the prime factors of 45. (NS 4.1, p. 300)

25. Test Prep The numbers in this pattern decrease by the same amount each time. What are the next three numbers in this pattern?

24, 21, 18, 15, ▪ , ▪, ▪

A 16, 17, 18

B 12, 13, 14

C 12, 9, 6

D 14, 13, 12

MATH POWER — Problem Solving and Reasoning

ALGEBRA Blaise Pascal, a French mathematician, made this math triangle popular about 350 years ago. Pascal's Triangle is known for its number patterns. Each row in the triangle is formed by the row above it.

What might the missing numbers in the pattern be?

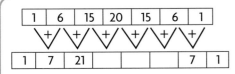

Rule: Each row starts and ends with a 1. Each of the other numbers is the sum of the two closest numbers above it.

So, the missing numbers in the pattern are 35, 35, and 21.

1. If you added three more rows to the triangle, what numbers would you include?

2. **WRITE Math** Look for another number pattern in the triangle and describe the pattern you found. **Explain** your answer.

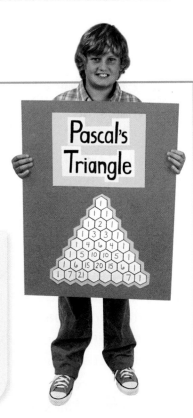

Problem Solving Workshop
Strategy: Find a Pattern

OBJECTIVE: Solve problems by using the strategy *find a pattern*.

Learn the Strategy

Patterns can be found everywhere in the real world. You can use math to talk about patterns in nature, architecture, music, dance, art, and language. You can use patterns to solve problems.

Geometric patterns can be based on color, size, shape, position, or number of figures.

What might be the next floor tile to be put down?

The last tiles were two rhombuses. So the next tile might be an octagon.

Pattern unit:

Number patterns can increase, decrease, repeat, or stop.

What is the date of the third Wednesday in May?

Rule: Start at 3. Add 7. 3, 10, 17, 24, 31
So, the third Wednesday in May is the 17th.

May						
Sun	Mon	Tue	Wed	Thu	Fri	Sat
	1	2	③	4	5	6
7	8	9	⑩	11	12	13
14	15	16	17	18	19	20
21	22	23	㉔	25	26	27
28	29	30	㉛			

Some visual patterns can be described using numbers.

Erin is building a model of a skyscraper with square tiles. She will build one more array for the base of the skyscraper. How many squares might be in the base if the pattern continues?

Rule: Increase the number of rows and columns of tiles by 1.

So, the base will be a 5-by-5 array, with 25 tiles.

Design	Number of Tiles
▢	1
▦	4
▦	9
▦	16

TALK Math
How can finding a rule help you predict what comes next?

NS 3.0 Students solve problems involving addition, subtraction, multiplication, and division of whole numbers and understand the relationships among the operations. *also* MR 1.0, MR 1.1, MR 2.0, MR 2.3, MR 2.4, MR 3.0, MR 3.1, MR 3.2, MR 3.3

Use the Strategy

PROBLEM Claire's family is putting a wall with a stair-step pattern in their bathroom. If they want the wall to be 5 cubes tall, how many cubes will they need?

Read to Understand

• **What information is given?**

Plan

• **What strategy can you use to solve the problem?**
You can find a pattern to solve the problem.

Solve

 Reading Skill

• **How can you use the strategy and graphic aids to solve the problem?**
Write a rule for the pattern.

Design	Pattern Description	Number of Cubes
	1-cube base, 0 on top	1
	2-cube base, 1 on top	3
	3-cube base, then 2, then 1 on top	6
	4-cube base, then 3, then 2, then 1 on top	10

Rule: For each new design, the base has 1 more cube than the design before.

Use the rule to find the number of cubes in a wall that is 5 cubes tall.

So, a wall that is 5 cubes tall has 15 cubes.

Check

• **Look at the Number of Cubes column. What is a number pattern for the number of cubes in each figure?**

Guided Problem Solving

1. Parker is building a model of a ziggurat wall with blocks. How many blocks might he place in the next row?

   Write a rule for the pattern.

   Rule: Subtract ▮ from the previous row.

   Use the rule to find the number of blocks in the next row.

   $9 - ▮ = ▮$

▲ A ziggurat is a kind of ancient temple.

9 blocks
11 blocks
13 blocks
15 blocks

2. **What if** Parker continued the pattern? Could the pattern continue without end? **Explain.**

3. The table shows the number of windows on each floor of a skyscraper. How many windows might be on the tenth floor?

Floor	1	2	3	4	5	6	7	8	9
Number of Windows	4	8	6	10	8	12	10	14	12

Problem Solving Strategy Practice

Find a pattern to solve.

4. Draw a pattern unit for two center rings of the tree grate. How many large trapezoids might be in the whole circle?

5. Many brick columns use this pattern. Write a number pattern that describes the lengths of the bricks in each row.

|← 24 in. →|

6. The mailboxes in Hannah's apartment building are in an array. Some of the numbers have fallen off the mailboxes. Look for a pattern in the rows. Look for a pattern in the columns. What might be the missing numbers?

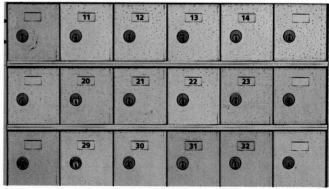

Height: 1,483 ft
Petronas Tower
Kuala Lumpur
Malaysia

Height: 986 ft
Eiffel Tower
Paris
France

Height: 1,046 ft
Chrysler
Building
New York City

Height: 1,250 ft
Empire State
Building
New York City

Choose a
STRATEGY

Draw a Diagram or Picture

Make a Model or Act It Out

Make an Organized List

Find a Pattern

Make a Table or Graph

Predict and Test

Work Backward

Solve a Simpler Problem

Write an Equation

Use Logical Reasoning

Mixed Strategy Practice

USE DATA For 7–10, use the information in the picture.

7. Two buildings have a difference in height of 60 feet. Which are the two buildings?

8. The U.S. Bank Tower in Los Angeles is x feet taller than the Eiffel Tower. The U.S. Bank Tower is 1,018 feet tall. What is x?

9. **Pose a Problem** Look back at Problem 7. Write a similar problem by changing the difference in height.

10. **WRITE Math** ▸ One mile is 5,280 feet. Estimate to find if all four skyscrapers put together would be about one mile high. **Explain** how you estimated.

11. **Open-Ended** Use grid paper to draw a picture of a skyscraper. Include a numerical pattern in your drawing. For example, the number of windows on each floor might increase by 3. Write a rule for your pattern.

CHALLENGE YOURSELF

The Eiffel Tower, at 986 feet tall, was the tallest building in the world when it was built in 1889 in Paris, France. It takes 50 tons of paint to cover the Eiffel Tower.

12. Before the Eiffel Tower was completed, the Washington Monument was the world's tallest building. The Washington Monument stands 185 yards tall. Is the Eiffel Tower about 3 times as tall as the Washington Monument? **Explain.**

13. The Eiffel Tower is painted every 7 years. How many tons of paint were used between the year the Eiffel Tower opened and 2008?

Extra Practice

Set A Use arrays to find all the factors of each product. (pp. 288–291)

1. 24
2. 35
3. 41
4. 56
5. 32

List the first ten multiples of each number.

6. 2
7. 5
8. 4
9. 11
10. 12

11. Emma paid $24 for some key chains. If each one cost the same amount, how many could she have bought?

Set B Write *prime* or *composite* for each number. (pp. 292–295)

1. 33
2. 17
3. 40
4. 43
5. 27
6. 49
7. 21
8. 18
9. 19
10. 37

Set C Write an equation for the arrays shown. (pp. 296–297)

1.
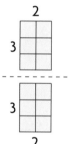
2.
3.
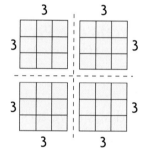

Set D Make a factor tree to find the prime factors. (pp. 298–299)

1. 20
2. 28
3. 31
4. 40
5. 50

Set E Find a rule. Then find the next two numbers in your pattern. (pp. 300–303)

1. 38, 41, 44, 47, 50, ■, ■
2. 211, 216, 221, 226, 231, ■, ■
3. 986, 886, 786, 686, 586, ■, ■
4. 29, 36, 33, 40, 37, 44, 41, ■, ■
5. 59, 54, 56, 51, 53, 48, 50, ■, ■
6. 15, 3, 15, 3, 15, 3, ■, ■

7. Shawna is passing out programs in the auditorium. She places the first program on the second chair and then puts a program on every third chair. On which chair does she place the fifth program?

Technology
Use Harcourt Mega Math, Ice Station Exploration, *Arctic Algebra,* Level O.

Factor Farm

On Your Mark!
2 to 3 players

Get Set!
- Number cards (2–10)
- 2-color counters

21	35	18	16	6
32	40	12	10	3
20	4	9	27	8
39	28	5	15	22
2	25	14	7	36

Go!

- Shuffle the number cards and place them facedown in a stack.

- Draw a number card from the stack. If the number is a factor of one of the numbers on your grid, put a counter on that number.

- You may put a counter on only one number for each number card drawn.

- The first player to place counters on 5 numbers in a horizontal, vertical, or diagonal line wins.

 # Chapter 12 Review/Test

Check Vocabulary and Concepts

Choose the best term from the box.

> **VOCABULARY**
>
> composite number
> factor tree
> prime factor
> prime number

1. A whole number greater than 1 that has only two factors, 1 and itself, is called a __?__. (O┱ NS 4.2, p. 292)

2. A __?__ can be used to find all the factors of a number. (O┱ NS 4.2, p. 298)

3. A __?__ is a factor that is a prime number. (O┱ NS 4.2, p. 298)

Check Skills

Use arrays to find all the factors of each product. (NS 4.0. pp 288–291)

4. 45   **5.** 27   **6.** 42   **7.** 25   **8.** 36

Write *prime* or *composite* for each number. (O┱ NS 4.2, pp. 292–295)

9. 25   **10.** 53   **11.** 39   **12.** 41   **13.** 26

Write an equation for the arrays shown. (NS 4.1, pp. 296–297)

14.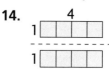

15.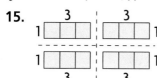

16.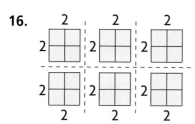

Make a factor tree to find the prime factors. (O┱ NS 4.2, pp. 298–299)

17. 12   **18.** 26   **19.** 42   **20.** 35   **21.** 27

Find a rule. Then find the missing numbers in your pattern. (O┱ NS 3.0, pp. 300–303)

22. 34, 38, 42, ▨, 50, 54, ▨   **23.** 89, 84, 79, 74, ▨, 64, ▨

Check Problem Solving

Solve. (O┱ NS 3.0, MR1.1, pp. 304–307)

24. Andy went jogging on Monday, and every other day after that. On what day did Andy go jogging for the tenth time?

25. 〔WRITE Math〕 The table shows the number of stickers on each page of Rosie's notebook. Write a rule to describe her pattern. **Explain** how you found her pattern.

Page Number	1	2	3	4	5	6
Number of Stickers	3	6	9	12	15	18

GO **Technology** Use *Online Assessment.*

Enrich • Find Common Factors
A Day at the Beach

Emily's class spent the day at Sea Glass Beach. They found 8 green and 12 blue pieces of sea glass at the beach. They want to put the same number of pieces in bags, with the same color in each bag. How many pieces can they put in each bag?

You can solve the problem by finding the **common factors** of 8 and 12.

List the factors of 8 and 12.

Factors of 8: 1, 2, 4, 8
Factors of 12: 1, 2, 3, 4, 6, 12

The **common factors** in both lists are 1, 2, and 4.

So, Emily's class can put their sea glass into bags with 1, 2, or 4 pieces in each bag.

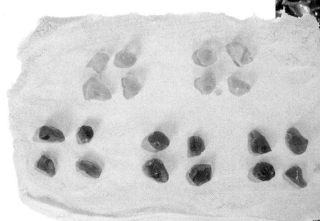

Sea Glass Beach near Fort Bragg, California, is famous for the amount of sea glass that can be found there. ▶

Break It Down

A List the common factors of 2 and 10.

2: 1, 2
10: 1, 2, 5, 10

The common factors are 1 and 2.

B List the common factors of 6 and 9.

6: 1, 2, 3, 6
9: 1, 3, 9

The common factors are 1 and 3.

Give It a Tumble

Write the common factors for each set of numbers.

1. 3 and 9
2. 8 and 10
3. 6 and 12
4. 5 and 10

5. Roy has 9 baseball cards and 12 football cards. He wants to arrange all of the cards in equal rows, and he wants each row to have the same type of card. How many cards can Roy put in each row?

6. **Challenge** Kara has 4 wooden beads, 8 metallic beads, and 12 glass beads. She wants to make necklaces with the same number of beads. She wants only one type of bead on each necklace. What is the greatest number of beads she can put on each necklace?

WRITE Math ▶ **Explain** how you can find the common factors of any two prime numbers.

Unit Review/Test
Chapters 10–12

Multiple Choice

1. Which number is both a multiple of 4 and a factor of 4? (NS 4.0, p. 288)

   A 1

   B 2

   C 4

   D 8

2. A pack of 52 cards is divided equally into 4 piles. How many cards are in each pile? (O—¬ NS 3.4, p. 244)

   A 13

   B 21

   C 23

   D 26

3. What is the hundreds digit of the quotient? (O—¬ NS 3.2, p. 258)

   $$5\overline{)952}$$

   A 1

   B 2

   C 3

   D 5

4. Ming has $99. He decides to spend an equal amount of money on music, books, and computer games. How much will he spend on music? (O—¬ NS 3.2, p. 248)

   A $3   **C** $102

   B $33   **D** $297

5. Which number is a factor of 10? (NS 4.0, p. 288)

   A 30

   B 20

   C 15

   D 5

6. Which pair of numbers completes the equation? (O—¬ NS 3.4, p. 246)

   $$\bigcirc \div \square = 10$$

   A 80 and 8

   B 2 and 12

   C 6 and 12

   D 8 and 11

7. Which statement is true? (NS 4.0, p. 288)

   A 1 is a factor of only odd numbers.

   B 1 is not a factor of any number.

   C 1 is a factor of only 0.

   D 1 is a factor of every number.

GO ONLINE **Technology** Use *Online Assessment.*

8. Mr. Rodrigues has 126 stickers for the students in his class. If there are 9 students in the class, how many stickers does each student receive?

(O⊓ NS 3.4, p. 270)

A 12

B 13

C 14

D 15

9. The number 1,423 is a prime number. Which number is a factor of 1,423?

(O⊓ NS 4.2, p. 292)

A 4

B 3

C 2

D 1

10. Neena has 97 cents. What is the greatest number of nickels she could have? (O⊓ NS 3.4, p. 248)

A 20

B 19

C 18

D 17

11. 108 ÷ 5 =   (O⊓ NS 3.2, p. 274)

A 21 r3

B 21

C 20 r3

D 19 r3

Short Response

12. Lynn needs 3 tablespoons of chocolate powder to make 1 cup of chocolate milk. There are 45 tablespoons of chocolate powder left in the box. How many cups of chocolate milk can Lynn make?

(O⊓ NS 3.4, p. 246)

13. Make arrays to find all the factors of 32.

(NS 4.0, p. 288)

14. The table shows the number of students in the summer basketball league.

Summer Basketball League	
Grade	Number of Students
Third	84
Fourth	91
Fifth	73

Each team has 9 students. How many complete teams of fourth graders are there? How many fourth graders will be left over? (O⊓ NS 3.4, p. 246)

Extended Response ⟦WRITE Math⟩

15. **Explain** how you know that 2 is a prime number. (O⊓ NS 4.2, p.292)

16. Dwayne has 43 books. If each storage box holds 9 books, how many boxes does he need to store all of his books? **Explain** your answer. (O⊓ NS 3.4, p. 268)

17. **Explain** how to find the prime factors for 16 by using a factor tree. (NS 4.1, p. 298)

Amazing Collectibles

COLLECTING CRATE LABELS

Millions of people have hobbies that involve collectibles. Some people collect items from their state, such as signs or license plates.

From the 1880s to the 1950s, many fruits and vegetables grown in California were packed in wooden crates with colorful labels. Today, many people collect those labels. More than 8,000 different labels have been used to advertise the fruits and vegetables.

Amazing Collections	
Type of Collection	**Number**
California orange crate labels	750
Colored vinyl records	1,180
Handmade walking canes	639
Model cars	3,711
Retired traffic signs	600

FACT·ACTIVITY

Use the Amazing Collections table to answer the questions.

❶ If the walking-cane collector took 9 years to collect the canes and collected the same number each year, how many were collected each year?

❷ If the California orange crate collector decides to sell 5 labels a month, in how many months will the whole collection be sold?

❸ If the collector of retired traffic signs collected 8 signs a year, how many years did it take to collect 600 signs?

❹ A collector finds 4 colored vinyl records per month. Estimate how many years it would take to collect the number of records listed in the table.

❺ **Pose a Problem** Write a division problem about the model car collection.

WHAT DO YOU COLLECT?

There is no limit to what you can collect! Many adult collectors began collecting when they were children. Kids all over the world collect objects that are interesting to them.

Bottle caps

Penguins

Stamps

FACT·ACTIVITY

Think of something you would like to collect. Answer the questions about planning your collection.

► What do you want to collect? How many items would you like to have in your collection?

► Where will you keep the items? Will you arrange them in equal groups, such as 8 items per shelf? Will there be items left over?

► Write division sentences to show how your collection might be arranged in equal groups. Try a few different ways to arrange them.

5 Data and Algebra

Math on Location

1

The National Agricultural Statistics Service collects, organizes, and represents data to help farmers decide how much of each crop should be grown each year.

2

Grains, such as barley, corn, and wheat, are grown in regions where the weather patterns and seasons are favorable for these crops.

3

Floating cranberries in a bog are moved to pumps that load them onto trucks. Data about production costs are also tracked to help farmers.

VOCABULARY POWER

TALK Math

What math do you see in the **Math on Location** photographs? How could data be organized to help farmers decide how much of each crop should be grown each year? What types of graphs could be used?

READ Math

REVIEW VOCABULARY You learned the words below when you learned how to organize and analyze data. How do these words relate to **Math on Location**?

bar graph a graph that uses bars to show data

data information collected about people or things

range the difference between the greatest number and the least number in a set of data

tally table a table that uses tally marks to record data

WRITE Math

Copy and complete the semantic map below. Use what you know about organizing and analyzing data to complete the semantic map.

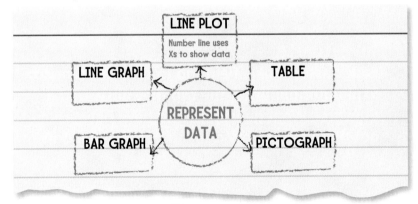

Technology
Multimedia Math Glossary link at
www.harcourtschool.com/hspmath

13 Collect, Organize, and Represent Data

The Big Idea Data can be collected in various formats and analyzed.

CALIFORNIA FAST FACT

The Exploratorium is a special museum in San Francisco. It has more than 650 hands-on science and art exhibits. More than 500,000 people visit it each year.

Investigate

Four classes took a field trip to the San Francisco Exploratorium. After the trip they answered a question. What question could have been asked to get these data? How can you describe the data?

Exploratorium Field Trip	
Exhibit	**Number of Students**
Bubble hoops	卌 卌 卌 卌 卌 II
Geyser	卌 IIII
Shadow box	卌 卌 卌 III
Spinning blackboard	卌 III
Remember that taste	卌 卌 II

Technology
Student pages are available in the Student eBook.

Check your understanding of important skills needed for success in Chapter 13.

▶ **Make and Use a Tally Table**

Use the data.

1. Use the data to make a tally table.

2. Which grade has the most students on the bus?

3. What is the total number of first- and second-grade students on the bus?

4. How many more third-grade than fourth-grade students are on the bus?

> The school bus from Tara's neighborhood carries 7 first–grade students, 12 second–grade students, 15 third–grade students, and 8 fourth–grade students.

▶ **Use Symbols in a Pictograph**

Use the pictograph.

5. How many cats are on the Horton farm?

6. How many more dogs than rabbits are there?

7. How many Guinea pigs and rabbits are there altogether?

8. How many pets are on the Horton farm?

Horton Farm Pets	
Dogs	🐾 🐾
Cats	🐾 🐾🐾
Guinea pigs	🐾 🐾
Rabbits	🐾
Key: Each 🐾 = 2 animals.	

VOCABULARY POWER

CHAPTER VOCABULARY

categorical data	outlier
frequency	range
interval	scale
line plot	survey
median	Venn
mode	diagram
numerical data	

WARM-UP WORDS

survey a method of gathering information to record data

categorical data data that can be sorted into different groups

frequency the number of times an event occurs

numerical data data that can be counted or measured

Collect and Organize Data

OBJECTIVE: Collect and organize data by conducting a survey and using a frequency table.

Learn

A **survey** is a method of gathering information.
Follow these rules to take a survey:

- Decide on a question about which you want to gather data.

- Ask each person the question only one time.

- Use a tally mark to record each person's response.

Max took a survey by asking his classmates the question "What is your favorite subject in school?" He recorded their responses in a tally table.

Favorite Subject Survey	
Subject	**Tally**
Reading	IIII
Math	IIII II
Science	IIII
Social Studies	IIII II

Since this set of data can be sorted into different groups, it is called **categorical data.** The groups in the table above are school subjects.

Quick Review

According to the tally table, who got the most votes?

Votes for Class President	
Student	**Tally**
Anna	IIII IIII
Dan	IIII II
Horatio	IIII III

Vocabulary

survey

categorical data

frequency

numerical data

HANDS ON

Activity Take a survey and record the results in a tally table.

Step 1

Write a question for your survey. Make the question clear and simple.
Decide on the response choices.

Organize your question and response choices in a table like the sample survey to the right.

Step 2

Survey your classmates.
- Be sure each classmate gives only one response.
- Use a tally mark to record each response.

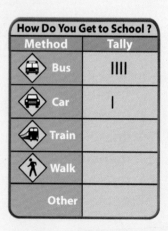

How Do You Get to School ?	
Method	**Tally**
Bus	IIII
Car	I
Train	
Walk	
Other	

• Why do you ask each person the question only one time?

SDAP 1.1 Formulate survey questions; systematically collect and represent data on a number line; and coordinate graphs, tables, and charts. *also* NS 3.0, SDAP 1.0, MR 2.3, MR 2.4, MR 3.2

Frequency Tables

A frequency table helps you organize the data from a tally table. The **frequency** is the number of times a response occurs. In a frequency table, numbers are used instead of tally marks.

Jenna asked her classmates to pick their favorite tool for drawing pictures. First, she made a tally table to show the results of her survey. Then Jenna showed the same data in a frequency table.

The table below shows numerical data. **Numerical data** are data that are counted or measured.

Favorite Drawing Tool	
Drawing Tool	Tally
Color Pencil	III
Crayon	IIII III
Marker	IIII II

Favorite Drawing Tool	
Drawing Tool	Frequency
Color Pencil	3
Crayon	8
Marker	7

Time It Takes to Write Your Name	
Time (in seconds)	Frequency
3	7
6	3
7	7
8	2

• How are numerical data different from categorical data?

Guided Practice

1. Copy and complete the frequency table with the following data: eggs, toast, cereal, cereal, eggs, eggs, cereal, cereal, cereal.

Favorite Breakfast Food			
Food	Eggs	Cereal	Toast
Frequency			

For 2–3, use Jenna's data in the Favorite Drawing Tool table above. Tell whether each statement is true or false. Explain.

2. More students chose markers than crayons.

✓ 3. More students chose markers than color pencils.

For 4–6, use the School Population frequency table.

4. How many students are in fourth grade?

5. How many more students are in the grade with the greatest number of students than in the grade with the least number?

✓ 6. If 2 sixth graders move away and 5 fifth graders enroll, how many students will the fifth and sixth grades have in all?

7. **TALK Math** Explain how you can use a tally table to make a frequency table.

School Population (Washington Elementary)	
Grade	Number of Students
K	45
1	42
2	54
3	58
4	41
5	55
6	50

Independent Practice and Problem Solving

For 8–10, use the Favorite Types of TV Show frequency table. Tell whether each statement is true or false. Explain.

8. More students chose comedies than mysteries as their favorite.

9. More students chose sports and comedy as their favorite than chose cartoons and mysteries.

10. Cartoons are the students' favorite choice to watch.

Students' Favorite Types of TV Show	
Type of Show	Votes
Comedy	8
Cartoons	9
Sports	7
Mysteries	6

For 11–14, use the Heights of Seedlings frequency table.

11. How many seedlings are 7 centimeters?

12. How many more seedlings are 10 centimeters than 9 centimeters?

13. What height are the least number of seedlings?

14. **Reasoning** When the seedlings reach 8 centimeters they can be transplanted. How many seedlings can be transplanted? **Explain** your answer.

Heights of Seedlings	
Height (in centimeters)	Frequency
7	2
8	3
9	6
10	8
11	4

Tell whether the data are numerical or categorical.

15. color of your eyes   16. test scores   17. favorite bird

Write a survey question and response choices. Survey your classmates. Record the responses in a frequency table. For 18–19, use the survey results to answer each question.

18. What conclusions can you make about the data?

19. How might the survey results change if you surveyed your teachers instead of your classmates?

For 20–23, use the Lessons for Wind Instruments bar graph.

20. Describe the data set used to make this graph.

21. How many more students take trumpet lessons than tuba lessons?

22. How many students are taking wind instrument lessons in all?

23. **Reasoning** Suppose 3 more students take flute lessons and 3 students stop taking tuba lessons. How will this change the graph?

24. Use a factor tree to find the prime factors of 40. (⊶ NS 4.2, p. 298)

25. Which of the following polygons always has exactly one right angle? (Grade 3 MG 2.4)

pentagon, square, right triangle, parallelogram

26. Test Prep How many people were surveyed about their favorite color?

Favorite Colors			
Color	Red	Blue	Yellow
Votes	6	4	5

A 4 **C** 6

B 5 **D** 15

27. What is the value of the expression below? (⊶ AF 1.2, p. 142)

$$(12 + 3) \times 4 - 3$$

28. Test Prep Patsy surveyed her friends about their favorite school subjects. She made a tally table to show her results.

Favorite Subject	
Subject	Number of Students
Science	|||
Math	~~||||~~ ~~||||~~ |||
English	~~||||~~ |||

How many students chose math?

A 3 **C** 13

B 8 **D** 15

 **Problem Solving and Reasoning**

LOGICAL REASONING Using the results of a survey is a good way to predict how people will respond to a decision. An *unbiased survey* is one where everyone has an equal chance of being asked to respond. A *biased survey* is one where some people are more likely to be asked than others.

The booster club raised $400 from a bake sale. The money will be used for either a new basketball hoop or costumes for a play. Three students did surveys to find out which item most students want.

Use the survey results to answer the questions.

1. Whose results are biased? Whose are unbiased? **Explain.**

2. What other group could be surveyed to obtain unbiased results?

Jared asked members of the drama club.

Which should the school buy?
Costumes ~~||||~~ ~~||||~~
Basketball hoop ||

Miko asked members of the basketball team.

Which should the school buy?
Costumes ~~||||~~
Basketball hoop ~~||||~~ ~~||||~~ ||

Sara asked the first 20 students who came to school on Monday.

Which should the school buy?
Costumes ~~||||~~ ~~||||~~ |||
Basketball hoop ~~||||~~ ||

Make and Interpret Venn Diagrams

OBJECTIVE: Interpret and construct Venn diagrams to sort and describe data.

Quick Review

Carl's scores on his math tests are 75, 80, 85, 97, 86, 99, 89, 79, 86, and 90. Sort and classify his scores by letter grades. Use A for 90 to 100, B for 80 to 89, and C for 70 to 79.

Vocabulary

Venn diagram

Learn

You can use Venn diagrams to sort information. A **Venn diagram** shows relationships among sets of things.

PROBLEM Every state has its own flag. Look at the state flags shown. What is one way these flags can be sorted?

Example Make a Venn diagram.

Step 1

Decide how you will sort the flags. Some of the flags have symbols of **animals**, some have symbols of **people**, and some have **both**.

Step 2

Draw two overlapping ovals. Label each section with the description of each set. The data inside the area where the sets overlap are described by both labels.

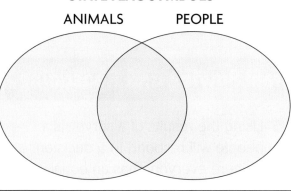

STATE FLAG SYMBOLS

ANIMALS   PEOPLE

Step 3

Sort the state flag names.

STATE FLAG SYMBOLS

ANIMALS   PEOPLE

Pennsylvania   New York   Massachusetts
Illinois   New Jersey
                Michigan

Write the states of the flags that have only animals in the section of the diagram labeled ANIMALS and the states that have only people in the section labeled PEOPLE. Write the states that have both animals and people in the section where the sets overlap.

So, one way to sort these flags is by their symbols.

• How can you check that your answer is correct?

Pennsylvania

New York

Illinois

Massachusetts

New Jersey

Michigan

SDAP 1.0 Students organize, represent, and interpret numerical and categorical data and clearly communicate their findings. *also* **SDAP 1.1, MR 2.3, MR 2.4, MR 3.2**

Guided Practice

Copy the Venn diagrams. Place the numbers where they belong.

1.
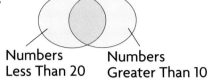
Numbers Less Than 20   Numbers Greater Than 10

2, 14, 33, 19, 5, 79, 21, 50, 6

2.
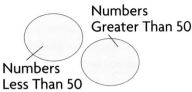
Numbers Greater Than 50

Numbers Less Than 50

1, 22, 53, 89, 49, 13, 57, 4, 32

3.
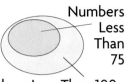
Numbers Less Than 75

Numbers Less Than 100

99, 24, 7, 63, 86, 24, 70, 12, 31

For 4–5, use the Venn diagram.

✓ **4.** What label should you use for Section C?

✓ **5.** Why are the numbers 6 and 12 sorted in the Section B of the diagram?

6. [TALK Math] **Explain** how a Venn diagram can help you understand relationships.

A Multiples of 2   B ___?___   C ___?___

2 4
8
14 10
6
12
3 9
15

Independent Practice and Problem Solving

For 7–8, use the Venn diagram.

7. What label can you use for Section B?

8. **Reasoning** Can there be a section for numbers that fit both A and B? Why or why not?

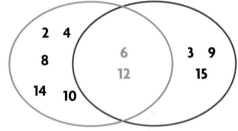
A Odd   B ___?___

5 7
9

4 12
18

For 9–10, use the table.

9. Copy and complete the table by surveying 10 classmates. Show the results in a Venn diagram.

10. [WRITE Math] **Explain** whether to use a Venn diagram with 2 overlapping ovals or 2 separate ovals for the table.

Toppings Liked on Pizza

Topping	Names of Students
Pepperoni Only	?
Sausage Only	?
Pepperoni and Sausage	?

Achieving the Standards

11. $18 \div 2 =$ (⊶ NS 3.0, p. 116)

12. How many people voted for bird if 22 people voted in all? (SDAP 1.0, p. 320)

Favorite Animal

Animal	Cat	Dog	Horse	Bird
Votes	6	4	5	■

13. What type of triangle has 3 equal sides?
(Grade 3 ⊶ MG 2.2)

14. **Test Prep** Look at the Venn diagram for Problems 7–8. Which number belongs in Section B?

A 30   B 27   C 33   D 55

Find Mode and Median

OBJECTIVE: Find the mode and median of a set of data.

Quick Review

1. 56 ÷ 8   2. 24 ÷ 3
3. 45 ÷ 9   4. 28 ÷ 7
5. 35 ÷ 5

Vocabulary

median   mode

Learn

The **median** is the middle number in an ordered set of data.

PROBLEM The table shows the record high temperatures in California for August through February. What is the median temperature?

Extreme High Temperatures in California							
Month	August	September	October	November	December	January	February
Temperature (in °F)	127	126	117	105	100	97	100

ONE WAY Use a model to find the median.

Materials ■ index cards

Step 1	
Write the 7 temperatures on index cards.	127 100 126 117 97 100 105

Step 2	
Arrange the cards from least to greatest.	97 100 100 105 117 126 127

Step 3	
Remove one card from each end. Keep doing this, moving toward the middle until only one number is left. This number is the median, or middle number.	105 ← Middle number 97 100 100 117 127 126

So, the median temperature is 105°F.

ERROR ALERT

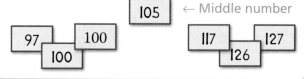

The frequency tells you how many times to list each number of points scored.

ANOTHER WAY Use paper and pencil to find the median.

Points Scored by Basketball Starters					
Points	4	6	8	10	12
Frequency	3	2	3	1	1

Step 1	**Step 2**	**Step 3**
Order the data from least to greatest. Cross out values on each end. 4̶, 4̶, 4̶, 6̶, 6, 8, 8̶, 8̶, 1̶0̶, 1̶2̶	There is an even number of data. Add the two middle numbers. 6 + 8 = 14	Divide the sum by 2. 14 ÷ 2 = 7

So, the median of the data is 7 points.

SDAP 1.2 Identify the mode(s) for sets of categorical data and the mode(s), median, and any apparent outliers for numerical data sets. *also* SDAP 1.0, SDAP 1.1, MR 2.3, MR 2.4, MR 3.2

Find the Mode

The **mode** is the number or item that occurs most often.

Much of California's rainfall occurs between November and March. The table shows the number of inches of rain over five months at the Mount Hamilton water station. What is the mode for the data?

| Rainfall to the Nearest Inch at Mount Hamilton, California ||
Month	Rain (in inches)
November 2004	2
December 2004	7
January 2005	5
February 2005	6
March 2005	6

Activity 2

Materials ■ index cards

Find the mode.

Write the data on index cards. Sort the cards by numbers. Find the number that occurs most often. This number is the mode. There may be more than one mode. If no number is repeated, there is no mode.

| 2 | 7 | 5 | 6 |
| 6 |

So, the mode for the data is 6 inches.

Examples Find the mode using frequency tables.

A Numerical Data

Ages of Children in Cooking Club					
Age	7	8	9	10	11	12
Frequency	1	3	4	3	0	4

Find the data that have the greatest frequency.

For these data, there are 2 modes. Ages 9 and 12 both have the greatest frequency, 4.

So, the modes are 9 and 12.

B Categorical Data

winter, fall, fall, spring, summer, winter, fall, summer, summer, fall, spring, summer, winter, summer, fall, fall

Organize the data in a table to find the mode.

FAVORITE SEASON			
Season	Winter	Spring	Summer	Fall
Frequency	3	2	5	6

So, the mode is fall.

- **What if** one more person chose summer as a favorite season in Example B? What would the mode be?

- What is the median age of the children in Example A?

Guided Practice

1. Tara used index cards to find the median for the number of students at each of 6 lunch tables. Order the numbers from least to greatest. What is the median number of students at each table?

| 6 | 4 | 5 |
| 5 | 4 | 6 |

Find the median and mode.

2.

Snowfall						
Month	Nov	Dec	Jan	Feb	Mar	Apr
Number of Inches	6	12	10	8	4	1

3.

Art Club				
Age	8	9	10	12
Frequency	3	4	2	2

✔ 4.

Books Read				
Month	Jan	Feb	Mar	Apr
Books	6	5	4	5

✔ 5.

Rainfall						
Month	Apr	May	Jun	Jul	Aug	Sep
Number of Inches	10	6	8	6	4	9

6. **TALK Math** **Explain** the difference between the median and mode of a set of data.

Independent Practice (and Problem Solving

Find the median and mode.

7.

Computers in Each Computer Lab					
Lab	A	B	C	D	E
Computers	6	8	4	6	10

8.

Goals Scored per Game				
Goals	1	2	3	4
Frequency	3	4	1	0

9.

Plants Sold				
Plant	Tomato	Pepper	Bean	Cucumber
Number	1	2	5	4

10.

Miles Jogged					
Week	1	2	3	4	5
Number of Miles	3	6	5	8	8

11. Alana kept a record of her math quiz scores: 8, 10, 10, 9, 8, 8, 9. Find the median and the mode of her quiz scores.

For 12–13, use the graph.

12. What is the median number of animals adopted on Monday?

13. How many animals were adopted in all?

14. A class voted on their favorite snacks. Muffins received 12 votes, peanuts received 12 votes, and fruit received 10 votes. What is the mode for these data?

15. ⭐**Algebra** The median of the set of data 6, 8, 8, *b*, 10, and 12 is 9. What is the missing number from the data?

16. **WRITE Math** **What's the Question?** The data listed are the ages of the players on the youth basketball team: 7, 6, 7, 8, 6, 8, 8, 6, and 8. The answer is 8.

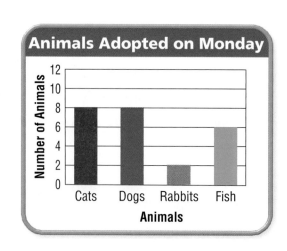

17. Make a frequency table for the following data. (SDAP 1.1, p. 320)

Favorite Kind of Fruit Juice

Fruit Juice	Tally
Apple	卌 ||
Orange	卌
Pineapple	卌 卌

18. Copy the Venn diagram. Place the numbers where they belong. (SDAP 1.1, p. 324)

Numbers Less than 30

Numbers Greater than 10

45, 21, 7, 4, 3, 27, 32, 15

19. What is the greatest value in the data set 32, 19, 28, 23, 30, and 28? (⊶ NS 1.2, p. 16)

20. **Test Prep** What is the median of the following set of test scores?

75, 86, 72, 93, 85, 97, 80, 93, 84

A 72   **C** 93

B 85   **D** 97

21. **Test Prep** Look back at the *Animals Adopted on Monday* graph on page 328 for Problems 12–13. What would the mode be if one more dog was sold?

A 8   **C** 10

B 9   **D** no mode

MATH POWER   Problem Solving and Reasoning

LOGICAL REASONING You can construct a data set with a given median and mode.

A data set has five numbers. The median is 6, and the mode is 8. What are five possible numbers in the data set?

Step 1	Step 2	Step 3
The median is the middle number. Write the median.	The next two numbers must be the mode, 8.	Choose two different numbers less than 6 to complete the data.
□, □, 6, □, □ ↑ median	□, □, 6, 8, 8 ↑ ↑ mode	3, 5, 6, 8, 8 You could have used 1, 2, or 4.

So, five possible numbers are 3, 5, 6, 8, and 8.

Find possible numbers for each set of data.

1. A data set has seven numbers. The median is 24. The mode is 21.

2. A data set has six numbers. The median is 5, and the mode is 7.

LESSON 4 Read Line Plots

OBJECTIVE: Use line plots to read and organize data.

Learn

PROBLEM The table below shows the shuttle missions that NASA launched between 1998 and 2002. During this period, in how many years did NASA launch 5 or more shuttles?

You can use a line plot to solve the problem. A **line plot** is a graph that shows the frequency of data along a number line.

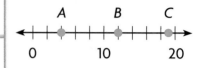

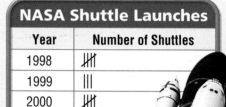
Activity

Materials ■ grid paper

Step 1	Step 2
Use grid paper to draw a number line starting from the least value of data to the greatest. 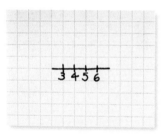	Plot an X above the number line for each piece of data. Write a title for the line plot. 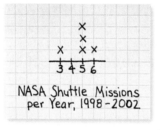

NASA Shuttle Launches

Year	Number of Shuttles
1998	₩
1999				
2000	₩
2001	₩|
2002	₩

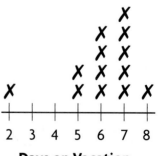

▶ NASA Shuttle

So, in 4 different years NASA launched 5 or more shuttles per year.

The **range** is the difference between the greatest and least values in a set of data.

In one year there were 3 shuttle missions, and in one year there were 6 shuttle missions. So, the range for these data is 6 − 3, or 3.

Look at the line plot of the number of days spent on vacation. Most of the data form a cluster, or group, from 5 through 8. The value 2 is an outlier. An **outlier** is a value separated from the rest of the data.

Days on Vacation

• What does the outlier suggest about vacations that last 2 days?

SDAP 1.1 Formulate survey questions; systematically collect and represent data on a number line; and coordinate graphs, tables, and charts. *also* SDAP 1.0, SDAP 1.2, MR 2.3, MR 2.4, MR 3.2

1. Make a line plot to show the number of models owned by students in Space Club. Start by ordering the data. Then draw X's above the numbers on a number line to show the data.

Number of Rocket Models:
2, 7, 3, 5, 1, 9, 7, 3, 2, 6, 4, 2, 1, 7, 8.

For 2–5, use the Number of Hours line plot.

2. The line plot shows the results of a tourist survey. How many people surveyed spent more than 2 hours visiting NASA?

☑3. What is the range of the hours spent visiting?

☑4. For how long did most tourists visit NASA? How can you tell?

5. **TALK Math** Explain what the outlier in these data shows.

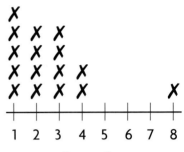

Numbers of Hours

For 6–8, use the Dollars Spent line plot.

6. The line plot shows how many souvenirs Mimi bought at each price. How much money did Mimi spend on souvenirs in all?

7. Find the median of the dollars spent on souvenirs.

8. **Reasoning** Explain why there is no outlier in these data.

Dollars Spent

For 9–10, use the Tourist Photo Survey data.

9. Make a tally table and line plot to show the data.

10. **WRITE Math** Explain how to find the range of the data.

Tourist Photo Survey

Question: How many pictures did you take while at Kennedy Space Center Visitor Complex?

Responses: 10, 12, 12, 8, 4, 12, 10, 13, 15, 14, 14, 15, 10, 11, 13, 15, 10, 11, 10

Achieving the Standards

11. Order the numbers from least to greatest. (O┳ NS 1.2, p. 16)

  3,310; 3,204; 3,104; 3,014

12. What is the number 1,012,060 in word form? (O┳ NS 1.1, p.10)

13. The length of a square frame is 8 inches. What is the perimeter? (Grade 3 MG 1.3)

14. **Test Prep** What is the mode for the data in the Dollars Spent line plot?

  A 1   **C** 3

  B 2   **D** 4

Technology
Use Harcourt Mega Math, The Number Games, *Arachnagraph*, Levels E, F.

Extra Practice on page 336, Set D

5 Choose a Reasonable Scale

OBJECTIVE: Choose a reasonable scale and interval for a set of data.

Quick Review

Make a frequency table for the following survey results.

Question: What is your favorite pet?

Responses: dog, dog, dog, cat, bird, dog, cat, hamster, cat, dog, hamster, dog, bird

Learn

You can use different graphs to compare the same data.

A **scale** of a graph is a series of numbers placed at fixed, or equal, distances. The highest value on the scale should be greater than the greatest value of the data.

The **interval** of a graph is the difference between one number and the next on the scale of a graph.

Vocabulary

scale   interval

Graph A

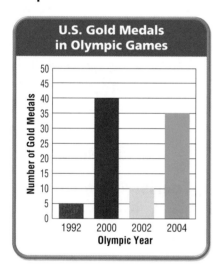

Graph B

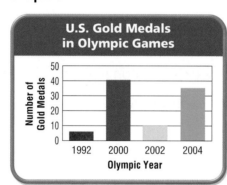

Math Idea

The interval should be small enough to show the data clearly, but large enough to fit all the data on the graph.

• Which graph makes it easier to compare the data? Why?

Guided Practice

1. Would you use an interval of 1 to show the data in Graph A? **Explain.**

For 2–4, choose 5, 10, or 100 as the most reasonable interval for each set of data. Explain your choice.

2. 25, 30, 20, 10, 15   ✓3. 200, 350, 100, 250, 500   ✓4. 25, 79, 50, 45, 90

5. **TALK Math** **Explain** how to decide which scale to use in graphs for the data in Problems 2, 3, and 4.

332

SDAP 1.0 Students organize, represent, and interpret numerical and categorical data and clearly communicate their findings. *also* **SDAP 1.1, SDAP 1.3, MR 2.3, MR 2.4, MR 3.2**

For 6–9, choose 5, 10, or 100 as the most reasonable interval for each set of data. Explain your choice.

6. 45, 79, 30, 80, 21

7. 4, 16, 6, 15, 30

8. 80, 490, 920, 550, 150

9. 92, 70, 12, 45, 60

Favorite Winter Olympic Events

For 10–11, use the Favorite Winter Olympic Events graph.

10. What is a better interval to use to show these data?

11. **Reasoning** Why wouldn't 1 and 100 be reasonable intervals to use for the data shown in the graph?

For 12–14, use the Favorite Summer Olympic Events graph.

12. What are the scale and interval used in the graph?

13. About how many more votes did gymnastics get than basketball and diving combined?

14. **Pose a Problem** Use the information in the graph to write a problem. Explain how to find the answer to your problem.

15. ☰**FAST FACT** The Winter Olympic Games were held in Lake Placid, New York, in 1932. They were held in Lake Placid again in 1980. How many years later was this?

16. ▐WRITE Math▶ **What's the Question?** Haley made a graph for the data in a problem. The answer is 0–100.

Favorite Summer Olympic Events

17. Which number is greater: 23,212 or 23,221? (○┑ NS 1.2, p. 12)

18. What is the value of the expression below? (○┑ AF 1.2, p. 146)

$$(12 + 3) - (6 \times 2)$$

19. Allan, Tim, and Tara are in the band. Grace and Paul are in the chorus. Sophie is in the band and the chorus. Draw a Venn diagram to show this information.

(SDAP 1.1, p. 324)

20. **Test Prep** What is the scale for the graph below?

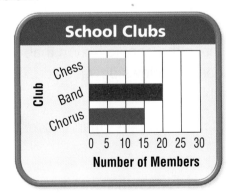

School Clubs

A 0–5

C 0–20

B 0–10

D 0–30

Problem Solving Workshop
Skill: Make Generalizations

OBJECTIVE: Solve problems by using the skill *make generalizations*.

Use the Skill

PROBLEM A heart rate is the number of times the heart beats per minute. Grace has a resting heart rate of 85 beats per minute. Sara's resting heart rate is 77 beats per minute. Use the bar graph to find who is probably older, Grace or Sara.

A **generalization** is a conclusion based on given or known information. To help make a generalization, you can summarize data.

Identify the information in the bar graph.

Look at the graph. Write a paragraph identifying the known information.

> The heart rate at rest for newborns is up to 140 beats per minute. For children, it is about 90 beats per minute. For adult females, it is about 80 beats per minute. For adult males, it is about 75 beats per minute. For adults over 65, it is about 65 beats per minute.

Look for patterns or connections in the information.

• The age groups go from younger to older.
• The beats per minute decrease, or go from faster to slower.

Make a generalization and use it to make a prediction or draw a conclusion.

You can make the generalization that, as people get older, their resting heart rate slows down. Since $77 < 85$, Sara's heart rate is slower than Grace's.

So, Sara is probably older than Grace.

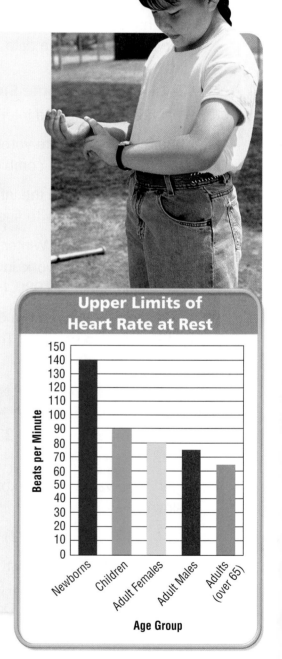

Think and Discuss
Make a generalization. Then solve the problem.

a. Jack and Mary are both 30 years old. Who probably has a faster heart rate, Jack or Mary?

SDAP 1.0 Students organize, represent, and interpret numerical and categorical data and clearly communicate their findings. *also* SDAP 1.3, MR 2.0, MR 2.3, MR 2.4, MR 3.0, MR 3.1, MR 3.2, MR 3.3

For 1–3, use the table. Make a generalization. Then solve the problem.

1. When you exercise, your heart beats faster. The table shows maximum target heart rates for different ages. Copy and complete the chart with the data from the graph.

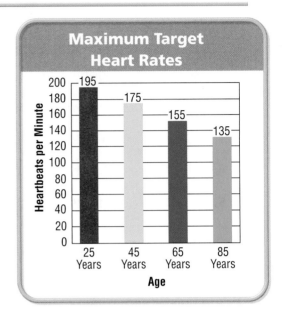

Maximum Target Heart Rates

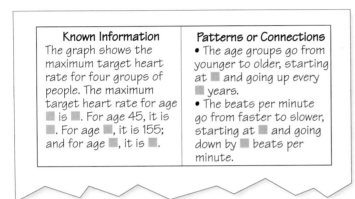

Known Information	Patterns or Connections
The graph shows the maximum target heart rate for four groups of people. The maximum target heart rate for age ▨ is ▨. For age 45, it is ▨. For age ▨, it is 155; and for age ▨, it is ▨.	• The age groups go from younger to older, starting at ▨ and going up every ▨ years. • The beats per minute go from faster to slower, starting at ▨ and going down by ▨ beats per minute.

2. What might the target heart rate be for age 35?

3. Miyu is 25 years old. She does aerobics for a half hour and then measures her heart rate. If it is 180 beats per minute, should Miyu slow her exercising, or can she continue at the same pace? **Explain** your answer.

Mixed Applications

USE DATA For 4–6, use the table.

4. How many more calories does an 11-year-old male need than a 9-year-old female?

5. Beth and Travis are 12-year-old twins. Helena is 8 years old, and her sister Marta is 10 years old. List the names of the children in order from the one who needs the least calories to the one who needs the greatest calories. **Explain.**

6. Based on the data in the table, about how many calories might a 15-year-old male need?

7. **Algebra** Peter's dog weighs 24 pounds. His cat weighs n pounds. If his dog weighs 3 times as much as his cat, what is n?

8. **WRITE Math** On a hot, sunny day, bamboo can grow about an inch an hour. Ben's bamboo was 3 inches tall when he went to school. Now it is 11 inches tall. How can you use a generalization to decide about how long Ben was gone?

Calories Needed by Active Children

Age	Male	Female
8	2,000	1,800
9	2,000	1,800
10	2,200	2,000
11	2,200	2,000
12	2,400	2,200
13	2,400	2,200

 **Extra Practice**

Set A Use the Favorite Colors frequency table. (pp. 320–323)

1. How many students said orange was their favorite color?

2. Which two colors were chosen by the same number of students?

3. How many more students chose blue than orange?

4. Which color was chosen most often?

5. How many students were surveyed?

Favorite Colors	
Color	**Number of Students**
Blue	36
Green	28
Orange	11
Purple	41
Red	28

Set B Use the Venn diagram. (pp. 324–325)

1. List the fourth-grade students who are chorus members.

2. List the fourth-grade students who are band members.

3. Why are some of the students' names in the middle section of the diagram?

Fourth-Grade Musicians

Chorus Members   Band Members

Toshi   Lui   Taylor
Alice   Rosa
Jordan   Anton
Marion
Leesa

Set C Find the median and mode. (pp. 326–327)

1.
Neighborhood Pets				
Family	Walker	Chen	Damiano	Smith
Number of Pets	1	3	9	3

2.
Hours of Sleep Per Night					
Student	Andrew	Sheryl	Max	Shameka	Doria
Number of Hours	11	11	8	9	11

Set D Use the line plot. (pp. 330–331)

1. How many students have 4 letters in their first name?

2. How many more students have 7 letters in their first name than have 5 letters in their first name?

3. How many students were surveyed in all?

Student First Names

```
                        X
              X         X
              X   X     X
              X   X  X  X
          X   X   X  X  X  X
      X   X   X   X  X  X  X
    +---+---+---+--+--+--+--+--+--+
    1   2   3   4  5  6  7  8  9
```

Number of Letters

Set E Choose 5, 10, or 100 as the most reasonable interval for each set of data. Explain your choice. (pp. 332–333)

1. 201, 450, 550, 600, 799

2. 19, 25, 15, 31, 20

3. 51, 20, 28, 90, 60

4. 94, 25, 70, 49

5. 300, 199, 420, 690

6. 9, 14, 30, 15, 45

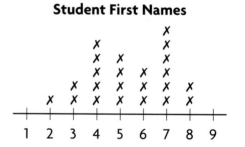 **Technology**
Use Harcourt Mega Math, The Number
Games, *ArachnaGraph,* Levels E, F.

Sort It Out

On Your Mark!
2 players

Get Set!
- Sorting cards
- Number cards (1–50)

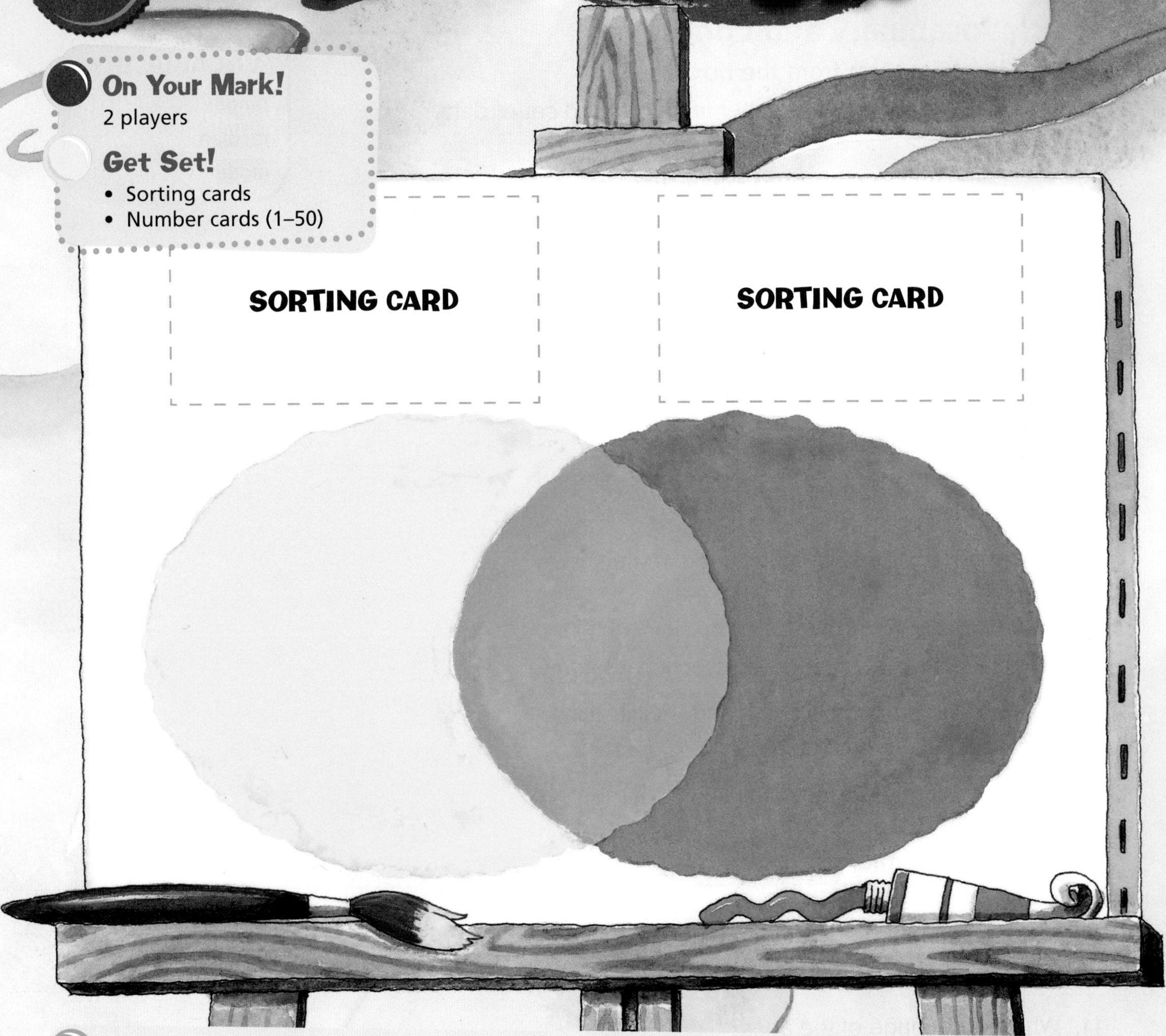

SORTING CARD

SORTING CARD

Go!

- Without looking, choose two sorting cards. Place each card above the Venn diagram.

- Mix up the number cards. Place them facedown in a stack. Decide who will play first, and take turns.

- Turn over the top number card. Place it in the correct circle of the Venn diagram. If it belongs to more than one circle, place it in the section that overlaps. If it does not belong, place it outside the circles.

- When all the number cards have been placed, count your cards in the center section. Whoever has more cards wins.

Chapter 13 Review/Test

Check Vocabulary and Concepts

Choose the best term from the box.

1. The __?__ is the middle number in an ordered set of data.
(SDAP 1.2, p. 326)

2. The __?__ is the difference between the greatest and the least values of a set of data. (SDAP 1.1, p. 330)

Check Skills

For 3–5, use the Favorite Music frequency table.

(SDAP 1.1, pp. 320–323)

3. How many students prefer rhythm and blues over classical music?

4. Which type of music is the most popular among the students surveyed?

5. How many students were included in the survey?

Favorite Music	
Type of Music	Number of Students
Rock	23
Classical	7
Jazz	11
Hip-Hop	12
Rhythm and Blues	17

For 6–8, use the Venn diagram. (SDAP 1.0, pp. 324–325)

6. What labels should you use for sections B and C?

7. Why are the numbers 12, 24, and 36 listed in section B of the Venn diagram?

8. In which section would you write the number 40?

Multiples of 4   **B**   **C**

28 8   16   12   18   30
    4   24 36   6   42
20

For 9–11, use the table.

(SDAP 1.2, pp. 362–329, SDAP 1.1, pp. 330–331)

9. Make a line plot of the team members' ages.

10. Find the median and mode of the ages.

11. What is the range of the ages?

Gymnastics Team							
Age	8	9	10	11	12	13	14
Frequency	5	8	8	7	5	3	4

Check Problem Solving

Solve. (SDAP 1.0, MR 2.3, pp. 334–335)

12. Use the *Gymnastics Team* table to make a generalization about the ages of the team members.

13. What interval would you choose if you were making a bar graph using the data from the *Favorite Music* survey? Why?

14. **Explain** how you know that all multiples of 12 are both multiples of 4 and multiples of 6.

15. **WRITE Math** Write a set of data that has the same median and mode.

GO ONLINE **Technology** Use *Online Assessment.*

Enrich • Glyphs
Signs and Symbols

Glyphs are a way of using pictures or symbols to represent data. At the right are two glyphs that you may have seen. The glyph on the left with the H tells you how to get to a hospital. The other glyph uses a picture of students to tell you that a school is near.

Glyphs can also tell a story with data. Just writing your name can reveal some information about you.

Students used these tables to show how to make their own personal glyphs. This table shows the color to use to show how you get to school most days.

Common glyphs

Hospital

School

If you	walk	take a bus	take a car	ride a bicycle
Write your name in	blue	red	black	green

This table shows how to write your name to show the number of brothers and sisters you have.

If you	0	1	2	3 or more
Write your name	printed in capital letters	printed in all lowercase letters	printed with the first letter capital and the others lowercase	in cursive

Examples

A Jeremy walks to school and has 2 brothers and/or sisters.

Jeremy

B Anna rides a bus and has no brothers or sisters.

ANNA

Try It

1. Use the tables above to create your own personal glyph on an index card.

2. **Challenge** What do you know about a student who uses a black marker to write her name in all lowercase letters?

WRITE Math **Explain** how you could make a glyph for a student who rides his bike to school and has 4 brothers.

Number Sense

1. The Figueroa at Wilshire in Los Angeles was completed in 1989. In 2005, the building was sold for three hundred fifty-six million, seven hundred thousand dollars. What is this number in standard form? (O⊓ NS 1.1)

   A 356,700,000   **C** 3,567,000

   B 300,056,700   **D** 356,700

Test Tip **Decide on a plan.**

See Item 2. Think about what the problem is asking you to do. You know the number of cookies in a batch. You want to know how many are in 28 batches. You need to multiply.

2. A bakery makes 28 batches of cookies per day. If there are 36 cookies in each batch, how many cookies does the bakery make each day? (O⊓ NS 3.3)

   A 64   **C** 350

   B 90   **D** 1,008

3. $6,785 - 3,409 =$ (O⊓ NS 3.1)

   A 3,384   **C** 3,374

   B 3,376   **D** 3,276

4. **WRITE Math** **Explain** why 2 is the only even prime number. (O⊓ NS 4.2)

Algebra and Functions

5. If $m + 8 = n + 8$, which of the following statements is true? (O⊓ AF 2.1)

   A $m = n$

   B $m < n$

   C $m + 8 < n$

   D $n + 8 = m$

6. What is the value of the expression if $g = 5$? (O⊓ AF 1.2)

   $$13 - (g + 2)$$

   A 10

   B 7

   C 6

   D 4

7. Look at the equation below. (O⊓ AF 1.5)

   $$\square = \triangle + 6$$

   If $\square = 8$, what is $\triangle$?

   A 2

   B 8

   C 14

   D 48

8. **WRITE Math** **Explain** how you know that the value of d is the same in both equations. (O⊓ AF 2.2)

Statistics, Data Analysis, and Probability

9. What is the mode of this data set? (SDAP 1.2)

$$3, 3, 3, 6, 6, 7, 8$$

A 8   **C** 6

B 7   **D** 3

10. Use the line plot below. How many baseball team members have at least 5 caps? (SDAP 1.3)

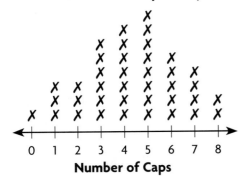

Baseball Team Cap Survey

Number of Caps

A 8   **C** 17

B 13   **D** 19

11. Gloria surveyed the fourth-grade students about their favorite subject. She wants to make a bar graph to show her results. The data values range from 19 to 35. What is the most reasonable interval for Gloria to use for her bar graph? (SDAP 1.1)

A 1   **C** 10

B 5   **D** 50

12. **WRITE Math** **Explain** how to find the median of a set of data if there is an even number of values. (SDAP 1.2)

Measurement and Geometry

13. What is the area of the figure on the grid? (Grade 3 O▬ MG 1.2)

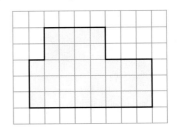

A 32 square units

B 34 square units

C 36 square units

D 40 square units

14. Which figure is a hexagon? (Grade 3 O▬ MG 2.1)

A

B

C

D

15. **WRITE Math** **Explain** how a rectangle is different from a square. (Grade 3 O▬ MG 2.3)

14 Interpret and Graph Data

The Big Idea Data can be analyzed and displayed in various graphical formats.

CALIFORNIA FAST FACT

From May 1 to November 1, no more than 100 people are allowed to visit Mount Whitney during the day. No more than 60 people may visit overnight.

Investigate

The table shows some of the mountains in California. Mount Whitney is the tallest mountain in the 48 states south of Canada. How can you show the data another way? Show the data your way.

Mountains in California

Mountain	Height (in feet)
Mount Diablo	3,849
Mount Lassen	10,457
Mount Shasta	14,163
Mount Tamalpais	2,571
Mount Whitney	14,494

GO ONLINE

Technology
Student pages are available in the Student eBook.

Show What You Know

Check your understanding of important skills needed for success in Chapter 14.

▶ **Classify Data**

Tell whether the data are categorical or numerical.

1. hours worked
2. hair colors
3. plant heights

▶ **Parts of a Graph**

Use the bar graph.

4. What is the title of this graph?
5. What interval is used for the vertical scale?
6. What label would you place at the bottom?
7. What is the label for the vertical scale?

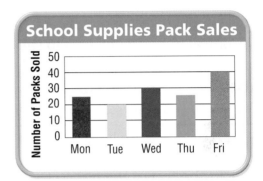

▶ **Choose a Reasonable Interval**

Choose 5, 10, or 100 as the most reasonable interval for each set of data. Explain your choice.

8. 10, 15, 22, 35, 24
9. 10, 27, 30, 75, 90
10. 115, 350, 480, 525, 660
11. 15, 32, 47, 80, 100

VOCABULARY POWER

CHAPTER VOCABULARY

bar graph
circle graph
data
double-bar
   graph
grid
interval
line graph

median
mode
ordered pair
pictograph
range
scale
trend

WARM-UP WORDS

bar graph a graph that uses bars to show data

double-bar graph a graph used to compare similar types of data

circle graph a graph in the shape of a circle that shows data as a whole made up of different parts

Interpret Bar Graphs

OBJECTIVE: Read and interpret bar graphs.

Learn

PROBLEM NASA has a school for astronauts. The bar graph shows how many students were in each class.

Use a **bar graph** to compare categorical data, or data about different groups. A bar graph can use vertical or horizontal bars to show data.

Example 1 Use a vertical bar graph.

How many students were in the 2004 class?

> Find the bar for the year 2004.
>
> Follow the top of the bar to the left to the scale. The number on the scale that matches the bar is 14.

So, the 2004 class had 14 students.

• How could you find how many students were in the 2000 class?

Example 2 Use a horizontal bar graph.

What is the range of the number of students in the classes?

> Find the greatest bar. Follow the end of the bar down to the scale.
>
> The greatest number of students is 25.
>
> Find the least bar. Follow the end of the bar down to the scale.
>
> The least number of students is 14.
>
> Subtract the least value from the greatest value to get the range.
>
> 25 − 14 = 11

So, the range of the number of students is 11.

• Write the data shown in the bar graph from least to greatest.

scale → **title**

NASA Astronaut Classes

Number of Students (26, 24, 22, 20, 18, 16, 14, 12, 10, 8, 6, 4, 2, 0)

1998 2000 2004

labels → **Year**

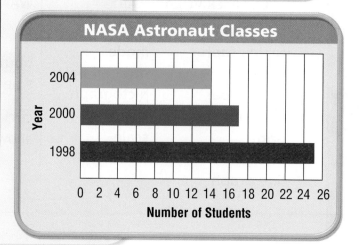

NASA Astronaut Classes

Year: 2004, 2000, 1998

0 2 4 6 8 10 12 14 16 18 20 22 24 26
Number of Students

SDAP 1.3 Interpret one- and two-variable data graphs to answer questions about a situation. *also* **SDAP 1.0, MR 2.3, MR 2.4, MR 3.2**

Guided Practice

For 1–4, use the Camp Choices graph.

1. Which camp do most students prefer? Find the tallest bar. This bar has the greatest value. Follow the bar to the left to find the value.

✓ 2. Which camp was chosen by the fewest students?

✓ 3. How many students chose space camp?

4. **TALK Math** How many more students chose space camp than sports camp? **Explain.**

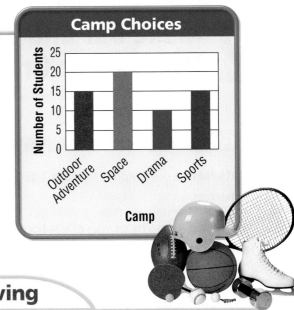

Camp Choices

Independent Practice and Problem Solving

For 5–8, use the Camp Choices bar graph above.

5. What is the range of votes for different camps?

6. Which two camps were chosen by the same number of students?

7. What interval is used on the scale?

8. What is the mode of the data?

For 9–11, use the Moons graph.

9. What is the median number of moons for the planets shown?

10. Which planet has more moons than Mars but fewer than Uranus?

11. **WRITE Math** **Sense or Nonsense** Jorge says that the interval for this bar graph is 34. Is Jorge correct? **Explain.**

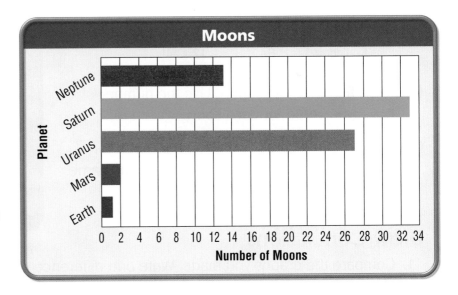

Moons

Achieving the Standards

12. What is $1,000,000 + 20,000 + 5$ in standard form? (○━ NS 1.1, p. 10)

13. $61 \times 55 =$ (○━ NS 3.2, p. 220)

14. Look at the Moons graph above. Why would it not make sense to use an interval of 20? (SDAP 1.0, p. 332)

15. **Test Prep** Look at the Moons graph above. Which planet has 1 more than 2 times as many moons as Neptune?

   A Uranus   **c** Saturn

   B Mars   **D** Earth

2 Make Bar and Double-Bar Graphs

OBJECTIVE: Make and interpret bar graphs and double-bar graphs.

Investigate

Materials ■ bar-graph patterns ■ 2 different-color crayons or markers

Mrs. Lyon's fourth grade class took a survey of their favorite sports. Use the data in the table to make two bar graphs.

A Make a bar graph of the boys' favorite sports to watch. Decide on a title, labels, and a scale for the graph.

Favorite Sports to Watch		
Sport	**Boys**	**Girls**
Football	17	5
Gymnastics	4	14
Ice Skating	6	12

B Draw a bar for each sport. Use the number of boys who voted for each sport.

C Use the same steps to make a bar graph for the girls' favorite sports to watch. Use the same scale and interval.

Draw Conclusions

1. Compare the graphs you made. Write one difference the graphs show between the girls' and boys' votes for sports.

2. **Evaluation** Suppose the scales and intervals of the two bar graphs were different. Would it be more or less difficult to compare how many girls and boys voted for football? Explain.

Quick Review

How many more students have dogs than cats?

What Pet Do You Have?	
Animal	**Tally**
Dog	IIII II
Cat	IIII
Bird	I
No pet	IIII I

Vocabulary

double-bar graph

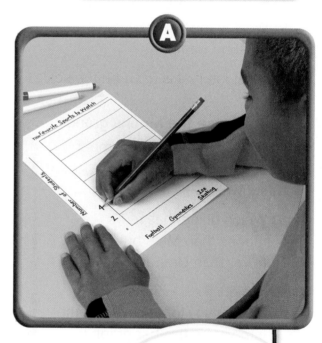

Math Idea

You can use a bar graph to show categorical data.

SDAP 1.0 Students organize, represent, and interpret numerical and categorical data and clearly communicate their findings. *also* **SDAP 1.1, SDAP 1.3, MR 2.0, MR 2.3, MR 2.4, MR 3.2**

A **double-bar graph** is a graph used to compare similar types of data. This double-bar graph shows the same information as the two bar graphs you made on page 346.

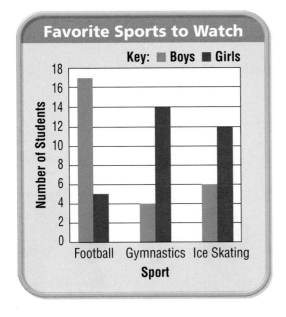

Favorite Sports to Watch

Key: ■ Boys ■ Girls

(Number of Students vs Sport: Football, Gymnastics, Ice Skating)

The key in the graph uses different colors to show the different data.

TALK Math

Which makes it easier to compare the data, the double-bar graph or the two single-bar graphs? Explain.

Practice

For 1–2, use the data in each table to make two bar graphs. Then make a double-bar graph.

1.

Average High Temperature (°F)			
City	Jan	Feb	Mar
Canton, Ohio	33	37	48
Detroit, Michigan	33	36	46

✓ 2.

Favorite Time of Day		
Time	Boys	Girls
Morning	6	8
Afternoon	20	17
Evening	33	31

For 3–6, use the double-bar graph.

✓ 3. Which city gets less rainfall from July through September?

4. Which city has a greater range of inches of rainfall during the three months? **Explain.**

5. How much more rain does Tampa get than Tucson in August?

6. ▮WRITE Math▮ Do you predict that Tucson or Tampa will have more rainfall in September next year? **Explain.**

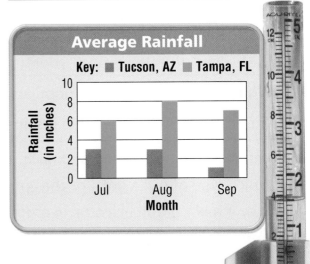

Average Rainfall

Key: ■ Tucson, AZ ■ Tampa, FL

(Rainfall in Inches vs Month: Jul, Aug, Sep)

3 Interpret Circle Graphs

OBJECTIVE: Read and interpret circle graphs.

Learn

Use a **circle graph** to compare data as parts of a whole. You can use a circle graph to show categorical data, or data about different groups.

PROBLEM Aisha took a survey of favorite summer activities. She recorded her data in a circle graph. Which activity got the most votes?

	Favorite Summer Activity			
Activity	Hiking	Fishing	Visit Theme Park	Beach Activities
Votes	4	3	4	5

Example 1 Understand a circle graph.

Each color represents one category.

The size of each section represents the number of people who voted for that category.

Favorite Summer Activities

Hiking — Beach Activities — Fishing — Theme Park

The circle represents the whole, or all the categories.

Beach activities have the greatest amount shaded.

So, beach activities received the most votes.

Example 2 Interpet a circle graph.

Which type of pizza is least popular?

The smallest part of the circle is spinach.

So, the least popular pizza is spinach.

Favorite Pizza

Pepperoni 15 — Spinach 10 — Cheese 25

- Which type of pizza got $\frac{1}{2}$ of the votes?
- How is a bar graph like a circle graph? How is it different?

SDAP 1.3 Interpret one- and two-variable data graphs to answer questions about a situation. *also* SDAP 1.0, MR 2.0, MR 2.3, MR 2.4, MR 3.2

Guided Practice

For 1–4, use the Favorite Breakfast graph.

1. Did waffles, eggs, or cereal receive the most votes?

✓ 2. Which type of breakfast received the least number of votes?

✓ 3. Which type of breakfast received less than $\frac{1}{4}$ of the votes?

4. **TALK Math** What does the whole circle represent?

Independent Practice and Problem Solving

For 5–7, use the Favorite Fruit graph.

5. Which fruit received the greatest number of votes?

6. Which fruit received the least number of votes?

7. How many more people voted for oranges than pears?

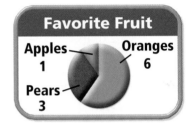

For 8–9, use the Favorite Dog graph.

8. Which dog received the least number of votes?

9. Which dog received almost half the votes?

10. **Reasoning** Raymond's allowance is $10. He spends $5 for a movie ticket and $2 on snacks. He saves the rest. How would you show this in a circle graph?

11. **WRITE Math** **What's the Error?** Joey earns $1 on Monday, $4 on Wednesday, and $5 on Friday. He says Graph A matches the data. Describe Joey's error. Tell which graph matches the set of data.

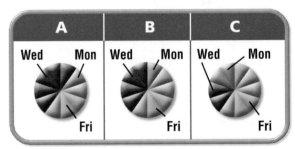

Achieving the Standards

12. What polygon has 3 sides?

(Grade 3 ⚬━━ MG 2.1)

13. Write the missing number. (⚬━━ NS 3.0, p. 16)

100 120 140 160 ■

14. Make a bar graph using the data from the Favorite Fruit graph above. (SDAP 1.0, p. 346)

15. **Test Prep** Look at the Favorite Dog graph above. Which dog received the most number of votes?

A retriever   **C** terrier

B bulldog   **D** poodle

Extra Practice on page 366, Set B

ALGEBRA

Graph Ordered Pairs

OBJECTIVE: Describe the relationship between two sets of related data shown as ordered pairs.

Quick Review

Write the missing number.

0 2 a 6 8 b 12 c d 18 e

1. a   **2.** b   **3.** c

4. d   **5.** e

___

Vocabulary

ordered pair

Learn

An **ordered pair** is a pair of numbers that names a point on a grid. The first number shows how many units to move horizontally. The second number shows how many units to move vertically.

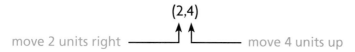

(2,4)

move 2 units right   move 4 units up

ERROR ALERT

The first number shows how to move horizontally and the second number shows how to move vertically when graphing an ordered pair.

Example 1 Graph an ordered pair.
Graph (2,5).

- Start at 0.
- Count 2 units right.
- Count 5 units up.
- Graph a point.
- Label the point (2,5).

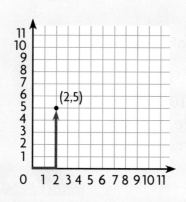

(2,5)

So, the point is located at (2,5).

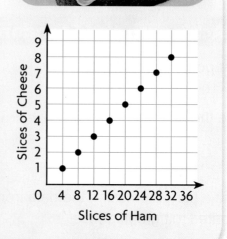

You can also graph ordered pairs from a table to solve a problem.

Example 2 Graph ordered pairs from a table.

Pablo uses 4 slices of ham and 1 slice of cheese for each sandwich. How many cheese slices does he use if he uses 32 ham slices?

Slices of Ham	4	8	12	16	20	24	28	32
Slices of Cheese	1	2	3	4	5	6	7	8

Graph each ordered pair.

(4,1), (8,2), (12,3), (16,4), (20,5), (24,6), (28,7), (32,8)

So, Pablo needs 8 slices of cheese.

O→ **MG 2.0** Students use two-dimensional coordinate grids to represent points and graph lines and simple figures. *also* **MR 1.1, MR 2.3, MR 2.4, MR 3.2**

Guided Practice

1. To graph the point (5,8), in which direction and how many units will you move first? What will you do next?

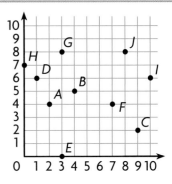

For 2–6, use the grid. Write the ordered pair for each point.

2. *A*   3. *B*   ✓ 4. *C*   ✓ 5. *D*

6. [TALK Math] **Explain** how to write ordered pairs from a table.

Independent Practice and Problem Solving

For 7–12, use the grid above. Write the ordered pair for each point.

7. *E*   8. *F*   9. *G*   10. *H*   11. *I*   12. *J*

For 13–14, write ordered pairs for each table. Then use grid paper to graph the ordered pairs.

13.
Number of Pages	1	2	3	4
Number of Photos	4	8	12	16

14.
Miles Traveled	20	40	60	80
Gallons of Gas	1	2	3	4

For 15, complete the table to help solve. Then use grid paper to graph the ordered pairs.

15. Carter buys 32 slices of turkey. If he uses 8 slices of turkey for each sandwich, how many sandwiches can he make?

Number of Sandwiches	1	2	▨	4
Number of Turkey Slices	8	▨	24	▨

16. **Pose a Problem** Look at Problem 15. Write a similar problem by changing the number of slices of turkey.

17. [WRITE Math] ▸ **What's the Question?** You start at (0,0). You move 6 units right and then 2 units up.

Achieving the Standards

18. Jack made 3 rows of crackers with 3 in each row. He ate 2 crackers. How many are left? (O┳ NS 3.0, p. 114)

19. $500 - 276 =$ (O┳ NS 3.1, p. 64)

20. Order the numbers from greatest to least.
(NS 1.2, p. 16)

5,400   5,040   5,041   5,410

21. **Test Prep** What is the ordered pair for point A?

A (2,2)

B (6,3)

C (3,6)

D (4,5)

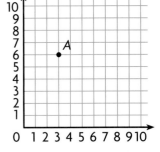

5 Interpret Line Graphs

OBJECTIVE: Interpret line graphs.

Learn

A **line graph** uses line segments to show how data change over a period of time. Even when there are no numbers in a line graph, the shape of the graph can tell you about the data. You can think of the shape of a line graph as telling you a story.

PROBLEM Paige measured the distance from the seawall to the water at different times of day. What story does the graph tell about the distance over time?

Example 1 Understand a line graph.

This line graph shows the relationship between time and distance from the seawall to the water.

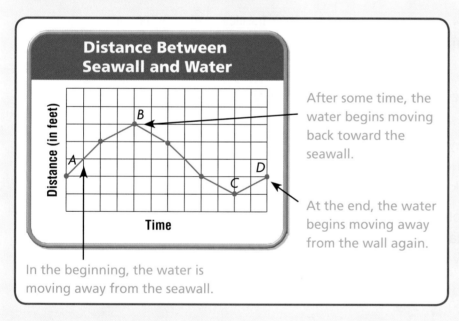

Distance Between Seawall and Water

After some time, the water begins moving back toward the seawall.

At the end, the water begins moving away from the wall again.

In the beginning, the water is moving away from the seawall.

▲ Ocean Beach in San Diego, California

Math Idea
A line graph shows a relationship.

So, the water was moving away from the wall when Paige started her experiment. Then the water began to move closer to the wall. Finally, the water began to move away again.

• What happened to the distance between points *A* and *B*?

• High tide is when the distance between the water and the seawall is at its lowest point. What point shows high tide?

SDAP 1.3 Interpret one- and two-variable data graphs to answer questions about a situation. *also* SDAP 1.0, MR 1.1, MR 2.0, MR 2.3, MR 2.4, MR 3.2

Line Graphs and Trends

Example 2 Find the height of the bean plant at Week 3.

For 4 weeks, Caroline kept track of the growth of a bean plant in her family's garden. How tall was the bean plant at Week 3?

Step 1

Find the line labeled Week 3. Follow that line up to the point (•).

Step 2

Follow that line to the scale on the left to locate the height at Week 3.

So, the bean plant was 11 inches tall at Week 3.

- What do the numbers on the left side of the graph stand for?

- If there were no numbers on this graph, what story would it tell about the data?

You can think of the points on a line graph as ordered pairs. The point (Week 2,9) shows that at Week 2 the plant was 9 inches.

- What ordered pair shows the height of the plant at Week 1?

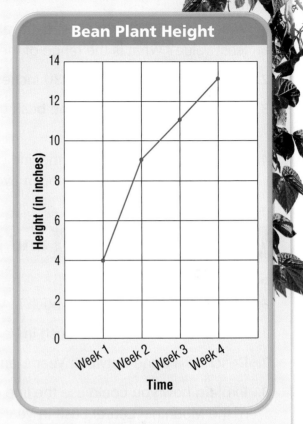

Bean Plant Height

Each line segment shows the change in the bean plant's height each week.

Areas of a line graph where data increase, decrease, or stay the same over time are called **trends**.

Example 3 Describe trends.

The graph shows the average rainfall for Livermore, California between January and April. Does rainfall increase or decrease?

The line moves downward between January and April.

So, rainfall decreases between January and April.

- Look at the trend between March and April. If the trend continues, do you think rainfall will increase, decrease, or stay the same in May?

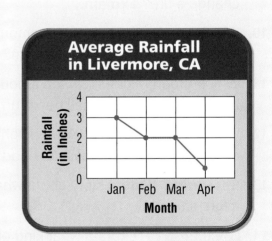

Average Rainfall in Livermore, CA

Each line segment shows the change in the average rainfall for each month.

For 1–4, use the Growth of a Mountain Laurel Bush graph.

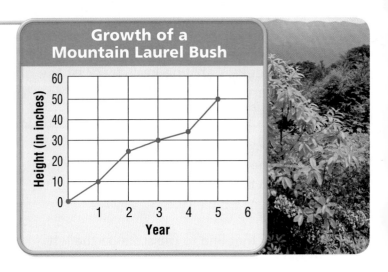

Growth of a Mountain Laurel Bush

☑ **1.** Which year has the greatest data value? the least value? What is the range of the data?

☑ **2.** At what year was the bush 30 inches tall?

3. Between which years did the bush grow more slowly? How can you tell?

4. [TALK Math] **Explain** what the line graph tells you about the height of the bush over 5 years.

Independent Practice and Problem Solving

For 5–8, use the graph above.

5. What was the height of the bush in Year 5?

6. How much taller was the bush in Year 5 than in Year 3?

7. Describe a trend between Year 1 and Year 5.

8. **Explain** how you could use the line graph to predict the height of the Mountain Laurel Bush in Year 6.

For 9–13, use Graph 1 and Graph 2. Explain your choice and write a label for the left side of each graph.

9. Which graph might show that a bicyclist stopped to change a tire? **Explain.**

10. Which graph might show the amount of water in a bucket left out during a rainstorm? **Explain.**

11. Which graph might show the amount of water in a bathtub once the tap has been turned off? **Explain.**

12. Which graph might show the height of a baby elephant until it reaches adulthood? **Explain.**

13. **Reasoning** Write a story about what Graph 2 might show.

14. [WRITE Math] ▸ **Explain** what kind of data you might show in a line graph.

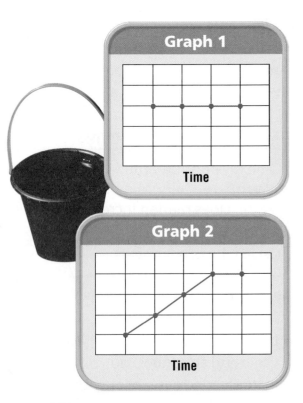

Graph 1

Time

Graph 2

Time

Technology
Use Harcourt Mega Math, The Number Games, *ArachnaGraph*, Levels I, J.

15. Describe how to find the ordered pair (4,9) on a grid. (⚷ MG 2.0, p. 350)

16. Jerry has read the first 48 pages of a 212-page book. Write an equation that can be used to find the number of pages he must read to finish the book. (AF 1.1, p. 84)

17. What is the mode of this set of numbers? the median? (SDAP 1.2, p. 326)

$$6, 18, 13, 12, 9, 6, 9, 6$$

For 18–19, use the graph below.

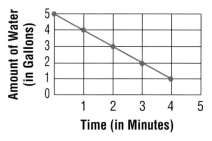

Water in a Draining Bathtub

18. Test Prep How many gallons were in the bathtub when the water had drained for 2 minutes?

A 5 gallons **C** 3 gallons

B 4 gallons **D** 2 gallons

19. Test Prep The graph shows that the data are following which trend?

A increasing **C** staying the same

B decreasing **D** none of these

Problem Solving [connects to] **Science**

What a Panda Eats

The giant panda depends on one plant, bamboo, for its survival. Giant pandas live in bamboo forests in the mountains of China. A panda eats for about 12 hours each day. One panda can eat up to 84 pounds of bamboo in one day.

For 1–2, use the graph.

1. About how many more pounds of bamboo did the panda eat in Week 2 than Week 1?

2. **What if** the graph sloped downward sharply between Week 4 and Week 5? What might this show about the panda's health? **Explain.**

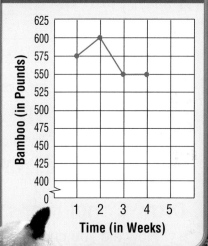

Bamboo Eaten by a Giant Panda

6 Make Line Graphs

OBJECTIVE: Make line graphs.

Investigate

Materials ■ line-graph pattern or grid paper

Use the line-graph pattern to make a line graph to show the data in the table.

A Write a title for the graph. Choose a scale and interval for the data. Write the label and scale numbers along the left side of the graph. The last number on the scale should be one interval more than the greatest data value.

Average Daily Temperature in January, 2006, in Chicago, IL	
Day	Temperature (in Degrees Fahrenheit)
1	35
2	41
3	40
4	42
5	36
6	30
7	32

B Write the labels for the days along the bottom of the graph.

C Plot each point. Then draw line segments to connect the points from left to right.

Draw Conclusions

1. How did you choose the scale and interval for your graph?

2. Compare your graph with those of your classmates. Are there any differences in your graphs? Explain.

3. **Application** Think of some other kind of data that you could show in a line graph. Explain how you would make your graph.

356

SDAP 1.0 Students organize, represent, and interpret numerical and categorical data and clearly communicate their findings. *also* SDAP 1.1, MR 1.1, MR 2.0, MR 2.3, MR 2.4, MR 3.2

Connect

Some line graphs show a rule. When a line graph shows a rule, you can extend the pattern to find information not shown on the graph.

The graph below shows the relationship between your distance from lightning and the number of seconds that pass until you hear thunder.

Math Idea
The information in a line graph showing a rule can be extended to find information not shown on the graph.

How far away is the lightning strike if thunder is heard 15 seconds later?

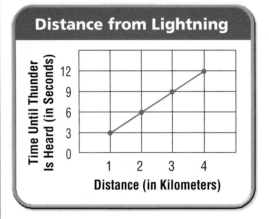

Think: The rule is, divide the number of seconds by 3 to get the number of kilometers.

TALK Math
How do you know where to place each point on a line graph?

Continue a pattern on the line graph.
Divide 15 by 3 to get the distance in kilometers.

So, 15 seconds between lightning and thunder means lightning is 5 kilometers away.

Practice

For 1–2, use the data to make a line graph.

1.

Rainfall				
Month	Jun	Jul	Aug	Sep
Amount (in Inches)	3	5	6	4

✔ 2.

My Plant's Growth				
End of Week	1	2	3	4
Height (in Inches)	6	9	13	15

✔ 3. Copy the graph. Use the data to make a line graph. How far will Aaron swim in 5 minutes if he continues at the same rate?

Aaron's Swim-a-Thon				
Time (in Minutes)	1	2	3	4
Distance (in Meters)	25	50	75	100

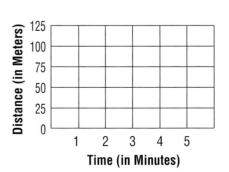

4. **WRITE Math** ▸ **Explain** how to use the data in a table to make a line graph.

Problem Solving Workshop
Strategy: Make a Graph

OBJECTIVE: Solve problems by using the strategy *make a graph*.

Learn the Strategy

Making a graph can help you organize and display data.
Different types of graphs show different types of information.

Make a bar graph or pictograph.

Ms. Fedders' class took a survey of the states they have visited.

Use a bar graph or pictograph to compare categorical data, or data about different groups.

States Students Have Visited	
State	**Number of Students**
Florida	11
California	10
New York	7
Nevada	6

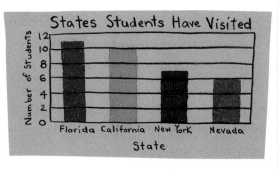

Make a line graph.

Ava recorded the height of her tomato plant each week.

Use a line graph to show how data change over time.

Height of Tomato Plant	
Week	**Height (in Inches)**
1	3
2	5
3	8
4	11

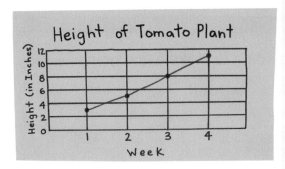

Make a circle graph.

Shane spent 20 minutes on homework after school. He spent 5 minutes reading a short story, 10 minutes doing math homework, and 5 minutes studying for a spelling test.

Use a circle graph to compare data as parts of a whole.

TALK Math

What type of data would you not display in a circle graph?

SDAP 1.1 Formulate survey questions; systematically collect and represent data on a number line; and coordinate graphs, tables, and charts. *also* **SDAP 1.0, SDAP 1.3, MR 1.0, MR 1.1, MR 2.0, MR 2.3, MR 2.4, MR 2.6, MR 3.0, MR 3.1, MR 3.2, MR 3.3**

Use the Strategy

PROBLEM The table shows about how many tourists from New Zealand came to California between February and June in 2004. What is the greatest monthly difference in the number of New Zealand tourists visiting California between February and June?

Read to Understand

- **What information is given?**
- **Is there information you will not use? If so, what?**

Plan

- **What strategy can you use to solve the problem?**
  You can make a graph to help you see the information clearly.

New Zealand Tourists in California (2004)

Month	Number of Tourists
February	5,000
March	6,000
April	8,000
May	9,000
June	11,000

Solve

- **How can you use the strategy to solve the problem?**
  The data set includes different groups. Make a bar graph or pictograph to compare the number of New Zealand tourists visiting California each month.

  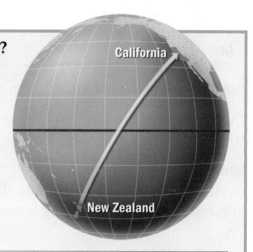

  Reading Skill Classify and categorize the information you will use to solve the problem.

  Write a label for each row.

  Look at the numbers. Choose a key to tell how many each symbol stands for.

  February has the least number of symbols, and June has the most. June has 6 more symbols than February.

  So, the greatest difference is 6,000 tourists.

New Zealand Tourists in California (2004)

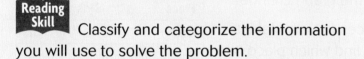

February	🏃🏃🏃🏃🏃
March	🏃🏃🏃🏃🏃🏃
April	🏃🏃🏃🏃🏃🏃🏃🏃
May	🏃🏃🏃🏃🏃🏃🏃🏃🏃
June	🏃🏃🏃🏃🏃🏃🏃🏃🏃🏃🏃

Key: Each 🏃 = 1,000 tourists.

Check

- **How can you check to see whether your solution is correct?**

Guided Problem Solving

1. The table shows about how much money visitors spent in New York City each year from 2000 to 2004. Which two years had the greatest difference in the amount of money visitors spent?

   To compare information, you can use a pictograph or a bar graph. Make a pictograph to compare the amount of money visitors spent each month.

   Decide on a symbol and a key for the pictograph.

   Visitor Spending in New York City

2000	
2001	
2002	
2003	
2004	
Key: ▪	

   Visitor Spending in New York City

Year	Billions of Dollars
2000	17
2001	14
2002	15
2003	18
2004	21

   Copy and complete the graph. Then solve the problem.

2. **What if** you add the data for 1999, when visitors spent $16 billion in New York City? How would the graph change?

3. Manuel's class voted for their favorite places to visit. Make a double-bar graph to show the data. Then find which place had the greatest difference in votes between girls and boys.

   Places Manuel's Class Would Like to Visit

Place	Girls	Boys
Lake	3	1
Ocean	5	4
National Park	2	7
Amusement Park	6	8

Problem Solving Strategy Practice

For 4–6, use the Exhibit Attendance table.
Make a graph to solve.

4. A museum is keeping track of the number of people who visit each exhibit. What is the range of the data?

5. What is the mode of the data? **Explain.**

6. **Reasoning** To save money, the museum is thinking of closing one exhibit. Which exhibit might it make sense to close? **Explain.**

7. **WRITE Math** ▶ Suppose the museum made another table to show the amount of money that was spent to set up each exhibit. Would it make more sense to make a circle graph or a line graph of the data? **Explain.**

   Exhibit Attendance

Exhibit	Number of People
Dinosaurs	90
Ancient Egypt	50
Titanic	45
Star Gallery	60
Machines	90

Mixed Strategy Practice

For 8–11, use the information in the map.

8. New York City is made up of 5 boroughs. Which borough is about twice the size of Manhattan?

9. The sum of the areas of two boroughs in New York City is 104 square miles. Which two boroughs are they?

10. **Pose a Problem** Look back at Problem 8. Write a similar problem about two different boroughs. Solve the problem.

11. Craig, Jim, and Pedro live in three different boroughs—Brooklyn, Queens, and Manhattan. Neither Craig nor Pedro lives in Brooklyn. Craig does not live in Queens. In which borough does each friend live?

12. Grace arrived at the museum at 9:15 A.M. It took 15 minutes to walk from her house to the subway. She waited 10 minutes for the train. The train ride was 20 minutes. Then she walked 10 minutes from the train station to the museum. At what time did Grace leave her house to go to the museum?

13. **Open-Ended** Molly walks 3 blocks east to get from her house to her school in Brooklyn. Use grid paper to make a coordinate grid. Graph a point for Molly's house at (0,0). Then graph a point for her school. Decide on a point for the library so Molly's path from her house to school to the library and back home is a right triangle.

CHALLENGE YOURSELF

Central Park is in the center of the island of Manhattan. It is a rectangle that is $2\frac{1}{2}$ miles long and $\frac{1}{2}$ mile wide. There are 26,000 trees and over 9,000 benches in Central Park.

14. If you were going to jog around Central Park, how many miles would you jog?

15. American elms make up 1,700 of the trees in Central Park. How many trees are not American elms?

Choose a STRATEGY

Make a Table or Graph
Draw a Diagram or Picture
Make a Model or Act It Out
Make an Organized List
Find a Pattern
Predict and Test
Work Backward
Solve a Simpler Problem
Write an Equation
Use Logical Reasoning

The Size of the 5 Boroughs of New York City

Bronx: 44 square miles

Manhattan: 24 square miles

Queens: 112 square miles

Brooklyn: 82 square miles

Staten Island: 60 square miles

▲ New York City is broken into five different areas called *boroughs*.

Choose an Appropriate Graph

OBJECTIVE: Choose an appropriate graph.

Learn

The type of graph used to display data depends upon the type of information you want to show.

Quick Review

Ronnie is making a pictograph to show the data below. What key should he use?

Favorite Car Color				
Color	Red	Blue	Green	Pink
Votes	5	10	5	20

Examples

A

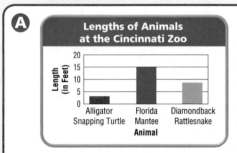

Use a bar graph or double-bar graph to show and compare data about different categories, or groups.

B

Use a pictograph to show and compare data about different categories, or groups.

C

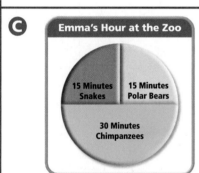

Use a circle graph to compare parts of a group to a whole group.

D

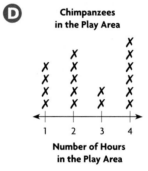

Use a line plot to show the frequency of the data along a number line.

E

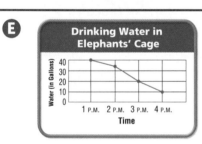

Use a line graph to show how data change over time.

Math Idea

Choosing the correct graph makes it easier to see trends, make predictions, and compare data to solve problems.

• Which types of graph or plot show categorical data? Which types show only numerical data?

SDAP 1.0 Students organize, represent, and interpret numerical and categorical data and clearly communicate thier findings. *also* **SDAP 1.1, MR 1.1, MR 2.0, MR 2.3, MR 2.4, MR 3.0, MR 3.1, MR 3.2**

The Best Graph for the Data

Harrison and Kiyo made graphs to show the data in the table. Which is the better graph?

Sales on Sunday

Item	Number Sold
Key Chains	3
Stuffed Animals	5
Toy Tractors	7
Inflatable Bats	8

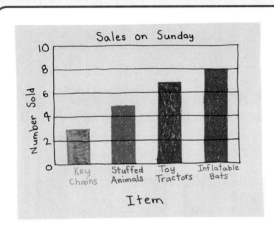

A bar graph compares different groups of data. A bar graph is the better choice.

The data do not show changes over a period of time. So, a line graph is **not** the better way to show the data.

- **Reasoning** What other kind of graph could be used to show the data? Explain.

Guided Practice

1. To show how many days Ali worked 5 hours, would you use a line plot or a line graph? **Explain** your choice.

Hours Ali Worked

Day	1	2	3	4	5	6
Hours Worked	5	5	6	7	8	5

For 2–7, choose the best type of graph or plot for the data. Explain your choice.

2. how Ana spent $5.00 at the zoo

3. the number of workers at each food booth

4. the temperature at the zoo between noon and 5 P.M.

5. how many classmates bought different numbers of drinks at the zoo

✓ 6. the number of inches of rain over 5 days

✓ 7. the number of people taking different types of transportation to the zoo

For 8, use the Hours Ali Worked table.

8. **TALK Math** **Explain** what kind of display would be easiest to find the median hours Ali worked.

For 9–14, choose and explain the best type of graph or plot for the data.

9. height of a sunflower plant over time

10. how Jason spends 8 hours working

11. number of points scored at a basketball game by different players

12. number of people who scored different numbers of points at a hoop game

13.

Monday Lemonade Sales				
Size	Small	Medium	Large	X-Large
Number Sold	7	13	9	11

14.

Cars Washed by Students				
Students	4	6	3	1
Cars	1	2	4	5

For 15–16, use the line graph and bar graph.

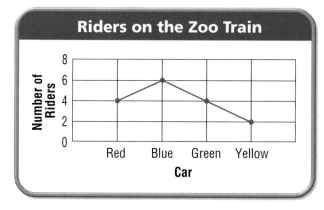

Riders on the Zoo Train

Growth of a Leopard Gecko

15. Why is a line graph not the best choice to show the riders on the zoo train?

16. Why is the bar graph not the best choice to show the growth of a gecko?

17. Collect data about the color of shoes in your class. Choose the best graph to display your data. Make the graph.

18. **WRITE Math** Write a type of data that you could show in a line graph. Explain why the data work in a line graph.

Achieving the Standards

19. What is the median of the data shown in the table in Problem 13? (SDAP 1.2, p. 326)

20. What is the perimeter of a square with a side of 4 centimeters? (Grade 3 ⦿ MG 1.3)

21. Owen had 53 prize tickets. He won 3 more then gave 12 to his brother. How many tickets did he have left?

(⦿ NS 3.0, p. 58)

22. **Test Prep** Which type of graph or plot would best display daily high temperatures at the zoo?

   A bar graph   **C** line graph

   B circle graph   **D** line plot

Write a Conclusion

Some graphs show relationships, such as the relationship between time and distance. This graph shows the relationship between the distance Steven rode his bike and the time his trip took.

What does the graph show about the bike trip?

Read Deja's description of Steven's ride and her conclusions about the relationships in the graph.

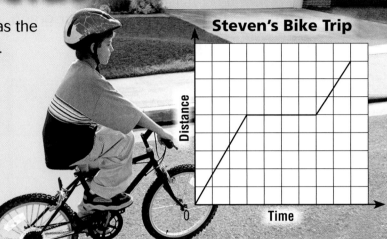

Steven's Bike Trip

The graph shows the relationship of distance and time during Steven's bike trip.

At the beginning of the ride, the line moves up. That means he is moving some distance. In the middle, the line is straight. That shows he is not moving any distance. He has stopped. Then the line moves up again. That means he is moving again.

The graph shows that Steven started to ride his bike, then stopped, maybe to talk to a friend, then began riding again.

Tips

To analyze a graph:
- Read the title and find out what the graph is about.
- Look at the labels to find out what relationship the graph shows.
- Describe and explain each change in the data.
- Write a conclusion to explain the action the data show.

Problem Solving Analyze and describe the data. Write a conclusion to explain the actions that the data show.

1. **Money in Ally's Savings Account**

2. **Rita's 100-Meter Swimming Race**

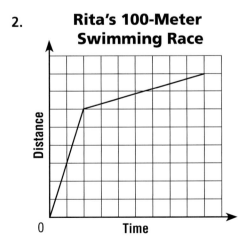

Extra Practice

Set A Use the Favorite Type of Movie bar graph. (pp. 344–345)

1. How many more students chose comedies than cartoons as their favorite?

2. What is the range of the data?

3. Which types of movies were chosen by the same number of students?

4. What is the interval used on the scale?

5. What is the mode of the data?

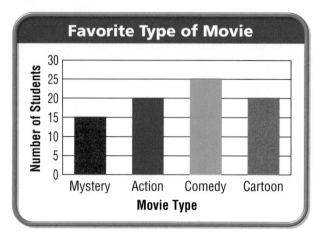

Set B Use the After-School Activities graph. (pp. 348–349)

1. In which after-school activity do the greatest number of students participate?

2. In which after-school activity do the least number of students participate?

3. In which activities did one-fourth of the students participate?

4. Write an activity that is not the most popular or the least popular.

Set C Use the grid.
Write the ordered pair for each point. (pp. 350–351)

1. A   2. B

3. C   4. D

5. E   6. F

7. G   8. H

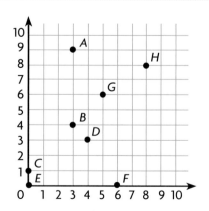

Technology
Use Harcourt Mega Math, The Number Games,
ArachnaGraph, Levels A, B, C, D, H, I, J.

Write ordered pairs for each table. Use grid paper to graph the ordered pairs.

9.

Time (in hours)	1	2	3	4
Miles traveled	50	100	150	200

10.

Time (in minutes)	1	2	3	■	5
Miles traveled	18	■	■	72	■

11. Dee has 72 cookies. Use ordered pairs to find how many 12-packs of cookies she can make.

12. A recipe calls for 3 cups of flour to make 2 loaves of bread. Use ordered pairs to find how many cups of flour are needed to make 8 loaves of bread.

Set D Use the April Rain graph. (pp. 352–355)

1. Between which two weeks was there the greatest increase in rainfall?

2. By how many inches did the rainfall decrease between Week 1 and Week 2?

3. During which week was there no rain?

4. Is the total rainfall for the 4 weeks greater than or less than 6 inches?

5. What was the trend in rainfall between Week 1 and Week 3?

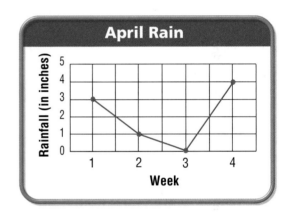

Set E For 1–6, choose the best type of graph or plot for the data. Explain your choice. (pp. 362–365)

1.

Favorite Baseball Team		
Team	Mets	Cubs	Reds
Votes	18	16	14

2.

Temperature on Monday			
Time	8:00	9:00	10:00	11:00
Temp (°F)	81	86	90	91

3. Ray tossed 2 number cubes labeled 1 to 6 twenty times. He recorded the sum for each toss.

4. types of sandwiches sold in the cafeteria for 1 week

5. height of a sunflower plant during 12 weeks

6. how Jody spent her allowance last month

7. Collect data about the weather in your area for one week. Choose the best graph to display your data. Make the graph.

Check Vocabulary and Concepts

Choose the best term from the box.

VOCABULARY

ordered pair

line graph

1. An __?__ is a pair of numbers that names a point on a grid. (O–π MG 2.0, p. 350)

Check Skills

For 2–3, use the bar graph at the right. (SDAP 1.3, pp. 344–345)

2. On which days were the same number of tickets sold?

3. What is the interval of the scale?

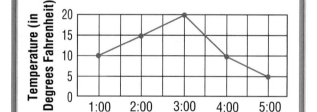

Talent Show Tickets

Write ordered pairs for each table. Then use grid paper to graph the ordered pairs. (O–π MG 2.0, pp. 350–351)

4.

Time (in hours), x	1	2	3	4
Pages Read, y	15	30	45	60

For 5–6, use the line graph at the right.

(SDAP 1.3, pp. 352–355)

5. At what hours was the temperature the same?

6. What was the trend from 3:00 to 5:00?

Temperature on January 15

For 7–9, write the type of graph or plot you would choose. Explain your choice. (SDAP 1.3, pp. 362–365)

7. growth of a lizard   8. how Ana spent 1 hour at school   9. votes for favorite colors

Check Problem Solving

Solve. (SDAP 1.1, MR 2.3, pp. 358–361)

10. Make an appropriate graph to display the data.

Favorite Vacation	
Destination	**Number of Votes**
Beach	6
Amusement Park	9
Water Park	15
Mountains	3

GO Technology Use *Online Assessment.*

Enrich • Interpret Data
Making the Grade

These line plots show the grades on a test taken by two classes. At lunch, the students talked about which class did better.

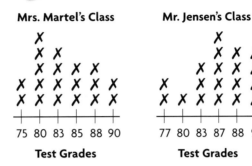

Compare the median scores of the classes.

Mrs. Martel's class: median = 83
Mr. Jensen's class: median = 87

Compare the modes of the two classes.

Mrs. Martel's class: mode = 80
Mr. Jensen's class: mode = 87

The median and mode for Mr. Jensen's class are greater than the median and mode for Mrs. Martel's class. So, Mr. Jensen's class did better on the test than Mrs. Martel's class.

Try It

1. Two groups of students were surveyed about how many days per week they have after-school activities. Find and compare the medians and modes for the two groups. In which group do the students have fewer after-school activities?

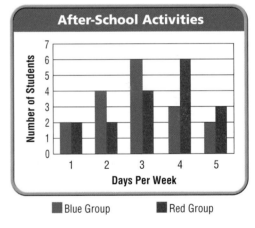

WRITE Math ▶ Two sports teams were asked how many hours a week they spend practicing. Find the median and mode for each team. Which team do you think spends more time practicing? **Explain.**

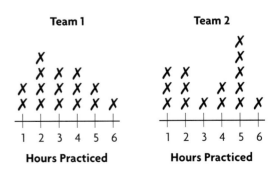

Achieving the Standards
Chapters 1–14

Measurement and Geometry

1. Tanya used four 3-inch toothpicks to make a square. What is the perimeter of her square? (Grade 3 O⊣ MG 1.3)

   A 6 inches   **C** 12 inches

   B 9 inches   **D** 15 inches

Test Tip Look for important words.

See Item 2. The word *isosceles* tells you that the triangle must have 2 equal sides.

2. Which figure is an isosceles triangle? (Grade 3 O⊣ MG 2.2)

   A

   B

   C

   D

3. Which figure has 2 pairs of parallel sides and might not have any right angles? (Grade 3 O⊣ MG 2.3)

   A trapezoid

   B square

   C rectangle

   D parallelogram

4. **WRITE Math** **Describe** a pentagon, and draw an example. (Grade 3 O⊣ MG 2.1)

Algebra and Functions

5. What number goes in the box to make this number sentence true? (O⊣ AF 2.2)

   $$(8 - 3) \times 7 = 5 \times \blacksquare$$

   A 3

   B 4

   C 5

   D 7

6. Which number is represented by m? (AF 1.1)

   $$16 \times m = 144$$

   A 3   **C** 12

   B 9   **D** 128

7. What is the value of the expression if $n = 5$? (O⊣ AF 1.2)

   $$12 - (6 + n)$$

   A 1

   B 6

   C 11

   D 13

8. **WRITE Math** Add parentheses to each expression so that the value of each is 18. **Explain** how you know. (O⊣ AF 1.3)

   $$3 \times 5 + 1$$
   $$7 \times 4 - 1 + 9$$
   $$9 \times 2 + 2 \div 2$$

Statistics, Data Analysis, and Probability

9. How far did the students ride each hour? (SDAP 1.3)

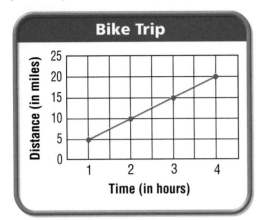

A 1 mile   **C** 6 miles

B 5 miles   **D** 10 miles

10. Jessica surveyed 50 students. She asked them to name their favorite after-school activity. What type of graph is the most appropriate to display her results? (SDAP 1.1)

A line graph

B Venn diagram

C circle graph

D line plot

11. ▐WRITE Math▌ ▸ Find possible numbers for a data set that has the following.

$$mode = 8$$

$$median = 12$$

$$range = 10$$

Explain your thinking. (SDAP 1.2)

Number Sense

12. Which set of data is listed in order from least to greatest? (O—n NS 1.2)

A 300,026; 302,206; 300,006

B 300,026; 300,206; 302,006

C 302,026; 302,206; 302,006

D 302,006; 300,206; 300,026

13. The population of Bakersfield, California, was 247,057 in 2000 according to the U.S. Census. In 2003, the population of Bakersfield was 271,035. How many more people lived in Bakersfield in 2003 than in 2000? (O—n NS 3.1)

A 24,978

B 24,078

C 23,978

D 23,078

14. Jerry bought a dozen packages of copy paper. Each package holds 400 sheets of paper. How many sheets of paper did he buy? (O—n NS 3.3)

A 4,800

B 4,400

C 4,000

D 2,400

15. ▐WRITE Math▌ ▸ **Explain** why 7 is a prime number. Give the next prime number after 7. (O—n NS 4.2)

15 Algebra: Explore Negative Numbers and Graphing

The Big Idea The number line can be extended to show negative numbers; the coordinate plane can be used to graph relationships.

CALIFORNIA FAST FACT

Lake Tahoe is the second-deepest lake in the United States— as much as 1,645 feet deep. It has 72 miles of shoreline and is about 22 miles long and 12 miles wide.

Investigate

Tahoe City is on the shore of Lake Tahoe. The sun shines there often, but the temperature varies a lot. What are some ways to compare the temperatures shown in the table by using a number line?

Tahoe City, California, Temperatures (in °F)												
Month	Jan	Feb	Mar	Apr	May	Jun	Jul	Aug	Sep	Oct	Nov	Dec
Record High	59	60	67	74	81	90	93	94	87	80	70	60
Record Low	−14	−15	−6	5	9	24	22	29	21	9	1	−16

GO ONLINE

Technology
Student pages are available in the Student eBook.

Show What You Know

**Check your understanding of important skills
needed for success in Chapter 15.**

▶ Locate Numbers on a Number Line

Write the number each letter represents on the number line.

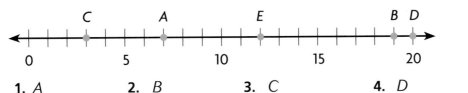

1. A 2. B 3. C 4. D 5. E

▶ Read a Thermometer

Write the temperature shown on the thermometer.

6. 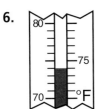   7. 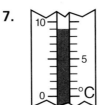   8.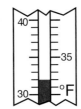

▶ Graph Ordered Pairs

Write ordered pairs for each table. Then use grid paper
to graph the ordered pairs.

9.

Tables	1	2	3	4
Legs	4	8	12	16

10.

Pennies	10	20	30	40
Dimes	1	2	3	4

VOCABULARY POWER

CHAPTER VOCABULARY

coordinate plane	negative numbers
degree Celsius (°C)	ordered pair
	origin
degree Fahrenheit (°F)	positive numbers
	x-axis
	x-coordinate
function table	y-axis
	y-coordinate

WARM-UP WORDS

degree Fahrenheit (°F) a standard unit
for measuring temperature

degree Celsius (°C) a metric unit for
measuring temperature

negative numbers all the numbers to
the left of zero on the number line; negative
numbers are less than zero

1 Temperature

OBJECTIVE: Measure temperatures and change in temperatures in degrees Fahrenheit and degrees Celsius.

Quick Review

Draw a number line to show the order of the numbers from least to greatest: 5, 1, 12, 21, and 15.

Vocabulary

degree Fahrenheit (°F)

degree Celsius (°C)

Learn

Degrees Fahrenheit (°F) are customary units for measuring temperature. The United States uses the Fahrenheit scale. Water freezes at 32°F and boils at 212°F.

Read 32°F as "thirty-two degrees Fahrenheit."

Temperatures less than 0°F are negative temperatures. On a thermometer, negative temperatures are located below the zero. The record low temperature in Chicago, Illinois was ⁻27°F.

Read ⁻27°F as "twenty-seven degrees below zero Fahrenheit."

Example 1 Find the change in temperature.

If the temperature drops from a high of 19°F to a low of ⁻12°F, what is the change in temperature?

Step 1

Count the change in temperature from 19°F to 0°F. The change is 19°F.

Step 2

Count the change in temperature from 0°F to ⁻12°F. The change is 12°F.

Step 3

Add the two changes. 19° + 12° = 31°

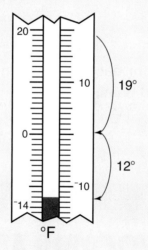

So, the temperature drops 31°F.

Example 2 Estimate the temperature.

Sometimes you do not need to know the exact temperature. You can estimate temperature to the nearest 5 degrees.

Think: The temperature is closer to 80°F than to 85°F.

So, the estimated temperature is about 80°F.

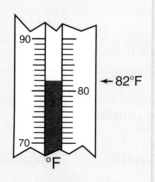

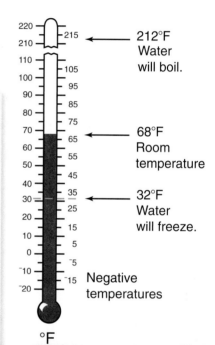

212°F
Water
will boil.

68°F
Room
temperature

32°F
Water
will freeze.

Negative
temperatures

°F

NS 1.8 Use concepts of negative numbers (e.g., on a number line, in counting, in temperature, in "owing"). *also* NS 1.0, MR 1.1, MR 2.3, MR 2.4, MR 3.2

Degrees Celsius

Degrees Celsius (°C) are metric units for measuring temperature. Many countries use the Celsius scale. Water freezes at 0°C.

You can read temperatures in degrees Celsius the same way as in degrees Fahrenheit. Read 10°C as "ten degrees Celsius." Read ⁻5°C as "five degrees below zero Celsius."

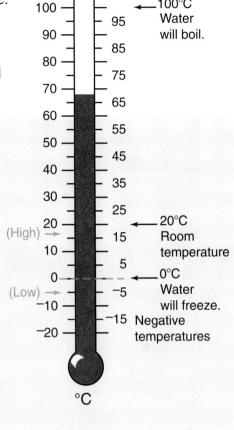

Example 3 Find the change in temperature.

The temperature rose from a low of ⁻5°C to a high of 17°C. By how many degrees did the temperature rise?

Step 1

The change in temperature from ⁻5°C to 0°C is 5°C.

Step 2

The change in temperature from 0°C to 17°C is 17°C.

Step 3

Add the two changes. 5° + 17° = 22°

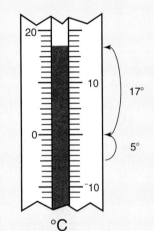

So, the temperature rose 22°C.

• How do you find a drop in temperature from 80°C to 45°C?

Activity Measure and compare temperatures.

Materials ■ Fahrenheit and Celsius thermometers

• Estimate and measure the temperatures of a few places around your school in the morning in degrees Fahrenheit or degrees Celsius. Copy the table and record the places, times, estimated temperatures, and your measured temperatures.

• How do your estimated temperatures compare with your measured temperatures?

• Find the change in temperature. Estimate, measure, and record the temperatures in the afternoon. Measure the temperatures in the same places and with the same unit as your first measurement.

		Temperature Readings at School		
Place	Time	Estimated Temperature (in °F or °C)	Measured Temperature (in °F or °C)	Change
?		■	■	■

1. Letter A shows a temperature of 4°C. What is the temperature that is 10 degrees warmer?

Use the thermometer to find the temperature shown by each letter.

2. B   ✓ **3.** C   ✓ **4.** D

5. [**TALK Math**] **Explain** how you can estimate the temperatures of hot soup and a cold drink using temperatures you already know.

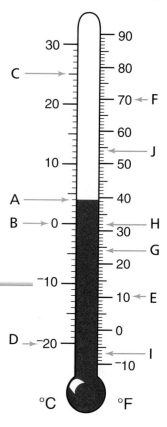

Independent Practice (and Problem Solving)

Use the thermometer to find the temperature shown by each letter.

6. E   7. F   8. G

9. H   10. I   11. J

Write each temperature. Then estimate to the nearest 5 degrees.

12.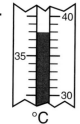

13.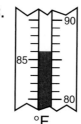

14.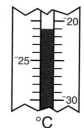

Use a thermometer to find the change in temperature.

15. 4°F to 12°F   16. ⁻8°C to 15°C   17. ⁻2°F to ⁻14°F

18. 32°F to 17°F   19. ⁻24°C to 3°C   20. ⁻47°F to ⁻32°F

Choose the better estimate.

21. ice cube: 32°F or 45°F   22. classroom: 20°C or 35°C   23. snow: ⁻5°C or 15°C

24. hot day: 65°F or 85°F   25. bedroom: 78°F or 92°F   26. hot cocoa: 20°C or 90°C

27. **Reasoning Explain** why zero degrees Fahrenheit is not the same temperature as zero degrees Celsius.

28. [**WRITE Math**] ▶ Write a paragraph about temperatures in your area during spring, fall, summer, and winter.

USE DATA For 29–31, use the table.

29. Order the cities from the greatest to least change in temperature.

30. Which city has a greater difference between its January and July temperatures, Fairbanks or Madison?

31. Draw a thermometer and show the January and July temperatures in Baltimore. Find the difference.

Average Monthly Temperatures in U.S. Cities		
City	January (in °F)	July (in °F)
Baltimore, MD	32	77
Fairbanks, AK	⁻10	62
Jackson, MS	45	81
Madison, WI	17	72

 Achieving the Standards

32. Order from least to greatest: 5,032; 5,320; 5,203; 3,502. (○⊓ NS 1.2, p. 16)

33. What is the mode for the numbers 2, 2, 7, 4, 6, 7, 9, 7, 7? (SDAP 1.2, p. 328)

34. **Test Prep** The temperature rose from ⁻1°F to 5°F. What was the change in temperature?

35. Which the following has the greater value? 36,945 or 36,459? (○⊓ NS 1.2, p. 12)

36. **Test Prep** The high temperature was 22°C and the low temperature was 4° lower. What was the low temperature?

    A ⁻18°C   **B** ⁻4°C   **C** 18°C   **D** 26°C

 **Problem Solving and Reasoning**

VISUAL THINKING You can use thermometers to help you compare temperatures with the same units.

In Pittsburgh, Pennsylvania, temperatures have reached lows of ⁻2°F and ⁻19°F. Which temperature is colder?

On a Fahrenheit or Celsius thermometer, the greater or warmer temperature is closer to the top. The lesser or cooler temperature is closer to the bottom of the thermometer. The arrow for ⁻19°F is closer to the bottom of the thermometer.

So, ⁻19°F is colder than ⁻2°F.

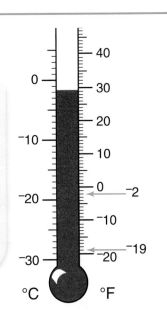

Use a thermometer to compare the temperatures. Write < or >.

  1. ⁻16°C ● ⁻11°C   **2.** ⁻10°F ● 10°F   **3.** ⁻15°C ● 2°C   **4.** ⁻1°F ● ⁻4°F

Explore Negative Numbers

OBJECTIVE: Locate and name negative numbers by using a number line and counting techniques.

Quick Review

Order from least to greatest.

1. 25, 15, 35
2. 86, 84, 87
3. 1,556; 1,565; 1,555
4. 997, 996, 979
5. 1,763; 1,673; 1,765

Vocabulary

positive numbers

negative numbers

Learn

PROBLEM People in Fosston, Minnesota, enjoy outdoor winter sports such as skiing and snowmobiling. The normal low temperature in winter is 5°F. However, the coldest recorded temperature is ⁻25°F.

Look at the thermometer. **Positive numbers** are greater than 0, so they are above the 0 on a thermometer. **Negative numbers** are less than 0, so they are located below the 0. The number 0 is neither positive nor negative.

So, ⁺5 is a positive number and is read as "positive five," and ⁻25 is a negative number read as "negative twenty-five."

There are different ways to use negative and positive numbers.

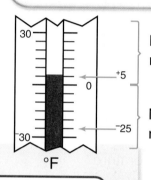

Positive numbers

Negative numbers

°F

Example 1

A Count up

Count: ⁺1, ⁺2, ⁺3, ⁺4, ⁺5, and ⁺6

B Count back

Count: ⁻1, ⁻2, ⁻3, ⁻4, ⁻5, and ⁻6

So, the quarterback gained 6 yards.
Positive number: ⁺6
Read: positive six

So, the quarterback lost 6 yards.
Negative number: ⁻6
Read: negative six

▲ Usually, the air temperature must be less than 41°F, or 5°C, for snow to stay on the ground.

Example 2

A Earn money

Pam earns $8 for weeding the neighbor's garden.

B Owe money

Paco pays his sister the $7 he owes her.

So, Pam has $8 more in her pocket.
Positive number: ⁺8
Read: positive eight

So, now Paco has $7 less in his wallet.
Negative number: ⁻7
Read: negative seven

• Leo deposited $20 into his bank account. Is 20 a positive or a negative number in this situation?

NS 1.8 Use concepts of negative numbers (e.g., on a number line, in counting, in temperature, in "owing"). *also* NS 1.0, SDAP 1.0, MR 1.1, MR 2.3, MR 2.4, MR 3.0, MR 3.2, MR 3.3

Compare and Order

Elevations are measured by their relationship to sea level. Our nation's capital in Washington, D.C., is 1 foot below sea level. Part of Japan is 13 feet below sea level. You can use the negative numbers ⁻1 and ⁻13 to represent these elevations. Locate these negative numbers on a number line.

Elevations Above and Below Sea Level		
Place	Location	Elevation (in feet)
Death Valley, CA	U.S.	-282
Dead Sea	Israel	-1,372
Hachiro-gata	Japan	-13
Mt. Arvin, MI	U.S.	1,979
Mt. McKinley, AK	U.S.	20,320
Mt. Everest	Nepal	29,035
Washington, D.C.	U.S.	-1

Example 3 **Locate negative numbers on a number line.**

On a number line, negative numbers are to the left of 0. Positive numbers are to the right of 0.

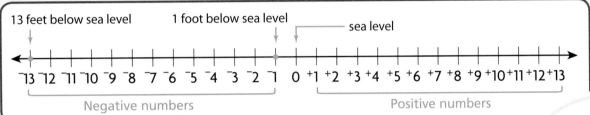

- How do you read the numbers representing the elevations listed in the table?

Example 4 **Use a number line to compare the numbers.**

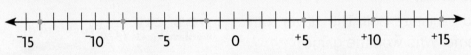

> **Math Idea**
> As you move to the left on a number line, the numbers decrease. As you move to the right, the numbers increase.

A Compare ⁺15 and ⁺5.
Since ⁺15 is to the right of ⁺5, ⁺15 > ⁺5.

B Compare ⁻2 and ⁻14.
Since ⁻2 is to the right of ⁻14, ⁻2 > ⁻14.

C Compare ⁺10 and ⁻8.
Since ⁻8 is to the left of ⁺10, ⁺10 > ⁻8.

- Order the numbers representing the elevations in the table above from least to greatest.

Guided Practice

1. Write the missing numbers from left to right on the number line.

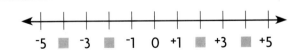

Name the number represented by each letter.

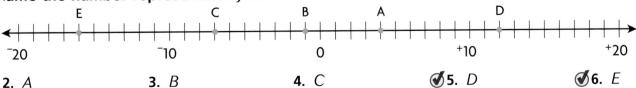

2. *A*

3. *B*

4. *C*

✓5. *D*

✓6. *E*

7. [**TALK Math**] Explain how to use a number line to describe negative numbers.

Name the number represented by each letter.

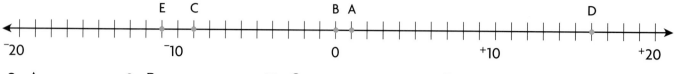

8. A   9. B   10. C   11. D   12. E

Draw a number line and graph the numbers. Compare using < or >.

13. $^+4$ and $^+7$ 14. $^-12$ and 0 15. $^+2$ and $^-2$ 16. $^-10$ and $^+10$ 17. $^-15$ and $^-18$

Write a positive or negative number to represent each situation.

18. Amy owes a friend $5.

19. Sunil earns $10.

20. Marvin added 12 cards to his collection.

21. Jacque dropped 7 pencils.

★ **Algebra** Write the missing numbers to complete a possible pattern.

22. $^+15, ^+12, ^+9, ^+6, ^+3, ▨, ▨, ▨$

23. $^+18, ^+14, ^+10, ^+6, ^+2, ▨, ▨, ▨$

USE DATA For 24–26, use the table.

24. Abby and her family played Miniature Golf. The player with the least score wins the game. Who won the game?

25. Order their scores from least to greatest?

26. Which players had total scores that were greater than Buddy's?

27. **WRITE Math** ▸ **Sense or Nonsense** Lee says that since $^+10$ is greater than $^+7$, then $^-10 > ^-7$. **Explain** why you agree or disagree.

Foston Miniature Golf Score Card

Player	Hole 1	Hole 8	Hole 9	Total Score
Abby	+1	-2	+1	-9
Riley	-1	+2	-1	+6
Cassie	+1	+2	-2	+3
Buddy	+1	-1	-1	-3
Kelly	-1	-1	-1	+5

Achieving the Standards

28. The temperature rose from 45°F to 53°F. What was the change in temperature? (O━┓ NS 1.8, p. 376)

29. What is the missing number in the input/output table? (O━┓ AF 1.5, p. 96)

Input, x	2	5	10	17
Output, y	9	12	17	▨

30. $54 \times 791 =$ (O━┓ NS 3.2, p. 224)

31. **Test Prep** Use the number line to find which number sentence is false.

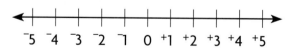

A $^+2 > ^-3$ C $^-2 > ^+1$

B $^-5 < ^-3$ D $^-1 < ^+4$

Race to the Finish

 Reading Skill **Summarize**

Death Valley Trail Marathon

Leadfield (ruins)
CALIFORNIA *NEVADA*
Titus Canyon Road
Start
Titus Canyon
El. 3,460 feet
374
Red Pass Summit El. 5,250 feet
White Pass Summit El. 4,900 feet
Finish
El. 200 feet

The Death Valley Trail Marathon is a race run every year in Death Valley National Park. The race trail follows an unpaved road through Titus Canyon. From the map, you can see that the 26.2-mile marathon course starts at an elevation of 3,460 feet. In February, the average temperature in Death Valley is 15°C. The record low temperature for February is ⁻3°C. How much less than the average temperature is the record low temperature?

You can *summarize*, or restate in a shortened form, the given information to help you understand the problem.

Rewrite the paragraph in shortened form.
Summary: The Death Valley Trail Marathon is run in Death Valley National Park. It goes through Titus Canyon. The race is 26.2 miles long and starts at an elevation of 3,460 feet. The average temperature in February in Death Valley is 15°C, but the record low for February is ⁻3°C.

▲ In 2006, the race was held on February 4. There were runners from more than 30 states and 6 foreign countries.

Problem Solving **Summarize to understand the problem.**

1. Solve the problem above.

2. Mt. McKinley, Alaska, is 20,320 feet above sea level, Death Valley, California, is 282 feet below sea level, and Chicago, Illinois, is 580 feet above sea level. Order the numbers representing the elevations from least to greatest.

Problem Solving Workshop
Strategy: Act It Out

OBJECTIVE: Solve the problem using the problem solving strategy *act it out.*

Learn the Strategy

Acting out a problem can help you understand the problem and see how the problem is solved. You can act out a problem by performing each step or using a model.

Act it out with your classmates.

Jim, Mark, and Hannah are finalists in a spelling bee. Before the last round starts, they will all shake hands once. How many handshakes will there be in all?

Act it out using models.

Ken buys a puzzle for $3.50, a bag of trail mix for $0.79, and a pack of markers for $1.24. He gives the cashier $10.00. How much change should he get back?

> **TALK Math**
> Explain how you can use the information in the problem to help you decide which way to act it out.

O─┓ NS 1.8 Use concepts of negative numbers (e.g., on a number line, in counting, in temperature, in "owing"). *also* NS 1.0, MR 1.0, MR 1.1, MR 2.0, MR 2.1, MR 2.3, MR 2.4, MR 3.0, MR 3.1, MR 3.2, MR 3.3

Use the Strategy

PROBLEM In the evening, the temperature was 4°C. During the night, the temperature fell to ⁻9°C. What was the change in temperature?

Read to Understand

Reading Skill
- Visualize what you are asked to find.
- What information is given?

Plan

- **What strategy can you use to solve the problem?**

  You can act out the problem with a model of a thermometer.

Solve

- **How can you use the strategy to solve the problem?**

  Use index cards to act out the change in temperature.

  Write ⁻9° on an index card. Use a new index card for each degree from ⁻9° to 4°. Next, use masking tape to place the cards on a wall to look like a thermometer.

  Place your hand on 4°. Now move your hand down one index card at a time, and count the number of cards or degrees until you get to ⁻9°.

  You counted 13.

  So, the change in temperature was 13°C.

Check

- **How can you check your answer?**
- **What other strategy could you use to solve the problem?**

Guided Problem Solving

1. A group of friends want to go ice fishing Saturday morning, but only if the temperature is 4°C or below. It was ⁻8°C on Friday night. Saturday morning, the temperature rose 11°C. Did they go fishing? If not, how many degrees greater than 4°C was it?

   First, write each temperature from ⁻8°C to 4°C on an index card and place the cards in a column with ⁻8°C on the bottom.

   Next, start at ⁻8°C and count up 11 cards.

   Finally, compare the temperatures to find out if they went fishing.

2. **What if** the Friday night temperature in Problem 1 was ⁻9°C and had risen 15°C? Would the group of friends have been able to go fishing? If not, how many degrees greater than 4°C would it have been?

3. A special tool called an auger is used to drill through ice so that people can ice fish. If the ice is 28 inches thick and the tool can reach 8 inches below the ice, how many inches long is the auger?

Problem Solving Strategy Practice

Act it out to solve.

4. Cara and her friends are hiking to a snow fort. When they leave in the morning, the temperature is ⁻7°C. When they arrive at the snow fort at 2:00 P.M., the temperature has risen to 12°C. What is the change in temperature?

5. Al went to the skating rink with his sister, Kay. They each paid $1.25 to rent skates. Al bought a drink for $0.55 and a muffin for $0.75. Kay bought a slice of pizza for $1.50. How much more did Kay spend than Al?

6. Four students are in line at the sink. Shannon is ahead of Alfonso. Theodore is behind Alfonso. Shannon is behind Cecily. Who is first in line?

7. Amelia recorded a temperature of 11°C on January 1. On January 15, the temperature was 13°C colder than it had been on January 1. What was the temperature on January 15?

8. **WRITE Math** ▶ Joan, Reba, and Phillip are playing freeze tag. Each person must tag the others twice to end the game. **Explain** how to find the number of tags needed to end the game.

384

Mixed Strategy Practice

USE DATA For 9–10, use the table.

Mens Individual Olympic Speed-Skating Records (Rounded Times)		
Event	Long-Track Race	Short-Track Race
500 m	34 sec	42 sec
1,000 m	1 min 7 sec	1 min 27 sec
1,500 m	1 min 44 sec	2 min 16 sec
5,000 m	6 min 15 sec	
10,000 m	12 min 59 sec	

Choose a
STRATEGY

Draw a Diagram or Picture

Make a Model or Act It Out

Make an Organized List

Find a Pattern

Make a Table or Graph

Predict and Test

Work Backward

Solve a Simpler Problem

Write an Equation

Use Logical Reasoning

9. **Open-Ended** Some races started exactly on the minute. When might the races have started and when might the races have stopped?

10. In short-track skating, a 500-meter race is about 4 laps, and a 1,500-meter race is about 13 laps. About how many laps is a 1,000-meter race?

11. **Pose a Problem** Look back at Problem 4. Write a similar problem by changing the temperatures.

12. Rosalia went to winter fun day at the ski hill. First, she won a ski race. She drank cocoa before she made a snow globe but after she built the snow fort. In what order did she do the activities?

▲ Short-track speed skating

CHALLENGE YOURSELF

In the winter, tickets for the chair lift at the Lake Placid, New York, Olympic area cost $9.00 for adults and $6.00 for children.

13. Jake and his family visited the Olympic area in January. They took the chair lift to the top of the 120-meter ski jump. They paid a total of $45.00. How many adults and how many children could there have been?

14. In the spring, tickets cost $5.00 for adults and $3.00 for children. How much less does it cost a family of 2 adults and 3 children to take the chair lift in the spring than a family of 1 adult and 3 children to take the chair lift in the winter? **Explain** how you found your answer.

Use a Coordinate Plane

OBJECTIVE: Identify, locate, and graph points on a coordinate grid and describe paths.

Learn

A grid formed by a horizontal line called the **x-axis** and a vertical line called the **y-axis** is a **coordinate plane**. The point where the x-axis and the y-axis meet is the **origin**, or (0,0).

You can use ordered pairs to locate a points on a coordinate plane. The **x-coordinate** tells how far to move horizontally, and the **y-coordinate** tells how far to move vertically.

$(^+1, ^+4)$

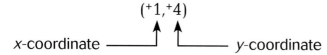

x-coordinate   y-coordinate

PROBLEM The coordinate plane shows the location of the activities at the school carnival. What ordered pair gives the location of the trampoline?

Example 1 Name the ordered pair for the trampoline.

Step 1

Start at the point labeled Trampoline. Look down at the x-axis. It is 4 units to the right of the origin. The x-coordinate is $^+4$.

Step 2

Then look to the left at the y-axis. It is 3 units up from the origin. The y-coordinate is $^+3$.

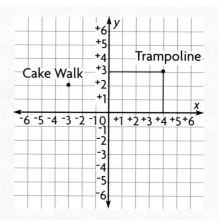

So, the trampoline is located at $(^+4, ^+3)$.

Example 2 What activity is located at $(^-3, ^+2)$?

Step 1

Start at the origin. Count 3 units to the left.

Step 2

Then count 2 units up.

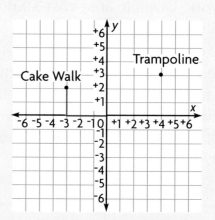

So, the cake walk is located at $(^-3, ^+2)$.

• How is $(^-3, ^+2)$ different from $(^+2, ^-3)$?

MG 2.0 Students use two-dimensional coordinate grids to represent points and graph lines and simple figures. *also* MR 2.3, MR 2.4, MR 3.2

Example 3 Graph points.

A Graph a point at (⁻6,⁻4) to show the Prize Booth.

Start at the origin. Count 6 units left. Count 4 units down. Graph a point and label it.

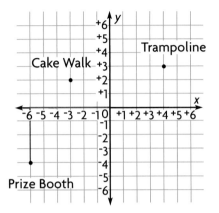

B Graph a point at (0,⁻3) to show the Hay Ride.

Start at the origin. Since the x-coordinate is 0, do not move right or left. Count 3 units down. Graph a point and label it.

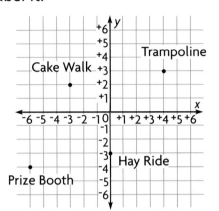

Example 4 Graph plane figures.

The fourth grade students are making a fenced area for parking their bikes. If the fence poles are placed at (⁻2,⁻5), (⁻2,⁺1), and (⁻4,⁺1), where should the fourth fence pole be located to form a rectangle?

ERROR ALERT

The first number is the number of units right or left and the second number is the number of units up or down from the origin.

Step 1	Step 2
Graph the three points. Connect them with line segments.	Place a point that will form a rectangle. Connect the line segments.

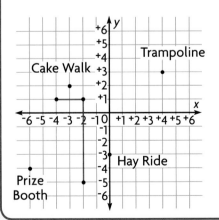

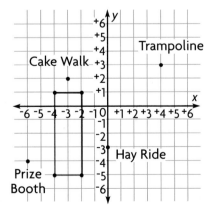

So, the fourth pole should be located at (⁻4,⁻5).

1. To graph (⁻4,⁺3) on a coordinate plane, tell how many units and in which direction you move first. What will you do next?

Write the point for each ordered pair on the coordinate plane.

2. (⁺2,⁻2)

3. (0,⁺5)

4. (⁻3,⁻4)

✓ 5. (⁺5,⁺3)

✓ 6. **TALK Math** **Explain** how to move horizontally and vertically from point A to point H using *left*, *right*, *up*, or *down*.

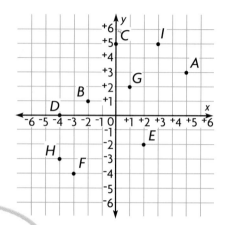

Independent Practice and Problem Solving

Write the point for each ordered pair on the coordinate plane above.

7. (⁻2,⁺1)   8. (⁺1,⁺2)   9. (⁻4,⁻3)   10. (⁻4,0)   11. (⁺3,⁺5)

Use grid paper. Graph each point and label it using the ordered pair.

12. (⁺4,⁻5)   13. (⁻3,⁺1)   14. (⁺4,⁺1)   15. (⁻3,⁻5)   16. (⁺3,⁻5)

17. What polygon is formed by the points (⁺4,⁻5), (⁻3,⁺1), (⁺4,⁺1), and (⁻3,⁻5)?

18. What polygon is formed by the points (⁻3, ⁺1), (⁺4,⁺1), and (⁺4,⁻5)?

For 19–21, use the map.

19. Emily is at the lemonade stand. She moves 4 units right and 3 units up. Then she moves 1 unit left and 4 units up. Where is she now? Name the ordered pair.

20. Which booth is located 2 units left and 1 unit down from the balloon pop?

21. There are flags at 4 of the booths. The flags are the vertices of a rectangle. What ordered pairs describe where the flags are located?

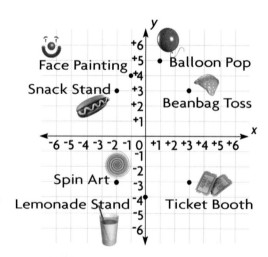

22. **Reasoning Explain** how you know that the line segment joining (12,0) and (0,12) is not a horizontal line segment.

23. **WRITE Math** **What's the Question?** You start at (0,0). You move 8 units right and then 5 units down.

24. Chris rode his bike 19 miles on Monday and 15 miles on Tuesday. How many more miles did he ride on Monday than on Tuesday? (O—n NS 3.0, p. 44)

25. **Test Prep** How many units to the left of the origin is ($^-$4,$^+$9)?

  A 13

  B 9

  C 5

  D 4

26. What is the mode of this set of numbers? (SDAP 1.2, p. 326)

10, 12, 34, 12, 14, 10, 12

27. Lisa's DVD is 133 minutes long. How many hours and minutes is the DVD? (Grade 3 MG 1.4)

28. **Test Prep** What is the origin on a coordinate grid?

  A the *y*-axis   **C** the point (0,0)

  B the *x*-axis   **D** a trend

Problem Solving [connects to] Music

The Romley High School marching band is learning a routine. The grid shows where each member should stand to form the letter F. The next letter they will form is a T.

1. **Explain** which band members must move to form the letter T. For each member that must move, describe the path he or she must take and give an ordered pair to show that member's new location. Use *north*, *south*, *east*, and *west* in your description.

2. Use grid paper to make a map like the one shown. Use a different formation for the band members. Describe how they could move to make a new formation. Use *north*, *south*, *east*, and *west* and ordered pairs in your description.

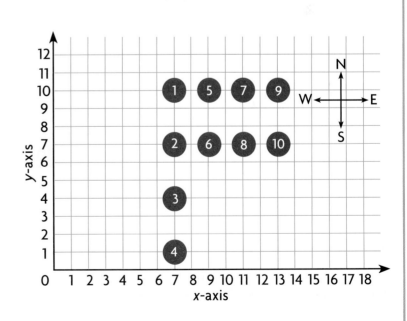

5 Length on a Coordinate Plane

OBJECTIVE: Find the distance between two points on a coordinate plane.

Learn

At Adventure Playground in Berkeley, California, children use saws and hammers to make their own projects.

PROBLEM Charlie and his uncle are working on a fort. Charlie hammers one nail 6 inches from the end of a plank of wood and another nail 13 inches from the same end. How far apart are the nails?

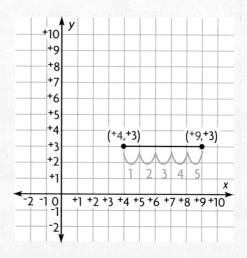

Example 1 Use a number line.

You can count units or subtract to find the distance between two points on a number line.

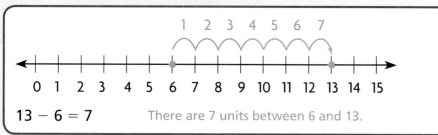

$13 - 6 = 7$ There are 7 units between 6 and 13.

So, the nails are 7 inches apart.

To find the horizontal distance between two points on a coordinate plane, look at the *x*-coordinates.

Example 2 Find the length of a horizontal line segment on a coordinate plane.

A playground design shows a swing at $(^+4, ^+3)$ and a slide at $(^+9, ^+3)$. Find the distance from the swing to the slide.

Step 1

Graph the ordered pairs $(^+4, ^+3)$ and $(^+9, ^+3)$. Then connect the points.

Step 2

Count the units between the two points, or subtract the *x*-coordinates. $9 - 4 = 5$

So, the distance from the swing to the slide is 5 units.

• What is the distance between $(^+5, ^+2)$ and $(^+8, ^+2)$?

MG 2.2 Understand that the length of a horizontal line segment equals the difference of the *x*-coordinates.
MG 2.3 Understand that the length of a vertical line segment equals the difference of the *y*-coordinates.
also MG 2.0, MR 2.2, MR 2.3, MR 2.4, MR 3.2

Vertical Distance and Perimeter

You can also find the vertical distance between two points on a coordinate plane. To find a vertical distance, look at the *y*-coordinates.

Example 3 Find the length of a vertical line segment.

Climbing tires are placed on the playground at ($^+$2,$^+$3) and ($^+$2,$^+$9). Find the distance between the climbing tires.

Step 1

Graph the ordered pairs ($^+$2,$^+$3) and ($^+$2,$^+$9). Then connect the points.

Step 2

Count the units between the two points, or subtract the *y*-coordinates.

$9 - 3 = 6$

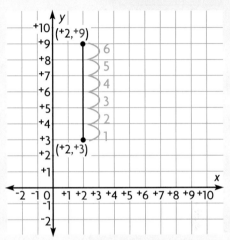

So, the distance between the climbing tires is 6 units.

• What is the distance between ($^+$3,$^+$2) and ($^+$3,$^+$10)?

Activity

Materials ▪ ruler ▪ grid paper

Find the perimeter of a rectangle with vertices at ($^+$2,$^+$2), ($^+$2,$^+$5), ($^+$6,$^+$5), and ($^+$6,$^+$2).

> **Remember**
> To find perimeter, count the number of units around the figure.

• Graph the ordered pairs. Connect the points to make a rectangle.

• Find the distance around the rectangle by counting the units between each point.

Horizontal distances:	($^+$2,$^+$2) to ($^+$6,$^+$2) = 4 units
	($^+$2,$^+$5) to ($^+$6,$^+$5) = 4 units
Vertical distances:	($^+$2,$^+$2) to ($^+$2,$^+$5) = 3 units
	($^+$6,$^+$2) to ($^+$6,$^+$5) = 3 units

Add the units.

$4 + 4 + 3 + 3 = 14$

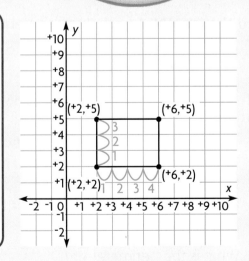

So, the perimeter is 14 units.

Guided Practice

Find the length of each line segment.

1.

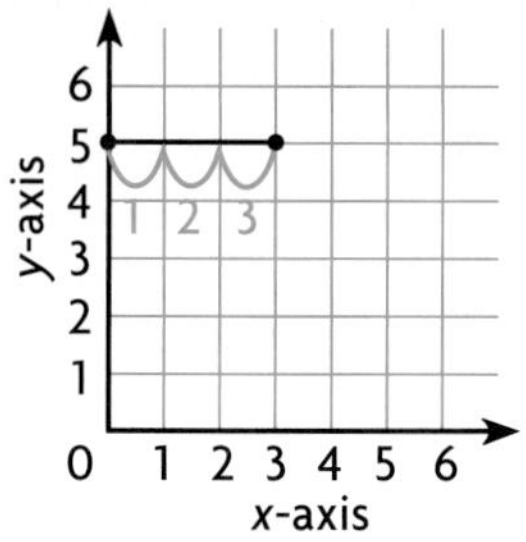

```
6
5 ∩∩∩
4 1 2 3
3
2
1
0  1 2 3 4 5 6
      x-axis
```
(y-axis labeled on vertical)

2.

```
6
5        •
4
3
2
1        •
0  1 2 3 4 5 6
      x-axis
```
(y-axis labeled on vertical)

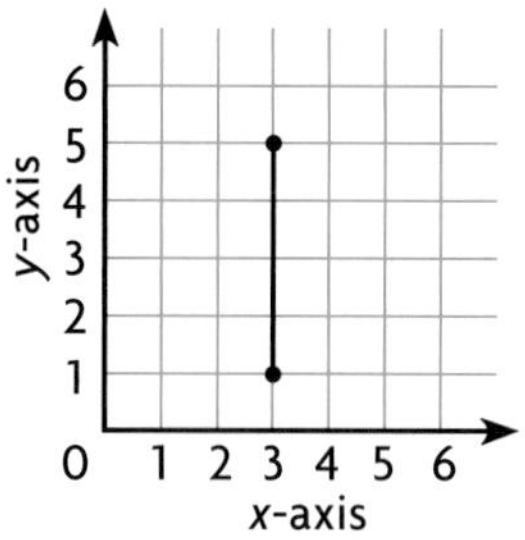

Graph the ordered pairs and connect the points.
Find the length of each line segment.

3. (5,3) and (5,8)   **4.** (7,9) and (10,9)   **5.** (3,5) and (3,8)   ✓**6.** (2,2) and (6,2)

Find the length of each line segment.

7. (4,6) and (0,6)   **8.** (6,3) and (6,6)   **9.** (3,5) and (8,5)   ✓**10.** (2,6) and (2,4)

11. [TALK Math] **Explain** how you could find the length of a line segment between (3,1) and (3,3).

Independent Practice (and Problem Solving

Graph the ordered pairs and connect the points.
Find the length of each line segment.

12. (2,9) and (10,9)   **13.** (4,3) and (10,3)   **14.** (5,7) and (5,2)   **15.** (3,6) and (3,7)

Find the length of each line segment.

16. (1,0) and (1,3)   **17.** (1,4) and (6,4)   **18.** (3,1) and (6,1)   **19.** (2,2) and (2,8)

For 20–21, use the Pearson Park Bike Path map.

20. Tina rides her bike from the start of the path to the first resting area. Then she rides back to the start. Keenan rides from the start to the water fountain. How much farther does Tina ride?

21. What is the perimeter of the bike path?

Pearson Park Bike Path
Each unit = 1 kilometer

```
9
8  Start      Resting
7             Area 3
6
5             Resting
4             Area 2
3
2  Resting    Water
1  Area 1     Fountain
0  1 2 3 4 5 6 7 8 9
        x-axis
```
(y-axis labeled on vertical)

Extra Practice on page 402, Set D

22. Algebra What is the missing x-coordinate for a rectangle with vertices at $(3,3)$, $(3,6)$, $(7,3)$, and $(\blacksquare,6)$? Graph the ordered pairs and draw the rectangle.

23. **WRITE Math** **What's the Error?** Erin says that the horizontal distance from $(3,7)$ to $(7,7)$ is 0. What error did Erin make? What is the correct answer?

24. What is the value of $5 \times n$ if $n = 6$?
(AF 1.1, p. 146)

25. What is the median of this set of numbers? (SDAP 1.2, p. 326)

18, 15, 20, 17, 15, 19, 14, 15, 18

26. Test Prep Look at the graph. Point A is at $(1,1)$. Point B is at $(1,5)$.

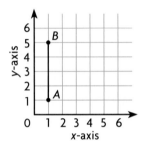

How can you find the number of units from point A to point B?

A Add: $1 + 5$ **C** Subtract: $5 - 1$

B Add: $1 + 1$ **D** Subtract: $5 - 5$

27. Suki owes her friend Will $8. Write a positive or negative number to represent this situation. (O—┐ NS 1.8, p. 378)

28. Test Prep What is the length of the line segment joining the points $(2,2)$ and $(5,2)$?

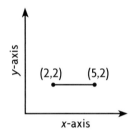

A 0 units

B 2 units

C 3 units

D 8 units

 **Problem Solving and Reasoning**

MEASUREMENT You can find the vertical and horizontal distances between points on a coordinate plane by counting the units between the points.

The distance between $(^-2,^+3)$ and $(^+4,^+3)$ is 6 units.

Graph the ordered pairs and connect the points. Find the length of each line segment.

1. $(^+5,^-2)$ and $(^+5,^+5)$

2. $(^-4,^-2)$ and $(^+4,^-2)$

Use an Equation

OBJECTIVE: Use a function table to find a second number when a first number is given.

Vocabulary

function table

Learn

You can think of an equation as a rule.

$y = 5x$ is the same as $y = 5 \times x$.

Rule: To find y, multiply x by 5.

Input, x	Output, y
1	5
2	10
3	15

You can use a function table to find values for y. A **function table** is a table that matches each input value to an output value. The output values are determined by the function.

PROBLEM To skateboard at the park, Courtney can rent a helmet for the day for $3. The skateboard rents for $2 per hour. How much will it cost to rent the skateboard and helmet for 1, 2, 3, or 4 hours?

Write an equation:
$$y = 2x + 3$$
$$\downarrow \quad \downarrow$$
y = total cost x = number of hours rented

Example 1 Use an equation to complete a function table.

Step 1

List values for the input, x.

Hours, x	1	2	3	4
Total Cost, y	■	■	■	■

Step 2

Replace x in the equation with the values in the table.

$x = 1$	$x = 2$	$x = 3$	$x = 4$
$y = 2x + 3$	$y = 2x + 3$	$y = 2x + 3$	$y = 2x + 3$
$y = (2 \times 1) + 3$	$y = (2 \times 2) + 3$	$y = (2 \times 3) + 3$	$y = (2 \times 4) + 3$
$y = 2 + 3$	$y = 4 + 3$	$y = 6 + 3$	$y = 8 + 3$
$y = 5$	$y = 7$	$y = 9$	$y = 11$

Step 3

Record in the function table the values you found for y.

Hours, x	1	2	3	4
Total Cost, y	5	7	9	11

So, renting the skateboard and helmet for 1, 2, 3, or 4 hours will cost Courtney $5, $7, $9, or $11.

○━ **AF 1.5** Understand that an equation such as $y = 3x + 5$ is a prescription for determining a second number when a first number is given. *also* **AF 1.0, AF 1.1, MR 1.1, MR 2.3, MR 2.4, MR 2.6, MR 3.0, MR 3.2**

Example 2 Use an equation to complete a function table.

Use the equation $y = (x \div 3) + 1$.

Step 1

List values for the input, x.

Input, x	3	6	9	12
Output, y	■	■	■	■

Step 2

Replace x in the equation with the values in the table.

$x = 3$	$x = 6$	$x = 9$	$x = 12$
$y = (x \div 3) + 1$	$y = (x \div 3) + 1$	$y = (x \div 3) + 1$	$y = (x \div 3) + 1$
$y = (3 \div 3) + 1$	$y = (6 \div 3) + 1$	$y = (9 \div 3) + 1$	$y = (12 \div 3) + 1$
$y = 1 + 1$	$y = 2 + 1$	$y = 3 + 1$	$y = 4 + 1$
$y = 2$	$y = 3$	$y = 4$	$y = 5$

Step 3

Record in the function table the values you found for y.

Input, x	3	6	9	12
Output, y	2	3	4	5

So, the ordered pairs for this function table are (3,2), (6,3), (9,4), and (12,5).

Example 3 Use ordered pairs to check the values of a function table.

Caydon made a function table for $y = 4 - x$.
Are the values in the table correct?

Input, x	1	2	3	4
Output, y	3	2	3	0

The ordered pairs for this function table are
(1,3), (2,2), (3,3), and (4,0).
Check each pair of values given. Replace x and y
in the equation with the numbers.

Remember

In an ordered pair (x,y), the first number is always x and the second number is always y. In the ordered pair (3,5), x is 3 and y is 5.

Try (1,3).	**Try (2,2).**	**Try (3,3).**	**Try (4,0).**
$y = 4 - x$	$y = 4 - x$	$y = 4 - x$	$y = 4 - x$
$3 \stackrel{?}{=} 4 - 1$	$2 \stackrel{?}{=} 4 - 2$	$3 \stackrel{?}{=} 4 - 3$	$0 \stackrel{?}{=} 4 - 4$
true	true	not true	true

So, (1,3), (2,2), and (4,0) make the equation $y = 4 - x$ true.
(3,3) is incorrect.

• Does (6,22) make the equation $y = 4x - 2$ true? Explain.

1. The function table shows values for the equation $y = 2x - 3$. Complete the function table.

Input, x	3	4	5	6
Output, y	3		7	

$\downarrow$ $\downarrow$
$(2 \times 3) - 3$ $(2 \times 5) - 3$

Use the equation to complete each function table.

2. $y = 3x + 5$

Input, x	1	2	3	4
Output, y				

✅ 3. $y = (x \div 2) - 1$

Input, x	4	6	8	10
Output, y				

Does the ordered pair make the equation $y = 4x - 1$ true? Write *yes* or *no*.

4. $(1,3)$ 5. $(4,16)$ 6. $(3,11)$ 7. $(6,20)$ ✅ 8. $(5,19)$

9. **TALK Math** Explain how to write an ordered pair for the equation $y = 3x - 4$ if $x = 5$.

Independent Practice and Problem Solving

Use the equation to complete each function table.

10. $y = 2x - 6$

Input, x	3	4	5	6
Output, y				

11. $y = (x \div 5) + 2$

Input, x	5	10	15	20
Output, y				

Does the ordered pair make the equation $y = (x \div 4) + 2$ true? Write *yes* or *no*.

12. $(4,3)$ 13. $(20,7)$ 14. $(12,6)$ 15. $(24,8)$ 16. $(8,4)$

For 17–19, use the table.

17. How much does it cost to rent a mountain bike and a helmet for 1, 2, or 3 hours?

18. How much does it cost to rent a skateboard and pads for 2, 3, or 4 hours?

19. Does it cost more to rent a skateboard and a helmet for 2 hours or a scooter and pads for 3 hours? **Explain.**

20. **Reasoning** In the equation $y = 3x - 2$, how can you find the x value if $y = 16$?

21. **WRITE Math** Explain how to make a function table for the equation $y = 2x + 2$.

Board & Bike Rentals

Hourly Rate	Day Rate
Pads $2	Mountain bike $4
Helmet $3	Scooter $3
	Skateboard $2

22. What number is represented by n?

$$n \times 5 = 35 \text{ (AF 1.1, p. 126)}$$

23. Which representation of 12 includes only prime numbers? (O━ⁿ NS 4.2, p. 298)

3×4 6×2 $3 \times 2 \times 2$ 1×12

24. The temperature yesterday was 1°C. Today it dropped 4°C. What is the temperature today? (O━ⁿ NS 1.8, p. 378)

25. Test Prep What is the value of y if $x = 3$ in the equation $y = 2x + 5$?

A 6   C 13

B 11   D 28

26. Test Prep The sum of x plus y equals 14. If $x = 5$, which equation can be used to find the value of y?

A $y - 5 = 14$ C $x + 14 = 5$

B $5 + y = 14$ D $x - y = 5$

Problem Solving [connects to] Science

Avocado trees can be grown year-round in California because of the warm climate. These trees need lots of sun and water. A full-grown avocado tree uses about 20 gallons of water daily, and produces around 150 avocados a year.

You can write an equation to show how many gallons of water an avocado tree uses.

Let x represent the number of days, and let y represent the total number of gallons.

$y = 20x$

1. Complete the function table using the equation $y = 20x$.

Number of Days, x	1	2	3	4
Total Gallons, y	▨	▨	▨	▨

2. What if an avocado farmer has 80 gallons of water per day for one area of an orchard? How many avocado plants might the farmer plant in that area?

3. Reasoning Would an avocado farmer expect to use more than or less than 100 gallons of water on an avocado tree in one week? **Explain.**

◀ You can grow your own avocado tree by placing the wide end of the pit in water in a sunny spot.

Graph Relationships

OBJECTIVE: Use an equation to graph relationships.

Quick Review

Multiply each
number by 3.

1. 2   2. 5
3. 6   4. 7
5. 9

Learn

You can graph an equation on a coordinate grid.

HANDS ON

Activity

Materials ■ coordinate grid with the x-axis labeled 0–11
and the y-axis labeled 0–26 ■ ruler

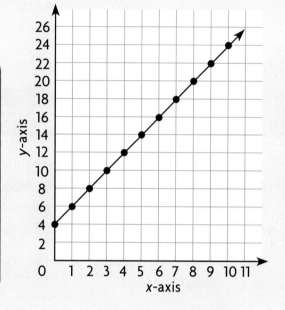

- Copy and complete the table for the
  equation $y = 2x + 4$.

Input, x	0	1	2	3	4	5	6	7	8	9	10
Output, y	4	6	8	10	■	■	■	■	■	■	■

- Write the values of x and y as ordered pairs (x,y).

  (0,4), (1,6), (2,8), (3,10), (4,12), (5,14),

  (6,16), (7,18), (8,20), (9,22), (10,24)

- Graph the ordered pairs on the coordinate grid.
  Use a ruler to connect the points.

- Look at the graph of the equation $y = 2x + 4$.
  What happens to y as x increases?

Example Graph the equation $x = 3$.

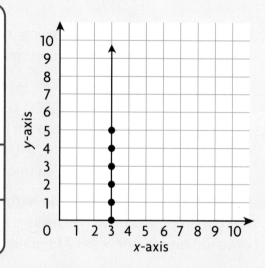

Step 1

Make a table. The values for x are always 3. Choose any
values for y.

Input, x	3	3	3	3	3	3
Output, y	0	1	2	3	4	5

Step 2

Write the ordered pairs. (3,0), (3,1) (3,2), (3,3), (3,4), (3,5)

Step 3

Graph the points. Use a ruler to connect the points.

- What kind of line is made by graphing $x = 3$?

○━ MG 2.1 Draw the points corresponding to linear relationships on graph paper (e.g., draw 10 points on
the graph of the equation $y = 3x$ and connect them by using a straight line). *also* **AF 1.0, AF 1.1, AF 1.4,**
○━ **AF 1.5, MR 1.1, MR 2.3, MR 2.4, MR 3.2**

Guided Practice

1. The table at the right shows values for the equation $y = 2x - 1$. Find the missing value. Then list the ordered pairs in the table.

Input, x	1	2	3	4	5
Output, y	1	3	5	7	▦

Make a table using values of 1 through 10 for x. Then graph the equation on a coordinate grid.

2. $y = x + 4$ 3. $y = x + 2$ ✓4. $y = 2x$ ✓5. $y = 2x - 2$

6. **TALK Math** **Explain** how to graph the equation $y = x + 1$.

Independent Practice and Problem Solving

Make a table using values of 1 through 10 for x. Then graph the equation on a coordinate grid.

7. $y = x + 8$ 8. $y = x - 1$ 9. $y = 3x$ 10. $y = 3x - 2$

For 11–12, use the table.

11. In the equation $d = r \times t$, d represents distance, r represents rate or speed, and t represents time. Write an equation to show the distance, d, that Emma can bike in 2 hours. Then solve.

12. Make a table to show the distance Emma can bike in 1, 2, or 3 hours. Graph the ordered pairs on a coordinate grid.

13. **WRITE Math** **Explain** what kind of line is made by graphing $y = 1$.

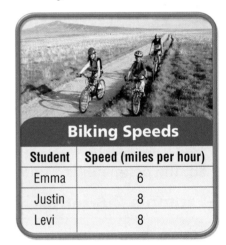

Biking Speeds

Student	Speed (miles per hour)
Emma	6
Justin	8
Levi	8

Achieving the Standards

14. What is the value of the expression below if $a = 2$? (AF 1.1, p. 82)

$$12 + (a - 2)$$

15. What is the value of the expression below? (O━┓ AF 1.2, p. 142)

$$(17 + 5) - (3 \times 4)$$

16. Does the ordered pair $(3,11)$ make the equation $y = 2x + 5$ true? Write *yes* or *no*. (O━┓ AF 1.5, p. 394)

17. **Test Prep** Lee graphed the equation $y = 4x + 2$. Which could be the coordinates of a point on his graph?

A $(1,7)$ C $(3,14)$

B $(2,4)$ D $(4,16)$

Technology
Use Harcourt Mega Math, The Number Games, *ArachnaGraph*, Level L.

Identify Linear Relationships

OBJECTIVE: Identify and graph linear relationships on a coordinate grid.

Quick Review

Find the value of the expression.

1. $3 \times a$ if $a = 4$
2. $15 \div b$ if $b = 5$
3. $9t$ if $t = 6$
4. $24 \div v$ if $v = 3$
5. $7 \times k$ if $k = 7$

Learn

PROBLEM Marta drew squares of different sizes to plan her garden. How is the length of the side of the garden related to the perimeter of the garden?

Example 1 Make a table to find a rule.

Length of One Side, x	1	2	3	4
Perimeter, y	4	8	12	16

$\downarrow$ $\downarrow$ $\downarrow$ $\downarrow$

$1 \times 4 = 4$ $2 \times 4 = 8$ $3 \times 4 = 12$ $4 \times 4 = 16$

Rule: Multiply x by 4 to find y.

So, the perimeter is 4 times the length of one side.

Remember
You can find the perimeter of a figure by counting the units around the figure.

Example 2 Graph the ordered pairs on a coordinate grid.

Step 1

Write the ordered pairs for the table.
(1,4), (2,8), (3,12), (4,16)

Step 2

Graph the ordered pairs.

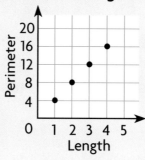

Guided Practice

1. The table shows the perimeters of different equilateral triangles. Use the table to complete the rule.

Length of One Side (in inches), x	1	2	3	4
Perimeter (in inches), y	3	6	9	12

Rule: Multiply x by ■ to find y.

AF 1.4 Use and interpret formulas (e.g., area = length × width or $A = lw$) to answer questions about quantities and their relationships *also* **AF 1.0, AF 1.1, ○┓ AF 1.5, ○┓ MG 2.0, ○┓ MG 2.1, MR 1.1, MR 2.3, MR 2.4, MR 3.2**

Write a rule. Graph the ordered pairs.

2.

Input, x	1	2	3	4	5
Output, y	1	2	3	4	5

3.

Input, x	2	4	6	8	10
Output, y	1	2	3	4	5

4. **TALK Math** Explain how the perimeter of an equilateral triangle is related to the length of one side. Use the table in Problem 1 to help.

Independent Practice and Problem Solving

Write a rule. Graph the ordered pairs.

5.

Input, x	1	2	3	4	5
Output, y	2	3	4	5	6

6.

Input, x	2	3	4	5	6
Output, y	1	2	3	4	5

For 7–8, use the graph.

7. The graph shows the relationship between the lengths and widths of tiles sold at a garden shop. How is the length related to the width?

8. If a customer buys a tile with a length of 8 inches, what is the width of the tile?

9. **Reasoning** Graph ordered pairs for the rule $y = 6$. What type of line did you graph?

10. A graph has points at (3,7), (5,9), (11,15), and (15,19). Write an ordered pair that would belong on this graph. **Explain** your choice.

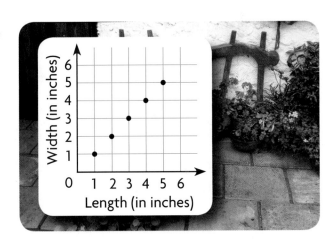

11. **WRITE Math** **Sense or Nonsense** Latisha says that a rule for this table is to multiply the value of x by itself to find y. Does Latisha's statement make sense? **Explain.**

Input, x	1	2	3	4	5
Output, y	1	4	9	16	25

Achieving the Standards

12. Draw a picture, and shade it to show 2 out of 5 parts. (Grade 3 NS 3.0)

13. What is the length of the line segment connecting the points (3,5) and (3,9)?

    (⊶ MG 2.3, p. 390)

14. 2 feet 1 inch = ▇ inches (Grade 3 MG 1.4)

15. **Test Prep** Look at the graph for Problems 7–8. What would the length be if the width were 10 inches?

    A 10 inches   **C** 22 inches

    B 20 inches   **D** 24 inches

Extra Practice on page 403, Set G

 **Extra Practice**

Set A Write each temperature. Then estimate to
the nearest 5 degrees. (pp. 374–377)

1.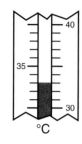
°C

2.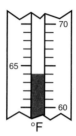
°F

3.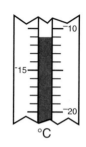
°C

Use a thermometer to find the change in temperature.

4. 12°F and 21°F

5. 6°C and 26°C

6. 18°F and 27°F

7. ⁻1°F and 15°F

8. ⁻3°C and 9°C

9. ⁻1°C and ⁻20°C

Set B Name the number represented by each letter. (pp. 378–381)

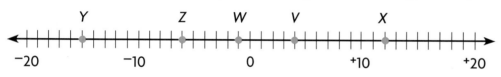

1. V

2. W

3. X

4. Y

5. Z

**Draw a number line and graph the numbers.
Compare using < or >.**

6. ⁺2 and ⁻8

7. ⁻4 and 0

8. ⁺3 and ⁻3

9. ⁻6 and ⁺6

10. ⁻9 and ⁻16

Set C Write the point for each
ordered pair on the coordinate plane. (pp. 386–389)

1. (⁻4,⁺2)

2. (⁺1,⁺6)

3. (⁺4,⁻2)

4. (⁻5,0)

5. (⁻3,⁻5)

6. (⁺2,⁻4)

7. Jan graphed the points (⁺2,⁺1), (⁺2,⁺4), and (⁺4,⁺4) on a coordinate grid. What point should she graph next if she wants the points to be vertices of a rectangle?

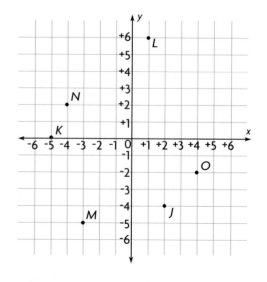

 Technology
Use Harcourt Mega Math, The Number
Games, *ArachnaGraph*, Levels H, L.

Set D Graph the ordered pairs and connect the points.
Find the length of each line segment. (pp. 390–393)

1. (7,2) and (7,7)
2. (2,5) and (9,5)
3. (6,4) and (6,1)
4. (6,1) and (0,1)
5. (2,9) and (10,9)
6. (4,3) and (10,3)

Set E Use the equation to complete each function table. (pp. 394–397)

1. $y = 3x - 2$

Input, x	2	3	4	5
Output, y	▣	▣	▣	▣

2. $y = (x \div 3) + 1$

Input, x	3	6	9	12
Output, y	▣	▣	▣	▣

**Does the ordered pair make the equation
$y = 5x + 3$ true? Write *yes* or *no*.**

3. (2,13)
4. (7,35)
5. (5,22)
6. (12,63)

Set F Make a table using values of 1 through 10 for *x*.
Then graph the equation on a coordinate plane. (pp. 398–399)

1. $y = x + 4$
2. $y = 3x + 5$
3. $y = 2x$
4. $y = 3x - 1$
5. $y = 4x + 3$
6. $y = x + 6$

Set G Write a rule. Graph the ordered pairs. (pp. 400–401)

1.
Input, x	1	2	3	4
Output, y	4	5	6	7

2.
Input, x	2	3	4	5
Output, y	0	1	2	4

For 3–4, use the graph.

3. The graph shows the relationship between the number of stools and the number of legs a craftsman makes. How is the number of legs related to the number of stools?

4. How many legs would be needed for 5 stools?

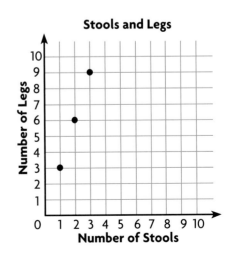

Stools and Legs

 # Chapter 15 Review/Test

Check Vocabulary and Concepts

Choose the best term from the box.

1. The ordered pair (0,0) is called the __?__.

   (O━┓ MG 2.0, p. 386)

2. __?__ are always less than zero. (O━┓ NS 1.8, p. 378)

3. The __?__ tells how far to move horizontally.

   (O━┓ MG 2.0, p. 386)

Check Skills

Use a thermometer to find the change in temperature. (O━┓ NS 1.8, pp. 374–377)

4. 6°F and 32°F

5. ⁻9°C and 12°C

6. 18°F and 43°F

7. 0°C and ⁻19°C

Write the point for the ordered pair on the coordinate plane. (O━┓ MG 2.0, pp. 386–389)

8. (⁺4,⁺3)

9. (⁺6,0)

10. (⁻2,⁻1)

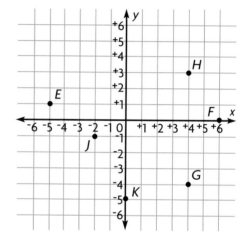

Graph the ordered pairs and connect the points. Find the length of the line segment.

(O━┓ MG 2.2, 2.3, pp. 390–393)

11. (4,7) and (10,7)

12. (2,3) and (2,6)

Does the ordered pair make the equation $y = 4x + 2$ true? Write *yes* or *no*. (O━┓ AF 1.5, pp. 394–397)

13. (0,2)

14. (2,10)

15. (3,11)

Make a table using values of 1 through 10 for *x*. Then graph the equation on a coordinate grid. (O━┓ MG 2.1, pp. 398–399)

16. $y = x + 5$

17. $y = 2x + 1$

18. $y = 4x - 1$

Check Problem Solving

Solve. (O━┓ MG 2.0, MR 2.3, pp. 382–385)

19. In the evening, the temperature was 12°C. Overnight, the temperature fell 14 degrees. What was the temperature in the morning?

20. ▐WRITE Math▶ **Explain** how to find the change in temperature between ⁻3°C and 8°C.

GO ONLINE **Technology** Use *Online Assessment.*

Enrich • Graph Clues
Scavenger Hunt

Dean and Tina are on a scavenger hunt. Here is a riddle they have to answer by drawing: I can be found in your eye, on TV, or in the sky. What am I?

You can plot ordered pairs on a coordinate grid and connect the points to see what Dean and Tina found.

Use clues 1 and 2 to find the first two ordered pairs. Then plot these ordered pairs on the coordinate grid.

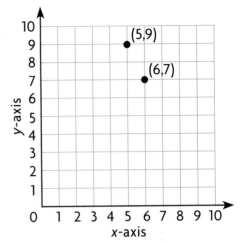

- Clue 1: The first coordinate is the prime number between 3 and 7. The second coordinate is 4 more than the first coordinate.

So, the first ordered pair is (5,9).

- Clue 2: The first coordinate is the first even number greater than 5. The second coordinate times the first coordinate is 42.

So, the second ordered pair is (6,7).

Try It

Copy the grid shown above. Use the following clues to name ordered pairs. Then plot the ordered pairs on the grid.

1. The first coordinate equals $56 \div 7$. The second coordinate is 1 less than the first coordinate.

2. The first coordinate equals 2×3. The second coordinate is the first coordinate divided by 1.

3. The first coordinate is 3 more than the second coordinate. The sum of the coordinates is 11.

4. The first coordinate is the same as the second coordinate. The product of the coordinates is 25.

5. The second coordinate is 1 more than the first coordinate. The first coordinate equals $18 \div 6$.

6. The second coordinate is 2 more than the first coordinate. The first coordinate is the second even number after 1.

7. The first coordinate equals $14 \div 7$. The second coordinate equals 1×7.

8. The first coordinate is 2 times itself. The second coordinate equals $2 + 5$.

9. Connect the points in order of the clues. What is the answer to the riddle?

WRITE Math ▸ **Explain** how you found the ordered pair in Problem 3.

Multiple Choice

1. The line on the coordinate grid shows the equation $y = 3x$. Which ordered pair represents a point that is not on that line?
(O━▪ AF 1.5, p. 398)

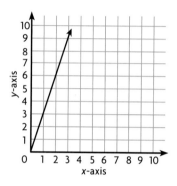

A (1,3)

B (2,6)

C (3,9)

D (0,5)

2. How many more runs did Huang score than Steve during June? (SDAP 1.3, p. 344)

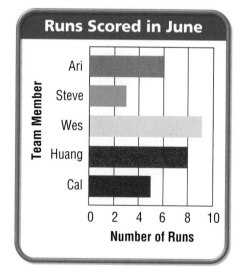

A 3   **C** 5

B 4   **D** 6

3. The table shows the heights of all the Pearson family members. (SDAP 1.2, p. 326)

Pearson Family Heights (in inches)				
Mom	Dad	Jenny	Julie	Jack
64	72	53	51	66

Which is the median height?

A 72 inches   **C** 63 inches

B 64 inches   **D** 61 inches

4. What is the length of the line segment on the coordinate grid? (O━▪ MG 2.2, p. 390)

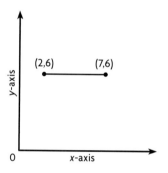

A 8 units   **C** 6 units

B 7 units   **D** 5 units

5. Look at the Venn diagram. Which numbers should be shown in section **Y**?
(SDAP 1.3, p. 324)

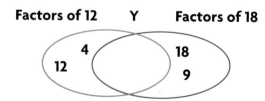

A 1, 2, 3, 6   **C** 6, 9

B 2, 3, 4   **D** 1, 2, 3, 4

GO Technology Use *Online Assessment.*

6. When was the greatest increase in rainwater in the bucket? (SDAP 1.3, p. 352)

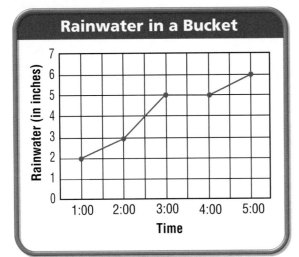

A from 1:00 to 2:00

B from 2:00 to 3:00

C from 3:00 to 4:00

D from 4:00 to 5:00

7. Which statement describes how to find the length of a vertical line segment? (O⟍ MG 2.3, p. 390)

A Find the difference between the *y*-coordinates of the endpoints.

B Find the sum of the *y*-coordinates of the endpoints.

C Find the sum of the *x*-coordinates of the endpoints.

D Find the difference between the *x*-coordinates of the endpoints.

8. Choose the most reasonable interval for this set of data. (SDAP 1.1, p. 332)

$$10, 15, 40, 95, 150$$

A 1   **C** 10

B 5   **D** 100

Short Response

9. The high temperature yesterday was 2°C. The low temperature was ⁻1°C. Find the difference between the high and low temperatures. (O⟍ NS 1.8, p. 374)

10. Draw 5 points on the graph of the equation $y = 2x + 3$. Connect the points with a straight line. (O⟍ MG 2.1, p. 398)

11. Mr. Gupta kept a record of the growth of his puppy each month from September through April. What type of graph is the most appropriate to display the data? (SDAP 1.1, p. 362)

Extended Response 🖊 WRITE Math ▸

12. The line plot shows the numbers of matches won by all the tennis team members.

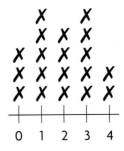

Tennis Team Matches Won

How many team members won at least 3 matches? **Explain** how you found your answer. (SDAP 1.3, p. 330)

13. James plots two points on a coordinate grid and connects the points with a straight line. The length of the line is 7. Could the points be (1,8) and (4,8)? **Explain** how you know. (O⟍ MG 2.2, p. 390)

Waves and Weather

WAVE HEIGHTS

California has about 840 miles of coastline and many beautiful beaches. In order to help keep people safe on the beach, scientists have been keeping track of how high the waves are in different weather conditions, storms, and seasons. Small floating objects called buoys are used to measure the wave heights.

FACT·ACTIVITY

Use the table to answer the questions.

❶ Find the difference between the highest and lowest wave heights in the graph. What is this number called?

❷ What is the mode of this set of data? **Explain**.

❸ At which beach are the wave heights twice as high as the waves at Hammond's Reef?

❹ Which beach has waves less than 3 feet high?

❺ **WRITE Math** Find the median height of the waves on October 6, 2006. **Explain** how you found your answer.

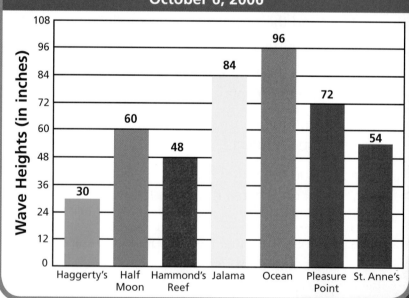

**Wave Heights for California Beaches
October 6, 2006**

Wave Heights (in inches)

Beach	Height
Haggerty's	30
Half Moon	60
Hammond's Reef	48
Jalama	84
Ocean	96
Pleasure Point	72
St. Anne's	54

SURFING SENSE

The height of a wave as it nears the beach depends on the wind speed, the area over which the wind blows, and the shape of the ocean floor. Surfers also judge the period, or time between the peak of one wave and the next, the wind direction, and the angle at which the wave hits the beach.

The table shows more data on the conditions at some of the beaches on the opposite page. Surfers look for light winds less than 8 mph, waves of 32 inches or greater, and periods of 10 seconds or greater.

Conditions at Some Southern California Beaches, October 6, 2006				
Name of Beach	Wave Height (in inches)	Period (in seconds)	Wind Speed (in mph)	Water Temperature (in °F)
Half Moon	60	11	5	55
Hammond's Reef	48	12	17	64
Ocean	96	7	13	57
Pleasure Point	72	11	5	55
St. Anne's	54	13	9	60

FACT·ACTIVITY

Use the table and the information above to answer the questions.

1 Which do you think was the least favorable beach for surfing on October 6th? **Explain.**

2 Which column of data, besides the wave height, helped you decide which beach was the least favorable to surf at? Did more than one column help you decide?

3 Make a graph or another display of the data for each column that helped you decide. Find the range, median, and mode of the data in those columns.

4 Which beach do you think is the best beach for surfing? **Explain** your choice.

5 If you were not a surfer, and you like warm days with little wind, which beach would you choose? Which data helped you decide? How could you display the data that helped you decide?

6 Fractions and Decimals

Math on Location

① Customers choose the components of a skateboard by their size and color.

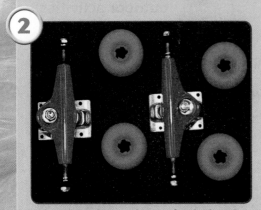

② A skateboard is made up of a deck, grip tape, 2 trucks, 4 wheels, and 8 bearings.

③ The deck is 7 layers of $\frac{1}{16}$-inch maple veneer. Its strength is tested by measuring the amount of flex to a fraction of an inch.

VOCABULARY POWER

TALK Math

What math is used in making a skateboard? Look at the green, pink, red, clear, and white wheels in the **Math on Location** photographs. How could you represent what fraction of the wheels are each color?

READ Math

REVIEW VOCABULARY You learned the words below when you first learned about fractions. How do these words relate to **Math on Location**?

denominator the part of a fraction below the bar, that tells how many equal parts are in the whole or in the group

equivalent fractions two or more fractions that name the same amount

fraction a number that names part of a whole or part of a group

WRITE Math

Copy and complete the chart below, using what you know about fractions. Use your own words to write the definition. Write as many facts, examples, and nonexamples as you can think of.

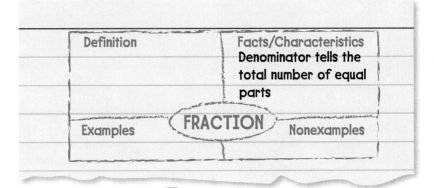

Definition	Facts/Characteristics
	Denominator tells the total number of equal parts
Examples	FRACTION	Nonexamples

GO ONLINE

Technology
Multimedia Math Glossary link at
www.harcourtschool.com/hspmath

16 Understand Fractions and Mixed Numbers

The Big Idea Fractions and mixed numbers can be expressed in equivalent forms and be compared and ordered.

CALIFORNIA FAST FACT

Every year about 150,000 people ride the carousel at Tilden Regional Park, located in the Berkeley hills. Visitors can also do outdoor activities.

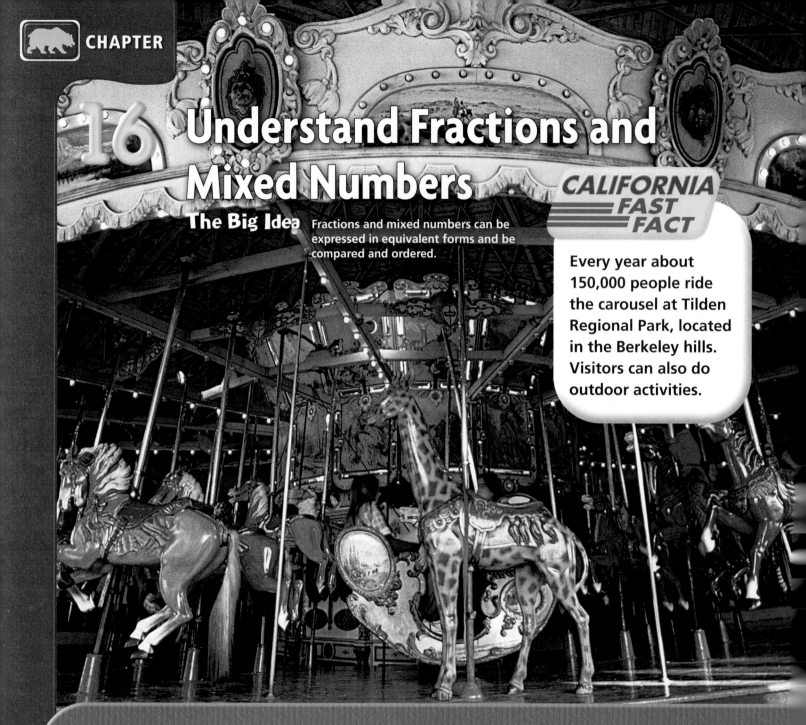

Investigate

Use the animals on the carousel. Using fractions, compare the number of each animal to the number of each type. Then compare the number of each type of animal to the total number of animals on the carousel. Write as many fractions as you can.

Carousel at Tilden Park											
Type of Animal	Horse	Big cat	Frog	Giraffe	Cat	Chicken	Duck	Dragon	Goat	Pig	Reindeer	Stork
Number	40	2	2	2	1	1	1	1	1	1	1	1

Technology
Student pages are available in the Student eBook.

Show What You Know

Check your understanding of important skills
needed for success in Chapter 16.

▶ **Parts of a Whole**

Write a fraction for each shaded part.

1. 2. 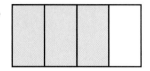 3. 4.

▶ **Parts of a Set**

Write a fraction for each shaded part.

5. 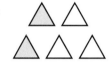 6. 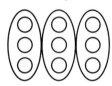 7. 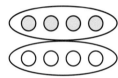 8.

▶ **Locate Numbers on a Number Line**

Write the number that names the point.

9.  10.  11.

VOCABULARY POWER

CHAPTER VOCABULARY

denominator numerator
equivalent   simplest
  fractions   form
fourths   thirds
fraction   whole
group
halves
mixed number

WARM-UP WORDS

fraction a number that names part of a whole or part of a group

numerator the number above the bar in a fraction that tells how many parts of the whole or group are being considered

denominator the number below the bar in a fraction that tells how many equal parts are in the whole

1 Read and Write Fractions

OBJECTIVE: Read and write fractions.

Quick Review

Name the number each letter represents.

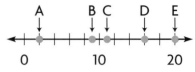

A   B C   D   E

0   10   20

1. A   **2.** D   **3.** E
4. C   **5.** B

Learn

PROBLEM For lunch Ben had an orange with 8 equal sections. He ate 2 of the sections. What fraction expresses the amount of orange Ben ate?

A **fraction** is a number that names part of a whole or part of a group.

Vocabulary

fraction	denominator
numerator	unit fraction

Example 1 Name part of a whole.

The number of sections Ben ate were part of the total number of sections in the orange.

number of parts Ben ate $\rightarrow$ 2 $\leftarrow$ numerator
total equal parts $\rightarrow$ 8 $\leftarrow$ denominator

Read: two eighths   **Write:** $\frac{2}{8}$
     two out of eight
     two divided by eight

So, Ben ate $\frac{2}{8}$ of the orange.

Example 2 Count equal parts of a whole.

You can count equal parts, such as eighths, to make one whole.

$\frac{1}{8}$ $\frac{2}{8}$ $\frac{3}{8}$ $\frac{4}{8}$ $\frac{5}{8}$ $\frac{6}{8}$ $\frac{7}{8}$ $\frac{8}{8}$

$\frac{8}{8}$ = one whole, or 1

Each equal part of the whole is $\frac{1}{8}$. The fraction $\frac{1}{8}$ is a unit fraction.

A **unit fraction** has a numerator of 1.

• In Example 1, how can you count equal parts to find the fraction of the orange Ben did not eat?

NS 1.5 Explain different interpretations of fractions, for example, parts of a whole, parts of a set, and division of whole numbers; explain equivalents of fractions. *also* NS 1.7, MR 1.1, MR 2.3, MR 2.4, MR 3.2, MR 3.3

Example 3 Show division.

ONE WAY Use a model.

Ben's 4 sisters share 3 waffles equally. How much waffle will each sister get?

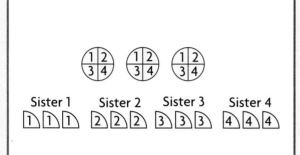

Sister 1   Sister 2   Sister 3   Sister 4

So, each sister will get $\frac{3}{4}$ of a waffle.

ANOTHER WAY Use a number line.

Emma's 3 brothers share a box of cereal equally. What fraction of the cereal will each brother get?

A number line can be used to represent one whole. The line can be divided into any number of equal parts.

This number line is divided into three equal parts, or thirds.

$$\begin{array}{ccccc} 0 & & \frac{1}{3} & \frac{2}{3} & 1 \end{array}$$

The point shows the location of $\frac{1}{3}$.

So, each brother will get $\frac{1}{3}$ of the box of cereal.

• What do the numerator and the denominator in $\frac{3}{4}$ represent?

Example 4 Name part of a group.

Kelly baked 12 lemon-poppyseed muffins in one pan. She gave 5 of the muffins to her neighbor. What fraction of the muffins did Kelly give away?

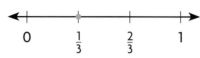

number given away → $\frac{5}{12}$ ← numerator
total number in the group → $\phantom{\frac{5}{12}}$ ← denominator

Read: five twelfths   **Write:** $\frac{5}{12}$
five out of twelve
five divided by twelve

So, $\frac{5}{12}$ of the muffins were given away.

Guided Practice

1. Sam drew a rectangle with four equal parts. He shaded $\frac{3}{4}$ of the rectangle. Which rectangle could he have drawn?

A   B   C

Write a fraction for the shaded part. Write a fraction for the unshaded part.

2.

3.

✓ 4.

✓ 5.

6. TALK Math Explain what a fraction can represent.

Independent Practice and Problem Solving

Write a fraction for the shaded part. Write a fraction for the unshaded part.

7.

8.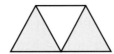

9.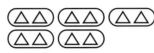

10.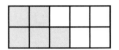

Draw a picture and shade part of it to show the fraction. Write a fraction for the unshaded part.

11. $\frac{7}{8}$

12. $\frac{5}{9}$

13. $\frac{12}{12}$

14. $\frac{8}{10}$

Write the fraction for each.

15. one seventh

16. six out of six

17. three divided by four

18. two thirds

Write the fraction that names the point.

19.

0   1

20.

0   1

★Algebra Write the missing fraction.

21. $\frac{1}{8}, \frac{2}{8}, \blacksquare, \frac{4}{8}, \frac{5}{8}$

22. $\frac{5}{12}, \frac{6}{12}, \frac{7}{12}, \frac{8}{12}, \frac{\blacksquare}{\blacksquare}$

23. $\frac{7}{16}, \frac{6}{16}, \frac{5}{16}, \frac{\blacksquare}{\blacksquare}, \frac{3}{16}$

USE DATA For 24–26, use the picture.

24. What fraction of the items on the tray is fruit?

25. What fraction of the items on the tray is neither muffins nor apples?

26. Write the total number of items on the tray as a fraction.

27. Mike bought 15 apples, 5 bananas, and 10 pears for a party. What fraction of the fruit Mike bought is pears?

28. WRITE Math Explain how you can model the same fraction three different ways. Then give examples of your explanation.

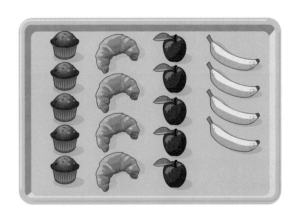

29. The monthly normal temperature in January in Barrow, Alaska is ⁻14°F. For the same month in Fresno, California, it is 46°F. How much warmer is it in Fresno?

(⬤━┓ NS 1.8, p. 374)

30. Of the 6 soccer balls, 5 are red and white. What fraction of the soccer balls are red and white? (NS 1.5, p. 414)

31. Use a coordinate grid to find the length of the line segment joining the points (3, ⁻7) and (12, ⁻7). (⬤━┓ MG 2.2, p. 390)

32. Test Prep Five friends share 3 pizzas equally. What fraction of the pizzas will each friend get?

A $\frac{1}{5}$ **B** $\frac{1}{3}$ **C** $\frac{1}{2}$ **D** $\frac{3}{5}$

33. Test Prep Of the 8 buses taking students to a play, 5 are full. What fraction of the buses are NOT full?

A $\frac{1}{8}$ **B** $\frac{1}{5}$ **C** $\frac{3}{8}$ **D** $\frac{5}{8}$

MATH POWER — Problem Solving and Reasoning

NUMBER SENSE You can find a fraction of a group or a collection, even if the denominator of the fraction is not the same as the number in the group.

A Find $\frac{2}{3}$ of 6.

Draw 6 objects.

The denominator is 3. Make 3 equal groups.

The denominator is 3. Make 3 equal groups.

Then shade 2 groups. Count the total objects shaded.

So, $\frac{2}{3}$ of 6 is 4.

B Find $\frac{3}{4}$ of 16.

Draw 16 objects.

The denominator is 4. Make 4 equal groups.

Then shade 3 groups. Count the total objects shaded.

So, $\frac{3}{4}$ of 16 is 12.

Draw a picture to solve.

1. $\frac{1}{2}$ of 6   **2.** $\frac{1}{4}$ of 8   **3.** $\frac{2}{3}$ of 15   **4.** $\frac{5}{6}$ of 12   **5.** $\frac{3}{8}$ of 24

Model Equivalent Fractions

OBJECTIVE: Model equivalent fractions in simplest form.

Learn

PROBLEM As of 2005, there were 10 giant pandas in zoos in the United States and Mexico. The National Zoo, in Washington, D.C., had 2 of these pandas. What fraction of the pandas is this?

$\frac{2}{10}$ ← National Zoo pandas
← total pandas

$\frac{1}{5}$ ← National Zoo pandas
← total pandas

So, $\frac{2}{10}$, or $\frac{1}{5}$ of the giant pandas are at the National Zoo. $\frac{2}{10}$ and $\frac{1}{5}$ are **equivalent fractions** because they name the same amount.

Activity Find equivalent fractions for $\frac{2}{3}$.

Materials ■ fraction bars ■ number lines

ONE WAY Use fraction bars.

Step 1

Line up two $\frac{1}{3}$ bars for thirds with the bar for 1 to show $\frac{2}{3}$.

1

| $\frac{1}{3}$ | $\frac{1}{3}$ |

Step 2

Line up other bars of the same type to show the same amount as $\frac{2}{3}$.

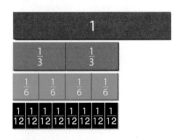

So, $\frac{4}{6}$ and $\frac{8}{12}$ are equivalent to $\frac{2}{3}$.

ANOTHER WAY Use number lines.

Fractions that line up with $\frac{2}{3}$ are equivalent to $\frac{2}{3}$.

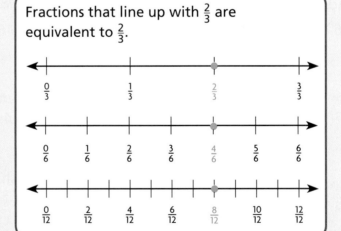

Remember
There are many ways to write 1 as a fraction. In every case, the numerator and denominator are the same.

NS 1.5 Explain different interpretations of fractions, for example, parts of a whole, parts of a set, and division of whole numbers; explain equivalents of fractions. *also* NS 1.7, MR 1.1, MR 2.3, MR 2.4, MR 3.2, MR 3.3

Multiply or Divide

You can multiply both the numerator and denominator of a fraction by any number except zero to find equivalent fractions.

If the numerator and denominator have a common factor, you can also divide both by that factor to find an equivalent fraction.

Find fractions that are equivalent to $\frac{4}{16}$.

ONE WAY Multiply the numerator and the denominator by the same number.

Try 2. $\frac{4}{16} = \frac{4 \times 2}{16 \times 2} = \frac{8}{32}$

So, $\frac{4}{16}$ is equivalent to $\frac{8}{32}$.

ANOTHER WAY Divide the numerator and the denominator by the same number.

Try 4. $\frac{4}{16} = \frac{4 \div 4}{16 \div 4} = \frac{1}{4}$

So, $\frac{4}{16}$ is equivalent to $\frac{1}{4}$.

You can also find equivalent fractions for whole numbers.

$1 = \frac{1}{1} = \frac{1 \times 10}{1 \times 10} = \frac{10}{10}$

$4 = \frac{4}{1} = \frac{4 \times 3}{1 \times 3} = \frac{12}{3}$

So, $\frac{10}{10}$ is equivalent to 1.

So, $\frac{12}{3}$ is equivalent to 4.

A fraction is in **simplest form** when the only number that can be divided into the numerator and the denominator evenly is 1.

ONE WAY Use a model.

Find the simplest form of $\frac{8}{10}$.

Line up eight $\frac{1}{10}$ bars with the bar for 1 to show $\frac{8}{10}$.

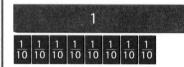

Then line up other bars of the same type with denominators smaller than 10 to show the same amount as $\frac{8}{10}$.

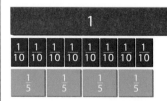

Fifths are the largest fraction pieces that are equal to tenths.

ANOTHER WAY Divide.

Find the simplest form of $\frac{36}{48}$.

Try 6. Divide the numerator and denominator by 6.

$\frac{36}{48} = \frac{36 \div 6}{48 \div 6} = \frac{6}{8}$

Next, try 2. Divide the numerator and denominator by 2.

$\frac{6}{8} = \frac{6 \div 2}{8 \div 2} = \frac{3}{4}$

Now the only number that can be divided into the numerator and denominator of $\frac{3}{4}$ is 1.

So, the simplest form of $\frac{36}{48}$ is $\frac{3}{4}$.

So, the simplest form of $\frac{8}{10}$ is $\frac{4}{5}$.

1. What two equivalent fractions are shown by these models? Which fraction is in simplest form?

Write two equivalent fractions for each model.

2.

☑ 3.
$\frac{1}{4}$

☑ 4.
$\frac{0}{6}$ $\frac{1}{6}$ $\frac{2}{6}$ $\frac{3}{6}$ $\frac{4}{6}$ $\frac{5}{6}$ $\frac{6}{6}$

5. **TALK Math** **Explain** why equivalent fractions are equal. Use fraction bars.

Independent Practice and Problem Solving

Write two equivalent fractions for each model.

6.
$\frac{0}{9}$ $\frac{1}{9}$ $\frac{2}{9}$ $\frac{3}{9}$ $\frac{4}{9}$ $\frac{5}{9}$ $\frac{6}{9}$ $\frac{7}{9}$ $\frac{8}{9}$ $\frac{9}{9}$

7.
| $\frac{1}{8}$ | $\frac{1}{8}$ | $\frac{1}{8}$ | $\frac{1}{8}$ | $\frac{1}{8}$ | $\frac{1}{8}$ |

8.

Write two equivalent fractions for each.

9. $\frac{1}{4}$ 10. $\frac{12}{16}$ 11. $\frac{3}{5}$ 12. $\frac{7}{8}$ 13. $\frac{4}{12}$ 14. $\frac{9}{9}$

Tell whether the fractions are equivalent. Write *yes* or *no*.

15. $\frac{3}{4}, \frac{8}{10}$ 16. $\frac{2}{18}, \frac{1}{9}$ 17. $\frac{4}{12}, \frac{1}{3}$ 18. $\frac{9}{12}, \frac{4}{6}$ 19. $\frac{10}{25}, \frac{3}{5}$ 20. $\frac{8}{16}, \frac{1}{2}$

Tell whether the fraction is in simplest form. If not, write it in simplest form.

21. $\frac{12}{18}$ 22. $\frac{12}{20}$ 23. $\frac{8}{15}$ 24. $\frac{8}{8}$ 25. $\frac{11}{12}$ 26. $\frac{15}{25}$

⭐ Algebra **Find the missing numerator or denominator.**

27. $\frac{3}{5} = \frac{\blacksquare}{15}$ 28. $\frac{10}{16} = \frac{5}{\blacksquare}$ 29. $\frac{4}{4} = \frac{\blacksquare}{8}$ 30. $\frac{7}{14} = \frac{\blacksquare}{2}$ 31. $\frac{6}{9} = \frac{24}{\blacksquare}$ 32. $\frac{5}{6} = \frac{20}{\blacksquare}$

33. **WRITE Math** **What's the Question?** If you multiply the numerator and denominator by 4, you get $\frac{12}{24}$.

34. **Reasoning** What is one way that you know that a fraction is in simplest form without dividing the numerator and denominator? **Explain.**

USE DATA For 35–37, use the graph.

35. What fraction of the cubs are cheetahs? Write the amount in simplest form.

36. What fraction of the cats are tigers? Write an equivalent fraction for the amount.

37. **Pose a Problem** Look back at Problem 36. Write a similar problem by changing the numbers.

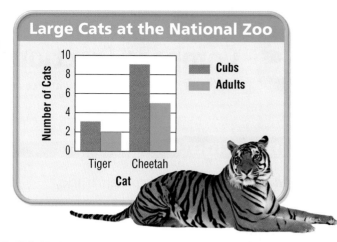

Large Cats at the National Zoo

Number of Cats — Tiger, Cheetah — Cat — Cubs, Adults

Achieving the Standards

38. Nina has 6 cousins. All but one of her cousins are boys. What fraction of her cousins are boys? (NS 1.5, p. 414)

39. Look at the bar graph above. How many more cheetahs are there than tigers at the National Zoo? (SDAP 1.3, p. 346)

40. What is the remainder when you divide 13 by 5? (○━ NS 3.2, p. 244)

41. **Test Prep** What is $\frac{12}{16}$ in simplest form?

   A $\frac{3}{4}$ B $\frac{6}{8}$ C $\frac{1}{2}$ D $\frac{1}{4}$

42. **Test Prep** Which fraction is equivalent to $\frac{5}{10}$?

   A $\frac{1}{5}$ B $\frac{5}{20}$ C $\frac{10}{20}$ D $\frac{15}{20}$

MATH POWER — Problem Solving and Reasoning

VISUAL THINKING The charge to park a car at the National Zoo is $3 per car. You can use a ratio to compare the charge to the number of cars. A **ratio** compares two amounts.

A ratio can be shown as a picture.

Read: $3 per car

The ratio can be written three ways.　　3:1　　$\frac{3}{1}$　　3 to 1

Read: three to one

The ratio of the charge to park to the number of cars will be equivalent to 3:1 no matter the amount of money collected or number of cars parked.

Draw a picture and write a ratio to compare the cost to park and the number of cars.

1. 2 cars　　　2. $15　　　3. 6 cars　　　4. $24　　　5. 7 cars

3 Compare Fractions

OBJECTIVE: Compare fractions with like and unlike denominators.

Quick Review

Find the missing number.

1. $\frac{1}{2} = \frac{4}{\blacksquare}$ 2. $\frac{6}{12} = \frac{\blacksquare}{6}$

3. $\frac{1}{3} = \frac{\blacksquare}{12}$ 4. $\frac{4}{16} = \frac{2}{\blacksquare}$

5. $\frac{6}{8} = \frac{3}{\blacksquare}$

Investigate

Materials ■ counters ■ pattern blocks

You can use counters and pattern blocks to compare fractions.

A Use counters to compare $\frac{3}{4}$ and $\frac{1}{4}$. Use yellow counters to show the numerators.

$\frac{3}{4}$ ●●●● $\frac{1}{4}$ ●●●●

B Which fraction has more yellow counters? Which fraction is greater? Complete by using $<$, $>$, or $=$. $\frac{3}{4}$ ⬤ $\frac{1}{4}$

C Use pattern blocks to compare $\frac{1}{3}$ and $\frac{2}{6}$. Remember that if one yellow hexagon = 1, then one green triangle = $\frac{1}{6}$ and 1 blue rhombus = $\frac{1}{3}$.

Now use the green triangles to show $\frac{2}{6}$ on your model.

D How do $\frac{2}{6}$ and $\frac{1}{3}$ compare? Complete by using $<$, $>$, or $=$. $\frac{2}{6}$ ⬤ $\frac{1}{3}$

Draw Conclusions

1. How would you use counters to compare $\frac{2}{6}$ and $\frac{5}{6}$?

2. How would you use pattern blocks to compare $\frac{2}{3}$ and $\frac{4}{6}$?

3. **Synthesize** What conclusion can you draw about comparing fractions that have the same denominator?

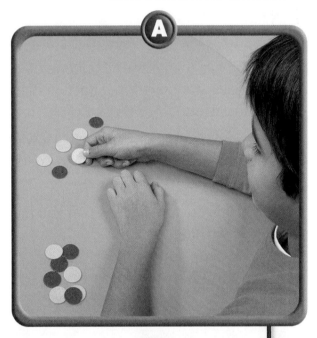

0⟳ NS 1.9 Identify on a number line the relative position of positive fractions, positive mixed numbers and positive decimals to two decimals places. *also* NS 1.5, NS 1.7, MR 2.0, MR 2.3, MR 2.4, MR 3.2

Connect

You can also compare fractions by using number lines.

Activity Compare fractions using number lines.

A Like Denominators

Compare $\frac{2}{8}$ and $\frac{5}{8}$.
Use a number line divided into eighths.
Locate $\frac{2}{8}$ and $\frac{5}{8}$ on a number line.

$$\begin{array}{ccccccccc} 0 & \frac{1}{8} & \frac{2}{8} & \frac{3}{8} & \frac{4}{8} & \frac{5}{8} & \frac{6}{8} & \frac{7}{8} & 1 \end{array}$$

The fraction farther to the left is the lesser fraction.

So, $\frac{2}{8} < \frac{5}{8}$.

B Unlike Denominators

Compare $\frac{3}{4}$ and $\frac{5}{8}$.
Divide one number line into fourths and locate $\frac{3}{4}$ on it. Divide the other number into eighths and locate $\frac{5}{8}$.

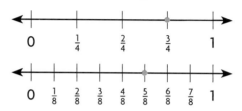

$$\begin{array}{ccccc} 0 & \frac{1}{4} & \frac{2}{4} & \frac{3}{4} & 1 \end{array}$$

$$\begin{array}{ccccccccc} 0 & \frac{1}{8} & \frac{2}{8} & \frac{3}{8} & \frac{4}{8} & \frac{5}{8} & \frac{6}{8} & \frac{7}{8} & 1 \end{array}$$

The fraction farther to the right is the greater fraction.

So, $\frac{3}{4} > \frac{5}{8}$.

When you compare fractions with like denominators, compare only the numerators. Use the symbols $<$, $>$, $=$, and $\neq$ to compare fractions.

TALK Math

How could you compare fractions by finding equivalent fractions?

Practice

Model each fraction to compare. Write $<$, $>$, or $=$ for each ●.

1. $\frac{1}{5}$ ● $\frac{4}{5}$

2. $\frac{2}{8}$ ● $\frac{4}{8}$

☑ 3. $\frac{1}{2}$ ● $\frac{2}{6}$

4. $\frac{4}{10}$ ● $\frac{1}{2}$

5. $\frac{2}{3}$ ● $\frac{7}{9}$

6. $\frac{3}{8}$ ● $\frac{5}{6}$

Use number lines to compare.

7. $\frac{4}{6}$ ● $\frac{5}{6}$

8. $\frac{1}{4}$ ● $\frac{1}{8}$

☑ 9. $\frac{1}{6}$ ● $\frac{1}{5}$

10. $\frac{5}{8}$ ● $\frac{1}{4}$

11. $\frac{3}{4}$ ● $\frac{6}{8}$

12. $\frac{9}{16}$ ● $\frac{2}{4}$

13. **WRITE Math** ▸ **Explain** the difference between comparing fractions with like denominators and comparing fractions with unlike denominators.

CD ROM **Technology**
Use Harcourt Mega Math, Fraction Action, *Fraction Flare Up*, Level F.

4 Order Fractions

OBJECTIVE: Order fractions.

Quick Review

Compare. Write <, >, or = for each ●.

1. $\frac{2}{6}$ ● $\frac{5}{6}$

2. $\frac{11}{18}$ ● $\frac{7}{18}$

3. $\frac{2}{3}$ ● $\frac{3}{5}$

4. $\frac{3}{4}$ ● $\frac{4}{12}$

5. $\frac{3}{8}$ ● $\frac{6}{16}$

Learn

PROBLEM Seth, Ryan, and Antonio each ride their bikes to school. Seth rides $\frac{1}{2}$ mile, Ryan rides $\frac{3}{10}$ mile, and Antonio rides $\frac{3}{5}$ mile. Which boy rides his bike the shortest distance to school?

Activity Use fraction bars.

Materials ■ fraction bars

Order $\frac{1}{2}$, $\frac{3}{10}$, and $\frac{3}{5}$ from greatest to least.

Step 1

Start with the bar for 1. Line up fraction bars for $\frac{1}{2}$, $\frac{3}{10}$, and $\frac{3}{5}$ below it.

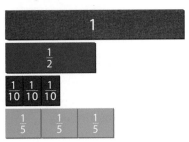

Compare the rows of fraction bars.

Step 2

Move the rows until you have them in order from longest to shortest.

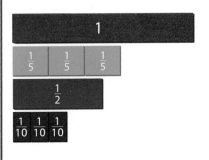

So, the order from greatest to least is $\frac{3}{5}$, $\frac{1}{2}$, $\frac{3}{10}$. Since $\frac{3}{10}$ is the least, Ryan rides his bicycle the shortest distance to school.

Example Use number lines.

Order $\frac{1}{2}$, $\frac{1}{8}$, and $\frac{1}{4}$ from least to greatest.

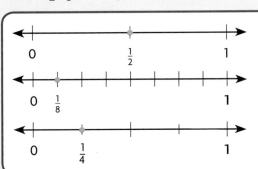

Locate $\frac{1}{2}$, $\frac{1}{8}$, and $\frac{1}{4}$ each on a number line.

The fraction farthest to the left is the least fraction.

So, the order from least to greatest is $\frac{1}{8}$, $\frac{1}{4}$, $\frac{1}{2}$.

O━ NS 1.9 Identify on a number line the relative position of positive fractions, positive mixed numbers, and positive decimals to two decimal places. *also* NS 1.5, NS 1.7, MR 1.1, MR 2.3, MR 2.4, MR 3.2, MR 3.3

1. Use the fraction bars to order $\frac{2}{5}$, $\frac{3}{4}$, and $\frac{6}{10}$ from least to greatest.

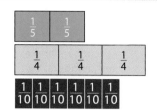

Order the fractions from greatest to least.

2. $\frac{1}{2}$, $\frac{7}{8}$, $\frac{4}{6}$

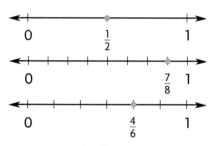

☑ 3. $\frac{3}{8}$, $\frac{12}{12}$, $\frac{1}{6}$

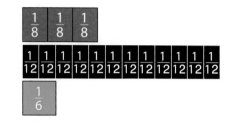

☑ 4. $\frac{4}{10}$, $\frac{1}{3}$, $\frac{3}{5}$

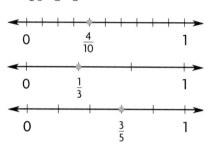

5. **TALK Math** **Explain** how you would use number lines to order $\frac{2}{3}$, $\frac{1}{2}$, and $\frac{4}{5}$ from least to greatest.

Independent Practice and Problem Solving

Order the fractions from least to greatest.

6. $\frac{1}{2}$, $\frac{1}{8}$, $\frac{1}{4}$

7. $\frac{8}{16}$, $\frac{1}{5}$, $\frac{3}{10}$

8. $\frac{5}{6}$, $\frac{2}{3}$, $\frac{1}{2}$

9. $\frac{3}{5}$, $\frac{2}{4}$, $\frac{8}{12}$

Order the fractions from greatest to least.

10. $\frac{2}{4}$, $\frac{8}{10}$, $\frac{3}{12}$

11. $\frac{1}{6}$, $\frac{1}{8}$, $\frac{1}{2}$

12. $\frac{2}{6}$, $\frac{9}{9}$, $\frac{1}{12}$

13. $\frac{2}{3}$, $\frac{2}{4}$, $\frac{2}{5}$

14. Lily used $\frac{3}{4}$ cup seeds, $\frac{5}{8}$ cup berries, and $\frac{3}{10}$ cup raisins to make trail mix. Order the ingredients from least to greatest.

15. **WRITE Math** **Explain** how you know which fraction is least or greatest using fraction bars.

Achieving the Standards

16. There are 4 red marbles and 2 green marbles in a bag. The marbles are all the same size. If you pull a marble without looking, is it *more likely* or *less likely* you will pull red? (Grade 3 SDAP 1.1)

17. $(7 + 4) \times 8 =$ (O┑ AF 1.3, p. 142)

18. Draw and shade part of a figure to represent a fraction equivalent to $\frac{1}{3}$.
(NS 1.5, p. 424)

19. **Test Prep** Esteban jogged for $\frac{2}{3}$ hour, swam for $\frac{5}{6}$ hour, and biked for $\frac{1}{2}$ hour. Which activity took the longest? **Explain.**

OBJECTIVE: Read and write mixed numbers and express fractions greater than one as mixed numbers.

Learn

PROBLEM Carlos made a large candle from one and two-thirds cups of wax. Write a mixed number for the number of cups of wax.

A **mixed number** is made up of a whole number and a fraction.

The picture shows one and two-thirds cups of wax.

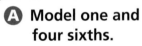

Read: one and two thirds

Write: $1\frac{2}{3}$

Activity 1 Use pattern blocks.

Materials ■ pattern blocks

A Model one and four sixths.

$1 + \frac{4}{6} = 1\frac{4}{6},$ or $1\frac{2}{3}$

B Model two and one half.

$2 + \frac{1}{2} = 2\frac{1}{2}$

C Model one and one third.

$1 + \frac{1}{3} = 1\frac{1}{3}$

• Look at Example A. How many sixths make two wholes?

You can locate mixed numbers on a number line.

Activity 2 Use a number line.

Materials ■ number line

Draw a number line to locate $1\frac{4}{5}$ and $3\frac{2}{5}$.

First, divide the number line into four equal parts. Label the whole numbers.

Then, mark five equal parts between each whole number. Each part represents one fifth.

Locate $1\frac{4}{5}$ and $3\frac{2}{5}$.

NS 1.9 Identify on a number line the relative position of positive fractions, positive mixed numbers, and positive decimals to two decimal places. *also* NS 1.5, NS 1.7, MR 2.0, MR 2.3, MR 2.4, MR 3.2

Rename Fractions and Mixed Numbers

Sometimes the numerator of a fraction is greater than the denominator. These fractions have a value greater than 1. They can be renamed as mixed numbers.

ONE WAY — Use fraction bars.

Rename $1\frac{3}{8}$ as a fraction.
Use fraction bars to rename the mixed number as a fraction. Model $1\frac{3}{8}$.

| 1 | $\frac{1}{8}$ | $\frac{1}{8}$ | $\frac{1}{8}$ |

Place $\frac{1}{8}$ bars under the bars for $1\frac{3}{8}$.

| 1 | $\frac{1}{8}$ | $\frac{1}{8}$ | $\frac{1}{8}$ |

| $\frac{1}{8}$ | $\frac{1}{8}$ | $\frac{1}{8}$ | $\frac{1}{8}$ | $\frac{1}{8}$ | $\frac{1}{8}$ | $\frac{1}{8}$ | $\frac{1}{8}$ | $\frac{1}{8}$ | $\frac{1}{8}$ | $\frac{1}{8}$ |

The total number of $\frac{1}{8}$ bars is the numerator of the fraction. The numerator of the fraction is 11.

ANOTHER WAY — Use division.

Rename $\frac{11}{3}$ as a mixed number.

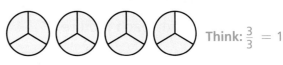 Think: $\frac{3}{3} = 1$

Since $\frac{11}{3}$ means $11 \div 3$, you can use division to rename a fraction greater than 1 as a mixed number.

$$\text{denominator} \rightarrow 3\overline{)11}^{\;3r2} \leftarrow \text{numerator}$$
$$\underline{-9}$$
$$2 \leftarrow \text{number of thirds left over}$$

Write the quotient as the whole number part. Then write the remainder as the numerator and the divisor as the denominator.

So, $1\frac{3}{8}$ renamed as a fraction is $\frac{11}{8}$.

So, $\frac{11}{3}$ renamed as a mixed number is $3\frac{2}{3}$.

A fraction greater than 1 is sometimes called an *improper fraction*.

So, $\frac{11}{8}$ and $\frac{7}{5}$ are examples of improper fractions.

• How can you use multiplication to rename a mixed number as a fraction?

• What does a mixed number represent?

Guided Practice

1. Complete to name the mixed number shown by the picture.

$1 + \dfrac{\blacksquare}{3} = \blacksquare$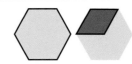

Write a mixed number for each picture.

2.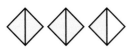

✓ 3.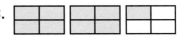

✓ 4.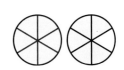

Rename each fraction as a mixed number and each mixed number as a fraction. You may wish to draw a picture.

5. $\frac{15}{2}$　　6. $2\frac{3}{4}$　　7. $\frac{12}{7}$　　8. $9\frac{1}{3}$　　9. $\frac{26}{8}$　　✓10. $5\frac{5}{6}$

11. **TALK Math** Explain how to model $3\frac{1}{6}$.

Independent Practice and Problem Solving

Write a mixed number for each picture.

12. 　　13. 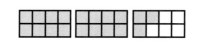　　14.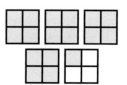

For 15–20, use the number line to write the letter each mixed number or fraction represents.

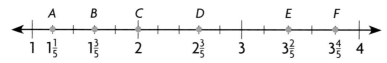

15. $\frac{6}{5}$　　16. $2\frac{3}{5}$　　17. $\frac{8}{5}$　　18. $3\frac{2}{5}$　　19. $\frac{19}{5}$　　20. $\frac{10}{5}$

Rename each fraction as a mixed number and each mixed number as a fraction. You may wish to draw a picture.

21. $\frac{13}{5}$　　22. $1\frac{1}{6}$　　23. $\frac{21}{4}$　　24. $2\frac{1}{2}$　　25. $\frac{13}{6}$　　26. $\frac{19}{3}$

27. $6\frac{2}{9}$　　28. $\frac{17}{8}$　　29. $7\frac{2}{7}$　　30. $\frac{35}{6}$　　31. $\frac{28}{12}$　　32. $5\frac{3}{4}$

33. Jodi cut a piece of ribbon $3\frac{3}{8}$ inches long. Draw a number line and locate $3\frac{3}{8}$.

34. **Reasoning** Adam needs 1 cup of wax to make a pear-shaped candle. Is this more than or less than $\frac{15}{8}$ cup, the amount of wax needed to make an apple-shaped candle? **Explain.**

35. Miguel takes a craft class that lasts $2\frac{1}{2}$ hours. Draw a picture to represent the length of the class.

36. Madeleine buys six and a half dozen candles. Write the number of dozens she bought as a mixed number and a fraction.

37. **WRITE Math** Jack thinks $4\frac{1}{3} = \frac{13}{3}$. Is he correct? You may use models or draw a picture. **Explain.**

Technology
Use Harcourt Mega Math, Fraction Action,
CD ROM *Number Line Mine*, Levels F, H, J.

38. Show tickets cost $18 for adults and $13 for children. What is the total cost for 2 adults and 3 children? (O⚏ NS 3.0, p. 184)

39. Emilia has to read 10 pages for homework. She has read 7 of them already. Write a fraction to show what part she has left to read. (NS 1.5, p. 414)

40. Ahmed drank $\frac{1}{2}$ cup of milk for breakfast and $\frac{2}{3}$ cup of milk for lunch. Use a number line to find out if he drank more milk for breakfast or for lunch. (O⚏ NS 1.9, p. 426)

41. Test Prep Drew's class ate $4\frac{5}{8}$ pizzas. How many slices of pizza did they eat if each slice was $\frac{1}{8}$ of a pizza?

   A 5   **C** 32

   B 8   **D** 37

42. Test Prep Melanie used $\frac{7}{4}$ cups of flour to make bread. Which shows $\frac{7}{4}$ as a mixed number?

   A $1\frac{1}{4}$ **C** $1\frac{3}{4}$

   B $1\frac{4}{7}$ **D** $4\frac{1}{3}$

 **Problem Solving and Reasoning**

MEASUREMENT A ruler is a type of number line. You can locate mixed numbers on a ruler.

The longest marks on the ruler below show whole numbers. The shortest marks show eighths. Notice that some eighths marks are longer than others. These marks show quarters and halves.

Find $3\frac{7}{8}$ on the ruler.

Draw a line segment $3\frac{7}{8}$ inches long.

Start at the left edge of the ruler. Draw the line segment to reach $3\frac{7}{8}$ inches.

$3\frac{7}{8}$

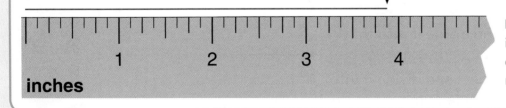

inches

From 3, count seven $\frac{1}{8}$ inch marks to the right of the 3-inch mark to reach $3\frac{7}{8}$ inches.

Use a ruler. Draw a line segment for each length.

1. $2\frac{3}{8}$ inches   **2.** $4\frac{1}{8}$ inches   **3.** $1\frac{3}{4}$ inches   **4.** $3\frac{1}{2}$ inches   **5.** $5\frac{1}{4}$ inches

6 Compare and Order Mixed Numbers

OBJECTIVE: Compare and order mixed numbers.

Learn

PROBLEM Amanda spent some of her time last week doing different after school activities. The table shows the amount of time she spent doing each activity. Did she spend more time working on her science project or at soccer practice?

Amanda's After School Activities Last Week	
Activity	Time (in hours)
Homework	$2\frac{2}{3}$
Piano lessons and practice	$2\frac{1}{4}$
Science project	$1\frac{2}{3}$
Soccer practice	$1\frac{1}{3}$

Activity 1
Materials ■ fraction bars

A **Compare mixed numbers with like denominators.**

Compare $1\frac{2}{3}$ and $1\frac{1}{3}$ using fraction bars.

Model $1\frac{2}{3}$, then line up the bars for $1\frac{1}{3}$ below it.

| 1 | $\frac{1}{3}$ | $\frac{1}{3}$ |
| 1 | $\frac{1}{3}$ | |

Compare the two rows of fraction bars. The longer row represents the greater mixed number.

$1\frac{2}{3} > 1\frac{1}{3}$, so Amanda spent more time on her science project than at soccer practice.

• When you compare $1\frac{2}{3}$ and $1\frac{1}{3}$, why do you have to compare only the fraction parts?

B **Compare mixed numbers with unlike denominators.**

Did Amanda spend less time doing homework or at piano lessons and practice?

Compare $2\frac{2}{3}$ and $2\frac{1}{4}$ using number lines.

Draw a number line, and divide it into thirds between each whole number. Locate $2\frac{2}{3}$.

Draw another number line, and divide it into fourths between each whole number. Locate $2\frac{1}{4}$.

The mixed number farther to the right is the greater number.

$2\frac{2}{3} > 2\frac{1}{4}$, so Amanda spent less time at piano lessons and practice.

O—π NS1.9 Identify on a number line the relative position of positive fractions, positive mixed numbers, and positive decimals to two decimal places. *also* **NS 1.5, NS 1.7, MR 1.1, MR 2.3, MR 2.4, MR 3.2, MR 3.3**

Activity 2 Compare and order mixed numbers.

ONE WAY Use drawings.

Compare and then order $2\frac{1}{2}$, $1\frac{1}{6}$, and $1\frac{3}{4}$ from greatest to least.

Draw pictures for $2\frac{1}{2}$, $1\frac{1}{6}$ and $1\frac{3}{4}$.

$2\frac{1}{2}$

$1\frac{1}{6}$

$1\frac{3}{4}$

First, compare the whole numbers. Since $2 > 1$, $2\frac{1}{2}$ is the greatest.

Then compare the other two fractions by finding equivalent fractions.

$1\frac{1}{6} = 1\frac{2}{12}$ $1\frac{3}{4} = 1\frac{9}{12}$

Since, $2 < 9$, $1\frac{3}{4}$ is greater than $1\frac{1}{6}$.

So, the order from greatest to least is $2\frac{1}{2}$, $1\frac{3}{4}$, $1\frac{1}{6}$.

ANOTHER WAY Use a number line.

Order $\frac{5}{2}$, $2\frac{3}{4}$, and $2\frac{3}{8}$ from least to greatest using a number line.

> **Math Idea**
> To order mixed numbers, compare the whole number parts first. Then compare the fraction parts.

Find equivalent fractions. $\frac{5}{2} = 2\frac{1}{2} = 2\frac{4}{8}$ $2\frac{3}{4} = 2\frac{6}{8}$

Draw a number line showing 2 and 3 with the distance between them divided into eighths. Place each mixed number on the number line.

The mixed number farthest to the right is the greatest number.
The mixed number farthest to the left is the least number.

$2 \quad \frac{1}{8} \quad \frac{2}{8} \quad \frac{3}{8} \quad \frac{4}{8} \quad \frac{5}{8} \quad \frac{6}{8} \quad \frac{7}{8} \quad 3$

So, the order from least to greatest is $2\frac{3}{8}$, $\frac{5}{2}$, $2\frac{3}{4}$.

Guided Practice

1. Use the number line. Is $3\frac{4}{5}$ greater than or less than $3\frac{2}{5}$?

$3 \quad \frac{1}{5} \quad \frac{2}{5} \quad \frac{3}{5} \quad \frac{4}{5} \quad 4$

Compare the mixed numbers. Use <, >, or =.

2.

$1\frac{1}{3} \bullet 1\frac{1}{2}$

3.

$1\frac{3}{4} \bullet 1\frac{3}{8}$

4.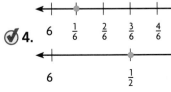

$6\frac{1}{6} \bullet 6\frac{1}{2}$

Order the mixed numbers from greatest to least.

5. $4\frac{1}{6}$, $3\frac{2}{3}$, $4\frac{3}{4}$

6. $5\frac{1}{4}$, $6\frac{3}{8}$, $5\frac{1}{12}$

7. $3\frac{3}{4}$, $3\frac{2}{5}$, $3\frac{1}{2}$

✓8. $1\frac{7}{9}$, $1\frac{1}{2}$, $1\frac{12}{18}$

9. [TALK Math] **Explain** how you would compare the mixed numbers $4\frac{5}{12}$ and $2\frac{7}{8}$.

Independent Practice and Problem Solving

Compare the mixed numbers. Write $<$, $>$, or $=$ for each ●.

10.

$1\frac{3}{4}$ ● $1\frac{2}{5}$

11.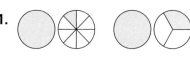

$1\frac{1}{8}$ ● $1\frac{1}{3}$

12.

```
←—+————————+————————+————→
   4         1         2         5
             3         3
```

$4\frac{2}{3}$ ● $4\frac{1}{3}$

Order the mixed numbers from least to greatest.

13. $8\frac{3}{4}$, $7\frac{3}{10}$, $8\frac{1}{2}$

14. $3\frac{1}{2}$, $3\frac{2}{3}$, $2\frac{4}{16}$

15. $4\frac{2}{6}$, $4\frac{2}{3}$, $4\frac{2}{12}$

16. $5\frac{2}{5}$, $5\frac{6}{10}$, $5\frac{2}{7}$

★ **Algebra** Find the missing number.

17. $1\frac{1}{4} < 1\frac{1}{\blacksquare} < 1\frac{1}{2}$

18. $2\frac{5}{6} > 2\frac{\blacksquare}{5} > 2\frac{1}{3}$

19. $4\frac{\blacksquare}{6} < 4\frac{2}{5} < 4\frac{3}{4}$

20. $2\frac{1}{5} < 2\frac{3}{10} < 2\frac{\blacksquare}{2}$

USE DATA For 21–23, use the table.

21. Which activity takes Amanda the most time? the least time?

22. Which activity does Amanda spend $\frac{11}{4}$ hours doing? Which activity does she spend almost as much time doing?

How Amanda Spends Her Day			
Activity	Free Time	Homework	Sleep
Time (in hours)	$2\frac{3}{4}$	$2\frac{2}{3}$	$9\frac{1}{4}$

23. **Pose a Problem** Use the information in the table to write a problem involving ordering mixed numbers. Have a classmate solve the problem.

24. [WRITE Math] ▸ **What's the Error?** Amy says that $3\frac{1}{2}$ is less than $\frac{13}{4}$ because a denominator of 2 is less than a denominator of 4. Describe her error.

Achieving the Standards

25. Alex took 3 oranges from a full box. Write an expression to show how many oranges are left. (AF 1.1, p. 82)

26. Marin read 8 of the 10 books on her reading list. Write the fraction of the books she has read in simplest form.
(NS 1.5, p. 418)

27. Julia hiked $\frac{14}{3}$ miles. Write the distance as a mixed number. (NS 1.5, p. 427)

28. **Test Prep** Which of the following has the greatest value?

A $2\frac{1}{3}$ **B** $2\frac{1}{6}$ **C** $2\frac{2}{3}$ **D** $2\frac{1}{2}$

Write Number Riddles

Ms. Owens asked her students to write a riddle about fractions and mixed numbers. She told them to explain how they used what they knew about fractions and mixed numbers to write a riddle that had only one answer.

Elena's group wrote this riddle and explanation.

○ I am a mixed number between 1 and 2.

My fraction part is greater than $\frac{1}{2}$.

○ My denominator is 8 and my numerator is an even number.

What number am I?

First, we drew a number line and located a mixed number on it.

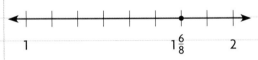

1                              $1\frac{6}{8}$ 2

Our first clue tells about the whole number part of the answer to our riddle.

Next, we decided to give clues about the numerator and denominator in our riddle.

Finally, we checked our riddle. $\frac{5}{8}, \frac{6}{8}, \frac{7}{8}$ are greater than $\frac{1}{2}$. 6 is the only even numerator. The answer is $1\frac{6}{8}$.

Tips

- Use a drawing or model to understand what is being asked.
- You may want to use comparisons in the riddle.
- Include clues about the numerator and the denominator of a fraction.
- Put the clues together to write the riddle.
- Solve your riddle to check that there are enough clues. Make sure the clues make sense and there is only one correct answer.

Problem Solving Write a number riddle for each answer given.

1. a fraction less than $\frac{1}{2}$

2. a fraction greater than $\frac{1}{2}$

3. a mixed number between 2 and 3

4. any fraction or mixed number written in simplest form

LESSON 7

Problem Solving Workshop
Skill: Sequence Information

OBJECTIVE: Solve problems by using the skill *sequence information*.

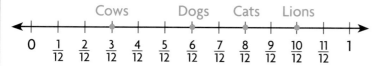

Read to
Understand

Plan

Solve

Check

Use the Skill

PROBLEM Cats can spend $\frac{2}{3}$ of a day sleeping. Cows can spend $\frac{1}{4}$ of a day sleeping. Dogs can sleep for $\frac{1}{2}$ of a day. Lions can sleep for $\frac{5}{6}$ of a day. Which animal can spend the greatest amount of time sleeping? Which can spend the least?

To solve the problem, you can sequence the information. One way to sequence information is to put it in order on a number line.

Step 1

Find equivalent fractions with a denominator of 12.

$$\frac{2 \times 4}{3 \times 4} = \frac{8}{12} \qquad \frac{1 \times 3}{4 \times 3} = \frac{3}{12} \qquad \frac{1 \times 6}{2 \times 6} = \frac{6}{12} \qquad \frac{5 \times 2}{6 \times 2} = \frac{10}{12}$$

Step 2

Use a number line to sequence the equivalent fractions. Draw a number line and divide it into twelfths. Locate each of the equivalent fractions on the number line.

```
       Cows        Dogs    Cats   Lions
◄──┼───┼───┼───┼───┼───┼───┼───┼───┼───┼───┼───┼──►
   0   1   2   3   4   5   6   7   8   9   10  11  1
      12  12  12  12  12  12  12  12  12  12  12
```

The order from greatest to least is $\frac{10}{12}, \frac{8}{12}, \frac{6}{12}, \frac{3}{12}$.

So, lions spend the most time sleeping and cows spend the least time sleeping.

▲ Different animals have different sleeping patterns.

Think and Discuss

Sequence the information to solve.

a. Jan bought $1\frac{1}{3}$ yards of ribbon, Monica bought $1\frac{1}{4}$ yards, and Sheila bought $1\frac{1}{8}$ yards. Which girl bought the most ribbon?

b. Mike, Scott, and David used a total of 10 stamps. Scott used $\frac{1}{2}$ of the total, and David used $\frac{1}{5}$. Who used the least number of stamps?

434

○━ NS 1.9 Identify on a number line the relative position of positive fractions, positive mixed numbers, and positive decimals to two decimal places. *also* NS 1.7, AF 1.1, MR 1.0, MR 1.1, MR 2.0, MR 2.3, MR 2.4, MR 3.0, MR 3.1, MR 3.2, MR 3.3

Sequence information to solve.

1. Newborn babies spend $\frac{2}{3}$ of a day sleeping. School-age children sleep for $\frac{5}{12}$ of a day. Adults sleep for $\frac{1}{4}$ of a day. Which age group spends the least time sleeping? Which spends the greatest time?

   First, find equivalent fractions.
   Then, use a number line to sequence the equivalent fractions.

   Finally, find the age group for the least and greatest fractions.

2. **What if** one piece of data is added to the number line? Add the following information to the number line: Teenagers sleep for $\frac{1}{3}$ of a day.

3. Gloria gives her youngest cat $1\frac{1}{2}$ cups of food. She gives the oldest cat $\frac{7}{8}$ cup of food and the second-oldest cat $1\frac{3}{4}$ cups of food. Draw a number line to represent the amounts of food. Which cat gets the most food?

Mixed Applications

4. After school, Abby ran $\frac{2}{3}$ mile, Kyle ran $\frac{1}{2}$ mile, and Matt ran $\frac{3}{4}$ mile. Order the distances from least to greatest.

5. Jose and his friend made cookies. They each ate 2 cookies. Jose took 10 cookies to school and gave 6 to his neighbor. What fraction of the cookies did Jose take to school?

6. Bart spent $\frac{8}{6}$ hours at his friend's house. Dana spent $\frac{5}{4}$ hours at her friend's house. Who stayed longer?

7. Lisa bought 2 rolls of film. Each roll holds 24 pictures. If Lisa has $\frac{1}{3}$ of a roll left, how many pictures did she take?

8. Viv, Troy, and Ming check out library books. Each reads half a book but a different number of pages. For each student, write a fraction that could show the number of pages read and the number of pages in the book.

9. **WRITE Math** ▶ Find the pattern in this set of fractions. **Explain** your pattern.

$$\frac{1}{2}, \frac{1}{4}, \frac{1}{8}, \frac{1}{16}$$

 **Extra Practice**

Set A Write a fraction for the shaded part.
Write a fraction for the unshaded part. (pp. 414–417)

1.

2.

3.

4.

Set B Find two equivalent fractions for each. (pp. 418–421)

1. $\frac{3}{4}$

2. $\frac{2}{10}$

3. $\frac{8}{12}$

4. $\frac{5}{8}$

5. $\frac{3}{9}$

6. $\frac{5}{5}$

7. Pam baked 20 cupcakes. She took 15 of them to school.
   Write the fraction of cupcakes she took to school in simplest form.

Set C Order the fractions from least to greatest. (pp. 424–425)

1. $\frac{1}{3}, \frac{1}{8}, \frac{1}{6}$

2. $\frac{3}{4}, \frac{6}{12}, \frac{2}{3}$

3. $\frac{7}{8}, \frac{1}{2}, \frac{12}{12}$

4. $\frac{3}{5}, \frac{9}{10}, \frac{1}{2}$

5. Haley jogged $\frac{7}{8}$ mile. Luke jogged $\frac{5}{6}$ mile.
   Rosa jogged $\frac{1}{4}$ mile. Who jogged farthest?

Set D Write a mixed number for each picture. (pp. 426–429)

1.

2.

3.

4.

Rename each fraction as a mixed number and each mixed
number as a fraction.

5. $\frac{9}{5}$

6. $1\frac{2}{3}$

7. $\frac{7}{3}$

8. $3\frac{1}{4}$

9. $\frac{12}{5}$

10. $4\frac{1}{10}$

Set E Compare the mixed numbers. Use <, >, or =. (pp. 430-433)

1.

2.

3.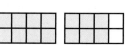

$1\frac{1}{3} \bullet 1\frac{1}{2}$

$3\frac{1}{4} \bullet 3\frac{3}{4}$

$1\frac{3}{6} \bullet 1\frac{5}{8}$

Order the mixed numbers from greatest to least.

4. $4\frac{5}{6}, 4\frac{3}{9}, 4\frac{2}{3}$

5. $6\frac{3}{8}, 5\frac{3}{4}, 6\frac{1}{2}$

6. $1\frac{2}{3}, 1\frac{5}{6}, 1\frac{5}{12}$

7. $2\frac{1}{2}, 2\frac{7}{10}, 2\frac{3}{5}$

CD ROM **Technology**
Use Harcourt Mega Math, Fraction Action,
Fraction Flare Up, Levels B, C, D, E, F.

Fraction Action

Heroes!
2 players

Get Set!
Fraction domino cards

Action

- Place the domino cards face down in a stack. You and your partner each take five domino cards and hold them in your hands.

- Place a domino card on the desk. Your partner must match a fraction circle picture with its name or a fraction name with its picture.

- Take turns with your partner. If you need to, take cards from the stack until you get a domino card that can be played.

- The player with the fewest domino cards when the stack is gone is the winner.

Chapter 16 Review/Test

Check Vocabulary and Concepts

Choose the best term from the box.

1. A __?__ is made up of a whole number and a fraction. (O⊸ NS 1.9, p. 426)

2. Two or more fractions that name the same amount are __?__.
   (NS 1.5, p. 418)

3. A __?__ is a number that names part of a whole or part of a set.
   (NS 1.5, p. 414)

Check Skills

Write the fraction or mixed number for each picture. (NS 1.5, pp. 414–417, O⊸ NS 1.9, pp. 426–429)

4.    5. 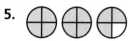   6. 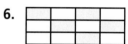   7.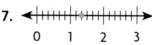

Tell whether the fraction is in simplest form. If not, write
it in simplest form. (NS 1.5, pp. 418–420)

8. $\frac{2}{12}$ 9. $\frac{15}{20}$ 10. $\frac{6}{9}$ 11. $\frac{9}{16}$

Model to compare. Write <, >, or = for each ●. (O⊸ NS 1.9, pp. 424–425, 430–433)

12. $\frac{2}{3}$ ● $\frac{9}{12}$ 13. $4\frac{1}{3}$ ● $4\frac{1}{4}$ 14. $\frac{9}{10}$ ● $\frac{3}{5}$ 15. $2\frac{2}{6}$ ● $2\frac{3}{9}$

Order the fractions or mixed numbers from greatest to least. (O⊸ NS 1.9, pp. 424–425, 430–433)

16. $\frac{1}{7}, \frac{1}{9}, \frac{1}{3}$ 17. $2\frac{2}{3}, 2\frac{1}{6}, 2\frac{5}{12}$ 18. $\frac{7}{8}, \frac{12}{12}, \frac{3}{4}$ 19. $1\frac{2}{3}, 1\frac{3}{4}, 1\frac{5}{6}$

Rename each fraction as a mixed number and each mixed
number as a fraction. (O⊸ NS 1.9, pp. 426–429)

20. $4\frac{1}{4}$ 21. $\frac{17}{5}$ 22. $2\frac{7}{8}$ 23. $\frac{14}{9}$

Check Problem Solving

Solve. (O⊸ NS 1.9, MR 1.1, pp. 434–435)

24. Reggie has a set of measuring cups. Three of the sizes are $\frac{1}{2}$, $\frac{1}{4}$ and $\frac{1}{3}$ cup. Which measuring cup holds the greatest amount?

25. **WRITE Math** ▸ Meg ran $3\frac{1}{2}$ laps, Jill ran $3\frac{3}{8}$ laps, and Randy ran $3\frac{1}{4}$ laps around a track. Explain how to use a number line to find who ran the greatest distance.

GO ONLINE Technology Use *Online Assessment.*

Enrich • Interpret Fractions
Fraction Puzzles

When you know what part of a whole looks like, you can figure out what the whole looks like. When you know what the whole looks like you can figure out what parts of the whole look like.

You can use pattern blocks to find the whole or parts of the whole.

Activity
Find the value of ▲ **if the value of** ◇ **is 1.**

Materials ■ pattern blocks

Use the ◇ as 1 whole.

Place ▲ on top of it to make 1 whole.

How many ▲ did you use?

What part of the ◇ is equal to one ▲ ?

So, 1 ▲ has a value of $\frac{1}{2}$.

Piece it Together
Use pattern blocks to solve.

1. If ▱ has a value of 1, what is the value of ▲ ?

2. If ◇ has a value of 1, what is the value of ⬡ ?

3. If ▱ has a value of 1, what is the value of ⬡ ?

4. If ▲ has a value of $\frac{1}{3}$, which pattern block has a value of 1?

5. If ⬡ has a value of $\frac{1}{4}$, how many ⬡ would you need to have a value of 1?

6. If ◇ has a value of $\frac{1}{6}$, how many ◇ would you need to have a value of 1?

Complete the Puzzle

WRITE Math ▶ Explain how using pattern blocks can help you find the whole or parts of the whole.

Number Sense

1. Amanda makes bead necklaces. She uses 25 beads in each necklace. How many beads does she need to make 36 necklaces? (0━ⁿ NS 3.3)

A 61

B 90

C 610

D 900

 Test Tip **Look for important words.**

In Item 2, an important word is *prime*. Determine which number is prime.

2. Robert says his age is a prime number. Which could be Robert's age? (0━ⁿ NS 4.2)

A 19

B 20

C 21

D 22

3. Which fraction represents the smallest part of a whole? (NS 1.5)

A $\frac{1}{2}$

B $\frac{1}{3}$

C $\frac{1}{4}$

D $\frac{1}{5}$

4. **WRITE Math** **Explain** how to find 12×26. (0━ⁿ NS 3.2)

Measurement and Geometry

5. Look at the line segment below.

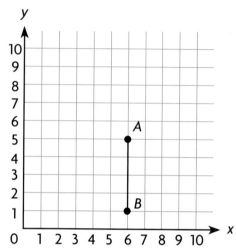

What is the length of the line segment? (0━ⁿ MG 2.3)

A 6 units   **C** 4 units

B 5 units   **D** 1 units

6. The temperature at 8:00 A.M. is ⁻2°F. It rises 5° by noon. What is the temperature at noon? (0━ⁿ NS 1.8)

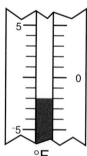

A ⁻7°F   **C** 3°F

B ⁻3°F   **D** 7°F

7. **WRITE Math** **Explain** how to find the length of the line segment in Item 5. (0━ⁿ MG 2.3)

Algebra and Functions

8. Look at the problem below.

$$\blacktriangle - 7 = \blacksquare$$

If $\blacktriangle = 12$, what is $\blacksquare$? (O━━ AF 1.5)

A 19

B 5

C 4

D 3

9. What is the value of the expression below if $k = 5$? (O━━ AF 1.2)

$$(2 \times k) + 5$$

A 5

B 12

C 15

D 20

10. What number goes in the box to make this number sentence true? (O━━ AF 2.2)

$$6 \times \blacksquare = 9 \times 6$$

A 3

B 9

C 15

D 54

11. **WRITE Math** ▶ **Explain** how to use the order of operations to evaluate the expression. (SDAP 1.3)

$$(12 - 8) \times 5$$

Statistics, Data Analysis, and Probability

12. The bar graph shows the number of medals won on field day by the students in each fourth-grade class.

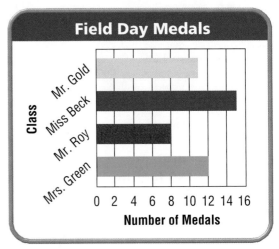

How many more medals were won by the students in Mr. Gold's class than by the students in Mr. Roy's class?

(SDAP 1.3)

A 1   **C** 4

B 3   **D** 8

13. What type of graph would be best to show your height each year since birth?

(SDAP 1.1)

A line plot

B pictograph

C bar graph

D line graph

14. **WRITE Math** ▶ **Explain** how to find the median of this set of numbers.

(SDAP 1.2)

$$6, 7, 10, 8, 6, 5, 9$$

17 Add and Subtract Like Fractions and Mixed Numbers

The Big Idea Addition and subtraction of fractions and mixed numbers is based on understanding equivalent fractions.

CALIFORNIA FAST FACT

The Pizza Farm, in Fresno, is 150 feet in diameter. It grows wheat for pizza crust and tomatoes for the sauce. Milk from the dairy cows is used to make cheese.

Investigate

After visiting the Pizza Farm, students were asked how much pizza they would like for lunch. Their responses are shown on the line plot. Each small pizza is divided into eighths. Use the data in the line plot to write a word problem that can be solved with this number sentence: $\frac{2}{8} + \frac{2}{8} + \frac{2}{8} = \frac{6}{8}$.

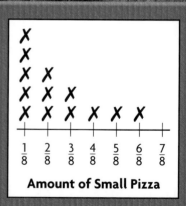

Amount of Small Pizza

Technology
Student pages are available in the Student eBook.

Show What You Know

Check your understanding of important
skills needed for success in Chapter 17.

▶ **Model Fractions and Mixed Numbers**

Write a fraction or mixed number for each picture.

1.   2.   3.

▶ **Equivalent Fractions**

Write two equivalent fractions for each picture.

4.   5. 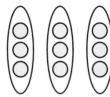   6.

▶ **Simplest Form**

Tell whether each fraction is in simplest form.
If it is not, write it in simplest form.

7. $\frac{8}{12}$ 8. $\frac{8}{10}$ 9. $\frac{3}{8}$ 10. $\frac{10}{12}$ 11. $\frac{12}{3}$ 12. $\frac{6}{12}$

VOCABULARY POWER

CHAPTER VOCABULARY

denominator
equation
equivalent
  fractions
like fractions
mixed
  number

numerator
simplest
  form
variable
fraction

WARM-UP WORDS

like fractions fractions with the same denominator

mixed number an amount given as a whole number
and a fraction

equivalent fractions two or more fractions that
name the same amount

1 Model Addition

OBJECTIVE: Use models to add like fractions.

Quick Review

Jamie drew the model shown. What fraction of the model is shaded?

Vocabulary

like fractions

Investigate

Materials ■ pattern blocks

You can use pattern blocks to explore adding like fractions. **Like fractions** are fractions with the same denominator.

A The yellow hexagon represents 1 whole. Use a fraction to describe the value of each pattern block shown.

    1           $\frac{1}{2}$ $\frac{1}{3}$ $\frac{1}{6}$

B The model shows $\frac{1}{3}$.

Show how to model $\frac{1}{3} + \frac{1}{3}$. Then, record the sum.

C Model $\frac{4}{6} + \frac{2}{6}$. Record the sum.

Draw Conclusions

1. Explain how the pattern blocks show the numerator of the sum.

2. Compare your model with those of other classmates. What can you conclude? Explain.

3. What rule could you write to add fractions with like denominators?

4. **Formulation** How could you use pattern blocks to find $\frac{1}{6} + \frac{3}{6}$?

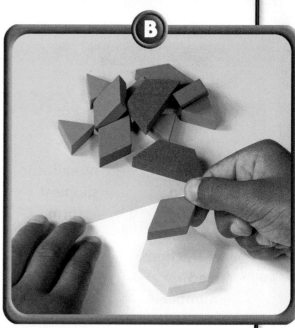

Preparing for Grade 5 〇━ℸ **NS 2.3** Solve simple problems, including ones arising in concrete situations, involving the addition and subtraction of fractions and mixed numbers (like and unlike denominators of 20 or less), and express answers in the simplest form. *also* **Grade 4 MR 2.0, MR 2.3, MR 2.4, MR 3.2**

Connect

You can use drawings to add fractions.

Step 1

Draw a number line and divide it into 8 equal parts. Model the fraction $\frac{1}{8}$ by shading 1 part of the line green.

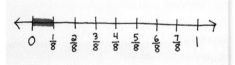

Step 2

Add the fraction $\frac{5}{8}$ by shading 5 more parts of the line red.

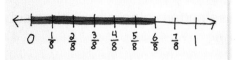

Step 3

Add the fractions. Since there are 8 equal parts, the denominator stays the same. Add the numerators and record the sum over the denominator.

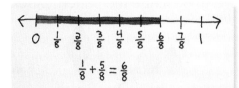

$\frac{1}{8} + \frac{5}{8} = \frac{6}{8}$

So, $\frac{1}{8} + \frac{5}{8} = \frac{6}{8}$.

To add like fractions, add the numerators. Use the same denominator as in the like fractions.

TALK Math

How does using a number line help you add like fractions?

Practice

Find the sum.

1.

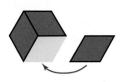

$\frac{2}{3} + \frac{1}{3}$

2.

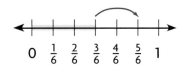

$\frac{3}{6} + \frac{2}{6}$

✓ **3.**

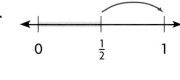

$\frac{1}{2} + \frac{1}{2}$

Model the sum. Record your answer.

4. $\frac{4}{6} + \frac{1}{6}$

5. $\frac{1}{4} + \frac{3}{4}$

6. $\frac{1}{8} + \frac{3}{8}$

✓ **7.** $\frac{5}{12} + \frac{2}{12}$

8. $\frac{4}{10} + \frac{3}{10}$

9. $\frac{5}{6} + \frac{1}{6}$

10. $\frac{4}{12} + \frac{9}{12}$

11. $\frac{2}{5} + \frac{1}{5}$

12. **WRITE Math** ▸ Would you use pattern blocks or a number line to find $\frac{2}{9} + \frac{5}{9}$? **Explain** your choice.

Technology
Use Harcourt Mega Math, Ice Station Exploration, *Arctic Algebra*, Levels Y, S.

2 Model Subtraction

OBJECTIVE: Use models to subtract like fractions.

Quick Review

Ryan modeled the fraction shown with pattern blocks. Write the fraction.

Investigate

Materials ■ pattern blocks

You can use pattern blocks to explore subtracting like fractions.

A The yellow hexagon represents 1 whole. Use fractions to describe the pattern blocks shown.

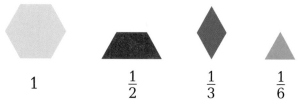

1	$\frac{1}{2}$	$\frac{1}{3}$	$\frac{1}{6}$

B Use a take away model. Place 5 triangle pattern blocks on the hexagon. Take away 3 of the 5 blocks. What do you notice? What is $\frac{5}{6} - \frac{3}{6}$?

C Use a compare model. Place 5 triangle pattern blocks on a hexagon. Then use 3 triangle blocks to cover 3 of the triangle blocks. Compare the groups of blocks. What do you notice? What is $\frac{5}{6} - \frac{3}{6}$?

Draw Conclusions

1. Explain how you used the pattern blocks to subtract in part B.

2. Explain how you used the pattern blocks to subtract in part C.

3. What rule could you write to subtract fractions with like denominators?

4. **Synthesis** How does subtraction of fractions compare to addition of fractions?

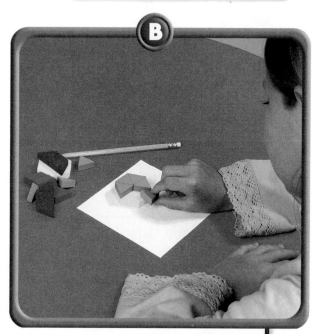

Preparing for Grade 5 0━ NS 2.3 Solve simple problems, including ones arising in concrete situations, involving the addition and subtraction of fractions and mixed numbers (like and unlike denominators of 20 or less), and express answers in the simplest form. *also* **Grade 4 MR 2.0, MR 2.3, MR 2.4, MR 3.2**

Connect

You can solve $\frac{7}{10} - \frac{3}{10}$ using a number line.

Step 1	Step 2	Step 3
Draw a number line divided into 10 equal parts. Model the fraction $\frac{7}{10}$ by shading 7 parts of the line green.	To subtract on a number line, move left. To subtract $\frac{3}{10}$ from $\frac{7}{10}$, start at $\frac{7}{10}$ and move 3 parts to the left.	Record your answer. Since there are 10 equal parts, the denominator stays the same. Subtract the numerators and record the difference over the denominator.

So, $\frac{7}{10} - \frac{3}{10} = \frac{4}{10}$

TALK Math

What other ways could you find the difference?

Practice

Find the difference.

1.

$\frac{2}{3} - \frac{1}{3}$

2.

$\frac{5}{6} - \frac{1}{6}$

✔ 3.

$\frac{1}{2} - \frac{1}{2}$

Model the difference. Record your answer.

4. $\frac{3}{4} - \frac{2}{4}$

5. $\frac{11}{12} - \frac{5}{12}$

6. $\frac{5}{8} - \frac{3}{8}$

✔ 7. $\frac{2}{3} - \frac{1}{3}$

8. $\frac{9}{10} - \frac{3}{10}$

9. $\frac{3}{6} - \frac{1}{6}$

10. $\frac{7}{12} - \frac{5}{12}$

11. $\frac{7}{8} - \frac{4}{8}$

12. **WRITE Math** **Explain** how to find $\frac{5}{12} + \frac{1}{12}$ by using a number line.

Technology
Use Harcourt Mega Math, Ice Station
Exploration, *Arctic Algebra*, Levels Z, S.

Record Addition and Subtraction

OBJECTIVE: Model and record addition and subtraction
of fractions with like denominators.

Learn

PROBLEM Rory's herb garden is in a window box. He divided it
into 4 equal parts. He used 1 part for mint, 1 part for basil, and
2 parts for thyme. What part of Rory's garden is either basil or mint?

Example 1 Use fraction bars. Add. $\frac{1}{4} + \frac{1}{4}$

MODEL	THINK	RECORD
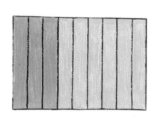	Count the $\frac{1}{4}$ fraction bars. There are two $\frac{1}{4}$ fraction bars.	$\frac{1}{4} + \frac{1}{4} = \frac{2}{4}$ Write the sum in simplest form. $\frac{2}{4} = \frac{1}{2}$

So, $\frac{2}{4}$, or $\frac{1}{2}$ of Rory's garden is either basil or mint.

Example 2 Use drawings. Add. $\frac{3}{9} + \frac{6}{9}$

MODEL	THINK	RECORD
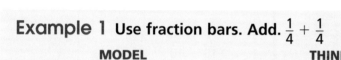	Count the number of dark green sections and the number of light green sections. There are 3 dark green sections and 6 light green sections.	$\frac{3}{9} + \frac{6}{9} = \frac{9}{9}$ Write the sum as a whole number. $\frac{9}{9} = 1$

So, $\frac{3}{9} + \frac{6}{9} = \frac{9}{9}$, or 1.

Example 3 Use paper and pencil. Add. $\frac{2}{5} + \frac{4}{5}$

THINK	RECORD
The denominators are the same. Add the numerators.	$\frac{2}{5} + \frac{4}{5} = \frac{6}{5}$ Write the sum as a mixed number. $\frac{6}{5} = \frac{5}{5} + \frac{1}{5} = 1\frac{1}{5}$

So, $\frac{2}{5} + \frac{4}{5} = 1\frac{1}{5}$.

Preparing for Grade 5 ⊶ **NS 2.3** Solve simple problems, including ones arising in concrete situations,
involving the addition and subtraction of fractions and mixed numbers (like and unlike denominators of 20
or less), and express answers in the simplest form. *also* **Grade 4 AF 1.1, MR 2.0, MR 2.3, MR 2.4, MR 3.2**

Subtract Like Fractions

Tia's garden is divided into 10 equal sections. $\frac{7}{10}$ of her garden has various leafy herbs, and $\frac{3}{10}$ of her garden has chives. How much more of her garden is leafy herbs than chives?

Example 1 Compare.

Subtract. $\frac{7}{10} - \frac{3}{10}$

MODEL	THINK	RECORD
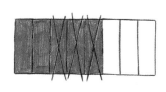	Compare the rows of $\frac{1}{10}$ bars. Find the difference. The difference is four $\frac{1}{10}$ bars.	$\frac{7}{10} - \frac{3}{10} = \frac{4}{10}$ Write the answer in simplest form. $\frac{4}{10} = \frac{2}{5}$

So, $\frac{2}{5}$ more of Tia's garden space has leafy herbs than chives.

Example 2 Take away.

Subtract. $\frac{5}{8} - \frac{3}{8}$

MODEL	THINK	RECORD
	Cross out 3 of the shaded parts. There are 2 shaded parts not crossed off.	$\frac{5}{8} - \frac{3}{8} = \frac{2}{8}$ Write the answer in simplest form. $\frac{2}{8} = \frac{1}{4}$

So, $\frac{5}{8} - \frac{3}{8} = \frac{2}{8}$.

- Find the difference in the numerators of $\frac{5}{8} - \frac{3}{8}$. How does this compare to the numerator of the difference, $\frac{2}{8}$, found in Example 2?

Example 3 Use paper and pencil.

Subtract. $\frac{5}{6} - \frac{2}{6}$

THINK	RECORD
The denominators are the same. Subtract the numerators.	$\frac{5}{6} - \frac{2}{6} = \frac{3}{6}$ Write the answer in simplest form. $\frac{3}{6} = \frac{1}{2}$

So, $\frac{5}{6} - \frac{2}{6} = \frac{3}{6}$.

1. Make the model shown. Then use your model to find and record the sum.

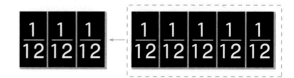

Find and record the sum or difference.

2. $\frac{5}{8} + \frac{2}{8}$

3. $\frac{9}{10} - \frac{2}{10}$

✓ 4. $\frac{4}{6} + \frac{3}{6}$

✓ 5. $\frac{3}{4} - \frac{1}{4}$

6. **TALK Math** Explain why the denominator does not change when you add or subtract like fractions.

Independent Practice and Problem Solving

Find and record the sum or difference.

7. $\frac{5}{8}$
   $-\frac{4}{8}$

8. $\frac{8}{10}$
   $-\frac{3}{10}$

9. $\frac{27}{100}$
   $+\frac{48}{100}$

10. $\frac{5}{8}$
    $+\frac{5}{8}$

11. $\frac{5}{10} + \frac{7}{10}$

12. $\frac{7}{12} - \frac{6}{12}$

13. $\frac{3}{4} + \frac{1}{4}$

14. $\frac{7}{100} - \frac{2}{100}$

Compare. Write <, >, or = for each ●.

15. $\frac{2}{3} + \frac{2}{3}$ ● 1

16. $\frac{1}{2}$ ● $\frac{7}{8} - \frac{3}{8}$

17. $\frac{1}{5} + \frac{2}{5}$ ● $\frac{4}{5}$

18. $\frac{2}{3}$ ● $\frac{11}{12} - \frac{1}{12}$

★ **Algebra** Find the value of n.

19. $\frac{5}{9} + \frac{2}{n} = \frac{7}{9}$

20. $\frac{n}{7} - \frac{2}{7} = \frac{4}{7}$

21. $\frac{n}{5} - \frac{1}{5} = \frac{3}{5}$

22. $\frac{3}{n} + \frac{9}{n} = 1$

USE DATA For 23–24, use the graph.

23. How much taller is the sage plant than the marjoram plant?

24. If the basil plant grows another $\frac{7}{8}$ inch by the end of next week, how tall will it be?

25. The height of the mint plant at two weeks measured $\frac{4}{8}$ inch. If the plant continues to grow at this rate, how tall will the plant be at 4 weeks?

26. **Pose a Problem** Look back at Problem 25. Write a similar problem by changing the numbers.

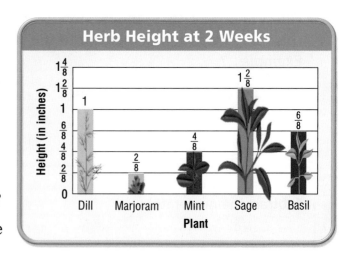

27. Ron has 3 equal-sized jars. One has $\frac{2}{8}$ cup paint, one has $\frac{4}{8}$ cup paint, and the other has $\frac{6}{8}$ cup paint. Which jar has the least amount of paint?

28. **What's the Error?** Ken wrote $\frac{1}{5} + \frac{2}{5} = \frac{3}{10}$. Dora wrote $\frac{1}{5} + \frac{2}{5} = \frac{3}{5}$. Who is correct? **Explain** your reasoning.

Achieving the Standards

29. What mixed number does the model show? (NS 1.7, p. 426)

30. Use a model to find $\frac{5}{8} - \frac{2}{8}$. (Grade 3 ⚼ NS3.2)

31. Test Prep Barnie jogged $\frac{5}{8}$ mile in the morning and $\frac{6}{8}$ mile in the afternoon. How far did he jog in all?

A $\frac{1}{8}$ mile   **C** $1\frac{3}{8}$ miles

B 1 mile   **D** $1\frac{1}{2}$ miles

32. The sides of a triangle are 5 meters, 8 meters, and 9 meters long. What is the perimeter of the triangle? (Grade 3 ⚼ MG 1.3)

33. Test Prep Ana bought $\frac{3}{8}$ pound of ham and $\frac{7}{8}$ pound of roast beef. How much more roast beef than ham did he buy?

A $\frac{3}{8}$ pound   **C** $\frac{7}{8}$ pound

B $\frac{1}{2}$ pound   **D** $1\frac{1}{4}$ pounds

Problem Solving connects to Social Studies

Regions of the United States

The map shows the five regions of the United States. Of the 50 states, what part makes up the Northeast and the Middle West?

Find the fraction of states that make up the Northeast: $\frac{11}{50}$

Find the fraction of states that make up the Middle West: $\frac{12}{50}$

Add to find the total part: $\frac{11}{50} + \frac{12}{50} = \frac{23}{50}$

So, $\frac{23}{50}$ of the states make up the Northeast and the Middle West.

Legend:
- Northeast
- Southeast
- Middle West
- Southwest
- West

Solve.

1. How much greater is the fraction of states in the Southeast than in the Southwest?

2. Reasoning Do a larger fraction of the states have coastline along the Pacific Ocean or the Atlantic Ocean? **Explain.**

Problem Solving Workshop
Strategy: Write an Equation

OBJECTIVE: Solve problems using the strategy *write an equation*.

Learn the Strategy

Writing an equation can help you understand how the facts in a problem are related. Remember that an equation is a number sentence that shows that two quantities are equal.

Write an addition equation.

Greg walks $\frac{5}{8}$ mile to the store from his home. Then he continues in the same direction and walks to the library. The library is $\frac{7}{8}$ mile from his home. How far is it from the store to the library?

Let *b* represent the distance from the store to the library.

$$\frac{5}{8} + b = \frac{7}{8}$$

Write a subtraction equation.

Raven had 5 yards of fabric. She used some of the fabric to make a banner. She has 2 yards left. How much fabric did Raven use to make the banner?

Let *f* represent the amount of fabric she uses to make the banner.

$$5 - f = 2$$

Write a multiplication equation.

Len's class has set up seats for the play. There are 7 seats in each row. There are 56 seats in all. How many rows of seats are there?

Let *s* represent the number of rows of seats.

$$s \times 7 = 56$$

Write a division equation.

Mrs. Hall has 24 stickers. She gives the same number of stickers to each of 8 students. How many stickers does each student receive?

Let *t* represent the number of stickers each student receives.

$$24 \div 8 = t$$

To write an equation, choose a variable to represent an unknown quantity. Then choose the operation that relates the unknown quantity to the known quantities.

TALK Math

What are some questions that you can ask yourself to help choose the correct operation?

AF 1.1 Use letters, boxes, or other symbols to stand for any number in simple expressions or equations (e.g., demonstrate an understanding and the use of the concept of a variable). *also* **MR 1.0, MR 2.0, MR 2.3, MR 2.4, MR 3.2**

Use the Strategy

PROBLEM During her dance class, Maria spends $\frac{3}{6}$ of the class on ballet. The rest of the class is spent on tap. The class lasts 1 hour. What fraction of the class is spent on tap?

Read to Understand

• Identify the details in the problem.
• What details will you use?

Plan

• **What strategy can you use to solve the problem?**
You can write an equation. An equation can show how the information in the problem is related.

Solve

• **How can you use the strategy to solve the problem?**
Choose a variable to represent the unknown time. Tell what the variable represents. Let *x* stand for the time Maria spends on tap during her dance class. Choose the operation you will use.

Write an equation.

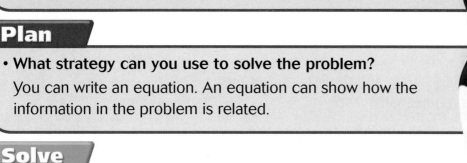

fraction of an hour spent on ballet		fraction of an hour spent on tap		total length of class
↓		↓		↓
$\frac{3}{6}$	+	x	=	$\frac{6}{6}$

Use mental math to solve the equation.

$$\frac{3}{6} + x = \frac{6}{6}$$ **Think:** $\frac{3}{6}$ plus what fraction equals $\frac{6}{6}$?

$$x = \frac{3}{6}, \text{ or } \frac{1}{2}$$

So, $\frac{3}{6}$, or $\frac{1}{2}$ of the class is spent on tap.

Check

• **How can you check your answer?**
• **What other ways can you solve the problem? Explain.**

Guided Problem Solving

1. Monday's dance class lasts for $\frac{3}{4}$ hour and consists of ballet and jazz. The first part of the class is ballet. After ballet, jazz lasts for $\frac{1}{4}$ hour. How long does ballet last?

   First, choose a variable. Tell what the variable represents.

   Let b stand for the fraction of the hour spent on ballet.

   Then, choose the operation and then write an equation.

   $b + \frac{1}{4} = \frac{3}{4}$

   $b = \blacksquare$

   Finally, use mental math to solve the equation.

2. **What if** the dance class lasts $\frac{11}{12}$ hour, and the jazz part of the class lasts $\frac{4}{12}$ hour. How long does ballet last?

3. Jen takes a dance class of hip-hop and jazz. The class lasts $\frac{9}{10}$ hour. Hip-hop lasts $\frac{4}{10}$ hour. Which part lasts longer?

Problem Solving Strategy Practice

Write an equation to solve.

4. Camille bought $\frac{7}{8}$ foot of elastic for her ballet slippers. She used some elastic for her slippers and had $\frac{5}{8}$ foot of elastic left. How much elastic did she use for her slippers?

5. In Wednesday's class, $\frac{3}{5}$ of the students are boys. What fraction of the students are girls?

USE DATA For 6–8, use the table.

6. At Level C, students dance to a CD for $\frac{2}{6}$ hour. A pianist plays for the rest of the class. How long does the pianist play?

7. Meg is in Level A. She takes two classes a week. How many hours does she spend in class each week?

8. **WRITE Math** At Level B, students take tap for $\frac{3}{10}$ hour, jazz for $\frac{3}{10}$ hour, and hip-hop for the rest of the class. **Explain** how to write and solve an equation to find how long the students take hip-hop in the class.

Academy Dance Classes

Level	Class Length (in hours)
A	$\frac{11}{12}$
B	$\frac{9}{10}$
C	$\frac{5}{6}$

Mixed Strategy Practice

USE DATA For 9–12, use the
circle graph.

9. **Reasoning** Beth takes 4 hours of ballet each week. How many hours does she spend taking jazz?

10. Does Beth spend more time taking ballet and tap or ballet and jazz each week? How much more time?

11. **Pose a Problem** Look back at Problem 9. Write a similar problem comparing the types of dance lessons that Beth takes.

12. **Open-Ended** Write three different equations that can be solved by using the circle graph. Use at least one addition equation and one subtraction equation. Ask a question that can be answered by solving one of your equations.

13. Nate, Sean, and Jonah take chorus, drama, and band. Jonah and Sean do not like drama best. Jonah's favorite is not band. What is each boy's favorite type of class?

14. Gavin spends 90 minutes each week taking violin lessons. How many hours each week does he spend taking violin lessons? Express your answer as a mixed number.

Choose a STRATEGY

Draw a Diagram or Picture

Make a Model or Act It Out

Make an Organized List

Find a Pattern

Make a Table or Graph

Predict and Test

Work Backward

Solve a Simpler Problem

Write an Equation

Use Logical Reasoning

Beth's Weekly Dance Lessons

CHALLENGE YOURSELF

Lara is a member of a community orchestra. One half of its members play string instruments, $\frac{1}{6}$ of its members play brass instruments, $\frac{2}{12}$ of its members play woodwind instruments, and $\frac{1}{6}$ of its members play percussion instruments.

15. What part of the orchestra do the string, woodwind, and brass sections make up? How does this compare to the whole orchestra?

16. Next year, the conductor expects only $\frac{1}{3}$ of the members to play string instruments. How would the fraction of the members in each of the other sections need to change in order to make one whole?

5 Add and Subtract Mixed Numbers

OBJECTIVE: Add and subtract mixed numbers with like denominators.

Learn

PROBLEM Keoni and Jack are making puppets for the library puppet show. The thigh of each puppet is $1\frac{1}{4}$ inches longer than the forearm. How long is the thigh if the forearm is $3\frac{2}{4}$ inches long?

Example 1 Add. $1\frac{1}{4} + 3\frac{2}{4}$

MODEL	THINK	RECORD
Step 1 Draw a picture for each mixed number. Add the fractions first. 	Count the number of fourths shaded.	$\begin{array}{r} 1\frac{1}{4} \\ + 3\frac{2}{4} \\ \hline \frac{3}{4} \end{array}$
Step 2 Then add the whole numbers. 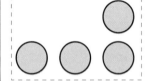	Count the number of whole circles shaded.	$\begin{array}{r} 1\frac{1}{4} \\ + 3\frac{2}{4} \\ \hline 4\frac{3}{4} \end{array}$

ERROR ALERT

Remember to add the additional whole number if the fractional part of a sum is greater than 1.

So, the thigh is $4\frac{3}{4}$ inches long.

More Examples

A Like Fractions

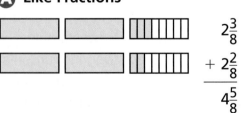

$\begin{array}{r} 2\frac{3}{8} \\ + 2\frac{2}{8} \\ \hline 4\frac{5}{8} \end{array}$

B Like Fractions

$\begin{array}{r} \frac{4}{6} \\ + 1\frac{3}{6} \\ \hline 1\frac{7}{6} = 1 + 1\frac{1}{6} = 2\frac{1}{6} \end{array}$

Preparing for Grade 5 ⊶ NS 2.3 Solve simple problems, including ones arising concrete situations, involving the addition and subtraction of fractions and mixed numbers (like and unlike denominators of 20 or less), and express answers in the simplest form. *also* **Grade 4 AF 1.1, MR 2.0, MR 2.3, MR 2.4, MR 3.2**

Subtract Mixed Numbers

Subtracting mixed numbers is similar to adding mixed numbers.

The body of an eagle puppet is $1\frac{1}{3}$ feet shorter than its wingspan. The wingspan of the puppet is $3\frac{2}{3}$ feet long. How long is the puppet's body?

$3\frac{2}{3}$ feet

Example 2 Subtract. $3\frac{2}{3} - 1\frac{1}{3}$

MODEL	THINK	RECORD
Step 1 Draw a model for the first mixed number. Subtract the fractions first.	Cross off 1 of the shaded parts.	$\begin{array}{r} 3\frac{2}{3} \\ -\ 1\frac{1}{3} \\ \hline \frac{1}{3} \end{array}$
Step 2 Then subtract the whole numbers.	Cross off 1 whole.	$\begin{array}{r} 3\frac{2}{3} \\ -\ 1\frac{1}{3} \\ \hline 2\frac{1}{3} \end{array}$

So, the puppet's body is $2\frac{1}{3}$ feet long.

More Examples

A Like Fractions

$\begin{array}{r} 4\frac{4}{5} \\ -\ 1\frac{1}{5} \\ \hline 3\frac{3}{5} \end{array}$

B Like Fractions

$\begin{array}{r} 3\frac{3}{7} \\ -\ 3\frac{1}{7} \\ \hline \frac{2}{7} \end{array}$

• How do models help you add or subtract mixed numbers?

Guided Practice

1. Use the model. Subtract. $2\frac{7}{10} - 1\frac{4}{10}$

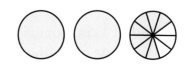

Model and record the sum or difference.

2. $1\frac{3}{4}$
$+2\frac{1}{4}$

3. $4\frac{5}{8}$
$-3\frac{1}{8}$

4. $2\frac{1}{3}$
$+2\frac{1}{3}$

5. $5\frac{3}{4}$
$-1\frac{2}{4}$

✓ 6. $3\frac{1}{6}$
$+1\frac{3}{6}$

✓ 7. $1\frac{4}{5}$
$-\frac{2}{5}$

8. **TALK Math** Explain how to use models to find $3\frac{2}{12} + 1\frac{4}{12}$.

Independent Practice and Problem Solving

Model and record the sum or difference.

9. $3\frac{4}{10}$
$+2\frac{3}{10}$

10. $6\frac{3}{5}$
$-2\frac{1}{5}$

11. $2\frac{7}{12}$
$+2\frac{3}{12}$

12. $5\frac{5}{8}$
$-3\frac{1}{8}$

13. $\frac{2}{5}$
$+1\frac{3}{5}$

14. $3\frac{6}{8}$
$-2\frac{5}{8}$

15. $3\frac{9}{12} - 1\frac{5}{12}$

16. $4\frac{5}{6} + \frac{2}{6}$

17. $3\frac{1}{2} + 1\frac{1}{2}$

18. $4\frac{2}{3} - 4\frac{1}{3}$

★ **Algebra** Find the value of *n*.

19. $5\frac{n}{4} + 2\frac{1}{4} = 7\frac{3}{4}$

20. $2\frac{n}{6} + 1\frac{1}{6} = 3\frac{5}{6}$

21. $3\frac{1}{8} + 1\frac{n}{8} = 4\frac{6}{8}$

22. $4 - n = 3\frac{2}{5}$

USE DATA For 23-24 and 27, use the table.

23. A $3\frac{3}{4}$ inch rod is used to extend the length of a rod puppet. How long is the puppet with the extension?

24. Order the types of puppets from longest to shortest. How much longer is the longest puppet than the shortest puppet?

25. Pablo stores the hand puppets in boxes of 18 and the marionettes in boxes of 15. He has 4 boxes filled with hand puppets and 3 boxes filled with marionettes. How many hand puppets and marionettes does he have in all?

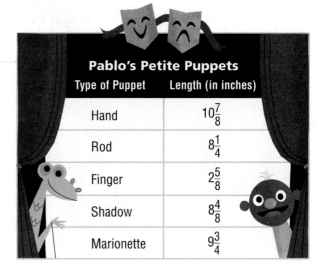

Pablo's Petite Puppets

Type of Puppet	Length (in inches)
Hand	$10\frac{7}{8}$
Rod	$8\frac{1}{4}$
Finger	$2\frac{5}{8}$
Shadow	$8\frac{4}{8}$
Marionette	$9\frac{3}{4}$

26. **≡FAST FACT** The first puppet show in Boston, Massachusetts, was in 1768. How many years ago was this?

27. **WRITE Math** What's the Question? Compare the lengths of two of Pablo's puppets. The answer is this puppet is $1\frac{1}{2}$ inches longer.

28. **Reasoning** Nilda needs $1\frac{3}{4}$ cups of milk for one recipe and $2\frac{3}{4}$ cups of milk for another recipe. Will Nilda have enough milk if she buys a quart? **Explain.**

29. Of the tiles Mark used in his design, $\frac{3}{8}$ were red and $\frac{5}{8}$ were black. Use a number line to find out if he used more red or more black tiles. (O─ NS 1.9, p. 424)

30. What is the mode of this set of numbers? 20, 15, 25, 20, 30, 18, 24 (SDAP 1.2, p. 322)

31. **Test Prep** Toby has hiked $2\frac{1}{4}$ miles. The trail to the lake is $2\frac{3}{4}$ miles long. How much further does Toby have to hike to reach the lake?

    A $\frac{1}{4}$ mile   **C** $1\frac{1}{2}$ miles

    B $\frac{1}{2}$ mile   **D** 5 miles

32. What fraction is represented by the model? (NS 1.7, p. 416)

33. **Test Prep** Kylie painted for $1\frac{4}{6}$ hours in the morning. In the afternoon she painted for $1\frac{5}{6}$ hours. How long did she paint altogether?

    A $\frac{1}{6}$ hour   **C** $2\frac{1}{2}$ hours

    B $2\frac{1}{6}$ hours   **D** $3\frac{1}{2}$ hours

MATH POWER   **Problem Solving and Reasoning**

NUMBER SENSE Rounding fractions to 0, $\frac{1}{2}$, or 1 can help you estimate fraction sums and differences. Rounding mixed numbers to the nearest whole number can help you estimate mixed number sums and differences.

Estimate. $\frac{1}{8} + \frac{2}{3}$

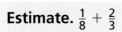

Think: $\frac{1}{8}$ is close to 0.
      $\frac{2}{3}$ is close to 1.

$0 + 1 = 1$

So, $\frac{1}{8} + \frac{2}{3}$ is about 1.

Estimate. $4\frac{9}{10} - 1\frac{3}{5}$

Think: $\frac{9}{10}$ is close to 1. So, $4\frac{9}{10}$ is close to 5.
      $\frac{3}{5}$ is close to $\frac{1}{2}$. So, $1\frac{3}{5}$ is close to $1\frac{1}{2}$.

$5 - 1\frac{1}{2} = 3\frac{1}{2}$

So, $4\frac{9}{10} - 1\frac{3}{5}$ is about $3\frac{1}{2}$.

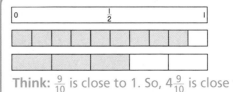

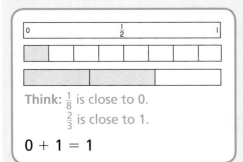

Use models to estimate the sum or difference. Then find the actual sum or difference and compare it to the estimate to determine whether your answer is reasonable.

1. $\frac{5}{12} + \frac{2}{5}$ **2.** $\frac{5}{8} + \frac{5}{6}$ **3.** $\frac{7}{8} - \frac{1}{5}$ **4.** $3\frac{11}{12} - 1\frac{3}{8}$ **5.** $2\frac{1}{4} + 4\frac{1}{10}$

🐻 Extra Practice

Set A Find and record the sum or difference. (pp. 448–451)

1. $\frac{3}{5}$
$+\frac{1}{5}$

2. $\frac{7}{8}$
$-\frac{4}{8}$

3. $\frac{7}{10}$
$+\frac{4}{10}$

4. $\frac{3}{4}$
$-\frac{1}{4}$

5. $\frac{12}{100}$
$+\frac{19}{100}$

6. $\frac{5}{6}$
$-\frac{2}{6}$

7. $\frac{3}{8}$
$+\frac{2}{8}$

8. $\frac{9}{12}$
$-\frac{6}{12}$

Compare. Write $<$, $>$, or $=$ for each ⬤.

9. $\frac{8}{10} + \frac{3}{10}$ ⬤ 1

10. $\frac{2}{3} - \frac{1}{3}$ ⬤ $\frac{1}{2}$

11. $\frac{5}{8} + \frac{3}{8}$ ⬤ $\frac{7}{8}$

12. $\frac{11}{12} - \frac{5}{12}$ ⬤ $\frac{1}{2}$

13. Lisa brings home a pizza for dinner. The pizza is divided into 12 equal slices. If Lisa eats 3 slices and her sister eats 4 slices, what part of the pizza do Lisa and her sister eat.

14. Hunter buys $\frac{2}{3}$ pound of Swiss cheese and the same amount of mozzarella cheese. How many pounds of cheese does he buy in all?

Set B Find the sum or difference. (pp. 456–459)

1. $3\frac{1}{4}$
$+1\frac{3}{4}$

2. $6\frac{5}{8}$
$-2\frac{3}{8}$

3. $9\frac{7}{10}$
$-1\frac{4}{10}$

4. $3\frac{5}{6}$
$+2\frac{1}{6}$

5. $4\frac{5}{12}$
$+3\frac{2}{12}$

6. $2\frac{3}{4}$
$-1\frac{1}{4}$

7. $2\frac{3}{5}$
$+\frac{4}{5}$

8. $6\frac{2}{3}$
$-4\frac{1}{3}$

9. $2\frac{3}{5} + 4\frac{1}{5}$

10. $3\frac{6}{7} + 4\frac{1}{7}$

11. $6\frac{3}{5} - 2\frac{2}{5}$

12. $10 - 9\frac{1}{3}$

13. Barb baby-sat for $2\frac{1}{2}$ hours yesterday and $1\frac{1}{2}$ hours today. How many hours did she baby-sit?

14. Grant volunteered $3\frac{3}{4}$ hours this week and $1\frac{1}{4}$ hours last week. How many more hours did he volunteer this week than last?

Technology
Use Harcourt Mega Math, Fraction Action, *Fraction Flare Up,* Levels G, H.

FRACTION CONCENTRATION

Get Ready!
2 players and a host

Get Set!
- Magazines with color photos
- 20 sticky notes (2-inch by 2-inch)

The host has found a photo and covered it with the sticky notes.

1	2	3	4	5
6	7	8	9	10
11	12	13	14	15
16	17	18	19	20

Six of the sticky notes have been removed. Can you guess what is in the photo?

1	2	3	4
6	8	9	10
13	14	15
16	17	19

Play the Game!

- On the sticky side of each of 10 sticky notes, write an addition or subtraction problem involving fractions and mixed numbers. On the sticky side of 10 other notes, write the solutions. Then randomly number all the notes from 1 through 20.

- The host finds a magazine picture of something that both players will recognize, and sticks the notes on the picture so that it is completely covered.

- Players take turns. The first player turns over any two sticky notes. If the notes show a problem and its solution, the

player takes both notes and gets another turn. If not, the player puts the notes back in place and does not try to identify the photo.

- The winner is the first player to correctly identify the photo.

- If a player tries to identify the photo but is wrong, the other player wins the round.

- If neither player can identify the photo after all the notes have been taken, the winner is the player with more notes.

Chapter 17 Review/Test

Check Vocabulary and Concepts

Choose the best term from the box.

VOCABULARY

like fractions
mixed numbers
simplest form

1. A fraction is in __?__ if the numerator and denominator cannot be divided by any common factor other than 1. (NS 1.5, p. 418)

2. Fractions with the same denominator are called __?__.

   (Grade 5 O—n NS 2.3, p. 444)

Check Skills

Model the sum or difference. Record your answer. (Grade 5 O—n NS 2.3, pp. 444–445, 446–447)

3. $\frac{2}{5} + \frac{3}{5}$

4. $\frac{3}{6} - \frac{1}{6}$

5. $\frac{5}{8} + \frac{1}{8}$

6. $\frac{7}{12} - \frac{3}{12}$

Find and record the sum or difference. (Grade 5 O—n NS 2.3, pp. 448–451, 456–459)

7. $\frac{1}{8} + \frac{4}{8}$

8. $\frac{3}{7} - \frac{1}{7}$

9. $\frac{4}{9} + \frac{4}{9}$

10. $\frac{7}{12} + \frac{1}{12}$

11. $\begin{aligned} \frac{2}{6} \\ + \frac{1}{6} \\ \hline \end{aligned}$

12. $\begin{aligned} \frac{2}{3} \\ - \frac{1}{3} \\ \hline \end{aligned}$

13. $\begin{aligned} \frac{7}{10} \\ + \frac{2}{10} \\ \hline \end{aligned}$

14. $\begin{aligned} \frac{37}{100} \\ - \frac{26}{100} \\ \hline \end{aligned}$

15. $\begin{aligned} 2\frac{2}{12} \\ + 4\frac{8}{12} \\ \hline \end{aligned}$

16. $\begin{aligned} 3\frac{5}{8} \\ - 1\frac{1}{8} \\ \hline \end{aligned}$

17. $\begin{aligned} 6\frac{5}{8} \\ + 7\frac{3}{8} \\ \hline \end{aligned}$

18. $\begin{aligned} 1\frac{11}{12} \\ - \frac{7}{12} \\ \hline \end{aligned}$

Check Problem Solving

Solve. (AF 1.1, MR 2.3, pp. 452–455)

19. Allison practices piano for $\frac{1}{3}$ hour on Monday. She practices for $\frac{1}{2}$ hour on Tuesday. How long does she practice piano during the two days?

20. **WRITE Math** ▸ Mia and Brady picked strawberries to sell at a fruit stand. Brady picked $1\frac{1}{3}$ quarts. Together, they picked $4\frac{2}{3}$ quarts. How many quarts did Mia pick? **Explain** how you know.

GO ONLINE Technology Use *Online Assessment.*

Enrich • Properties and Fractions
Properties in Action

In whole number operations, you have used the properties of addition shown below. The properties of addition also apply to fractions.

Property	Whole Number	Fraction
Identity	$94 + 0 = 94$ $0 + 94 = 94$	$\frac{3}{8} + 0 = \frac{3}{8}$
Commutative	$55 + 67 = 67 + 55$	$\frac{3}{10} + \frac{4}{10} = \frac{4}{10} + \frac{3}{10}$
Associative	$(21 + 37) + 52 = 21 + (37 + 52)$	$\frac{1}{4} + \left(\frac{1}{4} + \frac{3}{4}\right) = \left(\frac{1}{4} + \frac{1}{4}\right) + \frac{3}{4}$

Examples

Apply the properties of addition to fractions to find a missing number.

A Identity Property

$\blacksquare + \dfrac{5}{6} = \dfrac{5}{6}$

$0 + \dfrac{5}{6} = \dfrac{5}{6}$

So, $\blacksquare = 0$.

B Commutative Property

$\dfrac{6}{10} + \dfrac{\blacksquare}{\blacksquare} = \dfrac{1}{10} + \dfrac{6}{10}$

$\dfrac{6}{10} + \dfrac{1}{10} = \dfrac{1}{10} + \dfrac{6}{10}$

So, $\dfrac{\blacksquare}{\blacksquare} = \dfrac{1}{10}$.

C Associative Property

$\dfrac{2}{7} + \left(\dfrac{1}{7} + \dfrac{3}{7}\right) = \left(\dfrac{2}{7} + \dfrac{\blacksquare}{\blacksquare}\right) + \dfrac{3}{7}$

$\dfrac{2}{7} + \left(\dfrac{1}{7} + \dfrac{3}{7}\right) = \left(\dfrac{2}{7} + \dfrac{1}{7}\right) + \dfrac{3}{7}$

So, $\dfrac{\blacksquare}{\blacksquare} = \dfrac{1}{7}$.

Try It

Write the missing number. Name the property you used.

1. $\dfrac{2}{3} + \dfrac{1}{3} = \dfrac{\blacksquare}{\blacksquare} + \dfrac{2}{3}$

2. $\dfrac{3}{5} + \dfrac{\blacksquare}{\blacksquare} = \dfrac{3}{5}$

3. $\left(\dfrac{1}{6} + \dfrac{2}{6}\right) + \dfrac{\blacksquare}{\blacksquare} = \dfrac{1}{6} + \left(\dfrac{2}{6} + \dfrac{3}{6}\right)$

4. $\dfrac{3}{9} + \left(\dfrac{1}{9} + \dfrac{4}{9}\right) = \left(\dfrac{3}{9} + \dfrac{\blacksquare}{\blacksquare}\right) + \dfrac{4}{9}$

5. $\dfrac{\blacksquare}{\blacksquare} + \dfrac{4}{8} = \dfrac{4}{8} + \dfrac{3}{8}$

6. $0 + \dfrac{\blacksquare}{\blacksquare} = \dfrac{5}{12}$

Change the order or group the addends so that you can add mentally. Find the sum. Name the property you used.

7. $\dfrac{3}{25} + \dfrac{10}{25} + \dfrac{7}{25}$

8. $\dfrac{7}{100} + \dfrac{14}{100} + \dfrac{16}{100}$

9. $\dfrac{15}{18} + \dfrac{25}{18} + \dfrac{24}{18}$

10. $\dfrac{10}{16} + \dfrac{18}{16} + \dfrac{4}{16}$

11. $\dfrac{9}{12} + \dfrac{5}{12} + \dfrac{11}{12}$

12. $\dfrac{313}{1,000} + \dfrac{250}{1,000} + \dfrac{150}{1,000}$

WRITE Math ▶ Compare and contrast using the Associative and Commutative Properties of Addition to add fractions.

Achieving the Standards
Chapters 1–17

Number Sense

Test Tip **Get the information you need.**

See item 1. You need to know the number of weeks in a year. Multiply that number by the amount saved per week.

1. Karen plans to save $28 each week for a year. How much will she have saved by the end of the year?

   (O━┓ NS 3.2)

   A $80

   B $336

   C $1,456

   D $2,800

2. On the number line below, what number does point *P* represent?

   (O━┓ NS 1.9)

   A $5\frac{2}{5}$

   B $5\frac{3}{5}$

   C $6\frac{2}{5}$

   D $6\frac{3}{5}$

3. **WRITE Math** **Explain** how you could model the fraction $\frac{3}{4}$ using a circle. How could you model $\frac{3}{4}$ using 4 squares? (NS 1.7)

Algebra and Functions

4. Which expression has the same value as the expression below?

   (O━┓ AF 1.2)

   $$3 \times (8 - 5) + 9$$

   A $(3 \times 3) + 9$

   B $(3 \times 24) - 14$

   C $3 \times (24 - 14)$

   D $3 \times (3 + 9)$

5. What is the value of the expression below if $x = 7$? (AF 1.1)

   $$18 - x$$

   A 25

   B 11

   C 7

   D 1

6. Which expression shows the sum of 8 and 10 divided by 6? (AF 1.3)

   A $6 \div 8 + 10$

   B $8 + 10 \div 6$

   C $6 \div (8 + 10)$

   D $(8 + 10) \div 6$

7. **WRITE Math** **Explain** how to solve the equation below. (O━┓ AF 1.5)

   $$4 + y = 12$$

Statistics, Data Analysis, and Probability

8. The library held a summer reading contest and made a bar graph of the results.

Who read twice as many books as Randy? (SDAP 1.3)

A Kayla

B Randy

C Pablo

D Madison

9. Which event is equally likely to happen as tossing an even number on a number cube labeled 1 to 6? (Grade 3 SDAP 1.1)

A tossing a 2

B tossing a 6

C tossing an odd number

D tossing a multiple of 3

10. **WRITE Math** Would you use a bar graph, a circle graph, or a line graph to show the results of the election for student council president? **Explain.**

(SDAP 1.1)

Measurement and Geometry

11. Which figure includes an angle that is greater than a right angle? (Grade 3 MG 2.4)

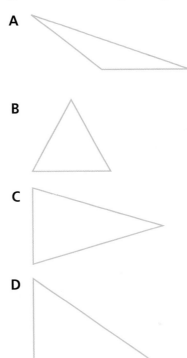

12. What is the perimeter, in centimeters, of the rectangle below? (Grade 3 MG 1.3)

A 23 centimeters

B 46 centimeters

C 56 centimeters

D 112 centimeters

13. **WRITE Math** **Explain** how to graph the equation $y = 2x + 1$. What should the graph look like? (0—n MG 2.1)

18 Understand Decimals and Place Value

The Big Idea The place values to the right of the decimal point in the base-ten system name numbers less than one.

CALIFORNIA FAST FACT

Amanda Bailey competed on the trampoline during the U.S. Olympic Trials for Rhythmic Gymnastics and Trampoline in June 2004. These Olympic trials took place at the San Jose State University Events Center in San Jose, California.

Investigate

In 2003, the National Trampoline and Tumbling championships were held in Sacramento. The scoreboard shows the top five trampoline scores for girls ages 9–10, level 5. You are reporting the scores in the school newspaper. What can you write about the outcome of the meet?

Trampoline Scores	
Kiley Belcher	25.00
Carly Filip	26.10
Kaci Kent	25.50
Mikayla McMahan	25.00
Kristen Sayre	25.40

GO ONLINE

Technology
Student pages are available in the Student eBook.

Show What You Know

Check your understanding of important skills
needed for success in Chapter 18.

▶ **Model Fractions and Mixed Numbers**

Write the fraction or the mixed number for the shaded part.

1.   2.    3.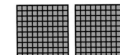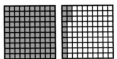

▶ **Fractions with Denominators of 10 and 100**

Write a fraction for each. You may wish to draw a picture.

4. six tenths   5. eight hundredths   6. thirty-three hundredths

Complete to show equivalent fractions. You may wish to draw a picture.

7. $\dfrac{1}{10} = \dfrac{\blacksquare}{100}$ 8. $\dfrac{4}{10} = \dfrac{\blacksquare}{100}$ 9. $\dfrac{8}{10} = \dfrac{\blacksquare}{100}$

▶ **Money Notation**

Name the amount shown.

10.   11.

Write a decimal for the money amount.

12. five dollars and twenty-eight cents   13. twelve dollars and five cents

VOCABULARY POWER

CHAPTER VOCABULARY

decimal
  point
equal to (=)
equivalent
  decimals
fraction

decimal
hundredth
mixed
  number
not equal to (≠)
tenth

WARM-UP WORDS

decimal a number with one or more digits to the right of the decimal point

decimal point a symbol used to separate dollars from cents in money amounts and to separate the ones and the tenths places in a decimal

equivalent decimals two or more decimals that name the same amount

Relate Fractions and Decimals

OBJECTIVE: Model, read, and write fractions as decimals.

Learn

PROBLEM Ty is reading a 100-page book about metamorphic rocks. He has read $\frac{7}{10}$ of the book. Only 1 page has a picture. What decimal part of the book has Ty read? What decimal part has pictures?

A **decimal** is a number with one or more digits to the right of the **decimal point.**

ONE WAY   Use models.

A Use decimal models.

Shade the model to show 1.	Shade $\frac{7}{10}$ of the model.	Shade $\frac{1}{100}$ of the model.

Fraction	**Decimal**	**Fraction**	**Decimal**	**Fraction**	**Decimal**
Read: one	**Read:** one	**Read:** seven tenths	**Read:** seven tenths	**Read:** one hundredth	**Read:** one hundredth
Write: $\frac{1}{1}$	**Write:** 1.0	**Write:** $\frac{7}{10}$	**Write:** 0.7	**Write:** $\frac{1}{100}$	**Write:** 0.01

So, Marvin has read 0.7 of the book, and $\frac{1}{100}$, or 0.01 of the book has pictures.

B Use money.

1 dollar	10 dimes = 1 dollar	100 pennies = 1 dollar
	1 dime = $\frac{1}{10}$, or 0.1, of a dollar	1 penny = $\frac{1}{100}$, or 0.01 of a dollar
$1.00	$0.10	$0.01

NS 1.6 Write tenths and hundredths in decimal and fraction notations and know the fraction and decimal equivalents for halves and fourths (e.g., $\frac{1}{2}$ = 0.5 or .50; $\frac{7}{4}$ = $1\frac{3}{4}$ = 1.75). *also* NS 1.7, AF 1.1, MR 2.3, MR 2.4, MR 3.0, MR 3.2, MR 3.3

Use place value.

C Decimals, like whole numbers can be written in standard form, word form, and expanded form.

Ones	.	Tenths	Hundredths
0	.	2	8

0 × 1	.	2 × 0.1	8 × 0.01
0	.	0.2	0.08

Standard Form	Word Form	Expanded Form
0.6	six tenths	0.6
0.28	twenty-eight hundredths	0.2 + 0.08
$0.14	Fourteen cents	$0.10 + $0.04

ERROR ALERT

Always place the decimal point between the ones digit and the tenths digit.

decimal point
↓
0.1
↑

A zero is used to show there are no ones

A number line divided into 100 equal parts can be used to model fractions and decimals. You can also write a fraction that has a denominator other than 10 or 100 as a decimal.

Examples

D Use a number line.

Locate the point 0.75. What fraction names this point on the number line?

$\frac{75}{100}$

$\frac{0}{100}$ $\frac{10}{100}$ $\frac{20}{100}$ $\frac{30}{100}$ $\frac{40}{100}$ $\frac{50}{100}$ $\frac{60}{100}$ $\frac{70}{100}$ $\frac{80}{100}$ $\frac{90}{100}$ $\frac{100}{100}$

0   0.1 0.2 0.3 0.4 0.5 0.6 0.7 | 0.8 0.9   1
0.75

So, 0.75 names the same amount as $\frac{75}{100}$ and $\frac{3}{4}$.

E Use a model.

First write the fraction using a denominator of 10 or 100.

What decimal shows the amount as $\frac{1}{5}$?

$\frac{1}{5} = \frac{1 \times 2}{5 \times 2} = \frac{2}{10}$, or 0.2

So, 0.2 shows the same amount as $\frac{1}{5}$.

Guided Practice

1. Copy the model and shade to show $\frac{8}{10}$. Write the amount as a decimal.

Write the decimal and fraction shown by each model.

2.

✓ 3. $\frac{0}{10}$ $\frac{5}{10}$ $\frac{10}{10}$

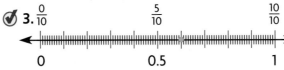

0   0.5   1

4.

te each fraction as a decimal. You may draw a picture.

5. $\frac{2}{10}$ **6.** $\frac{80}{100}$ **7.** $\frac{3}{5}$ **8.** $\frac{2}{4}$ ✓ **9.** $\frac{5}{100}$

10. [TALK Math] **Explain** how the models that represent one whole, one tenth, and one hundredth are related.

Independent Practice and Problem Solving

Write the decimal and fraction shown by each model.

11. 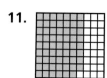   **12.**    **13.**

$\frac{0}{10}$ \qquad $\frac{5}{10}$ \qquad $\frac{10}{10}$

0 \qquad 0.5 \qquad 1

Write each fraction as a decimal. You may draw a picture.

14. $\frac{9}{10}$ **15.** $\frac{3}{4}$ **16.** $\frac{4}{10}$ **17.** $\frac{42}{100}$ **18.** $\frac{4}{5}$

Write the amount as a fraction of a dollar, as a decimal, and as a money amount.

19. 8 dimes   **20.** 3 dimes, 5 pennies   **21.** 6 pennies   **22.** 1 dollar, 2 dimes, 6 pennies

⭐ **Algebra** **Find the missing number.**

23. 6 tenths + 2 hundredths = 0.■2   **24.** 0 tenths + ■ hundredths = 0.04

25. $0.58 = ■ dimes + ■ pennies   **26.** 0.04 = ■ tenths + ■ hundredths

USE DATA **For 27–28, use the table.**

27. Write a decimal to show what part of the rocks listed in the table are igneous.

28. Sedimentary rocks make up 0.3 of Ramon's collection. Write this decimal as a fraction and in word form.

29. Josh paid for three books with two $20 bills. He received $1 in change. Each book was the same price. How much did each book cost?

30. [WRITE Math] ▸ **Explain** how to use a model to write the fraction $\frac{12}{100}$ as a decimal.

Classifying Rocks	
Name	**Type**
Basalt	Igneous
Rhyolite	Igneous
Granite	Igneous
Peridotite	Igneous
Shale	Sedimentary
Limestone	Sedimentary
Sandstone	Sedimentary
Gness	Metamorphic
Slate	Metamorphic
Scoria	Igneous

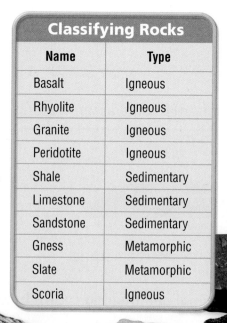

(Extra Practice) on page 484, Set A)

31. Are the fractions equivalent? Write *yes* or *no*. (NS 1.5, p. 418)

$$\frac{1}{2}, \frac{3}{8}$$

32. What digit is in the hundreds place of 53,029? (NS 1.0, p.4)

33. Test Prep Which decimal means the same as $\frac{8}{10}$?

A 0.08   **C** 0.810

B 0.8   **D** 8.1

34. Round 8,423,562 to the nearest thousand. (O━ NS 1.3, p. 34)

35. Test Prep Which decimal is shown by the model?

A 0.04   **C** 0.4

B 0.06   **D** 0.6

Problem Solving [connects to] Science

Soil Texture

Max is learning about types of soil. He is using the table to help classify the particles in a soil sample he collected.

Soil Texture	
Particle	**Size in (millimeters)**
Very coarse sand	2.0 to 1.0
Coarse sand	1.0 to 0.5
Medium sand	0.5 to 0.25
Fine sand	0.25 to 0.10
Very fine sand	0.10 to 0.05
Silt	0.05 to 0.002
Clay	Less than 0.002

1. In his soil sample, Max has particles that measure 0.4 mm, 0.18 mm, 0.09 mm, and 0.01 mm. What types of particles are in his soil sample?

2. Write the size range of medium sand particles as fractions.

3. Max's sample is $\frac{3}{10}$ sand, $\frac{45}{100}$ silt, and $\frac{25}{100}$ clay. Write the fractions in decimal form.

2 Equivalent Decimals

OBJECTIVE: Find equivalent decimals.

Investigate

Materials ■ tenths and hundredths models

Equivalent decimals are decimals that name the same number.

Use shading and paper folding of tenths and hundredths models to find equivalent decimals.

Are 0.3 and 0.30 equivalent decimals?

Ⓐ Shade 0.3 of the tenths model and 0.30 of the hundredths model.

0.3   0.30

Ⓑ Fold 0.3 of the tenths model and 0.30 of the hundredths model.

Ⓒ Compare the models for both decimals. What can you conclude?

Ⓓ Use shading and paper folding to find whether 0.5 and 0.60 are equivalent. What can you conclude?

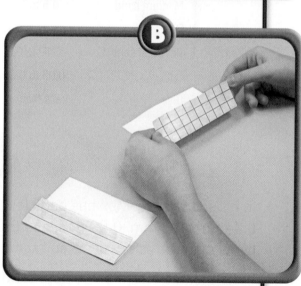

Draw Conclusions

1. How do you write 0.3 and 0.30 as fractions?

2. How much did you fold in each of the models?

3. How can you tell when a tenths decimal and a hundredths decimal are equivalent?

4. **Application** Is 0.03 equivalent to 0.3? Explain.

NS 1.6 Write tenths and hundredths in decimal and fraction notations and know the fraction and decimal equivalents for halves and fourths (e.g., $\frac{1}{2}$ = 0.5 or .50; $\frac{7}{4}$ = $1\frac{3}{4}$ = 1.75). *also* **AF 1.1 MR 2.0, MR 2.3, MR 2.4, MR 3.0, MR 3.2, MR 3.3**

Connect

You can use money amounts to model tenths and hundredths.

Example 1

Use dimes to model 1 tenth.

$1 \text{ dime} = \frac{1}{10} = \frac{10}{100} = 0.10 \text{ of } \$1.00$

Use dimes to model 10 tenths.

$10 \text{ dimes} = \frac{10}{10} = \frac{100}{100} = \$1.00$

Example 2

Use dimes to model 4 tenths.

$4 \text{ dimes} = \frac{4}{10} = \frac{40}{100} = 0.40 \text{ of } \$1.00$

Use pennies to model 4 tenths.

$40 \text{ pennies} = \frac{40}{100} = 0.40 \text{ of } \$1.00$

TALK Math
How can you use pennies to show $0.60? How can you use dimes to show the same amount?

Practice

Use a tenths model and a hundredths model. Are the two decimals equivalent? Write *equivalent* or *not equivalent*.

1. 0.4 and 0.44
2. 0.50 and 0.5
3. 0.71 and 0.17
4. 0.20 and 0.2
5. 0.60 and 0.06
6. 0.57 and 0.75

Write an equivalent decimal for each. You may use decimal models.

7. 0.4
8. 0.3
9. 0.70
10. 0.20
11. 0.90
12. 0.1
13. $\frac{1}{2}$
14. $\frac{1}{4}$

Algebra Write an equivalent decimal. Use the models to help.

15.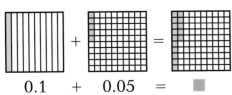

$0.1 + 0.05 = \blacksquare$

16.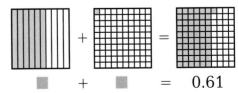

$\blacksquare + \blacksquare = 0.61$

17. **WRITE Math** Explain why models can help you find if two decimals are equivalent.

LESSON 3

Relate Mixed Numbers and Decimals

OBJECTIVE: Model, read, and write mixed numbers as decimals.

Learn

PROBLEM Many pocket-sized toy cars are about two and six tenths inches long. How can you write this length as a mixed number and as a decimal?

 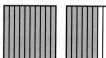

Activity 1 **Use a model.**
Materials ■ tenths models

Use models to write and read mixed numbers as decimals.

> Shade the whole number and the fraction of the mixed number.
>
>
>
> **Mixed Number:** $2\frac{6}{10}$
>
> **Decimal:** 2.6
>
> **Read:** two and six tenths

So, you can write the length as $2\frac{6}{10}$, or 2.6, inches.

Examples

Ⓐ **Write and read the value of the model as a mixed number and as a decimal.**

Mixed Number: $1\frac{27}{100}$

Decimal: 1.27

Read: one and twenty-seven hundredths

Ⓑ **Write and read the value of the model as a mixed number and as a decimal.**

Mixed Number: $2\frac{4}{100}$

Decimal: 2.04

Read: two and four hundredths

• What model other than the one used in Activity 1 could you use to show 2.6?

 NS 1.6 Write tenths and hundredths in decimal and fraction notations and know the fraction and decimal equivalents for halves and fourths (e.g., $\frac{1}{2}$ = 0.5 or .50; 7/4 = $1\frac{3}{4}$ = 1.75). *also* NS 1.7, ⊶ NS 1.9, AF 1.1, MR 2.3, MR 2.4, MR 3.0, MR 3.1

Activity 2 Use a number line.
Materials ■ number line

Find the decimal equivalent for $1\frac{25}{100}$

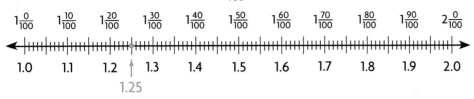

First, locate $1\frac{25}{100}$ on the number line.
Next, name the decimal that names this point.
Locate and label three other points on your number line.
Name the decimal and the mixed number that names each point.

Example 1 Use place value.

Decimals, like whole numbers, can be written in standard form, word form, and expanded form.

Ones	.	Tenths	Hundredths
2	.	7	
3	.	6	5

Standard Form	Word Form	Expanded Form
2.7	two and seven tenths	2 + 0.7
3.65	three and sixty-five hundreths	3 + 0.6 + 0.05

Example 2 Use models to show mixed numbers and decimals that are equivalent.

 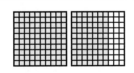 

$1.75 = 1\frac{75}{100} = 1\frac{3}{4} = \frac{7}{4}$ $1.70 = 1\frac{70}{100} = 1\frac{7}{10} = \frac{17}{10}$ $1.60 = 1\frac{60}{100} = 1\frac{6}{10} = 1\frac{3}{5}$

Guided Practice

1. Look at the model at the right. What whole number part is modeled? What fraction is modeled? Write the mixed number as a decimal.

Write an equivalent decimal and a mixed number for each model.

2.

3.

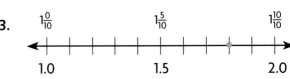

Write an equivalent mixed number or decimal for each.
Then write the word form. You may use a model.

4. $1\frac{8}{10}$ **5.** 3.1 **6.** $1\frac{57}{100}$ **7.** 4.05 ✓**8.** $2\frac{3}{4}$

9. [TALK Math] Explain how a decimal equivalent for a mixed number
is like a decimal equivalent for a fraction and how it is different.

Independent Practice (and Problem Solving

Write an equivalent decimal and mixed number for each model.

10. 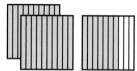   **11.**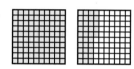

12. 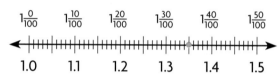   **13.**

Write an equivalent mixed number or decimal for each.
Then write the word form. You may use a model.

14. 2.3 **15.** $7\frac{1}{2}$ **16.** 3.45 **17.** $3\frac{3}{4}$ **18.** 4.01

⭐**Algebra** Write the missing number for each ▦.

19. $7.16 = 7 + \blacksquare + 0.06$ **20.** $1.58 = 1 + 0.5 + \blacksquare$ **21.** $4.02 = \blacksquare + 0.02$

22. Nate is thinking of some decimals between 1 and 2. What might they be? Give at least 15 answers.

23. **Reasoning Sense or Nonsense** Tara said her temperature was 10.15 when she was sick. Does this make sense? **Explain.**

24. ≣**FAST FACT** The smallest camera is only 1.65 centimeters thick. Write this measure as a mixed number.

25. [WRITE Math] ▸ What's the Question? The answer is one and six hundredths.

🐻 Achieving the Standards

26. What is the equivalent fraction for the decimal 0.50 in simplest form? (NS 1.6, p. 468)

27. What number makes this number sentence true? (O━┓ AF 2.2, p. 154)

$$(9 - 5) \times 8 = 4 \times \blacksquare$$

28. Round 3,291 to the nearest hundred.
(O━┓ NS 1.3, p. 34)

29. **Test Prep** Which mixed number is equivalent to 2.05?

A $2\frac{1}{5}$ **C** $2\frac{5}{100}$

B $2\frac{5}{10}$ **D** $2\frac{1}{500}$

(**Extra Practice**) on page 484, Set B)

Tiny Trains

 Reading Skill **Identify the Details**

The Golden State Model Railroad Museum displays model train layouts in O, HO, and N scales. The layouts cover 10,000 square feet. The Valley Division layout models the tracks that connect California's Bay Area to Sacramento. It is in HO scale. Every 3.5 millimeters of train length in HO scale is 1 foot in real life. What mixed number can you write for a length in HO scale that is 1 foot in real life?

In order to solve this problem, you must identify the details. Then choose only the details you need to answer the question.

▲ The Golden State Railroad Museum is located in the San Francisco Bay Area.

Make a list of the details you are given in the problem.	3 model train layouts Layouts cover 10,000 square feet. HO scale is 3.5 millimeters for every 1 foot in real life.
↓	
Think about what you are asked to find.	Write a mixed number for the HO scale length for 1 foot.
↓	
Choose the details you need to solve the problem.	Write a mixed number for 3.5 millimeters.

Problem Solving **Identify the details to understand the problem**

1. Solve the problem above.

2. A railroad track's gauge is the distance between the edges of the rails. HO gauge rails are 16.5 millimeters apart. The train car is 11 inches long. What mixed number can you write for the track's gauge?

4 Compare Decimals

OBJECTIVE: Compare decimals.

Quick Review

Write an equivalent decimal for each.

1. 0.20
2. 0.4
3. 0.5
4. 0.10
5. 0.9

Investigate

Materials ■ hundredths models ■ number line

Which decimal is greater: 1.20 or 1.25?

A Shade decimal models.

     1.20   1.25

B Compare the models. What do you notice?

C Locate the points 1.20 and 1.25 on a number line to compare the decimals.

    1.0   1.1   1.2   1.3   1.4   1.5

D Compare the location of the points on the number line. What do you notice?

Draw Conclusions

1. How do decimal models help you compare decimals?

2. How does a number line help you compare decimals?

3. How are both methods alike? How are they different?

4. **Application** Explain which method you would use to compare 1.01 and 1.9. Tell why you would use that method.

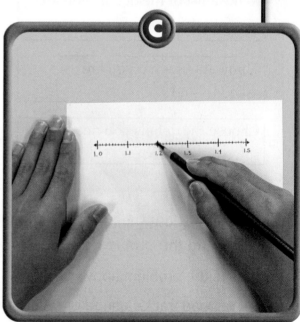

O━┓ NS 1.2 Order and compare whole numbers and decimals to two decimal places. *also* O━┓ NS 1.9,
NS 1.7, MR 2.0, MR 2.3, MR 2.4, MR 3.2

Connect

You can use a place-value chart to compare decimals.

Compare 2.89 and 2.8.

Ones	.	Tenths	Hundredths
2	.	8	9
2	.	8	0

Think: 2.8 and 2.80 are equivalent decimals.

$2 = 2$ $8 = 8$ $9 > 0$

Compare the digits beginning with the greatest place value.

Since $9 > 0$, $2.89 > 2.8$.

Be sure to write a 0 in the hundredths place of the decimals with tenths only to help you correctly line up the decimal places.

TALK Math

How is using a place-value chart to compare decimals like using a model? How are the methods different?

Practice

Compare. Write $<$, $>$, or $=$ for each ●.

1.

0.40 ● 0.4

2.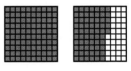

1.65 ● 1.56

3.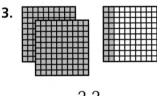

2.2 ● 2.15

4.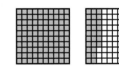

0.38 ● 1.27

Use the number line to determine whether the number sentences are *true* or *false*.

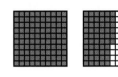

A number line from 1.0 to 2.0 marked in tenths.

5. $1.07 > 1.70$ **6.** $1.3 < 1.30$ **7.** $1.54 > 1.45$ **8.** $1.82 = 1.8$ **9.** $1.65 > 1.6$

10. $1.72 < 1.27$ **11.** $1.18 < 1.20$ **12.** $1.78 > 1.09$ **13.** $1.9 < 1.90$ **14.** $1.08 > 1.11$

15. **WRITE Math** **What's the Error?** Erin says that $4.5 < 4.49$ because the last digit in 4.5 is less than the last digit in 4.49. Describe and correct her error.

5 Order Decimals

OBJECTIVE: Order decimals.

Quick Review

Compare. Write <, >, or = for each ●.

1. 3.3 ● 3.30
2. 1.75 ● 1.7
3. 0.48 ● 0.84
4. 0.7 ● 0.70
5. 0.06 ● 0.11

Investigate

Materials ■ string ■ clothespins

Order 1.2, 1.9, 1.6 from least to greatest.

A Use your marker to mark the location of the points 1.0, 1.5, and 2.0 on your string.

B Use clothespins to label the points you marked.

C Now locate the points 1.2, 1.9, and 1.6 on your string by using labeled clothespins.

D Draw a picture of the number line you modeled.

E Compare your drawing and your model. What do you notice?

Draw Conclusions

1. What do you notice about the two number lines you made?

2. Use the drawing or model to order the decimals 1.4, 1.35, and 1.43 from least to greatest.

3. **Application** Explain how you can use a number line to compare and order decimals.

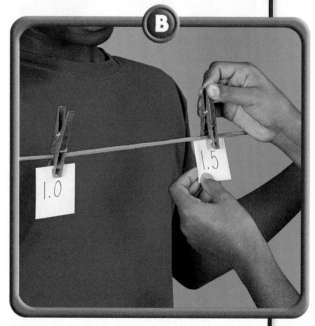

NS 1.2 Order and compare whole numbers and decimals to two decimal places.
also NS 1.9, MR 2.0, MR 2.3, MR 2.4, MR 3.2

Connect

You can also use place value to order decimals.

Order 1.52, 0.87, and 1.56 from least to greatest.

Step 1	Step 2	Step 3
Line up the decimal points.	Compare the tenths.	Compare the hundredths.
Think: Compare the digits in the greatest place.		
1.52	1.52	1.52
↓ $0 < 1$	↓ $5 = 5$	↓ $2 < 6$
0.87	1.56	1.56
↓		
1.56	0.87	0.87
Since $0 < 1$, 0.87 is the least.	There are the same number of tenths.	So, the order from least to greatest is 0.87, 1.52, 1.56.

TALK Math

How is using place value to order decimals different from using a number line?

Practice

Use the number line to order the decimals from least to greatest.

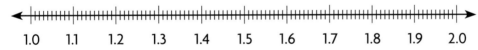

1.0 1.1 1.2 1.3 1.4 1.5 1.6 1.7 1.8 1.9 2.0

1. 1.11, 1.2, 1.01, 1.1

2. 1.32, 1.23, 1.3, 1.2

3. 1.9, 1.09, 1.5, 1.55

4. 1.65, 1.56, 1.6, 2.0

5. 1.15, 1.1, 1.51, 1.3

✓6. 1.7, 1.75, 1.5, 1.05

Order the decimals from greatest to least.

7. $1.41, $0.14, $1.14, $1.40

8. 7.03, 7.3, 6.98, 6.89

✓9. $2.15, $1.89, $1.09

10. 1.04, 0.96, 1.4, 0.9

11. 5.5, 5.55, 5.05, 5.15

12. $0.95, $0.80, $1.00

13. 3.8, 3.06, 3.97, 3.61

14. $1.35, $3.15, $1.53, $3.51

15. 6.25, 7.2, 6.93, 7.11

16. **WRITE Math** ▶ **Explain** how a number line helps you order decimals.

Technology
Use Harcourt Mega Math Fraction Action, *Number Line Mine*, Levels P, R.

Problem Solving Workshop
Skill: Draw Conclusions

OBJECTIVE: Solve problems by using the skill *draw conclusions*.

Read to Understand
Plan
Solve
Check

Use the Skill

PROBLEM The newspaper ads show the cost of basketball trading cards at three different sporting goods stores. Which store has the lowest price for a box of cards?

Sports Palace: The basketball players you want: 1 box of cards $6.59

Special buy ~~2300~~

You can draw conclusions to help you solve the problem. To draw conclusions, combine the facts from the problem with what you know from your own experience.

Facts from the Problem	What You Know
Angelo's Sports: $6.95 per box Sports Palace: $6.59 per box Town Sports: $5.95 per box	• Bills and coins can be used to model decimals. • You can order decimals by comparing the place value of each digit, beginning with the greatest place value. • The best price is the lowest price.

~~Best optns bspu, $13,~~

Town Sports: Basketball trading cards $5.95 per box of cards

~~w:~~ Accordian with ca~~s~~

To draw a conclusion about the lowest price, use models and place value to order the money amounts. Then choose the lowest price.

Ones	.	Tenths	Hundredths
6	.	9	5
6	.	5	9
5	.	9	5

~~superc~~ ~~best offer~~

Angelo's Sports: Hottest new basketball stars: $6.95 per box of cards

Brand new soc~~ks~~

Order of prices from least to greatest: $5.95, $6.59, $6.95.
So, Town Sports has the lowest price for a box of cards.

Think and Discuss

Tell which facts from the problem and what information you know can be used to draw conclusions. Solve the problem.

a. Ted can run a mile in 7.25 minutes. Rick runs it in 7.05 minutes, and Leroy runs it in 7.5 minutes. Who can run the fastest mile?

b. At the store, Power Thirst costs $3.98. Sports Power sells for $3.89, and Zoom! costs $3.90. Which drink costs the most?

NS 1.2 Order and compare whole numbers and decimals to two decimal places. *also* AF 1.1, MR 1.0, MR 2.0, MR 2.3, MR 2.4, MR 3.0, MR 3.1, MR 3.2, MR 3.3

Guided Problem Solving

1. The ads to the right show the price of a new best-selling book at three different bookstores. Which bookstore has the best price for the book?

   Copy and complete the chart.

Facts from the Problem	What You Know
Bob's Bookstore: ▦ Books Are Us: ▦ Books on Broadway: ▦	• _?_ can be used to model decimals. • You can order decimals by _?_. • The best price is the _?_ price.

   How can you use the information in the chart to draw a conclusion?

✔2. **What if** Open Page Bookstore sells the same book for $9.80? Then which store has the best price?

✔3. Megan lives 2.4 miles from Bob's Bookstore. Josh lives 2.15 miles away, and Sam lives 2.09 miles away. Who lives closest to Bob's Bookstore?

Mixed Applications

USE DATA For 4–5, use the map.

4. Who walks farther to school, Morgan or Dan?

5. Greg lives 2.8 miles from the mall. Warren lives 2.54 miles from the mall. Use the map and this information to list the four students in order from nearest to farthest distance from the mall.

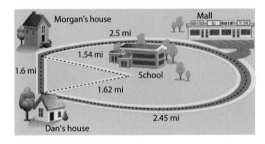

6. A basketball jersey at a sporting goods store costs $45. Sharif paid for the jersey with three $20 bills. How much change did he get back? Do you need an estimate or an exact answer?

7. The school needs 150 boxes of juice to give to the students going to the baseball game. If the juice comes in packages of 4 boxes, how many packages must the school buy?

8. [WRITE Math] ▸ Ezra jogged 125 miles in 3 weeks of training. He jogged 32 miles during the first week and 39 miles during the second week. **Explain** how to choose the more reasonable answer for the number of miles he jogged during the third week: 54 miles or 34 miles.

9. Hannah ran the 50-yard dash in 8.23 seconds. Tarika ran the dash in 7.95 seconds, and Rita ran the dash in 8.2 seconds. Who ran the dash the fastest?

Extra Practice

Set A Write the decimal and fraction shown by each model. (pp. 468–471)

1.

2.

3. $\frac{0}{10}$ $\frac{5}{10}$ $\frac{10}{10}$

   0   0.5   1

Write each fraction as a decimal. You may draw a picture.

4. $\frac{9}{10}$

5. $\frac{17}{100}$

6. $\frac{7}{10}$

7. $\frac{5}{100}$

8. $\frac{14}{100}$

9. $\frac{4}{10}$

10. $\frac{1}{2}$

11. $\frac{1}{4}$

12. $\frac{6}{100}$

13. $\frac{65}{100}$

Write the amount as a fraction of a dollar, a decimal, and a money amount.

14. 3 quarters

15. 2 dimes, 2 pennies

16. 1 quarter, 1 nickel

17. 2 quarters, 3 dimes, 4 pennies

18. 9 nickels, 8 pennies

19. 2 dollars, 6 nickels, 5 pennies

20. Jane is reading a book that has 100 pages. She has read 56 pages. What part of the book has Jane read? Write the answer as a decimal.

21. Spencer has 10 math problems to do for homework. He has done 8 of the problems. Which part of his math homework has Spencer done? Write the answer as a decimal and as a fraction.

Set B Write an equivalent decimal and mixed number for each model. (pp. 474–477)

1.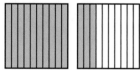

2.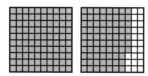

3.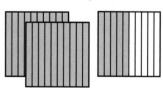

Write an equivalent mixed number or a decimal for each. Then write the word form. You may use a model.

4. $2\frac{9}{10}$

5. 3.17

6. $4\frac{9}{100}$

7. $3\frac{1}{10}$

8. 6.5

9. 5.75

10. $4\frac{1}{4}$

11. 6.03

12. $3\frac{6}{10}$

13. 5.21

14. Rachael has $5\frac{1}{2}$ jars of beads. Write this amount as a decimal.

15. Morris runs 2.25 miles each day. Write the distance as a mixed number.

CD ROM

Technology
Use Harcourt Mega Math, Fraction Action, *Number Line Mine*, Levels P, Q, R.

ORDER, PLEASE!

● **Get Ready!**
2 or 3 players and a dealer

○ **Get Set!**
Set of index cards with these decimal numbers: 0.1–0.9, 0.15–0.25, 0.01–0.09

● **Play the Game!**

■ The object of the game is to have 5 decimal cards in order from least to greatest.

■ The dealer shuffles the cards and places 5 cards faceup in front of each player and places the remaining cards facedown in a stack. The cards should remain in this order throughout the game.

■ At each turn, a player chooses one card to replace, and places it in the discard stack. The dealer gives the player a new card from the top of the stack to be placed in the same spot as the card that was just given to the dealer.

■ A player who thinks all 5 of his or her cards are in order from least to greatest calls out "Order!"

■ If the cards are in order, that player wins.

■ When all the cards in the stack have been used, the dealer shuffles the cards in the discard stack, places them facedown, and starts a new stack.

■ Whoever wins becomes the dealer for the next round.

 Chapter 18 Review/Test

Check Vocabulary and Concepts

Choose the best term from the box.

1. The ___?___. separates the ones place and the tenths place. (NS 1.6, p. 468)

2. ___?___ are decimals that name the same number. (NS 1.6, p. 474)

Check Skills

Write each fraction or mixed number as a decimal. *You may draw a picture.*

(NS 1.6, pp. 468–471, 474–477)

3. $\frac{9}{10}$

4. $\frac{17}{100}$

5. $\frac{9}{100}$

6. $\frac{12}{100}$

7. $\frac{3}{100}$

8. $5\frac{6}{10}$

9. $3\frac{5}{100}$

10. $6\frac{1}{100}$

11. $2\frac{81}{100}$

12. $9\frac{9}{100}$

Write the amount as a fraction of a dollar, as a decimal, and as a money amount. (NS 1.6, pp. 468–471)

13. 1 dime

14. 1 quarter, 1 dime

15. 2 pennies

16. 4 dimes, 1 penny

Write an equivalent decimal for each. You may use decimal models. (pp. 472–473)

17. 0.9

18. 0.20

19. $\frac{1}{4}$

20. $\frac{1}{2}$

Compare. Write <, >, or = for each ●. (O→n NS 1.2, pp. 478–479)

21. 4.6 ● 4.06

22. $3.70 ● $4.00

23. 4.40 ● 4.4

24. 6.8 ● 6.08

Order the decimals from greatest to least. (O→n NS 1.2, pp. 480–481)

25. 8.06, 8.4, 7.89, 8.89

26. 1.35, 0.89, 1.05, 0.09

27. $4.20, $4.16, $4.41

28. 0.78, 7.08, 8.70

29. 5.24, 4.25, 5.44

30. 0.16, 6.01, 1.61

Check Problem Solving

Solve. (O→n NS 1.2, MR 3.0, pp. 482–483)

31. Kate swam the 50-meter freestyle race in 30.05 seconds. Which of the girls listed in the table beat Kate in the race?

32. Of the results listed in the table, who swam the fastest?

33. ⌷WRITE Math▸ If Kate and the four girls listed in the table were the only ones in the race, who came in fourth place? **Explain** how you know.

50–Meter Freestyle Results	
Swimmer	**Time (in seconds)**
Larisa	31.02
Michelle	30.2
Sara	30.52
Rebecca	30.01

GO ONLINE **Technology** Use *Online Assessment.*

Enrich • Interpret Decimal Models
RADIO SURVEY

A radio station asked 500 students whether they listen to the radio each morning. Fifty students said they listen to the radio in the morning.

500 students

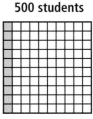

▲ **50 students**

The decimal model represents the 500 students in the survey. Each square then represents $500 \div 100 = 5$ students. To represent 50 students, shade $50 \div 5 = 10$ squares.

Examples

A What part of the decimal model would you shade to represent 125 students?

Think: What number times 5 equals 125? Use a related division sentence to find the missing factor: $125 \div 5 = 25$, so $25 \times 5 = 125$.

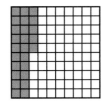

So, shade 25 squares to represent 125 students.

B What number of students does the shaded part of the decimal model represent?

Think: 50 squares are shaded. 50 is $\frac{1}{2}$ of 100 and 250 is $\frac{1}{2}$ of 500.

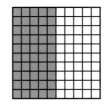

So, the shaded part represents 250 students.

Try It

Write the whole number the shaded part of the model represents.

1. 200 dogs

2. 400 toys

3. 600 birds

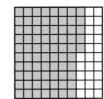

4. 300 trucks

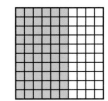

WRITE Math ▸ **Explain** how showing 100 balls in a decimal model that represents 200 balls would be different than showing it in a decimal model that represents 400 balls.

Achieving the Standards
Chapters 1–18

Number Sense

1. Which of the following has the greatest value? (O—¬ NS 1.2)

   A 11.05

   B 3.25

   C 1.63

   D 0.97

2. On the number line below, what number does point *P* represent? (O—¬ NS 1.9)

   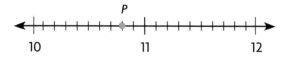

   A $11\frac{8}{10}$

   B $11\frac{2}{10}$

   C $10\frac{9}{10}$

   D $10\frac{8}{10}$

3. Which is a prime number? (O—¬ NS 4.2)

   A 9

   B 14

   C 17

   D 21

4. **WRITE Math** Compare. Use >, <, or =. **Explain** your answer. (NS 1.6)

   $0.65 \,\bullet\, \frac{3}{4}$

Measurement and Geometry

5. Stephen practiced his guitar for $3\frac{1}{2}$ hours. For how many minutes did he practice? (Grade 3 MG 1.4)

   A 100 minutes

   B 210 minutes

   C 240 minutes

   D 360 minutes

6. Which figure appears to have no right angles? (Grade 3 O—¬ MG 2.4)

   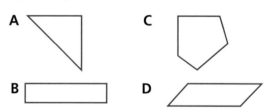

7. Find the perimeter of the swimming pool? (Grade 3 O—¬ MG 1.3)

   A 627 feet

   B 297 feet

   C 104 feet

   D 52 feet

8. **WRITE Math** Mitch drew an obtuse scalene triangle. **Describe** what you know about the sides and angles of his triangle. (Grade 3 O—¬ MG 2.2)

Algebra and Functions

9. There were 12 students in the Chess Club. Then some more students joined. Which expression represents the number of students in the Chess Club now? (AF 1.1)

   A $12 + s$

   B $12 - s$

   C $12 \times s$

   D $12 \div s$

10. What is the value of y when $x = 7$? (O—¬ AF 1.5)

$$y = (5x - 3)$$

   A 15

   B 21

   C 32

   D 35

11. What number makes this number sentence true? (O—¬ AF 2.2)

$$(9 - 6) \times 8 = 3 \times \blacksquare$$

   A 8   C 5

   B 6   D 4

12. **WRITE Math** Evaluate each expression. Are the values the same? **Explain** why or why not. (O—¬ AF 1.2)

$$(4 + 9) \times 2 - 15$$
$$4 + 9 \times 2 - 15$$

Statistics, Data Analysis, and Probability

13. How many more students participated in the backward race than in the spoon race on Field Day? (SDAP 1.3)

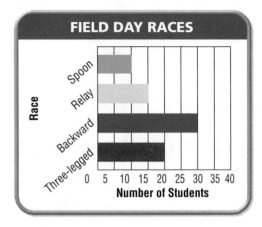

   A 10   C 20

   B 15   D 25

Test Tip Eliminate choices.

See item 14. Determine the mode. Then eliminate choices that are incorrect.

14. What is the median of this set numbers? (SDAP 1.2)

$$6, 7, 8, 9, 10$$

   A 6

   B 7

   C 8

   D 9

15. **WRITE Math** Kenji wants to make a graph to show the results of an election. What type of graph should he use? **Explain** how you decided. (SDAP 1.1)

CHAPTER

19 Add and Subtract Decimals and Money

The Big Idea Addition and subtraction of decimals are based on place value and addition and subtraction with whole numbers.

Investigate

Farmers markets sell fresh fruits and vegetables that are locally grown. Suppose you have $10.00 to spend at the market. What foods could you buy without spending more than $10.00? How much money would you have left?

Tomatoes $1.99/pound

Carrots $1.29/pound

Okra 75¢/pint

Plums $2.29/pound

Watermelons $2.80 each

Fresh orange juice $1.75/pint

Prickly-pear Cactus $4.50/pound

CALIFORNIA FAST FACT

On an average day, visitors to the Los Angeles Farmers Market toss $35 into the Wishing Well. The money collected is given to charity.

GO ONLINE

Technology
Student pages are available in the Student eBook.

Show What You Know

Check your understanding of important skills
needed for success in Chapter 19.

▶ Count Bills and Coins

Write the amount.

1.

2.

3.

▶ Model Decimals

Write the decimal for the shaded part.

4.

5.

6.

7.

8.

9.

▶ Decimal Place Value

Write the value of the underlined digit in each decimal.

10. 0.2<u>3</u>   11. 0.<u>5</u>7   12. 0.1<u>4</u>   13. 0.6<u>3</u>

14. 0.3<u>8</u>   15. 0.<u>9</u>4   16. 0.<u>4</u>6   17. 0.8<u>7</u>

VOCABULARY POWER

CHAPTER VOCABULARY		WARM-UP WORDS
decimal	hundredth	**decimal** a number with one or more digits to the right of the decimal point
decimal point	round	
digit	tenth	**round** to replace a number with another number that tells about how many or how much
estimate		
		digit any one of the ten symbols 0, 1, 2, 3, 4, 5, 6, 7, 8, or 9 used to write numbers

1 Round Decimals

OBJECTIVE: Round decimals.

Learn

PROBLEM The amount of wool cut from one sheep is called a fleece. In the United States the average weight of one fleece is 8.2 pounds. What is this weight to the nearest pound?

ONE WAY Use a number line.

```
        8.2
         ↓
  ◄──┼──┼┼──┼──┼──┼──┼──┼──┼──┼──┼──►
     8              9
```

8.2 is between 8 and 9, but it is closer to 8.

So, the weight of a fleece to the nearest pound is 8 pounds.

OTHER WAYS Use place value and rounding.

Example 1 Round to the nearest whole number.

> 32.89
> Look at the tenths place.
> Since 8 > 5, the digit 2 increases by 1.

So, 32.89 rounded to the nearest whole number is 33.

Example 3 Round to the nearest dollar.

> $23.49
> Look at the tenths place.
> Since 4 < 5, the digit 3 stays the same.

So, $23.49 rounded to the nearest dollar is $23.

Example 2 Round to the nearest tenth.

> 6.73
> Look at the hundredths place.
> Since 3 < 5, the digit 7 stays the same.

So, 6.73 rounded to the nearest tenth is 6.7.

Example 4 Round to the nearest tenth.

> 12.97
> Look at the hundredths place.
> Since 7 > 5, the digit 9 increases by 1. It becomes 0 and the ones digit increases by 1.

So, 12.97 rounded to the nearest tenth is 13.0.

Remember
To round a number you can:
• Find the place to which you want to round.
• Look at the digit to its right.
• If that digit is less than 5, the digit in the rounding place stays the same.
• If that digit is 5 or greater, the digit in the rounding place increases by 1.

• **What if** you round 32.89 in Example 1 to the nearest tenth? Explain how to round 32.89 to the nearest tenth.

NS 2.2 Round two-place decimals to one decimal or the nearest whole number and judge the reasonableness of the rounded answer. *also* **NS 1.9, MR 2.3, MR 2.4, MR 2.5, MR 3.1, MR 3.2**

Guided Practice

1. In which numbers is the digit in the tenths place 5 or more? Which numbers will round to 15 when rounded to the nearest whole number?

| 14.9 | 15.23 |
| 15.5 | 14.49 |

Round each number to the nearest tenth and each money amount to the nearest dollar.

2. 45.67   3. 8.23   4. $19.35   ✓ 5. 5.55   ✓ 6. $48.92

7. **TALK Math** Explain how to use a number line to round 7.33 to the nearest tenth.

Independent Practice and Problem Solving

Round each number to the nearest tenth and each money amount to the nearest dollar.

8. 4.56   9. 5.87   10. 12.97   11. 123.08   12. 645.55

13. $3.57   14. $9.98   15. $32.12   16. $87.55   17. $123.68

Round each number to the nearest whole number.

18. 6.78   19. 5.24   20. 15.8   21. 32.51   22. 57.98

USE DATA For 23–24, use the map.

23. For each state shown, round the weight per fleece to the nearest whole number. Then make a bar graph for the data.

24. Order the states shown according to the lightest weight per fleece to the heaviest.

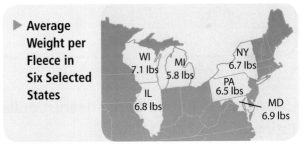
► Average Weight per Fleece in Six Selected States

WI 7.1 lbs
MI 5.8 lbs
NY 6.7 lbs
PA 6.5 lbs
IL 6.8 lbs
MD 6.9 lbs

25. **Reasoning** For what digits will 3.9▉ rounded to the nearest tenth be 4? **Explain.**

26. **WRITE Math** What's the Question? A skein of wool, or wool wrapped in a loose coil, costs $3.75. The answer is $4.

Achieving the Standards

27. $6{,}291 - 2{,}748 =$ (O━n NS 3.1, p. 58)

28. $\frac{1}{12} + \frac{5}{12} =$ (Preparing for Grade 5 O━n NS 2.3)

29. Graph the ordered pairs (5,6) and (5,⁻4) on a coordinate grid. Then find the length of the line segment joining the points. (O━n MG 2.3, p. 392)

30. **Test Prep** Jack drove 25.68 miles to work. Which is the distance he drove rounded to the nearest tenth?

   A 25.6 miles   **C** 26 miles

   B 25.7 miles   **D** 26.7 miles

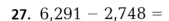 Extra Practice on page 506, Set A

OBJECTIVE: Estimate decimal sums and differences.

Learn

PROBLEM The table shows the number of students enrolled by grade span during the 2003–2004 California school year. About how many total students were enrolled?

Example 1 Round to the nearest whole number.
Estimate. 20.9 + 41.8 + 46.6

20.9 → 21	
41.8 → 42	Line up the decimal points. Round
+46.6 → +47	to the nearest whole number.
110	

So, about 110 thousand students were enrolled.

Example 2 Round to the nearest ten.
Estimate. 63.59 + 75.13

63.59 → 60	Line up the decimal points.
+75.13 → +80	Round to the nearest ten.
140	

So, 65.39 + 75.13 is about 140.

Example 3 Round to the nearest dollar.
Estimate. $45.72 − $12.09

$45.72 → $46	Line up the decimal points.
− 12.09 → −$12	Round to the nearest dollar.
$34	

So, $45.72 − $12.09 is about $34.

• Do you think the estimate in Example 1 is greater than or less than the exact answer? Explain.

California Elementary School Enrollment

Grade Span	Students Enrolled (in thousands)
K–2	20.9
K–3	41.8
K–4	46.6

▲ Schools in California are organized by grade span.

ERROR ALERT

Look at the digit in the ones place when rounding to the nearest ten.

Guided Practice

1. Round each addend to the nearest whole number. Add both rounded numbers. What is the estimated sum?

$$34.56 → 3\blacksquare$$
$$+25.19 → \underline{2\blacksquare}$$
$$\blacksquare\blacksquare$$

NS 2.1 Estimate and compute the sum or difference of whole numbers and positive decimals to two places. *also* NS 2.2, MR 2.3, MR 2.4, MR 3.2

Estimate the sum or difference.

2.	3.	4.	✓5.	✓6.
6.9	48.78	$84.54	$91.24	4.09
+5.8	−23.92	+ 15.97	− 39.87	8.98
				+1.43

7. **TALK Math** Explain how you can tell whether 127.79 is a reasonable answer for 29.38 + 98.41.

Independent Practice and Problem Solving

Estimate the sum or difference.

8. 3.8 − 2.5   9. 5.68 − 2.19   10. $72.94 + $49.57   11. 8.92 + 6.58

12. 65.54 + 32.09   13. $56.18 − $12.83   14. 12.6 + 32.8 + 49.5   15. 65.12 − 21.78

Estimate to compare. Write <, >, or = for each ⬤.

16. 56.12 − 14.78 ⬤ 17.03 + 13.98   17. 45.89 + 42.70 ⬤ 87.01 − 10.90

USE DATA For 18–19, use the table.

18. About how many more students were enrolled in 6–8 middle schools than the combined enrollment of 5–8 and 7–8 middle schools?

19. The total enrollment in middle schools was about 26.5 thousand more than for the middle schools in the table. About how many students, in thousands, were enrolled in middle schools?

2003-2004 California Middle School Enrollment

Grade Span	Students Enrolled (in thousands)
5–8	40.1
6–8	815.4
7–8	290.0

20. **≡FAST FACT** The total enrollment for California schools in 2003–2004 was 6,298,774 students. What is this number in word form?

21. **WRITE Math** Explain how to determine if the sum 79.3 is reasonable for the following addition problem:
29.5 + 30.4 + 19.4

Achieving the Standards

22. Round 16.74 to the nearest whole number. (NS 2.2, p. 494)

23. What is the median for the set of data shown in the table for problems 18 and 19? (SDAP 1.2, p. 328)

24. $423 + $125 =   (O⟶ NS 3.1, p. 58)

25. **Test Prep** The Cruz family drove 78.75 miles on Monday and 59.25 miles on Tuesday. About how many more miles did they drive on Monday than on Tuesday?

A 10 miles   C 30 miles

B 20 miles   D 130 miles

3 Model Addition

OBJECTIVE: Model addition of decimals.

Quick Review

1. 13 + 45
2. 48 + 123
3. 378 + 298
4. 32 + 47 + 89
5. 145 + 678 + 324

Investigate

Materials ■ decimal models ■ color pencils

Use decimal models to find 0.34 + 0.66.

Ⓐ Shade 34 squares on a decimal model red to represent 0.34.

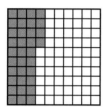

Ⓑ Shade 66 squares on the same decimal model blue to represent 0.66.

Ⓒ Make three more models with addends whose sum is 1.00.

Draw Conclusions

1. What is the sum of 0.34 and 0.66?

2. How did the decimal models help you find the sum?

3. What are two decimals you could add by using tenths models?

4. **Synthesis** If you add two decimals that are both less than 0.5, will the sum be less than or greater than 1?

NS 2.1 Estimate and compute the sum or difference of whole numbers and positive decimals to two places. also AF 1.1, MR 2.0, MR 2.3, MR 2.4, MR 3.0, MR 3.2, MR 3.3

Connect

You can draw a picture to help you add decimals.

Add. 0.5 + 0.8

Step 1

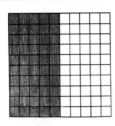

Shade 5 columns red.

Step 2

Shade 8 columns blue.
Count the total number
of columns shaded.

So, 0.5 + 0.8 = 1.3.

TALK Math

How would you model
the sum of 1.42 and 0.36?

Practice

Use models to find the sum.

1.	2.	3.	✓4.
0.45	0.9	0.92	1.66
+0.89	+0.7	+0.47	+1.07

5. 3.71 + 0.54   6. 1.05 + 0.98   7. 2.75 + 0.84   ✓8. 2.3 + 0.59

★Algebra Use the models to find the missing addend.

9.

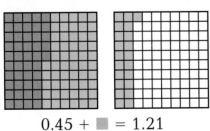

0.45 + ■ = 1.21

10.

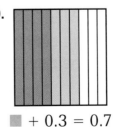

■ + 0.3 = 0.7

11. **WRITE Math** ▸ Summarize how you can use decimal
models to find the sum of any two decimals.

Technology
Use Harcourt Mega Math, Fraction Action,
Fraction Flare Up, Level L.

4 Model Subtraction

OBJECTIVE: Model subtraction of decimals.

Quick Review

1. 67 − 25
2. 90 − 13
3. 313 − 210
4. 562 − 278
5. 400 − 164

Investigate

Materials ■ decimal models ■ color pencils

Use decimal models to find 0.8 − 0.5.

A Shade 8 columns on a decimal model red.

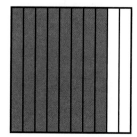

B Cut out 5 columns from the shaded model.

C Make three more models to show subtracting a decimal from 1.0.

D Use decimal models to find 0.81 − 0.46.

Draw Conclusions

1. How did the decimal model help you find the difference?

2. What are two decimals you could find the difference of by using tenth grids?

3. **Synthesis** If two decimals are both less than 1, what can you say about the difference between them?

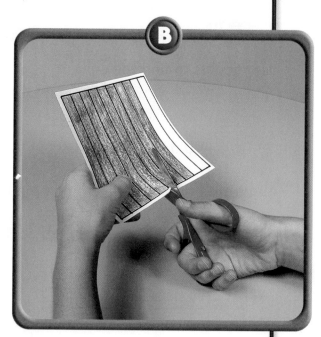

NS 2.1 Estimate and compute the sum or difference of whole numbers and positive decimals to two places. *also* AF 1.1, MR 2.0, MR 2.3, MR 2.4, MR 3.0, MR 3.2, MR 3.3

You can draw a picture to help you subtract decimals.

Subtract. 0.75 − 0.29

Step 1

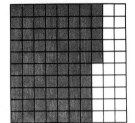

Shade 75 squares.

Step 2

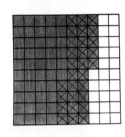

Draw X's on 29 squares of the shaded part. Then, count the shaded squares that do not have X's.

So, 0.75 − 0.29 = 0.46.

TALK Math

How would you use models to find the difference of any two decimals?

Practice

Use models to find the difference.

1. 0.56 − 0.32	**2.** 0.8 − 0.2	**3.** 0.72 − 0.37	✓**4.** 1.12 − 0.45

5. 2.71 − 1.34   **6.** 0.62 − 0.18   **7.** 4.05 − 1.61   ✓**8.** 1.3 − 0.52

Algebra Use the models to find the missing number.

9.

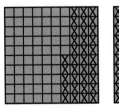 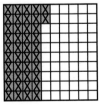

1.42 − ■ = 0.65

10.

■ − 0.73 = 0.23

11. **WRITE Math** **Explain** how you can use models to find 0.6 − 0.45.

Technology
Use Harcourt Mega Math, Fraction Action, *Fraction Flare Up*, Level L.

CD ROM

5 Record Addition and Subtraction

OBJECTIVE: Record addition and subtraction of decimal amounts and money.

Learn

PROBLEM Each year, the average American eats about 3.36 pounds of peanut butter and about 2.21 pounds of fruit spread, per person. How many pounds of peanut butter and fruit spread does each person eat per year?

Example 1 Add. $3.36 + 2.21$ **Estimate.** $3 + 2 = 5$

MODEL	THINK	RECORD
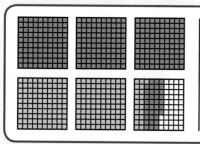	Count the number of squares in the partially shaded models. Then count the number of models that are completely shaded.	3.36 + 2.21 ——— 5.57

So, each person eats about 5.57 pounds of peanut butter and fruit spread per year. Since the sum 5.57 is close to the estimate of 5, it is reasonable.

Math Idea
You can add decimals the same way you add whole numbers if you line up the decimal points first.

Example 2

Subtract. $3.36 - 2.21$ **Estimate.** $3 - 2 = 1$

MODEL	THINK	RECORD
	Cross out 21 squares on the partially shaded model and 2 completely shaded models. Count the number of squares not crossed out to find what is left.	3.36 − 2.21 ——— 1.15

So, $3.36 - 2.21 = 1.15$.

Example 3 Count up on a number line.

Subtract. $2.5 - 0.7$

Count up from 0.7 to 2.5. Add the amounts you counted up by: $0.3 + 1.0 + 0.5 = 1.8$.

$0.3 + 1.0 + 0.5$

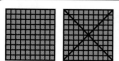

0 ↑ 1   2 ↑ 3
   0.7   2.5

So, $2.5 - 0.7 = 1.8$.

NS 2.1 Estimate and compute the sum or difference of whole numbers and positive decimals to two places. *also* NS 2.2, AF 1.1, MR 2.1, MR 2.3, MR 3.1

Use Equivalent Decimals

Sometimes one number has more decimal places after the decimal point than the other. Write equivalent decimals with the same number of decimal places before adding or subtracting.

Allan buys a 2.5-pound jar of peanut butter. He has 0.75 pound left in another jar. How much peanut butter does he have in all?

Example Add. 2.5 + 0.75   **Estimate.** 3 + 1 = 4

Step 1	Step 2
Line up the decimal points. Place zeros to the right of the last digit after the decimal point so each number has the same number of digits after the decimal point.	Add as you do with whole numbers. Place the decimal point in the sum.
2.5**0** + 0.75	1 2.50 + 0.75 3.25

So, Allan has 3.25 pounds of peanut butter. Since 3.25 is close to the estimate of 4, it is reasonable.

More Examples

A Use equivalent decimals to subtract.

5.8 − 2.94   Estimate. 6 − 3 = 3

$$\begin{array}{r} \overset{\overset{17}{4\ \cancel{7}\ 10}}{\cancel{5}.\cancel{8}\,\emptyset} \\ -\ 2.94 \\ \hline 2.86 \end{array}$$

Place a zero to the right of the digit 8 in 5.8.

B Add money amounts.

$12.00 + $34.98
Estimate. $12 + $35 = $47

$$\begin{array}{r} \$12.00 \\ +\ \$34.98 \\ \hline \$46.98 \end{array}$$

C Subtract money amounts.

$52.07 − $11.45
Estimate. $52 − $11 = $41

$$\begin{array}{r} \overset{1\ 10}{\$5\cancel{2}.\cancel{0}7} \\ -\ 11.45 \\ \hline \$40.62 \end{array}$$

Guided Practice

1. Which of the choices shows how to record what is shown in the model?

   a. 1.00 − 0.67   **b.** 0.10 + 0.67   **c.** 1.00 + 0.67

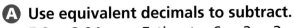

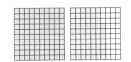

Estimate. Then record the sum or difference.

2. 4.8
    + 2.4

3. 35.83
    − 12.18

✓ 4. $23.44
      + 19.85

✓ 5. 67.1
      − 9.98

6. (TALK Math) **Explain** how using equivalent decimals helps you add and subtract.

Independent Practice and Problem Solving

Estimate. Then record the sum or difference.

7. 6.5
    + 3.9

8. 71.82
    − 52.39

9. $42.13
    + 81.32

10. $31.50
     − 19.17

11. $2.03 + $27.89

12. 8.75 − 6.43

13. 3.5 + 42.32

14. 12.64 − 5

Compare. Write <, >, or = for each ●.

15. $1.00 + $1.10 ● $1.00 + $0.40

16. 57.1 − 25.09 ● 3.4 + 32.75

★ **Algebra** Find the missing decimals. The sums are given at the end of each row and bottom of each column.

17–20.

21.5	0.64	▓	33.83
▓	17.16	65.2	85.34
58.7	▓	9.34	70.24
83.18	20	86.23	▓

21–24.

▓	14.5	6.03	24.33
7.56	▓	74.68	99.89
61.98	10.01	▓	93.29
73.34	42.16	102.01	▓

USE DATA For 25–27, use the nutrition label.

25. How many grams of fat in 2 tablespoons of this peanut butter are not saturated fat, polyunsaturated fat, or monounsaturated fat?

26. Write an equation to show how many more grams of sugar than grams of dietary fiber are in 2 tablespoons of peanut butter. Then solve.

27. **Pose a Problem** Write a problem that uses the nutrition label.

28. ≡**FAST FACT** The world's largest peanut butter and jelly sandwich measured 2.44 meters long by 2.44 meters wide. It was made on September 7, 2002, in Oklahoma City, OK. Do you need an estimate or an exact answer to determine whether the sandwich was longer than 2.03 meters? **Explain.**

Nutrition Facts
Serving Size 2 tbsp (32.0g)

Amount Per Serving

Calories	190
Calories from Fat	147

% Daily Value*

Total Fat 16.3g	25%
Saturated Fat 3.6g	18%
Polyunsaturated Fat 4.4g	
Monounsaturated Fat 7.8g	
Cholesterol 0mg	0%
Sodium 5mg	0%
Total Carbohydrates 6.2g	2%
Dietary Fiber 1.9g	8%
Sugars 2.5g	
Protein 8.1g	

Vitamin A 0%

Vitamin C 0%

Calcium 1%

Iron 3%

Nutritional Units 5

* Based on a 2000 calorie diet

29. Reasoning Two packages of peanuts weigh 1.74 pounds and 2.68 pounds. Is 1.7 + 2.7 a reasonable estimate of the combined weights, to the nearest tenth of a pound? **Explain.**

30. **WRITE Math** **Explain** how adding and subtracting decimals is like adding and subtracting whole numbers. Then tell how it is different.

Achieving the Standards

31. Write the name of the figure. (Grade 3 MG 2.0)

⟵————————⟶

32. $114 \div 6 =$ (**O⊓** NS 3.2, p. 270)

33. Round 13.75 to the nearest whole number (NS 2.2, p. 494)

34. Test Prep Alda is 62.5 inches tall. Her younger brother is 3.75 inches shorter than she is. How tall is Alda's younger brother?

A 59.75 inches **C** 58.25 inches

B 58.75 inches **D** 57.75 inches

35. Test Prep Dale bought a pair of sneakers on sale for $33.95. This was $12.95 less than the original price. What is the original price of the sneakers?

A $21.00

B $22.00

C $46.80

D $46.90

Problem Solving [connects to] Science

Protein Power
The recommended amount of protein for children ages 4 to 8 is 19 grams and 34 grams for ages 9 to 13.

Grams of Protein per Serving	
Item	Protein (in grams)
1 scrambled egg	6.76
1 cup shredded wheat cereal	5.56
1 oat bran muffin	3.99
1 cup low-fat milk	8.22

USE DATA For 1–2, use the table.

1. Gianna is 12 years old. She had a scrambled egg, an oatbran muffin, and a cup of low-fat milk for breakfast. How much more protein does she need to eat to reach the recommended level for a day?

2. Ming is 8 years old. His mom wants him to eat between 12 and 15 grams of his recommended amount of protein for breakfast. What items would make a good breakfast for Ming? How many grams of protein will he need to eat during the rest of the day?

Problem Solving Workshop
Strategy: Compare Strategies

OBJECTIVE: Compare different strategies to solve problems.

Use the Strategy

PROBLEM The vending machine at the community center takes exact change only, including bills and coins. Anthony wants to buy a bottle of water that costs $1.50. He has a $1 bill, 2 quarters, 2 dimes, and 3 nickels. What are all the different ways that Anthony can pay for the bottle of water?

Read to Understand

Reading Skill

• Visualize the types of coins available.

• Is there information you will not use? If so, what?

Plan

• **What strategy can you use to solve the problem?**
You can make a table or you can predict and test.

Solve

• **How can you use each strategy to solve the problem?**

Make a Table
Start with the greatest values of bill and coins.

$1 Bills	Quarters	Dimes	Nickels	Total
1	2			1 $1, 2 Q

Predict and Test
Make an organized list to record your prediction. To test your prediction, add to check the total.

So, Anthony can pay for the water in three different ways: one $1 bill, 2 quarters or one $1 bill, 1 quarter, 2 dimes, and 1 nickel or one $1 bill, 1 quarter, 1 dime, and 3 nickels.

1 $1 and 1 Q = $1 + $0.25 = $1.25
1 $1 and 2 Q = $1 + $0.50 = $1.50
1 $1, 1 Q, 1 D, and 1 N = $1 + $0.25 + $0.10 + $0.05 = $1.40
1 $1, 1 Q, 2 D, and 1 N = $1 + $0.25 + $0.20 + $0.05 = $1.50
1 $1, 1 Q, 1 D, and 3 N = $1 + $0.25 + $0.10 + $0.15 = $1.50
1 $1, 2 Q, 2 D, and 3 N = $1 + $0.50 + $0.20 + $0.15 = $1.85

Check

• **Which strategy was more helpful, *Make a Table* or *Predict and Test*? Explain.**

NS 2.1 Estimate and compute the sum or difference of whole numbers and positive decimals to two places. *also* AF 1.1, MR 1.0, MR 2.0, MR 2.3, MR 2.4, MR 2.6, MR 3.0, MR 3.1, MR 3.2, MR 3.3

Guided Problem Solving Practice

Choose a
STRATEGY

Draw a Diagram or Picture

Make a Model or Act It Out

Make an Organized List

Find a Pattern

Make a Table or Graph

Predict and Test

Work Backward

Solve a Simpler Problem

Write an Equation

Use Logical Reasoning

1. Sara wants to buy a can of apple juice from the vending machine. She needs exactly $2.30. She has two $1 bills, 5 quarters, 2 dimes, and 2 nickels. What are all the different ways that Sara can pay for the juice?

   First, decide whether to make a table or predict and test which bills and coins to use.

   Predict and Test
   2 $1, 1 Q, and 1 D = $2.00 + $0.25 + $0.10 = $2.35
   2 $1, 1 Q, and 1 N = $2.00 + $0.25 + $0.05 = ■
   1 $1, 5 Q, and 1 N = $1.00 + ■ + $0.05 = ■
   1 $1, 4 Q, 2 D, and 2 ■ = ■

   Fill in the boxes to predict and test the different possible combinations to make $2.30.

2. **What if** Sara wants to buy grape juice that costs $1.85? What are all the different ways she can make exactly $1.85 with the bills and coins she has? Solve and explain the strategy you used.

3. The vending machine has 10 drinks left. Some are juice and some are water. There are more cans of juice left than bottles of water. What possible combinations of water and juice could be left in the machine?

Mixed Strategy Practice

USE DATA For 4–5, use the table.

4. The community center has a swimming pool. Henry paid the entrance fee with 8 coins. What coins did Henry use?

5. How many different ways can you pay the exact amount for a towel if you have the following bills and coins?

6. Kay is swimming in the lap lane 12 feet behind Lee and 6 feet in front of Mindy. Mindy is swimming an equal distance between Paul and Alan. How far is the first swimmer from the last?

COMMUNITY CENTER POOL	
Item	Price
Entrance Fee	$1.50
Bathing Cap	$2.75
Towel	$5.55

Extra Practice

Set A Round each number to the nearest tenth and each money amount to the nearest dollar. (pp. 492–493)

1. 5.48
2. 42.07
3. 412.11
4. $56.72
5. 5.16
6. $8.08
7. 4.53
8. 5.82
9. $65.61
10. $248.92

Round each number to the nearest whole number.

11. 5.90
12. 5.28
13. 25.89
14. 23.17
15. 413.07

16. David says that the mass of his bag of fruit is 3.46 kilograms. Round this mass to the nearest whole number.

17. Margaret is trying to lift a box weighing 28.94 pounds. Round this weight to the nearest whole number.

Set B Estimate the sum or difference. (pp. 494–495)

1. $6.5 - 3.4$
2. $9.31 - 5.26$
3. $58.36 + 29.99
4. $9.87 + 6.54$
5. $25.79 + 54.11$
6. $47.09 - 21.99
7. $23.5 + 21.9 + 63.7$
8. $72.74 - 38.09$

9. Domingo had $19.11. He bought a book for $16.09. About how much money does Domingo have left?

10. Gabriella had $24.75. Her mother gave her $13.06. About how much money does Gabriella have now?

Set C Estimate. Then record the sum or difference (pp. 500–503)

1. $\begin{array}{r} 8.6 \\ + 1.8 \\ \hline \end{array}$
2. $\begin{array}{r} 73.91 \\ - 19.68 \\ \hline \end{array}$
3. $\begin{array}{r} \$33.42 \\ + \$72.46 \\ \hline \end{array}$
4. $\begin{array}{r} \$53.28 \\ - \$27.34 \\ \hline \end{array}$
5. $\begin{array}{r} 63.97 \\ - 24.83 \\ \hline \end{array}$
6. $\begin{array}{r} 37.89 \\ + 24.09 \\ \hline \end{array}$
7. $\begin{array}{r} 56.29 \\ - 23.01 \\ \hline \end{array}$
8. $\begin{array}{r} 9.4 \\ - 2.37 \\ \hline \end{array}$

9. Nathan has $5.83 in his piggy bank. He has $6.41 in his pocket. Estimate how much Nathan has to the nearest dollar.

10. Isabelle had $15.85. She spent $5.41 on a necklace. Estimate how much Isabelle has left to the nearest dollar.

Technology
CD ROM
Use Harcourt Mega Math, Fraction Action, *Number Line Mine*, Levels P, Q.

Decimal Train

Pack your bags!
2 or more players

Buy your ticket!
Decimal cards

START

All aboard!

- Shuffle the decimal cards. Place them facedown in a stack. Players will take turns.

- The first player takes the top two decimal cards. Place one card on the engine and one card on the first car of the train. Find the sum of the two decimals. If the sum is correct, a player receives 1 point, and the cards stay on the train. If the sum is incorrect, the player receives no points, and the cards go to the bottom of the stack.

- After two cards are on the train, each player will choose one card from the stack and add it to the train. Each new decimal is added to the sum of all the previous decimals. Keep a running total. Do not forget to return a card to the stack if a sum is incorrect. Keep track of your scores, too.

- Repeat until the train is full of cards.

- The player with the most points wins.

FINISH

Check Concepts

1. **Explain** how you can use hundredths decimal models to find the sum of $0.15 + 0.81$. (NS 2.1, pp. 496–497)

2. Summarize how you can draw a picture to help you subtract 0.63 and 0.36. (NS 2.1, pp. 498–499)

Check Skills

Round each number to the nearest tenth and each money amount to the nearest dollar. (NS 2.2, pp. 492–493)

3. 34.91 4. $\$12.49$ 5. 7.53 6. $\$199.98$ 7. 439.17

Estimate the sum or difference. (NS 2.1, pp. 494–495)

8. $4.2 - 1.9$ 9. $\$44.29 + \$36.71$ 10. $\$11.94 - \$7.22$ 11. $10.6 + 9.4 + 13.7$

12. $21.2 - 19.7$ 13. $18.42 + 3.99$ 14. $66.67 + 33.37$ 15. $\$78.15 - \$59.99$

Estimate. Then record the sum or difference. (NS 2.1, pp. 500–503)

16. $\begin{array}{r} 3.9 \\ + 5.7 \\ \hline \end{array}$ 17. $\begin{array}{r} 14.65 \\ - 8.77 \\ \hline \end{array}$ 18. $\begin{array}{r} 26.88 \\ + 11.74 \\ \hline \end{array}$ 19. $\begin{array}{r} \$46.83 \\ - \$38.27 \\ \hline \end{array}$

20. $\begin{array}{r} 45.38 \\ - 26.97 \\ \hline \end{array}$ 21. $\begin{array}{r} 85.91 \\ + 23.05 \\ \hline \end{array}$ 22. $\begin{array}{r} \$27.51 \\ + \$36.99 \\ \hline \end{array}$ 23. $\begin{array}{r} 57.12 \\ - 38.09 \\ \hline \end{array}$

Check Problem Solving

Solve. (NS 2.1, MR 2.3, pp. 504–505)

24. Dante wants to buy a baseball. He has two $\$1$, 5 quarters, 3 dimes, and 4 nickels. What are all the different ways Dante can pay for the baseball?

25. **WRITE Math** Emma bought a baseball bat and chalk. **Explain** why Emma gave the cashier $\$20.08$, and tell how much change Emma should receive.

$29.99

$1.75

$16.09

$2.99

GO **Technology** Use *Online Assessment.*

Enrich • Properties and Decimals
Valuable Properties

Daniel has 5 dimes, 8 pennies, and 1 nickel. To find out how much money he has, he needs to add the value of the coins, or $0.50 + $0.08 + $0.05. Nicole has the same coins in her pocket. If she has 5 dimes and 1 nickel, what is the value of the pennies in her pocket?

▲ Built in 1926, the bank was San Jose's first skyscraper.

You apply the properties of addition to decimals.

Property	Whole Numbers	Decimals
Identity	$138 + 0 = 138$ $0 + 138 = 138$	$0.17 + 0 = 0.17$
Commutative	$13 + 24 = 24 + 13$	$2.9 + 1.7 = 1.7 + 2.9$
Associative	$(49 + 39) + 61 = 49 + (39 + 61)$	$(0.9 + 0.18) + 0.02 = 0.9 + (0.18 + 0.02)$

You can use the Commutative Property to find the value of the coins.

$0.50 + $0.08 + $0.05 = $0.05 + ■ + $0.50
$0.50 + $0.08 + $0.05 = $0.05 + $0.08 + $0.50

So, the value of the pennies in Nicole's pocket is $0.08.

Examples

Apply the properties of addition to decimals to find a missing number.

A Identity Property

$19.3 + ■ = 19.3$
$19.3 + 0 = 19.3$

So, ■ = 0.

B Associative Property

$■ + (1.45 + 1.89) = (2.55 + 1.45) + 1.89$
$2.55 + (1.45 + 1.89) = (2.55 + 1.45) + 1.89$

So, ■ = 2.55.

Try It

Write the missing number. Name the property you used.

1. $6.7 + 2.4 = ■ + 6.7$

2. $0.79 = 0 + ■$

3. $(1.29 + 0.17) + 3.33 = 1.29 + (■ + 3.33)$

4. $(\$4.02 + \$2.81) = (\$2.81 + ■)$

Change the order or group the addends so that you can add mentally. Find the sum. Name the property you used.

5. $0.53 + 0.8 + 0.07$ 6. $4.7 + 2.6 + 3.4$ 7. $5.2 + 9.9 + 1.8$ 8. $0.57 + 0.09 + 0.91$

WRITE Math Explain how the Commutative and Associative properties can help you add decimals.

 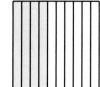
Multiple Choice

1. The model is shaded to represent $1\frac{4}{10}$.

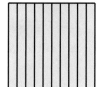

Which decimal represents the model?

(NS 1.6, p. 474)

A 0.4

B 1.0

C 1.4

D 1.6

2. On the number line below, what mixed number does point *P* represent?

(⊙━ NS 1.9, p. 426)

A $1\frac{1}{5}$

B $1\frac{1}{2}$

C $1\frac{3}{5}$

D $1\frac{4}{6}$

3. Laura was 21.65 inches long when she was born. What is her length rounded to the nearest inch? (NS 2.2, p. 492)

A 22

B 21.7

C 21

D 20

4. Molly lives 0.97 mile from the library. Karen lives 0.83 mile from the library. How much farther from the library does Molly live? (NS 2.1, p. 498)

A 0.07 mile

B 0.14 mile

C 0.70 mile

D 1.4 miles

5. Hiro bought one set of notebooks and one folder. He paid with a $5 bill. How much change did he receive?

(NS 2.1, p. 500)

School Supplies	
Item	**Price**
Set of notebooks	$3.79
Package of pencils	$1.29
Folder	$0.49

A $9.28

B $4.28

C $1.28

D $0.72

6. Which decimal means the same as $1\frac{1}{4}$?

(NS 1.6, p. 474)

A 1.14

B 1.25

C 1.4

D 1.5

Technology Use *Online Assessment.*

7. The table shows how much of each type of cheese Mindy bought.

Cheese Tray	
Cheese	**Weight (in pounds)**
American	$\frac{3}{8}$
Swiss	$\frac{4}{8}$
Muenster	$\frac{7}{8}$
Cheddar	$\frac{1}{8}$

How much cheese did Mindy buy in all?

(Grade 5 ⚬━ NS 2.3, p. 448)

A $1\frac{3}{8}$ pounds

B $1\frac{5}{8}$ pounds

C $1\frac{7}{8}$ pounds

D 2 pounds

8. Which equation is not represented by the model? (NS 2.1, p. 498)

A $0.51 + 0.28 = 0.79$

B $0.28 + 0.79 = 0.51$

C $0.79 - 0.28 = 0.51$

D $0.79 - 0.51 = 0.28$

9. Look at the number line.

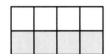

Which number sentence is true?

(⚬━ NS 1.9, p. 478)

A $1.54 < 1.5$ **C** $1.29 < 1.19$

B $1.4 < 1.40$ **D** $1.03 < 1.3$

Short Response

10. Nathan's soup recipe calls for $2\frac{3}{4}$ cups of tomato sauce. He has $2\frac{2}{3}$ cups of tomato sauce. Make a model to show whether Nathan has enough tomato sauce for the recipe. (NS 1.7, p. 430)

11. Yolanda is 41 inches tall. There are 12 inches in a foot.

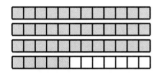

How many feet tall is Yolanda? Write your answer as a mixed number. (NS 1.7, p. 426)

12. Write two fractions that are equivalent to $\frac{4}{8}$. (NS 1.5, p. 418)

13. List these decimal numbers in order from least to greatest. (⚬━ NS 1.2, p. 480)

4.8, 4.18, 4.1, 4.81, 4.08

Extended Response [✏️WRITE Math]▶

14. Mihn added 3.19 and 2.4. He got a sum of 5.23. Is he correct? **Explain.**

(NS 1.6, p. 500)

15. Tonya says that 3.30 is greater than 3.3. Do you agree? **Explain** your thinking.

(NS 1.6, p. 472)

16. **Explain** how to use a model to find the missing number. (NS 2.1, p. 498)

$$0.42 - \blacksquare = 0.29$$

Cool Kites

KITE FESTIVALS AND COMPETITIONS

Each year, the state of California holds dozens of kite festivals and competitions. The largest are the Berkeley Kite Festival and West Coast Kite Championships. Two events in the West Coast Kite Championships are the kite ballet and fighter kites. Kite ballet is an event using graceful movements with multiple kites and music. The object of kite fighting is to get your opponent's kite out of the sky first.

FACT·ACTIVITY

Kite trains can also be seen at the Berkeley Kite Festival. A kite train is two or more kites flown together in a line. Kite trains have been used to pull boats across water or go-carts across sand. Most of the time, people fly kite trains just for fun.

Use the kite train photos to answer the questions.

❶ **WRITE Math** A student says that 3 kites in each kite train are red, so $\frac{3}{5} = \frac{3}{9}$. Is the student correct? **Explain** why or why not. Draw a diagram to support your answer.

❷ What fraction of the 5-kite train is yellow? Draw and color a kite train with 10 kites that shows the equivalent fraction.

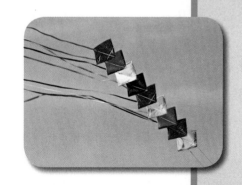

DESIGN A KITE

The earliest known kites had simple flat shapes, like squares, rectangles, and diamonds, but kites can be made in other shapes. In the early 1900s, Orville and Wilbur Wright studied box-shaped kites to help them design the first airplane. Kites can even be made in fun shapes, like birds or dragons.

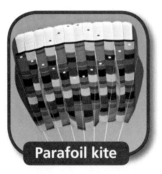
Parafoil kite

Box kite

Flat kite

FACT·ACTIVITY

Design your own flat kite.

► What shape will your kite be? What will its dimensions (length and width) be? Make at least one dimension a mixed number.

► Draw a diagram of your kite. Label its dimensions.

► Write a number sentence about the dimensions of your kite.

► Write a number sentence to compare the dimensions of your kite to those of a classmate's kite.

► **WRITE Math** ► Think about some different uses of kites. **Explain** how your kite alone or in a kite train might be useful. Then research and make a list of other ways kites can be useful.

7 Geometry

Math on Location

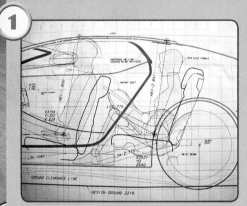

1

Designers and engineers use points, lines, angles, and plane figures in concept drawings.

2

The drawing is made into a 3-dimensional clay model to test its resistance to air.

3

A top-view drawing shows the symmetry in the car's design.

VOCABULARY POWER

TALK Math

What math do you see in the **Math on Location** photographs? What geometric words can you use to talk about car designs?

READ Math

REVIEW VOCABULARY You learned the words below when you learned about geometry. How do these words relate to **Math on Location**?

angle a figure formed by two rays or line segments that share an endpoint

polygon a closed plane figure with straight sides that are line segments

rectangle a quadrilateral with two pairs of parallel sides, two pairs of equal sides, and four right angles

WRITE Math

Copy and complete the degrees of meaning grid below for geometric figures. Use what you know about geometry to complete the grid.

General	Less General	Specific	More Specific
polygon			
solid figure			

Technology
Multimedia Math Glossary link at
www.harcourtschool.com/hspmath

20 Lines, Rays, Angles, and Plane Figures

The Big Idea Points, lines, planes, and their classifications and relationships are the building blocks of geometry.

Investigate

Barn, Cape Cod, Massachusetts, by Ansel Adams, hangs in the San Francisco Museum of Modern Art. What geometric figures do you see in the photo? Draw your own barn or building. Include as many different geometric figures as you can.

CALIFORNIA FAST FACT

The San Francisco Museum of Modern Art is the second-largest modern art museum in the United States. The building has 225,000 square feet of space.

GO ONLINE

Technology
Student pages are available in the Student eBook.

Check your understanding of important skills needed for success in Chapter 20.

▶ **Identify Geometric Figures**

Write the name of each figure.

1. •

2. •——•

3.

4. •——→

5. ⬜ (square)

6. ▭ (rectangle)

7. △ (triangle)

8. ○ (circle)

▶ **Types of Lines**

Describe the lines. Write *parallel* or *intersecting*.

9. ⇆

10.

11.

12. ⇗

▶ **Sides and Angles**

Write the number of sides and angles in each figure.

13. (right triangle)

14. (pentagon)

15. (rectangle)

16. (octagon)

17. (parallelogram)

18. (scalene triangle)

19. (hexagon)

20. (trapezoid)

VOCABULARY POWER

CHAPTER VOCABULARY		WARM-UP WORDS
chord	one-dimensional	**point** an exact location in space
decagon	plane	**line segment** is a part of a line that includes two points called endpoints and all the points between them.
degree (°)	radius	
diameter	regular polygon	**endpoint** the points at either end of a line segment
dimension	scalene triangle	
endpoint	trapezoid	
	vertex	

1 Points, Lines, and Rays

OBJECTIVE: Identify, describe, and draw points, lines, line segments, rays, and planes.

Quick Review

Draw a line segment.

Vocabulary

point	line
line segment	endpoint
ray	dimension
plane	one-dimensional
	two-dimensional

Learn

The vocabulary of geometry helps describe plane and solid figures you see both in nature and in the things people make. You can use the following geometric ideas and terms to describe the world around you.

TERM AND DEFINITION	DRAW IT	READ IT	WRITE IT	EXAMPLE
A **point** names an exact location in space.	A •	point A	point A	
A **line segment** is part of a line. It has two **endpoints**, the points at either end of the line segment, and all of the points between them.	D E	line segment DE or line segment ED	$\overline{DE}$ or $\overline{ED}$	
A **line** is a straight path of points that continues without end in both directions with no endpoints.	B C	line BC or line CB	$\overleftrightarrow{BC}$ or $\overleftrightarrow{CB}$	
A **ray** is part of a line that has one endpoint and continues without end in one direction.	F G	ray FG	$\overrightarrow{FG}$	EXIT →
A **plane** is a flat surface that continues without end in all directions.	K M L	plane KLM	plane KLM	

A plane is named by at least three points in the plane.

Dimension is a measurement along a straight line of length, width, or height of a figure. **One-dimensional** is a measure in only one direction, such as length. **Two-dimensional** is a measure in two directions, such as length and width. A rectangle is an example of a two dimensional figure. Its dimensions are length and width.

MG 3.0 Students demonstrate an understanding of plane and solid geometric objects and use this knowledge to show relationships and solve problems. *also* MR 1.1, MR 2.3, MR 2.4, MR 3.2

Guided Practice

1. Name the figure at the right. **Think:** It has 2 endpoints.

A •————————• B

Name a geometric term that best represents the object.

2. tip of a tack   3. train track rail   ✅ 4. flagpole   ✅ 5. laser beam

6. **[TALK Math]** **Explain** how lines, line segments, and rays are alike and different.

Independent Practice and Problem Solving

Name the geometric term that best represents the object.

7. one way arrow   8. tip of a marker   9. parking lot   10. edge of a desk

Name an everyday object that represents the term.

11. line   12. line segment   13. ray   14. plane

Draw and label an example of each.

15. line *XY*   16. point *H*   17. ray *MN*   18. plane *PQR*

USE DATA For 19–20, use the photo.

19. What geometric term describes where 2 walls and a floor meet?

20. What features on the building show line segments?

21. **Reasoning** Draw four points. What is the greatest number of line segments you can draw by connecting the points?

22. Write all the names for this ray.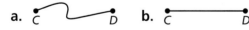

23. **[WRITE Math]** **Explain** how you know which path is the shortest distance between point C and point D.

   a. C •~~~~~~• D   b. C •————————• D

Achieving the Standards

24. Jake bought a bowling ball on sale for $56.79. To the nearest dollar, how much did it cost? (NS 2.2, p. 492)

25. Name the figure. (MG 3.0, p. 518) •————→

26. $7 \times (9 - 3) =$ (O▬ᴛ AF 1.2, p. 142)

27. **Test Prep** Which geometric term is a straight path of points that continues without end in both directions?

   A plane   **C** line

   B line segment   **D** ray

Extra Practice on page 538, Set A

2 Classify Angles

OBJECTIVE: Identify and describe right, acute and obtuse angles.

Quick Review

Write the name of each figure.

1. •   2. •——→

3. ←——→   4. •——•

5.

Learn

Two rays with the same endpoint form an **angle**. The shared endpoint is called a **vertex**.

DRAW IT	READ IT	WRITE IT
ray → A B• vertex ray C	angle *ABC* angle *CBA* angle *B*	∠*ABC* ∠*CBA* ∠*B*
	NOTE: The vertex is always the middle letter or the single letter that names the angle.	

Vocabulary

angle	acute angle
vertex	right angle
degree (°)	obtuse angle

PROBLEM In the Tower Bridge, angles are formed where the steel supports meet. The angle marked in yellow has the same measure as ∠*ABC* above. What type of angle is ∠*ABC*?

Example Classify angles by comparing.

The unit used for measuring angles is a **degree (°)**.

 right angle	 angle marker	 angle marker
A **right angle** measures 90°. The square marker shows a right angle forms a square corner.	An **acute angle** is an angle with a measure less than a right angle.	An **obtuse angle** is an angle with a measure greater than a right angle.

So, the angle in the photo is an acute angle.

▲ The Tower Bridge spans the Sacramento River to connect Sacramento with West Sacramento, California.

 HANDS ON

Activity Make a right angle.

Make a right angle by using a sheet of paper like this. Fold the paper twice evenly to make what appears to be a right angle.
• Use the right angle to classify these angles as right, acute, or obtuse.

a.

b.

c.

MG 3.5 Know the definitions of a right angle, an acute angle, and an obtuse angle. Understand that 90°, 180°, 270°, and 360° are associated, respectively, with $\frac{1}{4}$, $\frac{1}{2}$, $\frac{3}{4}$, and full turns. *also* **MG 3.0, MR 1.1, MR 2.3, MR 2.4, MR 3.1, MR 3.2**

1. Classify the angle as acute, right, or obtuse.
   Think: Compare the angle to a right angle.

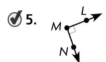

Classify each angle as *acute*, *right*, or *obtuse*.

2.

3.

✓ 4.

✓ 5.

6. [TALK Math] Describe the number and types of angles found in the letter **X**.

Independent Practice (and Problem Solving)

Classify each angle as *acute*, *right*, or *obtuse*.

7.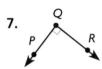

8.

9.

10.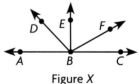

Draw and label an example of each.

11. right angle *ABC*   12. obtuse angle *DEF*   13. acute angle *MNO*   14. right angle *JKL*

For 15–16, use the picture of the bridge.

15. What type of angle does Angle *B* appear to be?

16. Which angle appears to be an obtuse angle?

17. [WRITE Math] ▸ **What's the Error?** Quan says there is 1 right angle in the letter **F**. What error is he making? Correct his error.

18. Name an obtuse angle, a right angle, and an acute angle in the Figure *X*. Name each type of angle.

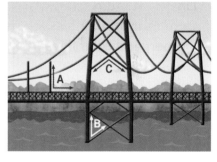

Figure *X*

Achieving the Standards

19. $19.7 + 25.6 =$ (NS 2.1, p. 500)

20. Do the lines appear to be parallel?
    (Grade 3 MG 2.0)

    ←——————————→
    ←——————————→

21. 3 hours = ▮ minutes (Grade 3 MG 1.4)

22. **Test Prep** At what time do the hands of a clock represent a right angle?

    A 12:30   **C** 3:15

    B 3:00   **D** 6:00

Line Relationships

OBJECTIVE: Identify, describe, and draw intersecting, parallel, and perpendicular lines

Quick Review

What is the name for the angle that forms a square corner?

Vocabulary

intersecting lines

parallel lines

perpendicular lines

Learn

PROBLEM Participants march in the Independence Day parade in Montclair, New Jersey. Use the terms below to identify an example of each type of line on the parade route map.

TERM AND DEFINITION	DRAW IT	READ IT	WRITE IT
Lines that cross each other at exactly one point are **intersecting lines**. They form four angles.		Line *AB* intersects line *CD* at point *E*.	$\overleftrightarrow{AB}$ intersects $\overleftrightarrow{CD}$ at point *E*.
Lines in the same plane that never intersect and are always the same distance apart are **parallel lines**.		Line *FG* is parallel to line *HJ*.	$\overleftrightarrow{FG} \parallel \overleftrightarrow{HJ}$ The symbol ‖ means "is parallel to."
Lines that intersect to form four right angles are **perpendicular lines**.		Line *KL* is perpendicular to line *MN*.	$\overleftrightarrow{KL} \perp \overleftrightarrow{MN}$ The symbol ⊥ means "is perpendicular to."

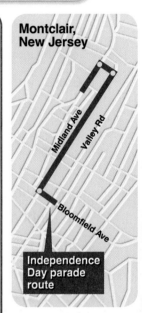

Montclair, New Jersey

▲ The red line shows the Independence Day parade route.

• What term identifies the relationship between Midland Avenue and Valley Road?

Activity **Materials** ■ paper ■ straightedge

Fold paper to make intersecting, parallel, and perpendicular lines.

• As shown in the diagram at the right, fold the paper in half twice so that the vertical edges meet. Which term best identifies the three crease lines after you unfold the paper?

• Now fold the paper in half the other way. When you open the paper, how do the crease lines appear? Which terms best identify the crease lines?

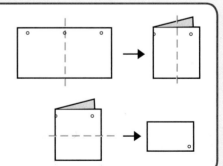

• Use grid paper to draw a pair of parallel lines, a pair of intersecting lines, and a pair of perpendicular lines.

MG 3.1 Identify lines that are parallel and perpendicular. *also* **MG 3.5, MR 1.1, MR 2.3, MR 2.4, MR 3.0, MR 3.2**

Guided Practice

1. How do you know if two lines are parallel? How do you know if two lines are perpendicular?

Name any line relationships you see in each figure.
Write *intersecting, parallel,* or *perpendicular*.

2.

3.

✓ 4.

✓ 5.

6. **TALK Math** How does the symbol ∥ help you remember its meaning?

Independent Practice and Problem Solving

Name any line relationships you see in each figure.
Write *intersecting, parallel,* or *perpendicular*.

7.

8.

9.

10.

USE DATA For 11–13, use the map.

11. Name a street that appears to be parallel to S 17th Street.

12. Name a street that appears to be parallel to Vernon Street and intersects S 17th Street. Classify the angle.

13. What street intersects both S 17th Street and S 19th Street and appears to be perpendicular to them? Classify the angles.

14. **WRITE Math** **What's the Error?** Trina says that all intersecting lines are perpendicular lines. Explain her error.

Achieving the Standards

15. Andy put 3 red and 5 blue marbles all the same size in a bag. Is it certain, likely, unlikely, or impossible that Andy will pull a green marble from the bag? (Grade 3 SDAP 1.1)

16. What geometric term best describes an edge of a photo? (MG 3.0, p. 518)

17. How many sides does the figure have? (Grade 3 MG 2.0)

18. **Test Prep** Which best describes perpendicular lines?

   A They never meet.

   B They form four right angles.

   C They form one acute angle.

   D They form one obtuse angle.

Extra Practice on page 538, Set C

Polygons

OBJECTIVE: Identify, classify, and describe polygons and determine whether polygons are regular or not regular.

Learn

A **polygon** is a closed plane figure formed by three or more straight sides that are connected line segments. There can be no breaks in the sides of the figure. Polygons are named by the number of sides or number of angles they have.

PROBLEM Name the polygons you see in this painting by artist Paul Klee.

Vocabulary

polygon	hexagon
triangle	octagon
quadrilateral	decagon
pentagon	regular polygon

Polygon	Example	Sides and Angles
triangle		3 sides 3 angles
quadrilateral		4 sides 4 angles
pentagon		5 sides 5 angles
hexagon		6 sides 6 angles
octagon		8 sides 8 angles
decagon		10 sides 10 angles

▲ Paul Klee, a Swiss painter who lived from 1879 to 1940, is considered one of the most original painters of modern art.

So, you can see triangles, quadrilaterals, a pentagon, and a hexagon in the painting.

• Can a polygon have a different number of sides than angles?

• Do any of the figures with curved paths in Klee's painting form polygons? Explain your answer.

• **What if** you cut a hexagon into 2 polygons? What 2 polygons could be formed?

MG 3.0 Students demonstrate an understanding of plane and solid geometric objects and use this knowledge to show relationships and solve problems. *also* MR 1.1, MR 2.3, MR 2.4, MR 3.2

Example Decide if each shape is a polygon.

Polygon	Not a Polygon	Not a Polygon	Not a Polygon

Closed plane figure with 5 sides and 5 angles	Sides intersect, but not at the endpoints.	Line segments do not connect.	A curved path is not a line segment.
So, it is a polygon.	So, it is not a polygon.	So, it is not a polygon.	So, it is not a polygon.

• How can you tell what kind of polygon a figure is?

• Find an example of a polygon in the classroom and tell what kind it is.

A **regular polygon** has all sides equal in length and all angles equal in measure.

Regular Polygons	Not Regular Polygons

All sides have equal length. All angles have equal measure.	Not all the sides have equal length. Not all the angles have equal measure.

• **What if** the quadrilateral had all sides equal? Would it be regular?

• **What if** the hexagon had all sides equal? Would it be regular?

Activity

Materials ■ dot paper ■ ruler

Draw a regular quadrilateral.

Step 1	Step 2
Mark four points that are all the same distance apart.	Connect the four points to form a regular quadrilateral.

Draw a quadrilateral that is not regular.

Step 1	Step 2
Mark four points that are not the same distance apart.	Connect the four points to form a quadrilateral that is not regular.

• How are the two quadrilaterals alike? How are they different?

Guided Practice

1. Does the figure have straight sides? Are any of the sides not connected? Is the figure a polygon?

Name the polygon. Tell whether it appears to be *regular* or *not regular*.

2.   3.   ✓ 4.    ✓ 5.

6. **TALK Math** **Explain** how you would draw a regular polygon with five sides and five angles on dot paper.

Independent Practice and Problem Solving

Name the polygon. Tell if it appears to be *regular* or *not regular*.

7.   8.    9.    10.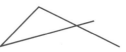

Tell if each figure is a polygon. Write *yes* or *no*. Explain.

11. 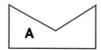   12.    13.    14.

Use dot paper to draw each polygon.

15. a triangle that is not regular

16. a pentagon that is not regular

17. a hexagon that is not regular

18. a regular quadrilateral

19. Choose the figure that does not belong. **Explain.**

USE DATA For 20–21, use the painting.

20. **Reasoning** Is the guitar in the center of Picasso's painting a polygon? **Explain** your thinking.

21. What polygons do you see in the painting?

22. **WRITE Math** **What's the Question?** Samir drew a picture with 2 triangles, 3 quadrilaterals, and 4 pentagons. The answer is 38.

▲ Pablo Picasso's
Mandolin and Guitar

 Technology
ROM Use Harcourt Mega Math, Ice Station Exploration, *Polar Planes*, Level D.

Extra Practice on page 538, Set D

23. Enrico bought a barbecue grill for $139 and a vacuum cleaner for $229. How much did Enrico spend to the nearest hundred dollars? (⊶ NS 2.1, p. 40)

24. $46.21 - 19.84 =$ (NS 2.1, p. 494)

25. Test Prep Which is a five-sided polygon?

   A triangle

   B pentagon

   C octagon

   D hexagon

26. Classify the angle as *acute*, *obtuse*, or *right*. (MG 3.5, p. 520)

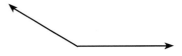

27. Test Prep How many angles does a decagon have?

   A 4

   B 5

   C 8

   D 10

Problem Solving [connects to] Art

Geometry

Architecture is the art and science of designing and building structures. Architects want to build structures that are pleasing to the eye. Architect I. M. Pei faced challenges when he designed the award winning East Wing of the National Gallery of Art on land shaped like a triangle.

Mr. Pei moved to the United States from Shanghai, China, to study architecture when he was 18. His designs won the Pritzker Prize in 1983. Mr. Pei works in the abstract form with stone, concrete, glass, and steel.

▲ I. M. Pei

1. Name the polygons you see in the aerial view of the East and West wings of the National Gallery.

2. How many sides does the polygon at the front of the photograph of the East Wing have?

▶ An aerial view of the East and West Wings

▶ The National Gallery of Art is located in Washington, D.C. This is a view of the East Wing.

OBJECTIVE: Classify triangles by the lengths of their sides and the measures of their angles.

Quick Review
Draw a regular polygon.

Vocabulary
equilateral triangle

isosceles triangle

scalene triangle

right triangle

acute triangle

obtuse triangle

Learn

PROBLEM Objects shaped like triangles are often found in nature. One example is the leaf of a cottonwood tree. What type of triangle does this cottonwood leaf appear to be?

Example Classify triangles.

Classify by the lengths of their sides.	Classify by the measures of their angles.
An **equilateral triangle** has 3 equal sides. 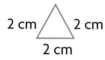 2 cm 2 cm 2 cm	A **right triangle** has 1 right angle.
An **isosceles triangle** has 2 equal sides. 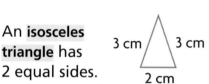 3 cm 3 cm 2 cm	An **acute triangle** has 3 acute angles.
A **scalene triangle** has no equal sides. 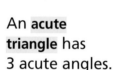 4 cm 2 cm 3 cm	An **obtuse triangle** has 1 obtuse angle. 

▲ The leaf of a cottonwood tree appears to be shaped like a triangle.

Math Idea
An equilateral triangle has 3 equal angles. An isosceles triangle has 2 equal angles. A scalene triangle has no equal angles.

So, the cottonwood leaf appears to look like an equilateral triangle and an acute triangle. You may use the corner of a piece of paper to check.

• Is the equilateral triangle above also a regular triangle?

• Which of the two sides of a right triangle are perpendicular?

Guided Practice

1. How many sides of the triangle are equal? What types of angles does the triangle have?

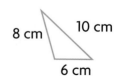

8 cm 10 cm 6 cm

MG 3.7 Know the definitions of different triangles (e.g., equilateral, isosceles, scalene) and identify their attributes. *also* MG 3.0, MG 3.5, MR 1.1, MR 2.3, MR 2.4, MR 3.2

Classify each triangle. Write *isosceles, scalene,* or *equilateral.*
Then write *right, acute,* or *obtuse.*

2. 3 in. 5 in. 4 in.

✓ 3. 9 ft 6 ft 7 ft

✓ 4. 9 yd 9 yd 9 yd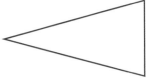

5. **TALK Math** **Explain** the difference between a right, an obtuse, and an acute triangle.

Independent Practice and Problem Solving

Classify each triangle. Write *isosceles, scalene,* or *equilateral.*
Then write *right, acute,* or *obtuse.*

6. 10 ft 10 ft 17 ft

7. 5 in. 13 in. 12 in.

8. 3 in. 3 in. 3 in.

Classify each triangle by the lengths of its sides.

9. 4 in., 4 in., 4 in.

10. 30 cm, 40 cm, 50 cm

11. 3 ft, 7 ft, 7 ft

Measure the sides of each triangle using a centimeter ruler. Then classify.

12.

13.

14.

USE DATA For 15, use the photograph.

15. **≡FAST FACT** The American crocodile's head appears to be shaped like a triangle. Classify the shape of the snout by the lengths of its sides. Write *isosceles, scalene,* or *equilateral.*

16. Draw 2 equilateral triangles that share a side. What polygon is formed? Is it a regular polygon?

17. **WRITE Math** **Explain** how a triangle can be isosceles and obtuse.

Achieving the Standards

18. Find the missing factor. (AF 1.1, p. 126)
$$\blacksquare \times 3 = 18$$

19. Which kind of polygon has 4 sides?
(MG 3.0, p. 524)

20. Round 67.83 to the nearest tenth.
(NS 2.2, p. 492)

21. **Test Prep** Which kind of triangle has 3 equal sides?

A square   **C** right

B scalene   **D** equilateral

Classify Quadrilaterals

OBJECTIVE: Identify and classify quadrilaterals.

Quick Review

Draw a quadrilateral.

Vocabulary

parallelogram

rhombus

trapezoid

Learn

Architects use quadrilaterals when designing buildings. A quadrilateral is a polygon with 4 sides and 4 angles. There are many kinds of quadrilaterals. They can be classified by their features.

Activity

Materials ■ geoboard ■ rubber bands ■ dot paper

Copy each quadrilateral on a geoboard. Use dot paper to record your work.

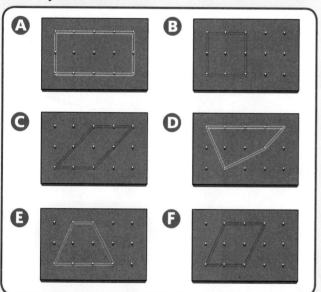

▲ PPG Place in downtown Pittsburgh, Pennsylvania has at least two special types of quadrilaterals.

• Which quadrilaterals shown above have 2 pairs of parallel sides? Which of these do you see in the photo?

• Which quadrilaterals shown above have 4 right angles? Which of these do you see in the photo?

• Which quadrilaterals shown above have 2 pairs of opposite sides that are equal? Which of these do you see in the photo?

• Which quadrilateral shown above has only 1 pair of parallel sides? Do you see this quadrilateral in the photo?

• Which quadrilateral shown above has no parallel sides? Do you see a quadrilateral with no parallel sides in the photo?

MG 3.8 Know the definition of different quadrilaterals (e.g., rhombus, square, rectangle, parallelogram, trapezoid). *also* MR 1.1, MR 2.3, MR 2.4, MR 3.2

Special Quadrilaterals

There are five special types of quadrilaterals: **parallelogram**, square, rectangle, **rhombus**, and **trapezoid**. Each has different features, and some can be classified in more than one way. Use the diagram to help you identify each type of quadrilateral.

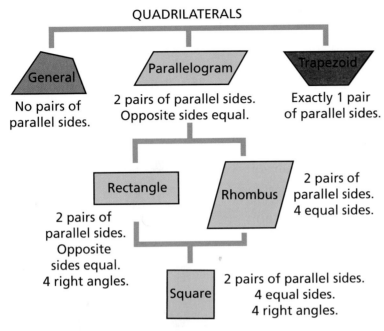

QUADRILATERALS

General
No pairs of parallel sides.

Parallelogram
2 pairs of parallel sides. Opposite sides equal.

Trapezoid
Exactly 1 pair of parallel sides.

Rectangle
2 pairs of parallel sides. Opposite sides equal. 4 right angles.

Rhombus
2 pairs of parallel sides. 4 equal sides.

Square
2 pairs of parallel sides. 4 equal sides. 4 right angles.

▲ *Geometrico* **by Mario Carreno**

- Which quadrilaterals are parallelograms? not parallelograms?
- Is a square a rhombus? a rectangle? **Explain.**

Guided Practice

1. Which are rectangles? Which is a trapezoid? Which are parallelograms?

A B C

Classify each figure in as many of the following ways as possible. Write *quadrilateral, parallelogram, rhombus, rectangle, square,* **or** *trapezoid.*

2.

3.

4.

 5.

Draw an example of each quadrilateral.

6. It has 2 pairs of equal and parallel sides.

7. It has 4 right angles.

 8. It has no parallel sides.

9. [TALK Math] **Explain** how quadrilaterals that are parallelograms are different from quadrilaterals that are not parallelograms.

Independent Practice and Problem Solving

Classify each figure in as many of the following ways as possible. Write *quadrilateral, parallelogram, rhombus, rectangle, square,* or *trapezoid.*

10. 11. 12. 13.

Draw an example of each quadrilateral.

14. It has 1 pair of parallel sides.

15. It has 4 equal sides.

16. It has 2 pairs of parallel sides.

USE DATA For 17–18, use the photograph.

17. What are the different ways to classify the quadrilateral shown on the side of the building?

18. **Pose a Problem** Write a problem using the photograph and solve it.

19. **Reasoning** Is a square also a parallelogram? **Explain.**

20. Draw three equilateral triangles. Arrange them so they form one quadrilateral. What type of quadrilateral do they form?

For 21–24, write the letters of the figures that answer the questions.

21. Which are parallelograms?

22. Which are rectangles?

23. Which are quadrilaterals?

24. **WRITE Math** **Explain** how a quadrilateral can be classified in more than one way. Give an example.

A   B   C   D

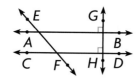 **Achieving the Standards**

25. Which line is perpendicular to $\overleftrightarrow{AB}$?
    (MG 3.1, p. 522)

26. Is a book about 8 inches wide or 8 feet wide? (Grade 3 MG 1.1)

27. $12 \div 2 =$ (O⊐ NS 3.0, p. 114)

28. Measure the length of the line segment to the nearest centimeter. (Grade 3 MG 1.1)

_____

29. **Test Prep** Which figure has only one pair of parallel sides?

    A rhombus   **C** trapezoid

    B parallelogram   **D** rectangles

CD ROM **Technology**
Use Hartcourt Mega Math, Ice Station Exploration, *Polar Planes,* Level G.

Building Models

Reading Skill Classify and categorize

◀ The historic Federal Building in the Palisades section of Balboa Park in San Diego, California, is now home to the San Diego Hall of Champions Sports Museum.

▲ The window above the entrance to the Federal Building

Students made a model of the window outlined in the photo at the right, which shows part of the Federal Building. First, they built a frame for the model. Then, they cut out squares, rectangles, and triangles for the window panes. Last, the students used a trapezoid for the window frame. How many types of quadrilaterals did the students need to make for their model?

Using the reading strategy *classify and categorize* can help you organize and understand information in math problems. Use the table to *classify and categorize* the plane figures.

Quadrilaterals			Not Quadrilaterals
No parallel sides	1 pair of parallel sides	2 pairs of parallel sides	
General			

Problem Solving Classify and Categorize to understand the problem.

1. Solve the problem above.

2. A student wants to cut out one large quadrilateral and draw smaller figures on it to make the model. How can he do this?

LESSON 7

Circles

OBJECTIVE: Identify, draw, and label parts of a circle.

Quick Review

1. 2×11
2. $14 \div 2$
3. 15×2
4. $10 \div 2$
5. $26 \div 2$

Vocabulary

circle   radius   diameter

center   chord   compass

Learn

PROBLEM A hurricane is a large tropical storm with winds that spin around the storm's "eye". The spinning winds of a hurricane form a shape that appears to look like a circle. Around what geometric point do the winds spin?

Example Identify parts of a circle.

A **circle** is a closed figure made up of points that are the same distance from the **center**. A circle can be named by its center, which is labeled with a capital letter.

center

P

Circle P

◄ A storm is called a hurricane if winds are more than 74 miles per hour.

Other parts of a circle:

A **chord** is a line segment that has its endpoints on the circle.	A **diameter** is a chord that passes through the center.	A **radius** is a line segment with one endpoint at the center of the circle and the other endpoint on the circle.
B ←endpoint, A, endpoint, P chord: $\overline{AB}$	C — P — D diameter: $\overline{CD}$	P K radius: $\overline{PK}$ The radius of a circle is half the length of the diameter.

So, the winds spin around the geometric point called the center, or eye, of the hurricane.

A **compass** is a tool used to construct circles.

HANDS ON

Activity Materials ■ compass ■ ruler

Step 1	Step 2	Step 3
Draw a point to be the center of the circle. Label it with the letter P.	Set the compass to the length of the radius you want.	Hold the compass point at point P, and move the compass to make the circle.

534

○━ MG 3.2 Identify the radius and diameter of a circle. *also* **MG 3.0, MR 1.1, MR 2.3, MR 2.4, MR 3.2**

1. A circle has a diameter of 12 inches. How would you find the length of the radius?

Construct circle J with a 5-centimeter radius. Label each of the following.

2. radius: $\overline{JA}$ ✓ 3. chord: $\overline{EF}$ ✓ 4. diameter: $\overline{BC}$

5. **TALK Math** **Explain** why a diameter can be a chord.

Independent Practice and Problem Solving

Construct circle L with a 2-inch radius. Label each of the following.

6. radius $\overline{LN}$ 7. diameter $\overline{XY}$ 8. chord $\overline{ST}$

For 9–12, use the drawing of circle Z and a centimeter ruler. Copy and complete the table.

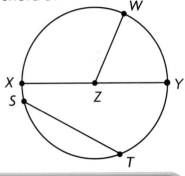

Name	Part of Circle	Length in cm
9. $\overline{ZY}$	?	
10. $\overline{ZW}$	?	

Name	Part of Circle	Length in cm
11. $\overline{ST}$	?	
12. $\overline{XY}$	?	

USE DATA For 13–15, use the diagram.

13. **≡FAST FACT** The strength of a hurricane is measured by its size and by the force of its winds. What is the radius of Hurricane A in miles?

14. What is the diameter of Hurricane B in miles?

15. How much greater is the diameter of Hurricane B than the diameter of Hurricane A?

16. **WRITE Math** **Explain** why a circle can have more than one radius.

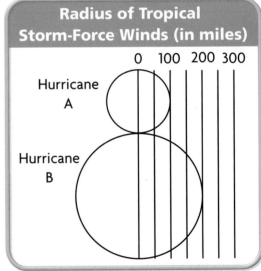

Radius of Tropical Storm-Force Winds (in miles)

Achieving the Standards

17. Make a bar graph that compares the diameters of the hurricanes in the diagram above. (SDAP 1.1, p. 346)

18. What kind of triangle always has 3 equal sides? (MG 3.7, p. 528)

19. What angle measure is $\frac{1}{4}$ of a circle? (MG 3.5, p. 520)

20. **Test Prep** What is the length of the radius of a circle with a diameter of 22 inches?

   A 11 inches   **C** 22 inches

   B 12 inches   **D** 44 inches

Problem Solving Workshop
Strategy: Use Logical Reasoning

OBJECTIVE: Solve problems by using the strategy *use logical reasoning*.

Use the Strategy

PROBLEM Jack's parents have five swimming pool diagrams shaped like plane figures. They ask Jack to sort the diagrams into two piles according to whether or not each pool has a right angle. How can the figures be sorted?

 A
 B
 C
 D
 E

Pentagon Swimming Pool Design

 Read to Understand

Reading Skill
• Classify and categorize the plane figures.
• What information is given?

Plan

• What strategy can you use to solve the problem?
  You can use logical reasoning.

Solve

• How will you solve the problem?
  Use logical reasoning.
  Make a Venn diagram with 2 overlapping ovals. Write the letter of the figure in a Venn diagram. Label one oval *2 or More Equal Sides* and the other oval *At Least 1 Right Angle*. In the area where the two ovals intersect, write the letter of the figure that fits both categories.

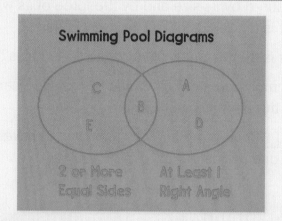

So, Jack sorted swimming pool diagrams C and E into the *2 or More Equal Sides* pile, diagrams A and D into the *At Least 1 Right Angle* pile, and diagram B into both piles.

Check

• How do you know your answer is correct?

 O━┓ **MG 3.0** Students demonstrate an understanding of plane and solid geometric objects and use this knowledge to show relationships and solve problems. *also* **MG 3.5, MG 3.7, MG 3.8, MR 1.1, MR 2.0, MR 2.3, MR 2.4, MR 3.2**

Guided Problem Solving

Choose a STRATEGY

Use Logical Reasoning

Draw a Diagram or Picture

Make a Model or Act It Out

Make an Organized List

Find a Pattern

Make a Table or Graph

Predict and Test

Work Backward

Solve a Simpler Problem

Write an Equation

1. Which of the swimming pool diagrams below have at least one set of parallel sides and at least one acute angle?

A   B   C   D   E

First, choose a strategy.

Next, draw and label a Venn diagram with overlapping ovals. Label one oval "At Least 1 Set of Parallel Sides" and the other oval "At Least 1 Acute Angle".

Then, use the diagram to classify and categorize the figures to help you organize and understand the information.

2. **What if** you were asked to find the swimming pool diagrams that had at least two sets of parallel sides and at least one obtuse angle? What would your answer be?

3. George wants to design a swimming pool that has at least two sets of parallel sides and and at least two sets of equal sides. Identify the figures shown above that appear to be like George's design?

Mixed Strategy Practice

4. Jack's aunt bought a new pool that was shaped like a diamond with two obtuse angles. Classify her pool in as many ways as possible.

USE DATA For 5, use the picture.

5. Jack and his sisters Rika and Daria combined their money to buy a snorkeling set to use in the new pool. The amounts they gave are shown in the picture. Jack gave more than Daria, and Rika gave more than Jack. How much did each person pay?

6. Rika threw 6 coins with a total value of $0.40 into the swimming pool. She had only two different kinds of coins. What coins did Rika throw into the pool?

7. *Swimmer* magazine costs $3 per issue at the newsstand. Daria will save $21 if she buys a 12-issue subscription. How much does a 12-issue subscription to the magazine cost?

8. **WRITE Math** ▶ Write down everything you know and everything you can find out about a rhombus and a square. Compare your two lists.

Set A Name the geometric term that best represents the object. (pp. 518–519)

1. fishing pole   **2.** the tip of a pen   **3.** table top   **4.** edge of ruler

Draw and label an example of each.

5. ray *AB*   **6.** plane *CDE*   **7.** line *NM*   **8.** point *P*

9. Which geometric term is a straight path of points that continues without end in both directions with no endpoints?

Set B Classify each angle as *acute*, *right*, or *obtuse*. (pp. 520–521)

1.    **2.** 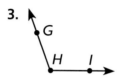   **3.** 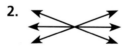   **4.**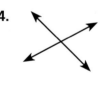

Draw and label an example of each.

5. right angle *HJW*   **6.** obtuse angle *CMG*   **7.** acute angle *RST*   **8.** obtuse angle *XYZ*

Set C Name any line relationship you see in each figure. Write *intersecting*, *parallel*, or *perpendicular*. (pp. 522–523)

1.    **2.**   **3.**   **4.**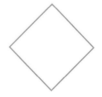

Set D Name the polygon. Tell if it appears to be *regular* or *not regular*. (pp. 524–527)

1.   **2.**    **3.**    **4.**

Tell if each figure is a polygon. Write *yes* or *no*.

5.   **6.**   **7.**   **8.**

CD ROM **Technology**
Use Harcourt Mega Math, Ice Station Exploration, *Polar Planes*, Levels A, B, D, F, G.

Set E Classify each triangle. Write *isosceles, scalene,* or
equilateral. Then write *right, acute,* or *obtuse.* (pp. 528–529)

1.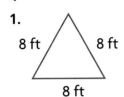
8 ft   8 ft

8 ft

2.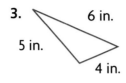
16 cm   10 cm

12 cm

3.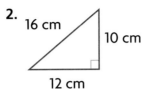
6 in.
5 in.
4 in.

4.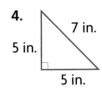
7 in.
5 in.
5 in.

Classify each triangle by the lengths of its sides.
Write *isosceles, scalene,* or *equilateral.*

5. 7 cm, 24 cm, 25 cm   6. 8 ft, 8 ft, 8 ft   7. 9 in., 9 in., 13 in.   8. 6 m, 8 m, 9 m

Set F Classify each figure in as many of the following
ways as possible. Write *quadrilateral, parallelogram,*
rhombus, rectangle, square, or *trapezoid.* (pp. 530–533)

1.

2.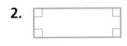

3.

4.

5. I have 4 sides and 4 angles. At least one of my angles is acute.
   What figures could I be?

Set G Use the drawing of circle Y and a centimeter ruler.
Copy and complete the table. (pp. 534–535)

	Name	Part of circle	Length in cm
1.	$\overline{AB}$	▨	▨
2.	$\overline{YA}$	▨	▨
3.	$\overline{YE}$	▨	▨
4.	$\overline{DE}$	▨	▨

5. A carousel has a diameter of 50 feet.
   What is the length of the carousel's
   radius?

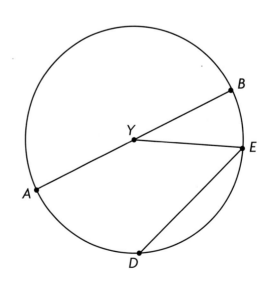

 Chapter 20 Review/Test

Check Vocabulary and Concepts

Choose the best term from the box.

1. A(n) _?_ is a polygon with 8 sides. (MG 3.0, p. 524)

2. A _?_ is a line segment with one endpoint at the center of the circle and the other endpoint on the circle. (MG 3.2, p. 534)

VOCABULARY

hexagon

octagon

radius

Check Skills

Classify each angle as *acute, right, straight,* or *obtuse.* (MG 3.5, pp.521–522)

3.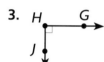

4.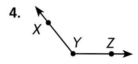

5.

6.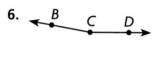

Name any relationship you see in each figure. Write *intersecting, parallel,* or *perpendicular.* (MG 3.1, pp. 522–523)

7.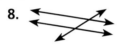

8.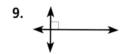

9.

10.

Classify each figure in as many ways as possible. (MG 3.7, MG 3.8, pp. 528–529, 530–533)

11.

12.

13.

14.

15.

16.

17.

18.

Check Problem Solving

Solve. (MG 3.0, MR 2.3, pp. 536–537)

19. Sort these polygons into a Venn diagram showing Regular Polygons and Quadrilaterals

20. [WRITE Math] **Explain** how to draw a Venn diagram showing 6 types of quadrilaterals sorted into two groups, one with *2 pairs of parallel sides* and one with *fewer than 2 pairs of parallel sides.*

GO ONLINE **Technology** Use *Online Assessment.*

Enrich • Use Visual Thinking
Look Closely

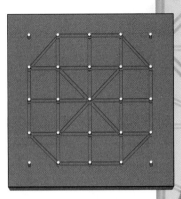

Kevin made this figure on his geoboard. How many triangles are in his figure?

To find the number of triangles in the figure, look for triangles that are made of one part, two parts, three parts, or four parts. Organize the information in a table to keep track of each type of triangle.

1 part

2 parts

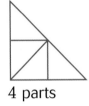

4 parts

Triangles	
Parts	Number
One Part	12
Two Parts	4
Three Parts	0
Four Parts	4

Types of triangles: $12 + 4 + 0 + 4 = 20$
So, the figure has 20 triangles.

Look Again!

What other polygons do you see in the figure? Do you see rectangles? trapezoids? pentagons? other polygons? You can find each of these polygons in the figure.

A How many squares are in the figure?

Think: Two triangles make a square.

Squares = $12 + 5 = 17$

Squares				
Parts	1	2	3	4
Number	12	0	0	5

B How many rectangles that are not squares are in the figure?

Rectangles = $16 + 8 + 4 + 4 + 2 = 34$

Rectangles that are not Squares.							
Parts	2	3	4	5	6	7	8
Number	16	8	4	0	4	0	2

Go Figure!

Copy and complete the table. Find the number of polygons in each figure.

1.

Parts	1	2	3	4	5	6
Rectangles						

2.

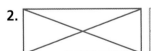

Parts	1	2	3
Triangles			

WRITE Math ▶ **Explain** how a table can help you keep track of the number of polygons in a figure.

Number Sense

1. What fraction is *best* represented by point *R* on the number line? (○━┓ NS 1.9)

   A $\frac{3}{8}$ C $\frac{6}{8}$

   B $\frac{5}{8}$ D $\frac{7}{8}$

2. The Arts Center has 28 rows of seats. There are 16 seats in each row. How many seats are in the Art Center?
   (○━┓ NS 3.3)

   A 448   C 280

   B 160   D 44

3. The table shows the changes in the population of a city during 10 years.

City Population	
Year	**Population**
1995	8,200,312
2000	8,259,417
2005	8,402,011

   What is the *best* estimate of the population in 2000 to the nearest hundred thousand? (○━┓ NS 1.3)

   A 8,000,000   C 8,300,000

   B 8,200,000   D 8,400,000

4. WRITE Math ▶ **Explain** how you could use a pattern to divide 20,000 by 5.
   (○━┓ NS 3.2)

Algebra and Functions

5. Which number is represented by *g*?
   (○━┓ AF 2.2)

   $$12 \times 6 = (7 + g) \times 6$$

   A 2   C 6

   B 5   D 12

6. Jack has two grocery bags of equal weight. Bag 1 has 4 large cans and Bag 2 has 3 small cans and 3 large cans. If he adds one large can to each bag, which bag will weigh more? (○━┓ AF 2.1)

   A bag 1

   B bag 2

   C They will both weigh the same.

   D Not enough information given

7. Look at the problem.

   $$x + y = 45$$

   If $x = 9$, what is y? (○━┓ AF 1.5)

   A 36

   B 34

   C 11

   D 5

8. WRITE Math ▶ Evaluate these expressions. **Explain** why their values are not the same. (○━┓ AF 1.2)

   $$7 \times 3 + 5 - 1 \times 10$$

   $$7 \times (3 + 5) - 1 \times 10$$

Measurement and Geometry

9. Rosa graphed ordered pairs on a grid representing the equation $y = x - 4$. She connected them with a straight line. Which ordered pair lies on that line?

   (O—π MG 2.1)

   A $(7,3)$ C $(3,7)$

   B $(8,5)$ D $(5,8)$

10. Classify this angle. (MG 3.5)

    A acute

    B right

    C obtuse

    D equilateral

11. Identify a radius of circle *T*. (MG 3.2)

    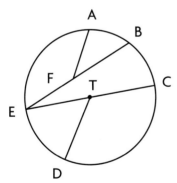

    A $\overline{AF}$ C $\overline{CE}$

    B $\overline{BE}$ D $\overline{DT}$

12. **WRITE Math** Nadia graphed the ordered pairs $(4,2)$ and $(4,9)$ on a coordinate grid. She connected the points with a line segment. **Explain** how to find the length of that line segment.

    (O—π MG 2.3)

Statistics, Data Analysis, and Probability

Test Tip **Get the information you need.**

See Item 13. Look at the answer choices to see what information is needed from the graph. You need to know how many students prefer magazines and how many prefer fiction.

13. Leonardo surveyed 32 of his classmates to find what they preferred to read. The bar graph shows his findings.

    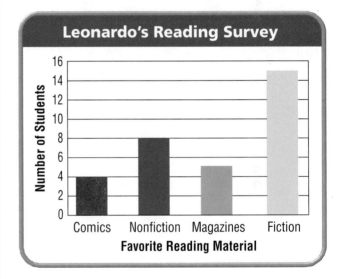

    Which statement is true? (SDAP 1.3)

    A 15 students prefer magazines.

    B 8 students prefer magazines.

    C 15 students prefer fiction.

    D 8 students prefer fiction.

14. **WRITE Math** **Explain** how to find the mode and median of a data set. How would you identify an outlier in a data set?

    (SDAP 1.2)

21 Motion Geometry

The Big Idea Two-dimensional figures can be classified according to their geometric properties.

CALIFORNIA FAST FACT

Although Death Valley is one of the hottest, driest places in North America, about 1,000 species of plants grow there. This photo shows the 100-year bloom.

Investigate

Study and describe the symmetry in each flower. Then draw a flower that has just one line of symmetry and a flower that has more than one line of symmetry. Explain how your two flowers are alike and how they are different.

Wooly daisy

Mariposa lily

GO ONLINE

Technology
Student pages are available in the Student eBook.

544

Show What You Know

Check your understanding of important skills
needed for success in Chapter 21.

▶ Compare Figures

Tell whether the two figures appear to be
the same size and shape. Write *yes* or *no*.

1.    2. 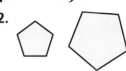   3.   4.

▶ Identify Symmetric Figures

Tell whether the blue line appears to be a line of symmetry. Write *yes* or *no*.

5. 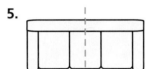   6.    7.   8.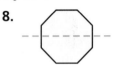

▶ Parts of a Whole

Write a fraction for each shaded part.

9.   10.   11.   12.

VOCABULARY POWER

CHAPTER VOCABULARY

angle
clockwise
congruent
counterclockwise
degree (°)

line symmetry
(bilateral
symmetry)
pattern
pattern unit
rotational symmetry
turns

WARM-UP WORDS

congruent having the same size and shape

line symmetry (bilateral symmetry) what a figure has if it can be folded about a line so that its two parts match exactly

rotational symmetry what a figure has if it can be turned around a central point and still look the same in at least two positions

1 Congruent Figures

OBJECTIVE: Identify congruent figures.

Quick Review

Identify the figure.

1. ▭ 2. ⬠

3. △ 4. ⬡

5. ⬠
_____

Vocabulary

congruent

Investigate

Materials ■ dot paper ■ scissors ■ ruler

You can place one figure on top of another figure to see whether they match.

A Draw the pairs of figures on dot paper.

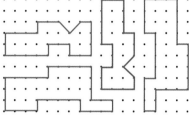

B Cut out each pair. Move them in any way to check for a match.

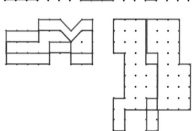

C On another piece of dot paper, draw two figures that you think will match. Cut one out and check to see if the figures match.

Draw Conclusions

1. How did you move the figures to check for a match?

2. Explain how matching pairs of figures are alike and different.

3. What can you conclude about matching pairs of figures?

4. **Application** Write a set of instructions that explains how to draw two figures on dot paper that have the same size and shape, but are turned in different directions.

A

B

MG 3.3 Identify congruent figures. *also* MR 2.0, MR 2.3, MR 2.4, MR 3.2

Connect

Figures that have the same size and shape are **congruent**.

Figures	Congruent or Not Congruent
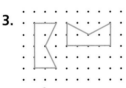 *A• •B C• •D*	Both line segments are 1 inch long. They have the same length and the same shape. They are congruent.
(two circles of different sizes)	The circles have the same shape, but their diameters are different lengths. The circles are not the same size. They are not congruent.
(two right angles F and G)	∠F and ∠G each measure 90°. The angles are the same size and shape. They will match exactly when one is placed on top of the other. They are congruent.
(two pentagons of different sizes)	The pentagons have the same shape, but they are different sizes. They are not congruent.
(two soccer balls)	The images of the soccer balls appear to be the same shape and size. They are congruent.

TALK Math

What are some objects in the classroom that are congruent and not congruent?

Practice

Tell whether the two figures are *congruent* or *not congruent*.

1. (triangle figures on dot grid)

2. (L-shape figures on dot grid)

3. (arrow/bowtie figures on dot grid)

4. (two leaves)

5. (two snowflakes)

6. (two starfish)

For 7–8, use the polygons A–E.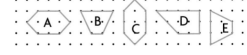

7. Which pairs of polygons are congruent? **Explain.**

8. Which pairs of polygons are not congruent? **Explain.**

9. [WRITE Math] ▶ **Explain** whether the statement *all circles are congruent* is true or false. You may include a drawing in your explanation.

2 Turns

OBJECTIVE: Relate angle measures to $\frac{1}{4}$, $\frac{1}{2}$, $\frac{3}{4}$, and full turns.

Quick Review

Name each angle. Write *acute*, *obtuse*, or *right*.

1.   2.

3.   4.

5.

Investigate

Materials ■ 2 paper strips ■ fastener

You can use turns of paper strips to explore the relationship between turns and angle measures.

The rays on a circle can be turned clockwise, the direction in which clock hands move, or counterclockwise, the opposite direction from the way clock hands move.

clockwise   counterclockwise

A

A Open the paper strip to form a 90° angle.

Is this a $\frac{1}{4}$, $\frac{1}{2}$, $\frac{3}{4}$, or full turn?

B Open the paper strip $\frac{1}{4}$ turn more to form a 180° angle.

Is this a $\frac{1}{4}$, $\frac{1}{2}$, $\frac{3}{4}$, or full turn?

C Make another $\frac{1}{4}$ turn to form a 270° angle.

Is this a $\frac{1}{4}$, $\frac{1}{2}$, $\frac{3}{4}$, or full turn?

D Move the paper strip $\frac{1}{4}$ turn to finish the circle.

Is this a $\frac{1}{4}$, $\frac{1}{2}$, $\frac{3}{4}$, or full turn?

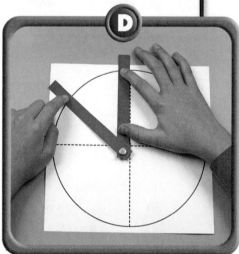
D

Draw Conclusions

1. How many degrees are in a full turn?

2. How many $\frac{1}{4}$ turns does it take to make a full turn?

3. **Synthesis** Explain the relationship between angle measures and turns.

MG 3.5 Know the definitions of a right angle, an acute angle, and an obtuse angle. Understand that 90°, 180°, 270°, and 360° are associated, respectively, with $\frac{1}{4}$, $\frac{1}{2}$, $\frac{3}{4}$, and full turns. *also* **MR 2.3, MR 2.4, MR 3.2, MR 3.3**

Connect

You can relate turns and angles measured in degrees to the hands of a clock. Let the hands of the clock represent the rays of an angle. Each minute mark on the clock represents 6°.

15 minutes elapsed   30 minutes elapsed   45 minutes elapsed

$15 \times 6° = 90°$ $30 \times 6° = 180°$ $45 \times 6° = 270°$

Minute hand has been turned 90°.

Minute hand has been turned 180°.

Minute hand has been turned 270°.

TALK Math

Explain how a 270° angle in a circle is like a $\frac{3}{4}$ turn and the span of 45 minutes on a clock.

Practice

Tell whether the rays on the circle show a $\frac{1}{4}$, $\frac{1}{2}$, $\frac{3}{4}$ or full turn. Then identify the number of degrees the rays have been turned clockwise or counterclockwise.

1.

2.

3.

4.

5.

6.

7.

✓ **8.**

Tell whether the figure has been turned 90°, 180°, 270°, or 360° clockwise or counterclockwise.

9.

10.

11.

12.

13.

14.

15.

✓ **16.**

17. **WRITE Math** ▶ **Explain** how the result of a 90° clockwise turn can look like the result of a 270° counterclockwise turn.

Symmetry

OBJECTIVE: Identify bilateral and rotational symmetry in geometric figures.

Quick Review

Lea needs two congruent tiles for a design. Which tiles appear to be congruent?

Vocabulary

line symmetry (bilateral symmetry)

rotational symmetry

Learn

PROBLEM Symmetry can be found all around us. It exists in nature, art, architecture, and music. One type of symmetry found in geometric figures is line symmetry. This sign is in the hills above Hollywood, California. Which letters in the Hollywood sign show line symmetry?

A figure has **line symmetry** if it can be folded about a line so that its two parts match exactly. Line symmetry is also called **bilateral symmetry**.

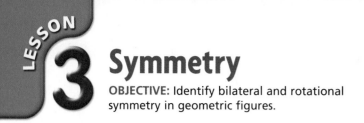

Activity 1 Explore bilateral symmetry.
Materials ■ pattern blocks ■ paper ■ scissors

Step 1	Step 2	Step 3	Step 4
Use pattern blocks or dot paper to make the letter W.	Trace the W.	Cut out the tracing.	Fold the tracing over itself.

The two parts of the folded W match exactly.

So, the W has bilateral symmetry.

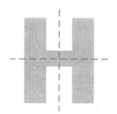   

H has 2 lines of symmetry.	L has 0 lines of symmetry.	Y has 1 line of symmetry.	O has 2 lines of symmetry.	D has 1 line of symmetry.

So, H, O, Y, W, and D have bilateral symmetry.

MG 3.4 Identify figures that have bilateral and rotational symmetry. *also* MG 3.3, MG 3.5, MR 2.3, MR 2.4, MR 3.2

Rotational Symmetry

A figure has **rotational symmetry** if it can be turned around a center point and still look the same in at least two positions.

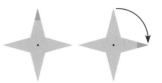

This is a $\frac{1}{4}$, or quarter, or 90° turn around a point.

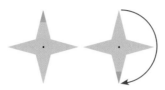

This is a $\frac{1}{2}$, or half, or 180° turn around a point.

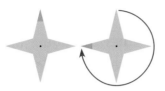

This is a $\frac{3}{4}$, or three quarter, or 270° turn around a point.

HANDS ON

Activity 2 Explore rotational symmetry.

Materials ■ tracing paper ■ pattern blocks

Step 1	Step 2	Step 3
Trace each pattern block. Place the tracing on top of the pattern block. Put an X at the top of the tracing. 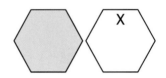	Keeping the center points together, turn the tracing to see if it matches exactly in another position.	Record the number of times the figure matches in another position until the X appears at the top of the tracing. If the X matches in more than one position, the figure has rotational symmetry.

- Which pattern blocks have rotational symmetry?
- Draw a figure that does not have rotational symmetry.

Examples Describe the symmetry each figure appears to have.

Ⓐ Bilateral Symmetry	Ⓑ Rotational Symmetry	Ⓒ Bilateral and Rotational Symmetry	Ⓓ No Lines of Symmetry
 The Transamerica Pyramid building in San Francisco has line symmetry but does not have rotational symmetry.	This letter Z has rotational symmetry. It can be turned about a central point and still look the same in at least two positions.	This triangle has 3 lines of symmetry. It can also be turned about a central point and still look the same in at least two positions.	 The shape of California on a map has no lines of symmetry.

Guided Practice

1. A line of symmetry is shown in the figure. Trace the figure on dot paper and draw 3 other lines of symmetry.

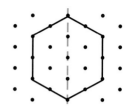

Tell whether the figure appears to have *bilateral symmetry (line symmetry)*, *rotational symmetry*, *both*, or *neither*.

2.

3.

4.

5.

6. **TALK Math** Explain how you can decide whether a figure has bilateral or rotational symmetry.

Independent Practice and Problem Solving

Tell whether the figure appears to have *bilateral symmetry (line symmetry)*, *rotational symmetry*, *both*, or *neither*.

7.

8.

9.

10.

Trace each figure. Then draw the line or lines of symmetry.

11.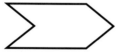

12.

13.

14.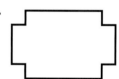

Draw a figure that has the following. Draw the line or lines of symmetry.

15. 0 lines of symmetry

16. 1 line symmetry

17. 2 lines of symmetry

18. rotational symmetry

USE DATA For 19–22, use the figures.

19. Which figure appears to have 6 lines of symmetry?

20. Which figures do not appear to have 90° rotational symmetry?

21. Which figure appears to have 180° rotational symmetry?

22. Which figure appears to have the most lines of symmetry?

A   B

C   D

Technology
Use Harcourt Mega Math, Ice Station Exploration, *Polar Planes*, Level J.

Extra Practice on page 558, Set A

23. Reasoning How could you finish this design so it would have at least one line of symmetry?

25. The word DOCK has a horizontal line of symmetry. Find two other words that have a horizontal line of symmetry.

24. What's the Error? Casey says that all regular polygons have bilateral symmetry but none have rotational symmetry. Describe and correct her error.

26. **WRITE Math** ▶ Choose and draw a figure with at least two lines of symmetry. Then write instructions that **explain** how to find the lines of symmetry.

Achieving the Standards

27. The numbers in the pattern decrease by the same amount each time. What are the next three numbers in this pattern? (**O—** NS 1.8, p. 96)

9, 7, 5, 3, 1, ■, ■, ■

28. Test Prep Which best describes the symmetry in the letter M?

  A horizontal   **C** rotational

  B vertical   **D** half turn

29. What type of lines meet at a square corner? (MG 3.1, p. 522)

30. $864 \div 6 =$ (**O—** NS 3.2, p. 270)

31. Test Prep Which best describes the symmetry in the letter Z?

  A horizontal   **C** rotational

  B vertical   **D** half turn

Problem Solving connects to Art

Kirigami

Materials ■ paper ■ scissors

Kirigami is the art of folding paper and then cutting it to make ornamental objects or designs. These designs were made by folding paper once.

Fold a sheet of paper in half and then in half again on the first fold. Cut out a hole in whatever shape you wish along the fold.

Use what you know about symmetry to predict what the design will look like. Then open the paper. Was your prediction right?

Predict what the figure will look like when the paper is unfolded. Check by folding and cutting.

1.   **2.**   **3.**   **4.**

Problem Solving Workshop
Strategy: Compare Strategies

OBJECTIVE: Compare strategies to solve problems.

Mein's Butterfly Design

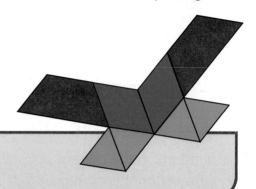

Use the Strategy

PROBLEM Mein used pattern blocks to make a butterfly. How can you prove that his butterfly has line symmetry?

Read to Understand

Reading Skill

• **Visualize what you are asked to find.**

• **What information is given?**

Plan

• **What strategies can you use to solve the problem?**

You can act it out or you can draw a diagram.

Solve

• **How can you use each strategy to solve the problem?**

Act It Out	*Draw a Diagram*
Use a mirror and pattern blocks to act it out. Copy the design and place the mirror where you think the line of symmetry is.	Trace around the pattern blocks, using a heavy dark line. Fold the design in half along the line you think is the line of symmetry.
Look into the mirror. Compare the reflection in the mirror to the side of the butterfly that is behind the mirror. If they are the same, the figure has line symmetry.	Hold the folded paper up to the light. If the two parts match exactly, the figure has line symmetry.

So, Mein's butterfly has line symmetry.

Check

• **Which strategy was more helpful, *act it out* or *draw a diagram*?**

MG 3.4 Identify figures that have bilateral and rotational symmetry. *also* MG 3.3, MR 1.0, MR 2.0, MR 2.3, MR 2.4, MR 3.0, MR 3.1, MR 3.2, MR 3.3

Guided Problem Solving

Choose a
STRATEGY

Draw a Diagram or Picture
Make a Model or Act It Out
Make an Organized List
Find a Pattern
Make a Table or Graph
Predict and Test
Work Backward
Solve a Simpler Problem
Write an Equation
Use Logical Reasoning

1. Cassie made a different butterfly, using pattern blocks. Does her butterfly have line symmetry?

   First, decide whether to act it out or to draw a diagram to check if the figure has line symmetry. Then use the strategy you choose to solve the problem.

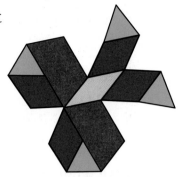

Act it Out	Draw a Diagram
Where do you think there is a line of symmetry? Place a mirror along the line and check for symmetry.	Trace around the pattern blocks to make the butterfly diagram on a sheet of paper. Fold the paper in half along the line you think is the line of symmetry.

2. **What if** Cassie wants to determine whether her design has rotational symmetry? Does her butterfly have rotational symmetry? **Explain.**

3. Buddy made the two rabbits shown at the right from pattern blocks. Are the rabbits congruent? **Explain.**

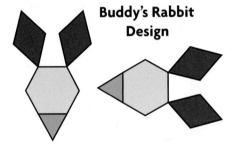

Buddy's Rabbit Design

Mixed Strategy Practice

For 4–7, use the pattern block design.

Robyn's Bat Design

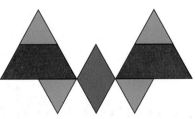

4. Robyn used pattern blocks to make a bat. Does her bat have line symmetry? **Explain.**

5. Does Robyn's bat have rotational symmetry? **Explain.**

6. Robyn wants to use this pattern block bat design to make a circle of 6 bats. How many green triangle pattern blocks does she need to make the circle of bats?

7. Robyn uses 20 red trapezoid pattern blocks to make copies of the bat design. How many bats does she make?

8. Zack made a butterfly by using 15 pattern blocks. He used one pattern block for the butterfly's body and two for antennas. How many pattern blocks did Zack use to make each wing?

9. Judy makes a bug by using 5 pattern blocks. How many pattern blocks does she use in all if she makes 5 more congruent bugs?

Geometric Patterns

OBJECTIVE: Identify, describe, extend, and make geometric patterns.

Quick Review

Write a rule for the pattern.

1. 2, 5, 8, 11
2. 2, 4, 8, 16
3. 30, 26, 22, 18
4. 80, 40, 20, 10
5. 7, 12, 9, 14, 11

Learn

PROBLEM Geometric patterns are often used as ornaments on buildings. They can be based on color, size, shape, position, and number of figures.

In geometric patterns, the pattern unit is repeated over and over. In this Victorian pattern, the unit is a leaf inside a border. The rule for this pattern is turn 180°, and then repeat.

Example Look for a possible pattern. Write a rule.

Color rule: yellow, orange, red
Size rule: small, large

So, the color rule is yellow, orange, red, and the size rule is small, large.

Activity Materials ■ 1-inch squares of tracing paper ■ colored pencils

Step 1

Draw the same simple design on five 1-inch squares of paper.

Step 2

Use turns to form a repeating pattern with the squares.

• What is the rule for this pattern?

• Where will the orange rectangle be in the eighth figure?

More Examples

A Write a rule for the pattern. Copy the pattern and draw the next figure.

■ ■■ ■■■ ■■■■

Rule: Increase the number of columns by 1.

So, the next figure is ■■■■■ .

B Write a rule for the pattern. Draw the missing figure.

○ ⬡ ⬡ __?__ ☐

Rule: Decrease the number of sides by 1.

So, the missing figure is ⬠ .

MG 3.5 Know the definitions of a right angle, an acute angle, and an obtuse angle. Understand that 90°, 180°, 270°, and 360° are associated, respectively, with $\frac{1}{4}$, $\frac{1}{2}$, $\frac{3}{4}$, and full turns. *also* MG 3.0, MR 1.1, MR 2.3, MR 2.4, MR 3.2

Guided Practice

1. Use the rule repeat *orange square, turn red trapezoid 90° clockwise* to make a repeating pattern. Then trace each figure, and color the figures to match the pattern you made.

Write a rule for the pattern. Then copy and draw the next two figures in your pattern.

2. 3.  4.

5. **TALK Math** Make a pattern that uses a rectangle and a dot. Write a rule for your pattern.

Independent Practice and Problem Solving

Write a rule for the pattern. Then copy and draw the next two figures in your pattern.

6. 7. 8.

Write a rule for the pattern. Then draw the missing figure in your pattern.

9. 10. 11.

USE DATA For 12–13, use the quilt.

12. Does a rule for the pattern appear to include color? **Explain.**

13. Write a rule for the bottom two rows of the quilt. If another row is added to the quilt, what might it look like?

14. **≡FAST FACT** Frieze patterns repeat in one direction. Describe the slides, flips, or turns in this frieze pattern.

Frieze Pattern

15. **WRITE Math** Make your own pattern. **Explain** the rule you used to make your pattern.

Achieving the Standards

16. Does the ordered pair (3,2) make $y = 2x - 4$ true? Write *yes* or *no*.
(O▬ AF 1.5, p. 394)

17. How many lines of symmetry does the letter **E** have? (MG 3.4, p. 550)

18. Name a polygon with 3 sides. (MG 3.0, p. 524)

19. **Test Prep** What will be the tenth figure in the pattern in Problem 9?

A   B   C   D

Extra Practice on page 558, Set B

 **Extra Practice**

Set A Tell whether the figure appears to have
line symmetry, rotational symmetry, both, or *neither.* (pp. 550–553)

1. 　　**2.** 　　**3.** 　　**4.**

Trace each figure. Then draw the line or lines of symmetry.

5. 　　**6.** 　　**7.** 　　**8.**

For 9–13, use figures A–F.

9. Which figure appears to have 6 lines of symmetry?

10. Which figures do not appear to have symmetry when turned 180°?

11. Which figures appear to have symmetry when turned 90°?

12. Which figure appears to have the most lines of symmetry?

13. Which figure does not appear to have either line symmetry or rotational symmetry?

A 　　B

C 　　D

E 　　F

Set B Write a rule for the pattern. Then copy and
draw the next two figures in your pattern. (pp. 556–557)

1. 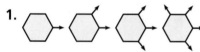　　**2.** 　　**3.**

Write a rule for the pattern. Then draw the missing figure in your pattern.

4. 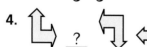　　**5.** 　　**6.**

7. What would be the eighth figure in the pattern in Problem 5?

Technology
Use Harcourt Mega Math, Ice Station
Exploration, *Polar Planes,* Levels H, I, J, M.

Congruent Match

🎾 **Volley!**

- One team is Red. The other is Yellow.

- A player from the Red team places a red counter on one figure on the game board. A teammate places a red counter on the figure that is congruent. You may then use the tracing paper to determine whether the chosen figures are congruent. If they are, leave the counters on the game board. If the figures are not congruent, remove the counters.

- Then the Yellow team places yellow counters on congruent figures.

- Teams take turns until all pairs of congruent figures have been claimed.

- The team with the greater number of counters on the game board wins.

 # Chapter 21 Review/Test

Check Vocabulary and Concepts

Choose the best term from the box.

1. **?** figures have the same shape and size. (MG 3.3, p. 546)

2. Figures that have **?** can be turned about a point and still look the same in at least two positions. (MG 3.4, p. 552)

Check Skills

Tell whether the two figures appear to be *congruent* or *not congruent*. (MG 3.3, pp. 546–547)

3.    4.    5.    6.

Tell whether the figure has been turned 90°, 180°, 270°, or 360°. (MG 3.5, pp. 548–549)

7. 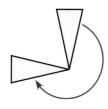   8.    9.    10.

Tell whether the figure has *line symmetry*, *rotational symmetry*, *both*, or *neither*. (MG 3.4, pp. 550–553)

11.   12.   13.   14.

Trace each figure. Then draw the line or lines of symmetry. (MG 3.4, pp. 550–553)

15.   16. 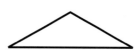   17. 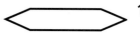   18.

Check Problem Solving

Solve. (MG 3.4, MR 1.1, pp. 554–555)

19. Write a rule for the pattern. Then copy and draw the next three figures in your pattern.

20. **WRITE Math** ► Draw the lines of symmetry for each regular polygon. Count the lines for each figure. **Explain** how to find the number of lines of symmetry in any regular polygon.

Go Technology Use *Online Assessment.*

Enrich • Use Visual Thinking
Writing in Symmetry Code

When letters are written as capitals, some have no lines of symmetry, some have 1 line, and some have 2 lines. If a letter has a line of symmetry, the line is either horizontal or vertical.

Can you read the word below by using line symmetry?

ABCDEFGHI
JKLMNOPQ
RSTUVWXYZ

Use a mirror to help you read a letter. Position the mirror along the line of symmetry. When the mirror is positioned correctly, either horizontally or vertically, the whole letter will appear.

> **Remember** A letter can have a horizontal or vertical line of symmetry or both. Some letters do not have a line of symmetry.

Activity

Read the word below.	Write the word **BABY** in symmetry code.
Draw the second half of each letter, or use a mirror. The word is **CAVE**.	Draw the top half, bottom half, right half, or left half of each letter.

Try It

Write each word in symmetry code.

1. **HAPPY**
2. **TODAY**
3. **FOOTBALL**
4. **PLAYGROUND**
5. Write a 3-letter word in which only one letter has line symmetry.
6. Write a 5-letter word in which each letter has line symmetry.

WRITE Math ▶ **Explain** how to read a word that is written in symmetry code.

Measurement and Geometry

1. How many lines of symmetry does this figure appear to have? (MG 3.4)

A 5   **C** 3

B 4   **D** 2

2. What is the length of line segment *AB* shown on the grid? (O━┓ MG 2.3)

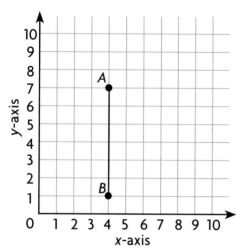

A 4 units

B 5 units

C 6 units

D 7 units

3. ⟦WRITE Math⟧ Gina draws the following triangles. (MG 3.7)

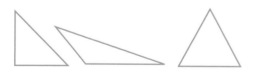

Explain two ways she can classify each triangle.

Number Sense

4. On this number line, what number does point *M* represent?

(O━┓ NS 1.8)

A ⁻4   **C** ⁺1

B ⁻3   **D** ⁺4

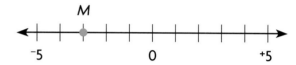

Test Tip Eliminate choices.

See item 5. Place the first digit. Since 7 is greater than 6, the first digit goes in the hundreds place. So, the quotient is a 3-digit number. Choices *C* and *D* are eliminated.

5. $7\overline{)6{,}053}$ (O━┓ NS 3.2)

A 864 r5   **C** 1,002 r3

B 954 r5   **D** 1,055 r2

6. Which statement is not true?

(O━┓ NS 4.2)

A The only factors of 9 are 1 and 9.

B The only factors of 7 are 1 and 7.

C The only factors of 5 are 1 and 5.

D The only factors of 3 are 1 and 3.

7. ⟦WRITE Math⟧ Mr. Sanchez sold 52 bike helmets at his bike store for $39 each. He estimated that he collected a total of about $2,000. Is this a reasonable estimate? **Explain** your answer. (O━┓ NS 3.3)

Algebra and Functions

8. Look at the problem below.

$$\blacksquare = \blacktriangle + 6$$

If $\blacktriangle = 9$, what is $\blacksquare$? (○━ AF 1.5)

A 27

B 18

C 15

D 3

9. What number goes in the box to make this number sentence true? (○━ AF 2.2)

$$(8 - 6) \times 7 = 2 \times \blacksquare$$

A 2

B 7

C 9

D 14

10. What is the value of the expression below?

(○━ AF 1.3)

$$(15 + 8) - (2 \times 9)$$

A 189

B 37

C 7

D 5

11. **WRITE Math** Make a function table for the equation.

$$y = 2x + 1$$

Graph the ordered pairs. **Explain** how x and y are related. (○━ AF 1.5)

Statistics, Data Analysis, and Probability

12. Hazel took a survey about the number of times students bought lunch in the cafeteria last week. The results of her survey are shown in the line plot.

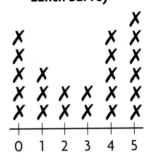

Lunch Survey

Lunches in Cafeteria

Find the median of the data above.

(SDAP 1.2)

A 1   **C** 3

B 2   **D** 4

13. **WRITE Math** Look at the line graph.

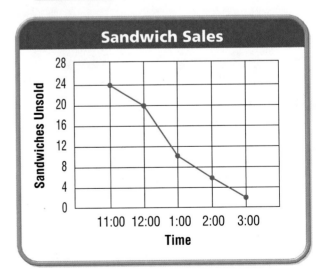

The Band Boosters' goal was to sell at least 20 sandwiches. Did they meet their goal? **Explain** how you know. (SDAP 1.3)

CHAPTER

22 Solid Figures

The Big Idea Three-dimensional figures can be classified according to their geometric properties.

Investigate

You can see three-dimensional solid figures in the design of Point Reyes National Seashore Lighthouse. Design your own lighthouse. Choose different geometric solid figures for each level.

Types of Solid Figures

cube	rectangular prism	triangular prism	triangular pyramid
square pyramid	cone	cylinder	sphere

Technology
Student pages are available in the Student eBook.

Check your understanding of important skills
needed for success in Chapter 22.

▶ **Identify Plane Figures**

Name each plane figure.

1.

2.

3.

4.

5.

6.

7.

8.

▶ **Identify Solid Figures**

Name each solid figure.

9.

10.

11.

12.

13.

14.

15.

16.

VOCABULARY POWER

CHAPTER VOCABULARY

base	rectangular pyramid
cone	sphere
cube	square pyramid
cylinder	three-dimensional
edge	triangular prism
face	triangular pyramid
net	two-dimensional
rectangular	vertex
prism	

WARM-UP WORDS

three-dimensional measured in three
directions, such as length, width, and height

face a polygon that is a flat surface of a
solid figure

edge the line segment where two faces
of a solid figure meet

vertex the point where three or more edges
meet in a solid figure; the top point of a cone

Faces, Edges, and Vertices

OBJECTIVE: Identify, classify, describe, and make solid figures.

Learn

Everywhere you look, you see solid figures—in buildings, in sculptures, and in everyday objects. Solid figures have length, width, and height, so they are **three-dimensional** figures.

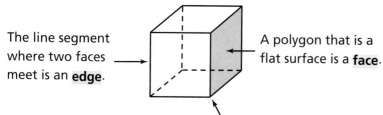

The line segment where two faces meet is an **edge**.

A polygon that is a flat surface is a **face**.

The point at which three or more edges meet is a **vertex**. The plural of *vertex* is *vertices*.

Math Idea

Solid figures can be classified by the shape and the number of their bases, faces, vertices, and edges.

Prisms and pyramids are named by the polygons that form their **bases**.

cube, square prism	rectangular prism	**triangular prism**	square pyramid	**rectangular pyramid**	**triangular pyramid**

Prisms have two congruent and parallel bases.   Pyramids have one base.

• Look at the photograph on page 567. What solid figure do you see? Look carefully at the faces of the rectangular pyramid below.

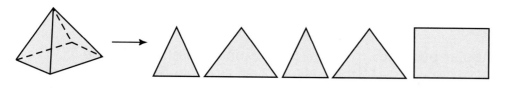

The faces are triangles and a rectangle. Name the plane figures found in the faces of the other solid figures above.

Some solid figures have curved surfaces. A cylinder has two circular bases. A cone has one circular base.

cylinder   cone   sphere

▲ The Mapparium, in Boston, Massachusetts, is a 3-story-tall stained-glass globe that has a diameter of 30 feet.

 MG 3.6 Visualize, describe, and make models of geometric solids (e.g., prisms, pyramids) in terms of the number and shape of faces, edges, and vertices; interpret two-dimensional representations of three-dimensional objects; and draw patterns (of faces) for a solid that, when cut and folded, will make a model of the solid. *also* MG 3.0, MG 3.1, MG 3.8, MR 1.1, MR 2.3, MR 2.4, MR 3.1, MR 3.2

Activity Make a cube.

Materials ■ straws ■ modeling clay or fastener material

Step 1	**Step 2**	**Step 3**
First, make a square.	Add a straw that is perpendicular to each vertex. Add a lump of clay on the other end of each straw you add.	To join the new straws, add 4 more straws to complete the cube.

- How many straws did you use to make the cube? How many edges does a cube have? How many vertices? How many faces?

- **What if** you wanted to make a triangular pyramid? How many straws would you need? How many edges does a triangular pyramid have? How many vertices? How many faces?

- Look at the edges of the cube at the right. Trace and extend $\overline{AB}$ and $\overline{DC}$ to make lines. Trace and extend $\overline{AB}$ and $\overline{BC}$ to make lines. Which pairs of lines appear to be parallel? Which pairs of lines appear to be perpendicular?

Guided Practice

1. What is the base of the solid figure at the right? Are the faces rectangles or triangles? Name the solid figure.

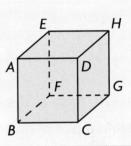

Name a solid figure that is described.

2. 12 edges

3. 4 vertices

✓ 4. fewer than 6 faces

✓ 5. 1 circular base

6. (**TALK Math**) **Explain** how cubes and rectangular prisms are alike. How are they different?

Technology
Use Harcourt Mega Math, Ice Station Exploration, *Frozen Solids*, Levels C, D, E.

Independent Practice and Problem Solving

Name a solid figure that is described.

7. 5 faces

8. all triangular faces

9. 2 circular bases

10. more than 5 vertices

Which solid figure or figures do you see in each?

11.

12.

13.

14.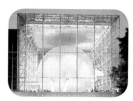

For 15–17, copy and complete the table.

	Name	Name of Faces and Number of Each	Number of Faces	Number of Edges	Number of Vertices
15.	Rectangular Prism	▦	▦	▦	▦
16.	Triangular Prism	▦	▦	▦	▦
17.	Square Pyramid	▦	▦	▦	▦

For 18–19, look at the edges of the triangular prism.

18. Name a pair of parallel line segments.

19. Name a pair of perpendicular line segments.

20. Which solid figure has more edges—a triangular prism or a triangular pyramid? How many more?

21. Reasoning If you remove a label from a soup can and look at the label, what plane figure do you see?

22. Reasoning Are all rectangular pyramids square pyramids? **Explain** your thinking.

23. **WRITE Math** ▸ **What's the Question?** The answer is 2 triangular faces and 3 rectangular faces.

 ## Achieving the Standards

24. What kind of a quadrilateral always has 4 right angles and 4 sides the same length?
(MG 3.8, p. 530)

25. $(10 - 4) + 8 = $ ▦ $+ 8$ (⟅🖛 AF 2.1, p. 88)

26. Which letter appears to have a line of symmetry?

A N R S (MG 3.4, p. 550)

27. Test Prep How many edges does a cube have?

A 6   **B** 8   **C** 9   **D** 12

Describe an Error

Y ou must understand a math concept before you can identify an error. To correct an error, you must be able to describe the error and explain how to correct it.

Michelle keeps her photographs in a box that is the shape of a rectangular prism. She told her friend that the box has 8 edges. What error did Michelle make?

Alberto wrote this description of Michelle's error.

> Michelle did not give the correct number of edges for a rectangular prism. There are 12 edges on a rectangular prism.
>
> First, I reviewed the definition of an edge. An edge is the line segment where two or more faces of a solid figure meet.
>
> Next, I counted the number of faces and vertices on the box to find the error she made. I know that a face is the flat surface of a solid figure and that it is a polygon. The box has 6 rectangular faces. I know that a vertex is a point in a solid figure at which three or more edges meet. I counted 8 vertices.
>
> So, since her answer is the number of vertices, not the number of edges, I think Michelle confused the meanings of *edge* and *vertex*.

Tips

To describe an error:

- Tell what the error is and give the correct answer.
- Review definitions of math terms that might cause the error.
- Describe what you did to figure out what the error was.
- In the last sentence of your description, state how the error happened.

Problem Solving Describe each error.

1. Edward counted the faces of a triangular prism. He counted 3 faces that are triangles.

2. Hannah says that a square pyramid has 4 faces and 4 vertices.

2 Patterns for Solid Figures

OBJECTIVE: Identify solid figures by their nets and make patterns to draw solid figures.

Quick Review

Tell the number of faces for each solid figure.

1. triangular pyramid
2. cube
3. rectangular prism
4. rectangular pyramid
5. triangular prism

Vocabulary

net

Learn

PROBLEM A **net** is a two-dimensional pattern that can be folded to make a three-dimensional figure. How can you make a net for the box shown?

You can cut apart a three-dimensional box to make a two-dimensional pattern.

  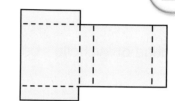

rectangular prism

a net for rectangular prism

Activity Make a net.

Materials ■ empty container, such as a cereal box ■ scissors ■ tape

Step 1	Step 2	Step 3
Cut along some of the edges until the box is flat. Be sure that each face is connected to another face by at least one edge.	Trace the flat shape on a sheet of paper. This shape is a net of the box.	Cut out the net. Fold it into a three-dimensional box. Use tape to hold it together.

• Compare your net with those of your classmates. What can you conclude?

Guided Practice

1. What shapes make up the net of a rectangular prism? How many of them are there?

MG 3.6 Visualize, describe, and make models of geometric solids (e.g., prisms, pyramids) in terms of the number and shape of faces, edges, and vertices; interpret two-dimensional representations of three-dimensional objects; and draw patterns (of faces) for a solid that, when cut and folded, will make a model of the solid. *also* **MG 3.0, MG 3.1, MR 2.0, MR 2.3, MR 2.4, MR 3.2**

Draw a net that can be cut to make a model of each solid figure.

2.   **3.**   ✅ **4.**   ✅ **5.**

6. (**TALK Math**) **Explain** how the nets for a cube and a rectangular prism are alike. How they are different?

Independent Practice and Problem Solving

Draw a net that can be cut to make a model of each solid figure.

7.   **8.**   **9.**   **10.**

Would the net make a cube? Write *yes* or *no*.

11.   **12.** **13.** **14.**

For 15–17, use the nets.

15. Which net can you use to make a triangular prism?

16. Identify the solid figure you can make with net B.

17. Which net can you use to make a triangular pyramid?

a.   **b.**   **c.**

18. Reasoning Look at the net at the right. When the net is folded, which face will be parallel to face *A*? Which faces will be perpendicular to face *B*?

19. (**WRITE Math**) **What's the Error?** Eric said the net at the right can be folded to make a triangular pyramid. Describe Eric's mistake. Then draw a net he could use to make a triangular pyramid.

Achieving the Standards

20. What is the mode of this set of data?
(SDAP 1.2, p. 326)

12, 9, 11, 9, 12, 7, 12

21. What shapes are the faces of a triangular prism? (MG 3.6, p. 566)

22. How many vertices does a square pyramid have? (MG 3.6, p. 566)

23. Test Prep What figure can you make when the net is folded on the dotted lines without overlapping?

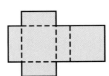

(Extra Practice) on page 578, Set B)

LESSON 3 Different Views of Solid Figures

OBJECTIVE: Identify and describe solid figures from different perspectives.

Quick Review

Antonio cuts out a net with 5 faces and tapes it together to make a triangular prism. What shapes are the faces?

Learn

PROBLEM Objects look different when viewed from different directions. If you draw the front view of the Capitol Records building, what shape would you draw?

HANDS ON

Activity Draw different views.

Materials ■ solid wooden cylinder

- Look at the top of the cylinder. Draw the top view.
- Look at the front of the cylinder. Draw the front view.
- Look at the side of the cylinder. Draw the side view.

So, you would draw a rectangle.

▲ The Capitol Records building in Hollywood, California is shaped like a cylinder.

You can identify solid figures by the way they look from different views.

Examples Use different views to identify each solid figure.

A top view   front view   side view

The top view shows that the base is a triangle and that the faces come together at a point.

The front and side views show the solid figure looks like a triangle.

So, this solid figure is a triangular pyramid.

B top view   front view   side view

The top view shows that the base is a circle and that the top comes to a point.

The front and side views show the solid figure looks like a triangle.

So, this solid figure is a cone.

ERROR ALERT

You cannot always identify a solid figure from just one view or two views.

- Which solid figure looks like a circle from any direction?
- How are the views of a rectangular prism and a cylinder alike? How are they different?
- **Reasoning** What plane figure could be used to describe the shadow of a building that is shaped like a rectangular prism?

 MG 3.6 Visualize, describe, and make models of geometric solids (e.g., prisms, pyramids) in terms of the number and shape of faces, edges, and vertices; interpret two-dimensional representations of three-dimensional objects; and draw patterns (of faces) for a solid that, when cut and folded, will make a model of the solid. *also* MG 3.0, MR 1.1, MR 2.0, MR 2.3, MR 2.4, MR 3.2

Guided Practice

1. All of the faces of a rectangular prism are rectangles. What is the top view of a rectangular prism? The front view? The side view?

Name the solid figure that has the following views.

✓2. top view   front view   side view   ✓3. top view   front view   side view

4. **TALK Math** Choose an object in your classroom. **Draw** the top, front, and side views.

Independent Practice and Problem Solving

Name the solid figure that has the following views.

5. top view   front view   side view   6. top view   front view   side view

Draw the top, front, and side views of each solid figure.

7.   8.   9. 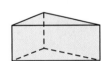   10.

For 11–12, use the different views.

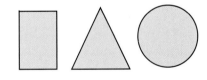

11. What solid figures have a rectangle as one of the views?

12. What solid figures have a triangle as one of the views?

13. **WRITE Math** **Explain** how you can identify whether a prism is a rectangular prism, a triangular prism, or a cube by its views.

Achieving the Standards

14. How many faces does a cube have?
(MG 3.6, p. 566)

15. Mark solved this problem. $9\overline{)218}$ with answer 24 r2
What expression can he write to check his answer? (O—n NS 3.4, p. 270)

16. Would you measure the length of a football field in yards or miles? (Grade 3 MG 1.1)

17. **Test Prep** Which figure does not have a circle as one of its views?

A cone   C cylinder

B cube   D sphere

Problem Solving Workshop
Strategy: Make a Model

OBJECTIVE: Solve problems by using the strategy *make a model.*

Learn the Strategy

It can be difficult to understand what is being described in a problem.
Sometimes you can use a model to show the actions in a problem.

A model can show the actions in a problem.

Amy baked 16 brownies. She took half of them to school for the bake sale. She gave Jamie half of what was left. She wants to know how many brownies are left.

Action 1
← Amy baked 16 brownies.

Action 2
← She took half to school.

Action 3

↑ She gave Jamie half of what was left.   ↑ Brownies left.

A model can show a situation before and after a change.

Tyrell built a prism that was 3 cubes long, 3 cubes wide, and 3 cubes high. Then he removed 6 cubes. What might his model look like now?

3 cubes   3 cubes

3 cubes

Before   **After**

A model can show the relationships in a problem.

Susan wants to know how many cubes she will need to make the next cube in this pattern.

1   2   3

When making a model, reread the problem to make sure that your model shows each part of the problem.

TALK Math
How is the strategy *make a model* like the strategy *act it out*? How are they different?

574

MG 3.6 Visualize, describe, and make models of geometric solids (e.g., prisms, pyramids) in terms of the number and shape of faces, edges, and vertices; interpret two-dimensional representations of three-dimensional objects; and draw patterns (of faces) for a solid that, when cut and folded, will make a model of the solid. *also* MG 3.0, MR 1.0, MR 1.1, MR 2.0, MR 2.3, MR 2.4, MR 3.0, MR 3.1

Use the Strategy

PROBLEM After John studied the buildings of architect Moshe Safdie, he used cubes to design a building. He drew a top view, a front view, and a side view of his building. How many cubes will John need to build his model?

top view   front view   side view

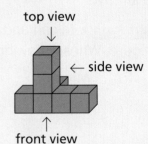

▲ Moshe Safdie designed these buildings for Expo 67, the 1967 World's Fair in Montreal, Canada. They were made from 354 stacked cubes.

Read to Understand

- **What are you asked to find?**
- **What information is given? Is there information you will not use? If so, what?**

Plan

- **What strategy can you use to solve the problem?**

Reading Skill

You can make a model to help you visualize the details in the problem.

Solve

- **How can you use the strategy to solve the problem?**

  You can use cubes to make a model of the building.

  First, build the top view. The model shows 5 cubes.

  Next, stack cubes to match the front view. The model now shows 7 cubes.

  Finally, decide whether the model matches the side view. If necessary, make any changes.

  Since the side view matches, no changes are needed.

  So, John will need 7 cubes to build his model.

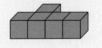

top view
↓
← side view
↑
front view

Check

- **How can you check your model?**
- **What other strategy could you use to solve the problem?**

1. Antoine made the model shown at the right by using 9 cubes. Draw a top view, a front view, and a side view on grid paper.

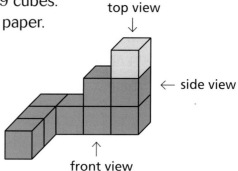

top view ↓

← side view

↑ front view

First, draw the top view.

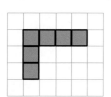

Next, look at the figure from the front, and draw what you see.

Finally, look at the figure from the side, and draw the side view.

2. **What if** the yellow cube was removed? Which of the three views would change? Draw each new view on grid paper, and label the view.

3. Alicia used the fewest possible cubes to make a building, whose views are shown at the right. How many cubes did she use?

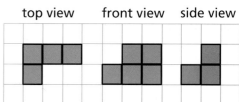

top view   front view   side view

Problem Solving Strategy Practice

Make a model to solve.

4. Sandra has 40 cubes. She uses half of them to make a building. She gives Jeffrey half of what is not used so that he can make a building. If Jeffrey uses 8 cubes in his building, how many of the 40 cubes are still not used?

5. Riko has 60 cubes. She builds a staircase beginning with 1 cube, then 3, then 6, then 10, and so on. When she has made the largest possible staircase, how many cubes will she have left over?

6. WRITE Math ▸ Micah and Natalie each drew the front view of this figure. Whose drawing is correct? **Explain.**

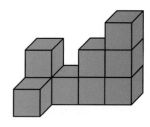

Micah   Natalie

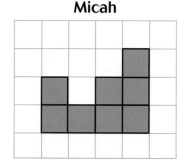
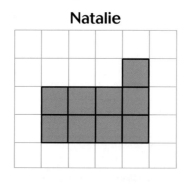

Mixed Strategy Practice

7. Ellie wants to sort the objects on the table according to their shapes. Make an organized list of how she can sort the objects.

USE DATA For 8–10, use the cube in the picture.

8. What if Rubik had designed a puzzle that was 6 cubes long, 6 cubes wide, and 6 cubes high, how many small squares would it have on one face?

9. The center of Rubik's puzzle is missing one small cube. How many small cubes make up the puzzle?

10. ≡FAST FACT When Rubik was designing his puzzle, he first used colored paper squares to cover each small square on the outside of the big cube. How many small paper squares did he need?

11. Pose a Problem Write a problem about a model made with 10 cubes.

12. Open-Ended Suppose you have 40 cubes. How could you make a pattern with some or all of the cubes? Describe the pattern.

CHALLENGE YOURSELF—
Use the figure at the right. There are no hidden cubes in the figure. Do not make a model to solve.

13. How many more cubes would be needed to change the model into a cube that has 16 small squares on each face? **Explain.**

14. Suppose you change the figure into a prism 2 cubes long, 2 cubes wide, and 2 cubes high. Would you need to add cubes or take cubes away? How many?

Choose a
STRATEGY

Draw a Diagram or Picture
Make a Model or Act It Out
Make an Organized List
Find a Pattern
Make a Table or Graph
Predict and Test
Work Backward
Solve a Simpler Problem
Write an Equation
Use Logical Reasoning

▼ Erno Rubik invented one of the best-selling puzzles in history in 1974. The small cubes can be arranged in more than 43,000,000,000,000,000,000, or 43 quintillion, different ways. Only 1 of the ways is correct.

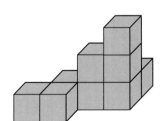

 **Extra Practice**

Set A Name a solid figure that is described. (pp. 566–569)

1. 6 congruent faces   **2.** 4 triangular faces   **3.** one circular base   **4.** 12 edges

Which solid figure or figures do you see in each?

5.    **6.**    **7.**    **8.**

9. All of my faces are triangles. What solid figure am I?

Set B Draw a net that can be cut to make a model of each solid figure. (pp. 570–571)

1.   **2.** 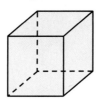   **3.** 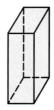   **4.**

For 5–6, use the nets.

5. Which net can you use to make a paperweight with a square base and 4 triangular faces.

6. Identify the solid figure you can make with net C.

a.   b.   c.

Set C Draw the top, front, and side views of each solid figure. (pp. 572–573)

1.   **2.**    **3.**    **4.**

5. What solid figures have a rectangle for all of the views?

6. What solid figures have a square for at least one of the views?

7. What solid figures have a circle for at least one of the views?

Technology
Use Harcourt Mega Math, Ice Station Exploration, *Frozen Solids*, Levels A, B, C, D, E, F, G, H, M.

Build the View

Builders!

2 teams, at least 2 players on each team

Building Blocks!

- Index cards (15)
- Centimeter cubes (15 for each team)
- Two-color counters

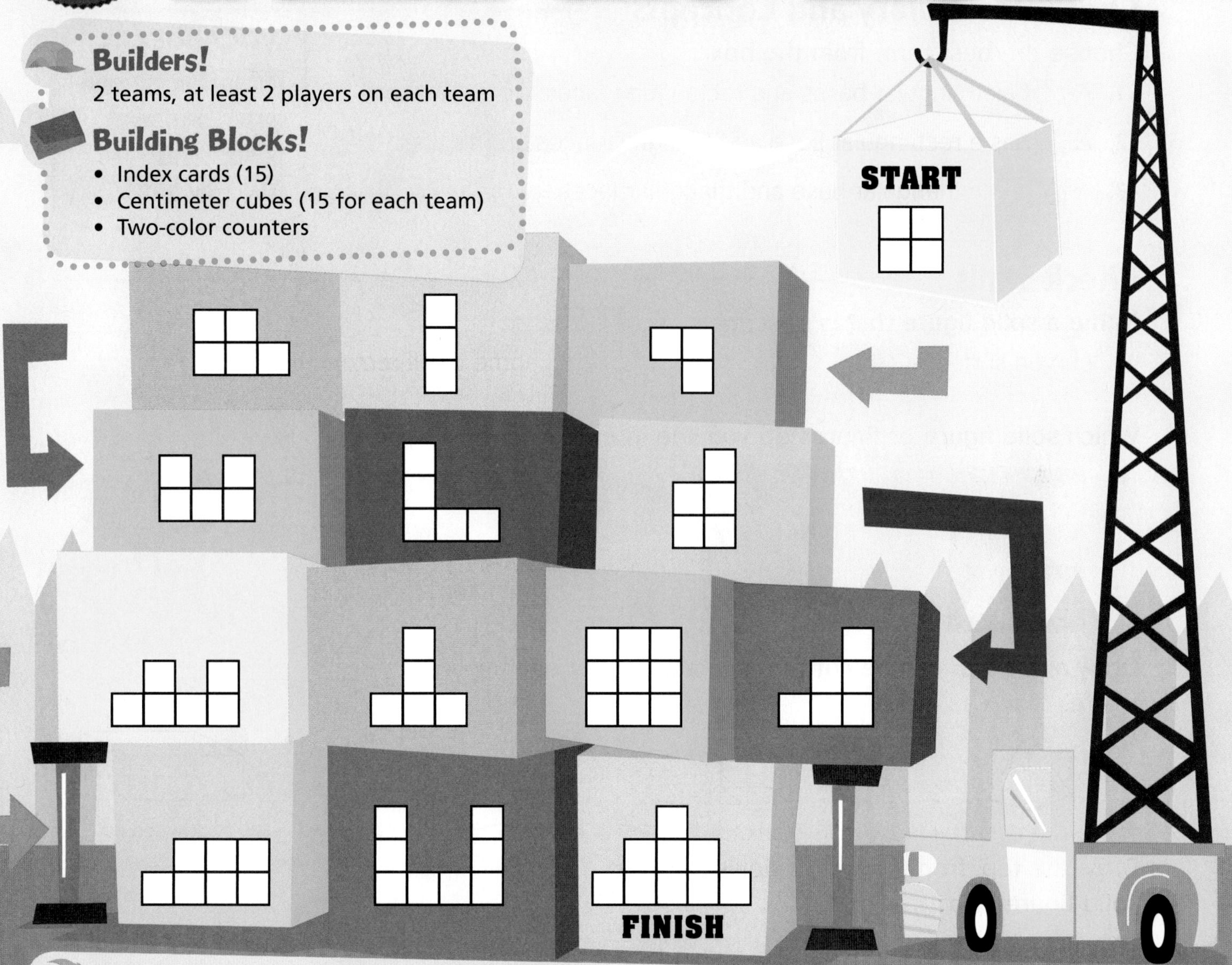

START

FINISH

Build!

- Shuffle the cards. Place them facedown in a stack.

- Begin with the space labeled START. Teams take turns drawing the top card. Teams use cubes to build a figure that has the view shown on the space and can be described by the view on the card.

- If both teams agree that the figure is correct, the team places a counter on that space. If the figure does not have that view, the other team draws the next view card and tries to build a figure. If neither team can build a figure with that view, the space is out of play.

- Move to the next space on the board. The team draws the top card and continues to play.

- Play ends with the space labeled FINISH. The team with the greater number of counters on the board wins.

 Chapter 22 Review/Test

Check Vocabulary and Concepts

Choose the best term from the box.

1. A _?_ has triangular bases and rectangular faces. (MG 3.6, p. 566)

2. A _?_ has a rectangular base and triangular faces. (MG 3.6, p. 566)

3. A _?_ has a triangular base and triangular faces. (MG 3.6, p. 566)

Check Skills

Name a solid figure that is described. (MG 3.6, pp. 566–569)

4. curved surfaces

5. some or all rectangular faces

Which solid figure or figures do you see in each? (MG 3.6, pp. 566–569)

6.

7.

8.

9.

Draw a net that can be cut to make a model of each solid figure. (MG 3.6, pp. 570–571)

10.

11.

12.

13.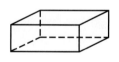

Draw the top, front, and side views of each solid figure. (MG 3.6, pp. 572–573)

14.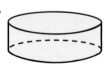

15.

16.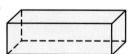

17.

Check Problem Solving

Solve. (MG 3.6, MR 1.0, pp. 574–577)

18. Byron built a rectangular prism with 24 cubes. Draw a top view, a front view and a side view on grid paper.

19. Melanie used 8 cubes to build this figure. Draw the top view, side view, and front view.

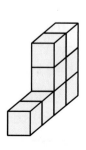

20. **WRITE Math** Explain how the views would change if the yellow cube were removed from this figure.

GO ONLINE Technology Use *Online Assessment.*

Enrich • Patterns in Prisms and Pyramids
Faces, Vertices, and Edges

Leonhard Euler was a Swiss mathematician who lived in the 1700s. He discovered that the numbers of faces, vertices, and edges in prisms and in pyramids are related.

▲ Leonhard Euler
(1707–1783)

Prisms	Pyramids
sides = number of sides on the base	sides = number of sides on the base
sides + 2 = faces	sides + 1 = faces
sides × 2 = vertices	sides + 1 = vertices
sides × 3 = edges	sides × 2 = edges

Examples

A Find the number of faces, vertices, and edges of a cube.

A cube has 4 sides on the base.

$4 + 2 = 6$ faces

$4 \times 2 = 8$ vertices

$4 \times 3 = 12$ edges

So, a cube has 6 faces, 8 vertices, and 12 edges.

B Find the number of faces, vertices, and edges of a square pyramid.

A square pyramid has 4 sides on the base.

$4 + 1 = 5$ faces

$4 + 1 = 5$ vertices

$4 \times 2 = 8$ edges

So, a square pyramid has 5 faces, 5 vertices, and 8 edges.

Try It

Tell how many faces, vertices, and edges each figure has.

1. rectangular pyramid

2. rectangular prism

3. triangular pyramid

4. triangular prism

5. **Challenge** If you read that a prism had 8 faces, 8 vertices, and 12 edges, how would you know that the information is incorrect?

WRITE Math ▶ **Explain** how to find the number of edges on any pyramid or prism if you know the number of sides on the base.

Multiple Choice

1. Which of the following appears to be an acute angle? (MG 3.5, p. 520)

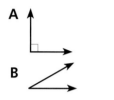
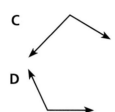

2. The figure below is an example of what type of quadrilateral? (MG 3.8, p. 530)

   A rectangle

   B square

   C parallelogram

   D trapezoid

3. A $\frac{1}{4}$ turn is equal to a turn of how many degrees? (MG 3.5, p. 548)

   A 90°   **C** 180°

   B 270°   **D** 360°

4. Which of the following figures appears to be congruent to this figure? (MG 3.3, p. 546)

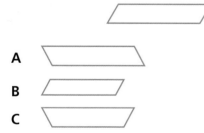

5. Which pair of lines appears to be perpendicular? (MG 3.1, p. 522)

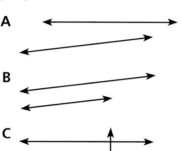

6. Which statement about this figure is true? (MG 3.4, p. 550)

   A The figure has no symmetry.

   B The figure has only line symmetry.

   C The figure has only rotational symmetry.

   D The figure has line and rotational symmetry.

7. Look at the pattern for the solid figure.

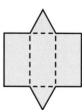

Which solid figure will it form when folded on the dotted lines without overlapping? (MG 3.6, p. 570)

 **Technology** Use *Online Assessment.*

8. Which of the following triangles is an equilateral triangle? (MG 3.7, p. 528)

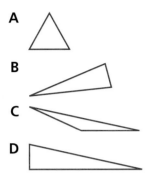

A

B

C

D

9. Elvis carved the model below from a bar of soap. How many edges does this figure have? (MG 3.6, p. 566)

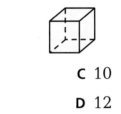

A 6   **C** 10

B 8   **D** 12

10. Jan drew a circle and measured the length of the radius. How can she find the length of the diameter of the circle?

(MG 3.2, p. 534)

A Add 2 to the length of the radius.

B Double the length of the radius.

C Triple the length of the radius.

D Divide the length of the radius by 2.

11. Which solid does this figure form?

(MG 3.6, p. 570)

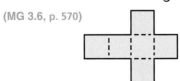

A triangular prism

B cube

C triangular pyramid

D square pyramid

Short Response

12. Classify this figure in as many ways as possible. (MG 3.8, p. 530)

13. Look at the figure below. Draw a line of symmetry. (MG 3.4, p. 550)

14. Draw a top view, front view, and side view of a rectangular prism. (MG 3.6, p. 572)

15. Draw a circle. Draw and label a diameter and a radius. (MG 3.2, p. 534)

16. Look at the map. Which streets appear to be parallel to each other? (MG 3.1, p. 522)

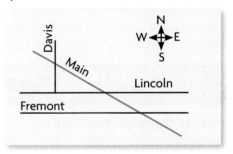

Extended Response ▏WRITE Math▏

17. **Explain** why it is not possible to draw an equilateral scalene triangle. (MG 3.7, p. 528)

18. **Explain** the differences between a triangular pyramid and a triangular prism. Draw an example of each. (MG 3.6, p. 566)

19. What time will it be when the minute hand has rotated 180°? **Explain** how you know.

(MG 3.5, p. 548)

Looking at Toys

SYMMETRIC TOYS

You can find board games about all kinds of topics, including California history. For example, there are games about the gold rush, California missions, and San Francisco. Many toys and games have symmetry. They may have line symmetry, rotational symmetry, both, or neither. What kind of symmetry does the Native American peg game board in the picture have?

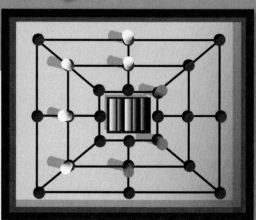

The game in the picture is a wooden peg board game based on a game played by California Native Americans.

FACT·ACTIVITY

Look at these pictures of toys. Tell whether each picture appears to have *line symmetry*, *rotational symmetry*, *both*, or *neither*.

1 Game piece

2 Electronic game

3 Number cube

Each picture shows part of a toy. Copy and complete each picture to show line symmetry.

4 Robot

5 Football

6 Guitar

7 [WRITE Math] Describe a toy or game not pictured here that has symmetry. **Explain** how you know.

GAME BOARDS

Chess and backgammon are games that have been played all over the world for centuries. Backgammon is one of the oldest games in recorded history. Early versions were played in Mesopotamia thousands of years ago. Chess was developed in India in the sixth century. Both are games of strategy for two people. Plane figures and solid figures were used in the design of these board games.

FACT·ACTIVITY

Suppose a large toy company asks you to design a new board game.

❶ Draw the game board. Decide what plane figures you want to use. Then color your design.

  ► Name the plane figures you used.

  ► Describe how you combined the plane figures to make your game board.

  ► Does your design show a pattern? Explain.

  ► Does your game board show symmetry? Explain.

❷ Draw one of your game pieces. Show the front and top views.

8 Measurement and Probability

Math on Location

① Different woods are cut to exact lengths, widths, and depths and glued together to form the guitar's body.

② Custom guitars have different shapes. Each surface has a different length and width or area.

③ Choices of shape, wood, finish, number of strings and electronics result in many different guitars.

VOCABULARY POWER

TALK Math

What math is used in the **Math on Location** photographs? What units would you use to measure the perimeter of a guitar? Why?

READ Math

REVIEW VOCABULARY You learned the words below when you learned about measurement. How do these words relate to **Math on Location**?

centimeter a metric unit for measuring length or distance; 100 centimeters = 1 meter

foot a customary unit used for measuring length or distance; 1 foot = 12 inches

perimeter the distance around a figure

WRITE Math

Copy and complete the word association tree below. Use what you know about measurement to complete the tree.

Technology
Multimedia Math Glossary link at
www.harcourtschool.com/hspmath

23 Perimeter and Area

The Big Idea Attributes of two- and three-dimensional figures can be measured.

CALIFORNIA FAST FACT

At Anderson Marsh State Historic Park, in California, you can see archaeological sites. Some are more than 10,000 years old. The sites tell us how ancient people lived.

Investigate

Archaeologists divide a dig area into smaller work sites. Suppose you are working on a dig. Your job is to lay out work sites with the areas shown in the table. Use models. In how many different ways could you set up each site?

Archaeological Dig Sites

Work Site	Area (in square feet)
A	20
B	24
C	30
D	36

Technology
Student pages are available in the Student eBook.

Check your understanding of important skills
needed for success in Chapter 23.

▶ **Add Whole Numbers**

Find the sum.

1. $5 + 6 + 8 =$ ▪
2. $9 + 4 + 2 + 7 =$ ▪
3. $2 + 6 + 9 + 1 + 5 =$ ▪

4. $11 + 27 + 18 =$ ▪
5. $5 + 46 + 28 + 31 =$ ▪
6. $53 + 21 + 66 + 34 =$ ▪

▶ **Multiplication Facts**

Find the product.

7. $8 \times 3 =$ ▪
8. $9 \times 8 =$ ▪
9. $12 \times 5 =$ ▪
10. $5 \times 6 =$ ▪

11. $6 \times 6 =$ ▪
12. $9 \times 7 =$ ▪
13. $8 \times 5 =$ ▪
14. $7 \times 4 =$ ▪

▶ **Expressions and Variables**

Find the value of the expression.

15. $a \times 3$ if $a = 9$
16. $7 + f + 18$ if $f = 13$

17. $7 \times c$ if $c = 5$
18. $s + 13 + 46$ if $s = 8$

19. $26 + 34 + r + 78$ if $r = 23$
20. $6 \times g$ if $g = 12$

21. $38 + h + 51$ if $h = 10$
22. $y \times 8$ if $y = 8$

VOCABULARY POWER

CHAPTER VOCABULARY

area	mass
capacity	perimeter
formula	square unit
length	weight

WARM-UP WORDS

perimeter the distance around a figure

formula a set of symbols that expresses a
mathematical rule

area the number of square units needed to cover
a surface

1 Customary Measurements

OBJECTIVE: Estimate, measure, and change customary units of length, weight, and capacity.

Learn

Linear units of measure are units used to measure length, width, height, and distance. The customary units of length include **inch (in.)**, **foot (ft)**, **yard (yd)**, and **mile (mi)**.

Common objects can be used as benchmarks for customary units of length. For example, the length of your thumb from the first knuckle to the tip is about 1 inch, the length of a license place is about 1 foot, the length of a baseball bat is about 1 yard, and the distance you can walk in 20 minutes is about 1 mile.

Activity 1 **Materials** ■ 5 classroom objects ■ inch ruler

- Estimate the lengths of 5 classroom objects to the nearest inch. Record your work in a table like the one shown.
- Use a ruler to measure the length of each object to the nearest $\frac{1}{2}$ inch and $\frac{1}{4}$ inch. Record your measurements.

Length			
Object	Estimate	Actual Measurement to the nearest	
		$\frac{1}{2}$ in.	$\frac{1}{4}$ in.
?	■	■	■

Weight is the measure of how heavy an object is. Customary units of weight include **ounce (oz)**, **pound (lb)**, and **ton (T)**.

Common objects can be used as benchmarks for customary units of weight. For example, 5 new pencils weigh about 1 ounce, 4 sticks of butter weigh about 1 pound, and a small car weighs about 1 ton.

1 ton

Activity 2 **Materials** ■ spring scale ■ classroom objects

- Estimate the weights of 5 classroom objects in ounces or pounds. Record your work in a table like the one shown.
- Now weigh each object using a spring scale. Record the actual weight in the table.

Weight			
Object	Unit (oz/lb)	Estimate	Actual measurement
dictionary	lb	3 lb	■
?	■	■	■

O─┒ AF 1.5 Understand that an equation such as $y = 3x + 5$ is a prescription for determining a second number when a first number is given. *also* **O─┒ NS 3.0, AF 1.1, MR 1.0, MR 1.1, MR 2.0, MR 2.3, MR 2.4, MR 2.5, MR 3.2**

More About Customary Measurement

Capacity is the measure of the amount a container can hold when filled. Customary units of capacity include **cup (c)**, **pint (pt)**, **quart (qt)**, and **gallon (g)**.

Commonly used containers can be used as benchmarks for customary units of capacity.

1 cup　　1 pint　　1 quart　　1 gallon

Activity 3

Materials ■ measuring cup ■ 1-pint, 1-quart and 1-gallon containers ■ other containers

- Estimate the capacity of 5 containers. Record your work in a table like the one shown.

- Now measure the capacity of each container. Record the actual capacity in the table.

Capacity			
Container	Unit	Estimate	Actual Measurement
basket	gallon	■	■
?	■	■	■

You can change from one customary unit of measure to another. To change from a larger unit to a smaller unit you need more smaller units, so multiply. To change from a smaller unit to a larger unit you need fewer larger units, so, divide.

 Use multiplication or division.

A Multiply.

6 lb = ■ oz　Think: 1 lb = 16 oz

6 × 16 = 96

6 lb = 96 oz

B Divide.

16 pt = ■ qt　Think: 1 qt = 2 pt

16 ÷ 2 = 8

16 pt = 8 qt

ANOTHER WAY　**Use an equation.**

You can use the equation $y = f \div 3$ to complete the table.

Feet, f	Yards, y
18	■
27	■
36	■

$y = f \div 3$

$y = 18 \div 3$, so $y = 6$

$y = 27 \div 3$, so $y = 9$

$y = 36 \div 3$, so $y = 12$

Feet, f	Yards, y
18	6
27	9
36	12

Customary Units of Length

1 foot (ft) = 12 inches (in.)
1 yard (yd) = 3 feet, or 36 inches
1 mile (mi) = 5,280 feet, or 1,760 yards

Customary Units of Weight

1 pound (lb) = 16 ounces (oz)
1 ton (T) = 2,000 pounds (lb)

Customary Units of Capacity

1 pint (pt) = 2 cups (c)
1 quart (qt) = 2 pints
1 gallon (gal) = 4 quarts

Guided Practice

1. How many pounds are equal to 5 tons?

Choose the more reasonable measurement.

2.

20 ft or 20 in.

3.

2 c or 2 qt

4.

6 oz or 6 T

Write an equation you can use to complete each table. Then copy and complete each table.

5.

Pints, *p*	8	10	12	14	16
Cups, *c*	16	▦	24	▦	▦

✓**6.**

Inches, *i*	36	72	108	144	180
Yards, *y*	▦	2	▦	▦	▦

7. **TALK Math** Which is greater, the number of cups needed to fill a pitcher or the number of quarts? **Explain.**

Independent Practice and Problem Solving

Choose the more reasonable measurement.

8.

5 gal or 5 pt

9.

200 lb or 2 T

10.

56 yd or 56 mi

Write an equation you can use to complete each table. Then copy and complete each table.

11.

Ounces, *o*	32	48	64	80	96
Pounds, *p*	▦	3	▦	▦	6

12.

Yards, *y*	4	5	6	7	8
Feet, *f*	12	15	▦	▦	▦

Estimate to the nearest inch. Then measure to the nearest $\frac{1}{2}$ inch and $\frac{1}{4}$ inch.

13.

14.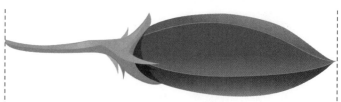

Order the measurements from least to greatest.

15. 30 in.; 2 ft; 3 yd; 1 mi

16. 4 pt; 3 qt; 1 gal; 9 c

17. 20 oz; 1 lb; 2,500 lb; 1 T

⭐**Algebra** Complete. Tell whether you *multiply* or *divide*.

18. 7 yd = ▦ in.

19. ▦ pt = 4 qt

20. 32 oz = ▦ lb

USE DATA For 21–24, use the journal entry.

21. About how many quarts of water were in the pool?

22. **Reasoning** Could the bristlecone pine tree have been 22 feet tall? **Explain** why or why not.

23. **Pose a Problem** Look back at Problem 22. Use the information in the journal to write another problem like it.

24. **WRITE Math** ▸ Did some of the fossils weigh more than 1 pound? **Explain.**

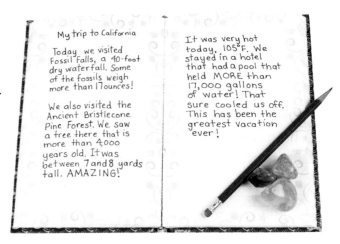

My trip to California

Today we visited Fossil Falls, a 40-foot dry waterfall. Some of the fossils weigh more than 17ounces!

We also visited the Ancient Bristlecone Pine Forest. We saw a tree there that is more than 4,000 years old. It was between 7 and 8 yards tall. AMAZING!

It was very hot today, 105°F. We stayed in a hotel that had a pool that held MORE than 17,000 gallons of water! That sure cooled us off. This has been the greatest vacation ever!

Achieving the Standards

25. $56 \times 100 =$ (⊶ NS 3.2, p. 202)

26. Matt spent 5 times as much on books than Ken spent. What expression shows how much Matt spent? (AF 1.1, p. 150)

27. How many faces, edges, and vertices does this figure have? (MG 3.6, p. 568)

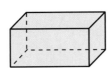

28. **Test Prep** How many pints are in 4 quarts?

A 2   C 8

B 6   D 16

29. **Test Prep** The length of Drew's bedroom is 21 feet. How long is Drew's room in yards? **Explain.**

MATH POWER   Problem Solving and Reasoning

MEASUREMENT It is important to use the right tool and know what unit to use when you are measuring.

An *odometer*, *trundle wheel*, or *pedometer* can be used to measure distances greater than 1 yard.

odometer

trundle wheel

pedometer

Tell which tool and which unit you would use to measure each.

1. distance across the U.S.
2. capacity of a pitcher
3. length of a marking pen
4. weight of a cell phone

Tools and Units	
Length	
• ruler	• inch
• odometer	• foot
• yardstick	• yard
• measuring wheel	• mile
• pedometer	
Weight	
• spring scale	• ounce
	• pound
	• ton
Capacity	
• measuring cup	• cup
• 1-pint, 1-quart, 1-gallon containers	• pint
	• quart
	• gallon

2 Metric Measurements

OBJECTIVE: Estimate, measure, and convert metric units of length, mass, and capacity.

Quick Review

Sally drank a glass of orange juice. Did she drink 250 mL or 120 L?

Learn

Length can be measured using metric units of measure. Metric units of length include **millimeter (mm)**, **centimeter (cm)**, **decimeter (dm)**, **meter (m)**, and **kilometer (km)**.

Common objects can be used as benchmarks for metric units of length. For example, the thickness of a dime is about 1 millimeter, the width of your index finger is about 1 centimeter, the width of an adult's hand is about 1 decimeter, the width of a door is about 1 meter, and the distance you can walk in 14 minutes is a kilometer.

Vocabulary

millimeter (mm)	meter (m)
centimeter (cm)	mass
decimeter (dm)	gram (g)
kilometer (km)	kilogram (kg)
liter (L)	milliliter (mL)

Activity 1 Materials ■ 5 classroom objects ■ centimeter ruler

- Estimate the length of 5 classroom objects to the nearest centimeter. Record your work in a table like the one shown.
- Use a ruler to measure the length of each object to the nearest centimeter and nearest millimeter. Record your measurements.

Length			
Object	Estimate	Actual Measurement to the nearest	
		cm	mm
desk	■	■	■

Mass is the amount of matter in an object. Metric units of mass include **gram (g)** and **kilogram (kg)**.

Common objects can be used as benchmarks for metric units of mass. For example, the mass of a dollar bill is about 1 gram, and the mass of a baseball bat is about 1 kilogram.

A dollar bill has the mass of about 1 gram.

Activity 2 Materials ■ balance ■ gram and kilogram masses ■ classroom objects

- Estimate the mass of 5 classroom objects in grams or kilograms. Record your work in a table like the one shown.
- Now find the mass of each object using a balance. Record the actual mass in the table.

Mass			
Object	Unit (g/kg)	Estimate	Actual Mass
chalk	g	■	■
?	■	■	■

 **AF 1.5** Understand that an equation such as $y = 3x + 5$ is a prescription for determining a second number when a first number is given. *also* **NS 3.0, AF 1.1, MR 1.0, MR 1.1, MR 2.0, MR 2.3, MR 2.4, MR 2.5, MR 3.2**

More About Metric Measurement

Capacity can be measured using metric units. Metric units of capacity include **milliliter (mL)** and **liter (L)**.

Commonly used containers can be used as benchmarks for metric units of capacity.

1 milliliter   1 liter

Activity 3

Materials ■ milliliter dropper ■ metric measuring cup ■ 1-liter container, other containers

- Estimate the capacities of 5 containers. Record your work in a table like the one shown.
- Now measure the capacity of each container. Record the actual capacity in the table.

Capacity			
Container	Unit (mL,L)	Estimate	Actual Capacity
spoon	mL	■	■
__?__	■	■	■

You can change from one metric unit of measure to another. Remember to multiply when changing from a larger unit to a smaller unit, since you need more smaller units, and to divide when changing from a smaller unit to a larger unit since you need fewer larger units.

Metric Units of Length

1 centimeter (cm) = 10 millimeters (mm)
1 decimeter (dm) = 10 centimeters (cm)
1 meter (m) = 1,000 millimeters
1 kilometer (km) = 1,000 meters

ONE WAY   Use multiplication or division.

A Multiply.

6 kg = ■ g

Think: 1 kg = 1,000 g

$6 \times 1,000 = 6,000$

6 kg = 6,000 g

B Divide.

900 cm = ■ dm

Think: 1 dm = 10 cm

$900 \div 10 = 90$

900 cm = 90 dm

Metric Units of Mass

1 kilogram (kg) = 1,000 grams (g)

Metric Units of Capacity

1 liter (L) = 1,000 milliliters (mL)

ANOTHER WAY   Use an equation to complete a table.

You can use the equation $d = m \times 10$ to complete the table.

Meters, m	Decimeters, d
7	■
8	■
9	■

$d = m \times 10$

$m = 7 \times 10$, so $d = 70$

$m = 8 \times 10$, so $d = 80$

$m = 9 \times 10$, so $d = 90$

Meters, m	Decimeters, d
7	70
8	80
9	90

Guided Practice

1. How many centimeters are in 35 decimeters?

Choose the more reasonable measurement.

2.

14 kg or 14 g

3.

5 mL or 5 L

✓4.

4 mm or 4 dm

Write an equation you can use to complete each table. Then copy and complete each table.

5.

Liters, *l*	7	8	9	10	11
Millimeters, *m*	7,000	▪	9,000	▪	▪

✓6.

Centimeters, *c*	1,100	1,000	900	800	700
Meters, *m*	▪	10	▪	▪	▪

7. **TALK Math** Which is more accurate, a measurement to the nearest half centimeter or nearest millimeter? **Explain.**

Independent Practice and Problem Solving

Write an equation you can use to complete each table. Then copy and complete each table.

8.

Grams, *g*	2,000	3,000	4,000	5,000	6,000
Kilograms, *k*	▪	3	▪	▪	▪

9.

Centimeters, *c*	9	10	11	12	13
Millimeters, *m*	90	▪	▪	120	▪

Estimate to the nearest centimeter. Then measure to the nearest half centimeter and nearest millimeter.

10.

11.

Order the measurements from greatest to least.

12. 1,500 g; 2 kg; 750 g; 1 kg   **13.** 70 dm; 2,000 mm; 500 cm   **14.** 2 L; 300 mL; 1 L; 100 mL

Choose the more reasonable measurement.

15.

8 cm or 8 m

16.

2 mL or 2 L

17.

5,000 kg or 5,000 g

★ **Algebra** Complete. Tell whether you *multiply* or *divide*.

18. 8,000 mL = ▪ L   **19.** ▪ cm = 4,000 mm   **20.** 16 kg = ▪ g

USE DATA For 21–23, use the table.

21. About how many milliliters of water would be needed for Tembo to fill her trunk twice?

22. How many grams less than 1 kilogram is Max ?

23. **What's the Error?** Lin thinks that one of Pocahontas's quills are about half the length of Dottie. Is he correct?

Animals at the San Diego Zoo	
Animal	**Fact**
Pocahontas the Porcupine	Quills are about 30 centimeters long.
Dotti and Tevi the Clouded Leopard Sisters	Each is about 1.5 meters long.
Max the Salmon Crested Cockatoo	Has a mass of about 550 grams.
Tembo the African Elephant	Can hold about 14 liters of water in her trunk.

Achieving the Standards

24. $56 + 68 + 101 =$ (⊙━ NS 3.1, p. 58)

25. When Stan's laptop is open, the angle between the screen and the keyboard makes a 95° angle. What type of angle is this? (MG 3.5, p. 520)

26. Jason drank 32 cups of water. How many quarts did he drink? (⊙━ AF 1.5, p. 590)

27. **Test Prep** Mara's desk is 50 decimeters long. How many centimeters long is her desk?

   A 5 centimeters   **C** 500 centimeters

   B 50 centimeters   **D** 5,000 centimeters

28. **Test Prep** Betsy is going on a trip. Her suitcase weighs 5 kilograms. How many grams does it weigh? **Explain.**

MATH POWER Problem Solving and Reasoning

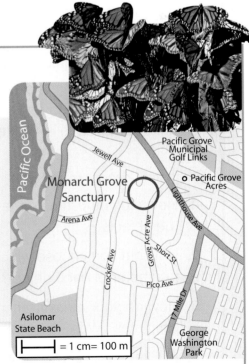

MEASUREMENT A map scale represents the relationship between distance shown on a map and the actual distance.

The map shows Pacific Grove, California, where the Monarch Grove Sanctuary is located. Every fall, thousands of monarch butterflies migrate to the sanctuary.

The scale on this map is 1 cm = 100 m. This means that every 1 centimeter shown on the map represents 100 meters of actual distance.

On the map, the distance from the sanctuary to Pacific Grove Acres is about 2 cm. So, the actual distance is about 200 m.

Find the actual distance from the sanctuary.

1. golf links
2. George Washington Park
3. Pacific Ocean

3 Estimate and Measure Perimeter

OBJECTIVE: Estimate and measure perimeter.

Quick Review

What is the length of the pen cap to the nearest centimeter?

Investigate

Materials ■ string ■ scissors ■ centimeter ruler ■ meterstick ■ 3 classroom objects

You can use string and a ruler to help you estimate and measure the perimeter of an object or a figure. **Perimeter** is the distance around a figure.

Vocabulary

perimeter

A Make a table to record the names, units, estimates, and actual measurements of 3 classroom objects.

Perimeter of Classroom Objects			
Object	Unit	Estimate	Actual Measurement
?	■	■	■
?	■	■	■

B Choose the unit you would use to measure the perimeter of each object. Then estimate and record the estimated perimeter of each object.

C Now use string to measure the perimeter of each object. Place string around the outside of the object. Cut or mark the string to show the perimeter of each object. Then measure and record the length of the string in the units you used to estimate.

Draw Conclusions

1. How did you estimate the perimeter of the objects?

2. How did you choose which unit to use to measure the perimeter of each object?

3. How do your measurements compare to your estimates? Were your estimates reasonable? Explain.

4. **APPLICATION** What unit would you use to meaure the perimeter of your classroom? Explain.

MG 1.0 Students understand perimeter and area. *also* MR 2.0, MR 2.3, MR 2.4, MR 2.5, MR 3.2

Connect

You can find the perimeter of a rectangle on a geoboard or dot paper by counting the number of units on each side.

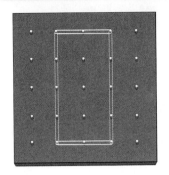

This rectangle is 2 units wide and 4 units long. So, the perimeter of the rectangle is 4 units + 2 units + 4 units + 2 units, or 12 units.

TALK Math
Explain how to find the perimeter of a square with sides 5 units long.

Practice

Use string to estimate and measure the perimeter of each object.

1. a sheet of notebook paper
2. an index card
3. a chalkboard eraser
✓ 4. your desk

Find the perimeter of each figure.

5.
6.
7.
8.
✓ 9.

Use dot paper or grid paper to draw a rectangle with the given perimeter. Then record the lengths of the sides.

10. 10 units
11. 20 units
12. 14 units
13. 12 units
14. 24 units
15. 16 units
16. 18 units
17. 26 units

Zach is helping his dad build a rectangular sandbox that has a perimeter of 24 feet.

18. On dot or grid paper, draw the different rectangular sandboxes that Zach and his dad could build. Label the length of each side.

19. **WRITE Math** Zach and his dad decide to make a sandbox that is square. What dimensions could they use? **Explain.**

ALGEBRA

Find Perimeter

OBJECTIVE: Use a formula to find perimeter.

Quick Review

1. $16 + 19 + 21$
2. $(2 \times 4) + (2 \times 10)$
3. $55 + 31 + 65 + 29$
4. $(2 \times 12) + (2 \times 11)$
5. $9 + 13 + 8 + 17 + 22$

Vocabulary

formula

Learn

Julio is putting a stone border around his garden. How many feet long is the border of Julio's garden?

To find how many feet of stones Julio needs, find the perimeter of the garden.

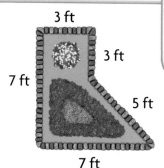

3 ft

3 ft

7 ft

5 ft

7 ft

ONE WAY Add the lengths of the sides.

$3 \text{ ft} + 3 \text{ ft} + 5 \text{ ft} + 7 \text{ ft} + 7 \text{ ft} = 25 \text{ ft}$

So, Julio needs 25 feet of stones.

A **formula**, or mathematical rule, can also be used to find perimeter. The number of variables used in a formula is the same as the number of sides in a figure.

ANOTHER WAY Use a formula.

A Since Figure A has 5 sides, there will be 5 variables in the formula.

$P = $ sum of the lengths of the sides
$P = a + b + c + d + e$
$P = 20 + 17 + 12 + 15 + 18$
$P = 82$

Think: Use a variable to represent the length of each side.

Figure A

17 cm   20 cm
    b   a
12 cm c   e 18 cm
      d
    15 cm

So, the perimeter of Figure A is 82 cm.

B Since Figure B has 6 sides, there will be 6 variables in the formula.

$P = $ sum of the lengths of the sides
$P = a + b + c + d + e + f$
$P = 15 + 12 + 16 + 20 + 17 + 10$
$P = 90$

Think: Use a variable to represent the length of each side.

Figure B

15 m
    a   f 10 m
             17 m
12 m b   e
      c   d 20 m
16 m

So, the perimeter of Figure B is 90 m.

MG 1.4 Understand and use formulas to solve problems involving perimeters and areas of rectangles and squares. Use those formulas to find the areas of more complex figures by dividing the figures into basic shapes. *also* O┓ NS 3.0, AF 1.1, AF 1.4, MG 1.0, MR 2.0, MR 2.3, MR 2.4, MR 3.2

Perimeter of Rectangles and Squares

You can use special formulas to find the perimeter of a rectangle and a square.

Polygon	Perimeter	Formula
Rectangle *w* *l* ▭ *l* *w*	Perimeter = length + width + length + width or Perimeter = 2 × length + 2 × width	$P = l + w + l + w$ or $P = (2 \times l) + (2 \times w)$
Square *s* *s* ▢ *s* *s*	Perimeter = side + side + side + side or Perimeter = 4 × side	$P = s + s + s + s$ or $P = 4 \times s$

Examples Use a formula.

A 5 in. / 9 in. / 9 in. / 5 in.
$P = (2 \times l) + (2 \times w)$
$P = (2 \times 9) + (2 \times 5)$
$P = 18 + 10$
$P = 28$

The perimeter is 28 in.

B 12 cm / 12 cm
$P = 4 \times s$
$P = 4 \times 12$
$P = 48$

The perimeter is 48 cm.

- If you know the perimeter of a square, how can you find the length of each side?

Guided Practice

1. Add the lengths of the sides. What is the perimeter of this figure?

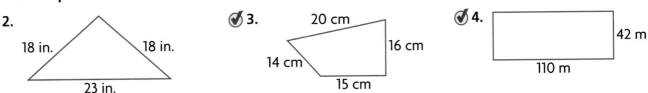

25 ft
13 ft
14 ft
13 ft
25 ft

Find the perimeter.

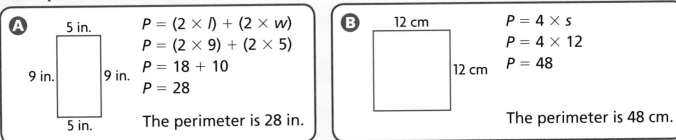

2. 18 in. / 18 in. / 23 in.

✓ 3. 20 cm / 16 cm / 14 cm / 15 cm

✓ 4. 42 m / 110 m

5. **TALK Math** All the sides of a pentagon are 6 decimeters long. **Explain** how you can use multiplication to find the perimeter.

Find the perimeter.

6.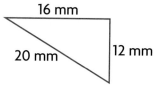
16 mm
20 mm 12 mm

7.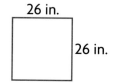
26 in.
26 in.

8.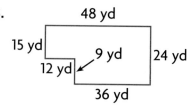
48 yd
15 yd
9 yd 24 yd
12 yd
36 yd

9.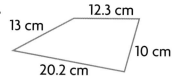
12.3 cm
13 cm
10 cm
20.2 cm

10.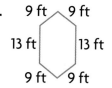
9 ft   9 ft
13 ft   13 ft
9 ft   9 ft

11.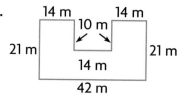
14 m   14 m
10 m
21 m   21 m
14 m
42 m

Use a formula to find the perimeter.

12.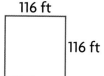
116 ft
116 ft

13. 11 dm
33 dm

14.
34 in.
20 in.

Measure with a centimeter ruler to find each perimeter.

15.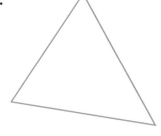

16.

17.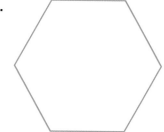

18. Reasoning A square and an equilateral triangle both have a perimeter of 36 centimeters. Draw and label the figures.

19. Reasoning The perimeter of a rectangle is 30 inches. The width of the rectangle is 5 inches. What is the length?

20. Mary is putting a brick edge around her patio. Her patio is shaped like a hexagon. Each side of the patio is 7 meters long. The bricks she is using are 50 centimeters long. How many bricks does Mary need? **Explain.**

21. WRITE Math ▸ **Sense or Nonsense** Tim wants to frame a square painting. One side of the painting is 4 feet long. He says 5 yards of frame is enough for the painting. Does this make sense? **Explain.**

Technology
Use Harcourt Mega Math, Ice Station Exploration, *Polar Planes,* Level P.
CD ROM

22. $9 \times 7 =$ ⬚ (⬚ NS 3.0, p. 116)

23. Jimmy cut 4 pieces of ribbon that were each 30 centimeters long. Does he have more or less than 1 meter of ribbon cut?

(Grade 3 ⬚ MG 1.4)

24. Kyle had $3.27. Then his mom gave him $7.50. How much money does Kyle have now? (NS 2.1, p. 500)

25. Test Prep What is the perimeter of this figure?

A 53 inches

B 66 inches

C 106 inches

D 520 inches

13 in.

40 in.

26. Test Prep What is the perimeter of a square with sides 16 centimeters long? **Explain.**

MATH POWER Problem Solving and Reasoning

ALGEBRA A **regular polygon** is a polygon that has all sides the same length. You can use a formula to find the perimeter.

Since all sides of a regular polygon are the same length, use the formula $P = n \times s$, in which n is the number of sides in the polygon and s is the length of each side.

Examples Find the perimeter.

A pentagon

12 in.

$P = n \times s$
$P = 5 \times 12$ ← There are 5 sides in a
$P = 60$ in.   pentagon so replace n with 5. The sides are each 12 inches long, so replace s with 12.

The perimeter is 60 inches.

B octagon

21 m

$P = n \times s$
$P = 8 \times 21$ ← There are 8 sides in an
$P = 168$ m   octagon so replace n with 8. The sides are each 21 meters long, so replace s with 21.

The perimeter is 168 meters.

Write a formula and use it to find the perimeter.

1.  35 mm

2. 16 ft

3. 25 yd

4. 19 km

Problem Solving Workshop
Skill: Use a Formula

OBJECTIVE: Solve problems by using the skill *use a formula*.

105 m

clocktowe

the palms marketplace

Use the Skill

PROBLEM Jonny is walking around the Palms Marketplace at the Los Angeles County Fair. The map shows the rectangular path Jonny walked. The perimeter of the marketplace is 490 meters. What is the length of the unknown side?

▲ Fairplex, in Pomona, California, has been the site of the LA County Fair since 1922.

Use a formula to find the length of a figure when you know the width and the perimeter.

$P = (2 \times l) + (2 \times w)$

$490 = (2 \times l) + (2 \times 105)$

Use the formula for the perimeter of a rectangle.
Replace *P* with 490 and *w* with 105.

$490 = (2 \times l) + 210$

Multiply.

$490 - 210 = (2 \times l)$

Work backward since subtracting 210 is the inverse operation to adding 210.

$280 = 2 \times l$

$280 \div 2 = l$

Work backward since dividing 2 is the inverse operation to multiplying by 2.

$140 = l$

So, the length of the unknown side is 140 meters.

140 m

broadwa

280 m

Think and Discuss
Use a formula to solve.

a. Marie jogged around her neighborhood square block. The perimeter of the block is 2,400 feet. What is the length of each side of the block?

140 m

b. Jonny is walking around the perimeter of the carnival. The map shows the distance he has already walked. The perimeter of the carnival is 1,050 meters. How many meters does Jonny have left to walk?

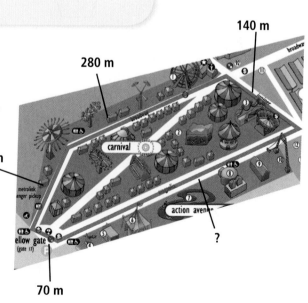

carnival

action avenue

metrolink
senger pickup

ellow gate
(gate 17)

?

70 m

O━ **AF 1.4** Use and interpret formulas (e.g., area = length × width or A = lw) to answer questions about quantities and their relationships. *also* O━ NS 3.0, O━ NS 3.1, AF 1.1, MG 1.4, MR 1.0, MR 2.0, MR 2.3, MR 2.4, MR 2.5, MR 2.6, MR 3.0, MR 3.1, MR 3.2, MR 3.3

Guided Problem Solving

Use a formula to solve.

1. The perimeter of the path around the museum's property grounds at Fairplex is about 1,120 meters. The property is about 70 meters wide. What is the length of the property?

    First, decide what formula to use.
    What is the formula for the perimeter of a rectangle?

    Then, replace the variables with the known values.
    What values are given in the problem?

    Finally, solve the equation for the unknown value.
    What operations do you need to use?

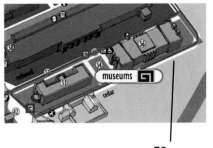

70 m

2. **What if** the museum property was a square with a perimeter of 360 yards? What would be the length of each side?

3. Stacy's bike path forms a pentagon. One side is 700 meters, one side is 650 meters, one side is 730 meters, and one side is 670 meters. The perimeter of the path is 3 km. What is the length of the fifth side of the bike path?

Mixed Applications

4. The perimeter of Loretta's rectangular room is 44 feet. The width of her room is 10 feet. What is the length?

5. Becky needs 5 yards of fabric to make curtains for her room. The fabric costs $7.00 per yard. How much will Becky spend?

USE DATA For 6–9 use the table.

6. The Van Ness family buys 2 sand dollars, 1 conch shell, and 3 king's crown shells. How much does the family spend?

7. **Reasoning** Harrison wants to buy 3 types of shells and spend the least amount of money. Should Harrison buy a bag of assorted shells or 3 individual shells? **Explain.**

8. Is $200 enough to buy 10 shell necklaces? **Explain** how you can use estimation to find out.

9. **WRITE Math** Mary buys 4 seashells. Is there enough information to find how much Mary spends? **Explain.**

Seashell Crafts Booths	
Item	Cost
Conch Shell	$13
Painted Sand Dollar	$15
King's Crown Shell	$10
Bag of Assorted Shells	$36
Shell Necklace	$21

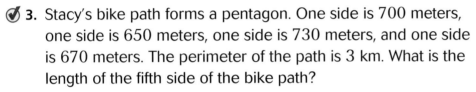
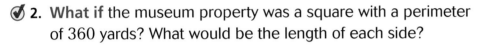

6 Estimate Area

OBJECTIVE: Estimate and find area.

Quick Review

1. $15 + 5 + 6$
2. $7 \div 2$
3. $8 + 5\frac{1}{2}$
4. $13 + 12 + 8$
5. $11 \div 2$

Investigate

Materials ■ centimeter square tiles

Area is the number of square units needed to cover a surface. A **square unit (sq un)** is a square that is 1 unit long and 1 unit wide.

1 unit
1 unit

Vocabulary

area   square unit (sq un)

To find the area of a figure, count the number of square units inside the figure.

You can use square tiles to estimate the area of a figure.

A Draw a right triangle.

B Use square tiles to fill the inside of the triangle. Each tile represents 1 square centimeter.

C Count the number of tiles. The area of the triangle is the number of tiles it took to exactly fill the inside of the triangle. What is the estimated area of your triangle in square centimeters?

D Draw 3 more triangles of different sizes and shapes. Repeat Steps A–C to estimate the area of the triangles. What is the estimated area of each triangle in square centimeters?

Draw Conclusions

1. Number your triangles 1–4. Then order the estimated areas from least to greatest.

2. What if you used square inch tiles? How would it affect the measure of estimated area of each triangle? **Explain.**

3. **Analysis** Were you able to cover the entire inside of each triangle with tiles? **Explain** what this tells you about the accuracy of your measurements.

MG 1.0 Students understand perimeter and area. *also* O—n NS 3.0, MG 1.1, MR 2.0, MR 2.3, MR 2.4, MR 2.5, MR 3.2

Connect

You can also estimate the area of a figure drawn on grid paper.

Sometimes a figure on a grid has units that are almost full or less than half full. To estimate the area, you can count each square that is full, almost full, and half-full.

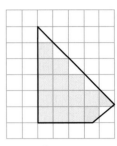

1 square unit = 1 square foot

Example Estimate the area.

The green squares are full. There are 13 full squares.

The orange squares are almost full. There are 2 almost-full squares.

The yellow squares are half-full.

There are 4 half-full squares. $4 \div 2 = 2$ full squares

The sum of the squares counted is $13 + 2 + 2 = 17$.

So, the area of Figure A is about 17 square feet.

TALK Math
Why is your answer an estimate rather than an exact answer? Explain.

Practice

Estimate the area of each figure. Each unit stands for 1 sq m.

1.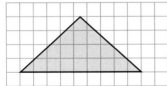

✓ 2.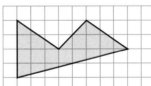

✓ 3.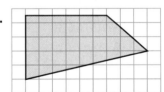

Draw each figure on grid paper. Then estimate the areas.

4. circle

5. triangle

✓ 6. oval

7. a figure with only straight lines

8. a figure with curved paths and straight lines

9. a figure with no straight lines

USE DATA For 10–12, use the diagram.

10. About how many square yards is the area of the closet?

11. Which is greater, the area of the family room or the area of the living room? **Explain.**

12. **WRITE Math** ▸ Rosa says the total area of the part of the house shown is 84 square yards. Is Rosa correct? **Explain.**

Floor Plan

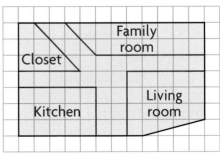

1 square unit = 1 square yard

LESSON 7

ALGEBRA

Find Area

OBJECTIVE: Measure and find area by counting, multiplying, and using a formula.

Quick Review

1. 16×10
2. 12×21
3. 44×23
4. 8×13
5. 23×11

Learn

PROBLEM Danny is tiling the floor in his kitchen. The floor is a rectangle 14 feet wide and 8 feet long. How many square feet of tile does Danny need?

To find how many square feet of tile Danny needs, find the area of the floor. There are different ways to find the area of a rectangle.

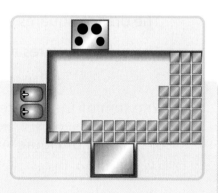

ONE WAY Count square units.

Step 1

To represent the floor, draw a rectangle 8 feet long and 14 feet wide on grid paper. Let each square represent 1 square foot.

Step 2

Estimate the number of squares inside the rectangle. Then count the squares. There are 112 squares, so the area of the floor is 112 feet.

So, Danny needs 112 square feet of tile.

- **What if** the rectangle was 12 feet long by 7 feet wide? How could you use grid paper to find the area?

OTHER WAYS

A Use multiplication.

To find the area of a rectangle, multiply the number of rows by the number of units in each row.

number of rows	number in each row	area
↓	↓	↓
3	× 5	= 15 square units

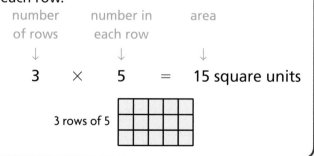

3 rows of 5

So, the area is 15 square units.

B Use a formula.

The formula for the area of a rectangle is Area = length × width, or $A = l \times w$.

Use the formula to find the area of the rectangle.

$A = l \times w$
$A = 3 \times 5$

$A = 15$

5 yd

3 yd   3 yd

5 yd

So, the area of the rectangle is 15 square yards.

MG 1.4 Understand and use formulas to solve problems involving perimeters and areas of rectangles and squares. Use those formulas to find the areas of more complex figures by dividing the figures into basic shapes.
also O—┑ NS 3.0, AF 1.4, MG 1.1, MR 2.3, MR 2.4, MR 3.2

Area of Rectangles and Squares

You can use special formulas to find the area of a rectangle and a square.

Polygon	Area	Formula
Rectangle 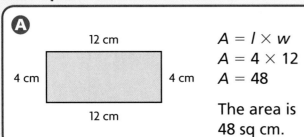	Area = length × width	$A = l \times w$
Square	Area = length × width or A = side × side	$A = l \times w$ or $A = s \times s$

Examples Use the formula.

A
12 cm
4 cm   4 cm
12 cm

$A = l \times w$
$A = 4 \times 12$
$A = 48$

The area is 48 sq cm.

B
4 cm
4 cm

$A = l \times w$
$A = 4 \times 4$
$A = 16$

The area is 16 sq cm.

Guided Practice

1. Use a formula to find the area of this square.

12 cm
12 cm

Find the area.

2.
10 in.
12 in.   12 in.
10 in.

✓ **3.**
9 mi
9 mi
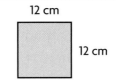

✓ **4.**
16 m
6 m
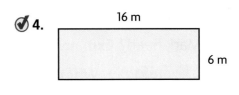

5. (**TALK Math**) **Explain** how can you find the area of a rectangle without counting each individual unit.

Find the area.

6.   6 km

6 km

7.   13 ft

5 ft   5 ft

13 ft

8.   20 cm

2 cm 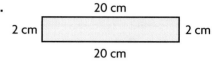 2 cm

20 cm

Use a centimeter ruler to measure each figure. Find the area and perimeter.

9.

10.

11.

⭐ **Algebra** **Find the unknown length.**

12.   ?

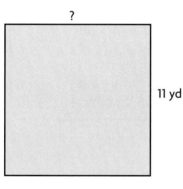

11 yd

Area = 121 sq yd

13.

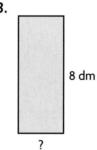

8 dm

?

Area = 24 sq dm

14.

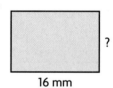

?

16 mm

Area = 80 sq mm

USE DATA **For 15–17, use the diagram.**

15. The gray brick area is a square. How many square feet of gray bricks does Mark need for that area?

16. Reasoning The area surrounding the patio is grass. How many square feet of grass does Mark need? **Explain.**

17. **WRITE Math** **What's the Question?** Mark compared the number of square feet of gray bricks to the number of square feet of red bricks needed for the patio. The answer is red bricks.

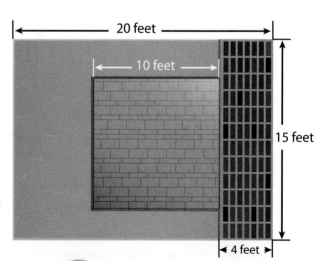

20 feet

10 feet

15 feet

4 feet

610 **Extra Practice** on page 620, Set D)

CD **Technology**
ROM Use Harcourt Mega Math, Ice Station Exploration, *Polar Planes*, Level Q.

18. What is 22 × 16? (O⚬ NS 3.2, p. 220)

19. Draw two perpendicular lines. (MG 3.1, p. 522)

20. Test Prep What is the area of this figure?

   A 20 square centimeters

   B 40 square centimeters

   C 60 square centimeters

   D 96 square centimeters

8 cm

12 cm

21. Kenny is framing a picture. The picture is 12 inches long and 14 inches wide. How many inches of framing material does Kenny need? (MG 1.4, p. 600)

22. Test Prep Use a formula to find the area of a square with sides 7 feet in length. **Explain.**

Problem Solving and Reasoning

MEASUREMENT The surface area of a solid figure is the number of square units it takes to cover the outside of the solid figure.

You can use grid paper to find the surface area of a cube and a rectangular prism.

Example 1 Find the surface area of a cube.

Make a cube that is 3 centimeters by 3 centimeters by 3 centimeters.

Cover the cube with centimeter grid paper.

There are 9 grid squares on each face.

There are 6 faces with 9 squares on each, so it takes 6 × 9 = 54 square centimeters to cover the cube.

So, the surface area of the cube is 54 square centimeters.

Example 2 Find the surface area of a rectangular prism.

Make a rectangular prism that is 4 centimeters by 2 centimeters by 2 centimeters.

Cover the prism with centimeter grid paper.

There are 8 grid squares on 4 faces.

There are 4 grid squares on 2 faces.

So, It takes 32 + 8 = 40 square centimeters to cover the prism.

So, the surface area of the prism is 40 square centimeters.

Make each figure. Then find the surface area.

   1. 4 cm by 5 cm by 3 cm rectangular prism

   2. 4 cm by 4 cm by 4 cm cube

   3. 2 cm by 3 cm by 5 cm rectangular prism

Problem Solving Workshop
Strategy: Solve a Simpler Problem

OBJECTIVE: Solve problems by using the strategy *solve a simpler problem*.

Learn the Strategy

Changing a problem to make it simpler is one way to help you understand and solve more difficult problems. There are different ways to make problems simpler to solve.

Make the numbers easier to work with.

A company makes 245 color copies a day. How many copies are made in 14 days?

Break apart 245 into numbers that are easier to multiply. Rewrite 245 as $200 + 40 + 5$, multiply each addend by 14, and add the partial products.

```
245 = 200 + 40 + 5
× 14          14
         2,800  ← 14 × 200
           560  ← 14 × 40
    +       70  ← 14 × 5
         3,430
```

Divide a figure into simpler parts.

The diagram shows the floor plan of a museum. What is the area of the entire museum?

Divide the shape into rectangles. Find the area of each rectangle and add.

```
      14ft
  ┌────────┐
  │        │16ft    ┌──── 14 ft ────┐
20ft│       │   10ft │               │
  │        └────────┘               │14ft
  │          10ft                   │
  └──────── 38ft ───────────────────┘
```

Find a pattern.

There are 8 students in a math league tournament. Each student will compete against every other student once. How many competitions will there be?

Solve the problem for 2 students, for 3 students, for 4 students, and for 5 students. Look for a pattern. Extend your pattern.

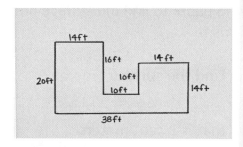

2 students – 1 competition
3 students – 3 competitions
4 students – 6 competitions
5 students – 10 competitions

The number of competitions increases by 2, 3, 4.

To solve a more difficult problem, decide how you can make the problem easier. Solve the simpler problem. Then solve the original problem.

TALK Math
Is there more than one way to divide the floor plan into simpler rectangles? Explain.

MG 1.4 Understand and use formulas to solve problems involving perimeters and areas of rectangles and squares. Use those formulas to find the areas of more complex figures by dividing the figures into basic shapes.
also O━n NS 3.0, MG 1.1, MR 1.0, MR 1.2, MR 2.0, MR 2.2, MR 2.3, MR 2.4, MR 3.0, MR 3.1, MR 3.2, MR 3.3

Use the Strategy

PROBLEM Ellie and her mom are attending a sand castle building competition. The diagram shows two sections of a beach that will be roped off for the competition. What is the total area of both sections? How much rope will be needed to enclose the whole area?

Read to Understand

Reading Skill

- **Read the graphic aid.**
- **Is there information you will not use? If so, what?**

Plan

- **What strategy can you use to solve the problem?**

  You can solve a simpler problem.

Solve

- **How can you use the strategy to solve the problem?**

  Divide the figure into sections.
  Then find the area and perimeter of each section.

Area of Each Section		Perimeter of Both Sections
Judging	**Supplies**	
$A = l \times w$	$A = l \times w$	$P = a + b + c + d + e + f$
$A = 5 \times 12$	$A = 6 \times 6$	$P = 12 + 5 + 6 + 6 + 6 + 11 = 46$
$A = 60$ sq m	$A = 36$ sq m	$P = 46$ m
Sum of the areas: $60 + 36 + 96$ sq m		

So, the area is 96 square meters, and 46 meters of rope is needed to enclose the two sections.

Diagram labels: 12 m · Judging · 5 m · 11 m · Supplies · ← 6 m · 6 m

Check

- **What other way could divide the diagram to find the total area?**

Solve a simpler problem to solve.

1. George is competing in a sand castle competition. The diagram shows part of the competition arena. What is the area of this part of the arena?

   First, divide the competition arena into sections

   Think: How can I divide the arena into rectangles and squares?

   Then, use a formula to find the area of each section.

   Think: What are the dimensions of each section?

   Finally, add the areas of the sections to get the total area.

   Think: What is the total area?

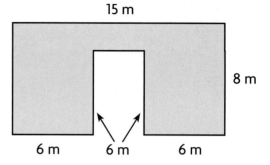

15 m

8 m

6 m   6 m   6 m

2. **What if** a rope was going to be placed around each section of the competition arena? How much rope would be needed?

3. The competition staff decides to put a fence around only the outside part of the arena shown. How much fencing is needed?

Problem Solving Strategy Practice

Solve a simpler problem to solve.

4. A diagram of Ryan's sand castle is shown. What is the total area of the sand castle?

5. Ryan is going to place shells along the perimeter of his castle. Each shell is 2 inches long. How many shells does Ryan need?

6. The diagram shows the floor plan of Mandy's sand castle. What is the total area of the sand castle?

7. Mandy is putting a moat around the outside of the castle. What will be the total length of the moat?

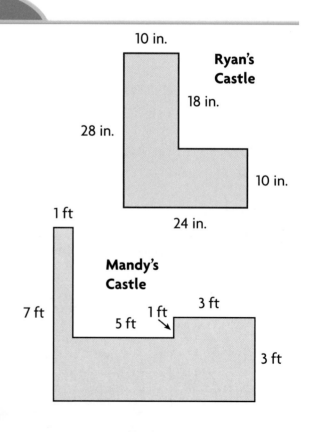

10 in.

Ryan's Castle

18 in.

28 in.

10 in.

24 in.

1 ft

Mandy's Castle

7 ft

5 ft   1 ft   3 ft

3 ft

Mixed Strategy Practice

8. Casey is building a sand castle in a space with 4 sides of equal length and a perimeter of 80 feet. What is the length of each side? What is area of this space?

9. ≡**FAST FACT** The weight of 1 cubic meter of dry sand is about 4,000 pounds. How many tons is this?

USE DATA For 10–13, use the table.

10. A gift shop usually sells 5 pails each day. How many pails will be sold in 12 days?

11. Janisa buys 2 different items from the list. How many different ways could she have chosen her supplies?

12. **Pose a Problem** Look back at problem 10. Write a similar problem by changing the number of items sold and the number of days.

13. **Open-Ended** Harry spent $40. List three different ways Harry could have spent the money on supplies.

Choose a
STRATEGY

Draw a Diagram or Picture
Make a Model or Act It Out
Make an Organized List
Find a Pattern
Make a Table or Graph
Predict and Test
Work Backward
Solve a Simpler Problem
Write an Equation
Use Logical Reasoning

Sand Castle Building Supplies	
Supply	**Cost**
Shovel	$3
Pail	$3
How-To Book	$9
Castle Tower Mold	$6
Spade	$2

CHALLENGE YOURSELF

The Sand Sculpture World Championships have strict rules. Single sculptors can build for 25 hours, pairs for 50 hours, and teams for 100 hours. If two people on a team each work 8 hours, they have worked a total of 16 hours.

14. There were 8 solo sculptors and 15 pairs in a competition. How many total hours could these sculptors spend building?

15. Yolanda is on a sand-sculpting team of 4 people. The team members each work 6 hours a day. How many days will it take for the team to have worked a total of 100 hours? **Explain.**

Relate Perimeter and Area

OBJECTIVE: Explore the relationship between area and perimeter.

Learn

PROBLEM Mr. Foster is framing three pictures. Does he need the same amount of framing for each picture? Does he need the same number of square inches of glass for each picture?

To find how much framing Mr. Foster needs, find the perimeter of each picture. To find how much glass he needs, find the area of each picture.

7 in.

3 in.

A

6 in.

5 in.

B
4 in.

C
5 in.

Activity 1 **Materials** ■ square tiles ■ grid paper

- Use square tiles to model Picture A. Make a rectangle 3 tiles long and 7 tiles wide. Trace the rectangle on grid paper.

- Copy the table and fill in the perimeter and area for Picture A.

- Repeat Steps 1 and 2 for the other pictures. Record your work in the table.

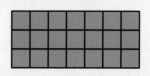

So, for each picture, Mr. Foster needs the same amount of framing but a different number of square inches of glass.

Perimeter and Area

Picture	Length	Width	Perimeter	Area
A	3 in.	7 in.	■	■
B	■	■	■	■
C	■	■	■	■

Activity 2 **Materials** ■ 24 square tiles ■ grid paper

- Use 24 square tiles to make a rectangle. Trace the rectangle onto grid paper. Copy the table and record the length and width. Find the perimeter and area, and record them in the table.

- Use the 24 tiles to make as many different rectangles as you can. Trace each rectangle and find the perimeter and area. Record each length, width, perimeter, and area in the table.

Perimeter and Area

Rectangle	Length	Width	Perimeter	Area
1	4 un	6 un	20 un	24 sq un
2	■	■	■	■
3	■	■	■	■

MG 1.2 Recognize that rectangles that have the same area can have different perimeters.
MG 1.3 Understand that rectangles that have the same perimeter can have different areas. *also* **AF 1.1,**
AF 1.4, MR 1.2, MR 2.0, MR 2.2, MR 2.3, MR 2.4, MR 3.2

Activity 3 **Materials** ■ square tiles ■ grid paper

Perimeter and Area				
Rectangle	Length	Width	Perimeter	Area
1	12	1	■	■
2	■	2	■	■
3	■	3	■	■

- Use square tiles to make a rectangle 12 tiles long and 1 tile wide. Trace the rectangle on grid paper.
- Find the perimeter and area. Copy and complete the table.
- Continue to make rectangles with 12 tiles by decreasing the length and increasing the width. Make as many rectangles as you can. Trace each rectangle, find the perimeter and area, and record your work in the table.

- What is the difference between area and perimeter? Explain.

Math Idea

Two figures can have the same area but different perimeters or different areas but the same perimeter.

Guided Practice

1. How can you change this rectangle so that it has the same perimeter, but a greater area? Model and then record your answer.

6 cm

2 cm

Find the area and perimeter of each figure. Then draw another figure that has the same perimeter but a different area.

2. 6 m

3 m

3. 9 mi

9 mi

✓ 4.   9 in.

1 in.

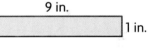

Find the area and perimeter of each figure. Then draw another figure that has the same area but a different perimeter.

5. 4 m

4 m

6. 9 ft

16 ft

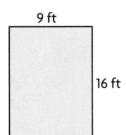

✓ 7. 10 mm

12 mm

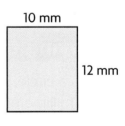

8. **TALK Math** **Explain** how knowing the factors of a number can help you find all the rectangles with an area of that number.

Find the area and perimeter of each figure. Then draw another figure that has the same perimeter but a different area.

9.

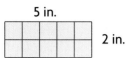

5 in.

2 in.

10.

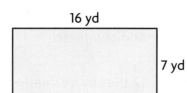

16 yd

7 yd

11.

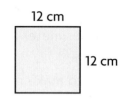

12 cm

12 cm

Find the area and perimeter of each figure. Then draw another figure that has the same area but a different perimeter.

12.

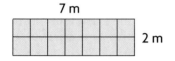

7 m

2 m

13.

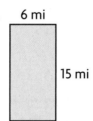

6 mi

15 mi

14.

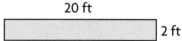

20 ft

2 ft

For 15–16, use figures a–d.

15. Which figures have the same area but different perimeters?

16. Which figures have the same perimeter but different areas?

a.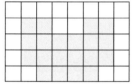

b.

c.

d.

17. Corynn paints a picture that has a perimeter of 22 centimeters. What are 3 possible areas for her picture?

18. **WRITE Math** Mia has two photos, both with an area of 36 square inches. One is a rectangle, and one is a square. Which has the greater perimeter? **Explain.**

 Achieving the Standards

19. Susie draws a circle. The diameter of the circle is 16 millimeters. What is the radius of the circle? (MG 3.2, p. 534)

20. Danny ate 3 pieces of a pie. There had been 8 pieces of pie in all. What fraction of the pie did Danny eat? (NS 1.5, p. 414)

21. Jenny's social studies scores are 95, 90, 95, 89, 88, 93, and 100. What is the mode of her scores? (SDAP 1.2, p. 326)

22. Test Prep The rectangles below have the same perimeter. Which has the greatest area?

A    C

B   D

Through the Lens

 Reading Skill **Sequence**

Leigh Ann took some photos of the Sierra Nevada during a photography workshop by the Ansel Adams Gallery. She wants to change the size of one of the photos she took during the workshop. She increases the size of a 2-inch by 3-inch photo by doubling the length and width. Then she triples the original dimensions. She wants to know how the length, width, perimeter, and area will change each time she changes the photo.

Knowing the sequence, or order, of the changes made to the picture will help you solve the problem. Use grid paper and a table to find how the dimensions will change.

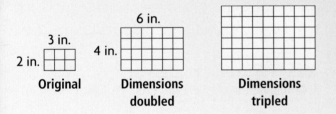

Picture	Length	Width	Perimeter	Area
Original	2 in.	3 in.	10 in.	6 sq in.
Doubled	4 in.	6 in.	20 in.	24 sq in.
Tripled	■	■	■	■

Perimeter and Area

Problem Solving Track the sequence of the changes in each problem to solve. Use grid paper and a table to record.

1. Solve the problem above.

2. Abby has a photo that is 2 inches by 4 inches. She doubles the dimensions. Then she triples the dimensions. Then she halves the dimensions. How does the area of the picture change as the dimensions change?

Extra Practice

Set A Choose the more reasonable measurement. (pp. 590–593)

1.

$2\frac{1}{2}$ c or $2\frac{1}{2}$ qt

2.

12 oz or 12 lb

3.

3 yd or 3 ft

Write an equation you can use to complete each table. Then copy and complete each table.

4.

Pints, p	4	6	8	10	12
Cups, c	8	▣	▣	20	▣

5.

Feet, f	1	2	3	4	5
Inches, i	▣	24	36	▣	▣

Estimate to the nearest inch. Then measure to the nearest $\frac{1}{2}$ and $\frac{1}{4}$ inch.

6.

7.

8. The length of Molly's bedroom is 18 feet. How long is her room in yards?

Set B Write an equation you can use to complete each table. Then copy and complete each table. (pp. 594–597)

1.

Kilometer, k	3	5	7	9	11
Meter, m	3,000	▣	7,000	▣	▣

2.

Decimeter, d	5	6	7	8	9
Centimeter, c	▣	▣	70	80	▣

Estimate to the nearest centimeter. Then measure to the nearest half centimeter and nearest millimeter.

3.

4.

Choose the more reasonable measurement.

5.

1,000 kg or 1,000 g

6.

15 dm or 15 cm

7.

200 L or 200 mL

8. Ryan has three containers. One holds 5L. Another holds 400 mL, and the other holds 3L. Order the size of containers from greatest to least.

 Technology
Use Harcourt Mega Math, Ice Station
Exploration, *Polar Planes*, Levels P, Q.

Set C Find the perimeter. (pp. 600–603)

1.
5 in.
2 in. [rectangle] 2 in.
5 in.

2.
17 yd
18 yd [trapezoid] 18 yd
9 yd

3.
2 mm [house shape] 2 mm
4 mm ↔1 mm
3 mm

4. The perimeter of Greg's garden is 18 feet. The width of the garden is 3 feet. What is the length?

5. Bella's painting is 15 inches long and 10 inches wide. What is the perimeter of her painting?

Set D Find the area. (pp. 608–611)

1.
11 in.
2 in. [rectangle]

2.
3 mm
3 mm [square]

3.
12 yd
2 yd [rectangle]

Use a centimeter ruler to measure each figure.
Find the area and perimeter.

4. [rectangle]

5. [rectangle]

6. [rectangle]

Set E Find the area and perimeter of each figure. Then draw another figure that has the same perimeter but a different area. (pp. 614–619)

1.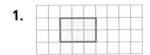

2.
13 mi
4 mi [rectangle]

3.
12 yd
1 yd [rectangle]

Find the area and perimeter of each figure. Then draw another figure that has the same area but a different perimeter.

4.

5.
9 in.
11 in. [rectangle]

6.
10 cm
10 cm [square]

Chapter 23 Review/Test

Check Vocabulary and Concepts

Choose the best term from the box.

1. Units used to measure length, width, height or distances are called __?__. (Grade 3 MG 1.1, p. 590)

2. The amount of matter in an object is called __?__. (Grade 3 MG 1.1, p. 594)

3. The distance around a figure is called the __?__. (MG 1.0, p. 598)

Check Skills

Choose the more reasonable measurement. (Grade 3 MG 1.1, pp. 590–593, 594–597)

4.

   5 ft or 5 in.

5.

   8 m or 8 cm

6.

   10 lb or 10 oz

Find the perimeter and area. (MG 1.4, pp. 600–603, 608–611)

7. 105 in. / 23 in.

8. 68 mi / 68 mi

9. 14 yd / 42 yd

Find the area and perimeter of each figure. Then draw another figure that has the same perimeter but a different area. (MG 1.2, MG 1.3, pp. 616–619)

10. 9 cm / 4 cm

11. 5 yd / 12 yd

12. 18 in. / 3 in.

Check Problem Solving

Solve. (MG 1.4, MR 1.2, pp. 604–605, 612–613)

13. The perimeter of an Olympic-sized swimming pool is 150 meters. The length of the pool is 50 meters. What is the width of the pool?

14. Shane helped his mom plant a vegetable garden. The diagram shows the plots where the vegetables were planted. What is the total area of the vegetable garden?

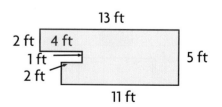

15. 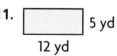 **Explain** how you can use a formula to help you solve Problem 14.

GO ONLINE Technology Use *Online Assessment.*

Enrich • Volume
Various Volumes

Marcus works at a grocery store. He is pulling small boxes of crackers out of a large box to place on the shelf to be sold. There are 20 small boxes of crackers. What is the volume of the large box?

Centimeter cubes can help you find the volume of objects. Remember, volume is the amount of space a solid figure takes up.

One Way
Find the volume of the large box.

| **Step 1** |
| Place the cubes in rows along the bottom of the large box. Make layers of cubes until the box is full. Count the cubes you use. |

| **Step 2** |
| Record how many cubes it took to fill the box. This is the volume of the box in cubic units. |

Another Way
Find the volume of one of the small boxes.

| **Step 1** |
| Place the cubes in rows along the bottom of the small box. Make layers of cubes until the box is full. Count the cubes you use. |

| **Step 2** |
| Multiply the volume of one box by 20, the total number of small boxes. This is the volume of the large box in cubic units. |

Try It
Count or multiply to find the volume. Write the volume in cubic units.

1.

2.

3.

4. Sam used connecting cubes to build a solid figure that was 6 cubes long, 2 cubes wide, and 4 cubes high. What is the volume of Sam's figure?

5. Richard built a rectangle that was 5 cubes by 4 cubes by 3 cubes. Joe built a rectangle that was 2 cubes by 4 cubes by 1 cube. What is the total volume of the two rectangles?

WRITE Math Ron built Figure A and Figure B out of connecting cubes. Which figure has the greater volume? **Explain.**

Figure A   Figure B

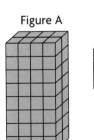

Achieving the Standards
Chapters 1–23

Number Sense

1. There are 192 students in the fourth grade. They are divided equally among 8 classes. How many students are in each class? (○¬ NS 3.4)

   A 18

   B 20

   C 24

   D 26

Test Tip **Understand the problem.**

See item 2. There are 12 groups with 25 in each group. You are asked to find the total. So to solve the problem, multiply.

2. Sarah bought 12 packs of erasers. There were 25 erasers in each pack. How many erasers did Sarah buy in all? (○¬ NS 3.3)

   A 75   C 215

   B 200   D 300

3. Nate had 3,102 baseball cards. He gave 1,487 to his brother. How many baseball cards does Nate have left? (○¬ NS 3.1)

   A 1,615

   B 2,385

   C 3,589

   D 4,589

4. **WRITE Math** Which is greater, 5.82 or 5.19? **Explain** how you found your answer. (○¬ NS 1.2)

Algebra and Functions

5. What is the value of the expression below? (○¬ AF 1.2)

   $$3 \times (4 + 7)$$

   A 11

   B 12

   C 19

   D 33

6. Which equation can be used to find the number of tags, y, given the number of dogs, x? (○¬ AF 1.5)

Dogs, x	Tags, y
6	12
7	14
8	16
9	18

   A $x = y \times 2$ C $y = x \times 2$

   B $y = x + 6$ D $x \div 2 = y$

7. Which statement *best* represents the expression $x + 9$? (AF 1.1)

   A 9 less than a number

   B 9 more than a number

   C a number divided by 9

   D a number times 9

8. **WRITE Math** What number goes in the box to make this number sentence true? **Explain**. (○¬ AF 2.2)

   $$4(5 + 3) = \blacksquare \times 8$$

Measurement and Geometry

9. What is the area of the floor? (MG 1.4)

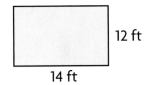

12 ft

14 ft

A 168 square feet

B 146 square feet

C 52 square feet

D 26 square feet

10. Len plotted 3 points on a grid. The 3 points were all in a straight line.

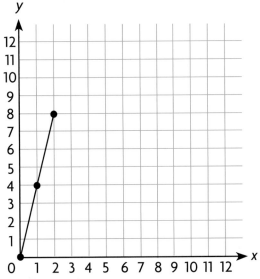

If he plots another point on the line, what could be its coordinates? (O▬ MG 2.1)

A (2,10)   **C** (3,12)

B (3,9)   **D** (4,11)

11. **WRITE Math** A horizontal line segment has one endpoint at (5,6) and the other endpoint at (3,6) on a coordinate grid. What is the length of the line segment? **Explain**. (O▬ MG 2.2)

Statistics, Data Analysis, and Probability

12. Jenna made this bar graph.

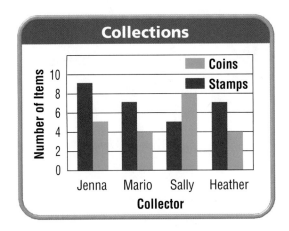

Which collector collected more coins than stamps? (SDAP 1.3)

A Heather   **C** Jenna

B Mario   **D** Sally

13. Which lists the different outcomes of pulling a marble of the same size from the bag? (Grade 3 O▬ SDAP 1.2)

A red, yellow, purple, black

B green, yellow, purple, black

C green, yellow, purple

D green, yellow

14. **WRITE Math** Marco plays basketball. The list below shows the points he scored in the last 5 games. What is the median of his scores? **Explain** how you got your answer. (SDAP 1.2)

14, 20, 16, 27, 23

24 Probability

The Big Idea Probability measures the likelihood of events and provides a basis for making predictions.

Investigate

Suppose you are waiting to ride a bumper car at the Orange County Fair. The cars may arrive in any order. Look at the graph below. Which color bumper car is most likely to be next? Which color bumper car would you like to ride in? What is the probability that it will come next? Explain how you know.

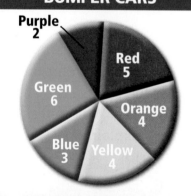

BUMPER CARS

Purple 2
Red 5
Green 6
Orange 4
Blue 3
Yellow 4

CALIFORNIA FAST FACT

The EuroSlide is at Orange County Fair. Every summer, the fair is held in Costa Mesa. It lasts 21 days. In 2006, almost 1,000,000 people came to the fair.

GO ONLINE
Technology
Student pages are available in the Student eBook.

Show What You Know

Check your understanding of important skills needed for success in Chapter 24.

▶ **Make and Use a Tally Table**

Use the data to make a tally table. Then answer each question.

> Kailynn surveyed her class about favorite colors. There were 9 students who chose purple, 12 who chose green, 4 who chose blue, and 2 who chose yellow.

1. How many students were surveyed?

2. Which color was the least favorite?

3. How many more students chose green than blue?

4. How many students did not choose blue?

▶ **Possible Outcomes**

List the possible outcomes for each experiment.

5. pulling a marble from this bag

6. spinning the pointer of this spinner

7. tossing a coin

▶ **Compare Parts of a Whole and a Group**

Write a fraction for the part of the whole named.

8. green sections

9. purple sections

Write a fraction for the part of the group named.

10. circles

11. circles or squares

VOCABULARY POWER

CHAPTER VOCABULARY

combinations   outcome
equally likely   predict
event   tree diagram
likely   unlikely

WARM-UP WORDS

outcome a possible result of an experiment

event an outcome or a combination of outcomes in an experiment

predict to make a reasonable guess about what will happen

1 List All Possible Outcomes

OBJECTIVE: List all possible outcomes of an experiment.

Quick Review

Write a fraction for the shaded part.

Vocabulary

outcome

Investigate

Materials ■ 4-part spinner colored red, blue, yellow, and green ■ coin

You can find the number of possible outcomes by doing an experiment.

When you do an experiment, the **outcomes** are the results.

A Spin the pointer of the spinner with 4 equal parts.

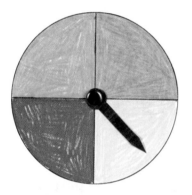

B Record your outcome.

C Repeat the activity 20 times. Each time you find a different possible outcome, record it in a list.

Draw Conclusions

1. Explain how you found the outcome of each spin.

2. How many colors are on the spinner? How many possible outcomes are there for this experiment? Name the possible outcomes.

3. **Application** Emma has a bag with 2 green marbles, 3 red marbles, and 2 blue marbles that are all the same size. How many possible outcomes are there for this experiment?

SDAP 2.1 Represent all possible outcomes for a simple probability situation in an organized way (e.g., tables, grids, tree diagrams). *also* MR 2.0, MR 2.2, MR 2.3, MR 2.4, MR 3.2

Connect

This table shows the possible outcomes of spinning a pointer on a spinner with 4 equal parts and tossing a coin.

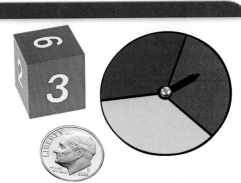

Coin	Color			
	Red	Blue	Green	Yellow
Heads	🪙 , ■	🪙 , ■	🪙 , ■	🪙 , ■
Tails	🪙 , ■	🪙 , ■	🪙 , ■	🪙 , ■

Do an experiment and record the results.

HANDS ON

Activity

Materials ■ 4-part spinner colored red, blue, yellow, and green ■ coin

- Make a table like the one above.

- Toss a coin and spin the pointer.

- Record the outcome in the table by using a tally mark.
  Repeat a total of 20 times, recording the outcome after each toss and spin.

TALK Math
How would the number of possible outcomes change if the spinner had five colors?

Practice

USE DATA For 1–4, use the pictures. List all the possible outcomes for each experiment.

1. tossing a dime

2. tossing a cube labeled 1 to 6

3. tossing a cube labeled 1 to 6 and spinning the pointer on a spinner with 3 equal parts

✔ 4. tossing a dime and spinning the pointer

USE DATA For 5–8, use the table.

✔ 5. List all the possible outcomes for the experiment.

6. How many possible outcomes are there?

7. How many times did the outcome *Heads, 3* occur?

8. **WRITE Math** Explain how to find the number of possible outcomes for an experiment by looking at a table of results.

Sally's Experiment
Roll a Number Cube and Toss a Coin

Coin	Number					
	1	2	3	4	5	6
Heads	II		III	I	III	II
Tails	I	II	I	II		IIII

Problem Solving Workshop
Strategy: Make an Organized List

OBJECTIVE: Solve problems by using the strategy *make an organized list.*

Learn the Strategy

Making an organized list is a good way to keep track of information. You can use different types of organized lists for different types of situations.

Make a list to sequence information.

Mr. Wong puts the daily schedule for his class on the board.

8:15 A.M. – Morning Meeting
8:30 A.M. – Spelling
9:00 A.M. – Math
10:15 A.M. – Reading
11:00 A.M. – Lunch

Make a list to organize information.

Each night, Kelly writes her homework assignments in a notebook. She organizes her homework by subject.

Daily Assignments
Date April 16   Year 2008
Read story and answer questions.

p. 210 Problems 1–15

Write each word 3 times.

Teacher Comments: Parent Comments:

Signed   Signed

Make a list to find possible outcomes.

A bakery offers 3 different flavors for their 2-layer cakes. Each cake uses 2 flavors.

yellow
chocolate

yellow
coconut

chocolate
coconut

> **TALK Math**
> Explain how using a list can help represent information.

When you make a list, organizing the list into categories or parts can help you make sure you don't forget anything.

SDAP 2.1 Represent all possible outcomes for a simple probability situation in an organized way (e.g., tables, grids, tree diagrams). *also* MR 1.0, MR 2.0, MR 2.2, MR 2.3, MR 2.4, MR 3.0, MR 3.1, MR 3.2, MR 3.3

Use the Strategy

PROBLEM Molly is playing a game at the fair. Without looking, she reaches into a bag and pulls out a marble. Then, she reaches into a different bag and pulls out another marble. All the marbles are the same size. If both marbles are the same color, Molly wins a prize. List and count the possible outcomes of the game. Then, name the way Molly can win a prize.

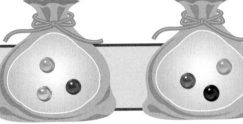

Read to Understand

Reading Skill

- Summarize what you are asked to find.
- What information will you use?

Plan

- **What strategy can you use to solve the problem?**

  You can make an organized list.

Solve

- **How can you use the strategy to solve the problem?**

  Make a list of all the possible outcomes. Organize your list by showing the outcomes that could result if the first marble is green. Then, list the outcomes that could result if the first marble is another color.

green, black	red, black	yellow, black
green, purple	red, purple	yellow, purple
green, green	red, green	yellow, green

  There is only one possible outcome in which both marbles are the same color, *green, green*.

  So, of the nine outcomes, there is only one in which Molly can win a prize with the outcome *green, green*.

Check

- **What other ways could you solve the problem?**

Guided Problem Solving

1. **USE DATA** Marianne is playing a game that uses two spinners. Each spinner has equal sections. She spins both pointers and adds the numbers. If the total is less than 4, she wins a prize. List the possible outcomes. Name the ways Marianne can win a prize.

   First, use a table to make an organized list.

   Then, find the total for two spins.

   Finally, find the totals that are less than 4.

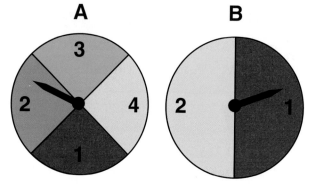

A   B

Spinner A	Spinner B	Sum
1	1	2
1	2	3
2	1	3
2	▨	▨

2. **What if** Spinner A had two equal sections labeled 1 and 2? How would the number of possible outcomes change?

3. Yuri is playing a game using a coin and Spinner A. He tosses the coin and spins the pointer. List all the possible outcomes.

Problem Solving Strategy Practice

Make an organized list to solve.

4. Lorrie is making tickets for the carnival. Each type of ticket will be a different color. There will be adult, child, and senior tickets. There will be one-day and two-day tickets. How many ticket colors will there be?

USE DATA For 5–6, use the information in the picture.

5. Robin plays a game in which she spins the pointer and picks one duck from the bag. How many possible outcomes are there?

6. To win a prize, Georgie must spin a number that is greater than 3 and pick the green duck. Name the ways Georgie can win.

7. **WRITE Math** Shelly wants to find the total number of possible outcomes of spinning a pointer and tossing a coin. **Explain** how Shelly can organize a list of the possible outcomes.

Mixed Strategy Practice

USE DATA For 8–12, use the pictures.

8. **≡FAST FACT** The Kentucky State Fair was started in 1902. Which state fair was started 61 years before that?

9. The Illinois State Fair was started after the Michigan and Indiana State Fairs, but before the California State Fair. In what year was the Illinois State Fair started?

10. **Pose a Problem** The California State Fair was started in 1854. Use this information and the years in which other state fairs were started to write a problem.

11. **Open-Ended** Make a table that shows the number of state fairs started during each decade from the 1840s to the 1880s. Name one fact your table shows.

12. My year is even. The sum of the first two digits is less than the sum of the last two. The number formed by the sum of the last two digits is 2 more than the number formed by the sum of the first 2 digits. What state fair am I?

CHALLENGE YOURSELF

One-day tickets to the California State Fair are $8 for adults and $5 for children.

13. An adult season pass is $4 more than 4 times the cost of a one-day ticket. A child season pass is $10 less than that. What is the cost of a season pass for a child?

14. **Algebra** A group of adults visited the California State Fair. Since they bought their tickets together, they got a $10 discount. What expression can you use to show the total cost of the group's tickets? **Explain** how to solve the problem.

Choose a STRATEGY

Draw a Diagram or Picture
Make a Model or Act It Out
Make an Organized List
Find a Pattern
Make a Table or Graph
Predict and Test
Work Backward
Solve a Simpler Problem
Write an Equation
Use Logical Reasoning

Nevada
Started: 1874

Gotta be there!

New York
Started: 1841

California
Started: 1854

West Virginia
Started: 1854

Arizona
Started: 1884

Indiana
Started: 1852

Michigan
Started: 1849

Texas
Started: 1886

3 Make Predictions

OBJECTIVE: Predict outcomes of experiments.

Quick Review

Name the possible outcomes of spinning both pointers.

Vocabulary

predict	impossible
event	equally likely
likely	certain
unlikely	

Learn

You can predict the likelihood of events. When you **predict**, you make a reasonable guess about what might happen.

An **event** can be one outcome or a set of outcomes. Sometimes, one event is more likely than another, but not certain. An event is **likely** if it has a greater than even chance of happening. An event is **unlikely**, but not impossible, if it has a less than even chance of happening.

Examples

Seven marbles of the same size are in a bag. What is the likelihood of each event?

A Pulling a yellow marble

An event is **impossible** if it is never able to happen. There are no yellow marbles in the bag, so pulling a yellow marble is impossible.

B Pulling a green or pulling a red marble

Two events are **equally likely** if they have the same chance of happening. There are the same number of red marbles as green marbles, so pulling a red marble and pulling a green marble are equally likely.

C Pulling a red, green, or purple marble

An event is **certain** if it will always happen. The bag has only red, green, and purple marbles, so pulling a red, green, or purple marble is certain.

• What is the difference between a certain and a likely event?

• This spinner has 3 equal sections. What is the likelihood of either spinning red or spinning yellow?

• What is the likelihood of tossing a number less than 10, if the number cube is labeled 1 to 6?

> **Math Idea**
> When you make a prediction, you decide which events are more likely to occur and which events are less likely to occur.

O—┑ SDAP 2.0 Students make predictions for simple probability situations. *also* SDAP 2.1, MR 1.1, MR 2.3, MR 2.4, MR 3.2

Activity

Materials ■ equal-sized color tiles ■ bag

Step 1

Place 6 blue tiles, 3 red tiles, and 1 yellow tile in the bag.

Step 2

Copy the table. Predict the outcomes for pulling one tile out of the bag 30 times. Write tally marks in the Predicted Outcomes column to show the number of times you think you will pull each color.

Experiment Results		
Color	Predicted Outcomes	Actual Outcomes
blue		
red		
yellow		

Step 3

Pull one tile from the bag. Record the outcome in the Actual Outcomes column of your table.

Step 4

Return the tile to the bag. Repeat 29 more times.

- How did your actual results compare to your predictions?
- List all possible outcomes. Which outcome is most likely? Explain.
- Which outcome is least likely? Explain.

Guided Practice

1. The bag has 7 marbles of the same size. Tim pulls one marble from the bag. Name an event that is likely, unlikely, and impossible.

Tell whether the event is *likely, unlikely, certain,* or *impossible*.

2. tossing a number greater than 1 on a cube labeled 1 to 6

3. spinning a multiple of 4 on a spinner with four equal parts labeled 4, 8, 12, and 16

4. **TALK Math** **Explain** the difference between an event that is unlikely and one that is impossible.

Independent Practice and Problem Solving

Tell whether the event is *likely, unlikely, certain,* or *impossible*.

5. tossing a number greater than 6 on a cube labeled 1 to 6

6. pulling a green marble from a bag that contains 22 red, 4 green, and 14 yellow marbles of the same size

USE DATA For each experiment, tell whether Events A and B are *equally likely* or *not equally likely*. If they are not equally likely, name the event that is more likely.

7. Experiment: Toss a coin.

Event A: heads
Event B: tails

8. Experiment: Toss a cube numbered 1 to 6.

Event A: tossing a number less than 3
Event B: tossing an even number

9. Experiment: Spin the pointer.

Event A: red
Event B: yellow

10. Experiment: Pull one tile from the bag if all tiles are the same size.

Event A: green
Event B: red

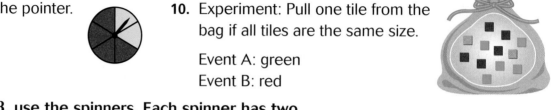

USE DATA For 11–13, use the spinners. Each spinner has two equal sections. In the experiment, each pointer is spun and the outcomes are added.

11. What are the possible sums? What is the most likely sum?

12. Copy the table. Record a prediction for how many times you will spin a sum of 3, if you do the experiment 20 times.

13. Make two spinners like the ones shown. Spin the pointers and add the results. Do the experiment 20 times. How do your results compare to the prediction you made in Problem 12?

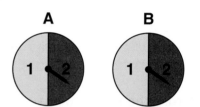

A   **B**

USE DATA For 14–16, use the spinner. The spinner has equal sections.

14. Which two events are equally likely?

15. Name an event that is impossible.

16. **WRITE Math** Harold is going to spin the pointer. Predict the outcome of his spin. **Explain** your choice.

Experiment Results		
Sum of 3	**Predicted Outcomes**	**Actual Outcomes**
▪	▪	▪

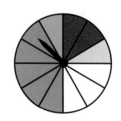

Achieving the Standards

17. What is the value of the expression below if $s = 12$? (AF 1.0, p. 142)

$$4 \times (s + 5)$$

18. What is the area of this figure? (MG 1.4, p. 608)

10 in.

5 in. ▭

19. Name a fraction that is the same as 0.5.

(NS 1.6, p. 468)

20. **Test Prep** The marbles in the bag are the same size. Without looking, which color marble are you most likely to pull from the bag?

A blue

B yellow

C green

D red

Technology
Use Harcourt Mega Math, Fraction Action, *Last Chance Canyon*, Level C.

Justify Your Answer

Sometimes you need to justify your answer by giving reasons to show that your answer is correct.

Molly's soccer coach will select one student to be team captain. She writes the names of each of the 23 players on a separate index card. Then, without looking, she selects one card. Is it likely, unlikely, certain, or impossible that Molly's name will be picked?

Molly wrote her answer and then gave reasons to justify it.

I think it is unlikely that my name will be picked.

1. Since there are other possible outcomes, it is not certain that my name will be picked.

2. Since my name is one of the possible outcomes, it is not impossible that it will be picked.

3. Each student has an equal chance of being picked. Since I have only a 1 out of 23 chance for my name to be picked, it is not likely that my name will be picked.

So, my reasons justify that it is unlikely my name will be picked.

Tips

To justify an answer:
- First, state your answer.
- Next, write statements to explain why other possible answers can't be true.
- Use correct math terms in your statements.
- Finally, tell whether your reasons justify your answer.

Problem Solving
Solve. Justify your answer.

1. One October morning, Ms. Morters says, "It is impossible that it will snow today." Do you agree with Ms. Morters?

2. Oscar tosses a number cube labeled 1 to 6 and tosses a nickel. How many possible outcomes are there?

3. Rodney tosses a number cube labeled 1 to 6 and tosses a penny. Name two outcomes that are equally likely to occur.

4. Melinda is going to toss a coin 50 times. How many times do you predict the coin will land heads up?

Probability as a Fraction

OBJECTIVE: Express probability as a fraction.

Quick Review

Tim tosses a number cube labeled 1 to 6. How many possible outcomes are there?

Vocabulary

mathematical probability

Learn

PROBLEM Pauline spins the pointer. Each section of the spinner is equal. How can she describe the likelihood that the pointer will stop on green?

Mathematical probability is a comparison of a number of favorable outcomes to the number of possible outcomes when the outcomes are equally likely. The probability of an event occurring is expressed as 0, 1, or a fraction between 0 and 1.

0	$\frac{1}{8}$	$\frac{1}{4}$	$\frac{3}{8}$	$\frac{1}{2}$	$\frac{5}{8}$	$\frac{3}{4}$	$\frac{7}{8}$	1
↑ impossible			less likely			more likely		↑ certain

So, Pauline can describe the likelihood that the pointer will stop on green as a fraction.

What is the mathematical probability of the pointer stopping on green?

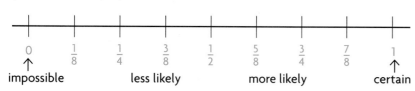

Probability of green = $\dfrac{\text{number of favorable outcomes (green)}}{\text{total number of possible outcomes (3 green, 4 red, 1 yellow)}} = \dfrac{3}{8}$

So, the mathematical probability of the pointer stopping on green is $\frac{3}{8}$, or 3 out of 8.

The closer a probability is to 1, the more likely the event is to occur. The closer it is to 0, the more unlikely it is to occur. A probability of $\frac{1}{2}$ means that the event is just as likely to happen as not to happen.

Suppose you want to find the likelihood that the pointer will stop on yellow.

• Which is more unlikely to occur: spinning red or spinning yellow? How do you know?

ERROR ALERT

The number of favorable outcomes is always the numerator. The total number of possible outcomes is always the denominator.

SDAP 2.2 Express outcomes of experimental probability situations verbally and numerically (e.g., 3 out of 4; $\frac{3}{4}$). *also* NS 1.7, SDAP 2.0, MR 1.1, MR 2.3, MR 2.4, MR 3.2

More Examples Find the probability of each event when all the marbles are the same size. Then, write the likelihood.

A Find the probability of pulling a marble that is not blue.

Probability of not blue = $\frac{5}{8}$ $\leftarrow$ $\frac{\text{favorable outcomes (4 red, 1 green)}}{\text{total possible outcomes (3 blue, 4 red, 1 green)}}$

The probability of pulling a marble that is not blue is **likely**.

B Find the probability of pulling a green marble.

Probability of green = $\frac{0}{9}$ $\leftarrow$ $\frac{\text{favorable outcomes (0 green)}}{\text{total possible outcomes (3 blue, 4 red, 2 yellow)}}$

The probability of pulling a green marble is **impossible**.

C Find the probability of pulling a red or green marble.

Probability of red or green = $\frac{5}{7}$ $\leftarrow$ $\frac{\text{favorable outcomes (2 red, 3 green)}}{\text{total possible outcomes (2 red, 3 green, 2 white)}}$

The probability of pulling a red or green marble is **likely**.

D Find the probability of pulling a black marble.

Probability of black = $\frac{8}{8}$ $\leftarrow$ $\frac{\text{favorable outcomes (8 black)}}{\text{total possible outcomes (8 black)}}$

The probability of pulling a black marble is **certain**.

Guided Practice

1. Use Spinner A, which has equal sections. What is the probability that the pointer will land on blue? Count the number of favorable outcomes. Count the total number of possible outcomes. Write the probability as a fraction.

A

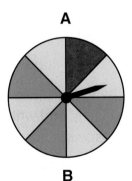

USE DATA For 2–6, use Spinner B. Spinner B has equal sections. Write the probability as a fraction.

2. spinning blue   3. spinning red or blue

B

4. spinning green   ✓5. not spinning red

6. spinning red   ✓7. not spinning blue or green

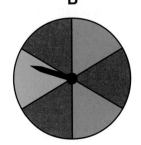

8. **TALK Math** Explain how you know that an event with the probability 11 out of 12 is likely to occur.

USE DATA For 9–13, use the equal-sized tiles. Write the probability as a fraction.

9. pulling a 1

10. pulling a 3

11. pulling a 5

12. pulling a 2 or 3

13. pulling a number that is not 6

USE DATA For 14–18, use the equal-sized cards. Write the probability as a fraction. Then, tell whether each event is *certain*, *impossible*, *likely*, or *unlikely*.

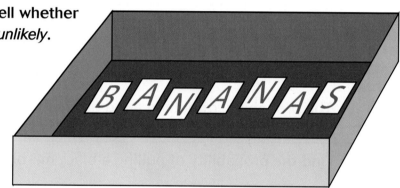

14. pulling a B

15. pulling an N or an A

16. pulling a T

17. pulling a B, A, N, or S

18. pulling a letter that is not A

Algebra Find the value of *n*.

19. Ron filled a bag with 12 equal-sized marbles. There are *n* blue marbles. The probability of pulling a blue marble from the bag is $\frac{1}{4}$.

20. Molly spins a pointer that has 3 equally likely outcomes: red, green, and blue. The probability of spinning yellow is *n*.

USE DATA For 22–24, use the spinner. The spinner has equal sections.

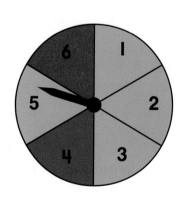

21. What fractions shows the probability of spinning green?

22. Write the following outcomes in order from least likely to most likely and write the probability of each as a fraction: *spinning green, spinning a 6, spinning an even number*

23. **Pose a Problem** Look back at Problem 21. Write a similar problem by changing the color.

24. **WRITE Math** ▸ **What's the Error?** Carlos says that the probability of spinning green is $\frac{1}{3}$ because green is one of three possible outcomes. Describe his error. Find the correct probability.

Technology
Use Harcourt Mega Math, Fraction
Action, *Last Chance Canyon*, Level F.

25. What are the possible outcomes of spinning the pointer on a spinner with three equal parts if 2 parts are red and 1 part is blue? (SDAP 2.1, p. 628)

28. Test Prep All the marbles are the same size. What is the probability of pulling a red marble?

A $\frac{1}{5}$ C $\frac{3}{5}$

B $\frac{2}{5}$ D $\frac{4}{5}$

26. What type of triangle has 1 right angle with no equal sides? (MG 3.7, p. 528)

29. Test Prep What is the likelihood of pulling a blue crayon from a box of red crayons? **Explain.**

27. Camille has a paperweight in the shape of a square pyramid. How many vertices does it have? (MG 3.6, p. 566)

MATH POWER — Problem Solving and Reasoning

FAIR OR UNFAIR In probability, an experiment is fair if each outcome is equally likely. An experiment is unfair if one or more outcomes are more likely than others.

Bob, Morgan, and Juanita are playing a game using a spinner. Each time the pointer stops on a player's name, that player gets 1 point.

Unfair

This spinner is unfair. Bob has a greater chance of scoring than the other players.

Fair

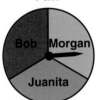

This spinner is fair. Each player has the same chance of scoring.

Tell whether each game is *fair* or *unfair*. Explain.

1. Oswaldo and Margie are tossing a number cube labeled 1 to 6. John wins if the outcome is 1, 2, or 3. Margie wins if the outcome is 4, 5, or 6.

3. Reggie and Pam are tossing a number cube labeled 1 to 6. Reggie wins if the outcome is less than 3. Pam wins if the outcome is greater than 3.

2. Lee and Walt are using the spinner below. Lee wins if the pointer stops on blue. Walt wins if the pointer stops on green or red.

5 Experimental Probability

OBJECTIVE: Find experimental probability of events.

Investigate

Materials ■ coin

The **experimental probability** of an event can be found by conducting repeated trials. Compare the number of times an event actually occurs to the total number of trials, or times you repeat the activity.

$$\text{Experimental probability} = \frac{\text{number of times event occurs}}{\text{total number of trials}}$$

You can use experimental probability to predict future events.

A Predict what you think will happen when you toss a coin 50 times.

B Toss the coin. Record the result in a tally table.

C Repeat for a total of 50 trials.

D Use your results to find the experimental probability of tossing heads.

$$\frac{\text{number of times heads occurs}}{\text{total number of tosses}} = \frac{\blacksquare}{50} \text{ or } \blacksquare \text{ out of } 50$$

E Find the mathematical probability of tossing heads.

$$\frac{\text{number of favorable outcomes (heads)}}{\text{total possible outcomes (heads, tails)}} = \frac{\blacksquare}{\blacksquare}$$

Draw Conclusions

1. Compare your prediction with the outcomes shown in the tally table. Was your prediction close? Explain.

2. Compare your experimental probability with that of your classmates. Did everyone get the same answer? Why do you think this is so?

3. **Analysis** Is your experimental probability the same as the mathematical probability? Why do you think this is so?

Quick Review

Find the probability when a number cube labeled 1 to 6 is tossed.

1. even number
2. 2 or 3
3. not 6
4. 1
5. 4, 5, or 6

Vocabulary

experimental probability

Coin Toss Experiment

	Prediction	Outcome	Tally
Heads			
Tails			

SDAP 2.2 Express outcomes of experimental probability situations verbally and numerically (e.g., 3 out of 4; $\frac{3}{4}$).
also NS 1.7, SDAP 2.0, SDAP 2.1, MR 2.0, MR 2.3, MR 2.4, MR 3.1, MR 3.2

Experimental probability comes closer to the mathematical probability as the number of trials increases. You can combine your results with those of your classmates to see this.

Yuri and nine classmates combined their results. The total number of trials is now 500 instead of 50.

The mathematical probability of heads is $\frac{1}{2}$. Look at the results for heads.

- Which experimental probability results came closer to $\frac{1}{2}$, Yuri's or the total combined results?

Coin Toss Experiment				
	Heads	Experimental Probability	Tails	Experimental Probability
Yuri	18	$\frac{18}{50}$	32	$\frac{32}{50}$
Total	230	$\frac{230}{500}$	270	$\frac{270}{500}$

TALK Math

Explain the difference between experimental probability and mathematical probability.

Practice

1. Toss a cube labeled 1 to 6 thirty times. Record the outcomes in a tally table. Write the experimental probability of rolling 1 as a fraction.

2. **USE DATA Reasoning** Mary plans to spin the pointer of Spinner A 30 times. Spinner A has equal sections. Mary predicts that the pointer will stop on red 3 times. Do you agree with Mary's prediction? Why or why not?

A

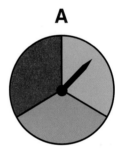

USE DATA For 3–6, use Spinner B and the table. Spinner B has equal sections.

3. How many times did Maryellen spin the pointer?

4. What is the experimental probability of spinning red? What is the mathematical probability?

5. What is the experimental probability of not spinning green? What is the mathematical probability?

6. **WRITE Math** What's the Question? Sue used the table to determine a probability. The answer is $\frac{14}{40}$.

B

Maryellen's Results				
Outcomes	Blue	Red	Green	Yellow
Tally	卌 卌 卌 III	卌 III	卌 卌 IIII	

Technology
Use Harcourt Mega Math, Fraction Action, *Last Chance Canyon*, Level I.

LESSON 6 — Tree Diagrams

OBJECTIVE: Use a tree diagram to determine all possible combinations.

Quick Review

What is the mathematical probability of tossing a number that is not a 2 on a cube labeled 1 to 6?

Learn

PROBLEM Mandy is playing a game. She pulls a marble out of the bag and tosses a number cube labeled 1 to 6. All the marbles are the same size. How many possible outcomes are there?

Vocabulary

tree diagram

You can use a **tree diagram** to make an organized list that shows all the possible outcomes of an event and the total number of outcomes.

Marble	Cube	Outcomes
red	1	red, 1
	2	red, 2
	3	red, 3
	4	red, 4
	5	red, 5
	6	red, 6
green	1	green, 1
	2	green, 2
	3	green, 3
	4	green, 4
	5	green, 5
	6	green, 6
yellow	1	yellow, 1
	2	yellow, 2
	3	yellow, 3
	4	yellow, 4
	5	yellow, 5
	6	yellow, 6

So, the total number of outcomes is 18.

• **Reasoning** What multiplication sentence can you write to find the total number of outcomes?

Guided Practice

1. How many outcomes in the tree diagram above show pulling a yellow marble and tossing a number less than 3?

Make a tree diagram to solve.

2. Tara tosses a coin and tosses a cube labeled 1 to 6. How many outcomes show tossing heads and an even number?

3. Tyrone tosses a penny and a nickel. How many possible outcomes are there?

4. **TALK Math** Explain how a tree diagram helps find all possible outcomes.

 SDAP 2.1 Represent all possible outcomes for a simple probability situation in an organized way (e.g., tables, grids, tree diagrams). *also* **MR 2.3, MR 2.4, MR 3.2**

USE DATA Make a tree diagram to solve. For 5–7, use the pictures.

5. Charlie spins the pointer and tosses the penny. How many outcomes show spinning red or blue and tossing heads?

6. Yolanda tosses the penny and pulls a marble from the bag. What are the possible outcomes?

7. Irma spins the pointer and pulls one marble out of the bag. How many possible outcomes are there?

For 8–9, choose one of each. Find the number of possible outcomes by making a tree diagram.

8. Clothing choices
Pants: blue, black, tan
Shirts: red, yellow

9. Snack choices
Cracker: wheat, graham
Topping: peanut butter, cheese

10. **Reasoning** Sam's team is choosing new baseball uniforms. They can choose red or yellow hats and white, black or grey shirts. List all posiible outcomes.

11. Ian tosses a coin and spins a pointer with black, white, and yellow sections. List all possible outcomes.

12. Using the information from Problem 11, how many outcomes show spinning white?

13. **WRITE Math** **Explain** how to find the outcomes of tossing a number cube labeled 1 to 6 and pulling a marble from a bag with 1 red, 1 green, 1 pink, and 1 orange marble.

Achieving the Standards

14. Bob surveyed students about their favorite subjects. The results were math—23, reading—18, and science—21. Display Bob's results in a bar graph. How many more students chose math and reading than science? (SDAP 1.1, p. 346)

15. Robin bikes a trail every weekend. The trail is 28 miles long. If she rode the trail for 52 weeks, about how many miles did she ride in all? (O—n NS 3.3, p. 220)

16. Which quadrilateral has only one set of parallel sides? (MG 3.8, p. 530)

17. **Test Prep** At summer camp, each camper has to choose one arts and crafts activity and one sports activity. How many different outcomes are possible?

Arts and Crafts	Sports
painting	soccer
woodworking	archery
ceramics	swimming

 **Extra Practice**

Set A Tell whether the event is *likely*, *unlikely*, *certain*, or *impossible*. (pp. 634–637)

1. pulling a blue tile from a bag that contains 26 green, 14 yellow, and 2 blue tiles of the same size

2. tossing a number less than 1 on a number cube labeled 1 to 6

For each experiment, tell whether Events A and B are equally likely or not equally likely. If they are not equally likely, name the event that is more likely.

3. Experiment: Spin the pointer

Event A: purple
Event B: green

4. Experiment: Pull one marble from the bag of marbles of the same size.

Event A: blue
Event B: red

Set B For 1–5, use the spinner to find the probability of each event. The spinner has equal sections. (pp. 638–649)

1. spinning orange
2. spinning purple

3. spinning red
4. spinning green or orange

5. spinning a color that is not blue

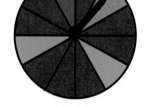

For 6–10, use the equal-sized cards. Write the probability as a fraction. Then, tell whether each event is *certain*, *impossible*, *likely*, or *unlikely*.

6. pulling an R
7. pulling an A or a C

8. pulling a H or a T
9. pulling a G

10. pulling an A, C, or R

C H A R A C T E R

Set C Make a tree diagram to solve.
For 1–2, use the pictures. (pp. 642–643)

1. Anita tosses the penny and spins the pointer. What are the possible outcomes?

2. Ian pulls one tile out of the bag of same-sized tiles and spins the pointer. How many possible outcomes are there?

Technology
Use Harcourt Mega Math, Fraction Action, *Last Chance Canyon*, Levels C, F, I.

PRACTICE GAME

Probably, Probably Not

 Players
2 teams of 2 players each

Materials
- 2 number cubes labeled 1 to 6
- Event cards

> The probability of tossing a 3 is $\frac{1}{6}$.

How to Play!

- Players shuffle the cards and place them facedown in a stack. The top card is turned face up.

- Each team determines the probability of the event shown on the card. Then they predict the results of tossing the cube 10 times.

- The team with the closest prediction scores 1 point.

- Play continues until one team scores 5 points to win the game.

Check Vocabulary and Concepts

For 1–3, choose the best term from the box.

1. An __?__ is the result of an experiment. (SDAP 2.1, p. 628)

2. When you __?__ , you make a reasonable guess about what might happen. (SDAP 2.0, p. 634)

3. A __?__ is an organized list that shows possible combinations of groups of objects or of an event. (SDAP 2.2, p. 644)

4. **Explain** the difference between experimental and mathematical probability. (SDAP 2.2, pp. 638–641, pp. 642–643)

Check Skills

Tell whether the event is *likely, unlikely, certain,* or *impossible.* (SDAP 2.0, pp. 634–637)

5. tossing a 0 on a number cube labeled 1 to 6

6. spinning an odd number on a spinner with three equal parts labeled 1 to 3

For 7–11, use the equal-sized cards. Write the probability as a fraction. Then, tell whether each event is *certain, impossible, likely,* or *unlikely.* (SDAP 2.2, pp. 638–640)

T R E A T M E N T

7. pulling a T

8. pulling a T, R, E, A, M, or N

9. pulling an A

10. pulling an M, E, or T

11. pulling an S

Make a tree diagram to solve. (SDAP 2.1, pp. 644–645)

12. James tossed a coin and pulled a marble out of a bag with one blue marble and one red marble. The marbles are the same size. How many possible outcomes are there?

13. Lonnie tosses a number cube labeled 1 to 6 and tosses a coin. How many possible outcomes are there?

Check Problem Solving

Solve. (SDAP 2.1, MR 2.0 pp. 630–633)

14. Amir is playing a game that uses two number cubes labeled 1 to 6. He earns an extra turn if he tosses 10 or greater. Name the ways Amir earn an extra turn.

15. **WRITE Math** **Explain** how Amir can organize a list to find all the possible combinations of tossing two number cubes labeled 1 to 6.

 Technology Use *Online Assessment.*

Enrich • Make Predictions
Guessing Games

Many popular games that you play use probability.

Most likely: the outcome that will occur the most.	If there are 5 red marbles and 1 blue marble in a bag, you are most likely to pull a red marble.
Least likely: the outcome that will occur the least.	If there are 5 red marbles and 1 blue marble in a bag, you are least likely to pull a blue marble.
Equally likely as: two outcomes have the same chance of happening.	If there are 2 red and 2 blue marbles in a bag, then red is equally likely as blue to be pulled.

Predict and Play

Alison and Jed are playing a number game. They each take turns tossing two number cubes. Then they add the numbers to find the score for each toss. Alison tosses a 3 and a 6, so they add 3 and 6 to get a total of 9.

When the results for tossing 2 number cubes are added, the least possible total is 2. The greatest possible total is 12.

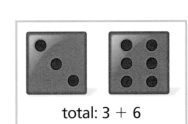

total: 3 + 6

Least possible total:

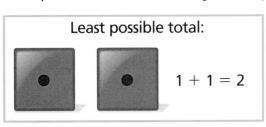

1 + 1 = 2

Greatest possible total:

6 + 6 = 12

• Predict which totals will occur most and least often. Why?

Game Toss

Materials ■ 2 number cubes

Play the number cube game with a classmate. Toss the number cubes 20 times. Record your totals in a tally table.

WRITE Math ▶ **Explain** how your prediction compares to your actual results and why.

Multiple Choice

1. Which statement about the figures is true?
(MG 1.3, p. 616)

A They have the same perimeter, but different areas

B They are the same length, but different heights.

C They have the same perimeter and the same area.

D They have the same area, but different perimeters.

2. What is the perimeter of the figure?
(MG 1.4, p. 600)

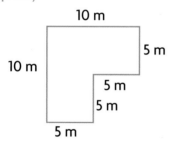

A 40 meters   **C** 75 meters

B 50 meters   **D** 100 meters

3. Tom wants to paint a wall with the dimensions of 10 feet long by 8 feet wide. What is the area of the wall Tom wants to paint? (MG 1.4, p. 608)

A 80 square feet

B 36 square feet

C 18 square feet

D 2 square feet

4. Which describes the probability of pulling a red marble from this bag of marbles of the same size? (SDAP 2.2, p. 642)

A $\frac{0}{8}$ **C** $\frac{2}{8}$

B $\frac{1}{8}$ **D** $\frac{3}{8}$

5. Which unit should be used to measure the area of Joni's patio? (MG 1.1, p. 608)

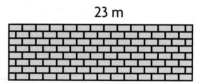

23 m

10 m

A meters

B square meters

C centimeters

D square centimeters

6. Which is not a possible outcome of spinning the spinner and tossing the coin? (SDAP 2.1, p. 628)

A red, heads

B green, tails

C tails, heads

D blue, heads

GO Technology Use *Online Assessment.*

7. Marta has a picture that is 12 inches long and 7 inches wide. What is the perimeter of Marta's picture? (MG 1.4, p. 600)

  A 84 inches

  B 38 inches

  C 19 inches

  D 5 inches

8. Without looking, which color marble are you most likely to pull from this bag of marbles of the same size?

(SDAP 2.0, p. 634)

  A green

  B yellow

  C red

  D blue

9. Mr. Van Ness is making a sandbox for his children. He wants the area of the sandbox to be 24 square feet. Which could not be the perimeter of the sandbox? (MG 1.2, p. 616)

  A 28 feet

  B 22 feet

  C 20 feet

  D 18 feet

Short Response

10. What is the probability, written as a fraction, that the pointer will stop on red? (SDAP 2.2, p. 638)

11. Stephanie has the shirts and pants shown below. How many different combinations of outfits can she choose? (SDAP 2.1, p. 644)

12. How many different outcomes are possible for tossing a number cube labeled 1 through 6 and tossing a coin? (SDAP 2.1, p. 628)

Extended Response ⟨ WRITE Math ⟩

13. Terry has a square table. The perimeter of the table is 92 inches. What is the length of each side of Terry's table? **Explain** how you found your answer. (MG 1.4, p. 600)

14. Nancy has a stuffed bear, a game, and a puzzle on her shelf. How many different ways are there for Nancy to place the toys on the shelf? Use a tree diagram to **explain** your answer. (SDAP 2.1, p. 644)

Birthday Rocks

BEAUTIFUL BIRTHSTONES

Do you know that many people buy jewelry based on the month they were born? Each month has its own birthstone. Many of the birthstones are found in mines. Topaz, which is November's birthstone, is mined in California.

Topaz

FACT·ACTIVITY

Birthstone Table			
Month	**Birthstone**	**Picture**	**Color**
January	Garnet		Red
February	Amethyst		Purple
March	Aquamarine		Blue
April	Diamond		Clear
May	Emerald		Green
June	Pearl		White
July	Ruby		Red
August	Peridot		Green
September	Sapphire		Blue
October	Opal		White
November	Topaz		Yellow
December	Turquoise		Blue

For 1–3, use the Birthstone Table.

❶ Make an organized list to see how many ways you can arrange stones on a ring that includes garnet, peridot, and topaz.

❷ If one of each birthstone is in a bag, what is the probability of selecting a red stone? What is the probability of selecting either a blue or a green stone?

❸ Survey and record 12 classmates' birthstones. If your results were placed in a bag, what would be the probability of choosing a green birthstone? **Explain.**

LIKELY GEMS

Most gems are mined from deep within Earth. Some people call gems like diamonds, emeralds, and rubies *precious gems* because they are rare. *Semiprecious gems* are found more often.

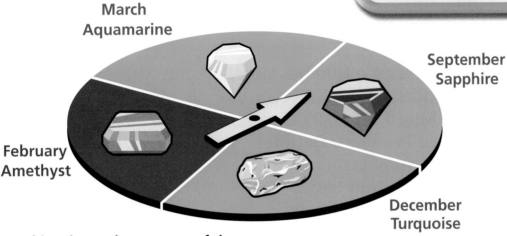

March
Aquamarine

September
Sapphire

February
Amethyst

December
Turquoise

This spinner shows some of the birthstones grouped by color.

FACT·ACTIVITY

For 1–2, use the spinner above.

❶ How many possible color outcomes are there for the spinner? Name them.

❷ On which color is the pointer more likely to land? **Explain.**

Make your own spinner and a birthstone game.

► Make a spinner with 8 or more sections of the same size. Place the 3 birthstone colors you like best in any arrangement on the spinner.

► Make up and write out the rules for a birthstone board game that uses your spinner. For example, players might move ahead depending on the color the pointer lands on.

Student Handbook

Review the Key Standards

These pages provide review of every state standard for your grade. They also help you avoid errors students often make.

🐻 Review the Key Standards

Read and Write Whole Numbers

O—π NS 1.1 Read and write whole numbers in the millions.

Use place value and periods to read and write numbers.

Read the number in each period, and put the period name at the end of each period when you read a number and write it in word form.

PERIODS

MILLIONS			THOUSANDS			ONES		
Hundreds	Tens	Ones	Hundreds	Tens	Ones	Hundreds	Tens	Ones
3	5	8,	3	0	2,	0	4	6

Standard Form: 358,302,046

Word Form: three hundred fifty-eight million,
three hundred two thousand, forty-six

Examples

A Write 3,470,509 in word form.

MILLIONS			THOUSANDS			ONES		
Hundreds	Tens	Ones	Hundreds	Tens	Ones	Hundreds	Tens	Ones
		3,	4	7	0,	5	0	9

So, 3,470,509 written in word form is three million, four hundred seventy thousand, five hundred nine.

ERROR ALERT

Be careful not to confuse periods and place value. The place value of a digit depends on its period.

B Write sixty-one million, four thousand, two hundred ninety in standard form.

MILLIONS			THOUSANDS			ONES		
Hundreds	Tens	Ones	Hundreds	Tens	Ones	Hundreds	Tens	Ones
	6	1,	0	0	4,	2	9	0

So, the number written in standard form is 61,004,290.

Try It

Write each number in word form.

1. 709,015

2. 3,084,900

3. 160,520,003

4. 19,007,201

5. 40,156,300

6. 5,601,192

Write each number in standard form.

7. forty-three million, one hundred two thousand, ten

8. five hundred million, ninety thousand, three hundred six

9. two hundred seventy-six thousand, three hundred twelve

10. eighteen million, nine hundred thousand, five

11. three million, seven hundred fifty thousand, eight hundred

12. ninety million, sixty-one thousand, two hundred forty-three

Solve.

13. A country's population is 50,736,000. Write this number in word form.

14. There were 7,309,500 people watching the program. Write this number in word form.

15. The budget for the movie was twenty-four million, eight hundred eleven thousand dollars. Write this number in standard form.

16. Three hundred four million, five hundred sixty thousand shirts were made at the factory. Write this number in standard form.

17. The Sequoia National Park covers 402,051 acres. Write this number in word form.

18. Mount Whitney is the tallest peak in California at fourteen thousand, four hundred ninety-four feet. Write this number in standard form.

19. Read the problem below. **COMMON ERROR** **Explain** why D cannot be the correct answer choice. Then choose the correct answer.

    Which of these is the number 6,030,020 written in word form?

    A six million, three thousand, twenty

    B six million, thirty thousand, twenty

    C six thousand, three hundred, twenty

    D six billion, thirty million, twenty

20. Read the problem below. **COMMON ERROR** **Explain** why C cannot be the correct answer choice. Then choose the correct answer.

    The estimated cost of a new stadium is eighty-five million dollars. What is this number in standard form?

    A $80,500

    B $85,000

    C $80,500,000

    D $85,000,000

🐻 Review the Key Standards

Order and Compare Whole Numbers

🔑 NS 1.2 Order and compare whole numbers and decimals to two decimal places.

Use place value to compare whole numbers. Begin at the greatest place value. Compare the digits in each place until the digits are different.

Use a place-value chart to order 2,317,209; 2,342,106; and 2,135,875 from least to greatest.

MILLIONS			THOUSANDS			ONES		
Hundreds	Tens	Ones	Hundreds	Tens	Ones	Hundreds	Tens	Ones
		2,	3	1	7,	2	0	9
		2,	3	4	2,	1	0	6
		2,	1	3	5,	8	7	5

ERROR ALERT

Be sure to compare digits in the same place-value position.

Step 1

2,317,209
↓   2 = 2
2,342,106
↓
2,135,875

The millions are the same.

Step 2

2,317,209
↓   1 < 3
2,342,106
↓
2,135,875

Since 1 < 3, the least number is 2,135,875.

Step 3

2,317,209
↓   4 > 1
2,342,106
↓

Since 4 > 1, the greatest number is 2,342,106.

So, 2,135,875 < 2,317,209 < 2,342,106.

Try It

Compare. Write <, >, or = for each ●.

1. 72,362 ● 72,329

2. 8,053 ● 8,071

3. 96,795 ● 528,614

4. 308,711 ● 30,785

5. 69,782 ● 69,900

6. 4,369,052 ● 4,396,052

7. Read the problem below. **COMMON ERROR** **Explain** why B cannot be the correct answer choice. Then choose the correct answer.

Which number is the greatest?

A 3,273,096

B 3,095,387

C 3,271,998

D 3,276,142

Review the Key Standards

Order and Compare Decimals

O→ NS 1.2 Order and compare whole numbers and decimals to two decimal places.

Use place value to compare decimals. Line up the decimal points. Then compare the digits beginning with the greatest place value.

Order 3.58, 3.54, and 3.7 from least to greatest. Write equivalent decimals to show the same number of places.

Step 1	**Step 2**	**Step 3**
Compare the ones.	Compare the tenths.	Compare the hundredths.
3.58 $\downarrow$ 3.54 $3 = 3$ $\downarrow$ 3.70	3.58 $\downarrow$ 3.54 $7 > 5$ $\downarrow$ 3.70	3.58 $\downarrow$ 3.54 $4 < 8$
The ones are the same.	Since $7 > 5$, the greatest number is 3.70, or 3.7.	Since $4 < 8$, the least number is 3.54.

So, from least to greatest the numbers are 3.54, 3.58, 3.7.

Examples

A Which number is greater: 6.2 or 6.08?

6.20 $2 > 0$
$\downarrow$
6.08

So, 6.2 is greater.

B Which is the least number: 1.47, 1.3, or 0.65?

1.47 $0 < 1$
$\downarrow$
1.30
$\downarrow$
0.65

So, 0.65 is the least number.

ERROR ALERT

Write a 0 in the hundredths place of decimals with tenths to correctly show an equivalent decimal.

$6.2 = 6.20$

Try It

Compare. Write $<$, $>$, or $=$ for each ●.

1. 6.42 ● 6.6

2. 1.05 ● 0.89

3. 0.05 ● 0.55

4. 7.84 ● 7.8

5. 8.71 ● 8.73

6. 0.89 ● 0.98

7. 9.9 ● 9.09

8. 3.7 ● 3.07

9. 5.3 ● 5.30

10. 0.72 ● 0.69

11. 0.19 ● 0.32

12. 2.51 ● 3.49

13. Read the problem below. **COMMON ERROR** **Explain** why C cannot be the correct answer choice. Then choose the correct answer.

Which number is the greatest?

A 4.6   **C** 4.08

B 4.8   **D** 3.99

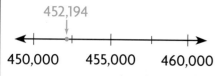

Review the Key Standards

Round Whole Numbers

NS 1.3 Round whole numbers through the millions to the nearest ten, hundred, thousand, ten thousand, or hundred thousand.

Use a number line or use rules to round a number to a given place.
Round 2,483,501 to the nearest hundred thousand.

Use a number line.

Locate the number on the number line.
2,483,501 is between 2,400,000 and 2,500,000.

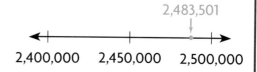

2,400,000   2,450,000   2,500,000

Find the hundred thousand to which the number is
closer. 2,483,501 is closer to 2,500,000 than to 2,400,000.

Use place value.

Find the place to which you want to round.
Look at the digit to the right of the
rounding place.

2,4**8**3,501
↑
rounding place

If the digit is *less than 5*, the digit in the
rounding place stays the same.

The digit to the right
of the rounding place is
greater than 5.

If the digit is *5 or greater*, the digit in the
rounding place increases by 1.

2,500,000

Change all the digits to the right of the
rounding place to zero.

ERROR ALERT

Be sure to look
only one place
to the right of
the digit of the
rounding place.

So, 2,483,501 rounded to the nearest hundred thousand
is 2,500,000.

Examples

Ⓐ What is 452,194 rounded
to the nearest ten thousand?

452,194
↓
450,000   455,000   460,000

So, 452,194 rounded to the
nearest ten thousand is 450,000.

Ⓑ What is 3,267,451 rounded
to the nearest thousand?

3,26**7**,451
↑
rounding place

So, 3,267,451 rounded to the
nearest thousand is 3,267,000.

Try It

Round each number to the place of the underlined digit.

1. 648,<u>2</u>09
2. 1,090,341 (underline under second 0 in 090)
3. 24,7<u>2</u>8,429
4. 6,4<u>8</u>5
5. 17,<u>3</u>46
6. 40,<u>1</u>56,397
7. 6<u>0</u>5,123
8. <u>3</u>9,092

Round each number to the nearest ten, hundred, and thousand.

9. 7,041
10. 21,529
11. 435,652
12. 19,327
13. 592,003
14. 2,584
15. 83,207
16. 299,380

Round each number to the nearest thousand, ten thousand, and hundred thousand.

17. 105,398
18. 27,945,928
19. 418,386,471
20. 2,148,503
21. 6,038,224
22. 95,309
23. 39,577,612
24. 772,047

Solve.

25. Two hundred sixty-one students attended the summer basketball camp. Round this number to the nearest hundred.

26. There were 15,392 people who attended the concert. Round this number to the nearest ten thousand.

27. There are 2,218 television stations in the United States. Round this number to the nearest thousand.

28. In 2005, the population of San Francisco was 739,426. Round this number to the nearest hundred thousand.

29. The state fair had 426,357 visitors during the first week. Round this number to the nearest ten thousand.

30. Dinner was served to 138 people at the restaurant. Round this number to the nearest ten.

31. Read the problem below. **COMMON ERROR** **Explain** why C cannot be the correct answer choice. Then choose the correct answer.

    What is 43,628,729 rounded to the nearest hundred thousand?

    A 43,000,000

    B 43,600,000

    C 43,630,000

    D 43,700,000

32. Read the problem below. **COMMON ERROR** **Explain** why D cannot be the correct answer choice. Then choose the correct answer.

    The total length of a vehicle is 215 inches. What is the length of the vehicle rounded to the nearest hundred inches?

    A 200

    B 210

    C 220

    D 300

Review the Key Standards

Rounded Solutions

O━ NS 1.4 Decide when a rounded solution is called for and explain why such a solution may be appropriate.

Sometimes only an estimate is needed to solve a problem. Use mental math to estimate when an exact answer is not needed. Rounding might be appropriate when you are trying to find about how much or about how many.

The Diaz family drove 212 miles on the first day of their vacation. On the second day, they drove 91 miles, and on the third day, they drove 64 miles. About how many miles did they drive in three days?

Estimate the total number of miles. Rounding is appropriate because the problem asks "about how many miles."

Round each number to the nearest ten.	Then add to estimate the total.
212 rounds to 210. 91 rounds to 90. 64 rounds to 60.	210 + 90 + 60 = 360

So, the Diaz family drove about 360 miles in three days.

Rounding might also be appropriate when comparing to solve a problem.

Julius has $20. He wants to buy a pair of sandals that costs $14.50, some socks that cost $5.25, and a magazine that costs $2.95. Does Julius have enough money to pay for all of these items?

Estimate the total cost. Rounding is appropriate because you can use an estimate to compare the approximate cost to the amount of money Julius has.

Round each amount to the nearest dollar.	Add to estimate the total cost.
$14.50 rounds to $15. $5.25 rounds to $5. $2.95 rounds to $3.	$15 + $5 + $3 = $23 $23 > $20

So, Julius does not have enough money to pay for all the items.

Examples

A There are 173 students in grade 3. There are 136 in grade 4, and 96 in grade 5. Are there more than 500 students?

173 rounds up to 180.

136 rounds to 140.

96 rounds to 100.

180 + 140 + 100 = 420

420 < 500

So, there are fewer than 500 students at the school.

B The jogging path around the park is 220 yards long. If Denisha runs around the track 4 times, will she run at least 800 yards?

220 rounds to 200.

200 × 4 = 800

800 ≥ 800

So, Denisha will run at least 800 yards.

> **ERROR ALERT**
>
> When estimating sums and differences, be sure to round each number to the greatest place value of the least number. Then use mental math to solve the problem.

Try It

Solve. Explain why a rounded solution might be appropriate.

1. There are 600 seats in the movie theater. Are there enough seats for 289 children and 214 adults to see a movie?

2. Amber has $15. She wants to buy some markers that cost $2.19, some crayons that cost $3.75, and an art pad that costs $6.97. Does she have enough money?

3. Students have set a goal to collect 1,000 cans of food for the food bank. The first graders have 145 cans, and the second graders have 183 cans. The third graders have 276 cans, and the fourth graders have 329 cans. Have the students reached their goal?

4. To train for a race, Mateo wants to ride his bike more than 400 miles during the week. He has ridden 72 miles each day for 6 days. Does he have to ride the seventh day to meet his goal of 400 miles?

5. Read the problem below. **COMMON ERROR** **Explain** why A cannot be the correct answer choice. Then choose the correct answer.

   A pilot flew 286 hours in the first month, 79 hours in the second month, and 114 hours in the third month. About how many hours did the pilot fly in three months?

   A 290 hours

   B 400 hours

   C 480 hours

   D 600 hours

6. Read the problem below. **COMMON ERROR** **Explain** why A cannot be the correct answer choice. Then choose the correct answer.

   Ling needs at least 275 ribbons for field day. She has 2 packages of 55 ribbons and 2 packages of 110 ribbons. Does she have enough ribbons?

   A No, she needs at least 100 more.

   B No, she needs only a few more.

   C Yes, she has just enough.

   D Yes, she has more than enough.

🐻 Review the Key Standards

Negative Numbers on a Number Line

🔑 NS 1.8 Use concepts of negative numbers (e.g., on a number line, in counting, in temperature, in "owing").

On a number line, negative numbers are to the left of 0. Positive numbers are to the right of 0. Use a number line to compare negative numbers.

The star is located at ⁻5, and the heart is located at ⁻2. The number ⁻5 lies to the left of the number ⁻2.

So, ⁻5 < ⁻2.

ERROR ALERT

Examples

> **A** What letter represents ⁻3 on the number line?
>
>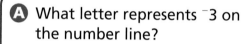
>
> The letter *K* is located at ⁻3.

> **B** Is this number sentence true or false? ⁻4 > ⁻1
>
>
>
> ⁻4 < ⁻1 because ⁻4 lies to the left of ⁻1 on the number line. So, the number sentence is false.

Be sure to count down from 0 as you label negative numbers on the number line.

Try It

Name the number represented by each letter.

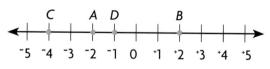

1. *A*   **2.** *B*   **3.** *C*   **4.** *D*

Use a number line. Tell whether the number sentence is *true* or *false*.

5. ⁻8 > ⁻12   **6.** ⁻15 < ⁻10

7. ⁻5 > ⁺1   **8.** 0 > ⁻7

9. Read the problem below. **Explain** why D cannot be the correct answer choice. Then choose the correct answer. **COMMON ERROR**

Which symbol is located at ⁻2 on the number line below?

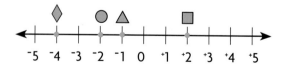

A ◇   **B** ◯   **C** △   **D** ▢

![bear] Review the Key Standards

Negative Numbers

○━┓ NS 1.8 Use concepts of negative numbers (e.g., on a number line, in counting, in temperature, in "owing").

A thermometer is a number line that shows temperatures. Temperatures less than 0°C are negative temperatures. On a thermometer, negative temperatures are located below the zero mark.

Use a thermometer to find temperature changes.

> The temperature was 5°C. Then it fell 8°. Find the new temperature. Start at 5°C. Count down 8° to find the new temperature: 4°, 3°, 2°, 1°, 0°, ⁻1°, ⁻2°, ⁻3° So, the new temperature is ⁻3°C.

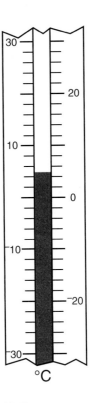

°C

Examples

Ⓐ Find the change in temperature from ⁻6°C to 9°C.

Change from ⁻6° to 0° is 6°.

Change from 0° to 9° is 9°.

6° + 9° = 15°

So, the change is 15°C.

Ⓑ Use a positive or negative number to represent a situation.

> Willie gave his brother 12 of his baseball cards.

⁻12 represents this situation in which Willie has 12 fewer baseball cards.

ERROR ALERT

Use zero as a point of reference when finding the change between positive and negative temperatures.

Try It

Use a thermometer to find the change in temperature.

1. 7°C to 12°C
2. ⁻5°C to 4°C
3. ⁻2°C to 9°C
4. ⁻1°C to ⁻8°C

Write a positive or negative number to represent each.

5. Darla saved $5.
6. Andy paid $5 for oranges.

7. Read the problem below. **Explain** why D cannot be the correct answer choice. Then choose the correct answer.   **COMMON ERROR**

At noon, the temperature was 4°C. By midnight, the temperature had dropped 10°. What was the midnight temperature?

A ⁻14°C   C ⁻6°C

B ⁻10°C   D 14°C

🐻 Review the Key Standards

Fractions and Mixed Numbers

○━🗝 NS 1.9 Identify on a number line the relative position of positive fractions, positive mixed numbers, and positive decimals to two places.

A fraction is a number that names a part of a whole. A mixed number is an amount given as a whole number and a fraction. Fractions and mixed numbers can be located on a number line.

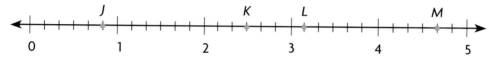

Determine the number of equal parts between whole numbers to find the number of equal parts in the whole. There are 6 equal parts marked between whole numbers.

So, point J is located at $\frac{5}{6}$, K at $2\frac{3}{6}$, L at $3\frac{1}{6}$, and M at $4\frac{4}{6}$.

ERROR ALERT

Check the number of equal parts between whole numbers to determine the denominator of the fraction.

Examples

A What fraction does point W represent?

Fractional parts are tenths.

So, point W is located at $\frac{7}{10}$.

B What mixed number does point H represent?

Fractional parts are fourths.

So, point H is located at $9\frac{1}{4}$.

Try It

Use the number line to write the fraction or mixed number represented by each letter.

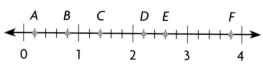

1. A **2.** B

3. C **4.** D

5. E **6.** F

7. Read the problem below. **Explain** why A cannot be the correct answer choice. Then choose the correct answer.   **COMMON ERROR**

On the number line below, what mixed number does point R represent?

A $24\frac{3}{4}$ **C** $26\frac{3}{8}$

B $25\frac{1}{4}$ **D** $27\frac{1}{8}$

Review the Key Standards

Fractions, Mixed Numbers, Decimals

NS 1.9 Identify on a number line the relative position of positive fractions, positive mixed numbers, and positive decimals to two places.

Fractions, mixed numbers, and decimals can be located on a number line. Use equivalent fractions or decimals to name each point as a fraction, mixed number, or decimal.

Point Q is located at 0.3, or $\frac{3}{10}$.

Point R is halfway between 1.7 and 1.8 at 1.75, and $1.75 = 1\frac{75}{100}$.

Point S is located at 2.5, and $2.5 = 2\frac{5}{10} = 2\frac{1}{2}$.

ERROR ALERT

Use equivalent fractions when renaming decimals as fractions or to simplify fractions.

Examples

A Which letter represents 2.6?

$2.6 = 2\frac{6}{10} = 2\frac{3}{5}$

So, *A* represents 2.6.

B Which letter represents the number closest to 0.4?

$\frac{2}{4} = \frac{1}{2} = 0.5$

So, *T* is closest to 0.4.

Try It

Write the letter that represents each number on the number line.

1. $\frac{1}{4}$

2. 1.75

3. $1\frac{1}{4}$

4. $1\frac{1}{2}$

5. 0.5

6. $\frac{7}{8}$

7. Read the problem below. **COMMON ERROR** **Explain** why D cannot be the correct answer choice. Then choose the correct answer.

Which letter represents the number *closest* to 3.5?

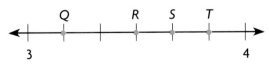

A Q

B R

C S

D T

🐻 Review the Key Standards

Add Multidigit Numbers

🔑 **NS 3.0** Students solve problems involving addition, subtraction, multiplication, and division of whole numbers and understand the relationships among the operations.
🔑 **NS 3.1** Demonstrate an understanding of, and the ability to use, standard algorithms for the addition and subtraction of multidigit numbers.

Use place value to add multidigit numbers. Line up the digits by place value. Remember to regroup when necessary.

Use place value to find the sum of 264,986 and 17,563.

Step 1	Step 2	Step 3	Step 4
Start by lining up like place values. Add the ones. Add the tens. Regroup.	Add the hundreds. Regroup.	Add the thousands. Regroup.	Add the ten thousands. Finally, add the hundred thousands.
$\begin{array}{r} ^{1} \\ 264,986 \\ +\ 17,563 \\ \hline 49 \end{array}$	$\begin{array}{r} ^{1\ 1} \\ 264,986 \\ +\ 17,563 \\ \hline 549 \end{array}$	$\begin{array}{r} ^{11\ 1} \\ 264,986 \\ +\ 17,563 \\ \hline 2,549 \end{array}$	$\begin{array}{r} ^{11\ 1} \\ 264,986 \\ +\ 17,563 \\ \hline 282,549 \end{array}$

So, 264,986 + 17,563 = 282,549.

Examples

A Add. 342,546 + 6,827 $\begin{array}{r} ^{1\ \ 1} \\ 342,546 \\ +\ \ \ \ 6,827 \\ \hline 349,373 \end{array}$	**B** Find the sum. 8,965 + 7,389 $\begin{array}{r} ^{1\ 11} \\ 8,965 \\ +\ 7,389 \\ \hline 16,354 \end{array}$

ERROR ALERT

Be sure to record the regrouping in each place every time you regroup to add.

Try It

Find the sum.

1. $\begin{array}{r} 69,028 \\ +\ 4,982 \\ \hline \end{array}$

2. $\begin{array}{r} 70,386 \\ +\ 28,438 \\ \hline \end{array}$

3. $\begin{array}{r} 196,935 \\ +\ 294,053 \\ \hline \end{array}$

4. $\begin{array}{r} 537,923 \\ +\ 24,278 \\ \hline \end{array}$

5. $\begin{array}{r} 8,973 \\ +\ 736 \\ \hline \end{array}$

6. $\begin{array}{r} 8,915 \\ +\ 320,143 \\ \hline \end{array}$

7. 2,156 + 7,895

8. 4,978 + 39,827

9. Read the problem below. **Explain** why A cannot be the correct answer choice. Then choose the correct answer.

COMMON ERROR

$\begin{array}{r} 25,374 \\ +\ 8,956 \\ \hline \end{array}$

A 23,220   **C** 34,330

B 34,230   **D** 34,430

🐻 Review the Key Standards

Subtract Multidigit Numbers

⊶ NS 3.0 Students solve problems involving addition, subtraction, multiplication, and division of whole numbers and understand the relationships among the operations.
⊶ NS 3.1 Demonstrate an understanding of, and the ability to use, standard algorithms for the addition and subtraction of multidigit numbers.

Use place value to subtract multidigit numbers. Line up the digits by place value. Remember to regroup when necessary.

Use place value to subtract $718,645 - 35,248$.

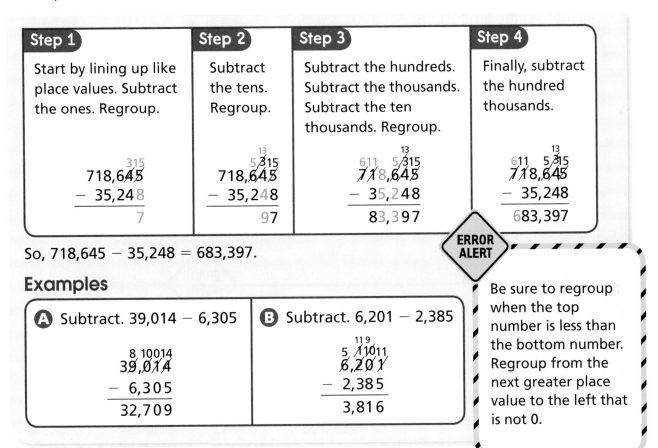

So, $718,645 - 35,248 = 683,397$.

Examples

A Subtract. $39,014 - 6,305$

$$\begin{array}{r} 39,014 \\ -\ 6,305 \\ \hline 32,709 \end{array}$$

B Subtract. $6,201 - 2,385$

$$\begin{array}{r} 6,201 \\ -\ 2,385 \\ \hline 3,816 \end{array}$$

ERROR ALERT

Be sure to regroup when the top number is less than the bottom number. Regroup from the next greater place value to the left that is not 0.

Try It

Find the difference.

1. $\begin{array}{r} 9,002 \\ -\ 4,371 \\ \hline \end{array}$

2. $\begin{array}{r} 42,073 \\ -\ 5,268 \\ \hline \end{array}$

3. $\begin{array}{r} 862,094 \\ -\ 124,182 \\ \hline \end{array}$

4. $\begin{array}{r} 703,825 \\ -\ 6,492 \\ \hline \end{array}$

5. $\begin{array}{r} 6,431 \\ -\ 579 \\ \hline \end{array}$

6. $\begin{array}{r} 80,075 \\ -\ 6,238 \\ \hline \end{array}$

7. Read the problem below. **COMMON ERROR** **Explain** why D cannot be the correct answer choice. Then choose the correct answer.

$$52,064 - 8,437$$

A 43,627   C 53,637

B 44,637   D 56,433

Review the Key Standards

Multiply by Two-Digit Numbers

NS 3.0 Students solve problems involving addition, subtraction, multiplication, and division of whole numbers and understand the relationships among the operations.
NS 3.2 Demonstrate an understanding of, and the ability to use, standard algorithms for multiplying a multidigit number by a two-digit number and for dividing a multidigit number by a one-digit number; use relationships between them to simplify computations and to check results.

Use place value to multiply by two-digit numbers. Align the digits by place value. Remember to regroup when necessary.

Use place value to find the product $46 \times 5{,}378$.

First, multiply the ones.	Then multiply the tens.	Finally, add the partial products.
2 44 5,378 $\times$ 46 32 268	1 3 3 2 44 5,378 $\times$ 46 32 268 215 120	1 3 3 2 44 5,378 $\times$ 46 32 268 +215 120 247,388

So, $46 \times 5{,}378 = 247{,}388$.

Examples

A Multiply. $3{,}007 \times 58$
Find the partial products.
Then add.

3,007	3,007	24,056
$\times$ 8	$\times$ 50	$+150{,}350$
24,056	150,350	174,406

B Find the product.

5
2
892
$\times$ 63
2 676
53 520
56,196

ERROR ALERT

Be sure to record the zero in the ones place when finding the partial product of the tens.

Try It

Find the product.

1. 846
   $\times$ 78

2. 3,952
   $\times$ 47

3. 1,908
   $\times$ 63

4. 291
   $\times$ 94

5. 2,753
   $\times$ 85

6. 2,672
   $\times$ 45

7. Read the problem below. **COMMON ERROR**
   Explain why A cannot be the correct answer choice. Then choose the correct answer.

   $39 \times 7{,}286$

   A 87,432   **C** 279,204

   B 273,054   **D** 284,154

🐻 Review the Key Standards

Divide by a One-Digit Divisor

🔑 **NS 3.0** Students solve problems involving addition, subtraction, multiplication, and division of whole numbers and understand the relationships among the operations.
🔑 **NS 3.2** Demonstrate an understanding of, and the ability to use, standard algorithms for multiplying a multidigit number by a two-digit number and for dividing a multidigit number by a one-digit number; use relationships between them to simplify computations and to check results.

Use long division to divide a multidigit number by a one-digit divisor. Use compatible numbers to determine where to place the first digit.

Estimate. $133 \div 6$

Think: $120 \div 6 = 20$
$180 \div 6 = 30$

The quotient is between 20 and 30.
So, place the first digit in the tens place.

Follow the process to divide 87 by 7.

ERROR ALERT

Step 1	Step 2	Step 3	
Divide the 8 tens.	Bring down the 7 ones. Divide the 17 ones.	To check, multiply the quotient by the divisor. Then add the remainder.	Place the first digit in the correct place.
$$\begin{array}{r} 1 \\ 7\overline{)87} \\ -7 \\ \hline 1 \end{array}$$ Divide. $8 \div 7$ Multiply. 7×1 Subtract. $8 - 7$ Compare. $1 < 7$	$$\begin{array}{r} 12 \text{ r3} \\ 7\overline{)87} \\ -7 \\ \hline 17 \\ -14 \\ \hline 3 \end{array}$$ Divide. $17 \div 7$ Multiply. 7×2 Subtract. $17 - 14$ Compare. $3 < 7$	$$\begin{array}{r} 1 \\ 12 \\ \times\ 7 \\ \hline 84 \\ +\ 3 \\ \hline 87 \end{array}$$ quotient divisor remainder dividend	INCORRECT: $$\begin{array}{r} 360 \text{ r1} \\ 4\overline{)145} \\ -12 \\ \hline 25 \\ -24 \\ \hline 1 \end{array}$$

So, $87 \div 7 = 12$ r3.

Try It

Divide.

1. $43 \div 8$
2. $37 \div 4$
3. $56 \div 9$
4. $67 \div 3$
5. $329 \div 9$
6. $217 \div 4$
7. $837 \div 5$
8. $722 \div 3$
9. $585 \div 7$
10. $825 \div 6$

11. Read the problem below. **Explain** why C cannot be the correct answer choice. Then choose the correct answer. **COMMON ERROR**

The team manager divided 126 baseball bats equally among 6 boxes. How many bats are in each box?

A 21
B 120
C 210
D 756

![bear] Review the Key Standards

Multiplication

O—π NS 3.0 Students solve problems involving addition, subtraction, multiplication, and division of whole numbers and understand the relationships among the operations.
O—π NS 3.3 Solve problems involving multiplication of multidigit numbers by two-digit numbers.

Use multiplication to solve problems about equal-size groups.

> There are 6,083 people who subscribe to a newsletter. The newsletter is mailed 24 times a year. How many newsletters were mailed last year?

Use multiplication to solve. Multiply. 24 × 6,083

Think: The same number of people received the newsletter for each mailing.

$$
\begin{array}{r}
\overset{1}{\underset{3\ 1}{}} \\
6,083 \\
\times \quad 24 \\
\hline
24\ 332 \\
+121\ 660 \\
\hline
145,992
\end{array}
$$

Estimate to be sure your answer is reasonable.
20 × 6,000 = 120,000
30 × 6,000 = 180,000

The product should be between 120,000 and 180,000.

So, 145,992 newsletters were mailed last year.

> Members of the math club sold banners for $7.95 each. They sold 63 banners. How much money did the math club raise from the banner sales?

Use multiplication to solve. Multiply. $7.95 × 63

Think: Each banner costs the same amount.

$$
\begin{array}{r}
\overset{5\ \ 3}{\underset{2\ 1}{}} \\
\$7.95 \\
\times \quad 63 \\
\hline
23\ 85 \\
+477\ 00 \\
\hline
\$500\,.85
\end{array}
$$

Estimate to be sure your answer is reasonable.
$8 × 60 = $480 $500.85 is close to the estimate of $480.

So, the math club raised $500.85.

Examples

A A citrus farmer has 128 rows of orange trees in his grove. Each row has 35 trees. How many orange trees are in the orange grove?

$$
\begin{array}{r}
\overset{2}{\underset{}{}} \\
\overset{1\,4}{128} \\
\times\ \ 35 \\
\hline
640 \\
+3\,840 \\
\hline
4{,}480
\end{array}
$$

So, there are 4,480 trees in the grove.

B Ms. Santos is ordering 36 rulers for her class. Each ruler costs $0.84. What is the total cost of her order?

$$
\begin{array}{r}
\overset{1}{\underset{}{}} \\
\overset{2}{\$0.84} \\
\times\ \ \ 36 \\
\hline
5\ 04 \\
+25\ 20 \\
\hline
\$30.24
\end{array}
$$

So, the total cost of Ms. Santos' order is $30.24.

ERROR ALERT

Be sure to place the decimal point in problems involving money amounts.

Try It

Solve.

1. A family zoo membership costs $65. The zoo sold 2,427 family memberships this year. How much money did the zoo raise from family memberships this year?

2. The football booster club wants to make 35 pennants for the game. They need 45 inches of material for each pennant. How much material do they need?

3. The theater holds 1,628 people. If a show was sold out for 74 performances, how many people saw the show?

4. There are 36 boxes of candles in the shop. If there are 24 candles in each box, how many candles are in the shop?

5. Jacque sold 41 bikes over the weekend. Each bike was on sale for $329. What were Jacque's total sales for the weekend?

6. There are 48 teams in a youth recreation club. Each team has 16 players. How many players are in the club?

7. Read the problem below. **Explain** why A cannot be the correct answer choice. Then choose the correct answer.   **COMMON ERROR**

   Mr. Ramirez bought 14 concert tickets to give to his employees. Each ticket cost $31.75. How much did he spend for the tickets?

   A $4,445.00   **C** $444.50

   B $476.25   **D** $317.50

8. Read the problem below. **Explain** why D cannot be the correct answer choice. Then choose the correct answer.   **COMMON ERROR**

   To raise money for the soccer team, players sold shirts for $13.79 each. They sold 52 shirts. How much money did they make from their sales?

   A $94.43   **C** $717.08

   B $581.98   **D** $51,798

🐻 Review the Key Standards

Division

O━┓ NS 3.0 Students solve problems involving addition, subtraction, multiplication, and division of whole numbers and understand the relationships among the operations.
O━┓ NS 3.4 Solve problems involving division of multidigit numbers by one-digit numbers.

Use division to solve problems about equal-size groups.

A shipping container contains 1,320 computers. The computers will be shared equally among 8 electronics stores. How many computers will each store get?

Divide. 1,320 ÷ 8

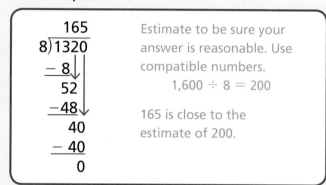

Estimate to be sure your answer is reasonable. Use compatible numbers.

$$1,600 \div 8 = 200$$

165 is close to the estimate of 200.

So, each store will get 165 computers.

Sometimes you must interpret the remainder to solve a division problem.

There are 405 people with reservations for cave tours. Tour rules allow only 6 people through the tunnel at a time. How many tours will have to be scheduled so everyone can pass through the tunnel?

Divide. 405 ÷ 6

```
      67 r3
  6)405
   −36↓
     45
   −42
      3
```

Estimate to be sure your answer is reasonable. Use compatible numbers.

$$360 \div 6 = 60$$
$$420 \div 6 = 70$$

The quotient should be between 60 and 70.

The quotient is 67, but 67 tours will not be enough since there will be 3 extra people. So, 68 tours will have to be scheduled.

Examples

A There are 2,160 DVDs in 3 storage cases. Each case holds the same number of DVDs. How many DVDs are in each case?

```
     720
3)2160
    21↓
     6
   − 6
     0
```

So, there are 720 DVDs in each storage case.

B Bridget has 815 postcards in her collection. She pastes 4 postcards on each page of her scrapbook. How many pages are full?

```
     203 r3
4)815
    8↓
    15
  −12
     3
```

So, 203 pages of her scrapbook are full.

ERROR ALERT

Be sure to check how a remainder affects the answer when you divide.

Try It

Solve.

1. There are 531 students in a basketball league. Each team has 9 players. How many teams are in the basketball league?

2. The coach spent $272 to buy 8 new soccer balls for the team. How much did each soccer ball cost?

3. A plane flew 828 miles in 4 hours. If it flew the same number of miles each hour, how many miles did the plane fly each hour?

4. There are 3,000 mugs in the warehouse. If each box holds 4 mugs, how many boxes are there?

5. Mrs. Chang has 435 feet of decorative cord. She needs 9 feet of cord to frame each bulletin board. How many complete bulletin boards can she frame?

6. Taylor has 1,736 stamps. He keeps them in 7 albums. Each album has the same number of stamps. How many stamps are in each album?

7. Read the problem below. **Explain** why C cannot be the correct answer choice. Then choose the correct answer. **COMMON ERROR**

The bakery baked 340 cupcakes. The cupcakes were packaged in boxes of 6. How many cupcakes were left over?

A 3

B 4

C 56

D 57

8. Read the problem below. **Explain** why B cannot be the correct answer choice. Then choose the correct answer. **COMMON ERROR**

Tickets have been sold to 335 people for scenic river trips. Each raft seats 8 people. How many rafts are needed?

A 40

B 41

C 42

D 43

Review the Key Standards

Prime Numbers

⊙¬ NS 4.2 Know that numbers such as 2, 3, 5, 7, and 11 do not have any factors except 1 and themselves and that such numbers are called prime numbers.

Every whole number greater than 1 is either prime or composite. A **prime** number has only two factors, 1 and itself. A **composite** number has more than two factors.

You can tell whether a number is prime or composite by making all the arrays you can for that number. Which number is prime, 9 or 11?

Number	Arrays	Factors
9		1, 3, 9
11		1, 11

So, 11 is a prime number since it has only two factors, 1 and itself.

ERROR ALERT

Remember that 2 is the only even prime number. All other multiples of 2 are composite numbers because every multiple of 2 can be divided by 2.

Examples

A Is 7 prime or composite?

7
1 ■■■■■■■

The factors of 7 are 1 and 7.
So, 7 is prime.

B Is 8 prime or composite?

8   4
1 ■■■■■■■■ 2 ■■■■
              ■■■■

The factors of 8 are 1, 2, 4, and 8.
So, 8 is composite.

Try It

Write *prime* or *composite* for each number.

1. 5
2. 12
3. 17
4. 10
5. 3
6. 27
7. 14
8. 23
9. 25
10. 4
11. 2
12. 35
13. 33
14. 29

15. Read the problem below. **Explain** why A cannot be the correct answer choice. Then choose the correct answer. **COMMON ERROR**

   Which statement is true?

   A The only factors of 6 are 1 and 6.

   B The only factors of 15 are 1 and 15.

   C The only factors of 19 are 1 and 19.

   D The only factors of 21 are 1 and 21.

⬤ Review the Key Standards

Expressions

○━ **AF 1.2** Interpret and evaluate mathematical expressions that now use parentheses.

An expression is a part of a number sentence that has numbers and operation signs but does not have an equal sign.

Sometimes an expression contains parentheses. Parentheses tell you which operation to complete first. An expression can have different values depending on where the parentheses are placed.

Evaluate $(35 - 15) - 12$.

$(35 - 15) - 12$
$\quad 20 \quad - 12$ Parentheses first.
$\qquad 8$

Evaluate $35 - (15 - 12)$.

$35 - (15 - 12)$
$35 - \quad 3$ Parentheses first.
32

So, $(35 - 15) - 12 = 8$, but $35 - (15 - 12) = 32$.

ERROR ALERT

Be sure to always complete the operations in the parentheses first.

Examples

Ⓐ Find the value of the expression.

$16 + (3 \times 2)$
$16 + \quad 6$
$\quad 22$

So, $16 + (3 \times 2) = 22$.

Ⓑ Find the value of the expression.

$(20 \div 4) \times 8$
$\quad 5 \quad \times 8$
$\qquad 40$

So, $(20 \div 4) \times 8 = 40$.

Try It

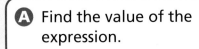

Find the value of each expression.

1. $40 - (9 - 6)$
2. $17 - (8 - 2)$
3. $12 - (2 \times 4)$
4. $(9 \times 5) \div 5$
5. $(12 - 9) - 3$
6. $26 - (12 - 6)$
7. $(35 - 11) \div 8$
8. $50 - (10 - 7)$
9. $72 \div (8 - 2)$
10. $24 + (15 \times 2)$
11. $(25 - 8) - 2$
12. $(64 \div 4) \div 2$
13. $(4 \times 7) - 9$
14. $(36 \div 4) - 2$
15. $(8 + 4) \div 3$
16. $42 \div (10 - 3)$
17. $20 + (18 - 4)$
18. $15 \times (24 \div 6)$

COMMON ERROR

19. Read the problem below. **Explain** why A cannot be the correct answer choice. Then choose the correct answer.

What is the value of the expression?

$$20 - (6 \times 3)$$

A 42

B 18

C 14

D 2

🐻 Review the Key Standards

Perform Operations with Parentheses

AF 1.3 Use parentheses to indicate which operation to perform first when writing expressions containing more than two terms and different operations.

Sometimes an expression contains more than one set of parentheses and more than one type of operation. Perform the operation in each set of parentheses first. Multiply and divide from left to right, and then add and subtract from left to right.

To find the value of $(16 + 2) - (3 \times 5) + (20 - 3)$

$$18 \quad - \quad 15 \quad + \quad 17 \qquad \text{Parentheses first.}$$

$$3 \quad + \quad 17 \qquad \text{Add and subtract from left to right.}$$

$$20$$

So, the value of the expression is 20.

Examples

A Find the value of the expression.

$$(9 \times 8) \div (6 + 2) - (9 \div 3)$$
$$72 \quad \div \quad 8 \quad - \quad 3$$
$$9 \qquad \quad - \quad 3$$
$$6$$

B Find the value of the expression.

$$(22 - 6) - (3 \times 2)$$
$$16 \quad - \quad 6$$
$$10$$

ERROR ALERT

If there is more than one set of parentheses, complete the operation in each set of parentheses first.

Try It

Find the value of each expression.

1. $100 - (10 + 2) \times (4 \times 2)$

2. $(18 + 6) \div 4 - (2 + 3)$

3. $(7 \times 8) \times (4 + 2) \div (16 - 10)$

4. $(32 - 17) + (16 + 15) - 10$

5. $(3 \times 6) - (4 + 8)$

6. $(10 \times 9) - (6 + 46) + (96 \div 8)$

7. Read the problem below. **Explain** why D cannot be the correct answer choice. Then choose the correct answer. **COMMON ERROR**

   What is the value of the expression?

   $$(10 \div 5) \times (6 \times 2) + (14 \div 7)$$

   A 4

   B 5

   C 26

   D 48

Review the Key Standards

Use an Equation

AF 1.5 Understand that an equation such as $y = 3x + 5$ is a prescription for determining a second number when a first number is given.

Think of an equation as a rule.

$y = 4x - 1$ is the same as $y = (4 \times x) - 1$.
Rule: To find y, multiply x by 4. Then subtract 1.

Use the equation to find the y-value for each x-value.

$x = 1$	$x = 2$	$x = 4$	$x = 5$
$y = (4 \times x) - 1$	$y = (4 \times x) - 1$	$y = (4 \times x) - 1$	$y = (4 \times x) - 1$
$y = (4 \times 1) - 1$	$y = (4 \times 2) - 1$	$y = (4 \times 4) - 1$	$y = (4 \times 5) - 1$
$y = 4 - 1$	$y = 8 - 1$	$y = 16 - 1$	$y = 20 - 1$
$y = 3$	$y = 7$	$y = 15$	$y = 19$

Examples

ERROR ALERT

A Find y when $x = 9$ for $y = x + 3$.

$y = x + 3$
$y = 9 + 3 = 12$

So, $y = 12$ when $x = 9$.

B Find y when $x = 8$ for $y = 6x + 2$.

$y = 6x + 2 = (6 \times x) + 2$

$y = (6 \times 8) + 2$
$y = 48 + 2 = 50$

So, $y = 50$ when $x = 8$.

Be sure to replace the value of x in the equation, then use the order of operations to find the value of y.

Try It

Solve.

1. Find y when $x = 3$ for $y = x - 1$.
2. Find y when $x = 5$ for $y = 2x$.
3. Find y when $x = 10$ for $y = x + 4$.
4. Find y when $x = 6$ for $y = 5x$.
5. Find y when $x = 4$ for $y = 3x - 1$.
6. Find y when $x = 15$ for $y = x - 10$.
7. Find y when $x = 8$ for $y = 2x + 6$.
8. Find y when $x = 2$ for $y = 4x - 3$.
9. Find y when $x = 14$ for $y = (x \div 2) + 1$.

10. Read the problem below. **Explain** why A cannot be the correct answer choice. Then choose the correct answer.

    COMMON ERROR

    Look at this problem.

    $y = 4x - 8$

    If $x = 20$, what is y?

    A 16   **C** 48

    B 32   **D** 72

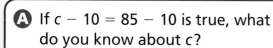 Review the Key Standards

Addition and Equations

🔑 **AF 2.0** Students know how to manipulate equations.

🔑 **AF 2.1** Know and understand that equals added to equals are equal.

An equation is a number sentence that shows two amounts are equal.

If you add or subtract the same number on both sides of an equation, the value of each side changes, but both sides are still equal.

$26 = 26$ is a true equation.

$26 + 4 = 26 + (2 + 2)$ is still true since the same number is added to both sides: $4 = (2 + 2)$.

Examples

A If $c - 10 = 85 - 10$ is true, what do you know about c?

Since the equation is true when the same number is subtracted from each side, $c = 85$.

B Find the missing number to make the equation true.

$7 + 9 = 7 + (3 \times \blacksquare)$

$7 = 7$ and $9 = 3 \times 3$

So, $\blacksquare = 3$.

ERROR ALERT

Be sure that the same number is added to or subtracted from both sides of an equation to keep the equation true.

Try It

Find the missing number to make each equation true.

1. $8 - 5 = 8 - (1 + x)$
2. $6 + \blacksquare = (3 \times 2) + 12$
3. $7 + (15 \div 3) = 7 + \blacksquare$
4. $20 - (4 \times 3) = 20 - x$
5. $35 + (9 - 5) = 35 + x$
6. $18 + x = (9 \times 2) + 8$
7. $30 + x = 30 + (12 \times 2)$
8. $24 - (5 \times 2) = 24 - x$
9. $40 - 18 = 40 - (\blacksquare \times 6)$
10. $57 + 35 = 57 + (5 \times \blacksquare)$
11. $100 - (25 - 5) = 100 - \blacksquare$

12. Read the problem below. **Explain** why B cannot be the correct answer choice. Then choose the correct answer.

COMMON ERROR

What value of y makes this number sentence true?

$$43 + (4 \times 5) = 43 + y$$

A 8

B 9

C 20

D 24

🐻 Review the Key Standards

Multiplication and Equations

🔑 **AF 2.0** Students know how to manipulate equations.

🔑 **AF 2.2** Know and understand that equals multiplied by equals are equal.

An equation is a number sentence that shows that two amounts are equal.

If you multiply or divide (except by 0) both sides of an equation by the same number, the value of both sides may change, but stay equal.

$11 = 11$ is a true equation.

$11 \times 12 = 11 \times (9 + 3)$ is still true since both sides are multiplied by the same number: $12 = (9 + 3)$.

Examples

A If $P \div 3 = 144 \div 3$ is true and P is not equal to 0, what do you know about P?

The equation is true when both sides of the equation are divided by the same number.

So, $P = 144$.

B Find the missing number to make the equation true.

$8 \times (6 + 3) = \blacksquare \times 9$

$6 + 3 = 9$

So, $\blacksquare = 8$.

ERROR ALERT

Be sure that both sides of an equation are multiplied or divided by the same number to keep the equation true.

Try It

Find the missing number to make each equation true.

1. $(2 + 5) \times y = 7 \times 3$

2. $18 \div y = 18 \div (3 + 3)$

3. $6 \times 25 = 6 \times (\blacksquare - 5)$

4. $20 \times y = 20 \times (12 - 5)$

5. $32 \div (2 + 2) = 32 \div \blacksquare$

6. $15 \times y = 15 \times (9 + 2)$

COMMON ERROR

7. Read the problem below. **Explain** why D cannot be the correct answer choice. Then choose the correct answer.

What value of y makes this number sentence true?

$$(9 - 5) \times 7 = 4 \times y$$

A $y = 4$ **C** $y = 7$

B $y = 5$ **D** $y = 9$

Review the Key Standards

Graph Lines

⊶ **MG 2.0** Students use two-dimensional coordinate grids to represent points and graph lines and simple figures.

⊶ **MG 2.1** Draw the points corresponding to linear relationships on graph paper (e.g., draw 10 points on the graph of the equation $y = 3x$ and connect them by using a straight line).

To graph an equation on a coordinate grid, make a function table. Then use the ordered pairs to graph the equation.

Graph $y = 2x$.

Make a function table of values. Choose input values for x. Use the equation to find the output values for y.

Input, x	0	1	2	3	4	5	6	7	8	9
Output, y	0	2	4	6	8	10	12	14	16	18

Write the values as ordered pairs:
(0,0), (1,2), (2,4), (3,6), (4,8), (5,10), (6,12), (7,14), (8,16), (9,18).

Graph the ordered pairs on the coordinate grid.
Then use a ruler to connect the points.

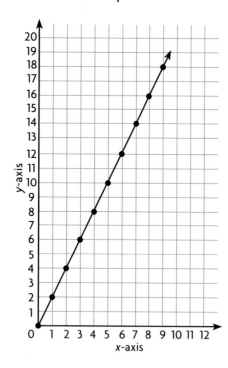

Examples

A Graph $y = 3x - 1$.

Input, x	1	2	3	4	5	6
Output, y	2	5	8	11	14	17

Write the ordered pairs.
(1,2), (2,5), (3,8), (4,11), (5,14), (6,17)

Graph the points. Use a ruler to
connect the points.

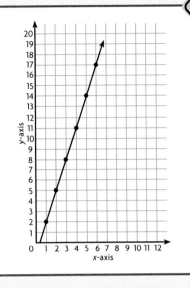

ERROR ALERT

Be sure to
always write
the x value first
in an ordered
pair. If $x = 7$
and $y = 6$, the
ordered
pair is (7,6),
NOT (6,7)

Try It

**Make and complete a function table for the equation. Then
graph the ordered pairs on a coordinate grid**

1. $y = x - 2$
   x-values: 2, 3, 4, 5, 6, 7, 8, 9, 10, 11

2. $y = 2x + 1$
   x-values: 0, 1, 2, 3, 4, 5, 6, 7, 8, 9

3. $y = x + 3$
   x-values: 0, 1, 2, 3, 4, 5, 6, 7, 8, 9

4. $y = 2x - 2$
   x-values: 1, 2, 3, 4, 5, 6, 7, 8, 9, 10

5. Read the problem below. **Explain**
   why B cannot be the correct
   answer choice. Then choose the
   correct answer.

   COMMON ERROR

   Maria graphed the equation $y = 3x + 1$.
   Which could be the coordinates of a point
   on her graph?

   A (2,6)

   B (7,2)

   C (3,10)

   D (3,8)

6. Read the problem below. **Explain**
   why A cannot be the correct
   answer choice. Then choose the
   correct answer.

   COMMON ERROR

   What could be the coordinates of
   a point on the line?

   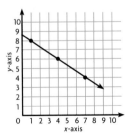

   A (2,10)

   B (8,3)

   C (9,2)

   D (10,2)

⬛ Review the Key Standards

Length of Horizontal Line Segments

○━ᴛ MG 2.0 Students use two-dimensional coordinate grids to represent points and graph lines and simple figures.

○━ᴛ MG 2.2 Understand that the length of a horizontal line segment equals the difference of the *x*-coordinates.

To find the length of a horizontal line segment on a coordinate grid, count the units on the grid, or subtract the *x*-coordinates.

The *y*-coordinates of a horizontal line segment on a coordinate grid are the same. To find the length of the horizontal line segment, find the difference of the *x*-coordinates.

Coordinates: (1,4) and (6,4). Subtract. $6 - 1 = 5$

So, the length of the line segment is 5 units.

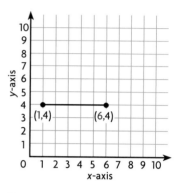

Examples

Ⓐ Find the length.

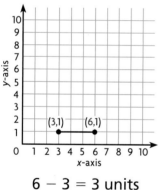

$6 - 3 = 3$ units

Ⓑ Find the length of the line segment from (4,8) to (9,8).

Subtract the *x*-coordinates

$9 - 4 = 5$ units

ERROR ALERT Be sure not to confuse the greater *x*-coordinate with the length of the line segment.

Try It

Find the length of each line segment.

1. (5,6) and (9,6)
2. (2,9) and (5,9)
3. (4,8) and (6,8)
4. (2,2) and (8,2)

5. Read the problem below. **Explain** why D cannot be the correct answer choice. Then choose the correct answer. **COMMON ERROR**

What is the length of the line segment?

A 3 units

B 4 units

C 6 units

D 8 units

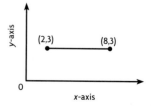

Review the Key Standards

Length of Vertical Line Segments

MG 2.0 Students use two-dimensional coordinate grids to represent points and graph lines and simple figures.

MG 2.3 Understand that the length of a vertical line segment equals the difference of the y-coordinates.

To find the length of a vertical line segment on a coordinate grid, count the units on the grid or subtract the y-coordinates.

The x-coordinates of a vertical line segment on a coordinate grid are the same. To find the length of the vertical line segment, find the difference of the y-coordinates.

Coordinates: $(2,1)$ and $(2,7)$. Subtract. $7 - 1 = 6$

So, the length of the line segment is 6 units.

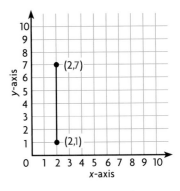

Examples

A Find the length.

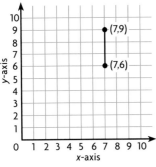

$9 - 6 = 3$ units

B Find the length of the line segment from $(4,8)$ to $(4,3)$.

Subtract the y-coordinates.

$8 - 3 = 5$ units

ERROR ALERT

Be sure to use only the y-coordinates to find the length of a vertical line segment.

Try It

Find the length of each line segment.

1. $(9,7)$ and $(9,0)$
2. $(6,3)$ and $(6,2)$
3. $(5,4)$ and $(5,1)$
4. $(10,9)$ and $(10,5)$

5. Read the problem below.
   Explain why A cannot be the correct answer choice. Then choose the correct answer.

   COMMON ERROR

   What is the length of the line segment?

   A 4 units

   B 5 units

   C 8 units

   D 9 units

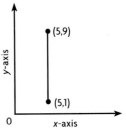

Test-Taking Strategies

Tips for Taking Math Tests

Being a good test-taker is like being a good problem-solver. When you answer test questions, you are solving problems. Remember to **Understand**, **Plan**, **Solve**, and **Check**.

Read to Understand

Read the problem

• Look for math terms and recall their meanings.

• Reread the problem and think about the question.

• Use the details in the problem and the question.

---

1. Ms. Lee has 270 pencils for her class. The pencils are in 9 boxes with the same number of pencils in each box. How many pencils are in each box?

   A 30

   B 40

   C 50

   D 60

Test Tip   **Understand the problem.**

When objects are separated into equal groups you can *divide* to find how many are in each group. Divide 270 pencils by 9 boxes to find how many are in each box. The answer is **A.**

• Each word is important. Missing a word or reading it incorrectly could cause you to get the wrong answer.

• Pay attention to words that are in all CAPITAL letters or italics like MUST, best, and closest.

---

2. An obtuse triangle MUST have?

   A 3 sides of different lengths.

   B 3 sides that are the same length.

   C 1 angle greater than a right angle.

   D 3 acute angles.

Test Tip   **Look for important words.**

The word *MUST* is an important word. An obtuse triangle may have 3 sides of different lengths, but it MUST have 1 angle greater than a right angle. The answer is **C.**

Plan

Think about how you can solve the problem

- Can you solve the problem with the information given?

- Pictures, charts, tables, and graphs may have the information you need.

- You may need to recall information not given.

- The answer choices may have information you need.

---

3. The numbers in the pattern increase by the same amount each time. What are the next three numbers in this pattern

$$^-10, \ ^-7, \ ^-4, \ ^-1, \ 2, \ 5, \ \blacksquare, \ \blacksquare, \ \blacksquare$$

A 10, 7, 4

B 8, 11, 14

C 2, $^-$1, $^-$4

D $^-$5, $^-$10, $^-$15

 Test Tip   **Get the information you need.**

Look at the number pattern to find by how much the numbers increase each time. Then use that rule to find the missing numbers. The answer is **B**.

- You may need to write a number sentence and solve it.

- Some problems have two steps or more.

- You may need to look at relationships rather than compute.

- If the path to the solution isn't clear, choose a problem solving strategy and use it to solve the problem.

---

4. There are 50 students in the high school band. Each student needs $600 to go to the state finals. How much money is needed in all?

A $30,000

B $35,000

C $42,000

D $50,000

 Test Tip   **Decide on a plan.**

You can use mental math and patterns instead of paper and pencil to multiply 50 and 600. $5 \times 6 = 30$, so $50 \times 600 = 30{,}000$. The answer is **A**.

Follow your plan, working logically and carefully

• Estimate your answer. Are any answer choices unreasonable?

• Use reasoning to find the most likely choices.

• Make sure you solved all steps needed to answer the problem.

• If your answer does not match any of the answer choices, check the numbers you used. Then check your computation.

---

5. Which statement about the figures is true?

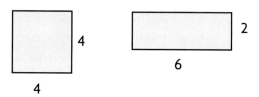

   A They both have the same area.

   B They both have the same perimeter.

   C They both have the same length.

   D They both have the same width.

Test Tip   **Eliminate choices.**

You can eliminate choices **C** and **D** because you can see that the lengths and widths of the two figures are not the same. You only need to check answer choices **A** and **B**. 4 + 4 + 4 + 4 = 16, and 2+2+6+6=16. The answer is **B**.

• If your answer still does not match, look for another form of the number such as a decimal instead of a fraction.

• If answer choices are given as pictures, look at each one by itself while you cover the other three.

• Read answer choices that are statements and relate them to the problem one by one.

• Change your plan if it isn't working. Try a different strategy.

---

6. Which statement is true?

   A A composite number has only two factors.

   B All odd numbers are prime numbers.

   C No even numbers are prime numbers.

   D A composite number has more than two factors.

Test Tip   **Choose the answer.**

Read each statement to decide if it is true. If you aren't sure if it is true, try to think of examples that would make the statement false. The answer is **D**.

Take time to catch your mistakes

• Be sure you answered the question asked.

• Check that your answer fits the information in the problem.

• Check for important words you might have missed.

• Be sure you used all the information you needed.

• Check your computation by using a different method.

• Draw a picture when you are unsure of your answer.

---

7. What is the value of x?

$$(8 + 2) \times 2 = 40 \div x$$

A 1

B 2

C 4

D 5

Test Tip Check your work.

Look at your answer choice. Replace the x with your answer choice and check that you did all the addition, multiplication, and division needed in the problem. The answer is **B**.

Don't Forget!

Before the test

• Listen to the teacher's directions and read the instructions.

• Write down the ending time if the test is timed.

• Know where and how to mark your answers.

• Know whether you should write on the test page or use scratch paper.

• Ask any questions you may have before the test begins.

During the test

• Work quickly but carefully. If you are unsure how to answer a question, leave it blank and return to it later.

• If you cannot finish on time, look over the questions that are left. Answer the easiest ones first. Then go back to answer the others.

• Fill in each answer carefully. Erase completely if you change an answer. Erase any stray marks.

• Check that the answer number matches the question number, especially if you skip a question.

Addition Facts

	K	L	M	N	O	P	Q	R
A	6 + 7	9 + 6	3 + 5	8 + 9	0 + 7	2 + 8	6 + 4	7 + 7
B	1 + 6	8 + 4	5 + 1	2 + 7	3 + 3	8 + 2	4 + 5	2 + 6
C	6 + 6	3 + 7	7 + 8	4 + 6	9 + 0	4 + 2	10 + 4	3 + 8
D	6 + 1	5 + 9	10 + 6	5 + 7	3 + 9	9 + 8	8 + 7	8 + 1
E	7 + 6	7 + 1	6 + 9	4 + 3	5 + 5	8 + 0	9 + 5	2 + 9
F	9 + 1	8 + 5	7 + 0	8 + 3	7 + 2	4 + 7	10 + 5	4 + 8
G	5 + 3	9 + 9	3 + 6	7 + 4	0 + 8	4 + 4	7 + 10	6 + 8
H	8 + 6	10 + 7	0 + 9	7 + 9	5 + 6	8 + 10	6 + 5	9 + 4
I	9 + 7	8 + 8	1 + 9	5 + 8	10 + 9	6 + 3	6 + 2	9 + 10
J	9 + 2	7 + 5	6 + 0	10 + 8	5 + 4	4 + 9	9 + 3	10 + 10

Division Facts

	K	L	M	N	O	P	Q	R
A	7)56	5)40	6)24	6)30	6)18	7)42	8)16	9)45
B	3)9	10)90	1)1	1)6	10)100	3)12	10)70	8)56
C	6)48	12)60	4)32	6)54	7)0	3)18	9)90	11)55
D	2)16	3)21	5)30	3)15	11)110	9)9	8)64	9)63
E	4)28	2)10	9)18	1)5	7)63	8)32	2)8	9)108
F	8)24	4)4	2)14	11)66	8)72	4)12	7)21	6)36
G	12)36	5)20	7)28	7)14	4)24	11)121	9)36	11)132
H	9)27	3)27	7)49	4)20	9)72	5)60	8)88	10)80
I	4)44	8)48	5)35	8)40	5)10	2)12	10)60	9)54
J	10)120	12)72	9)81	4)16	1)7	12)60	12)96	12)144

Table of Measures

Metric	Customary

Length

Metric	Customary
1 centimeter (cm) = 10 millimeters (mm)	1 foot (ft) = 12 inches (in.)
1 decimeter (dm) = 10 centimeters	1 yard (yd) = 3 feet, or 36 inches
1 meter (m) = 10 decimeters	1 mile (mi) = 1,760 yards, or 5,280 feet
1 kilometer (km) = 1,000 meters	

Capacity

Metric	Customary
1 liter (L) = 1, 000 milliliters (mL)	1 tablespoon (tbsp) = 3 teaspoons (tsp)
1 metric cup = 250 milliliters	1 cup (c) = 8 fluid ounces (fl oz)
	1 pint (pt) = 2 cups
	1 quart (qt) = 2 pints
	1 gallon (gal) = 4 quarts

Mass/Weight

Metric	Customary
1 gram (g) = 1, 000 milligrams (mg)	1 pound (lb) = 16 ounces (oz)
1 kilogram (kg) = 1, 000 grams	1 ton (T) = 2, 000 pounds

Time

1 minute (min) =	60 seconds (sec)
1 hour (hr) =	60 minutes
1 day =	24 hours
1 week (wk) =	7 days
1 year (yr) =	12 months (mo), or about 52 weeks
1 year =	365 days
1 leap year =	366 days

Money

1 penny =	1¢ or $0.01
1 nickel =	5¢ or $0.05
1 dime =	10¢ or $0.10
1 quarter =	25¢ or $0.25
1 half dollar =	50¢ or $0.50
1 dollar =	100¢ or $1.00

Symbols

$\perp$	is perpendicular to	$<$	is less than	$^\circ$	degree
$\parallel$	is parallel to	$>$	is greater than	$^\circ F$	degrees Fahrenheit
$\overleftrightarrow{AB}$	line AB	$\leq$	is less than or equal to	$^\circ C$	degrees Celsius
$\overrightarrow{AB}$	ray AB	$\geq$	is greater than or equal to	$^+8$	positive 8
$\overline{AB}$	line segment AB	$=$	is equal to	$^-8$	negative 8
$\angle ABC$	angle ABC	$\neq$	is not equal to	$(2,3)$	ordered pair (x,y)
		$\cent$	cent	$\$$	dollar

Formulas

Perimeter of polygon = sum of length of sides

Perimeter of rectangle $P = (2 \times l) + (2 \times w)$

Perimeter of square $P = 4 \times s$

Area of rectangle $A = l \times w$

Volume of rectangular prism $V = (l \times w \times h)$

By the end of grade four, students understand large numbers and addition, subtraction, multiplication, and division of whole numbers. They describe and compare simple fractions and decimals. They understand the properties of, and the relationships between, plane geometric figures. They collect, represent, and analyze data to answer questions.

Number Sense

1.0 Students understand the place value of whole numbers and decimals to two decimal places and how whole numbers and decimals relate to simple fractions. Students use the concepts of negative numbers:

○━ **1.1** Read and write whole numbers in the millions.

Which of these is the number 5,005,014?
(CST released test question, 2004)

1. Five million, five hundred, fourteen
2. Five million, five thousand, fourteen
3. Five thousand, five hundred, fourteen
4. Five billion, five million, fourteen

○━ **1.2** Order and compare whole numbers and decimals to two decimal places.

Which is bigger: 3.1 or 3.09?

○━ **1.3** Round whole numbers through the millions to the nearest ten, hundred, thousand, ten thousand, or hundred thousand.

Two hundred twenty-four students attend Green Street School. Round this number to the nearest hundred.

Lunch was served to 3,778 students. Round this number to the nearest thousand.

Each year it is estimated that 42,225 Canadian geese migrate south to warmer climates. Round this number to the nearest ten thousand.

○━ **1.4** Decide when a rounded solution is called for and explain why such a solution may be appropriate.

Norberto has ten dollars and he wants to buy some ballpoint pens, which cost $2.35; some notebooks, which cost $4.40; and a fancy eraser, which costs $1.45. He wants to make sure he has enough money to pay for all of them, so he rounds the cost of each item to the nearest dollar and adds them up: $2 + $4 + $1 = $7. He concludes that his ten dollars would be sufficient to buy all the items. Is he correct and, if so, why? If the estimate that he makes turns out to be $8 instead of $7, should he be concerned?

1.5 Explain different interpretations of fractions, for example, parts of a whole, parts of a set, and division of whole numbers by whole numbers; explain equivalence of fractions (see Standard 4.0).

1.6 Write tenths and hundredths in decimal and fraction notations and know the fraction and decimal equivalents for halves and fourths (e.g., $\frac{1}{2}$ = 0.5 or 0.50; $\frac{7}{4}$ = $1\frac{3}{4}$ = 1.75).

Which fraction means the same as 0.17?

(a) $\frac{17}{10}$ (b) $\frac{17}{100}$ (c) $\frac{17}{1000}$ (d) $\frac{17}{1}$

(CST released test question, 2004)

1.7 Write the fraction represented by a drawing of parts of a figure; represent a given fraction by using drawings; and relate a fraction to a simple decimal on a number line.

Which number represents the shaded part of the figure?
(Adapted from TIMSS gr. 3–4, M-5)

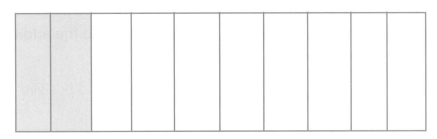

(a) 2.8   (c) 0.2
(b) 0.5   (d) 0.02

⊙¬ **1.8** Use concepts of negative numbers (e.g., on a number line, in counting, in temperature, in "owing").

Yesterday's temperature was 5 degrees Celsius, but the temperature dropped 9 degrees Celsius overnight. What is today's temperature?

Determine if the following number sentences are true or false by identifying the relative positions of each number on a number line:

$-9 > -10$ $-31 < -29$

⊙¬ **1.9** Identify on a number line the relative position of positive fractions, positive mixed numbers, and positive decimals to two decimal places.

Write a positive number for each letter on the number line shown below.

Which letter represents the number closest to 2.5?

Write the letter that represents where each number would go on the number line shown below:

$1\frac{1}{4}$ _____   2.50 _____ $\frac{3}{4}$ _____

```
0          1          2          3
|  ı  ı  ı  |  ı  ı  ı  |  ı  ı  ı  |
A  B  C  D  E  F  G  H  I  J  K
```

Determine if the following number sentences are true or false by identifying the relative positions of each number on a number line:

1. $\frac{1}{4} > 2.54$

2. $\frac{5}{2} < 2.6$

3. $\frac{12}{18} = \frac{2}{3}$ (Note the equivalence of fractions.)

4. $\frac{4}{5} < \frac{13}{15}$

2.0   Students extend their use and understanding of whole numbers to the addition and subtraction of simple decimals:

2.1   Estimate and compute the sum or difference of whole numbers and positive decimals to two places.

Solve $55.73 - 48.25 = ?$

2.2   Round two-place decimals to one decimal or to the nearest whole number and judge the reasonableness of the rounded answer.

In her science class Li Ping weighs two samples of quartz and determines that the first has a weight of 3.44 grams and the second has a weight of 2.39 grams. Her teacher wants Li Ping to report the combined weight of the two samples to the nearest tenth of a gram, and to the nearest gram; however, the scale cannot measure weights over 5 grams. Li Ping decides to round the numbers first and then to add them.

1. Is $3.4 + 2.4$ a reasonable estimate of the combined weights to the nearest tenth of a gram?
2. Is $3 + 2$ a reasonable estimate of the combined weights to the nearest gram?

o⌐ 3.0 Students solve problems involving addition, subtraction, multiplication, and division of whole numbers and understand the relationships among the operations:

o⌐ 3.1 Demonstrate an understanding of, and the ability to use, standard algorithms for the addition and subtraction of multidigit numbers.

Solve these problems using the standard algorithms:

1. 619,581 − 23,183 = ?
2. 6,747 + 321,105 = ?

3.2 Demonstrate an understanding of, and the ability to use, standard algorithms for multiplying a multidigit number by a two-digit number and for dividing a multidigit number by a one-digit number; use relationships between them to simplify computations and to check results.

Singh and Sepideh work independently to solve the problem 783 × 23 = ? They apply slightly different approaches, as shown below. Explain why both approaches are valid and give the same answer.

$$
\begin{array}{r}
783 \\
\times\ \ 3 \\
\hline
2{,}349
\end{array}
\qquad
\begin{array}{r}
783 \\
\times\ \ 20 \\
\hline
15{,}660
\end{array}
\qquad
\begin{array}{r}
2{,}349 \\
+15{,}660 \\
\hline
18{,}009
\end{array}
$$

Singh

$$
\begin{array}{r}
783 \\
\times\ \ 23 \\
\hline
2{,}349 \\
+15{,}660 \\
\hline
18{,}009
\end{array}
$$

Sepideh

3.3 Solve problems involving multiplication of multidigit numbers by two-digit numbers.

3.4 Solve problems involving division of multidigit numbers by one-digit numbers.

Solve each of the following problems and observe the different roles played by the number 37 in each situation:

1. Four children shared 37 dollars equally. How much did each get?

2. Four children shared 37 pennies as equally as possible. How many pennies did each get?

3. Cars need to be rented for 37 children going on a field trip. Each car can take 12 children in addition to the driver. How many cars must be rented?

4. There are 9 rows of seats in a theater. Each row has the same number of seats. If there is a total of 162 seats, how many seats are in each row? (CST released test question, 2004)

4.0 Students know how to factor small whole numbers:

4.1 Understand that many whole numbers break down in different ways (e.g., 12 = 4 × 3 = 2 × 6 = 2 × 2 × 3).

In how many distinct ways can you write 60 as a product of two numbers?

○━┓ (4.2) Know that numbers such as 2, 3, 5, 7, and 11 do not have any factors except 1 and themselves and that such numbers are called prime numbers.

Circle all the prime numbers in these different representations of 24:

(a) 2×12 (c) 4×6 (e) $2 \times 3 \times 4$ (g) 1×24

(b) 3×8 (d) $2 \times 2 \times 6$ (f) $2 \times 2 \times 2 \times 3$

Algebra and Functions

1.0 Students use and interpret variables, mathematical symbols, and properties to write and simplify expressions and sentences:

1.1 Use letters, boxes, or other symbols to stand for any number in simple expressions or equations (e.g., demonstrate an understanding and the use of the concept of a variable).

Tanya has read the first 78 pages of a 130-page book. Give the number sentence that can be used to find the number of pages Tanya must read to finish the book. (Adapted from TIMSS gr. 3–4, I-7)

1. $130 + 78 =$ ____

2. ____ $- 78 \square = 130$

3. $130 - 78 =$ ____

4. $130 -$ ____ $= 178$

○━┓ (1.2) Interpret and evaluate mathematical expressions that now use parentheses.

Evaluate the two expressions:

$(28 - 10) - 8 =$ ____ and $28 - (10 - 8) =$ ____.

Solve $5 \times (8 - 2) = ?$ (CST released test question, 2004)

○━┓ (1.3) Use parentheses to indicate which operation to perform first when writing expressions containing more than two terms and different operations.

What is the value of the expression below?

$(13 + 4) - (7 \times 2) + (31 - 17)$

(Adapted from CST released test question, 2004)

1.4 Use and interpret formulas (e.g., area = length $\times$ width or $A = lw$) to answer questions about quantities and their relationships.

Vik has a car that has a 16-gallon gas tank. When the tank is filled, he can drive 320 miles before running out of gas. How can Vik calculate his car's mileage in miles/gallon?

○━ **1.5** Understand that an equation such as $y = 3x + 5$ is a prescription for determining a second number when a first number is given.

○━ **2.0 Students know how to manipulate equations:**

○━ **2.1** Know and understand that equals added to equals are equal.

The letters S and T stand for numbers. If $S - 100 = T - 100$, which statement is true? (CST released test question, 2004)

$S = T$ $S > T$ $S = T + 100$ $S > T + 100$

○━ **2.2** Know and understand that equals multiplied by equals are equal.

What number goes into the box to make this number sentence true? $(7 - 3) \times 5 = 4 \times \square$ (CST released test question, 2004)

Measurement and Geometry

1.0   Students understand perimeter and area:

1.1   Measure the area of rectangular shapes by using appropriate units, such as square centimeter (cm^2), square meter (m^2), square kilometer (km^2), square inch ($in.^2$), square yard ($yd.^2$), or square mile ($mi.^2$).

1.2   Recognize that rectangles that have the same area can have different perimeters.

Draw a rectangle whose area is 120 and whose perimeter exceeds 50.
Draw another rectangle with the same area whose perimeter exceeds 240.

1.3   Understand that rectangles that have the same perimeter can have different areas.

Is the area of a 45×55 rectangle (in cm^2) smaller or bigger than that of a square with the same perimeter?

Draw a rectangle whose perimeter is 40 and whose area is less than 20.

1.4   Understand and use formulas to solve problems involving perimeters and areas of rectangles and squares. Use those formulas to find the areas of more complex figures by dividing the figures into basic shapes.

The length of a rectangle is 6 cm, and its perimeter is 16 cm. What is the area of the rectangle in square centimeters? (TIMSS gr. 7–8, K-5)

2.0 Students use two-dimensional coordinate grids to represent points and graph lines and simple figures:

2.1 2.1 Draw the points corresponding to linear relationships on graph paper (e.g., draw 10 points on the graph of the equation y = 3x and connect them by using a straight line).

1. Draw ten points on the graph of the equation $x = 4$.
2. Draw ten points on the graph of the equation $y = 71$.
3. Draw ten points on the graph of the equation $y = 2x + 4$.

2.2 Understand that the length of a horizontal line segment equals the difference of the x-coordinates.

What is the length of the line segment joining the points (6, −4) and (21, −4)?

2.3 Understand that the length of a vertical line segment equals the difference of the y-coordinates.

What is the length of the line segment joining the points (121, 3) to (121, 17)?

3.0 Students demonstrate an understanding of plane and solid geometric objects and use this knowledge to show relationships and solve problems:

3.1 Identify lines that are parallel and perpendicular.

(Teachers are advised to introduce the terms *intersecting lines* and *nonintersecting lines* when dealing with this standard.)

3.2 Identify the radius and diameter of a circle.

3.3 Identify congruent figures.

3.4 Identify figures that have bilateral and rotational symmetry.

Craig folded a piece of paper in half and cut out a shape along the folded edge. Draw a picture to show what the cutout shape will look like when it is opened up and flattened out. (Adapted from TIMSS gr. 3–4, T-5)

Let *AB*, *CD* be perpendicular diameters of a circle, as shown. If we reflect across the line segment *CD*, what happens to *A* and what happens to *B* under this reflection?

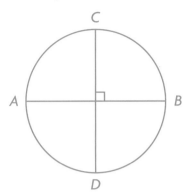

3.5 Know the definitions of a right angle, an acute angle, and an obtuse angle. Understand that 90°, 180°, 270°, and 360° are associated, respectively, with $\frac{1}{4}, \frac{1}{2}, \frac{3}{4}$, and full turns.

3.6 Visualize, describe, and make models of geometric solids (e.g., prisms, pyramids) in terms of the number and shape of faces, edges, and vertices; interpret two-dimensional representations of three-dimensional objects; and draw patterns (of faces) for a solid that, when cut and folded, will make a model of the solid.

3.7 Know the definitions of different triangles (e.g., equilateral, isosceles, scalene) and identify their attributes.

Name each of the following triangles:

1. No equal sides
2. Two equal sides
3. Three equal sides

3.8 Know the definition of different quadrilaterals (e.g., rhombus, square, rectangle, parallelogram, trapezoid).

Explain which of the following statements are true and why:

1. All squares are rectangles.
2. All rectangles are squares.
3. All parallelograms are rectangles.
4. All rhombi are parallelograms.
5. Some parallelograms are squares.

1.0   Students organize, represent, and interpret numerical and categorical data and clearly communicate their findings:

The following table shows the ages of the girls and boys in a club. Complete the graph by using the information for ages 9 and 10 shown in the table.
(Adapted from TIMSS gr. 3–4, S-1)

Ages	Number of Girls	Number of Boys
8	4	6
9	8	4
10	6	10

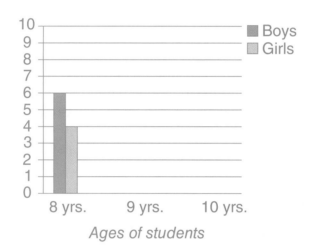

Ages of students

1.1   Formulate survey questions; systematically collect and represent data on a number line; and coordinate graphs, tables, and charts.

1.2   Identify the mode(s) for sets of categorical data and the mode(s), median, and any apparent outliers for numerical data sets.

1.3   Interpret one- and two-variable data graphs to answer questions about a situation.

2.0   Students make predictions for simple probability situations:

Nine identical chips numbered 1 through 9 are put in a jar. When a chip is drawn from the jar, what is the probability that it has an even number?
(Adapted from TIMSS gr. 7–8, N-18)

2.1   Represent all possible outcomes for a simple probability situation in an organized way (e.g., tables, grids, tree diagrams).

2.2 Express outcomes of experimental probability situations verbally and numerically (e.g., 3 out of 4; $\frac{3}{4}$).

Royce has a bag with 8 red marbles, 4 blue marbles, 5 green marbles, and 9 yellow marbles all the same size. If he pulls out 1 marble without looking, which color is he most likely to choose? (CST released test question, 2004)

Mathematical Reasoning

1.0 Students make decisions about how to approach problems:

1.1 Analyze problems by identifying relationships, distinguishing relevant from irrelevant information, sequencing and prioritizing information, and observing patterns.

1.2 Determine when and how to break a problem into simpler parts.

2.0 Students use strategies, skills, and concepts in finding solutions:

2.1 Use estimation to verify the reasonableness of calculated results.

2.2 Apply strategies and results from simpler problems to more complex problems.

2.3 Use a variety of methods, such as words, numbers, symbols, charts, graphs, tables, diagrams, and models, to explain mathematical reasoning.

2.4 Express the solution clearly and logically by using the appropriate mathematical notation and terms and clear language; support solutions with evidence in both verbal and symbolic work.

2.5 Indicate the relative advantages of exact and approximate solutions to problems and give answers to a specified degree of accuracy.

2.6 Make precise calculations and check the validity of the results from the context of the problem.

3.0 Students move beyond a particular problem by generalizing to other situations:

3.1 Evaluate the reasonableness of the solution in the context of the original situation.

3.2 Note the method of deriving the solution and demonstrate a conceptual understanding of the derivation by solving similar problems.

3.3 Develop generalizations of the results obtained and apply them in other circumstances.

Glossary

A.M. [ā•em′] **a.m.** The time between midnight and noon

acute angle [ə•kyōōt′ ang′əl] **ángulo agudo** An angle that measures less than a right angle (greater than 0° and less than 90°) (p. 520)
Example:

acute triangle [ə•kyōōt′ trī′ang•əl] **triángulo acutángulo** A triangle with three acute angles (p. 528)
Example:

addend [a′dend] **sumando** A number that is added to another in an addition problem
Example: 2 + 4 = 6;
2 and 4 are addends.

addition [ə•di′shən] **suma** The process of finding the total number of items when two or more groups of items are joined; the opposite operation of subtraction

angle [ang′əl] **ángulo** A figure formed by two line segments or rays that share the same endpoint (p. 520)
Example:

area [âr′ē•ə] **área** The number of square units needed to cover a surface (p. 606)
Example:

area = 9 square units

array [ə•rā′] **matriz** An arrangement of objects in rows and columns (p. 116)
Example:

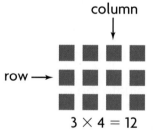

3 × 4 = 12

Associative Property of Addition [ə•sō′shē•ə•tiv prä′pər•tē əv ə•di′shən] **propiedad asociativa de la suma** The property that states you can group addends in different ways and still get the same sum (p. 78)
Example: 3 + (8 + 5) = (3 + 8) + 5

Associative Property of Multiplication
[ə•sō′shē•ə•tiv prä′pər•tē əv mul•tə•plə•kā′shən]
propiedad asociativa de la multiplicación The property that states you can group factors in different ways and still get the same product (p. 136)
Example: 3 × (4 × 2) = (3 × 4) × 2

bar graph [bär graf] **gráfica de barras** A graph that uses bars to show data (p. 344)
Example:

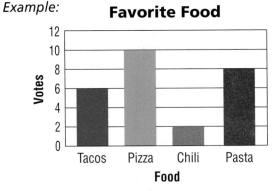

base [bās] **base** A polygon's side or a solid figure's face by which the figure is measured or named (p. 566)
Examples:

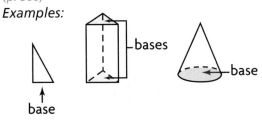

benchmark [bench′märk] **punto de referencia** A known number of things that helps you understand the size or amount of a different number of things (p. 15)

bilateral symmetry [bī•la′tə•rəl si′mə•trē] **simetría bilateral** See *line symmetry*.

capacity [kə•pa′sə•tē] **capacidad** The amount a container can hold when filled (p. 591)
1 half gallon = 2 quarts

categorical data [ka•tə•gôr′i•kəl dā′tə] **datos categóricos** Data that can be sorted into different groups (p. 321)

center [sen′tər] **centro** The point inside a circle that is the same distance from each point on the circle (p. 534)
Example:

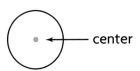
center

Word History

The word *center* comes from a Greek root, *kentrus*, meaning "spur, or sharp, pointed object." A sharp point was made at a center point to fix the spot and a duller object was dragged around the center to form the circle

centimeter (cm) [sen′tə•mē•tər] **centímetro (cm)** A metric unit for measuring length or distance (p. 594)
100 centimeters = 1 meter
Example:

1 centimeter

certain [sər′tən] **seguro** An event is certain if it will always happen (p. 634)

chord [kôrd] **cuerda** A line segment with endpoints on a circle (p. 534)
Example:

$\overline{AB}$ is a chord.

circle [sûr′kəl] **círculo** A closed figure made up of points that are the same distance from the center (p. 534)
Example:

circle C

circle graph [sûr′kəl graf] **gráfica circular** A graph in the shape of a circle that shows data as a whole made up of different parts (p. 348)
Example:

Today's Vegetables

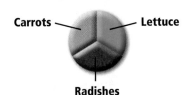

Carrots — — Lettuce

Radishes

closed figure [klōzd fi'gyər] **figura cerrada** A figure that begins and ends at the same point
Examples:

common factor [kä'mən fak'tər] **factor común** A number that is a factor of two or more numbers (p. 311)

Commutative Property of Addition [kə•myōō'tə•tiv prä'pər•tē əv ədi'shən] **propiedad conmutativa de la suma** The property that states that when the order of two addends is changed, the sum is the same (p. 78)
Example: $4 + 5 = 5 + 4$

Commutative Property of Multiplication [kə•myōō'tə•tiv prä'pər•tē əv mul•tə•plə•kā'shən] **propiedad conmutativa de la multiplicación** The property that states that when the order of two factors is changed, the product is the same (p. 136)
Example: $4 \times 5 = 5 \times 4$

compare [kəm•pär'] **comparar** To describe whether numbers are equal to, less than, or greater than each other (p. 12)

compass [kəm'pəs] **compás** A tool used to construct circles (p. 534)

compatible numbers [kəm•pa'tə•bəl num'bərz] **números compatibles** Numbers that are easy to compute mentally (p. 40)

composite number [kəm•pä'zət num'bər] **número compuesto** A whole number that has more than two factors (p. 293)
Example: 9 is composite since its factors are 1, 3, and 9.

cone [kōn] **cono** A solid, pointed figure that has a flat, round base (p. 566)
Example:

congruent [kən•grōō'ənt] **congruente** Having the same size and shape (p. 547)
Example:

coordinate grid [kō•ôr'də•nət grid] **cuadrícula de coordenadas** A grid formed by a horizontal line called the x-axis and a vertical line called the y-axis (p. 350)
Example:

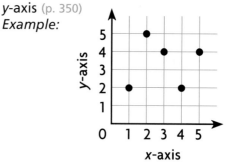

coordinate plane [kō•ôr'də•nət plān] **plano de coordenadas** A plane formed by two intersecting and perpendicular number lines called axes (p. 386)
Example:

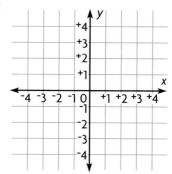

corner [kôr'nər] **esquina** See *vertex*.

cube [kyōōb] **cubo** A solid figure with six congruent square faces (p. 566)
Example:

cubic unit [kyōō'bik yōō'nət] **unidad cúbica** A unit of volume with dimensions of 1 unit $\times$ 1 unit $\times$ 1 unit

cup (c) [kup] **taza (t)** A customary unit used to measure capacity (p. 591) 8 ounces = 1 cup

cylinder [si'lən•dər] **cilindro** A solid figure that is shaped like a can (p. 566)
Example:

D

data [dā'tə] **datos** Information collected about people or things (p. 320)

decagon [de′kə•gän] **decágono** A polygon with ten sides and ten angles (p. 524)

decimal [de′sə•məl] **decimal** A number with one or more digits to the right of the decimal point (p. 468)

decimal point [de′sə•məl point] **punto decimal** A symbol used to separate dollars from cents in money amounts and to separate the ones and the tenths places in a decimal (p. 468)
Example: 6.4
↑ decimal point

decimeter (dm) [de′sə•mē•tər] **decímetro (dm)** A metric unit for measuring length or distance (p. 594) 10 decimeters = 1 meter

degree (°) [di•grē′] **grado (°)** The unit used for measuring angles and temperatures (p. 520)

degree Celsius (°C) [di•grē′ sel′sē•əs] **grado Celsius (°C)** A metric unit for measuring temperature (p. 375)

degree Fahrenheit (°F) [di•grē′ fâr′ən•hīt] **grado Fahrenheit (°F)** A standard unit for measuring temperature (p. 374)

denominator [di•nä′mə•nā•tər] **denominador** The number below the bar in a fraction that tells how many equal parts are in the whole (p. 414)
Example: $\frac{3}{4}$ ← denominator

diameter [dī•am′ə•tər] **diámetro** A line segment that passes through the center of a circle and has endpoints on the circle (p. 534)
Example:

diameter

difference [di′fər•əns] **diferencia** The answer to a subtraction problem (p. 38)

digit [di′jət] **dígito** Any one of the ten symbols 0, 1, 2, 3, 4, 5, 6, 7, 8, or 9 used to write numbers (p. 5)

dimension [də•men′shən] **dimensión** A measure in one direction (p. 518)

Distributive Property [di•stri′byə•tiv prä′pər•tē] **propiedad distributiva** The property that states that multiplying a sum by a number is the same as multiplying each addend by the number and then adding the products (p. 137)
Example: 5 × (10 + 6) = (5 × 10) + (5 × 6)

divide [di•vīd′] **dividir** To separate into equal groups; the opposite operation of multiplication (p. 110)

dividend [di′və•dend] **dividendo** The number that is to be divided in a division problem (p. 112)
Example: 36 ÷ 6; 6)36; the dividend is 36.

division [də•vi′zhən] **división** The process of sharing a number of items to find how many groups can be made or how many items will be in each group; the opposite operation of multiplication

divisor [də•vī′zər] **divisor** The number that divides the dividend (p. 112)
Example: 15 ÷ 3; 3)15; the divisor is 3.

double-bar graph [du′bəl bär graf] **gráfica de doble barra** A graph used to compare similar kinds of data (p. 347)
Example:

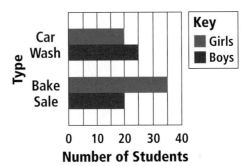

Fund Raiser Choices

doubles [du′bəlz] **dobles** Two addends that are the same number

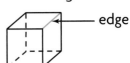

edge [ej] **arista** The line segment where two or more faces of a solid figure meet (p. 566)
Example:
edge

elapsed time [i•lapst′ tīm] **tiempo transcurrido** The time that passes from the start of an activity to the end of that activity (p. 53)

endpoint [end pôint] **extremo** The point at either end of a line segment (p. 518)

equal to (=) [ē′kwəl tōō] **igual a** Having the same value
Example: 4 + 4 is equal to 3 + 5

equally likely [ē′kwə•lē lī′klē] **igualmente probable** Having the same chance of happening (p. 634)

equation [i•kwā′zhən] **ecuación** A number sentence which shows that two quantities are equal (p. 84)
Example: $4 + 5 = 9$

equilateral triangle [ē•kwə•la′tə•rəl trī′ang•əl] **triángulo equilátero** A triangle with 3 equal, or congruent, sides (p. 528)
Example:

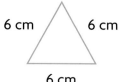

6 cm   6 cm

6 cm

equivalent [ē•kwiv′ə•lənt] **equivalente** Having the same value or naming the same amount

equivalent decimals [ē•kwiv′ə•lənt de′sə•məlz] **decimales equivalentes** Two or more decimals that name the same amount (p. 472)

equivalent fractions [ē•kwiv′ə•lənt frak′shənz] **fracciones equivalentes** Two or more fractions that name the same amount (p. 418)
Example: $\frac{3}{4}$ and $\frac{6}{8}$ name the same amount.

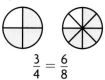

$$\frac{3}{4} = \frac{6}{8}$$

estimate [es′tə•māt] *verb* **estimar** To find an answer that is close to the exact amount

estimate [es′tə•mət] *noun* **estimación** A number close to an exact amount

even [ē′vən] **par** A whole number that has a 0, 2, 4, 6, or 8 in the ones place

event [i•vent′] **suceso** One outcome or a combination of outcomes in an experiment (p. 634)

expanded form [ik•span′dəd fôrm] **forma desarrollada** A way to write numbers by showing the value of each digit (p. 5)
Example: $253 = 200 + 50 + 3$

experimental probability [ik•sper•ə•men′tal prä•bə•bil′ə•tē] **probabilidad experimental** The ratio of the number of times the event occurs to the total number of trials or times the activity is performed (p. 642)

experimental probability $= \dfrac{\text{number of times event occurs}}{\text{total number of trials}}$

expression [ik•spre′shən] **expresión** A part of a number sentence that has numbers and operation signs but does not have an equal sign (p. 80)

face [fās] **cara** A polygon that is a flat surface of a solid figure (p. 566)
Example:

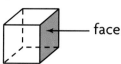

face

fact family [fakt fam′ə•lē] **familia de operaciones** A set of related multiplication and division, or addition and subtraction, equations (pp. 32, 112)
Example: $7 \times 8 = 56$; $8 \times 7 = 56$;
$56 \div 7 = 8$; $56 \div 8 = 7$

factor [fak′tər] **factor** A number that is multiplied by another number to find a product (p. 112)

factor tree [fak′tər trē] **árbol de factores** A diagram that shows the prime factors of a number (p. 298)
Example:

30
5 × 6
5 × 2 × 3

fairness [fâr′nəs] **equidad** Fairness in a game means that one player is as likely to win as another; each player has an equal chance of winning. (p. 641)

flip [flip] **inversión** A movement of a figure to a new position by flipping the figure over a line

Example:

foot (ft) [fōt] **pie** A customary unit used for measuring length or distance (p. 590)
1 foot = 12 inches

formula [fôr′myə•lə] **fórmula** A set of symbols that expresses a mathematical rule (p. 600)
Example: $A = l \times w$

fraction [frak′shən] **fracción** A number that names a part of a whole or part of a group (p. 414)
Example:

$\frac{1}{3}$

frequency [frē′kwen•sē] **frecuencia** The number of times an event occurs (p. 321)

frequency table [frē′kwen•sē tā′bəl] **tabla de frecuencia** A table that uses numbers to record data about how often something happens (p. 321)
Example:

Favorite Color	
Color	**Number**
blue	10
red	7
green	8
yellow	4

function table [funk′shən tā′bəl] **tabla de funciones** A table that matches each input value with an output value. The output values are determined by the function. (p. 394)

gallon (gal) [ga′lən] **galón (gal)** A customary unit for measuring capacity (p. 591)
4 quarts = 1 gallon

gram (g) [gram] **gramo (g)** A unit for measuring mass (p. 594) 1,000 grams = 1 kilogram

greater than (>) [grā′tər t͟han] **mayor que** A symbol used to compare two quantities, with the greater quantity given first
Example: 6 > 4

greater than or equal to (≥) [grā′tər t͟han ôr ē•kwəl tōō] **mayor que o igual a** A symbol used to compare two quantities when the first is greater than or equal to the second
Example: 4 + 5 ≥ 7

grid [grid] **cuadrícula** Evenly divided and equally spaced squares on a figure or flat surface

Grouping Property of Addition [grōō′ping prä′pər•tī əv ə•di′shən] **propiedad de agrupación de la suma** See *Associative Property of Addition.*

Grouping Property of Multiplication [grōō′ping prä′pər•tī əv mul•tə•plə•kā′shən] **propiedad de agrupación de la multiplicación** See *Associative Property of Multiplication.*

hexagon [hek′sə•gän] **hexágono** A polygon with six sides and six angles (p. 524)
Examples:

horizontal [hôr•ə•zän′təl] **horizontal** The direction from left to right (p. 386)

hour (hr) [our] **hora (hr)** A unit used to measure time; 60 minutes = 1 hour

hundredth [hən′drədth] **centésimo** One of one hundred equal parts (p. 468)
Example:

↳hundredth

Identity Property of Addition [ī•den′tə•tē prä′pər•tē əv ə•di′shən] **propiedad de identidad de la suma** The property that states that when you add zero to any number, the sum is that number (p. 78)
Example: 0 + 16 = 16

Identity Property of Multiplication [ī•den′tə•tē prä′pər•tē əv mul•tə•plə•kā′shən] **propiedad de identidad de la multiplicación** The property that states that the product of any number and 1 is that number (p. 136)
Example: 9 × 1 = 9

impossible [im•pä′sə •bəl] **imposible** Never able to happen (p. 634)

improper fraction [im•prä′pər frak′shən] **fracción impropia** A fraction greater than 1 (p. 427)

inch (in.) [inch] **pulgada (pulg)** A customary unit used for measuring length or distance (p. 590)
Example:

←—1 inch—→

inequality [in•i•kwol′ə•tē] **desigualdad** A mathematical sentence that shows two expressions do not represent the same quantity (p. 157)
Example: 4 < 9 − 3

intersecting lines [in•tər•sek'ting līnz] **líneas secantes** Lines that cross each other at exactly one point (p. 522)
Example:

interval [in'tər•vəl] **intervalo** The distance between one number and the next on the scale of a graph (p. 332)

inverse operations [in'vərs ä•pə•rā'shənz] **operaciones inversas** Operations that undo each other. Addition and subtraction are inverse operations. Multiplication and division are inverse operations. (pp. 32, 112)
Example: $6 \times 8 = 48$ and $48 \div 6 = 8$

isosceles triangle [ī•sä'sə•lēz trī'ang•əl] **triángulo isósceles** A triangle with two equal, or congruent, sides (p. 528)
Example:

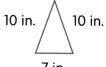

10 in.   10 in.

7 in.

Word History

When you look at the sides of an *isosceles* triangle, you see that the two sides are equal in length. The Greek root *iso-* means "same or equal," and *skelos* means "legs."

key [kē] **clave** The part of a map or graph that explains the symbols

kilogram (kg) [ki'lə•gram] **kilogramo (kg)** A metric unit for measuring mass (p. 595)
1 kilogram = 1,000 grams

kilometer (km) [kə•lä'mə•tər] **kilómetro (km)** A metric unit for measuring length or distance (p. 594) 1,000 meters = 1 kilometer

less than (<) [les than] **menor que** A symbol used to compare two numbers, with the lesser number given first (p. 12)
Example: $3 < 7$

less than or equal to (≤) [les than ôr ē'kwəl too] **menor que o igual a** A symbol used to compare quantities, when the first is less than or equal to the second *Example:* $8 \leq 14 - 5$

like fractions [līk frak'shənz] **fracciones semejantes** Fractions with the same denominator (p. 444)

likely [līk'lē] **probable** Having a greater than even chance of happening (p. 634)

line [līn] **línea** A straight path of points in a plane that continues without end in both directions with no endpoints (p. 518)
Example:

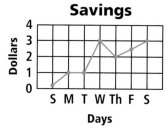

S   T

line graph [līn graf] **gráfica lineal** A graph that uses line segments to show how data changes over a period of time (p. 352)
Example:

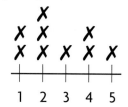

Savings

line plot [līn plät] **diagrama de puntos** A graph that shows the frequency of data along a number line (p. 330)
Example:

```
        X
 X  X       X
 X  X  X  X  X
 +--+--+--+--+
 1  2  3  4  5
```

Cookies Eaten

line segment [līn seg'mənt] **segmento** A part of a line that includes two points called endpoints and all the points between them (p. 518)
Example:

A   B

line symmetry [līn si'mə•trē] **simetría axial** What a figure has if it can be folded about a line so that its two parts match exactly (p. 550)
Example:

line of symmetry

linear units [li'nē•ər yoo'nəts] **unidades lineales** Units that measure length, width, height, or distance (p. 590)

liter (L) [lē′tər] **litro (L)** A metric unit for measuring capacity (p. 595)
1 liter = 1,000 milliliters

mass [mas] **masa** The amount of matter in an object (p. 595)

mathematical probability [math•ma′ti•kəl prä•bə•bi′lə•tē] **probabilidad matemática** A comparison of the number of favorable outcomes to the number of possible outcomes of an event (p. 638)

median [mē′dē•ən] **mediana** The middle number in an ordered set of data (p. 326)

meter (m) [mē′tər] **metro (m)** A metric unit for measuring length or distance (p. 594)
100 centimeters = 1 meter

mile (mi) [mīl] **milla (mi)** A customary unit for measuring length or distance (p. 590)
5,280 feet = 1 mile

milliliter (mL) [mi′lə•lē•tər] **mililitro (mL)** A metric unit for measuring capacity (p. 595)
1,000 milliliters = 1 liter

millimeter (mm) [mi′lə•mē•tər] **milímetro (mm)** A metric unit for measuring length or distance (p. 594) 1 centimeter = 10 millimeters

millions [mil′yənz] **millones** The period after thousands (p. 9)

minute (min) [mi′nət] **minuto (min)** A unit to measure short amounts of time
60 seconds = 1 minute

mixed number [mikst nəm′bər] **número mixto** An amount given as a whole number and a fraction (p. 426)

mode [mōd] **moda** The number(s) or item(s) that occur most often in a set of data (p. 327)

multiple [mul′tə•pəl] **múltiplo** The product of a given whole number and another whole number (p. 122)

multiplication [mul•tə•plə•kā′shən] **multiplicación** A process to find the total number of items in equal-sized groups, or to find the total number of items in a given number of groups when each group contains the same number of items; multiplication is the inverse of division

multiply [mul′tə•plī] **multiplicar** When you combine equal groups, you can multiply to find how many in all; the opposite operation of division (p. 110)

multistep problem [mul′ti•step prä′bləm] **problema de varios pasos** A problem requiring more than one step to solve (p. 208)

negative numbers [ne′gə•tiv num′bərz] **números negativos** All the numbers to the left of zero on the number line; negative numbers are less than zero (p. 378)

net [net] **plantilla** A two-dimensional pattern that can be folded to make a three-dimensional figure (p. 570)
Example:

not equal to (≠) [nät ē′kwəl tōō] **no igual a** A symbol that indicates one quantity is not equal to another (p. 13)
Example: 12 × 3 ≠ 38

number line [num′bər līn] **recta numérica** A line on which numbers can be located
Example:

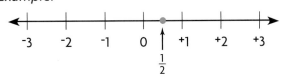

numerator [nōō′mə•rā•tər] **numerador** The number above the bar in a fraction that tells how many parts of the whole or group are being considered (p. 414)
Example: $\frac{2}{3}$ ← numerator

numericial data [nōō•mer′i•kəl dā′tə] **datos numéricos** Data that can be counted or measured (p. 321)

obtuse angle [äb•tōōs′ ang′əl] **ángulo obtuso** An angle that measures greater than a right angle (greater than 90° and less than 180°) (p. 520)
Example:

obtuse triangle [ăb•tōōs′ trī′ang•əl] **triángulo obtusángulo** A triangle with one obtuse angle (p. 528)
Example:

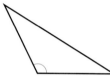

octagon [ăk′tə•gän] **octágono** A polygon with eight sides and eight angles (p. 524)
Examples:

odd [od] **impar** A whole number that has a 1, 3, 5, 7, or 9 in the ones place

one-dimensional [wən′ də•men(t)′shə•nəl] **unidimensional** A measure in only one direction, such as length (p. 518)
Examples:

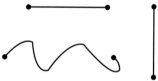

open figure [ō′pən fi′gyər] **figura abierta** A figure that does not begin and end at the same point
Examples:

order [ôr′dər] **orden** A particular arrangement or placement of things one after the other (p. 16)

order of operations [ôr′dər əv ä•pə•rā′shənz] **orden de las operaciones** A special set of rules which gives the order in which calculations are done in an expression (p. 141)

Order Property of Addition [ôr′dər prä′pər•tē əv ə•di′shən] **propiedad de orden de la suma** See *Commutative Property of Addition.*

Order Property of Multiplication [ôr′dər prä′pər•tē əv mul•tə•plə•kā′shən] **propiedad de orden de la multiplicación** See *Commutative Property of Multiplication.*

ordered pair [ôr′dərd pâr] **par ordenado** A pair of numbers used to locate a point on a coordinate grid. The first number tells how far to move horizontally, and the second number tells how far to move vertically. (p. 350)

origin [ôr′ə•jən] **origen** The point where the *x*-axis and the *y*-axis in the coordinate plane intersect, (0,0) (p. 386)

ounce (oz) [ouns] **onza** A customary unit for measuring weight (p. 591) 16 ounces = 1 pound

outcome [out′kum] **resultado** A possible result of an experiment (p. 628)

outlier [out′lī•ər] **valor atípico** A value separated from the rest of the data (p. 330)

P

P.M. [pē•em′] **p.m.** The time between noon and midnight

parallel lines [par′ə•lel līnz] **líneas paralelas** Lines in the same plane that never intersect and are always the same distance apart (p. 522)
Example:

parallelogram [par•ə•lel′ə•gram] **paralelogramo** A quadrilateral whose opposite sides are parallel and equal, or congruent (p. 531)
Example:

parentheses [pə•ren′thə•sēz] **paréntesis** The symbols used to show which operation or operations in an expression should be done first (p. 144)

partial product [pär′shəl prä′dəkt] **producto parcial** A method of multiplying in which the ones, tens, hundreds, and so on are multiplied separately and then the products are added together (p. 185)

pattern [pat′ərn] **patrón** An ordered set of numbers or objects; the order helps you predict what will come next (p. 38)
Example: 2, 4, 6, 8, 10

pattern unit [pat′ərn yoo′nət] **unidad de patrón** The part of a pattern that repeats (p. 556)
Example:

pattern unit

pentagon [pen′tə•gän] **pentágono** A polygon with five sides and five angles (p. 524)
Example:

perimeter [pə•ri′mə•tər] **perímetro** The distance around a figure (p. 598)

period [pir′ē•əd] **período** Each group of three digits separated by commas in a multidigit number (p. 5)
Example: 85,643,900 has three periods.

perpendicular lines [pər•pən•di′kyə•lər līnz] **líneas perpendiculares** Two lines that intersect to form four right angles (p. 522)
Example:

pictograph [pik′tə•graf] **pictografía** A graph that uses symbols to show and compare information (p. 362)
Example: **How We Get To School**

Walk	✹ ✹ ✹
Ride a Bike	✹ ✹ ✹ ✹
Ride a Bus	✹ ✹ ✹ ✹ ✹ ✹
Ride in a Car	✹ ✹

Key: Each ✹ = 10 students.

pint (pt) [pīnt] **pinta (pt)** A customary unit for measuring capacity (p. 591) 2 cups = 1 pint

place value [plās val′yoo] **valor posicional** The value of a digit in a number, based on the location of the digit (p. 5)

plane [plān] **plano** A flat surface that extends without end in all directions (p. 518)
Example:

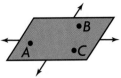

plane figure [plān fi′gyər] **figura plana** A figure in a plane that is formed by lines that are curved, straight, or both

point [point] **punto** An exact location in space (p. 518)

polygon [pä′lē•gän] **polígono** A closed plane figure formed by three or more straight sides that are connected line segments. (p. 524)
Examples:

Polygons   Not Polygons

positive numbers [pä′zə•tiv num′bərz] **números positivos** All the numbers to the right of zero on the number line; positive numbers are greater than 0 (p. 378)

pound (lb) [pound] **libra (lb)** A customary unit for measuring weight (p. 591) 16 ounces = 1 pound

predict [pri•dikt′] **predecir** To make a reasonable guess about what will happen (p. 492)

prime factor [prīm fak′tər] **factor primo** A factor that is a prime number (p. 298)

prime number [prīm num′bər] **número primo** A number that has only two factors: 1 and itself (p. 292)
Examples: 2, 3, 5, 7, 11, 13, 17, and 19 are prime numbers. 1 is not a prime number.

probability [prä•bə•bi′lə•tē] **probabilidad** The likelihood that an event will happen

product [prä′dəkt] **producto** The answer to a multiplication problem (p. 112)

pyramid [pir'ə•mid] **pirámide** A solid figure with a polygon base and triangular sides that meet at a single point
Example:

Q

quadrilateral [kwä•drə•la'tə•rəl] **cuadrilátero** A polygon with four sides and four angles (p. 524)

quart (qt) [kwôrt] **cuarto (ct)** A customary unit for measuring capacity (p. 591) 2 pints = 1 quart

quotient [kwō'shənt] **cociente** The number, not including the remainder, that results from dividing (p. 112)
Example: 8 ÷ 4 = 2; 2 is the quotient.

R

radius [rā'dē•əs] **radio** A line segment with one endpoint at the center of a circle and the other endpoint on the circle (p. 534)
Example:

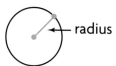

range [rānj] **rango** The difference between the greatest and the least number in a set of data (p. 330)

ratio [rā'shē•ō] **razón** The comparison of two numbers by division (p. 421)

ray [rā] **rayo** A part of a line; it has one endpoint and continues without end in one direction (p. 518)
Example:

rectangle [rek'tang•gəl] **rectángulo** A parallelogram with opposite sides that are equal, or congruent, and with four right angles (p. 531)
Example:

rectangular prism [rek•tang'gyə•lər pri'zəm] **prisma rectangular** A solid figure in which all six faces are rectangles
Example:

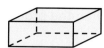

rectangular pyramid [rek•tang'gyə•lər pir'ə•mid] **pirámide rectangular** A pyramid with a rectangular base and with four triangular faces (p. 566)
Example:

regroup [rē•grōōp'] **reagrupar** To exchange amounts of equal value to rename a number (p. 58)
Example: 5 + 8 = 13 ones or 1 ten 3 ones

regular polygon [reg'yə•lər pä'lē•gän] **polígono regular** A polygon that has all sides that are equal in length and all angles equal in measure (p. 525)
Examples:

remainder [ri•mān'dər] **residuo** The amount left over when a number cannot be divided equally (p. 244)

rhombus [räm'bəs] **rombo** A parallelogram with four equal, or congruent, sides (p. 531)
Example:

right angle [rīt ang'əl] **ángulo recto** An angle that forms a square corner and has a measure of 90° (p. 520)
Example:

right triangle [rīt trī'ang•əl] **triángulo rectángulo** A triangle with one right angle (p. 528)
Example:

rotational symmetry [rō•tā'shən•əl si'mə•trē] **simetría rotacional** What a figure has if it can be turned about a central point and still look the same in at least two positions (p. 551)

round [round] **redondear** To replace a number with another number that tells about how many or how much (p. 34)

scale [skāl] **escala** A series of numbers placed at fixed distances on a graph to help label the graph (p. 332)

scalene triangle [skā′lēn trī′ang•əl] **triángulo escaleno** A triangle with no equal, or congruent, sides (p. 528)
Example:

30 cm
13 cm
18 cm

second (sec) [se′kənd] **segundo (seg)** A small unit of time (p. 96) 60 seconds = 1 minute

simplest form [sim′pləst fôrm] **mínima expresión** A fraction is in simplest form when 1 is the only number that can divide evenly into the numerator and the denominator (p. 419)

slide [slīd] **traslación** A movement of a figure to a new position along a straight line (p. 548)
Example:

solid figure [so′ləd fi′gyər] **cuerpo geométrico** A three-dimensional figure

sphere [sfēr] **esfera** A round object whose curved surface is the same distance from the center to all its points (p. 568)
Example:

square [skwâr] **cuadrado** A parallelogram with 4 equal, or congruent, sides and 4 right angles (p. 531)
Example:

square number [skwâr num′bər] **número cuadrado** The product of a number and itself (p. 122)
Example: 2 × 2 = 4, so 4 is a square number

square pyramid [skwâr pir′ə•mid] **pirámide cuadrada** A pyramid with a square base and with four triangular faces (p. 566)
Example:

square unit (sq un) [skwâr yōō′nət] **unidad cuadrada** A unit of area with dimensions of 1 unit × 1 unit (p. 606)

standard form [stan′dərd fôrm] **forma normal** A way to write numbers by using digits (p. 5)
Example: 3,540 ← standard form

subtraction [səb•trak′shən] **resta** The process of finding how many are left when a number of items are taken away from a group of items; the process of finding the difference when two groups are compared; the opposite operation of addition

sum [sum] **suma o total** The answer to an addition problem (p. 38)

surface area [sər′fəs âr′ē•ə] **área total** The sum of the areas of all the faces of a solid figure (p. 611)

survey [sûr′vā] **encuesta** A method of gathering information (p. 320)

T

tablespoon (tbsp) [tā′bəl•spōōn] **cucharada (cda)** A customary unit used for measuring capacity 3 teaspoons = 1 tablespoon

tally table [ta′lē tā′bəl] **tabla de conteo** A table that uses tally marks to record data (p. 320)

Word History

Some people keep score in card games by making marks on paper (IIII). These marks are known as tally marks. The word *tally* is related to *tailor*, from the Latin *talea*, meaning "one who cuts." In early times, a method of keeping count was by cutting marks into a piece of wood or bone.

teaspoon (tsp) [tē'spoon] **cucharadita (cdta)** A customary unit used for measuring capacity 1 tablespoon = 3 teaspoons

tenth [tenth] **décimo** One of ten equal parts (p. 468)
Example:

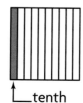

└── tenth

three-dimensional [thrē•də•men'shən•əl] **tridimensional** Measured in three directions, such as length, width, and height (p. 566)
Example:

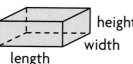

height
width
length

time line [tīm līn] **línea cronológica** A schedule of events or an ordered list of historic moments

ton (T) [tun] **tonelada (T)** A customary unit for measuring weight (p. 590) 2,000 pounds = 1 ton

trapezoid [tra'pə•zoid] **trapecio** A quadrilateral with exactly one pair of parallel sides (p. 531)
Examples:

tree diagram [trē dī'ə•gram] **diagrama de árbol** An organized list that shows all possible outcomes of an event (p. 644)
Example:

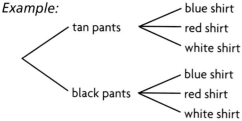

tan pants — blue shirt
— red shirt
— white shirt

black pants — blue shirt
— red shirt
— white shirt

trends [trendz] **tendencias** On a graph, areas where the data increase, decrease, or stay the same over time (p. 353)

triangle [trī'ang•gəl] **triángulo** A polygon with three sides and three angles (p. 524)
Examples:

triangular prism [trī•ang'gyə•lər pri'zəm] **prisma triangular** A solid figure that has two triangular bases and three rectangular faces (p. 566)
Example:

triangular pyramid [trī•ang'gyə•lər pir'ə•mid] **pirámide triangular** A pyramid that has a triangular base and three triangular faces (p. 566)
Example:

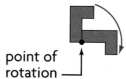

turn [tûrn] **giro** A movement of a figure to a new position by rotating the figure around a point (p. 548)
Example:

point of rotation ──

two-dimensional [too•də•men'shən•əl] **bidimensional** Measured in two directions, such as length and width (p. 518)
Example:

width
length

U

unit fraction [yoo'nit frak'shən] **fracción unitaria** A fraction that has a numerator of one (p. 414)

unlikely [un•lī'klē] **poco probable** Having a less than even chance of happening (p. 634)

V

variable [vâr'ē•ə•bəl] **variable** A letter or symbol that stands for a number or numbers (p. 82)

Venn diagram [ven dī′ə•gram] **diagrama de Venn** A diagram that shows relationships among sets of things (p. 324)

Example:

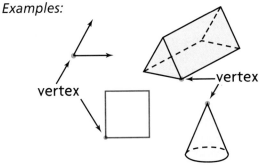

2-Digit Numbers   Even Numbers

vertex [vûr′teks] **vértice** The point at which two rays of an angle meet or two (or more) line segments meet in a plane figure, or where three or more edges meet in a solid figure; the top point of a cone (p. 520)

Examples:

vertex   vertex   vertex

vertical [vər′ti•kəl] **vertical** The direction from top to bottom (p. 386)

volume [väl′yо̄о̄m] **volumen** The measure of the amount of space a solid figure occupies (p. 623)

weight [wāt] **peso** How heavy an object is (p. 591)

whole number [hōl num′bər] **número entero** One of the numbers 0, 1, 2, 3, 4 . . . ; the set of whole numbers goes on without end

word form [wûrd fôrm] **en palabras** A way to write numbers by using words (p. 5)
Example: Sixty-two million, four hundred fifty-three thousand, two hundred twelve

x-axis [eks′ak′səs] **eje de la x** The horizontal line on a coordinate grid or plane (p. 386)

x-coordinate [eks′ kо̄•ôr′də•nət] **coordenada x** The first number in an ordered pair; it tells the distance to move horizontally (p. 386)

y-axis [wī′ ak′səs] **eje de la y** The vertical line on a coordinate grid or plane (p. 386)

y-coordinate [wī′ kо̄•ôr′də•nət] **coordenada y** The second number in an ordered pair; it tells the distance to move vertically (p. 386)

yard (yd) [yärd] **yarda (yd)** A customary unit for measuring length or distance (p. 590)
3 feet = 1 yard

Zero Property of Multiplication [zē′rō prä′pər•tē əv mul•tə•plə•kā′shən] **propiedad del cero de la multiplicación** The property that states that the product of 0 and any number is 0 (p. 136)
Example: $0 \times 8 = 0$

Index

make a model, 574–577
make an organized list, 630–633
make a table, 504–505
predict and test, 151, 158–161, 252–253, 504–505
solve a simpler problem, 612–615
use logical reasoning, 20–23, 536–537
work backward, 92–95
write an equation, 452–455
Products. *See* Multiplication
Properties
  Associative, 78–79, 136–139, 213, 463, 509
  Commutative, 78–79, 136–139, 213, 463, 509
  Distributive, 136–139, 197
  Identity, 78–79, 136–139, 463, 509
  Zero, 136–139
Pyramids
  square, 566–569
  rectangular, 566–569, 581
  triangular, 566–569, 581

Quadrilaterals, 524–527, 530–533
  parallelograms, 530–533
  rectangles, 530–533
  rhombuses, 530–533
  squares, 530–533
  trapezoids, 530–533
Quarts (qt), 590–593
Quotients, 112
  correcting, 275
  estimating, 274, 277
  placing the first digit in, 274, 258–259
  relationships with divisor, dividend, and
    remainder, 112, 244
  three-digit, 270–273, 274–277
  zeros in, 274–277
  See also Division

Radius, 534–535
Range, 330–331
Ray, 518–519
Read Math, xx–xxi, 1, 59, 107, 147, 157, 173, 241,
  317, 411, 515, 587
Read Math Workshop, 87, 119, 189, 251, 381, 477,
  533, 619
Reading skills
  cause and effect, 87
  classify and categorize, 533
  draw conclusions, 251
  identify the details, 477
  sequence, 619
  use graphic aids, 21, 189, 613
  visualize, 119, 575

Reasoning, 20–23, 48–49, 230–231, 536–537,
  612–615
  applying strategies from a simpler problem to
    solve a more complex problem, 612–615
  breaking a problem into simpler parts, 44,
    612–615
  choosing a problem solving strategy, 252–253,
    504–505, 554–555
  estimating, 40–43, 178–179, 206–207, 256–257,
    494–495, 598–599, 606–607
    using estimation to verify reasonableness of an
      answer, 58–61, 62–63, 190–191, 192–193,
      220–223, 230–231
  generalizing beyond a particular problem to
    other situations, 334–335
  identifying relationships among numbers,
    398–399, 400–401
  logical, 20–23, 73, 323, 329, 536–537
  observing patterns, 38–39, 96–97, 122–123,
    162–163, 176–177, 202–203, 254–255, 300–303,
    304–307, 556–557
  recognizing relevant and irrelevant information,
    68–69
  sequencing and prioritizing information, 434–435
  *Opportunities to explain reasoning are contained
  in every exercise set. Some examples are* 6, 15,
    19, 36, 60, 86, 111, 114, 123, 127, 141, 149, 152,
    153, 155, 157, 203, 207, 222, 226, 229, 259, 272,
    276, 277, 291, 294, 297, 299, 302, 303, 322, 325,
    333, 349, 354, 360, 363, 376, 377, 388, 393, 396,
    397, 401, 420, 428, 451, 455, 458, 459, 476, 493,
    503, 519, 526, 532, 553, 568, 571, 593, 597, 602,
    603, 605, 610, 611, 641, 643, 644, 645
Recording division, 248–251
Recording multiplication, 186–189, 220–223
Rectangles, 530–533
  area of, 608–611
  as face of solid figure, 566–569
  perimeter of, 600–603
  relationship between area and perimeter in,
    606–619
Rectangular prisms, 566–569
  volume of, 623
Rectangular pyramids, 566–569
Regular polygons, 524–527
Relational thinking, 101
Remainders, in division, 244–245, 268–269
Review/Test. *See* Chapter Review/Test
Review of Key Standards, H2–H31
Rhombuses, 530–533
Right angles, 520–521
Right triangles, 528–529
Roman numerals, 27
Rotational symmetry, 550–553
Rounding
  deciding when to round, 34–37, 492–493
  decimals, 492–493

Photo Credits

202 Kim Taylor/Dorling Kindersley; 203 James King-Holmes/Science Photo Library; 208 (t) Corbis; 208 (b) Gail Mooney/Masterfile; 213 Benjamin Rondel/Corbis; 216 AP Photo/Kathy Willens; 218 (tr) Jerry and Marcy Monkman/EcoPhotography.com/Alamy; 218 (b) Dennis MacDonald/PhotoEdit; 220 Kevin Dodge/Masterfile; 222 Holger Wulschlaeger/iStockPhoto; 224 Hulton-Deutsch Collection/Corbis; 225 Digital Vision Ltd./SuperStock; 227 Bob Daemmrich/The Image Works; 228 (t) Hulton Archive/Getty Images; 228 (b) David McNew/Getty Images; 230 SuperStock/age fotostock; 231 Drew Gardner; 235 (tr) AlanHaynes.com/Alamy; 235 (bg) Brand X Pictures/Alamy; 238 (t) Bettman/Corbis; 238 (c) NASA/ Science Photo Library; 238-239 (bg) Bettmann/Corbis.

Unit 4: 240 Karen Whylie/Masterfile; 241 (t) The Futures Channel; 241 (c) The Futures Channel; 241 (b) Movin' On Livestock; 242 Matthew Filar; 248 The Granger Collection, New York; 249 Photo File/MLB Photos via Getty Images; 251 Andy Mead/Icon SMI/NewsCom; 252 ML Harris/Getty Images; 253 (t) Yann Arthus-Bertrand/Corbis; 253 (tc) Imagebroker/Alamy; 253 (c) Yann Arthus-Bertrand/Corbis; 253 (bc) DK Limited/Corbis; 253 (b) Vario Images GmbH & Co.KG/Alamy; 254 Kelly-Mooney Photography/Corbis; 256 Michael & Patricia Fogden/Minden Pictures; 257 (tc) Michael Durham/Minden Pictures; 257 (tc) Stephen Dalton/Minden Pictures; 257 (bc) Tim Oram/Alamy; 257 (bc) Arco Images/Alamy; 258 Philip Krejcarek/JupiterImages; 259 Philip Krejcarek/JupiterImages; 263 (tr) Richard Hamilton Smith/Corbis; 263 (bg) Danita Delimont/Alamy; 263 (tl), (tc) PhotoDisc/Getty Images/Harcourt; 266 SeaPics.com; 268 Richard T. Nowitz/Corbis; 269 Sandro Vannini/Corbis; 270 Bettmann/Corbis; 271 (br) Ryan McVay/Getty Images (Royalty-free); 272 Chuck Eckert/Alamy; 273 Liu Liqun/Corbis; 274 (tc) Getty/Harcourt; 274 (tc) Getty/Harcourt; 274 (tr) Harcourt; 275 (tc) Brand X Pictures/Alamy; 275 (tr) Jack Cox - Travel Pics Pro/Alamy; 275 (br) Getty/Harcourt; 277 AM Corporation/Alamy; 278 Florian Graner/Nature Picture Library; 286 Bob Gibbons/Science Photo Library; 291 Harcourt /Corel Stock Photo Library - royalty free; 292 Lake County Museum/Corbis; 294 Norman Owen Tomalin/Bruce Coleman USA; 296 Mark Richards/PhotoEdit; 302 photolibrary.com pty. ltd./Index Stock; 304 Jeff Gynane/iStockPhoto; 305 Dynamic Graphics/Jupiterimages; 306 (tc) Chris Lisle/Corbis; 306 (cl) Tyler Olson/ShutterStock.com; 306 (cr) iStockphoto; 306 (br) Nancy Nehring/iStockphoto; 311 (bg) Betty Sederquist/California Stock Photo; 314 (t) Hulton Archive/Getty Images; 314 (cl) Hulton Archive/Getty Images; 314 (cr) Wesley Berry of Covina California; 314 (bcr) Swim Ink/Corbis; 314 (b) Hulton Archive/Getty Images; 314-315 (bg) ImageState/Alamy; 315 (t) California Statehood Stamp Design © 2002 United States Postal Service. All Rights Reserved. Used with Permission; 315 (tc) Tom Massung/Photographers Direct; 315 (cl) Anthony Nex/Jupiterimages; 315 (c) iStockphoto; 315 (c) Jupiterimages; 315 (cr) Bill Ross/Corbis; 315 (br) Robertstock.

Unit 5: 316 White Cross Productions/Getty Images; 317 (t) USDA; 317 (c) USDA; 317 (b) USDA; 318 Lawrence Migdale/PIX; 330 NASA/Harcourt Index; 332 Chris Trotman/Duomo/Corbis; 334 Michael Newman/Photo Edit; 339 (bg) Corbis/Harcourt; 342 Daryl Benson/Masterfile; 344 NASA; 345 Masterfile; 347 (tr) Jules Frazier/Getty Images; 347 (br) Tony Freeman/PhotoEdit; 348 (tr) Image Source/Getty Images; 348 (br) Envision/Corbis; 352 Ambient images; 353 Alamy; 354 Pat O'Hara/Corbis; 355 Jean-Paul Ferrero/AUSCAPE/Minden Pictures; 360 Joe Sohm/The Image Works; 361 Rudy Sulgan/Age Fotostock; 363 (tr) iStockphoto; 365 Nicole Katano/Age Fotostock; 369 Getty Images/PhotoDisc/Harcourt; 372 Dirk Yuricich; 374 Scott Olson/Getty Images; 377 Gay Bumgarner/Getty Images; 378 Macduff Everton/The Image Works; 381 AP Photo/Nathan Bilow; 384 (t) Annie Griffiths Belt/Corbis; 384 (b) Josef Fankhauser/Getty Images; 385 Jamie Squire/Getty Images; 387 Getty; 389 Dennis MacDonald/PhotoEdit; 391 Richard Hutchings/PhotoEdit; 396 Alamy; 397 (t) Mark Gibson/AGStock; 399 Michael DeYoung/Corbis; 400 Alamy; 401 Neil Sutherland/Alamy; 408 Alamy; 408-409 (bg) Les Walker/NewSport/Corbis.

Unit 6: 411 (t) The Futures Channel; 411 (c) The Futures Channel; 411 (b) The Futures Channel; 412 Ted Streshinsky/Corbis; 414 (r) Bob Daemmrich/PhotoEdit; 417 iStockphoto; 418 (cr) Taylor S. Kennedy/National Geographic/Getty Images; 419 AP Images/Jessie Cohen, National Zoo; 421 (b) AP Images/Evan Vucci; 424 Alamy; 426 Lisa Belleman courtesy of Ramsey House Plantation, Knoxville Tennessee; 434 INSADCO Photography/Alamy; 435 Dorling Kindersley; 442 Darren Schmall--Pizza Farm Agri-tainment Company; 448 (tr) JupiterImages; 449 The Garden Picture Library/Alamy; 453 ImageState/Alamy; 455 (cr) iStockphoto; 455 (c) Alamy; 455 (cl) Alamy; 463 Grant Faint/The Image Bank/Getty Images; 466 Jeff Gross/Getty Images; 470 (tr) Scientifica/Visuals Unlimited; 470 (cr) Joyce Photographics/Photo Researchers, Inc.; 470 (bc) Scientifica/Visuals Unlimited; 470 (br) Stephen J. Krasemann/Photo Researchers; 470 (bl) Andrew J. Martinez/Photo Researchers; 471 (l) Harcourt; 471 (r) Alamy; 477 (t) Courtesy Golden State Model Railroad Museum; 477 (b) Courtesy Golden State Model Railroad Museum; 487 Stuart Gregory/Photographer's Choice RF/Getty Images; 490 Bill Aron/Photo Edit; 492 Larry Lefever/Grant Heilman Photography; 494 Bill Aron/Photo Edit; 509 (tr) Tony Freeman/PhotoEdit; 512 (cl) Sal Maimone/SuperStock; 512 (cr) Audrey Gibson/Corbis; 512 (br) Robert Llewellyn/SuperStock;

512-513 (bg) age fotostock/SuperStock; 513 (tr) Alamy; 513 (cl) Chris Luneski/Alamy; 513 (c) Chris Luneski/Alamy; 513 (cr) photodisc/PunchStock.

Unit 7: 515 (t) The Futures Channel; 515 (c) Ford Motor Company; 515 (b) Ford Motor Company; 516 Richard Cummins/Corbis; 516 (inset) Ansel Adams Publishing Rights Trust/Corbis; 518 (t) Royalty-Free/Corbis; 518 (tc) Steve Gorton and Karl Shone/ Dorling Kindersley; 518 (c) Wesley Hitt/Alamy; 518 (bc) Kevin Britland/Alamy; 518 (b) Stockdisc/Getty Images; 519 Juptier Images; 520 Masterfile; 523 (tl) iStockphoto; 523 (tcl) Jon Shireman/Getty; 523 (tcr) Jupiter Images; 523 (tr) Age Fotostock; 524 Klee, Paul (1879-1940), *"Blue Mountain"* ("Blauer Berg"). 1919. Watercolor and pencil on paper, 28 x 18.5 cm. © 2007 Artists Rights Society (ARS), New York/VG Bild-Kunst, Bonn. Bildarchiv Preussischer Kulturbesitz/Art Resource, NY. ; 526 Picasso, Pablo (1881-1973) *"Mandolin and Guitar"*. Oil and sand on canvas, 1924. © 2007 Estate of Pablo Picasso/Artists Rights Society (ARS), New York. The Granger Collection, NY.; 527 (t) ERIC FEFERBERG/AFP/Getty Images; 527 (bl) TerraServer; 527 (br) Jim Pickerell/Alamy; 528 Neil Fletcher and Matthew Ward/DK Images; 529 ImageState/Alamy; 530 Jeffrey Greenberg/Photo Researchers, Inc.; 531 Kactus Foto/SuperStock; 532 Spencer Grant/PhotoEdit; 533 (tl) San Diego Historical Society; 533 (tr) San Diego Historical Society; 544 (t) Fred and Randi Hirschmann Photography; 544 (bl) David Carriere/Index Stock Imagery; 544 (br) Rod Planck/Photo Researchers Inc.; 547 Courtesy of Baden Sports, Inc.; 550 ImageState/Alamy; 551 Damir Frkovic/Masterfile; 552 (tl) Gene Chutka/iStockphoto; 552 (tcl) Hemera Technologies/Jupiter Images; 552 (cr) iStockphoto; 552 (cr) Steven Needham/Envision; 553 Syd M Johnson/The Image Works; 556 Tyrrell-Lewis Associates Limited; 557 *"98 Bright Dancing Squares"* (40" x 40") by Debby Kratovil. Published in Bold, Black & Beautiful Quilts (American Quilter's Society 2004). Photo by Charles R. Lynch.; 561 Diego Lezama Orezzoli/Corbis; 564 Bill Heinsohn/Alamy; 566 The Christian Science Monitor/Getty Images; 567 Stephen Johnson/Getty Images; 568 (tl) Bruce Chashin/Jupiter Images; 568 (tcl) Andrew Woodley/Alamy; 568 (tcr) Artefaqs Corporation; 568 (tr) Index Stock; 572 (r) Rodolfo Arpia/Age Fotostock; 575 SuperStock, Inc. /SuperStock; 577 (t) Klaus Hackenberg/zefa/Corbis; 577 (b) Stefano Bianchetti/Corbis; 578 (tl) Dynamic Graphics Group/Creatas/Alamy; 578 (tcl) Elvele Images/Alamy; 578 (tcr) Alex Bramwell/iStockPhoto; 578 (tr) P. Narayan/age fotostock; 580 (tl) Carolyn Ross/Jupiter Images; 580 (tcr) Christopher O Driscoll/iStock Photo; 580 (tr) SuperStock/Alamy; 581 (tr) HIP/Art Resource, NY; 581 (bg) Comstock Images/Alamy; 584 (cl) Alamy; 584 (c) Handout/NewsCom; 584 (cr) Steve Gorton/Getty Images; 584-585 (bg) World Almanac Books; 585 (tr) Getty Images/Harcourt.; 585 (c) Getty Images/Harcourt; 585 (cr) Glenn Mitsui/Photodisc/ Getty Images;

Unit 8: 586 Larry Gatz/Photographer's Choice/Getty Image; 587 (t) The Futures Channel; 587 (c) The Futures Channel; 587 (b) The Futures Channel; 588 Robert Holmes/Corbis; 593 (bl) Jim Cole, Photographer/Alamy; 593 (bc) Thomas Stevenson Grant; 593 (br) ST-images/Alamy; 597 Gordon & Cathy Illg/ Animals Animals; 599 imagebroker/Alamy; 604 Fairplex, Pomona, CA; 605 (t) Fairplex, Pomona, CA; 605 (c) lordsbaine/istockphoto; 605 (bl) Christophe Testi/istockphoto; 605 (bc) Hemera Technologies/ Jupiter Images; 605 (br) Stefan Glebowski/Shutterstock; 613 Corbis; 615 Bill Bachman/Alamy; 616 (tr) Thomas Henderson ABEL/Getty Images; 616 (cr) Alberto Biscaro/Masterfile; 616 (cl) Mike Powell/ Getty Images; 619 Masterfile Royalty Free; 620 (tl) Corbis/Harcourt; 620 (tc) Getty/Harcourt; 620 (bl) Zoomstock/Masterfile; 622 (tr) Getty/Harcourt; 623 Comstock Images/Alamy; 626 Larry Brownstein/ Ambient Images; 633 (tl) Nevada State Fair; 633 (tr) New York State Fair; 633 (cl) California Exposition & State Fair; 633 (cr) Corbis; 633 (bcl) Arizona State Fair; 633 (bcr) Indiana State Fair Commission; 633 (bl) Michigan State Fair & Expo Center; 633 (br) Alamy Images; 649 (bg) PhotoDisc/Getty Images/Harcourt; 652 (tr) Lawrence Lawry/Photo Researchers; 652 Garnet: Harry Taylor/Getty Images; 652 Amethyst: Lawrence Lawry/Photo Researchers; 653 Aquamarine: Lawrence Lawry/Photo Researchers; 652 Diamond: Charles D. Winters/Photo Researchers; 652 Emerald: Harry Taylor/Getty Images; 652 Pearl: Chip Forelli/ Getty Images; 652 Ruby: Harry Taylor/Getty Images; 652 Peridot: Harry Taylor/Getty Images; 652 Sapphire: Wayne Scherr/Photo Researchers; 652 Opal: Lawrence Lawry/Photo Researchers; 652 Topaz: Lawrence Lawry/Photo Researchers; 652 Turquoise: Lawrence Lawry/Photo Researchers; 652 (bg) Sandro Sodano/Getty Images; 653 (tr) Harry Taylor (c) Dorling Kindersley; 653 (tl) Colin Keates (c) Dorling Kindersley, Courtesy of the Natural History Museum, London.

Student Handbook: page H, Jim Brandenburg/Minden Pictures; H1 GK Hart/Vikki Hart/ Getty Images.

12 lights illuminate each tower.

24 lights illuminate the sidewalks.

128 lights are installed on the bridge roadway.

The weight of both main towers is **44,000** tons.

746 feet

Each tower rises above the water.